REFORMATIONS

From High Renaissance to Mannerism in the new
West of religious contention and colonial expansion

To Annes Tom with warmest regards

Christopher Carson

4/viii/2013

ARCHITECTURE IN CONTEXT is dedicated to my wife Juliet, without whose support – spiritual and material – it would never have been realized.
CT

REFORMATIONS

From High Renaissance to Mannerism in the new West of religious contention and colonial expansion

Christopher Tadgell

Routledge
Taylor & Francis Group

LONDON AND NEW YORK

ARCHITECTURE IN CONTEXT V

First published 2012 by Routledge
2 Park Square, Milton Park, Abingdon, Oxon, OX14 4RN

Simultaneously published in the USA and Canada by Routledge
711 Third Avenue, New York, NY10017

Routledge is an imprint of the Taylor & Francis Group, an informa business

© 2012 Christopher Tadgell

Series design by Claudia Schenk
Image processing and drawings by Mark Wilson

British Library Cataloguing in Publication Data
A catalogue record for this book is available from the British Library

Library of Congress Cataloging in Publication Data
Tadgell, Christopher, 1939-
Reformations : from High Renaissance to Mannerism in the new West of religious contention and colonial expansion / Christopher Tadgell. -- 1st ed.
p. cm. -- (Architecture in context ; 5)
Includes bibliographical references (p.) and index.
1. Architecture, Renaissance. 2. Mannerism (Architecture) 3. Architecture and society--Europe. I. Title.
NA510.T29 2012
724'.12--dc23
2011038857

ISBN: 978-0-415-40756-4 (hbk)

ISBN13 978–0–415–40754–0

PUBLISHER'S NOTE
This book has been prepared from camera-ready copy provided by the author.

Printed and bound in India by Replika Press Pvt. Ltd.

CONTENTS

In the text, AIC1 indicates a reference to *Antiquity: Origins, Classicism and the New Rome*, volume 1 in this series; AIC2 indicates a reference to volume 2, *The East: Buddhists, Hindus and the Sons of Heaven*; AIC3 indicates a reference to volume 3, *Islam: From Medina to the Maghreb and from the Indies to Istanbul*; AIC4 indicates a reference to volume 4, *The West: From the Advent of Christendom to the Eve of Reformation*.

›0.1 MICHELANGELO, SISTINE CHAPEL VAULT, CENTRAL BAY, from 1508: the Cumaean Sibyl.

DEFINITIONS

The achievements of the High Renaissance giants seemingly unsurpassable, progress in the arts demanded lateral endeavour beyond convention: supreme accomplishment prompted extreme accomplishment. Direction was various. A tendency towards heightened expressiveness was inspired by northern engraving – particularly the work of Martin Schongauer and Albrecht Dürer (AIC4, pages 708–709; and see page 36): following the latter, Raphael set a prominent example in his image of Christ carrying the cross. The projection of space on Albertian terms and the proportioning of realistic figures accordingly may continue to provide the context. The contrary tendency towards abstraction from reality – or the antique – in morphology and scale may be complemented by the renunciation of *sfumato* in favour of clear linear definition and brilliant contrasts of colour asserting the member against the group in bold subversion of *concinnitas* (AIC4, page 737).

The expected is disdained: self-conscious virtuosity springs surprise from countering convention, from sophistication in the knowing breach of rule, clearly appreciable to those – like the artist himself – whose expectations had been conditioned by convention. The wit to do the unexpected, not merely to assert sovereignty over the rules, is the prime faculty of 'Mannerism'.

The definition of Italian *maniera* (derived from late-medieval French courtly *manière*) begins in terms of personal deportment. In *Il cortegiano* (1528), his treatise on the courtier, Baldassare Castiglione described the consummate ease of manner – both physical and cerebral – which the Italians call *sprezzatura*, in terms of personal superiority rather than inherited status, of assiduity in service, of consummate excellence in the field of war and at the court of peace, of self-confidence but modesty in disdain for pedantry and affectation – of art concealing artifice.

To the well-disposed, ingenious virtuosity (from *virtù*, 'excellence', especially in mastering difficulty) was the key to the stylishness of the age: sophisticated, effortlessly accomplished, disdainful of revealed passion, its typical, but not invariable, characteristics were grace and elegance, inimical to strain, to brutality and to the overt assertion of emotion. To detractors, on the other hand, vain virtuosity descended to affectation and contrivance, to clever technique and convoluted abstrusion.

Affectation and contrivance, disdained by Castiglione, were far removed from the protean imagination and subtle intellect which stirred the cross-currents of genius soon after the turn of the new half-millennium. However, both detractors and devotees of the 'stylish style' use the epithet too widely in defining an era which itself both deployed and disclaimed it. That the art which acquired the label may not easily be defined in the unruffled terms favoured by the devotees – grace, elegance, even *sprezzatura* – is clear from the outset in the extreme agitation, the emotional and physical tension, the disturbed psychology of the seminal early works of the first master of the new age.

MICHELANGELO'S MANIERA

The origins of Mannerism are, of course, complex but prime responsibility for taking Italian art off at a tangent from its High Renaissance sensibility is not implausibly assigned to Michelangelo. His wayward complexity of thought was unprecedented, at least among the moderns. With him, virtuosity in invention and technique, springing from individual genius, triumphed in promoting the sovereignty of the artist over convention. The constraint of conventional iconography, certainly, is already relaxed in the first of his rare panel pictures, the 'Doni Tondo', and in his iconic statue of David – both begun c. 1501 and completed some four years later.**0.2, 0.3a**

›**0.2 MICHELANGELO, 'DONI TONDO',** from c. 1501.

›0.3 MICHELANGELO: (a) 'David' (from 1501); (b) 'S. Matthew' (from c. 1503).

After the expulsion of the Medici from Florence in 1494, Donatello's statue of Judith and Holofernes was removed from the private garden of the Medici palace to the Piazza della Signoria where it guarded the door to the seat of the restored republic as a public image of the city's brave confrontation of overweening power. On its completion in 1504 Michelangelo's colossal 'David', originally commissioned for an elevated position on the exterior of the cathedral, displaced Donatello's work as an even more persuasive image of heroic resistance.

Bathed in the strong, clear light essential to the full appreciation of contour in Classical bas-relief, Doni's Holy Family is welded together somewhat playfully as the Madonna turns in elevating her son. That is theologically appropriate on both counts, of course, yet there is caprice in the torsion – certainly it demonstrated self-conscious virtuosity in challenging sculpture with paint. In further virtuoso display – but less precision of focus – is the iconographically eccentric but compositionally crucial frieze of nude models ranged across the middle ground. These were soon to be brought to the fore.

David and Goliath

The statue was commissioned for the façade of the Florentine cathedral: it was destined to guard the door to the Signoria. The presentation of the hero as a nude youth had Donatello's precedent but Michelangelo's exercise is certainly one of self-assertive *virtù*. Donatello's prepubescent boy is found at rest after the event, in Polykleitan asymmetrical balance (AIC4, page 684). Michelangelo's older lad loses that ideal balance as he withdraws slightly in anxious anticipation of the unequal conflict to come: cold marble had been imbued with such vital psychological intensity by no-one since the Hellenistic author of the extraordinary sculpture group of 'Laocoön and his Sons', yet to be unearthed (AIC1, page 495). Moreover, whereas Donatello's figure – like Polykleitos's mature athlete (AIC1, page 402) – is harmonious in his proportions, Michelangelo's is too large in head and hands, suggesting neither boy nor man but late adolescent still in the course of gangling development. The ambivalence of the work is its psychological dimension but physical peculiarities compound the impression.

'David' and the 'Doni Tondo' had hardly been delivered to their patrons when Michelangelo was commissioned to carve a set of the twelve apostles for the Florentine cathedral and to paint a battle scene in the Palazzo della Signoria. Only one apostle approached completion and only the cartoon was produced for the Signoria.**0.3b, 0.4b** Both took physical tension and emotional intensity to heights unscaled since antiquity – and, indeed, fully apprehended only on the discovery of 'Laocoön and his Sons' in Rome early in 1506 (AICI, page 495).

Michelangelo's battle scene was to have been opposite one commissioned from Leonardo:**0.4a** competition was never fully engaged. In conception, both schemes departed from the Classical tradition of the commemorative frieze. Leonardo surpassed antique convention in the depth given to his Anghiari scrum of combatants, tightly knit by glance and gesture but above all by its swirling momentum in *chiaroscuro*: the violent movement and heightened emotion may have been seen as anti-Classical by his contemporaries – still unfamiliar with the Hellenistic achievement – yet a moment of ingrained unity had been won from chaotic diversity by sheer virtuosity. Michelangelo, representing the Florentines alarmed from bathing at Cascina, also gives naturalistic depth to his stage but to centripetal rather than centrifugal purpose: he ignores consistency of scale – abrogating Albertian rule – and deploys his flair for contriving contortion in a catalogue of postures to fracture the composition of his actors in their moment of confusion.

0.3b
Departing from the ambivalent stance and psychological insecurity of David – indeed, also departing from the languid disposition of the youth second from left in the 'Doni Tondo' – S. Matthew reacts in physical and emotional unison to divine revelation as to the galvanizing force of an electric shock. It has proven tempting to relate the apostle's expression, awful in the proper sense of the term, to the horror of Laocoön – but the discovery of the latter and the abandonment of the former seem to have been more or less contemporaneous. Intriguingly, too, it may be noted that the youth second from right in the 'Doni Tondo' shares his pose with Laocoön.

0.4a

>0.4 CONTENTION AT THE FLORENTINE PALAZZO DELLA SIGNORIA: (a) Leonardo's episode in the Battle of Anghiari (graphic copy by Rubens after the lost cartoon); (b) Michelangelo's prelude to the Battle of Cascina (engraving after a copy by Aristotile da Sangallo of the central group of the lost cartoon).

If Leonardo's formal intention is directed to the illustration of an episode germane to the violent nature of the subject, Michelangelo prefers the demonstration of personal virtuosity in the representation of the male nude to ingenuity in distilling the essence of the battle he was commissioned to depict. However, it may well be observed that the establishment of a canon of physical perfection *in extremis*, even in capricious reaction to self-imposed difficulty, was as important for the future direction of art as the idealization of violence in overt response to the subject. The range of male nude postures was once again to be explored graphically – on the vault of the Sistine Chapel.

0.4b

>0.5 RAPHAEL, 'MASSACRE OF THE INNO-CENTS', drawn to be engraved by Marcantonio Raimondi c. 1511 (London, British Museum).

The new medium of engraving was developed by the Germans as a means of proliferating popular images but also for original expressionistic purpose (AIC4, page 708). Importation of the publications into Italy informed the High Renaissance with a starkly different dimension of expressiveness. The profits to be made from the medium also appealed to the Italians, especially of course to artists of limited original genius. Marcantonio was in the van of a considerable movement: unauthorized, he published works after Dürer; Raphael contracted to provide him with specially composed works to forestall similar pillaging.

Though neither of the Signoria commissions was fully realized, the preliminary drawings were to be highly influential – Leonardo on the masters of the style which would be called Baroque, Michelangelo on his more immediate followers who knew the work through engraving. Within a decade Raphael had offered a virtuoso synthesis in his 'Massacre of the Innocents': drawing for engraving, of which he was the Italian pioneer, he projects a pristine grid for the positioning and proportioning of his Classicizing cast, avoiding disparity of scale in accordance with Alberti; he effects corporeality with Leonardesque *sfumato* but, eliciting frenzied terror from determined malignity, he propels the figures in diverse directions like Michelangelo.**0.5**

0.5

0.6a

(a) lateral elevation drawing after the project of 1505 (Florence, Uffizi Gallery); (b, c) 'Victory' (after 1520; Florence, Palazzo Vecchio); (d, e) 'Hercules and Cacus' (mid-1520s?; Florence, Casa Buonarroti).

The 'Victory' is associated – together with the celebrated unfinished slaves – with the project for the tomb of Julius II to which Michelangelo returned intermittently after the pope's death in 1513 – as and when the huge pressure of other work for the Medici and Farnese popes permitted. An object lesson in serpentine *contraposto*, valid in all-round view, it is also a key exercise of such finely tuned *maniera* that the violence of the subject cedes – in a moment of stasis in a complex cycle of movements – to perfectly pitched harmony and its inherent ugliness to supremely idealized beauty.

Of Michelangelo's several works which might have been presented in this connection, the *bozzetto* of fighting figures identified as Hercules and Cacus is obviously most relevant – but controversial. Reassembled from fragments in 1926, it is associated by some

0.6b,c

0.6d,e

with the Medici project for a colossal sculpture group to accompany 'David' at the entrance to the Palazzo Vecchio. Given to Michelangelo c. 1506, the commission was redirected to Baccio Bandinelli in 1525, returned to Michelangelo in 1528 (by the restored republic) and restored by the restored Medici to Bandinelli who completed the work in 1534. Other commentators, assessing discrepancies of proportion between the model and the block of marble reserved for the statue, have associated this work with the tomb of Julius II – perhaps as a pendant to the 'Victory' – and dated it to the mid 1520s.

Michelangelo had left Florence – and Cascina – for Rome in 1505 to produce a tomb for Pope Julius II. That was beset with difficulties, not least of location in the Vatican basilica whose projected rebuilding was currently in flux: revisions and studies were numerous well after the pope had died in 1513, even though Michelangelo had returned to Florence to work for the Medici at S. Lorenzo – where he effectively began his career as an architect in 1519 (see pages 105f).**0.6**

Frustrated by the lack of progress on his tomb, the pope fixed Michelangelo's attention on the vault of the Sistine Chapel in 1508 and held it to the development of a fresco scheme unprecedented in vastness and complexity: the exposition of Genesis across nine panels, defined by illusionistic architecture and supported by prophetic figures, promoted all the dimensions of the most complex of styles, ranging from the dramatic expressionism of the narratives, to the penetrating psychology of prophet or sibyl and on to the self-conscious artistry of the *ignudi*. Wide-ranging in sedentary posture, the last are deployed to abstract purpose in resolving the vertical thrust of the painted architecture but, beyond that, they are not unconvincingly explained in reference to their author's poetic commitment to the belief that the beauty of human form in the ideal was the manifestation of divine grace – the oversailing theme of the cycle from the creation through the fall to the redemption of man (AIC4, page 823).**0.1**

Michelangelo completed his gargantuan Sistine exercise in four years. Less than half-way through that period Raphael began working on his fresco of the 'School of Athens' in Pope Julius's stanze: having represented Euclid as Bramante and made Leonardo as Plato central to the congregation, within two years he had inserted Michelangelo as Heraclitus (AIC4, pages 826f). That

completed the acknowledgement of his principal debts –
to Bramante for architecture, of course, to Leonardo for
compositional and psychological vivacity, and to Michelangelo for physical power and grandeur. Like Michelangelo, the young genius from Urbino preferred not to cede
the clarity of forms to *sfumato* until his late years. Indeed,
after entering the service of Pope Julius II he concerted
with Michelangelo in translating the linear clarity of
Florentine draftsmanship – *disegno* – into the graver
idiom of Rome.

Leonardo's achievement of atmospheric integrity
through oil-based *sfumato* was paralleled by the Venetian
school of Giovanni Bellini in its essentially painterly
approach to the manipulation of pigment – *colore*. The
key to compositional coherence, it was developed to further expressive naturalism by Giorgione (c. 1476–1510)
and, in particularly vibrant brushstrokes, by Titian
(Tiziano Vecellio, 1488–1576) above all. As we shall see, it
was peculiarly appropriate to the genre of the *poesie*
derived from Bellini's introduction of the atmospheric
landscape whose colours might establish the radiant, the
sultry, the melancholy or the ambivalent mood of an
Ovidian metamorphosis.

The relative merits of the two modes – the analytical,
precisely delineated clarity of Florentine and Roman
disegno, the spontaneous, evocative impressionism of Venetian *colore* – would be the subject of debate in artistic acad-
emies for centuries to come, their parts being taken
respectively by those identified as 'ancients' and 'moderns'
– that is, of course, those whose artistic impulse was governed by reason drawn from antique models and those
whose genius had freer range. Naturally, the combination
of the two would be seen as the greatest objective (see also
AIC4, pages 830f).**⁰·⁷**

**›0.7 ROMAN DISEGNO AND VENETIAN
COLORE:** (a) Raphael, 'Sistine Madonna' (1514); (b)
Titian, 'Assumption of the Virgin' (1516–18).

Vasari defined the Florentine/Roman mode in the
determined terms of *disegno*, meaning sound analytical and compositional draftsmanship. *Colore*, on the
other hand, is the substantive from which the Venetians derived their preferred alternative term, the
participle *colorito* which has the verbal advantage of
process.

The 'Sistine Madonna' was commissioned by Pope
Julius II for the church of S. Sisto in Piacenza (a town
newly acquired for the papacy). The cruciform matrix of
Raphael's astonishing icon (with the triangle formed by
the three heads establishing the top and side extremities of the Cross, the putti its base) is the key, not only
to the structure, but to the psychology and the symbolism of the work. S. Sixtus (left, and sometimes identified with the patron) is pointing to something which is
clearly disturbing both mother and child: long
assumed to be fallen man (for whom the saints are
interceding), it now seems that it was a crucifix opposite the altar for which the work was designed. Thus, if
the scheme as a whole prefigures the Crucifixion, the
somewhat bemused jollity of the putti arising from the
base may relate to the mystery of the Resurrection.

Commissioned for the high altar of the great Franciscan basilica of S. Maria Gloriosa dei Frari, Titian's 'Assumption of the Virgin' has to compete – near and far – with the glowing colours of the circlet of stained glass in which it is set. There is the semblance of acute-angled geometric structure and dramatic hand gestures assert the soaring momentum of the subject between the zones of man and God. However, the coherence of the highly charged composition depends primarily on colour: the gold of the glory to which the Virgin is destined – explicit in the church's dedication and reflected in the flesh tones of the radiant putti – fills half the canvas as a foil for the penetrating red and green of her flowing dress. That associates her with, and distinguishes her from, the principals in the dense mass of apostles from which she is impelled.

0.7a

0.7b

RAPHAEL'S MANIERA

Michelangelo shares responsibility with Raphael for the generation of Mannerism – the one primarily formative, perhaps, the other seminal. Beyond imposition of stentorian will, beyond virtuosity in exhibiting the anatomical and psychological complexity of humanity, after the example of both Michelangelo and Leonardo, and beyond the whim to surprise by knowingly countering convention, Raphael inspired the complementary Mannerist trait of refined elegance. Above all, beyond assertion of sovereignty over the precepts of the ancients, his ambition led him to exceed them in Classicizing: his was the consummate example of Castiglione's *sprezzatura* and *sprezzatura* took him beyond the ideal in painting and architecture.**0.8**

Raphael would be promoted to the highest papal office in architecture after the death of his master, Bramante, in 1514 (AIC4, page 840). A year earlier, his architectural personality had clearly emerged in the Chigi Chapel in S. Maria del Popolo. The great crossing of Bramante's Vatican basilica, revised on a comparable scale for the 'School of Athens', is here echoed in miniature: but architecture, painting and sculpture complement one another with an integrity that is difficult to imagine on the scale of the original. In accordance with Classical precept, the paintings and sculptures inhabit voids in the scheme of the structure but, magnificent though it is, the architecture would be incomplete without them because they are all essential elements of a coherent iconography. Beyond that, however, the mouldings which may well relieve a Corinthian entablature have slipped down to fuse with the capitals into an extraneous frieze.**0.9**

After the Stanza della Segnatura, while working for Chigi, Raphael continued to develop his architectural personality in epochal painting. In the next room in the Vatican suite decorated to the order of Julius II, the Stanza di

›0.8 RAPHAEL, 'PORTRAIT OF BALDASSARE CASTIGLIONE': oil on canvas, 1515–16 (Paris, Louvre).

Castiglione's celebrated *Il cortegiano* (*The Book of the Courtier*; 1528) was conceived in the Montefeltro court of Urbino which had been cultivated to an exceptional degree by Duke Federico (AIC4, pages 767f) and sustained by his son Guidobaldo (died 1508).

Pope Julius II visited Guidobaldo's court after crushing the Bolognese rebellion in 1507: Castiglione records a discussion between his fellow courtiers and their guests from the papal entourage of the mental and physical accomplishments of the perfect gentleman (the courtier) and published the embellished account in 1528. Not a little indebted to Cicero, the book was translated into all the major European languages and provided the basis for the formation of the gentleman for centuries to come.

›0.9 ROME, S. MARIA DEL POPOLO, CHIGI CHAPEL, c. 1513: (a, b) general view and detail.

In this miniature exercise in monumentality, pendentives carry the dome over the octagonal space in the conventional way, as in the 'School of Athens'. Raphael provided the richness of materials and decorative detail which his archaeological work revealed as

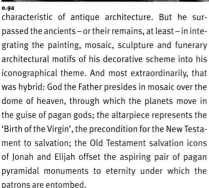

0.9a

0.9b

characteristic of antique architecture. But he surpassed the ancients – or their remains, at least – in integrating the painting, mosaic, sculpture and funerary architectural motifs of his decorative scheme into his iconographical theme. And most extraordinarily, that was hybrid: God the Father presides in mosaic over the dome of heaven, through which the planets move in the guise of pagan gods; the altarpiece represents the 'Birth of the Virgin', the precondition for the New Testament to salvation; the Old Testament salvation icons of Jonah and Elijah offset the aspiring pair of pagan pyramidal monuments to eternity under which the patrons are entombed.

Eliodoro (begun 1512), he upset the supreme rationality of the 'School of Athens' the better to communicate the sublime irrationality of a subject turning on the miracle of divine intervention. And that is invoked in a sombre space domed over columns contrary to the pendentive norm – and to the rational enlightenment evoked for the discourse of the assembled 'Athenians'. Irrationality with antique licence – real or supposed – is also provided to iconographic purpose by Raphael's representation of 'Solomonic columns' in his re-evocation of the temple as the setting for S. Peter's 'Healing of the Lame Man' in the series of Sistine Chapel tapestry cartoons produced to the order of Pope Leo X from about the middle of 1515.**0.10, 0.11**

Dynamics and the Temple

Heliodorus, commissioned to steal the treasure of the Temple of Jerusalem, was thwarted in response to priestly prayer and expelled by a mounted emissary of God: the energy generated by the praying priest propels the horseman and his attendants from centre back to right front. Julius II witnesses the dénouement across the plane but the two most prominent figures associated with his entourage direct their awe back to the priest. Albertian perspective provides the theatre for the event but the protagonists and their observers are not proportioned accordingly and the diagonal dynamic of the cataclysm divides the composition into three. Manipulation of scale for iconographic effect was a common device of anti-Classical Christian art, but to have the vanquished villain larger than the ministers of divinity was contrary to the conventions of both Christian and Classical art.

Anti-Classical manipulation of scale serves compositional purposes: the magnificent woman kneeling in the left foreground and the man peer-

›0.10 ROME, VATICAN PALACE, STANZA DI ELIODORO, 'EXPULSION OF HELIODORUS FROM THE TEMPLE': fresco from c. 1512.

The subject's raid on the treasure of the Temple was thwarted by divine intervention invoked by the high priest (2 Maccabees).

Francesco di Giorgio's S. Bernardino provides a precedent for columns supporting a dome but not without pendentives (AIC4, page 796).

ing in breach of decorum into the sanctuary from the pedestal of the column above her are the primary agents of unity on the left diagonal. Paradoxically, ingeniously, the figures most spectacularly anti-Classical in scale are the most Classical in derivation of form: the awestruck woman on the left recalls Michelangelo's Sistine Libyan sibyl but antique 'baroque' origins are affirmed by the recently recovered group of Laocoön and his Sons, one of whom was the model for Heliodorus (AIC1, page 495). There is virtuosity in the architecture too: Byzantium is recalled for the eastern style of the temple but it is Classicized inventively. Sovereignty over convention goes hand-in-hand with mastery of the antique – Classical and non-Classical.

The exploration of antiquity in his Classicizing mode led Raphael well beyond the canonical repertoire to a cardinal motif of the style later called Baroque. The quarry was close to hand in the theatre of his principal

›0.11 RAPHAEL, 'THE HEALING OF THE LAME MAN': distemper on paper, c. 1515 (London, Victoria and Albert Museum).

The image of ministry to the lame is the last in the cycle of four cartoons dedicated to S. Peter – there was a second cycle of six Pauline subjects – produced for tapestries to be hung below the suite of late-15th-century frescoes on the side walls of the Sistine Chapel.

preoccupation, the Constantinian basilica of S. Pietro: eight spiral columns screening the tomb of the apostle. Supposedly pillaged from the Temple of Solomon in Jerusalem (as rebuilt by Herod) after the future Emperor Titus had crushed the Jewish revolt of 66–70 CE, these informed Raphael's re-evocation of the portico of the Temple as the theatre of S. Peter's miracle in the tapestry cartoon. Giving life to dead masonry as Peter gave vitality back to the lame – the 'Solomonic' type was not unfamiliar to medieval builders but was first used wilfully to counter structural logic by Giulio Romano in Mantua – as we shall see. Kinetic energy, generating torsion no less than the diagonal dynamic of the force expelling Heliodorus, was to be essential to the style developed in Rome a century later.

By the time he succeeded Bramante at the Vatican, Raphael had acquired pre-eminent knowledge of antiquity through archaeology: in a letter to Castiglione of 1514 he asserted that, hoping to avoid the fate of Icarus, he aspired 'to find the beautiful forms of antique buildings' – the variety of which came as a revelation to him and his generation. Given official backing as *Commissario delle Àntichita* (1517), in the interest of preservation, he applied architectural method to archaeological purpose by recording ancient structures in plan, elevation, section and perspective with the aim of publishing a comprehensive survey.

The 'Incendio del Borgo', the main fresco in the Vatican stanza of that name, followed the work on Heliodorus after some three years: it is certainly no less significant in its architecture. It provides an invaluable record of the façade of S. Peter's Constantinian basilica (AIC1, pages 664–665). It provided a rich source of inspiration for the next generation in revising Bramante's Palazzo Caprini façade formula to incorporate the motif of an arch supported by a minor Order within a major one as the benediction loggia (AIC4, page 857). It is even more important as a record of archaeology informing its inventor's architecture – or, rather, urbanism.**0.12**

sustained but irregular medieval morphology is revised with redeployed Classical ruins.

In his comprehensive revision of the existing loggia – and Bramante's Caprini formula – Raphael recalls the Doric pilasters of his own Palazzo Jacopo da Brescia façade to frame the arcaded bays: the motif of an arch supported by a minor Order within a major one is usually known as the 'serliana' but Serlio (L' architettura, 1537–47) derived it from Bramante who bequeathed it to Raphael and his circle (AIC4, pages 837, 849, 857, and see below, pages 155f). The assertion of the horizontals in the courses of the protean rustication – without a relieving arch spanning the improbably split lintel – subverts the conventional articulation of structural forces.

In addition to the example of the moderns, particularly Bramante, and expanded comprehension of ancient practice, antique precept continued to inspire – especially as illustrated in the edition of Vitruvius published by Fra Giocondo in 1513. In the dado of the Stanza di Eliodoro – and subsequently elsewhere in the suite – the human figure was represented as a load-bearing agent in place of its conventional abstraction as a column from one of the Orders. Michelangelo condemned putti to ape Atlas in the architecture of his Sistine ceiling[0.1] and his slaves might have played a comparable part in the Julian tomb scenario. However, apart from the rich resource of antique

0.13b, c

0.13a

decorative motifs discovered in the cavernous remains of Roman imperial palaces, the immediate source for Raphael's Eliodoro caryatids seems to have been Fra Giocondo's image of the Vitruvian *persane*. Three years later, archaeology had provided herms as the inspiration for the Incendio dado.**0.13**

While furthering the embellishment of the Vatican stanze, Raphael set to work on decorating their extension into the loggias of the Cortile di S. Damaso. Leading a team of executive artists – trained as specialists in figural, abstract or illusionist painting – the master provided the design in whole and part. In the context of Bramante's pure Classicism here, he first adopted the antique style of ornament he had studied in the subterranean remains of the great thermae – a mixture of figural reliefs, Classical mouldings and stylized floral motifs often with human or animal forms incongruously sprouting from them, called 'grotesque' after their cavelike location. Under its Classicizing novelty, too, the main Vatican loggia reveals a new attitude to architectural morphology inspired by the operation of licence in the richly varied antique legacy. In the arcading of the inner wall is a series of pedimented windows: instead of an interruptive grand portal, a small door

›0.13 ANTHROPOMORPHIC SUPPORT: (a) Fra Giocondo's *persane*; (b, c) caryatids from the dadoes of the Stanza di Eliodoro (devised before 1514 when the main fresco cycle was substantially complete) and Stanza dell'Incendio del Borgo (from 1516).

Michelangelo had provided something of a precedent on the Sistine Chapel vault but the inspiration for the Eliodoro caryatids – probably realized to the master's direction by Francesco Penni – came from Fra Giocondo's illustration of Vitruvius's fanciful account of the origin of the caryatid and atlante as recording the condemnation of Persians to servitude by Alexander the Great's victorious Greeks. In the Leonine Stanza dell'Incendio del Borgo – again much realized by assistants to the master's direction – the caryatids have been displaced by herms extracted from the context of antique interior decoration.

Bookcases in the dado zone of the Stanza della Segnatura were replaced for Leo X with inlaid woodwork: destroyed during the Sack of Rome in 1527, that was replaced by Perino's extant grisaille frescoes with their caryatids after 1538 (see below, page 180). The dadoes in the other rooms, much restored, are essentially as Raphael conceived them in the three years to 1517. In the next two years herms appeared in the corners of his scheme for the Vatican loggia bays and in Peruzzi's Sala delle Prospettive in the Villa Farnesina (AIC4, page 859).

0.14a

›0.14 ROME, VATICAN PALACE, CORTILE DI S. DAMASO, begun by Bramante c. 1513, loggia decorated under Raphael's direction from 1518: (a, b) details of vault and of wall bay with door to the Sala dei Palafranieri.

The overall scheme of the thirteen vaults was designed by Raphael and executed largely by his assistants, notably Giovanni da Udine, Francesco Penni and above all Giulio Romano: the young Perino del Varga (born c. 1500) was added to the team on Giulio's recommendation and progressed from stucco work to narrative panel painting. The dominant *grotteschi* in the last four bays were clearly inspired by the decoration surviving in the Domus Aurea of Nero. The other nine bays each displays four Old Testament tableaux: these are represented not as a fresco in false perspective (*quadratura*) but as a framed easel picture (*quadro riportato*) set against illusionistic architecture open in the corners to glimpses of sky.

0.14b

breaches the base of one of these and pushes up the sill as its architrave. With one form penetrating another in this way, the Classical discretion of structural parts was rudely breached.**0.14** Raphael's playful approach to convention, his refusal to be awed by the greatest achievements of his master, was well demonstrated by his architecture at large, as we shall see.

0.15

›0.15 RAPHAEL, 'TRANSFIGURATION', begun c. 1518 and almost complete on the master's death in 1520 (Rome, Vatican Museums).

Far from capricious, Raphael's posturing and gesturing are as essential to the exposition of the subject as the Albertian grid which locates the proponents – as in his Massacre image.**0.5** However, it transcends compositional device for iconographic necessity: for example, while the monumentally beautiful figure of the woman in the foreground follows Alberti's advice in arresting us for direction into the scene, she also focuses the protagonists on their elusive goal; again, the silhouetted hands in the lower zone keep us at bay, externally, and indicate, internally, that even in the assembly of the elect it is Christ alone who can heal the breach between earth and heaven – and heal the deranged boy who seems alone to be aware of His transformation. Contemporaries claim that the picture remained as the dead master left it: modern scientific examination reveals that it was, in fact, never quite finished.

›0.16 ROME, VATICAN PALACE, SALA DI COSTANTINO: (a) 'Battle of the Milvian Bridge; (b) 'Baptism of Constantine' (Raphael, Giulio Romano and School; begun 1520, suspended by Adrian VI in 1522, completed at the behest of Clement VII in 1524).

Raphael was responsible for the overall scheme of the Sala di Costantino – his greatest in scale and complexity – and many drawings from his hand demonstrate his involvement in elucidating detail – at least of the Vision and Victory scenes on the east and south walls respectively. Giulio Romano led the executive team and presumably contributed to the elaboration of detail. Reference to antique reliefs – on Trajan's Column but especially on the Arch of Constantine – is combined with the inspiration of Michelangelo's command of human anatomy in general. In particular there are direct references to Cascina in the Milvian episode of the battle – but the complexity goes well beyond anything yet attempted in fresco by the older master – or anyone else. To complexity of content must be added complex richness of illusionism in form: the main scenes are presented as tapestries hung in the context of simulated marble and bronze and in startling contiguity with the simulated statuary of Virtues and popes

TRANSFIGURATION AND CATHARSIS

Increasingly preoccupied with architecture – and its Classicizing decoration (see below, pages 110f) – Raphael continued to accept commissions for both religious and secular paintings: many were realized to varying degrees by the

0.16a

- inspired by Michelangelo's prophets and sibyls. Both the visual richness of the conception – an innovative 'conceit' in the Italian sense of *concetto* or concerted theme – and the Classicizing intention of the adjacent Vatican loggie are furthered to unexcelled extent.

In the 'Incendio del Borgo', Raphael deploys antique remains in a context which had developed over the millennium between Leo IV and Leo X – the latter representing the former in a modern palace addressing the plausibly dilapidated scene of the eponymous ancient episode. Here in his last work, Raphael quotes meticulously from sources contemporary with the scene he is evoking.

0.16b

master's studio led by Giulio Romano (see page 111). The greatest of these were the 'Transfiguration' – the consummation of synthesis encompassing all the strands of modern painting – and the 'Battle of the Milvian Bridge', the central event in the cycle devised for the last of the Vatican stanze, the Sala di Costantino – the summation of his Classicizing powers. **0.15, 0.16** These two works – the one nearly finished, the other hardly begun on their author's untimely death – straddle one of the two poles between which Mannerism evolved in the figurative arts: standing at the other is Michelangelo's last great fresco, the 'Last Judgement' of 1534/41 on the altar wall of the Sistine Chapel. Neither admits of categorization in Mannerist terms but both offered rich resource to the Mannerists. **0.17**

In his last stupendous fresco, Michelangelo is self-conscious in his sovereignty over the conventions of spatial composition and the disposition of mass, as over the representation of the nude figure in a panoply of virtuoso

0.17

›ARCHITECTURE IN CONTEXT »FROM THE HIGH RENAISSANCE TO MANNERISM

Without the aid of an architectural framework –
God's House of Many Mansions, for example – and
reverting to the medieval technique of representing the
major players larger than the rest whatever their relationship to one another (in indeterminate space and
determined contradiction of Alberti), the sheer scale of
the exercise beggars comprehension – especially in a
work dedicated to architecture in context. Obviously,
however, the last trump has excited a cyclone which
whips the vast cast of saved and damned humanity into
circuitous tumult around the epicentre of the implaca-
ble Last Judge. The stupendous assertion of divine
power was never to be challenged but the no less stupendous assertion of the artist's sovereignty over the
representation of the male nude, in all its parts, was
soon seen as offensive to ecclesiastical decorum: the
genitals were covered in wisps of drapery mainly by
Daniele da Volterra at the behest of Pope Paul IV (1555–
59) – who pontificated during the penultimate phase of
the Council of Trent with notable rectitude.

The atmosphere of terrible foreboding induced by
deep depression, encapsulated in Michelangelo's
flayed self-portrait (right centre), has often been seen
in the light of his sonnet which ends with the lines:

> My face is shaped to strike terror.
> Precious art, once gratifying me with fame,
> Has reduced me to this condition,
> Poor, old and enslaved to others,
> I am lost if soon I do not die.

He lived to produce several of Rome's most important
buildings, as we shall see.

poses. The predominance of male flesh tones limits the
colour range but the rich chromaticism of the Sistine vault
– essentially structural and symbolic, rather than evocative of mood in the Venetian manner – was furthered by
Raphael in his major Roman works to complement the
complexities of posture. The 'Transfiguration' is the ultimate example on both counts: the splendid foreground
figure of Classicizing gravitas – recycled in reverse from
the context of Heliodorus – is the hallmark of *virtù*.[0.17]

FLORENTINE MANIERA IN DISEGNO

In the conventional genre of the *sacra conversazione*, stages
in the transition from Raphael's High Renaissance
achievement to Mannerism may be traced through the
comparison of three altarpieces produced within five years
of one another, the five years before the 'Transfiguration':
Raphael's own 'Madonna of the Fish' (c. 1513/14), his contemporary Andrea del Sarto's 'Madonna of the Harpies'
(1517) and the 'Visdomini Madonna' (1518) of Andrea's
pupil Jacopo Carrucci (Pontormo, 1494–1557). In the first,
the traditional calm symmetry is disturbed by the strong
diagonal momentum generated by the advent of the visitors from the left, returned in glance and gesture by the holy
pair backed by the solid authority of the Church. Andrea,
on the other hand, bravely eschews any physical or psychological interaction between his ideally beautiful entities, in their contrasting colours, but unites them in
symmetry, in rationally constructed context and, foremost,
in expressive engagement with us. Pontormo abrogates
convention in denying consistency of scale to his elegantly
elongated figures, obscuring the recession of their space
and somewhat disturbingly orientating them neither to
their observer nor to one another, except for the iconographically essential devotion of the donor's patron – and
the artifice of the holy hand gesture.[0.18, 0.19]

0.18a

0.18b

(a) 'Madonna of the Fish' ('Madonna and Child with
Tobias and the Angel and S. Jerome'; Raphael, 1513–14;
Madrid, Prado); (b) 'Madonna of the Harpies' (Andrea
del Sarto, 1517; Florence, Uffizi); (c) 'Visdomini
Madonna' (Pontormo, 1518; Florence, S. Michele
Visdomini).

0.18c

Mannerism in painting was at first essentially a manifestation of *disegno* – indeed it naturally transmuted into patterning defined by elegant line, enhanced by ravishing colour. Obsession with style was to eclipse concern with content but certainly not in the earliest works to encompass some of the traits of *maniera*. Thus, stylish elegance and wilful contrariness actually assist the eliciting of emotional and intellectual response at the highest level by Pontormo in his celebrated 'Deposition' of 1525 – which may be dubbed 'iconic' in both the traditional and modern senses of the term. Largely consistent in scale, though profiled against one another in clear light, the figures encircle an insignificant prop to the obliteration of rational space. However, uncertain standpoint compensates for the obviation of weighty *chiaroscuro* moulding in conveying the burden of Christ, on the one hand, and, on the other, the swooning of the Madonna. And the desolation of the grim scene, rather than deepened in Leonardesque *sfumato*, is heightened through irony – the disporting of joyful clothing in such a context, as though the players had dressed for carnival but were overtaken by the tragedy which their pathetic glance draws us to witness.[0.19a]

The contrast between Pontormo's masterpiece and the slightly earlier treatment of the subject by Rosso Fioren-

0.19a

›**0.19 MANNERIST DEPOSITION:** (a) Pontormo (1523–25; Florence, S. Felicita, Capponi Chapel); (b) Rosso (1521; Volterra, Art Gallery).

tino (Giovanni Battista di Jacopo, 1494–1540), another of Andrea del Sarto's pupils – is stark though both are spatially and structurally ambivalent: a base is delineated for muted mourners moulded in *chiaroscuro* but their feet are aligned on its edge, ladders are sent up for no-less corporeal protagonists but they seem to defy gravity in jarringly staccato disposition against the trabeation.**0.19b** And that is clearly contrary to the svelte fluidity and refinement which were to be accepted generally as essential to *maniera*.

0.19b

In Rosso's 'Dead Christ with Angels', painted in Rome some five years after his 'Deposition', penetrating *sfumato* obliterates the space beyond the frame-filling body but highlights the limp pallidity of death and the instruments of Passion which identify the subject; ironically, moreover, the *chiaroscuro* gave drained life to a model transposed from antique marble.**0.20a** Stylish, if not svelte, the work is *manieroso* in a mode quite foreign to its creator's friend and colleague: whereas heightened sensitivity informs the fluid artifice of Pontormo's 'Deposition' – and was not absent from Rosso's own rebarbative essay on that subject – here sophistication of form governs concern with content and the lamentable circumstances are represented

0.20a

›0.20 ROSSO, BRUTALITY AND THE EFFETE: (a) 'Dead Christ with Angels' (1526; Boston, Museum of Fine Arts); (b) 'Moses Defending the Daughters of Jethro' (1523; Florence, Uffizi); (c) 'Mars and Venus' (ink and wash, 1530; Boston, Museum of Fine Arts).

0.20b

0.20c

0.21a

›**0.21 AGNOLO BRONZINO:** (a) 'Eleanora di Toledo' (c. 1545; Florence, Uffizi); (b) 'Allegory with Venus and Cupid Attended by Folly and Time' (c. 1545; London, National Gallery).

The stunning clarity of Bronzino's mature style, inimical to High Renaissance *sfumato*, is demonstrated by his contemporary masterpieces in oil on panel: the new duchess's portrait and the allegory drawn with the connivance of 'Venus, Cupid, Folly and Time'. Mesmerizing in its ambivalence, abstracted from space, bordering on the surreal, its integrity of line serving brittle eroticism with porcelain sensuality, however, the latter is notoriously obscure of subject – and that was typical of later Mannerist painting. The following seems generally to be acknowledged: sensual love is personified by Venus and Cupid (identified respectively by the golden apple awarded to the goddess by Paris and the quiver of the boy who steps on the dove of love for good measure); these may retire to a bed of roses (strewn by Cupid's younger sibling, right, over the theatrical masks of illusion – or delusion) but are haunted by jealousy and deceit (behind the boys, left and right respectively, the latter with an innocent expression but wrong-handed) and overshadowed by time (Saturn) and truth (the last, top left, the least secure of the usual identifications).

only by the external symbols. Meanwhile, this capricious artist had taken the exposition of physical violence to an extreme of patterned abstraction in his 'Moses Defending the Daughters of Jethro' (1523): brutality is alien to *maniera* but not abstraction and the staging of the unexpected is typical – if not necessarily with the perversity of centring the composition on the hero's genitals.[0.20b] Stark indeed is the contrast between this and the paradisiacal 'Mars and Venus' (1530).[0.20c]

The principal Florentine court painter was Angnolo Bronzino (1503–72), Pontormo's pupil, who took Mannerism to its allegorical apogee, apart from evoking sumptuousness with unsurpassed clarity – which, ironically enough, derives from the study of sculpture ranging from the antique to Michelangelo.[0.21]

0.21b

0.22a

>0.22 FLORENCE, SCULPTURE IN THE
PIAZZA DELLA SIGNORIA:
(a) Benvenuto Cellini's
'Perseus with the Head of Medusa' (1554, in the Loggia
dei Lanzi with c), (b, c) Giambologna's 'Rape of the
Sabine' (1583 and 18th-century bronze reduction
respectively).

Following Polykleitos, the ultimate master of the
contrapposto mode, Cellini consciously emulates
Donatello's 'Judith and Holofernes' and 'David with the
Head of Goliath' but strips the one of clothing like the
other and, against the example of determination in execution, effects the transition to precarious vitality from
rest after achievement.

Giambologna consciously emulates the antique, the
later work of Praxiteles, Lysippos and their followers in

0.22b

0.22c

Sculptors vied with one another in elaborating the
ancient *contrapposto* technique to reveal characteristic
form not merely frontally or obliquely but all round – and
in the technical proficiency required to maintain both
visual and physical balance. Michelangelo set the standard
to be emulated in turning *contrapposto* to serpentine torsion – as we have seen (page 8). Most prominent in the
endeavour were the Florentine Benvenuto Cellini (1500–
71) and the Italianized Fleming Giovanni da Bologna
(Giambologna, 1529–1608), whose masterpieces are both
displayed in the Loggia dei Lanzi in Florence. Cellini con-
jures vitality from a transitory moment of instability when,
precariously perched on the victim, the victorious Perseus
raises his trophy aloft: rarely has the grizzly been so graced.
Forging his 'Rape of the Sabine' (1583), Giambologna's
brilliant resolution of the problem of perfecting asymmetrical balance in a marble group viewed from any angle
has never been surpassed but often reproduced.**0.22**

the 3rd century BCE but particularly the contortions of the Pergamene school represented by the 'Ludovisi' group (of a Gallic chief killing himself after having killed his wife, known in Rome through a 1st-century BCE copy now in the National Museum there) and above all by the great 'Laocoön and his Sons', recovered in Rome in 1506. Beyond the antique, the torsion of the Sabine rape was developed from Michelangelo's example: like the Madonna in the 'Doni Tondo', the 'Victory' in the Florentine Palazzo Vecchio seems devised to establish the primacy of the artist's *virtù*. Giambologna rose to the challenge: indeed, the subversive virility of his rapist – Romulus – demonstrates greater facility than any of his predecessors.

›0.23 CORREGGIO (Antonio Allegri da Correggio, c. 1489–1534): (a) 'Venus and Cupid with a Satyr' (1528; Paris, Louvre); (b) 'Adoration of the Shepherds' (1530; Dresden, Old Masters' Gallery); (c) 'Assumption of the Virgin', domical vault fresco over crossing, Parma cathedral (from 1522).

0.23a

PARMESAN HYBRIDS

Beyond Rosso's unorthodox Florentine circle, painterly style raised carnal sensuality to primacy in the work of the Parmesan Correggio. Responding to nature with consummate stylishness in a Leonardesque mode of atmospheric *sfumato*, he managed at once to promote sentiment without sentimentality, sensuality with uncontrived refinement, and elegance with apparently effortless fluency – especially in the evocation of the skin tone and texture of his mythological players in the bloom of their beautiful youth.**0.23a** Evoking the radiance of flesh – of spiritualized flesh – was his revolutionary achievement, most notably in the unprecedented literalness with which he responded to S. John's invocation of light as the substance of the divine.**0.23b**

0.23b

0.23c

Correggio's compositional technique, generating momentum along diagonal lines to engage the viewer, may be defined as proto-Baroque, rather than Mannerist. So too is his lighting – his sustained *sfumato* with which Florentine interests were soon to be in stark contrast. His contribution to the art of illusionism may be similarly defined, though of a higher order physically and iconographically: in the Camera di S. Paolo (1518) he opened oculii between vaulting ribs borrowed from Parma's great baptistery; at the epicentre of the vertical plane he spun his compositional lines into a vortex for the panoply of heaven and – mastering the foreshortened representation

The immediate – and not far distant – precedent for Correggio's illusionistic opening of the domical vault to the empyrean is Mantegna's illusionist vault in the Camera degli Sposi of the Mantuan ducal palace but the amplification of the medium was unparalleled – even in the Sistine Chapel. Raphael's limited excursion into the empyrean in the Vatican loggia shortly precedes Correggio's work. The simulated pergola of the Villa Farnesina's Psyche loggia is contemporary with the Camera di S. Paolo scheme.

0.24a

›0.24 PARMIGIANINO: (a) 'Frieze of Wise and Foolish Virgins', 1531–29 (Parma, S. Maria della Staccata, sanctuary vault); (b) 'Madonna with the Long Neck', 1534 (Florence, Uffizi).

0.24b

of figures from below (*di sotto in su*) – opened the domes of Parma's two greatest churches to the aspirations of the faithful in the congregation below.**0.23c**

Commissioned to decorate the vaults of Parma's third great church, S. Maria della Steccata, Correggio's young compatriot and probable pupil, Parmigianino (Francesco Mazzola, 1503–40), set a frieze of wise and foolish virgins dancing on the cornice before rich coffering: their fluid elegance is highly characteristic of his style.**0.24a** In his masterpiece, the icon of Mannerism known as the 'Madonna with the Long Neck', elegance is taken to an attenuated extreme and the worldly sensuality of Corregio's Olympians is drained from the sacred participants – especially the essentially human body of the naked Jesus prone on his mother's lap in stark *chiaroscuro*.**0.24b** The comparison with Raphael's treatment of the same subject is no less instructive but clearly Parmigianino owed more to Michelangelo, not only for the quirky background but also for the sibylline figure of the Madonna – though the attenuation purposely saps the power.

VENICE: THE APOGEE OF COLORE

Rosso introduced Mannerism to Venice with his 'Mars and Venus' of 1530 – a parody of sexploitation which could hardly be less potent than Correggio's exposition of Olympian eroticism. Not surprisingly the sensual Venetians preferred the latter: Correggio's painterly technique had more to do with their own sumptuous tradition of *colore* than with the clever complexities of Florentine *disegno*. Rosso took his new initiative to France instead and the Venetians pursued their native course to unrivalled achievement in all genres – most of it defying categorization in Mannerist terms. Though oligarchic, the Serenissima's republican constitution obviated the *manieroso* ambience of a princely court like that of Florence.

While Florentine painting was losing itself to abstruseness, the Venetians maintained their vibrant norm with rare lapses from immediacy. Under the direction of Titian, the secular lap of Venice's painterly course – furthering the evocation of the Ovidian *poesie* (AIC4, pages 830f) – took its naturalistic departure in parallel to Correggio, but descended from the feigned transcendence of mythological love to the immanence of gratification in the bedchamber and back again.**0.25a, b** On the other hand, if there is Mannerism in Titian's fecund response to the ethos of the *poesia* – a genre specifically invented to appease sophisticated court taste in its combination of the erotic and the erudite – it is in the virtuoso posturing of his players in unorthodox perspectives: his spontaneous, supremely painterly, ultimately impressionistic, approach was not finely calculated to meet a Michelangelesque analytical objective.**0.25c, d**

›0.25 TITIAN: (a) 'Danaë' (c. 1553; Naples, Capodimonte Museum); (b) 'Venus and Cupid with an Organist' (c. 1548; Madrid, Prado Museum); (c, d) 'Diana and Callisto' and 'Diana and Actaeon' (1556–59; London and Edinburgh, National Galleries), (e) 'Pietà' (with Palma Giovane, 1576; Venice, Gallery of the Academy of Art).

0.25b

0.25c

0.25d

0.25e

If Titian occasionally flirted – unhappily – with Mannerism in some of his secular works about mid-century, his response to nature, his ability to convey mood and express emotion are unsurpassed – as is the spiritual fervour of his greatest altarpieces.[0.25e] These last were approached in fervour, if not necessarily depth, only by Tintoretto (Jacopo Robusti, 1518–94). He may be seen as Mannerist in self-conscious *virtù*, especially in his secular exercises.[0.26a] Unconventional in composition, especially his dramatic, theatrically lit and sometimes erratic diagonals, he was certainly not Mannerist in the unrefined technique or the fervid content of his Biblical revelations.[0.26b]

›0.26 TINTORETTO: (a) 'Tarquin and Lucretia' (1578–80; Art Institute of Chicago); (b) 'Last Supper' (1592–94; Venice, S. Giorgio Maggiore).

0.26a

In his acres of religious work, Tintoretto (and/or his studio at his direction) must be seen as responding in good faith to Counter-Reformation ideals of decorum and direct spiritual communion which were quite inimical to the abstruse contortions of the latter-day Mannerists. On a very different plane, there is contortion enough in the vast panoply of figures congregated before Christ in the image of Paradise with which Tintoretto endowed the Grand Council Chamber of the Doge's Palace in reputed rivalry with Michelangelo's 'Last Judgement': reprovingly, he committed nothing to offend the post-Trentine sensibilities which masked the latter's multiple male organs in the most infamous exercise in bowdlerism in the history of art.

0.26b

If Titian catered for sublimation in an age of manifest decorum, Veronese (Paolo Caliari, 1528–88) staged the sumptuous display of that decorum. The *virtù* of the latter accords sublimely with the ethos of its age: in his great Biblical, historical or allegorical tableaux, Veronese distills the essence of the courtly ideal of *maniera* with gorgeous facility.**0.27**

After Raphael there was to be a bifurcation of the path in architecture, as in painting: one pursued by the devotees of the 'Ancients', the other promoted by the 'Moderns'. Leading the latter to the left, in the sophisticated subversion of Classical rule by sovereign genius, was

›0.27 VERONESE: 'The Feast at the House of Simon the Pharisee' (1570; Versailles, Museum of History).

0.27

Giulio Romano who took his jocular gravitas from Rome to the north: his impact was enhanced by the eclectic publicist Sebastiano Serlio but he was outlived by Michelangelo who translated his eccentricity from Florence to Rome and inspired the contrary movement. Leading to the right in the promotion of antique precept and the logic of structure – the rationalism of *disegno* in contrast to the emotionalism of *colore* – was Antonio da Sangallo the Younger: after his death, orthodoxy was most concisely articulated by Giacomo Vignola and even more accessibly by Andrea Palladio, neither of whom was entirely immune from the virus of Modernist genius.

Its paths bifurcated, 16th-century architecture may be defined as Mannerist inadequately. Elements of each are essential ingredients of the style which would dominate the 17th century – known as 'Baroque'. That is often defined in terms of opulent ornament, colossal scale, complexity, illusionism – all of which are germane to the era covered in this volume – but its essential characteristic is kinetic: movement in mass through the progressive projection of plane, articulated with an Order of progressive plasticity, or by undulation through convex and concave curvature – or, again, by the projection of propulsive perspectives on horizontal or vertical planes. The latter were forged from the diverse axes of the past. Producing a crescendo, the former was fully orchestrated only in the first Roman decade of the new century and it will be used as definitive in the transformation of the intricacies of our era into the overriding dynamic of the next.

0.28

›ARCHITECTURE IN CONTEXT »FROM THE HIGH RENAISSANCE TO MANNERISM

CONTEXT

The defining force of the modern world, which may be seen as issuing from the Renaissance, was the nation state galvanized by a centralizing monarchy. Essentially medieval in its emergence from the decay of Church, empire and feudalism – of the ideals of indivisible Christendom and universal imperium at the summit of a pyramidal hierarchy – it reached fruition with the renaissance of the antique ideal of commonweal and its translation into the terms of balance of power within a federation of different peoples, divergent in interests but common in culture. However, instead of the spiritual and temporal ascendancy of pope and emperor as guarantors of the moral orders of Christ and Caesar, hegemony in practice was the prize of the nation capable of asserting it by force. Machiavelli – with Guicciardini, originator of the modern science of history – clearly defined the new polity: indeed, his analysis of man as a political animal, his anatomy of constitutions, classification of governments, study of motives underlying public action and the causes of failure or success in the conduct of public affairs, exemplify the rigorous objectivity of Renaissance scholarship at its best – and most sinister.

With expanding secular literacy and assertive individuality immediately following an extended period of mass mobilization for ruinous war, political discontent was endemic by the early 15th century. It was stifled: as well as restored papal monarchy, the century culminated in the emergence of stronger monarchies in England, France, Spain and the other major Habsburg domains within the Empire (AIC4, pages 650, 818). The concept of the divine right of kings – derived mystically through unbroken lines of royal descent from the sanctification of the primitive king as the incarnation of a fertility deity – had long been invoked with varying degrees of sophistication by champions of the imperial power against the claims of papal pre-

Apocalyptic desolation, cryptically revealed to S. John on Patmos as consequent on the enigmatic 'Day of the Lord' (the Last Judgement of Christ at his Second Coming?), was widely expected in 1500: it came, of course, through human rather than divine agency, rending Catholic Church and Empire after the French rent Italy: the highly expressionistic late-Gothic style – soon to be superseded in the light of the author's experience of the High Renaissance in Italy – perfectly matches the Gothic horror of the mystical prediction. (On Dürer and the woodcut see AIC4, pages 708f.)

eminence: in modified recension, specifically in the confirmation by anointment that the birthright of the prince succeeding to a crown was God-given, it served equally to bolster the claims of 'national' monarchs against imperial pretension. Naturally, however, the idea met staunch opposition from national assemblies – as we shall see.

While conflict raged between Valois and Habsburg in the arena of Italian politics, and the standing of the pope was one of the main casualties of the ultimate imperial triumph, an even more damaging conflict had finally broken out in the Church itself. The bitter crop sown to sustain the restoration of papal supremacy in the mid-15th century, in the face of the humanist-inspired Conciliar Movement and its demand for Church reform (AIC4, page 259), had finally to be harvested before the new century was well advanced. Rome paid for stifling reform and western Christendom was ruptured: the nation state was further strengthened but the process was usually traumatic.**0.28**

POWER POLITICS

In the years around 1515, the principal *dramatis personae* on the stage of European politics changed for a new act. Pope Julius II died in 1513, having restored the Church of Rome to cultural preeminence, and was replaced with Giovanni de' Medici as Leo X (AIC4, pages 821, 824). Louis XII of France was succeeded in 1515 by his nephew François I. His English contemporary, Henry VIII, had succeeded his father in 1509 and married Catherine of Aragon. Her father, Ferdinand, died at the beginning of 1516 and was succeeded to effective power in Spain, Sicily, Naples and Sardinia by his grandson Charles of Habsburg in nominal co-regency with his mother – whose mental instability had forced her into retreat in 1509. Charles had succeeded his father, Philip the Fair, as titular duke of Burgundy – actual ruler of all the provinces of the 'Low Countries' (modern

›0.29 THE HABSBURG FRATERNITY IN BURGUNDY, SPAIN AND THE EMPIRE: (a) Duke-King-Emperor Charles V and his brother, the future Emperor Ferdinand I; (b) Isabella of Portugal (Titian; Madrid, Prado); (c) Anne of Hungary and Bohemia (Hans Maler, oil on panel c. 1518, Madrid, Thyssen Bornemisza Museum).

Isabella was the daughter of King Manuel I of Portugal: on the failure of the male succession with the demise of her great-nephew (and grandson), King Sebastian, her son, Philip II of Spain, claimed the throne of Portugal and united Iberia under his rule.

Anne Jagiello, the daughter of King Ladislaus II of Hungary and Bohemia (1456–1516), inherited the crown on the death of her twenty-year-old brother Louis II in 1526. Her marriage to Ferdinand reunited these two kingdoms with the Austrian archduchy.

The great trading towns of Burgundy – of the Flemish northern provinces especially – would be heavily taxed to fund the young duke's wars when, as Emperor Charles V, he was confronted with sectarian strife after the initiation of the Reformation – as we are about to see. That wealth had long also funded a court which, though ducal rather than royal, had been unsurpassed in opulence for much of the preceding century (AIC4, pages 242f). The splendour of Burgundian ceremony outshone its rivals in the estimation of its witnesses: indeed, the prestige claimed through the display of wealth was one of the main distinguishing features of the Burgundian court model as it had evolved by the end of the 15th century. Beyond dazzlingly impressive opulence and critical accountability, however, that model is often differentiated from its rivals, particularly the French from which it had derived, by virtue of its etiquette – the conventional rules of behaviour in respect of the privacy and security of a sacral ruler, the organization of audience, the service of the duke on dutiful display at table, etc. – which naturally affected the size and composition of the royal apartment.

Ruling over a disparate collection of provinces lacking geographical identity between France and the Empire, the dukes recognized an acute need to bind the regional elites to the court and overawe the restive bourgeoisie whose wealth they tapped. Hence increasingly intricate differentiations of hierarchy and commensurate degrees of privileged access to the ducal person: the process gained special impetus in 1430

0.29b

0.29a

0.29c

with the institution of the Order of the Golden Fleece restricted to knights who alone could fill many of the positions delegated by the four great officers of state – the steward, the chamberlain, the chancellor and the constable (AIC4, page 482), from the first of which the majordomo had emerged in overall control. Hence too part-time service to expand the number honoured. Hence, again, gradations of admission to multiple antechambers before the inner sanctum of the ducal bedroom and cabinet.

In attempting to define what was idiosyncratic of the Burgundian system – beyond the French legacy – modern scholarship has yet to determine conclusively whether its celebration by its familiars responded to qualitative or quantitative considerations. In any case, of course, there were equivalents in splendour, exclusiveness and chivalric aspiration: notably the Lancastrian court of England which the future Edward IV did little to diminish after he had returned from exile in Burgundy deeply impressed with the magnificence but also with the financial management promoted by Charles the Bold. More significantly, there was translation: the future Emperor Charles V had been formed at his grandmother's Burgundian court, sustained its traditions – not necessarily in disdain for those of his other realms – and imposed them formally on Spain in favour of his son Philip – as we shall see. From there a Burgundian-Spanish hybrid passed – in varying degrees – to supplement the local traditions of the Austrian Habsburgs, their clients or rivals, through affiliation and marriage.

Belgium and the Netherlands) – in 1506 under the regency of his aunt Margaret. He was elected emperor on the death of Maximilian I, his other grandfather, in 1519 – against the opposition of François I. His responsibilities were shared with his brother Ferdinand (AIC4, pages 248f, 821ff).**0.29**

The new emperor, who married Isabella of Portugal in 1526 with considerable political consequence, preferred his native Flanders and Spain to his eastern domains. He endowed Ferdinand with a vice-imperium based on the archduchy of Austria when he married the heiress of Bohemia and Hungary in 1521. Ten years later Ferdinand was installed as King of the Romans, heir to the Empire, but that was of fading significance in a Europe of nations contending with bitter enmity over Italy. With the failure of his grandfather's attempt to forge an effective imperial monarchy, the abstract concept of universal sovereignty had finally ceded to the reality of power based on territory – and through marriage Maximilian had ensured that his Habsburg heirs would have more of that than anyone else. Unhappily for Ferdinand, however, his major Hungarian holdings were soon lost to the forces of the Ottoman emperor Suleiman the Magnificent and his seat at Vienna was left dangerously exposed (AIC3, page 328).

François I, having restored French fortunes in Italy, exacted recognition from the pope and a concordat conceding him pre-eminence over the Gallican Church. In the attempt to mollify the emperor in return, he also called for a pan-Christian alliance against the Ottomans – not least to defend the Habsburg imperium in the east. Henry VIII, who had come to terms with France after a successful campaign, was induced by his adroit minister, Cardinal Wolsey, to espouse that cause. Peace was duly enshrined in the Treaty of London in 1518: the emperor came to Henry's court in May 1520; in June, Henry met François on the 'Field of the Cloth of Gold' in northern France.**0.30, 0.31**

His pacific professions notwithstanding, François launched a pre-emptive strike against the Empire. Henry supported his wife's nephew and an anglo-imperial force invaded northern France in 1523. There was little lasting profit for Henry but division of the French forces helped Charles: having consolidated his power over his dominions encircling France, he proceeded to drive the French from Italy during the brief pontificate of the Netherlandish Pope Adrian VI (1522–23) – who revived the attempt to deflect the energies of the contestants against the Turks but died without success mainly because it

›0.30 TRIUMPH OF FRANÇOIS I IN ITALY: Battle of Marignano, September 1515 (16th-century ms; Paris, National Library).

François I confined himself to reasserting his predecessors' claims to the duchy of Milan against the Sforza clients of the Emperor. His main adversary at Marignano was the Swiss Confederate allies of Massimiliano Sforza (the son of Lodovico il Moro).

›0.31 'FIELD OF THE CLOTH OF GOLD' (engraved by James Basire, 1781, after a watercolour by E. Edwards, 1771, after an anonymous contemporary painting).

›**0.32 TRIUMPH OF CHARLES V IN ITALY:**
Battle of Pavia, 1525 (engraved overview, Jörg Breu the
Elder, died 1537).

›**0.33 THE EMPEROR ACCOMPANIED BY THE
POPE IN CORONATION PROCESSION, BOL-
OGNA, 1530** (engraved after Robert Peril).

suited France to leave the Empire threatened by the
Ottomans in the east.

Fearful of the emperor's power, Pope Clement VII (1523–
34) – Leo X's cousin Giulio de' Medici – reaffirmed support for France. However, the latter's chief vassal, Charles
III, duke of Bourbon – appointed constable of France for
his service in the Milanese campaign of 1515 – had defected
to the emperor. The latter defeated and captured François
at Pavia in 1525, sent him prisoner to Madrid and exacted
a treaty renouncing all French claims to disputed territory
in Italy and the old duchy of Burgundy.**0.32** François repu-
diated the agreement on his release in March 1526, received
the assurance that the ceded Burgundians were loyal to
France and formed a new anti-imperial league. This
embraced the pope and the other leading Italian powers
and extended to alliance with the Poles and even the
Ottoman sultan who was then advancing through Hungary towards the imperial seat in Vienna.

Despite the emperor's parlous position in the north, his
forces advanced through Italy – under the command of the
duke of Bourbon – to chastise the pope: they sacked Rome
with appalling barbarity in May 1527. Henry VIII joined
the French in renewed war. Neither side could amass sufficient resources to pursue it. Negotiations at Cambrai
resulted in peace in August 1529. Charles married his sister Eleanor to François, conceded the latter's claims to
Burgundy but secured Milan for Francesco Maria Sforza
who married his niece.

Reconciled with the pope, the emperor was at last
crowned in February 1530.**0.33** The dukedom of Florence
was restored for Alessandro de' Medici, the illegitimate
son of the pope's cousin Lorenzo who was married to
Charles's illegitimate daughter Margaret in 1533. Dissolute
and tyrannical, Alessandero was assassinated in 1537 and
succeeded by his remote cousin Cosimo who was made

hereditary grand-duke by Pius V some thirty years later. Meanwhile the widowed Margaret was married to Ottavio Farnese, Duke of Parma. Mantua was raised to a duchy. Naples and Sicily had been Spanish – or Aragonese – since 1442, despite the French (AIC4, pages 652ff). Genoa enrolled its fleet in the imperial service. In decline, republican Venice had common cause with Vienna in the face of Ottoman aggression.

The Sack of Rome marked the end of Italian independence: Charles was master, Spain the principal beneficiary. The main concern of the administration was to protect its dominions (Naples, Sicily and Sardinia) and its clients, overawe the pope and suppress political and religious discord. But the conquerors – German and French as well as Spanish – were open to the cultural dominion of the conquered. And Italian culture soared from High Renaissance achievement to virtuoso mastery of its principles despite economic decline. The latter was caused partly by the political turmoil, partly by the expansion of mercantile economy and banking in central and western Europe, but above all by the shift of the main theatre of trade from the Mediterranean to the Atlantic at the primary behest of the Portuguese (AIC4, pages 250f, 488).

The Portuguese had penetrated east along the coast of Africa, the Spaniards west with Colombus across the Atlantic. At Tordesillas in 1494 the oceanic world was divided between them at the instigation of the Spanish Pope Alexander VI (AIC4, pages 248ff).**0.34a** Spain won most of the west without realizing that it was not Asia. Portugal's eastern sphere of influence was extended to India by Vasco da Gama in 1498 via a series of well-fortified trading posts. From their base at Goa on the west coast of the Indian peninsula, his compatriots quickly penetrated the 'East Indies' and reached southern China in 1517: by 1571 they had a string of 'factories' stretching to Nagasaki in Japan.

0.34a

›0.34 THE WORLD OF THE NAVIGATORS: (a) the 'Cantino' map of 1502; (b) Diego Ribero's map of 1529; (c) allegorical image of Ferdinand Magellan entering the Pacific Ocean from the straits of his name (c. 1590, from Theodorus de Bry's *Voyages*; London, British Library); (d) Portuguese in Japan (1593, Kano Naizen, Namban screen, Kobe).

Drafted in Lisbon, the so-called 'Cantino' map (after the commissioner) is centred on Jerusalem in accordance with medieval European tradition. It plots the Tordesillas line (270 leagues west of the Azores) which gave the 'Indies' to Spain. The shape of Africa is clear after Vasco da Gama completed his voyage to India where the earliest Portuguese bases are indicated. However, Asia is still hypothetical: there is no defined relationship between the western and eastern sides though the latter is speculatively represented as oceanic.

Pedro Álvares Cabral, en route to India in 1500, had made accidental landfall east of the Tordesillas line (on the coast which would be Pernambuco in Brazil). Dom Manuel of Portugal dispatched an expedition with the Italian navigator Amerigo Vespucci to explore the discovery. On the basis of Vespucci's report on the great extension of the new-found coast, the German cartographer Martin Waldseemüller published a map in 1507

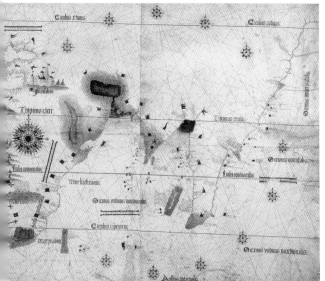

defining a new continental land mass with two (speculative) oceanic coasts and naming it America.

Ferdinand Magellan (c. 1480–1521), born in northern Portugal, had reached the Malay peninsula from Goa in the vice-regal expedition of 1511. Having failed to attract the patronage of Dom Manuel for a westward voyage in the Spanish hemisphere, he appealed to the King-Emperor Charles who equipped him with five ships (August 1519): passing from the Atlantic to the

The Portuguese navigator Pedro Álvares Cabral had landed on the coast of South America, east of the Tordesillas line, and claimed the land which would be Brazil for his king in 1500. To the north, west of the line, Diego Velázquez won Venezuela for Spain also in 1500: he went on to claim Cuba in 1511. Two years after that, Vasco de Balboa led the Spaniards across the isthmus of Panama and saw endless pacific sea. Ferdinand Magellan – a Portuguese sailing for Spain – found his way into and across the broadest of oceans, 1519–22: only then was the old world convinced that the new one of Columbus and his followers was a fourth great continent separating two great oceans though the southern landmass had already been named after its first coastal surveyor, the Italian Amerigo Vespucci.

By 1519 Hernando Cortés had embarked on the conquest of Mexico: a cathedral was rising over the cult centre of the Aztec capital by 1522. In 1532 Francisco Pizarro embarked on the conquest of Peru and the ruling Inca quickly fell to him – and to the diseases carried in his train (AICI, pages 322f, 342f). Except for Brazil, America was the preserve of the Spanish from Florida and the Mississippi delta to Tierra del Fuego by c. 1540.**0.34b** The settlers in the

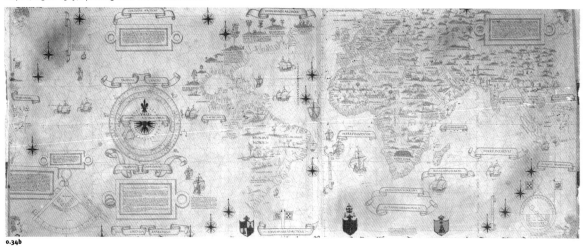

0.34b

wake of the Spanish conquistadors imported their own civilization – the worst and the best of it, of course – to supplant the less-sophisticated indigenous ones of under-populated America.

Mass emigration did not follow in the wake of da Gama to heavily populated India or China but more people were to travel between Europe and Asia than ever before. The transmission of ideas between the old-established worlds at either end of that journey was to be of considerable importance to the development of both. In the year of the Portuguese arrival, 1517, Ming China remained largely stable, despite a dissolute young emperor's wilful neglect of his responsibilities: despite a vigorous old emperor's assertiveness, the perceived profligacy of the pope provoked the proclamation of cataclysm in the west.

REFORMATION: ORIGINS RECAPITULATED

Disillusion and questioning sounded without and within the Church in the era of schismatism which issued from the Avignonese captivity of the papacy and its perceived degeneration. John Wycliffe (died 1384) maintained that legitimate lordship depends on divine grace and that papal claims to authority had no basis in scripture: he was soon followed by Jan Hus (c. 1372–1415) in Prague. Earlier, William of Ockham (1287–1347), pointing to the Bible as the supreme authority in Christendom, promoted the council of the whole Church as the supreme repository of Christian power. And, indeed, general councils were convened to address Church reform at various reprises in the 15th century. The challenge to papal authority was abortive in the short term but it reinforced the spirit of conflict with ecclesiastical authority among secular princes. Moreover, the failings of the councils frustrated the intellectual elite who had neither won the initiative

0.34c

Pacific through the straits which bear his name at the southern extremity of South America (October 1520), he died in the Philippine islands (April 1521). One of his ships (*Victoria*, commanded by Juan Sebastián Elcano), completing the western voyage home (September 1522), was the first to circumnavigate the world – though Magellan himself had passed through most of the two hemispheres in opposite directions. The conclusions were first drawn by the Portuguese cartographer Diego Ribero, working for the Spanish crown in 1529.

0.34d

for reform nor lost the critical spirit of their secular environment (AIC4, pages 234f, 252–261, 676).

Across the 15th century the critical study of ancient literature was broadened to include epic Greek as well as hitherto-neglected Latin authors – Cicero, for example – and extended, crucially, to the comparison of Greek and early Hebrew Biblical texts. Less secular in outlook than their Italian counterparts, perhaps, northern scholars tended to value antique texts primarily as aids to the progressive elucidation of scripture, to the reconstitution of a non-hierarchical Church on scriptural authority, to the resuscitation of early Christian purity.

The revival of the Catholic Church reform movement may not be disassociated from the humanist spirit of critical enquiry – and the printing press was important in setting the course which it was finally to take. By definition, however, that course could not be essentially humanist: the problem of co-ordinating the rational with the spiritual would exercise many great minds but definitive resolution was inevitably elusive and the dispassionate nature of humanism was a major casualty (AIC4, page 670).

REASON AND FAITH

Nowhere is intellectual and spiritual dichotomy – and its resolution – better demonstrated than by a digression into the future of scientific enquiry. One of the glories of the Renaissance, that was launched by astronomers in the spirit of dispassionate scholarship, indeed of antipathy to superstition and the blind acceptance of received ideas which exercised the radical Church reformers. The first major breakthrough was achieved in Poland by Nicolaus Copernicus (1473–1543): countering the prevailing view of the 2nd-century Alexandrine cartographer Ptolemy, of terrestrial centrality, elementary observation drew him to conclude that Earth was one of several spheres revolving about the sun (from 1513). A century later in England, Francis Bacon (1561–1626) was promoting induction from systematic experimentation as the sole means to knowledge. Tycho Brahe (1546–1601) and Johannes Kepler (1571–1630) in Prague were refuting the Aristotelian theory of the perfection of celestial spheres and comprehending the elliptical course of planetary motion aligned with the centre of the controlling sun. Then too, the Florentine Galileo Galilei (1564–1642) was observing the revolutionary course of planetary satellites and the imperfection of 'heavenly' bodies through a telescope of novel power (from 1610).**0.35** Adding that new dimension of verification to Copernicus's inductions, and articulating its defence with flair, Galileo earned proscription from the Inquisition and was forced to recant: at variance with scripture, heliocentricity seemed to deny the pivotal significance of God's manifestation as man in Christ. Yet in articulating the principle of force as the prime agent of mechanics, univalent and calculable, Galileo was hailed by liberal Christian apologists as having revealed the impetus of 'God's will': similarly, Kepler attributed all to the sentient being motivating the sun.

›0.35 GALILEO GALILEI instructing the allegories of Optics, Astronomy and Mathematics in the advantage of his telescope (anonymous engraving, 1656).

REFORMATION: ADVANCE

Beyond humanist rationalism, beyond assertion of sovereignty for the individual mind, Church reformers were, of course, motivated by many considerations – not least material. The cost of the Roman establishment to the taxpayer was a major issue especially as churchmen were the major landholders and claimed immunity from state taxation. And the rapacity of the papal agents ensured that the impetus for reform was boosted by the lower orders of commercial and industrial society, who bore the tax burden most onerously and who were now equipped to express themselves – and their nationalist aspirations – due to the great expansion of lay education.

›0.36 HIERONYMUS BOSCH, 'THE GARDEN OF EARTHLY DELIGHTS': triptych probably tracing the descent of man from 'Eden' to 'Hell' via the 'World Before the Flood' (c. 1505; Madrid, Prado).

Isolated in his Dutch provincial home town, the pioneering surrealist master (Jeroen van Aken of 's-Hertogenbosch, 1450–1516) provided this didactic exercise in the extreme manifestation of disgust with the world order on the eve of the Reformation: not a devotional image, it is a parody in the three-fold form of a panelled altarpiece and in the 16th-century Flemish iconic style of meticulously observed, etiolated realism (AIC4, page 706). Spheres float in a corrupting wilderness, even in Eden, and after the fall composite human, animal and/or vegetal forms – naturalistic in their parts but grotesque in their demonic transmogrification – are infused with visionary mysticism and the pessimistic essence of idiosyncratic north Burgundian parables largely incomprehensible to the post-medieval mind. Contorted realism damns in ugliness where the contemporary Italian Renaissance masters of anatomy ennobled in ideal beauty; where Italians celebrated civilizing potential, the instruments of pleasure – music in particular – are condemned by this prophet of Puritanism in the spirit of the strictest adherent to *Devotio Moderna*.

Universities were numerous by the beginning of the 16th century but more significant perhaps was information at the popular level which, naturally, promoted the vernacular and national identity. The clergy were the main purveyors of education but many charitable organizations were involved in teaching, not least under the auspices of the industrial and trade guilds, and it often began with vernacular Bible-reading in northern Europe. This was the concern of the Brothers and Sisters of the Common Life, for example: they instigated the new secular, individual, piety – *Devotio Moderna*. Suspicion of clerical institutions grew as books and preachers on popular piety proliferated. Unsurprisingly popular were mystical tracts: the most influential was *The Imitation of Christ* of Thomas à Kempis (c. 1380–1471) which provided a guide for the individual Christian mystically to accompany the Saviour in his mission through fervent study of the Gospels, prayer and

0.37a

contemplation of the Passion in all its brutality (AIC4, pages 256f). **0.36, 0.37**

With moral authority no longer the unquestioned preserve of the clergy, Church doctrine was debatable, especially the dogma of apostolic succession and intermediacy between the individual devotee and God. With preference for personal devotion over institutional worship, emphasis was shifting to service not office – office awarded on merit acknowledged even by the laity. A particular concern was the exclusion of the laity from full participation in the eucharist: this had been countered by the medieval establishment, especially after the promulgation in 1215 of the doctrine of transubstantiation – that the substance of bread and wine was transformed into the substance of Christ's body and blood in the mystery of Communion.

0.37b

›**0.37 IMITATION OF CHRIST:** (a) Grünewald (Mathis Gothart Neithart, c. 1470–1528), 'Crucifixion' (Isenheim altarpiece, c. 1515, Colmar, Unterlinden Museum); (b) Albrecht Dürer (1471–1528), self-portrait c. 1500 (Munich, Alte Pinakothek).

The imitation of Christ, at least in contemplation of his suffering, could hardly be more brutally served than by Grünewald's graphic depiction of the last extremity of a body distorted in torture – and the intense anguish it elicits from its devotees. Apart from the holy personages in attendance at the cataclysmic scene, these were specifically the patients in the Isenheim infirmary whose sight lines were focused on the chapel altar retable and whose suffering aligned them with their Saviour. The multi-shuttered construction, penetrated from paint to sculpture, takes the north European retable to its apogee of complexity: the contorted expressionism of the style is characteristic of German late-Gothic art, particularly in sculpture and in woodblock engraving (AIC4, pages 449 and 708).**0.28**

The late-Gothic German iconography of Christ – particularly as Salvator Mundi – is inescapably recalled by Dürer in a self-portrait which avoids blasphemy by overtly proclaiming that man is cast in the image of God and thus, through the contemplation of that image, contemplates God. It may well be noted that the sophistry of Scholasticism was anathema to the reformers in the age of the *Devotio Moderna* (AIC4, pages 252ff).

0.38a, b

PRIMARY PROTESTANTS

The cataclysm broke with the advent of Martin Luther in Germany but the Dutch-born itinerant Desiderius Erasmus (Gerhard Gerhards, c. 1466–1536) prepared the occasion.**0.38** He attacked superstition and worldliness and preached love, peace and simplicity of life as the true Christian vocation set out in the Gospels: he was committed to Church reform from within – to the irritation of many on both sides. He was the exemplary Christian humanist, reconciling the latter's anthropocentric motive with the theocratic imperative in the conjunction of faith and reason.

Like Luther, Erasmus was a pupil of the *Devotio Moderna* and matured in the characteristically northern context of Christian humanism which probed Scripture with the tools of Classical scholarship. Inspired particularly by extensive contact with his English contemporary John Colet (1467–1519), dean of S. Paul's in London, and with the Parisian Jacques Lefèvre d'Étaples (1455–1536), librarian of Saint-Germain, who presaged reformation in France, he turned back to the Gospel and the early Christian Fathers, subjecting the received Vulgate to comparison with original Greek and Hebrew sources – applying philology to the redefinition of Rome's fundamental tenets. After several visits to England, he spent six years there from 1509 teaching at Cambridge and preparing a

Greek edition of the New Testament which he published with his own Latin translation after his return to the Netherlands in 1516.

Exerting profound influence on the next generation of Protestant reformers, despite failing to join them, Erasmus and his works were condemned by the Catholic establishment as manifesting a dangerous freedom of thought. Yet, avoiding dogmatic denunciation of the establishment, he had promoted a personal religion, like the *Devotio Moderna*, but had not followed Colet in denying the priesthood competence to absolve sinners or maintaining that the eucharist was commemorative rather than sacrificial. His humanist belief that eloquent appeal against superstition and obscurantism would prevail proved vain. The alternative was force. The first blow was delivered in 1517 by the Augustinian friar Martin Luther (1483–1546) at Wittenberg, the seat of the Elector Frederick the Wise of Saxony (1486–1525).**0.39, 0.40**

›0.39 SALE OF INDULGENCES IN CHURCH: the pope as antichrist signing the sales note of indulgences (Lucas Cranach the Elder, woodcut from Martin Luther's *Passional Christi und Antichristi*, 1521).

Luther's mission

Protesting especially against the sale of indulgences by agents of the papacy, Luther initiated the Protestant Reformation in nailing ninety-five theses to the door of the church associated with the seat of the Elector of Saxony – who had banned the papal sales representative (Johann Tetzel) from his domain. The concept that, beyond mere temporal punishment, the pope could absolve sinners of their guilt for cash was naturally anathema to a preacher of S. Augustine's Pauline doctrine that man, totally corrupt, is redeemable only by divine grace – by faith not works, and certainly not by the intercession of priests or a heavenly hierarchy of saints. It was in accord with the Augustinian tradition that he expounded the doctrine of predestination: in contrast, Erasmus sustained his Catholic belief in free will.

Addressed to the German people and rapidly published, the ninety-five theses earned Luther enormous popular esteem in a country conditioned by anti-clericalism – in particular, antipathy to the mercenary Rome. Frederick the Wise supported the pastor who had brought notoriety to his new

0.40a

›0.40 MARTIN LUTHER: (a) portrait (Lucas Cranach the Elder, c. 1533); (b) Luther before the papal court in Augsburg (contemporary woodcut) .

The son of a miner, the young Martin was schooled by the Brothers and Sisters of the Common Life, earned a scholarship to school in Eisenach and progressed to the study of law at the University of Erfurt in 1501. Studying Latin, Greek and Hebrew sources of scripture, he abandoned law for theology and monastic servitude as an Augustinian eremite in 1505. In that circle, from which he emerged as a minister, he espoused the ideal that salvation is to be won solely through faith in Christ's passion rather than merit earned by good works or penance. In 1508 he was sent to Wittenberg to teach at the university founded by the Saxon Elector Frederick the Wise and took his doctorate after a year's absence in Rome (1510–11). Familiar with the works of the leading Christian humanists, past and present – especially Erasmus and Lefèvre – he developed lectures on the Epistles of S. Paul in part on the basis provided by Colet at Oxford from 1496.

Luther disseminated his Pauline thesis by publishing a sermon on the Apostle's affirmation that 'the righteous shall live by faith': maintaining that man's justification was to be found solely in divine grace, granted for reasons beyond human worth or comprehension, he announced a new evangelism. He acknowledged Hus as his precursor in the field and was clearly aware of Wycliffe. He was met with the Inquisition but its agents failed to enforce his summons to Rome. After refusing to recant at a papal court in Augsburg in 1518, he retreated into study of the papal claim to supremacy and demolished it next year in open debate with its Dominican champion, Johann Eck – not least in the light of the exposure of the 'Donation of Constantine' as fraudulent (AIC4, page 23).

0.40b

university and, with the elderly Emperor Maximilian fast failing, few in the hierarchy of Church or state dared counter a figure of potentially crucial influence in the forthcoming imperial election. In his tract *To the Christian Nobility of the German Nation* of 1520, Luther called for a comprehensive programme of social as well as ecclesiastical reform: the rejection of papal dogma and Roman rites in favour of evangelical observance and universal Bible study, the renunciation of clerical celibacy and the disenclosure of the religious orders the better to further Christ's humanitarian mission in society; schools everywhere for girls as well as boys, and parish poor laws. Complementing this, his pamphlet *The Babylonian Captivity of the Church* sustained the primacy of faith over observance and challenged the legitimacy of canon law. He reduced the traditional Catholic seven sacraments to three: baptism, confession and Eucharist. Rejecting the idea that the last was a sacrifice, he acknowledged the Bohemians (and Greeks) as orthodox in permitting the laity to communicate *sub utraque specie* ('in both kinds', bread and wine). After Wycliffe, he denied transubstantiation yet continued to maintain that the divine is ubiquitous, hence present in the bread and the wine as in the glorified body of Christ (AIC4, pages 252, 675f).

To much popular acclaim in Germany, before 1520 was out Luther had burnt a papal bull of excommunication condemning propositions attributed to him. His popularity earned him an imperial safe conduct to examination before the Diet of Worms in 1521, despite papal interdiction. He refused to recant there in the absence of scriptural testimony to error in his theses. Commitment to the primacy of faith and the sufficiency of grace in individual interpretation of scripture led him on to question the infallibility of Church councils and at that the emperor called a halt: Charles of Habsburg reasserted the supreme authority of council – not pope – but was bound to defend a millennium of Catholic orthodoxy against the private judgement of one friar – and reject the implication that the individual conscience was superior in moral authority to canon law.

Condemned as a heretic by the Edict of Worms but still under safe conduct, Luther retired to Wartburg at the behest of the Elector Frederick. There for nearly a year, he achieved the greatest monument of his Reformation: a German New Testament based on Erasmus's revised Greek version.

While Luther was preoccupied with his vernacular scripture, fundamentalist evangelical groups emerged to the detriment of his movement: to his dismay and vehement opposition, their radicalism issued in the anarchy of peasant revolt in 1524. However, disenchantment in the countryside was more than offset by admiration in the towns: their councils were as unenthusiastic about any manifestation of proletarian anarchy as they were about offending the emperor but shared Luther's ideals and saw solidarity behind him as a manifestation of independence from the imperial establishment. The ranks of Lutheran princes were swelling too: the heirs of Frederick the Wise, electors of Saxony from 1525 to 1554, were among the most powerful but so too was Philip of Hesse (1504–67), who played a leading part in crushing the peasant rebellion with Luther's support, and Albert of Hohenzollern (1490–1545), last grand-master of the Teutonic Order, who forged its territory into the Duchy of Prussia.**0.41, 0.42**

The majority of Germans remained Catholic but the orthodox establishment could as yet do little to stem the tide: the papacy was impotent under Clement VII; the emperor had instituted repression in his Netherlandish domains but he was too preoccupied with France in Italy to face the far more massive problem of imposing his will on Germany and his brother Ferdinand faced obliteration by the Turks at the gates of Vienna. The Catholic princes

0.41

›0.41 THREE ELECTORS OF SAXONY: Frederick the Wise (1486–25), John the Steadfast (1525–32), John Frederick the Magnanimous (1532–47) against the Elbe at Wittenberg (c. 1535, Lucas Cranach the Elder; Nuremberg, National Germanic Museum).

Saxony had been divided in 1485 between Ernestines (in most of the duchy of Saxe-Wittenberg and southern Thuringia) and the Albertines (in northern Thuringia and Dresden-Meissen-Leipzig). To rival the eminent university in the latter seat, Ernestine Frederick the Wise founded the University of Wittenberg in 1502: with the patronage of an enlightened prince, it became a crucible for religious reform. Frederick secured Luther's representation at Worms and protected him from the Edict which he did not enforce in Saxony. His successor earned his nickname by keeping faith with his brother's Lutheranism in his short reign: he established it as the state confession in Ernestine Saxony (1527). A regular correspondent with Luther, John Frederick reinforced the authority of the state Church: as we shall see, he built Germany's first significant specifically Lutheran church in his castle at Torgau and was a staunch supporter of Lutheran princely alliance.

›0.42 EMPEROR CHARLES V, c. 1530: (a) allegory with ideally defeated enemies (left to right), Sultan Suleiman, Pope Clement VII, François I, the Duke of Cleves, the Duke of Saxony and the Landgrave of Hesse (after Giulio Clovio); (b) 'Charles V with Hound' (Jacob Seisenegger; Vienna, Art-Historical Museum).

therefore formed themselves into an offensive league in July 1525 and Philip of Hesse responded by forming a defensive one which offered adherents the attractive promise of material gain from the secularization of monasteries.

Accord eluded a diet at Augsburg in late-1525 but next year at Speyer, under the shadow of the Turks threatening Vienna, freedom of conscience in matters of faith was conceded to each prince. This was denied when the emperor's fortunes recovered. Protest was lodged in 1529 at Speyer, the Protestants giving the reform movement its name.

Under imperial ban, Luther was represented at the Diet of Augsburg in 1530 by his deputy Philip Melanchthon who, more conciliatory than his master might have been, used the occasion to promote compromise with Rome: his Confession of Augsburg summarized Lutheran beliefs without specific denial of seven sacraments, transubstantiation, papal supremacy or even the validity of indulgences. Seeing this as a sign of weakness, however, the pope proved obdurate even in the face of the emperor's call for another general Church council.

Under the circumstances, the leading Lutheran princes, Saxony and Hesse, met at Schmalkalden in Thuringia to confirm their association in an armed league open to supporters of the Confession of Augsburg which they dedicated themselves to promoting (1531). They were joined by the rulers of Anhalt and Württemberg: the adherence of the majority of free imperial cities was led by Hanover, Frankfurt, Augsburg and Kempten in 1535. In that year, the ostensibly defensive complexion changed with the temporary adherence of France: Denmark followed in 1538, Brandenburg in 1539, the elector palatine in 1545.

Wary of Habsburg ambitions, meanwhile, the southern Catholic princes proved unready to enter the fray. With the emperor preoccupied by Ottoman aggression in the east, a truce had been called at Nuremberg in 1532, guaranteeing Protestant security until the convention of a general council. However, Clement VII was in no hurry to convene a body which would eclipse his authority.

REFORMATION ABROAD

The advance of the Reformation depended on politics and economics at least as much as on conscience and conviction. Dedicated to the ideal of restoring a united Europe under his Habsburg dynasty, Emperor Charles V was naturally the enemy of the enemies of Catholicism though, of course, the reformers saw themselves as restoring the supreme spiritual bonding agent. The lesser rulers – within and beyond the Empire – inevitably saw the Reformation in national terms, as a vehicle propelling them to independence of pope, emperor and, often, of a local establishment dominated by their rivals. That was the case in Saxony, where the conversion of the Albertine successors to Duke George from 1539 was a major Lutheran coup, and in Scandinavia where new kings were confronted by entrenched bishops and discontent with clerical extortion was sharpened by the readiness of the nobility to sell its support for confiscated monastic lands.

After the imperial truce of Nuremberg in 1532, the advance of Lutherism was impressive, not least due to missionaries from Wittenberg enthusiastically received by German trading communities round the Baltic. Of great significance was the tolerance of the elector of Brandenburg, whose eastern expansion was merchant-led: so too was the Protestantism of his relative, Albert of Hohenzollern who had made himself Duke of Prussia. Across the Baltic, national Lutheran Churches were established at the end of the 1530s in the united Danish-Norwegian kingdom and in Sweden. By then, too, Reformation was under way in England – taking a peculiar course at the behest of an essentially Catholic king, as we shall see.

›0.43 DESTRUCTION OF CHURCH IMAGES IN ZURICH (ms of 1524; Zurich, Central Library).
Ulrich Zwingli's rejection of episcopal authority was followed by the removal of images from churches, then by the disendowment of the monasteries and the arrogation of their assets to schools for the poor. Opposition from conservative rural cantons led to armed conflict in 1529 and Zwingli fell in battle at Kappel in 1531. The subsequent peace granted each canton freedom of choice in religion.

›0.44 ORIGINAL SIN: 'Adam and Eve' (Jan van Scorel, c. 1527; Haarlem, Frans Hals Museum).

The Bible begins the history of man with the fall through his original sin in defying God and it is in scripture – in the vernacular – that the strictest reformers find the sole path to redemption.

Scorel was born in 1495 in Schoorl, near Alkmaar. After apprenticeship with the Haarlem painter Cornelis Willemsz, he entered the studio of Jacob Cornelisz van Oostsanen in Amsterdam (1512): he was also registered in Utrecht as a pupil of Jan Mabuse who had visited Italy (1508–09) and returned to late-Gothic Flanders with an overtly Italianate style (AIC4, page 707). He went to Italy via Austria in 1518: among the first northern Netherlandish artists to study the High Renaissance masters of Venice and Rome, from 1522 he was retained by the Dutch Pope Adrian VI as curator of antiquities at the Vatican and recorded the extent of the great building works there. He made a pilgrimage to the Holy Land. He returned to Utrecht, entered the Church but maintained an extensive practice in which he introduced Italianate style to Dutch painting. His erstwhile pupil/colleague Martin van Heemskerck followed him to Rome where he made invaluable records of progress on great buildings – as we shall see.

ZWINGLI AND THE SWISS

Meanwhile in Switzerland, free of the Empire since 1499, there was much sympathy with the aspirations of Erasmus. A line of would-be reformers from Basel and Zurich led to Ulrich Zwingli (1484–1531), who is widely credited with initiating the Swiss Reformation in a series of evangelical sermons heavily indebted to the Erasmian Testament. Inspired by Luther in his opposition to the rule of canon law, he was prestigious enough by 1522 to prompt Zurich's city council to reject episcopal authority, remove images from churches and disendow monasteries.**0.43** In 1529 Catholic worship was proscribed but the mass had already been replaced in Zurich with Zwingli's Order of Communion: certainly not a sacrifice, this was presented as a commemoration in which the laity partook of both bread and wine. The difference with Luther over the nature of the latter proved irreconcilable.

CALVIN AND THE FRENCH

In 1530, while Zwingli and his radical urban followers were engaged in armed conflict with rural conservatives, the citizens of Geneva rebelled against their prince-bishop: they established an independent republic allied with Bern and declared for the reformed religion. In 1534 they provided the stage for a crucial new player, John Calvin (1509–64), who had fled from repression in France ready to promote a revised faith in redemption from original sin.**0.44**

In France, the ground for Reformation had been prepared by Jacques Lefèvre d'Étaples, whose commentaries on the Pauline epistles of 1512 anticipated much of Luther's evangelism and who produced a French New Testament twelve years later: his work was burned. Yet the king was ambivalent towards the Reformation: as unready as the emperor to admit the claims of personal judgement against those of established authority, he oscillated between the repression of Lutherans at home and the wooing of them abroad as anti-imperial allies. In 1534, however, Paris was placarded with tracts against the mass and popular outrage provoked repression. It was this which sent John Calvin, a radical ecclesiastical lawyer swayed by Lefèvre, to Switzerland.**0.45**

Calvin's mission

In his *Institutio Christianae Religionis* (*Institutes*), produced in Basel in 1536, Calvin went further than his predecessors in the clear ordering of Protestant thought. Man's wisdom can encompass only knowledge of himself and of God: contrary to the former, gleaned from observation of this world, the only way to the latter is through scripture. The certain knowledge of God in Christ is faith and only in this, through concomitant repentance, is man redeemed from the original sin bequeathed by Adam: his salvation predestined by God, man's justification is by faith alone.

The exposition of the Augustinian theme of the inscrutable omnipotence of God, determining the will of man, is shared with Luther as is faith solely in the gospel of Christ's saving mission. The guidance of the Church is not renounced – only the corruption of the path – but the need is seen for varied ways for various peoples. Luther is preferred to Zwingli but mediation between their positions on the doctrine of transubstantiation produced the proposition that the divine spirit does not imbue the physical substance of bread and wine but is communicated simultaneously in the mystery of the eucharist. Zwingli's followers accepted this subtlety but Luther did not.

In Geneva in 1541, Calvin was accorded control of the reformed Church. He then spent a decade developing his puritanical rule for the establishment of a model Protestant community pursuing the good, not in the belief that grace could be earned but as a sign that it had been disposed – and with strictly limited scope for free enquiry and none for frivolity. Though demanding the separation of Church and state, he endorsed civil government as divinely commissioned to enforce Christian morality. And in Geneva the ministers of his order dominated political, ecclesiastical and social life not without internal opposition but with decisive support from the swelling community of refugees. No fun, life in that quasi-theocratic

0.45a

›0.45 CALVIN AND HIS REFORMED CHURCH: (a) engraved portrait, (b) followers in context.

Son of a notary acting for the cathedral of Noyon, John Calvin (1509–64) first studied theology and philosophy in Paris. In 1528 he abandoned his plan to enter the priesthood in favour of studying law at Orléans and Bourges where he was taught Greek by the pro-Lutheran Swiss jurist Wolmar. In 1532 he abandoned law for Classical studies: the next year he converted to 'Protestantism' and joined Lefèvre back in Paris. He left France for Basel after the incident of the placards in 1534. Invited to Geneva by local reformers in 1536, he was expelled by the city council and proceeded to Strasbourg where he set up a church for French Protestant refugees. He was soon called back to develop his model reformed church in Geneva where he regularly preached. In addition to the *Institutes*, he wrote commentaries on most books of the Bible as well as theological treatises and confessional documents.

Refuting the pretensions of the papacy, he claimed that he and his fellow reformers were not schismatic but dedicated to the revival of the true Catholic Church – the body of the faithful in Christ. In the present day, long after its preparation by prophets and proclamation by apostles and evangelists, its necessary officers were only pastors (to preach) and doctors (to instruct) supplemented by elders (for the discipline of the congregation) and deacons (for ministry to the needy). The seven sacraments of Rome are reduced to two: baptism and eucharist.

The priest discounted as mediator, the altar at which the Roman rite had him officiating is displaced as the focus of the Calvinist service by the pulpit from which the word of God is proclaimed directly to the laity – with suitable commentary, of course. Strictly observing the commandments issued to Moses, the Calvinist Church bans images – not only of irrelevant saints, but especially of the only divinity – and focuses instead on tablets inscribed with those commandments.

0.45b

community was unrivalled in security – except for nonconformists. And the Calvinists did not fail to advertise their puritanical virtue abroad.

Within a decade of its publication Calvin's *Institutio* was burned in France and so too were many of its adherents (known as Huguenots). However, despite proliferating condemnation by special anti-heretical courts under the auspices of the *parlements* of Paris and the provinces, Calvinism spread among the bourgeoisie and even to the ruling class early in the reign of Henri II (1543–59). The ensuing cataclysm shook the French monarchy to its foundations.

Calvinism quickly took firm hold on the strong merchant class in the rich trading cities of the Netherlands. The emperor's Burgundian provinces – mainly imperial fiefs which he expanded, consolidated under rationalized administration – were encouraged in their industry but generally disaffected by insatiable taxation demands to pay for the incessant imperial wars. Like self-made men elsewhere, many of the most prominent citizens inclined to Protestantism and its concomitant political protest. However, though heresy was condemned, the regime was generally moderate until Ghent rebelled against imperial taxation in 1540 and paid a heavy price in fines and lost liberties: worse was to follow in the next reign.

Calvinism appealed to the bourgeoisie of north-west Europe, unsurprisingly, but it also won converts from the landed classes in central Europe and Poland. Its first significant princely gain in Germany was the elector palatine Frederick III in 1563: Saxony followed later in the century, Brandenburg early in the next. Meanwhile, in 1560, John Knox had introduced his version to Scotland where it would be dominant as Presbyterianism. At mid-century it was already making converts in England, especially at the great universities.

0.46a

0.46b

0.46c

0.46d

THE PECULIARITY OF ENGLAND

In England – which may claim to have been the progenitor of Reformation through Wycliffe and Colet (AIC4,
pages 234f) – economic and political expediency combined with doctrinal dispute to force change on a largely
apathetic populace, conventional in its religious obser-
vances, at the instigation of a conservative king who was
obsessed with the problem of dynastic succession but no
more keen to license freedom of thought against orthodoxy than the emperor or the king of France.**0.46** Yet, like
their continental contemporaries, the English were
increasingly critical of clerical shortcomings with the
advancement of lay education and they were no less resent-
ful than Germans or Scandinavians at the exactions of a

0.46e

**›0.46 THE PRINCIPALS IN THE QUEST FOR
TUDOR SUCCESSION:** (a) King Henry VIII (c 1537,
Hans Holbein the Younger; Rome, National Gallery of
Art); (b–d) Queen Catherine of Aragon, her successor,
Anne Boleyn, and her successor, Jane Seymour (anony-
mous, after Holbein); (e) Chancellor Cardinal Thomas
Wolsey (c. 1520, anonymous; London, National Portrait
Gallery); (f, g) Chancellors Thomas More and Thomas
Cromwell (chalk, c. 1526 and c. 1540 respectively,
Hans Holbein the Younger and school; Windsor, Royal
Collection).

Patronage proving sparse for German Protestant
artists in the era of contention centred on the Diets
of Augsburg, many emigrated in search of work:
born in Augsburg, active in Basel where he displaced
Matsys in the circle of Erasmus, Holbein (c. 1497–1543)
was in England from 1526–28 and again definitively
from c. 1532. The impact on the prevailing vernacular of
his incisive style, commanding of depth in perspective
and the *sfumato* of simulated relief as in psychological
penetration, is immediately manifest in the range of
royal portraits illustrated here: beyond that, displayed
in sumptuous fabrics with consummate skill exceeding
even that of his Flemish mentors, his variation on the
hieratic, yet virile, image of the king constitutes an icon
of monarchy which remains unsurpassed.

0.46f, g

rapacious Church or the precedence asserted for ecclesiastical jurisdiction over common law.

In the age of Luther, whose teaching infiltrated Oxford
and Cambridge and was soon adopted by London merchants with continental connections, the English reform
movement was assumed by William Tyndale (1494–1536):
he graduated from Oxford in 1515 but moved to the circle
of Erasmus in Cambridge before entering the Augustinian order. Viewed as heretical, he resorted to Germany
where he had translated the New Testament into English
by 1525: deemed seditious, it was suppressed and its author
succumbed to condemnation for heresy in 1536. By then,
however, the king's position had altered: in Germany
Reformation naturally appealed to the independently
minded prince; in England it appealed to an essentially
Catholic prince who wanted his own way on marriage in
his hope for a male heir – a way blocked by the pope under
the influence of the emperor.

Reformation of the 'Fidei Defensor'

Accorded the title of 'Defender of the Faith' by the pope for writing a repost
to Lutheranism in 1521, Henry VIII found himself forced into the radical
camp. The queen, Catherine of Aragon (1485–1536) – the emperor's aunt
who had first married Henry's older brother – had reached her mid-forties
after producing a daughter but not the male heir demanded by contemporary conceptions of national security. The king petitioned the pope for an
annulment in 1529 on the grounds that his marriage to his brother's wife
was uncanonical. Clement VII prevaricated before the risk of offending his
master the emperor and that prompted Henry to question papal supremacy
– which, of course, was a basic theme of the Protestant Reformation.

The king and his intended new queen, Anne Boleyn, who had developed evangelical sympathies while studying in France, entrusted their
cause to the wily lord chancellor, Cardinal Wolsey, but he failed and fell.
So too did his conservative Catholic replacement, Sir Thomas More.
Three years later the frustrated king, encouraged by scholars set to

quarry justification for his case, asserted supremacy over the Church in England and required the submission of the clergy. More resigned and was replaced by the pragmatic, reformist politician Thomas Cromwell (c. 1485–1540).

Legislation restraining appeal to Rome was enacted by parliament in February 1533 and in March a new archbishop of Canterbury, the reformist scholar Thomas Cranmer (1489–1556), prevailed upon the convocation of clergy to pronounce the king's marriage invalid, opening the way for his legal union with Anne Boleyn. She was crowned in May and produced Princess Elizabeth in September. Legislation confirming Elizabeth as the king's legitimate heir – in place of Catherine's daughter Mary – was passed in early 1534 at Cromwell's instigation and was followed in May by the Act of Supremacy – declaring the king head of the Church of England and requiring all his subjects to swear allegiance to him in his new stance.

Two years after the Act of Succession, Queen Anne fell to the king's fear of divine wrath as she had failed to produce a boy: her marriage was annulled by Cranmer, she was executed and her daughter declared illegitimate (like Princess Mary). The next queen, Jane Seymour (1508–37), produced the desired son, Prince Edward, in October 1537 but died in the effort.

0.47a

>**0.47 ENGLISH ADVANCE UNDER THE FIDEI DEFENSOR:** (a, b) the king reads his personal psalter (of c. 1540) in Latin (illuminated by Jean Mallard, 1540; London, British Library) but the populace was vouchsafed scripture in the vernacular, the Great English Bible of 1539, title page; (c) the fleet confronting the French beyond coastal defences at Portsmouth.

Tyndale's English New Testament was suppressed on both sides of the Channel but sufficient copies were smuggled into England to provide the single greatest inspiration to Reformation there. In the new climate of royal opposition to Rome, Miles Coverdale followed Tyndale's work with the Old Testament which he completed in the mid-1540s: jointly, they formed the basis for all future English translations.

Henry VIII's achievements in the defence of the realm, both on land and at sea, should not be overshadowed by his ecclesiastical record or the spectacular series of marriages prompted by the desire to secure the succession and avoid a recurrence of internecine strife. The longed-for son did not live to avoid the latter but the defences were to be proof against external hostility under the relegated daughter.

Sympathetic to the cause of the Protestants abroad, both Cromwell and Cranmer welcomed the opportunity for English reform provided by the king's detachment from Rome – though neither was a zealot. Henry himself had asserted his supremacy and denied the pope but he was essentially a reforming Catholic in the Erasmian mould.**0.47ª** Principles were required and some influence on their evolution was exerted by the Lutherans of the Schmalkaldic League with whom alliance was being sought in the later 1530s. Indulgences, pilgrimages to saintly shrines and the veneration of relics were condemned: the sacraments were reduced to three but the king did not accept the cardinal Lutheran proposition of justification by faith alone and he steadfastly believed that the eucharist was sacrificial. After considerable contention,

0.47b

the *King's Book* of 1543 followed the 'Six Articles' of 1539 which confirmed most of the Catholic creed and made it a capital offence to deny transubstantiation. In that year, however, Cromwell and Cranmer oversaw the production of the Great English Bible by Miles Coverdale and its distribution to all the parish churches in the land in the expectation that the old cults and superstitions would pale before widespread comprehension of the scriptures. **0.47b**

Promoting secular education and the reform of the secular clergy as vigorously as he countered entrenched opposition to the crown and its courts, Cromwell confronted the vast monastic establishment in the spirit of the Swiss – and in assertion of royal supremacy. He instituted a commission to assess the wealth of the enclosed orders initially for the purposes of taxation: as part of an important programme of administrative reforms, he introduced a general peacetime levy. However, perceived laxity ultimately led to the dissolution of the monasteries in 1539: the loss to England's cultural heritage in the process of secularization was enormous.

Much monastic land went to the new nobility of the Tudor reformed state and its administration: much remained with the crown. The proceeds from sales, enhanced revenues and the wealth of other seized treasures

0.47c

swelled the royal coffers. Contrary to Cromwell's intentions, much was squandered on rash wars with Scotland and France: Henry won against both but lost the peace with the former and the cost of holding his territorial gains from the latter was greater than their real worth. However, the defence of the southern coast against seaborne invasion was sophisticated and money was well spent on the development of the navy which Henry had promoted from his outset.[0.47c]

There was some opposition to the new English ecclesiastical establishment, especially in the north from whence came the 1536 'Pilgrimage of Grace' to crave indulgence for the old ways and the monasteries – with horrendous punishment for the adherents. However, a major consequence of the king's reformation was confirmation of English identity and most of the population saw no need to challenge the strong centralized government of crown and parliament in favour of Rome. Even the majority of clerics remained passive before parliament: the king's very ambivalence prompted many to accept his new position while maintaining the essence of Catholic dogma. But the situation was precarious: Protestants were executed for heresy, Catholics for treason. After Sir Thomas More, Cromwell was the major casualty: too evangelical for the prevailing conservatives, he fell fast in 1540 after mishandling the king's fourth marriage – to Anne of Cleves – in pursuit of alliance with Lutheran princes.

The vigorous growth of Protestantism in England in the last decade of his reign discouraged Henry from extreme reaction against the reformers: vernacular Bible studies were tolerated. Cranmer survived at Canterbury – though he was hardly less evangelical than Cromwell – and persisted in revising the liturgy for the English Church. Above all, Prince Edward was placed under the guardianship of his Protestant uncle and given Protestant tutors.

If 16th-century Florentine – and Roman – portraiture might effectively impress the attributes of sitters on idealizing formulae inspired by the antique, Venetian essays in the medium were typically freer and more spontaneous, more attuned to the individual personality of the sitter. Titian was the supreme master of the mode, paradoxically penetrating in perception through the lightness of his brush strokes – in both senses, but particularly that of 'Illumination' – as well as calculating psychological disposition from pose and, of course, status from attribute. The pose and attributes of his papal portrait follow those of Raphael's Julius II but it is not merely the character of the two pontiffs which differs: the remote preoccupation of the Raphael – time-honoured for state portraiture but eloquent of particular desolation – is firmly drawn as though in preparation for modelling in clay; the wily vitality, the imminence of the Titian could hardly be better conveyed than in paint. Thus this portrait of the aged pope, far less a state portrait than its model, may instructively be compared with those of the famously beautiful Queen-Empress Isabella in her early thirties, her husband Charles V determined on victory in battle in his late-forties, and their son Prince Philip in his mid-twenties – widowed but courting his cousin Queen Mary of England.

The brief reign of Edward VI (1547–53), saw the consolidation of the Reformation in England and the eclipse of Lutheranism by an influx of reformist refugees from official persecution under the Valois and Habsburgs. Action against the religious orders was extended to the dissolution of collegiate churches and religious guilds, which had long played a leading role in education. A new *Book of Common Prayer* discounted transubstantiation. Most regrettably, a wave of violent iconoclasm did incalculable damage to the medieval heritage. As elsewhere in the north, destruction was the first effect of Reformation on architecture: the second was design specifically for Protestant purposes – just as the Counter-Reformation developed its own church type (see below, page 182).

COUNTER-REFORMATION: INCEPTION

Charles V's dedication to the recovery of provinces lost to France by his predecessors – both Holy Roman imperial and Burgundian ducal – ensured that there would be no united Catholic challenge to the peripheral Protestant powers. On the contrary, faced with the rapid expansion of the Reformation, the emperor acknowledged Protestant support against the Turks – in contrast to the French king who concluded a formal alliance with the sultan in 1535. In face of impending disaster, Pope Paul III (1534–49) intervened to initiate internal Church reform and enforce Christian unity.**⁰·⁴⁸**

In 1538 a new accord between the French king and the emperor hinged on the proposed marriage of the former's second son to the latter's oldest daughter with Milan as the dowry – despite its strategic importance as the key to communication between the Austrian and Spanish halves of the Habsburg domains through the passes of the Alps. François I entertained Charles lavishly in Paris in 1540 but was finally alienated by the emperor's gift of Milan to his son Philip instead of to his betrothed daughter. To the consternation of Catholics and Protestants alike, the French navy concerted with the Turks to disrupt the sea routes between Spain and Italy while the emperor was preoccupied with rebellion in his native Ghent. There was also opposition to Habsburg dominion far to the east, in Transylvania, and disquiet in Bohemia. Thus, his rear secure and his prey distracted, the sultan advanced through Hungary and took the capital, Buda, from the emperor's brother. In 1543, however, Charles triumphed over François who had sought to exploit the situation in Flanders.

In the ascendant, the emperor had his way with the convening of the General Church Council at Trent in 1545: promoting internal Church reform at last, its deliberations were to last more than twenty years. It was promoted by the emperor – and the reformers – as the supreme ecclesiastical authority: it ended by entrenching papal supremacy.

RELIGIOUS STRIFE IN THE EMPIRE

The emperor had promoted the representation of reformers at Trent but the principal Protestants saw the purpose of the Council as offensive and rebuffed him. He declared war on the Schmalkaldic League and turned on its heartland when Duke Maurice of Albertine Saxony returned to the Catholic fold in the hope of winning the Electorate of Ernestine Saxony. As the Catholic forces advanced, Luther died in February 1546 – followed by the French king who supported the League. The emperor overcame the league's forces decisively at Mühlberg.**0.49a** His brother Ferdinand crushed the Czech rising of 1546.

The Protestants agreed to representation at Trent and the emperor formulated a compromise pending the outcome: the 'Interim of Augsburg' (May 1548).**0.49b** This conceded not enough to satisfy the Protestants but too much to mollify Rome: the latter disdained the author-

›0.49 EMPEROR CHARLES V: (a) victorious at Mühlberg in 1547 (Titian, 1548; Madrid, Prado); (b) at the Diet of Augsburg, May 1548.

The scene of the 1530 Augsburg Diet is recalled but now the alignment of princes in the foreground reflects the situation after the defeat of the Schmalkaldic allies at Mühlberg. The former co-leader of the Protestant princes, John Frederick of Ernestine Saxony, is displaced at the head of the row of electors in the foreground by his victor, Maurice of Albertine Saxony. Acceding to his dukedom in 1541, the latter had joined the emperor in war against the Ottomans the following year and against France in 1544. He confiscated Catholic Church property in his domains to finance his ambitions but refused to join the Schmalkaldic League at the instigation of its leader, his father-in-law, Philip of Hesse. On the contrary, he saw great advantage in agreeing to enforce the imperial ban on his Ernestine cousin, the Elector John Frederick, for his Reformist exertions. In the ensuing Schmalkaldic War the emperor and his brother triumphed with the duke's support and the latter was rewarded with the Saxon Electorate.

Next to Saxony is the elector of Brandenburg, Joachim II (1535–71). Unlike his father (Joachim I, 1499–1535), he was sympathetic to the Protestant cause but openly converted to Lutheranism only in 1555 – when it would no longer provoke his ally, the ailing emperor. The electorate, confirmed by Emperor Charles IV in 1356, had been granted to the house of Hohenzollern by Emperor Sigismund in 1415. Future division was proscribed by Albert Achilles (1471–86) with the disposition of the inheritance to the oldest son. The progenitor of Prussia with the extension of his rule to Pomerania in 1472, Albert diversified from agriculture (on the poor lands of his territory) to taxable industry boosted by imposts on riverine and Baltic coastal trade: he overawed the nobility and diminished the privileges of the towns not least through the considerable judicial independence conceded to him by Emperor Frederick III.

On the second bench from the left is the elector palatine Frederick II (Kurfürst von der Pfalz, 1544–56) and his ward Otto Heinrich, duke of Palatinate-Neuburg: when confirmed in 1356, the electoral domains ran from the Rhineland to Swabia and Franconia but by the beginning of the 16th century division of territory had left the elector largely the Rhineland ruled from Heidelberg. It was converted to Lutheranism after Frederick's accession in 1544: as a result he was outlawed until he submitted following Mühlberg. He was succeeded briefly by Otto Heinrich who reintroduced Lutheranism: his successor, Frederick III (1559–76), converted to Calvinism.

0.49a

izationof communion in the Protestant rite and the former objected to the restitution of Church jurisdiction. Maurice of Saxony abandoned the emperor and took several Protestant princes with him into alliance with the new king of France, Henri II. Maurice was killed in the

0.49b

campaign of 1553 but Henri took the imperial cities of Metz, Toul and Verdun on the west side of the Rhine valley – the route of communication between the emperor's northern and southern realms.

THE TUDOR SUCCESSION

The dauphin François was married to Mary Stuart, the Catholic queen of Scots, to the discomfort of the English establishment. Faced with religious discontent at home and depleted of resources by his father's unproductive wars with Scotland and France, Edward VI's protectors came to terms with France which left Henri II secure in his rear for his Rhine campaign. However, Edward died in 1553 before attaining his majority: his father's determination to secure the succession in the male line and the limited Reformation embarked upon in that cause were

›0.50 THE TUDOR SUCCESSION: (a) allegory of Henry VIII and Edward VI flanked by Mary I and King-Consort Philip attended by war (left), Elizabeth I attended by peace and plenty (after the lost original painting attributed to Lucas de Heere and Hans Eworth, c. 1590); (b) Queen Mary I (c. 1554, Antonis Mor; Madrid, Prado); (c) Prince Philip of Spain (c. 1550, Titian; Rome, National Gallery of Art at the Palazzo Barberini).

In 1544 Henry VIII had called on parliament to restore the right of succession to both his daughters: Elizabeth duly succeeded her childless sister in November 1558, having narrowly escaped execution. Just under five years earlier, Francisco de Eraso (secretary to the king-emperor) wrote to inform Prince Philip that a recent portrait of him by Titian, belonging to his aunt Mary of Hungary and Bohemia, had been sent secretly to Queen Mary for her perusal with a view to marriage. Describing it as a very good likeness which will please the prospective bride, Eraso notes that the prince is 'dressed in a furred sayo [buttoned coat] with

0.50a

0.50b, c

white wolfskin'. The English reciprocated with the queen's portrait by the Netherlandish artist Antonis Mor – perhaps a year earlier than the Prado version.

›0.51 EMPEROR AND EMPIRE C. 1570: (a) Emperor Maximilian II with Queen Maria, Archdukes Rudolf and Ernst and Archduchess Anna (c. 1563,

0.51a

foiled. Mary, the daughter of the Catholic queen Catherine, succeeded. Much initial popular enthusiasm waned after she was married to her cousin, Emperor Charles's son Philip, to counter France's Scottish alliance and, above all, to reinforce Catholicism in England. The blood spilt – or burned – in that failed endeavour stained her name and her death within five years was welcomed by the majority of the population: so was the accession of her half-sister, Elizabeth.**0.50**

The new queen's able team of ministers immediately turned to the consolidation of Thomas Cromwell's achievements in strengthening the royal government at the expense of the old nobility – underwritten by the wealth accruing to the new rulers and their clients from sequestered monastic property. Even more immediately, Elizabeth re-established a Protestant Church in England under her supreme governance, promoting a settlement designed to satisfy the moderate Protestant majority, rather than the radical Puritan minority, and not to excite armed reaction from the Catholics at home or invite intervention from their former co-ruler. As passed by the parliament of 1559, the Act of Supremacy required all public officials to swear an oath of loyalty to the monarch as the supreme governor but the heresy laws were repealed to obviate persecution and much superficially Catholic ritual was sustained. At the same time, a new Act of Uniformity was passed, which made attendance at church and the use of an adapted version of the 1552 *Book of Common Prayer* compulsory, though the penalties for recusancy, or failure to attend and conform, were not extreme.

THE HABSBURG SUCCESSION

Retiring to his Flemish homeland, the exhausted Charles V left his brother Ferdinand to effect a settlement. The Peace of Augsburg (1555) confirmed that the religion of a

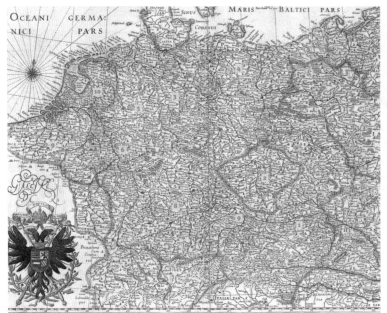

0.51b

Giuseppe Arcimboldo; Innsbruck, Schloss Ambras); (b) map with (1) Austria, (2) Bohemia, (3) Saxony, (4) Brandenburg, (5) Hesse, (6) the Palatinate, (7) Bavaria, (8) Württemburg, (9) County of Burgundy, (10) the Netherlands.

Charles V proffered his son Philip for election to his place as emperor but was prevailed upon to confirm the succession of his brother Ferdinand. On the latter's death, Philip put himself forward in opposition to his cousin Maximilian. Educated at the Spanish court, Emperor Ferdinand's heir-apparent had returned to Vienna in 1550 with his wife, the king-emperor's daughter, the infanta Maria. He was accorded a role in the government of Austria and as king of the Romans (of Germany) from 1562 he was in line for the imperial succession. To secure his position he flirted with Lutheranism and Protestant princes, assuring them of religious liberty. Whether this was from expediency or conviction is not clear: at his coronation he confirmed acceptance of the Confession of Augsburg and reassured the Catholic princes of his fidelity to Rome. Committed to reform, he was disappointed by the outcome of Trent and refused to publish its decrees but failed to satisfy the Protestants by countering its proscription of priestly marriage and communion in both species or granting them imperial fiefs when they administered prince-bishoprics. However, religious peace prevailed largely in the Empire.

Maximilian tried unsuccessfully to moderate Philip II's repression of dissent in the Netherlands but sent his daughter Anna off to Madrid as the Spanish king's fourth wife in 1570: in that same year he married his daughter Elizabeth to Charles IX of France. He secured German support for the protection of the eastern frontier but no acceptance of his demand for the right to veto German recruitment of foreign mercenaries. After indecisive action against them, in 1568 he accepted truce with the Turks which sustained his tributary obligations. He was elected king of Poland in 1571 against considerable opposition which he was unable to overcome.

principality would be that of its prince but guaranteed freedom of minority worship – explicitly to Catholics or Lutherans but not Calvinists. The ruling principle, defined in Latin as *cuius regio, eius religio,* underwrote claims to princely sovereignty: the emperor's aspiration to rule over a united Catholic Europe was foresworn. By the end of 1556, he had abdicated from all his realms: he died two years later.

In May 1558 Ferdinand was elected emperor: despite the efforts of his brother and grandfather, that dignity was insubstantial but he ruled a large portion of imperial territory as archduke of Austria, king of Bohemia and king of what was left of Hungary. Recognizing his imperial title but disclaiming his authority, the major regional powers were Bavaria, Saxony, Brandenburg, the Palatinate, Hesse and Württemberg. Apart from the three ecclesiastical electorates, there were also a vast number of minor independent duchies, free cities, abbeys and prince-bishoprics.**0.51b**

Sometime contender for office as principal painter to Philip II was the Greek immigrant Domenikos Theotokopoulos (El Greco, 1541–1614): he received only two major royal commissions but eclipsed his contemporaries in Spain with multiple works for ecclesiastical and private patrons – most of them eccentric in style, many of them peculiarly visionary. Notable, apart from the terrific drama lit from the

0.52a

cataclysmic sky, are the disregard for topographical reality both in the countering of spatial recession and in the dislocation of the major buildings, especially the cathedral and the alcázar which alone belong to the realm of tumult: it has, of course, prompted speculative interpretation in terms of the doleful influence of the Inquisition on the king's estate.

Prince Philip was represented to his prospective bride by Titian, Queen Mary by the Netherlandish artist Antonis Mor – as we have seen. The latter, active on emerging from the studio of Jan van Scorel

The problems of political fragmentation and sectarian differences were exacerbated with the advent of Calvinism which had not been officially recognized at Augsburg.

Emperor Ferdinand was succeeded by his son Maximilian (1564–76).[0.51a] Like his father, he was too preoccupied with problems in Bohemia and Hungary to espouse his uncle's cause of restoring imperial and ecclesiastical Catholicism. Towards the end of his life, however, as an heir to the Jagiellon rulers through his mother he was elected king of Poland by an assembly manipulated from Rome – but denounced by the Polish nobility. Worse, his attempt to regain Hungary after the death of Sultan Suleiman in 1566 had been rebuffed by the new sultan, Selim II, and Habsburg was humiliated as tributary to Ottoman. Taking Cyprus from the Venetians, along with much in the Aegean, the latter controlled the eastern Mediterranean: their vassals – and Barbary pirates – took the Spanish bases on the north coast of Africa and threatened commerce in the west.

In the west, on the other reach of Habsburg, the king-emperor's son Philip – king-consort of England – succeeded in Spain, Burgundy, the Italian dominions and America. He soon lost England with the death of the queen in 1558 but gained Portugal in 1580 following the death of his nephew Dom Sebastian in an ill-advised crusade against the Sultan of Morocco.[0.52]

King Philip's Spain

The Flemish-speaking king-emperor Charles had initially offended his Spanish subjects by importing Flemings to his government but absenting himself: reconciliation followed his successes abroad. His son Philip, trained for kingship in Spain, invited no resentment when he acceded to power as viceroy in the early 1540s and exercised it first mainly from Toledo. Before and after he was confirmed as king in 1556, his purpose was to unify the peninsula under his rule. Catholicism was his faith and his instrument but his political authority was not absolute: it was both furthered and inhibited by the lack of a single central consultative body. Each of the Spanish realms – Castile, Aragon, Catalonia, Valencia and Navarre – had its own assembly whose estates jealously guarded their feudal prerogatives against one another and against the centralization of government. However, the cause of the latter was furthered by the royal determination to limit the representation of the noble estates in the *cortes* and counter the convention of unanimity in decision-making. It was also furthered by the king's assertion of control over the appointment of chief ministers. And centralization was both symbolized and promoted by his removal of his court from Seville or Toledo to Madrid in 1561.

Seville, which had been favoured by King Charles, remained the commercial capital: in 1503 it had been granted virtual monopoly on trade with the Indies from whence came the wealth. Metropolitan Spain was poor and was further impoverished by the dispersal of the industrious Moors after they rebelled in Granada in 1568: the Turkish advance through the Mediterranean had sharpened fears of pro-Muslim subversion in Spain and prompted repressive measures. The *conversos* – former Muslims and Jews of suspect fidelity – were the prime concern of the Spanish Inquisition. Extended to Protestant 'heresies' imported from the printing presses of northern Europe, that infamous institution compounded impoverishment by stifling intellectual enquiry as well as inhibiting commercial activity. A royal commission which amounted to a centralized state within the royal estate, its tribunals were preferred to the civil courts when the latter proved intractable: that reinforced the power of the crown, in principle, but it left the civil authority – even the king – hostage to fortune as perceived by the Grand Inquisitor.

The merchants of the Spanish Netherlands were rich but inimical to subsidizing the belligerent exploits of a remote king; besides, as elsewhere in continental Europe, taxation was farmed to professional collectors to their profit. Moreover, as the treasury was regularly replenished with bullion imported from the Americas, little was done in Spain to encourage the development of industry – the true wealth of nations (as the 18th-century Scottish father of modern economics, Adam Smith, was to observe). Indeed, the minting of money from the imported bullion led to rampant

c. 1545, was appointed official court artist after the marriage and was in King Philip's train on its return to Spain in 1559. After his own return home to Utrecht in 1661, he was succeeded at the Spanish court by his pupil Alonso Sánchez Coello. The portrait of Queen Mary is conceived on the model of – but in opposition to – Titian's portrait of Prince Philip's mother, Empress Isabella: less painterly in the northern manner, stiffer, that established the hierarchy of the prospective wife in relatively austere formality. Mor's portrait of Philip himself may also be seen as a reversed paraphrase of the earlier full-length essay by Titian (1548; Madrid, Prado): another uncompromising assertion of status, it presents a mature commander, victor of (if not at) Saint-Quentin, instead of a somewhat diffident but engaging boy in martial dress.

0.52b

inflation on the one hand; on the other, high taxation of internal manufacturers crippled growth to the obvious advantage of foreigners.

Even the pillaging of Mexico and Peru was insufficient to defray the cost of the incessant wars against 'heresy' to which the late king-emperor dedicated his son. With that commitment Philip inherited and bequeathed bankruptcy – not least because Spain's resources in specie and troops were also extended to the emperor in Vienna. The two branches of the Habsburg family exchanged sisters and daughters as wives – to the ultimate decay of the Spanish branch.

The fortunes of Valois and Habsburg waxed and waned in the usual manner until a halt was called by the exhaustion of resources and by the threat of Protestant insurrection in their domains. Lasting accord was reached between the two great continental kings at Cateau-Cambrésis in the spring of 1559: late conquests were renounced but the French kept Metz, Toul and Verdun; the widowed Philip married Henri II's daughter Elisabeth.

THE VALOIS SUCCESSION

The last of the virile Valois, Henri II was killed in a jousting accident in Paris in July 1559: his oldest son, husband of Mary Queen of Scots, succeeded briefly as François II. Habsburg-Valois accord, sealed by the marriage of Philip and Elisabeth, was furthered by Henri II's widow, Catherine de' Medici, with the marriage of her second son, Charles IX (1560–74), to Elisabeth of Austria, daughter of Maximilian II. The Florentine queen-mother was the effective power during the minority of the new king: her regency was singularly unhappy for the Valois realm.**0.53, 0.54**

Religious war in France

During the twelve-year reign of Henri II, Calvinist conversions proliferated in all classes of French society: the most eminent were Louis de Bourbon, prince of Condé (1530–69) and Gaspard de Coligny (1519–72), admiral of

France since 1552. Persecution continued intermittently until the establishment of a new court to try heresy in 1559. On the king's accidental death that year, the Protestants faced the more vehement opposition of the pre-eminent Duc de Guise, uncle of the new king's wife, Mary Queen of Scots. A fervent Catholic, the queen-mother nevertheless viewed the power of the Guise faction as a threat to her own position as regent. She was initially moderate in her dealings with the Huguenots. In response, the Guise formed the Catholic League and opened negotiations with Spain.

The Estates-General was convened at Saint-Germain-en-Laye in 1561 to effect compromise. That proved elusive and the crown took the initiative at the beginning of the new year with the Edict of Saint-Germain which conceded limited rights of worship to the Huguenots. Within two months a Guise faction had massacred Protestants worshipping in accordance with the dispensation: naturally strife followed. Condé mobilized Huguenot forces and occupied several towns along the Loire. The Guise forced the revocation of the edict.

Under Charles IX the war passed through five main stages provoked by atrocities on alternating sides: no decisive victory was gained but the Protestants were confirmed in their limited freedom of worship. The loss of

›0.53 THE LATE-VALOIS AS REVEALED BY FRANÇOIS CLOUET: (a) Henri II (1559, oil on panel; Florence, Uffizi); (b–d) Catherine de' Medici, Charles IX and Elisabeth of Austria (chalk and wash on paper, b and d, Paris, National Library; c, S. Petersburg, Hermitage).

Following the Dutch miniaturist Corneille de Lyon (Cornelis van den Haag, naturalized French in 1547), whose elusive œuvre has been characterized in terms of sensitive naturalism on the basis of the rare definite attribution, and his father Jean, François Clouet (c. 1510–72) was open to influence from north and south. His full-length portrait of Henri II adapts the swarthy imperial model produced for Charles V by Seisenegger – unidealized at least in physiognomy (see page 57). The drawings, on the other hand, are readily appreciable for a lucidly incisive style not unrelated to contemporary Florentine *disegno* (see pages 23f). Not necessarily hieratic in motive, his forte in chalk and wash was the delineation of the presence of a sitter – and elaborate costume – rather, perhaps, than depth of character behind enigmatic glance. The latter was managed by Hans Holbein the Younger who alone among northerners challenges Clouet as a draftsman of portraiture.**0.46f,g**

›**0.54 'THE MASSACRE OF S. BARTHOLO-MEW'S DAY'** (François Dubois, oil on panel c. 1572; Lausanne, Cantonal Museum).

After the Bourbon-Valois wedding festivities, the leading Huguenots stayed in Paris to discuss their grievances with the king: a Huguenot force was camped outside Paris. On 22 August an attempt was made on the life of their leader, Admiral Coligny. The queen-mother was improbably implicated but discussed the crisis with the king and evidently secured his approval for a pre-emptive strike against the Huguenots on the grounds that Calvin's teaching had turned anti-monarchist: Coligny was dispatched forthwith. Estimates of the number of Huguenots killed thereafter range from 5000 to 30000.

Responsibility for the horror is disputed: it seems most likely that the queen's Italian advisers, backed by the Duc d'Anjou, won her approval to the elimination of the Huguenot leaders to pre-empt a *coup d'état*. The unforeseen escalation of popular mob violence in Paris was condemned by royal decree as soon as it became apparent. Guise was threatened with justice but the provocative role of the agents of the Duc d'Anjou compromised the royal family.

great figures to both camps culminated in the death of Condé in the third phase (1569): he was succeeded at the head of the Huguenot cause by his son Henri in concert with his cousin Henri of Navarre whose mother, Queen Jeanne III (Jeanne d'Albret) was the movement's spiritual leader. As both princes were minors, Admiral Coligny was in effective command: in league with the Protestants of the Netherlands and subsidized by Elizabeth I of England, he fought on against the Catholic forces of the Valois king's brother, the Duc d'Anjou, reinforced with Spanish troops.

An attempt at recalibration was made with the marriage of the king's sister, Marguerite, to Henri of Navarre who acceded to the throne on the death of his mother just before the wedding on 18 August 1572. In Paris for the event, Coligny was murdered by the Guise faction on the eve of the feast of S. Bartholomew. The next day thousands of Huguenots were slaughtered and the massacre spread to the provinces over the following weeks.**0.54** The forces of Anjou continued the repression until their master was called to Poland as king in May 1573. Two months later the Edict of Boulogne (or Peace of La Rochelle) curtailed Huguenot freedom of worship.

Philip II and Pope Gregory XIII welcomed the massacre as divine justice. Elizabeth of England and her fellow Protestant rulers were appalled, of course. So too were the king's father-in-law, Emperor Maximilian II, and even Tsar Ivan the Terrible. The fragile Charles IX himself, who reputedly blamed his mother and overweening brother, went into terminal decline and died within eighteen months.

THE PAPACY AND TRIDENTINE REFORM

With the Reformation spreading like wildfire in central, northern and western Europe, the Church council's protracted deliberations at Trent were concluded under the auspices of Pope Pius IV (1559–65). Rigorous in curbing excess at court, that wily diplomat had found his way through a morass of conflicting views: Emperor Ferdinand wanted doctrinal concessions to the Lutherans in the hope of enticing them back into the Catholic fold; the pope himself was prepared to sanction communion in both species and other less contentious doctrinal reforms as well as abrogation of abuses; the Roman Curia were prepared to concede the latter but not the former; Philip II was against any substantive change. The Curia's views prevailed with vague modification in terms of the papal and imperial views on communion. The Council was dissolved at the end of 1563, the pope confirmed its decrees forthwith and asserted the sole right to their interpretation. Trent restored discipline and reformed the organs for enforcing it: Rome retained them.[0.55]

›0.55 'THE CHURCH COUNCIL AT TRENT': concluding session in the cathedral, December 1563 (anonymous, traditionally attributed to Titian; Paris, Louvre).

The Protestant challenge was met both positively and negatively. The councillors sustained the contentions that the ecclesiastical authorities alone were competent to interpret the Bible and that ecclesiastical tradition was as valid as scripture in the information of faith – in particular the promotion of belief in the efficacy of prayer for the intercession of the Virgin Mary or the saints.[0.56] It asserted that the consecrated bread and wine of the eucharist became the body and blood of Christ. It authorized the revision of the Index of Prohibited Books promulgated by Paul IV in 1559. However, it reformed the Vatican offices and proscribed many of the practices which the Protestants deplored, in particular the sale of offices,

›0.56 'THE BURIAL OF COUNT ORGAZ' (with the panoply of heaven in prayer of intercession for the repose of his soul, El Greco, 1586; Toledo, S. Tomé).

Born in Crete, trained as a painter in the Byzantine tradition of the holy image, active in Venice from c. 1560, Domenikos Theotokopoulos effected the transition from the hieratic stylization of the highly formulaic traditional Greek icon to his adopted city's sensual *colore* mode in which spontaneity, furthered by a freeflowing painterly technique, is revealed in modulations of light to evoke atmosphere of wide-ranging mood (AIC4, pages 830f; see also above, page 73). Nicknamed in Spain where he arrived in 1571, El Greco drained any hint of the salacious in the sensuality of his Venetian style, retained the colour, and took painterly freedom from the constraints of Florentine *disegno* to a surreal expressive extreme in his visionary transformation of the physical into the spiritual, the immanent into the transcendental, the mundane concepts of space and relationship into the irrational: mannered, his style should not be confused with the Mannerism in contemporary Italy despite the coincidental predilection for the super-elongation of figures.

Don Gonzalo Ruíz, Count Orgaz, was a 14th-century knight of such piety that S. Stephen and S. Augustine descended personally to lift the body into the sepulchre and witness the ascent of his soul to heaven at the prayer of the attendant priest for the intercession of the Madonna and assembled saints. The representation of the legend for the Toledan parish church of S. Tomé is unexcelled in demonstrating its author's mesmerizing ability to effect mystical transition from the physical to the spiritual. It is thought that S. Augustine is represented by the Augustinian grand inquisitor Gaspar de Quiroga y Vela (1573–95).

the holding of multiple offices and absence from office. It prescribed the reaffirmation of monastic rule, tighter control over the training of clergy and, through preaching, the assiduous instruction of the laity. The Catholic liturgy was reformed, indulgences curtailed and sobriety ruled in Rome from moral high ground appreciable to reformers inside and outside the Roman Church.

Determined to regulate all aspects of the life of the Church, the council had surprisingly little to say on church planning. That was left to Pope Pius IV's nephew Cardinal Carlo Borromeo, archbishop of Milan, one of the most dedicated of reformers: he issued his *Instructiones fabricae et supellectilis ecclesiasticae* in 1577 to his subordinates in his archdioceses but its prescriptions were soon applied generally. The use of the 'heathenish' circle was proscribed in principle and in practice the rational, centralized, humanist forms favoured by Classical architects were found unsuitable to Christian liturgical purposes. Promoted instead was the symbolism of the True Cross – the Latin rather than the Greek version – and the form of the traditional early Christian basilica was recommended for general congregational worship: it projected a dynamic axis from entrance to altar in a clearly lit environment and the hierarchical distinction of the clergy in the sanctuary, beyond the crossing, from the laity in the nave. Aspiration to the awesome raised the church on an elevated site, removed from mundane pollution and detached from other buildings. Representing the defunct body of Christ, the exterior was to be austere – except for iconographically relevant sculpture on the façade. In complement, integrated iconographical programmes were prescribed for the interior. Drawn from scripture, the lives of the saints or the history of the Church, these were to be clearly intelligible, realistic and charged with emotional stimulus to devotion: there was to be 'nothing…that is foreign to Christian piety and religion or that is profane, ugly, sensual, lewd…'. **0.57**

›0.57 SACRED REALISM: (a, b) Christ crucified and dead (inlaid and polychromed wood, respectively by Juan Martínes Montañés, c. 1603, Seville cathedral; Gregorio Fernández, c. 1625, Madrid, Prado).

Fernández (1576–1636) – and the unidentified polychromist with whom he worked – ceded to none in the

0.57a

0.57b

Conciliatory, relatively enlightened, Pius IV was succeeded by the intolerant, ascetic Dominican Pius V (1566–72), whose career in the Inquisition had culminated in his appointment as Grand Inquisitor in 1558. That fearful institution, ever busier in this age of proliferating

representation of lacerated flesh oozing blood: his gory, unidealized representation of Christ's Passion at its various stages, but here at its end in approaching rigor mortis instead of heroic triumph over death, may well be seen as the consummate southern Catholic answer to the northern advocates of the *Devotio Moderna*, Grünewald in particular.

›0.58 'THE BATTLE OF LEPANTO', late-16th century: (H. Letter; Greenwich, National Maritime Museum).

The engagement was joined off the northern coast of the Gulf of Patras (western Greece). Commanded by the late-emperor's illegitimate son, the Holy League's fleet of 212 vessels was assembled from Philip II's Spain, Naples, Sicily and Sardinia together with flotillas sent by Venice, Genoa, Savoy and the Knights Hospitaller (established in Malta in 1530 by Charles V) – but not France. The last such engagement involving vessels powered mainly by rowers – the Christians confronted 222 Ottoman galleys supported by fifty-six lesser craft – it led to the retaking of strategic north African ports but a new Turkish naval force won them back three years later. However, Ottoman command of the sea was disrupted and the sultan's advance into southern Europe halted permanently.

'heresy', was rigorously supervised, its activities regularized, by the Holy Office which was established in 1542 as the highest court of appeal in ecclesiastical affairs: many were called to account for failings hitherto overlooked, many found it politic to inform. In 1571 the pope entrenched intolerance by instituting the Congregation of the Index to assume authority over the vetting of denounced works and the regular updating of prohibition; publishers fled.

Printing presses and intellectual enquiry were, perhaps, the main victims of Pius V's proscriptions but the net was wide-cast. Jews were expelled from the papal states in 1569. Imperial tolerance was deplored, Huguenots unequivocally proscribed, Elizabeth I of England excommunicated, Spain supported in the Netherlands and the Holy League formed for crusade against the Turks. This had initial success in the great naval battle at Lepanto in which the League's fleet, commanded by Philip II's half-brother Don John of Austria, overcame the Ottomans (October 1571).**0.58**

0.58

The Dominicans enhanced their traditional fanatical role in terrorizing the heterodox under their own pope, of course, but the Holy Office and its alter ego, the Office for the Propagation of the Faith, commanded several new orders of non-monastic clerks regular founded to fight heresy and indoctrinate worldwide from their headquarters in Rome. In particular, the example set by the Theatines of S. Gaetino di Thiene (1523) was followed by the Jesuits of S. Ignatius of Loyola (1540) and the Oratorians of S. Filippo Neri (1575). Of these, the Jesuits, organized on military lines by their soldier-founder, are generally seen as the most formidable – for their strict collegiate pedagogy but also for their sophistry.**0.59**

Pius V's three most important post-Tridentine successors, Gregory XIII (1572–85), Sixtus V (1585–90) and Clement VIII (1592–1605), sustained his zealous promotion of Catholic restoration through the implementation of reforms extending from the administration of the Church to its liturgy. Even more militant, less bigoted, just as irreproachable, the first had trained in law, was prominent at Trent and papal legate at the court of Philip II thereafter: he used his legal standing to secure the reversion to the papacy of disputed lands and devoted the revenue to finance anti-heretical powers abroad, especially Philip II and the queen-regent of France – whose lamentable operations we shall review in due course. More happily, he reformed canon law and the calendar (in 1582): devoting himself to developing the organs of Catholic education as a crucial aid to recovery, he favoured Jesuit colleges in particular.

Under the Franciscan Sixtus V, Gregorian subservience to Spain was countered in attitude – if not yet in decisive action. Ecclesiastical reform was not relaxed but it was complemented by measures to improve the administration, agriculture and commerce of the consolidated papal

0.59a

›0.59 DIDACTIC SAINTS: (a) 'S. Ignatius of Loyola'; (b) 'S. Dominic Flagellating' (Juan Martínez Montañés, respectively c. 1610 and 1606; Seville, Church of the Annunciation and Fine Art Museum).

0.59b

state, and by the great extension of previous papal drives to impose urban order on Rome.[0.60] As we shall see in the first section of this book, the brief pontificate also saw the completion of the stupendous centralized scheme for replacing the Constantinian basilica of S. Pietro. That, in turn, launched the great age of building for the Church Triumphant – of Protestantism defensive – which promoted the evocation of heaven by the masters of the Roman High Baroque – whose works will be the subject of our next volume.

ROMA
PER SACRAM B.PETRI SEDEM CAPVT ORBIS EFFECTA.

›0.60 ROME AT THE ACCESSION OF POPE SIXTUS V (Ignazio Danti, fresco; Rome, Vatican Galleries).

0.60

0.61 MAPS OF BALTIC STATES: (a) Poland with neighbouring Livonia, Estonia and parts of the Swedish and Finnish coasts (engraved c. 1645, J. and G. Blaeu, Amsterdam); (b) Prussia (engraved c. 1645, J. Janssonius, Amsterdam; (b)

0.61a

THE BALTIC AND THE EAST

While religious dissension was rife in most of Europe, contention raged in the north over trade in the Baltic. Sweden had emerged as a major power in the region after asserting its independence from Denmark – and from Rome – under the leadership of Gustav Vasa (1523–60). Occupying Tallinn (Estonia) later in his reign, Vasa offended the growing power of the Muscovite Tsar Ivan IV who had designs on Livonia (Latvia), the eastern Baltic domain of the Teutonic Knights. Claiming the Swedish crown, Denmark allied itself with Poland but that also offended the tsar who then reached accord with Sweden. In 1568, after seven years of war, the two western contenders were pacified by Emperor Maximilian who won recognition of his suzerainty over Teutonic lands. During the conflict, however, Muscovite ambition prompted the last of Livonia's Teutonic Brotherhood to place themselves under the protection of Sigismund II Augustus (1548–72), king of Poland and grand duke of Lithuania, and much of their domain was annexed to the Grand Duchy. The last grand master, Albrecht of Hohenzollern, retained the duchy of Prussia as a fiefdom

0.61b

0.62

›0.62 TAPESTRY WITH THE ROYAL MONO-GRAM S.A. (Sigismund II Augustus), 1555 (Brussels, circle of Frans Floris and Cornelis Bos).

The son of Sigismund the Old and his Sforza wife, who introduced the Renaissance into Poland from Lombardy (AIC4, page 886), Sigismund II Augustus achieved the culmination of his father's expansionist ambitions. But the legacy of the settlement he sponsored at Lubin was an elective monarchy, prone to bargain away privileges to an unruly nobility, and a bicameral central diet (upper house of nobles and clergy, lower house of burghers and landed commoners) whose delegates were bound to follow the dictates of the provincial diets and therefore could not coalesce.

of Poland but entailed its reversion to his cousins of Brandenburg (in 1618).**0.61**

The Lithuanian nobility, whose domains spread as far as Kiev, were highly vulnerable to the depredations of the tsar: in 1569 they agreed to join Poland in a federation under an elected monarch and parliament. The author of the accord, Sigismund II, had mediated successfully between Protestants and Catholics throughout his reign and had now to preside over merger with Orthodox peoples: the last of the Jagiellonian line, he had only three years to do so.**0.62**

The Poles first elected to replace Sigismund with Henri of Valois, heir to his fragile brother Charles IX. After little more than a year on the Polish throne, indeed, Henri was called back to Paris to rule under his mother. In his stead the election of Emperor Maximilian was overturned by the nobility in favour of the anti-Habsburg Hungarian patriot, Stephen Báthory, *voivode* of Transylvania, who had the support of the Ottoman sultan. With Russian support, Maximilian was preparing the enforcement of his claim when he died suddenly late in 1576.

The grand prince of Moscow, Ivan IV, had succeeded his father, Vasili III, at the age of three in 1533 and been crowned tsar in 1547. The early part of the reign was one of peaceful reforms and modernization: the latter part was dogged by reverse abroad.**0.63**

0.63a,b

Russian ascendancy under Ivan IV

The energetic, reforming tsar revised the law code, restricted the mobility of the peasants, created a standing army (the *streltsy*), established the Zemsky Sobor or assembly of the land, the council of the nobles. Appointing the first patriarch of Moscow, he asserted the independent identity of the Russian Orthodox Church and established the Council of the Hundred Chapters to regulate the rituals for the entire country. He decorated his new patriarchate by taking the vernacular tradition, crossed with elementary early Renaissance Classicism, to its apogee in Moscow's most iconic building (see also AIC4, pages 886f): those of us who persevere with this exercise will review the context of post-Renaissance Russian architectural development in the next volume.

The tsar pursued both peaceful and warlike foreign relations. He built a port on the Neva (near modern Saint Petersburg) to promote trade with the west but the Hanseatic traders refused to use it in preference to the established ports of Livonia. He also built Arkhangelsk at the head of the White Sea specifically to cater for the Muscovy Company of English merchants. On the other hand, in 1552 he defeated the Kazan Khanate, whose armies had repeatedly devastated the north-east of Russia, and annexed its territory. Four years later he annexed the Astrakhan Khanate. These conquests complicated relations with the aggressive nomadic hordes from Asia and transformed Russia into a multinational and multiconfessional state.

The later half of the reign was less successful: it turned on his near-fatal illness in 1553. The boyars were called on to swear allegiance to his infant son: many refused and were met with brutal reprisals. Within ten years Ivan had extended direct rule over much of the north and formed a personal police force (*oprichnik*). Directed against the boyars who opposed centralized absolutism, its deployment is also seen as a sign of the tsar's paranoia. With reverse, that increased and so did *oprichnik* excess.

0.63d

0.63c

The drive for expansion to the Baltic led Russia to the so-called Livonian War with the Swedes, Lithuanians, Poles and the Livonian Teutonic Knights: it dragged on for twenty-four years, damaging the Russian economy without territorial gain. In the 1560s and early 1570s the combination of drought, famine and plague, Polish-Lithuanian raids, Tatar invasions and the sea-trading blockade carried out by the Swedes, Poles and the Hanseatic League devastated the tsardom. With Báthory, Poland-Lithuania had acquired an energetic leader supported by Russia's Ottoman enemy. By 1579 he was advancing into the tsar's heartland and the Khan of the Crimea devastated Moscow. Five years later the deranged Tsar Ivan died in suspicious circumstances, leaving his ravaged kingdom to his unfit and childless son Feodor. After the latter's death in 1598, fifteen years of turmoil terminated the accession of the Romanovs who were to take tsarist Russia to its apogee.

RETURN WEST: THE NETHERLANDS AND ELIZABETHAN ENGLAND

The French Huguenots, led by Coligny, had been preparing to send armed support to the Protestants in the Netherlands on the eve of S. Bartholomew's Day, 1571. Discontent, widespread at the erosion of traditional liberties in the previous reign, was exacerbated in the mid-1560s by Philippine measures designed to enforce ecclesiastical uniformity on then seventeen provinces of the northern Burgundian domain. A consortium of Dutch magnates led by William of Orange (the Silent) sought religious toleration in the spirit of Augsburg but were rebuffed: rioting was suppressed by the viceroy, the duke of Alba, with great brutality from 1567. War followed and the rebels threatened inundation with the destruction of the dykes which held the sea at bay.**0.64, 0.65**

Masters at rebellion

Pieter Bruegel the Elder (c. 1525–69), starting his career in collaboration with didactic engravers, naturally first looked to expressionistic Gemans – rather than High Renaissance Italians, like many of his northern contemporaries – then to Bosch, then further back to the clear delineation of human status and the closely observed naturalistic detail of the Limbourg brothers. This eclectic mix, and his native facility for panoramic landscape enriched by Venetian experience, were forged into a style of deceptive simplicity deployed for cycles of religious and secular paintings: the latter no less didactic than the former, if sometimes humorously satirical, and the ostensible subject often ironically diminished by the topography of its cosmic setting, the appeal was primarily to affluent bourgeois clients with plenty of wall space. Like the celebrated cycle of the months, in which the seasonal scenes are acted out by a rude cast of rustics, 'The Massacre of the Innocents' in a peasant village was widely recognized as subversively allegorical. Reworked as a scene of plunder, the overpainted Biblical subject was the indiscriminate slaughter wreaked by a brutal tyrant – bent on exterminating every possible Christ-child – but the innocents were the aspirants

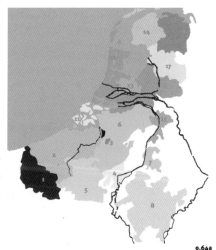

0.64a

›0.64 THE BURGUNDIAN 'LOW COUNTRIES', REPRESSION AND REBELLION: (a) map with (1) Artois, (2) Flanders, (3) Mechelen, (4) Namur, (5) Hainaut, (6) Brabant, (7) Limburg, (8) Luxembourg, (9) Ommelanden, (10) Drenthe-Westerwolde, (11) Zeeland, (12) Holland, (13) Utrecht, (14) Friesland, (15) Gelderland, (16) Groningen, (17) Overijssel; (b) 'The Massacre of the Innocents' (Peter Bruegel the Elder, 1565; London, Royal Collection); (c) 'The Fall of the Rebel Angels' (Frans Floris, c. 1554; Antwerp, Royal Museum of Religious Art).

The provinces, collectively ruled by the duke of Burgundy as nominal fiefs of France or the Empire, formed an Imperial Circle of the Holy Roman Empire (from 1512) at the instigation of Emperor Maximilian and the governor, his daughter the archduchess Margaret (regent for her nephew Charles who had succeeded his father Philip as duke in 1506). In addition to the free County of Burgundy (Franche-Comté) the circle roughly covered the modern kingdoms of the Netherlands and Belgium, the Grand-Duchy of Luxembourg and the two most northerly French *départements*. As a result of the emperor's victory over France in Flanders in 1543, the seventeen semi-autonomous provinces were forged into one hereditary entity (by the Pragmatic Sanction of 1549). That was reduced considerably with the secession of the Seven United Provinces in 1581 (recognized in 1648) and the annexation of the Franche-Comté by France in 1678.

0.64b

to Netherlandish freedom and the brutes were the agents of the absent Spanish king doubling for Herod.

In the decade before the horrors of Alba were surreptitiously recorded by Breugel, his Flemish contemporary Frans Floris (c. 1517–70) had provided an alternative view of suppressed rebellion – in an alternative style. In Italy from 1541 to 1545, Floris had studied the High Renaissance masters – like Jan van Scorel a generation earlier – and steeped himself in current Mannerist developments led by Michelangelo: that, of course, equipped him for importing to Antwerp a style – sculptural rather than painterly at first – attuned to the realization of his abiding interest in humanist and antique mythological themes as well heroic religious episodes such as the defeat and expulsion of the rebel angels from heaven. The patrons of his lucrative practice – and extensive workshop – were both ecclesiastical and secular, guild-masters and not least Spanish nobles with Flemish estates. His father was the mason/sculptor Cornelis I Floris de Vriendt (died 1538): his elder brother was the architectural designer Cornelis II (1514–75) with whom he collaborated on the decorations for the entry of Charles V and Prince Philip into Antwerp in 1549 – which we shall view in due course.

0.64c

Recalled, Alba was replaced by the more moderate Alexander Farnese, duke of Parma, in 1573. Ten southern provinces came to terms with their Catholic masters three years later but the seven Dutch-speaking, largely Calvinist northern provinces (Holland, Zeeland, Groningen, Friesland, Utrecht, Overijssel and Gelderland) formed the Union of Utrecht and fought on under the leadership of William the Silent, who had been elected *stadtholder* of Holland in 1572. Having declared their independence from the Spanish crown in July 1581, they agreed a confederal constitution in 1584: their representatives would meet in The Hague under the presidency of the prince of Orange as *stadtholder*. As the essential condition for reversing the situation, Parma was directed to prepare for the invasion of Protestant England.

Spain had maintained peace with England after Elizabeth's accession, if only to encourage her neutrality in the conflict with the Netherlandish Protestants. That was a vain hope. Moreover, Elizabeth's regime connived at attacks on Spanish shipping – especially the American treasure fleet – and even the plundering of Spanish ports: the Iberians called this piracy but the Protestant powers, denying the Tordesillas dispensation, claimed to be countering outrageous monopoly. Formal conflict was inevitable when England contracted to supply the Dutch with troops under the Treaty of Nonsuch in 1585, after Philip had allied Spain with the hostile French Catholic League.

As Elizabeth aged without issue the question of succession was a matter of international concern. The heir presumptive was her Stuart cousin, the Catholic Mary Queen of Scots, who allowed herself to be implicated in a Spanish-sponsored plot to overthrow the Protestant Tudor regime. Arrested, she was executed in prison in England in 1587. Her disaffected son and successor, James VI (1566–1625), was wise enough to offer no challenge. On the other

›0.65 'WILLIAM OF ORANGE' (the Silent, c. 1575, Adriaen Thomas Key; Amsterdam, National Museum).

William of Nassau (1533–84), prince of Orange in succession to a cousin in 1544, was born in Germany and raised as a Lutheran but was confirmed in his inheritance on condition of conversion to Catholicism. Serving in the regency court of Margaret of Parma, he was appointed governor (*Stadtholder*) of the northern provinces in 1559. As a member of the council of state he represented opposition to the centralizing policies of the predominantly Spanish administration. Further, appalled by the persecution of his Protestant compatriots, as a Catholic convert married to a Lutheran Saxon princess he promoted freedom of conscience and led the Dutch revolt against the oppression of the duke of Alba. Outlawed, dispossessed, in 1568 he allied himself with the French Huguenots and opened the war with the Spanish forces which culminated in the formation of the predominantly Protestant Union of Utrecht in 1579 and their declaration of independence in 1581. That followed alliance with the French king's brother, the duke of Anjou, who would assume the title of 'Protector of the Liberty of the Netherlands'. The duke ruined his cause by his brutal advent and left William discredited in 1582. Still *stadtholder*, he married Coligny's daughter in 1583 but was assassinated just over a year later.

0.66a

**›0.66 THE DEFEAT OF THE SPANISH
ARMADA:** (a) the battle joined (anonymous late-
16th-century English School; Greenwich, National Maritime Museum); (b) commemorative 'Armada' portrait
of Queen Elizabeth I flanked by details of the battle and
the stormy retreat of the Spanish ships (1588, attributed to George Gower; Woburn Abbey).

0.66b

hand, Philip II implemented his invasion plans: he dispatched his great armada to protect the passage of Parma's
army across the English Channel but it was badly mauled
and dispersed by the English navy – and hostile weather
on the return voyage around Scotland and Ireland.[0.66]
Attempts at revenge in the following decade were also disastrous – though the restored Spanish navy proved itself a
match for English privateers.

Unfortunately the Marian conspiracy, attended by
Spanish aggression, hardened attitudes to Catholics in
England. The rebellion of Catholic Ireland against Tudor
pretensions to supremacy there compounded the issue and
the Elizabethan reign ended far more repressively than it
had begun. However, triumph over vastly superior forces
at sea in 1588 boosted national morale already ascendant as
English navigators extended the national interest abroad:
claims to Virginia on the eastern seaboard of North America laid the foundations of great colonial power in 1597 –
though a permanent settlement was not established there
for another decade. Despite the dire financial consequences of protracted conflict in the anti-Catholic cause,
the reign ended with a stronger English realm, though one
in which the relative strengths of crown and parliament
remained to be tested under less charismatic monarchs.

FRANCE FROM VALOIS TO BOURBON

The creature of his mother, Henri III would have an even
unhappier reign than that of his brother.[0.67] During his
absence in Poland, his younger brother the Duc d'Alençon
had emerged as champion of the Huguenots – partly in his
bid to marry Elizabeth of England, partly out of antipathy
to his brother and mother. His coalition of forces forced
the issue of the Edict of Beaulieu which gave Huguenots
the limited right of public worship, representation in several *parlements*, and reparation for S. Bartholomew's Day.

Henri of Guise responded to perceived royal weakness by forming the Catholic League to defend the established Church, promote its spiritual renewal and also to further his personal ambition to gain the crown instead of the childless king's traitorous brother (now duc d'Anjou) or his Protestant brother-in-law, Henri of Navarre. Internally the League commanded a large urban following: externally it was supported by Pope Gregory XIII and Pope Sixtus V, the Jesuits and Philip II of Spain. Under its pressure, the Edict of Beaulieu was renounced at the end of 1576. Sporadic hostilities ensued.

Anjou was invited by William the Silent to be 'Protector of the Liberty of the Netherlands' but his installation early in 1582 met with considerable hostility from both the Flemish and the Dutch: he led his troops in a vicious assault on Antwerp early the next year but was routed. William the Silent was assassinated soon after. Anjou died of malaria in 1584, leaving the Protestant Henri of Navarre as heir apparent to France. Guise resorted to arms.

The so-called 'War of the Three Henries' – France, Navarre and Guise – went well for the League at first: it forced the king to suppress Protestantism and annul Navarre's right to the throne in favour of his cousin, the Cardinal of Bourbon. Paris turned against the widely discredited royal regime and the king fled. Afraid of assassination, he struck first: Guise was murdered at Blois at the end of 1588. Having joined forces with Henri of Navarre to retake Paris, the last of the Valois was himself assassinated by a Dominican friar loyal to the League in August 1589: he called for Navarre and begged him to become a Catholic to avoid further carnage. The dissident Leaguers could not agree on an alternative.

Conflict persisted until Henri IV converted in July 1593 and won Paris.**0.68a** He was granted absolution by Pope Clement VIII who thereby signalled the end of the papal

>**0.67 THE LAST OF THE VALOIS:** Henri III in 1577 (Paris, Louvre, Cabinet des Medailles).

0.68a

After Clouet – and Decourt – French royal portraiture
was briefly dominated by the Flemish Frans Pourbus
the Younger who was trained by his grandfather who
had been an assistant of Frans Floris. He developed his
style in Mantua for Eleanora de' Medici from 1600. Six
years later he was called to Paris by the latter's sister,
the French Queen Marie. Popular with most of the great
courts at the turn of the century, his formulaic courtly
mode is attuned to rarely relaxed formality of pose but
is notable for portraying individualism and for its
highly realistic recording of detail – sumptuous fabric
and jewelry in particular.

0.68b

subservience to Philipine interests which followed from
the foreign policy of Gregory XIII. Dissident Leaguers
retained the support of Spain: war with the latter – but not
hostility to the Habsburgs – ended to France's advantage
with the Peace of Vervins in May 1598. Philip II died four
months later. The League withered. The first step towards
rebuilding the shattered kingdom was the grant of limited
freedom to the Huguenots by the Edict of Nantes (April
1598) – without alienating the Catholics.

Over the first decade of the new century, the popular first
Bourbon and his great minister, the duc de Sully, achieved
much in restoring order to the country and reforming the
state: brooking no dissent from the *parlements* and dispensing with the Estates-General – discredited under the
late-Valois – he greatly furthered absolutism run by a
bureaucracy headed by his appointees at the centre and in
the provinces. Industry was encouraged and trade balanced
with protective tariffs on imports. Agriculture was restored
and peasants relieved of tax debts. Loss to the treasury was
offset by admission of the right to buy hereditary office.

Tragically, the king was assassinated in 1610: his heir was
his juvenile son, Louis XIII (1610–43); his widow, Queen
Marie de' Medici, ruled as regent.**0.68b** Her regime at first
favoured nobles pursuing lost privilege and Catholics promoting anti-Huguenot rapprochement with Spain –
sealed with the marriage of the king to Philip III's daughter, Anne of Austria. Bribes for support despoiled the treasury, Sully was sacked and the Estates-General was recalled
in 1614 – uselessly (and for the last time until 1789). Intrigue
ruled until the queen mother was banished by her alienated son in 1617 and the pro-Spanish policy renounced but
her minister, Cardinal Richelieu, emerged to effective rule
from 1624 to 1642. That propelled France along the road to
pre-eminence which would be achieved by the unlikely
product of the young royal couple's unhappy union.

IBERIAN EMPIRE

Spain had reached the peak of its power under Philip II, but his devotion to Catholicism – and the doleful effect of the Spanish Inquisition as both his servant and master – led him to intransigence and defeat in the English Channel, in the Netherlands, in his dream of restoring religious and secular unity to Europe.**0.69**

The dream of Philip II

Flourishing under Pius V, the Confraternity of the Most Holy Name of Jesus was founded by the Dominicans in accordance with the prescription of S. Paul (Epistle to the Philippians) that at the name of Jesus every knee should bow in heaven, on earth and below earth.**0.69b** El Greco shows the company of heaven in homage to the divine monogram at the top, the denizens of purgatory and hell bottom right, the faithful of earth bottom left. In the last group, the king is flanked by the pope (Pius V, facing out from the centre) and the doge (facing in from the foreground), the latter reconciled to the former in the pontiff's Holy League which prevailed at Lepanto (when the doge was Lodovico Mocenigo). Thus, while it pays homage to Pius V's Dominican order (Spanish in origin), the picture may be seen as an allegory of the Holy League, commemorative of the first triumph of the post-Tridentine Church under Christ's banner – to which the League was dedicated in perpetuity.

Enigmatic still are the other major figures in the terrestrial group: the king's half-brother Don John, the victor of Lepanto, has been proposed for the doge's neighbour and, indeed, that his death in 1578 was the immediate occasion for the commissioning of the picture. The cardinals flanking the pope may be Spain's two most important post-Tridentine Grand Inquisitors: Diego de Espinoza y de Arévalo, bishop of Siguenza, who was created cardinal by Pius V in 1568 and died the year after Lepanto, and the contemporary incumbent, the bearded Don Gaspar de Quiroga y Vela whose distinguished service as royal envoy to Rome and the Italian dominion earned him promotion to grand inquisitor (1573–94), archbishop of Toledo (from 1577) and cardinal (from 1578) – the artist's major non-royal patron, he is recognized as standing in for S. Augustine at 'The Burial of Count Orgaz'.

King Philip's major role in the Holy League of the Dominican pope is cer-

o.69a

›0.69 PHILIP II OF SPAIN: (a) in 1565 (Sofonisba Anguissola, formerly attributed to Alonso Sánchez Coello who was responsible for several other versions; Madrid, Prado); (b) c. 1579 with the Church hierarchy, the damned and all the panoply of heaven in 'Adoration of the Name of Jesus' (sometimes known as 'The Dream of Philip II', El Greco; El Escorial).

The medieval sources of El Greco's allegorical imagery are beyond us here except to note that they were shared by Bosch whose work, admired by Philip, would have been well known to El Greco: the latter's own is the ecstatic style but Correggio inspires the empyrean of angels elongated in the Mannerist mode of Parmigianino with a freedom exceeding even the most colouristic of Venetians.

0.69b

tainly consistent with an enhanced Inquisition throughout the Spanish Empire. The specific Spanish institution had been founded by the Catholic Monarchs in 1480 in a climate of clerical bigotry and nationalistic ambition: Rome protested but ultimately acquiesced, recognizing that its promotion of orthodoxy would be furthered by its secular motive. As that was to promote unity as the ecclesiastical arm of a centralizing monarchy, its organization was, of course, highly centralized: a network of provincial tribunals reported to a central supreme council which, though royal, was controlled by the grand inquisitor who held his office for life.

As Protestantism was not popular in Iberia, the main victims of the Inquisition were *conversos* – Muslims or Jews who chose, or were forced, to be baptized. Suspected of insincerity and denied access to public office but dominant commercially, they were resented, and prey to denunciation, fines or expropriation. That swelled the coffers of the tribunals: to curb abuse king and *cortes* proposed placing the financing of the institution on a regular basis as an arm of state but failed to overcome clerical opposition. King Charles had more success in protecting the natives of the American colonies, to which the Inquisition had been extended by his late grandfather: its jurisdiction was limited to Europeans in 1538. Three years later Prince Philip, as regent, increased its reach by formally establishing it in three new provinces controlled from Mexico City, Cartagena and Lima.

Unfortunate though it was at last, the severe reign may not be denied its triumphs: ending Valois ambitions in Italy in favour of Habsburg ascendancy and, through that, the ultimate success of the Counter-Reformation in checking the advance of Protestantism. Philip failed to deny France to the Bourbons but his intervention was crucial in prompting Henri IV's conversion, ensuring that Catholicism would remain the official Gallic faith. He annexed Portugal with its great Atlantic ports – and the second largest maritime empire. His officers played a major part in countering the threat posed to Europe by the Ottoman navy: they also succeeded in increasing imports from America despite English, Dutch and French privateers. His agents began the colonization of the Philippine islands in the western Pacific and established the first trans-Pacific trade route between America and Asia. He regulated the administration – and the urban development – of his kingdom and its colonies but insensitive determination on uniformity in the face of manifest differences, hardly less acute in Iberia than in the Netherlands, was bound for disaster.

›0.70 THE DUKE OF LERMA, 1603 (Peter Paul Rubens).

Francisco Gómez de Sandoval was born in Seville c. 1522, nephew of the archbishop. He gravitated to the court of Philip II where he endeared himself to the indolent – but pious – heir. Soon after the latter's accession in 1598, he was raised to his dukedom and entrusted with much of the government as chief minister. He had himself made cardinal in 1618, the year of his downfall. His mismanagement and corruption had provoked opposition which was spearheaded by his son, Cristóbal de Sandoval, duke of Uceda, but fomented by Gaspar de Guzmán, later count-duke of Olivares, favourite of Philip IV who terminated the brief ascendancy of the younger Sandoval on his accession in 1621.

Rubens clearly acknowledges the mastery of Titian's 'Charles V at Mühlberg', as would any artist bent on projecting an heroic equestrian image. However, the enhanced expressionism (not ignorant of Dürer), the dramatic lighting, the startling palette and the turning of the trajectory on to a more pronounced diagonal sets the work off on a dynamic course which leads straight to the Baroque – as we shall see in the context of complementary developments elsewhere.

Despite the wealth of the Indies and ruinous taxation, Philip II left a bankrupt kingdom. He also left an ineffective successor in thrall to an incompetent minister: Philip III (1598–1621) and the rapacious duke of Lerma (c. 1552–1625).**⁰·⁷⁰** The regime did achieve peace with England in 1604 and truce in the Netherlands in 1609. The latter had been bequeathed by Philip II to his daughter Isabella Clara Eugenia and her husband, Archduke Albert. By the end of the first decade of the new regime both sides to the Dutch war were exhausted. Lasting for twelve years, the truce allowed the south to recover under the relatively benign archducal couple but it amounted to *de facto* recognition of the Dutch republic – whose newly chartered East India Company was busily engaged on supplanting King Philip's Portuguese subjects in their worldwide trading posts.

The benefits of Lerma's peaceful foreign policy were not matched at home. In 1609, the regime decreed the expulsion of the industrious – but antipathetic – Moriscos from Iberia: that further undermined an economy already overdependent on imported treasure, rather than on industry, and reeling from the debasement of the currency to reduce debt. Further centralization was attempted at the expense of the constituent kingdoms and their quasi-independent *cortes*. However, the financial situation left the king dependent on the latter and, of course, the overwhelming majority of their members opposed supreme monarchical power: stultification ensued. Towards the reign's unhappy end, the corruption of Lerma and his cronies sapped tax revenues with such flagrance that the supine king had no option but to dispense with the duke in 1618. He was replaced by his son who undid his one achievement, peace abroad, by involving Spain in the conflict which would engulf Europe for the next thirty years. Left to Philip IV (1621–65) and another favourite, the count-duke of Olivares, that legacy's dividend would be ruination.

THE EMPIRE

Habsburg dreams of unity in the west evaporating, the situation in the Empire was certainly no better. In a chronically fissiparous polity, sectarian difference exacerbated political rivalry: of magnate against emperor or one another; of Habsburg against Bourbon; of Baltic states for hegemony in their region; of maritime powers for colonies. The condition, initially, was the erosion of the Augsburg settlement: as we have noted, neither Lutherans nor Catholics were satisfied with the 'Interim' and the intrusion of Calvinism into Germany took the strain to breaking point as the rival rite attracted great magnates, in particular the elector palatine (1560).

Open warfare followed the conversion of the Electoral archbishop of Cologne in 1583 which threatened to subvert the imperial electoral college: Spanish troops from the Netherlands were diverted to depose him in favour of the Catholic Ernest of Bavaria. The subsequent exertions of Duke Maximilian of Bavaria on behalf of his fellow Catholics, especially against the Protestants of Swabian Donauwörth in 1607, naturally alarmed both Calvinists and Lutherans. The Calvinists formed the League of Evangelical Union (1608) to which the duke responded with the Catholic League (1609). Having lost Nassau, Hesse and Brandenburg to the Calvinists early in the new century, the Lutherans found themselves confined largely to the north where they attracted Scandinavian support.

Like his father, Emperor Maximilian II had largely honoured the spirit of the Augsburg settlement with religious tolerance but this was reversed by his mentally unstable son Rudolf II (1576–1612). Humanist in inclination, he evinced little personal commitment to either Protestant or Catholic rites: he opposed repression of either at first but he was increasingly fractious with the Protestant powers in Germany, which he saw as threatening his hegemony.

0.71a

›0.71 EMPEROR RUDOLF II (1552–1612) and his artistic patronage: (a) as Vertumnus (god of the seasons, c. 1590, Giuseppe Arcimboldo; Skokloster, Sweden); (b, c) 'Bacchus and Ceres Leave Venus', 'Venus and Adonis' (Bartholomaeus Spranger, c. 1590–95; Vienna, Museum of Art History); (d–g) 'Rocky Landscape' (Roelandt Savery, c. 1608; Budapest, Museum of Fine Art), 'Dodo Study' (Vienna Belvedere), Noah's Ark (c. 1620; Warsaw, National Museum), and 'Still-life with Lizards' (1603; Utrecht, Central Museum); (h) 'Psyche with Pandora's Box' (Adriaen de Vries, c. 1600; Stockholm, National Museum).

The future emperor spent his adolescence in Spain, at the court of his uncle Philip II, returning to Vienna in 1571 aloof in the Spanish manner: melancholia supervened and he withdrew, in Prague Castle (from the early 1580s), into the occult, especially astrology and alchemy, into the patronage of scientists and artists and into collecting. He entered into several politically motivated bouts of marriage negotiation but, sexually unorthodox perhaps, he remained single.

Eccentricity certainly made Rudolf's reign problematic but its failures followed his pursuit of Christendom's lost unity with a fecklessness which exasperated both Catholics and Protestants. However, as a patron he was a resounding success in developing his father's advanced interests in the arts and sciences: ironically,

0.71b, c

And he opposed renewed threat from the Ottomans by attempting a new crusade in 1593: inconclusive, the conflict had exhausted the rump of Hungary by 1604 and provoked revolt. That was ended only when his brother Matthias took control of negotiations with the Hungarian estates on the one hand, the Turks on the other: by 1608 Matthias had claimed supremacy in Hungary, Austria and Moravia.

The emperor had moved the court to Prague Castle, where he was a notable patron of science and an obsessive collector of Mannerist art.**0.71** Balking at his brother's enhanced power, he sought support from Bohemia by

the most lasting memorial to this deranged emperor are the 'Rudolphine Tables', the astronomical tables compiled by Kepler and dedicated in gratitude for the sustenance and security provided at the imperial court. The art collection was the greatest of its age but pillage in the Thirty Years' War left only a fraction as the nucleus for accession to Vienna's Museum of Art History.

The most important artists represented in Rudolf's collection of paintings ranged from the greatest Germans, Dürer and Bruegel, to Correggio, Parmigianino and even Leonardo. The emperor was also patron to leading contemporary artists: he preferred the highly Mannerist eroticism of Bartholomaeus Spranger (drawn from Bronzino, softened after Correggio), the innovative *plein air* landscapes and complementary still-lives of the Dutch master Roelandt Savery (1576–1639) and the bizarre, surrealist allegorical confections of the Milanese Mannerist Giuseppe Arcimboldo (1527–93). His principal sculptor was Adriaen de Vries, the Dutch follower of Giambologna who produced major works for the church of S. Lorenzo at Philip II's Escorial and was first called to Prague c. 1590.

Rudolf commissioned decorative objects of all kinds, in particular mechanical moving devices and superb scientific instruments, astrolabes, compasses and telescopes for Kepler and his colleague, the Dane

0.71d

0.71g

0.71e

0.71h

0.71f

granting the 'Letter of Majesty' which guaranteed religious freedom (1609): not satisfied and sensing weakness, the Protestants rebelled. Met with force, the rebels called on Matthias and Rudolf was stripped of all but the imperial title to which his brother was duly elected after Rudolf's death in 1612.

The short reign of Matthias (1612–19) was destabilized by League rivalry and the issue of succession. The first in line, Archduke Ferdinand of Styria, was an ardent Jesuit-educated Catholic who was bent on restoring Catholic supremacy: his confirmation as crown prince of Bohemia in 1617 countered the will of the Hussite populace and nobility, many of whom preferred the elector palatine Frederick V, head of the League of Evangelical Union. The clash of Protestant and Catholic, of state and empire, of Frederick and Ferdinand, first favoured the latter who had duly been elected emperor after Matthias. However, it unleashed prolonged war which would destroy the old imperial order, lay the foundations of a new construct based on state sovereignty in central Europe – and leave dominance with France.

BRITAIN: DIVINE RIGHT AND PARLIAMENT

Protestant England, initially the staunchest supporter of the Dutch Republic, was ultimately to become its fiercest rival. Meanwhile the contention between crown and parliament, unresolved at the death of Queen Elizabeth, issued in rupture under pressure from revived religious contention.

The succession passed to the Catholic Queen Mary Stuart's Protestant son who ruled as James VI of Scotland and I of England (1603–25):**0.72** he sought reconciliation at home, peace and expansion abroad. The East India Company (founded 1601) completed its first voyage at the begin-

Tycho Brahe. Otherwise, his avid collecting ranged widely from ceremonial swords, musical instruments and clocks to animals – which Savery lost no opportunity to depict in his landscapes, real and ideal.

0.72

›0.72 JAMES I AND HIS ROYAL PROGENY
(mezzotint of 1814 after the engraved image by Willem
de Passe from after 1624).

James, son of Mary Queen of Scots, succeeded to
the throne vacated by his exiled mother in mid-1567,
when he was just over one year old: he attained his
majority in 1578 but was not free of regents until three
years later. On succeeding his mother's cousin Elizabeth I of England and Ireland in 1603 he ruled the three
kingdoms separately – each retaining its own parliament, judiciary and laws. He was married to Anne,
daughter of Frederick II of Denmark, in 1589: the progeny here include the princes of Wales, Henry (died
1612) and Charles (acceded 1625), to the right of the
royal couple and to the left, Princess Elizabeth and her
husband the elector palatine, Frederick V ('winter' king
and queen of Bohemia 1619–20) and their children
including Princes Frederick Henry, Charles, Rupert and
Maurice, Princesses Elisabeth, Louise and Sophie. The
last, married to Elector George Louis of Hanover, was
heir presumptive to the British thrones at her death in
1714, her claim passing to her son George.

ning of the reign. Virginia was settled in 1607 and British
'Puritans' began the colonization of New England in 1620.
Ireland was pacified. War with Spain had ended within a
year of the succession and a Spanish match sought for the
heir. Yet James supported the Protestants against the Habsburgs and married his daughter to the elector palatine,
Frederick V. As we shall see, the latter's championship of
the anti-Catholic cause was a major factor in the opening
phase of the Thirty Years' War and Britain was called to his
defence when his ambitions were thwarted.

At home, tension between Catholics and Protestants was
exacerbated by the Anglican Church establishment's measures against non-conformity. In 1605 the king and parliament had narrowly escaped obliteration by Catholics
alienated by perceived failure to ameliorate their lot. On the
other hand, the Puritans were alienated by royal backing for
episcopal enforcement of conformity in hostility to the
theocratic tendencies inherited by their sects from Calvin.
The House of Commons was offended by assertion of the
divine right of kings: objecting to court extravagance, it
nevertheless approved tax rises in 1611 but further increases
were proscribed. Dispensing with parliament largely thereafter, the king raised revenue irregularly through the sale of
titles, offices and monopolies. In 1621, however, he had to
appeal for war funds and received an inadequate grant on
condition that there would be no Spanish marriage. By 1624
parliamentary prescription on the disposition of funds
severely curtailed the royal prerogative.

The Elizabethan establishment had imposed bishops
on the Church of Scotland and the process of assimilating
the latter with the English Church was pressed by the Stu-
arts to culmination under Charles I (1625–49). **0.73** The
imposition of a quasi-Anglican liturgy by royal decree in
1637 provoked rebellion: 'Covenanters', sworn to resist the
perversion of their Church, took up arms and launched an

invasion of England in 1640. All Britain was soon convulsed: the occasion was the recurrence of religious discord – primarily between Protestant sects – but the condition was the opposition of political principle.

The venerable concept of the divine right of kings, compounded with the Biblical sanctification of the Lord's anointed, was of great potential in bolstering claims to national sovereignty. It was the aspiration of the late-Valois, though their way to its achievement in abrogation of the consultative rights of the Estates-General was as yet unclear. It was similarly elusive even for Philip II as he faced the *cortes* of Spain's disparate constituent elements. It sat particularly uncomfortably at the summit of the English political edifice founded on the Magna Carta. As interpreted by the end of the 13th century, that was a contract between king and commoner which conceded the rights of parliament (AIC4, page 228). A very different contract was postulated by the leading English political theorist of the mid-Stuart period, Thomas Hobbes: anticlerical and no proponent of divine right, he claimed that necessity forced the subject to surrender his uninhibited freedom to the authoritarian state – the Leviathan characterized as a monstrous man with the king as the head – in return for protection; that was regrettable but the insupportable alternative was chaos, literally uncivilized, and the life of man 'nasty, brutish and short'. At the end of the Tudor era, on the other hand, no social contract was recognized in the circle of Sir Walter Raleigh: chosen by 'God and the law divine', kings were not subject to the laws of men.**0.74**

Usurpers, the Tudors ruled by force – not least of personality. Lacking the latter, but the heir to usurpation, James I oscillated between extra-parliamentary prerogative, respect for common law and rule by and in virtue: ambivalent about his supra-legal authority, he had preten-

0.73

›0.73 CHARLES I (1631, Daniel Mijtens).

Born in The Hague to a family which had moved north from Flanders in escape the religious strife of the mid-16th century, Mijtens (or Mytens, c. 1590–1647) was the heir to the Netherlandish tradition developed by Pourbus from Antonis Mor. In England by 1618, he crossed his native inheritance with the late reflection of the Anglo-German tradition descended from Holbein: formality persists, but not to the obviation of individual characterization, and so too does mastery of detail, particularly the textures of fabrics and leather.

0.74a

›0.74 THE BRITISH PARLIAMENT AND THE LEVIATHAN: (a) Elizabeth I presiding over the assembled Lords and Commons (late-16th century); (b) title page of Hobbes's political treatise.

0.74b

sions to 'mystical reverence' as the Vicar of God. Claiming sanctity for the royal prerogatives, King Charles articulated no pretension to personal divine right but the contention between opposed interpretations of his status ruined his realm. That opened a new era, not only in British politics: while the tide of absolutism was on the flow in much of Europe, across the Channel it had already begun its ebb.

PART 1 SEMINAL ITALIANS

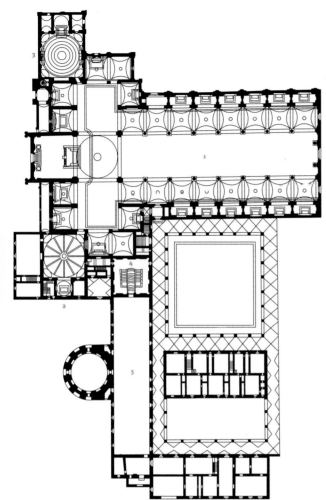

MICHELANGELO'S INITIATIVE

The sources of Michelangelo's architectural inspiration are unfathomable but, as we know, the ancients were adept at countering structural logic with wit (AICI, page 603). His wilful ambiguity infuses his delineation of form and space, frame and framed, load and support. In the New Sacristy at S. Lorenzo in Florence, for example, scrupulously observed Classical detail and flagrantly uncanonical mouldings are freely juxtaposed and in the design of the niches it is impossible to distinguish frame and framed from the complex interpenetration of forms or to isolate a single base for the projection and recession of planes.

The vestibule of the library which forms part of the S. Lorenzo complex is even more disturbing. It reverses the accepted conventions of articulation in which the wall is passive and the Order applied to it is the active agent of the forces implicit in structure; the main mass pushes through to engulf the columns and any residual virility is denied to the latter by their apparent reliance on consoles for support – yet the wall is largely lost to void. Energized in this way, the tall, narrow enclosure draws the visitor through a concertina of portal frames to release in the long, harmonious reading room.**1.1**

1.1a @ 1:1000

›1.1 FLORENCE, MICHELANGELO AT S. LORENZO: (a) plan with (1) Brunelleschi's basilica, (2) Old Sacristy, (3) New Sacristy, (4) library vestibule, (5) reading room, (b) basilica façade drawing, 1518, (c, d) New Sacristy (1519–34), axonometric (after Ackerman) and general view, (e–k) Laurentian Library, vestibule, staircase, section and plan, reading room, (i, j) project drawings for vestibule portal.

Michelangelo at S. Lorenzo

Michelangelo was back in Florence by 1516 to compete with Giuliano da Sangallo and others on the design for a façade for Brunelleschi's Laurentian basilica. He succeeded in 1518 with a revision of Giuliano's latest scheme of superimposed 'rhythmic bays' which extended the superstructure to the whole width, instead of expressing the basilican section (AIC4, page 849). Most significantly – ambiguously – he broke the Orders forward through two planes to assert the derivation of the intermediate bays from the piers of a triumphal arch but retained the temple-front pediment.

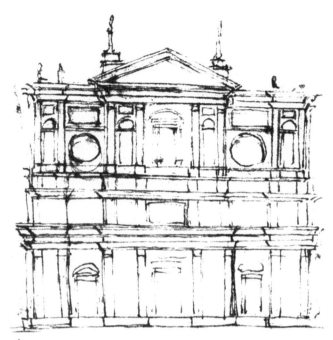

1.1b

On the death of Pope Leo X's brother Giuliano and nephew Lorenzo de'
Medici in 1516 and 1519 respectively, Michelangelo was commissioned to
provide a mortuary chapel for them and for their namesakes from the previous generation – Lorenzo the Magnificent and his brother Giuliano who
had died in 1492 and 1478 respectively. Specifically required to balance
Brunelleschi's sacristy, the New Sacristy retained the Corinthian ordonnance but the pendentives were raised between lunettes with trapezoidal
windows over an interpolated clerestory in which the truncated Order has
a contracted entablature. The semi-circular arch cedes to the ellipse for the
square altar chapel – opposite the entrance, as in the original – and for the
recessions containing the tombs on either side. In each of these simplicity
is reserved for the central niche containing the statue of the younger
deceased over the recumbent figures of Day and Night, Dawn and Dusk, on
their sarcophagi: the empty niches to the sides benefit only from pediments on consoles but the parapet is bizarre in its combination of inverted
balusters, swags and an isolated central console pretending to support
the entablature. The tightly packed minor bays in the corner are the richest

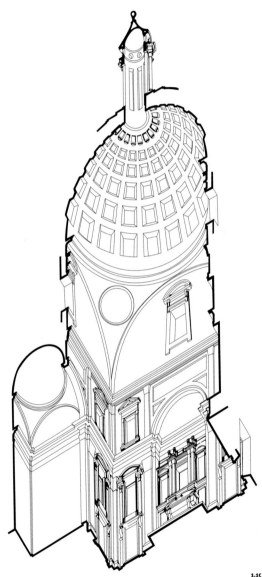

1.1c

in the uncanonical detailing of the blind aedicular niches: spatially ambiguous at the expense both of the vertical and horizontal planes, these are integrated with mainly blind doors through the agency of a horizontal moulding which at once provides base to the former and lintel to the latter. The tombs of the older dukes, projected for the entrance wall, were never finished.

In 1524 Pope Clement VII ordered the resumption of work on the New Sacristy, halted with the death of his Medici predecessor, and commissioned a library associated with the monastic cloister of the S. Lorenzo complex. The space available was tall and narrow for access, long and narrow for the reading room. Vestibule (*ricetto*) and staircase were combined for the former, the expansive organism of the latter oozing into most of the

1.1d

1.1e

1.1f

1.1g, h @ 1:1000

former to disturbingly enticing effect. That is enhanced by the drama enacted above through the reversal of convention in the articulation of exterior and interior and, further, in the deployment of column and wall by sinking the former and advancing the latter in apparent denial of active and passive norms. This is echoed by the dissonant subversion or displacement of structural detail – such as pilasters tapering from the top down or triglyphs transposed as consoles or consoles supporting nothing unless they support supposedly supportive columns – all in concert with an un-Classical medley of multiple mouldings on a stage of jostling planes.

1.1i

1.1k

RAPHAEL'S TESTAMENT

Raphael's playful approach to convention, his refusal to be awed by the greatest achievements of his master, was well demonstrated by his architecture at large. For the Palazzo Branconio dell'Aquila on the Vatican Borgo, now sadly lost, he canvassed all the major current palace façade types and everything is disposed against expectation. The Order of the Caprini piano nobile has slipped down to the shops at street level and was apparently to support only statues in the niches between the aedicules of the Pandolfini type on the principal storey. Horizontals counter verticals and the ratio of solid to void – heavy to light – increases from bottom to top, contradicting apparent necessity: the densest mass of the attic, panelled in the Alberini-Cicciaporci manner, is floated over a diaphanous mezzanine zone of stucco reliefs where a Florentine palazzo might have had *sgraffito* decoration. Little is known of the internal distribution but the site was not irregular. This was not the case

›1.2 ROME, RAPHAEL'S LATE PALACES: (a, b) Branconio dell'Aquila (1518), engraved façade, project drawing of court (attributed to Giulo Romano); (c) his own, ground-floor plan (attributed to Benvenuto della Volpaia).

The palace of the papal chamberlain, Giambattista Branconio, disappeared in the 17th century when its site at the opening of the Via Alessandrina was incorporated into a piazza. Richness of decorative detail *all' antica* is as characteristic of Raphael's late work as extending architrave and frieze into a stringcourse – or sustaining the integrity of the piano nobile ordonnance with niches in the corners at the expense of apparent strength. Characteristic too is precise quotation from the antique: for instance, the alternation of niches and aedicules derives from the remains of the Forum of Trajan and there too aesthetic logic denies apparent structural necessity (AIC1, page 625).

Raphael's own site faced streets to all four sides, none meeting at a right angle. The surviving plan indicates shops on the ground floor in bays defined by a colossal Order: no less significantly, it provides an object lesson to Classicists bent on denying irregularity. The axial entrance leads to a square nuclear court

1.2a

1.2b

surrounded by loggias: to the right – in the rear wing –
the main staircase doubled back in parallel ramps to
the upper loggias which served the patron's accommodation in the two longest ranges. Joined at an acute
angle by the reception rooms in the entrance wing, the
range of personal apartments – presumably – overlooked the Via Giulia: the awkward junction was skilfully masked by an antechamber which, like the
adjacent court, was rectangular with an apsidal extension into mass from which service stairs and ducts were
won. The secondary accommodation, bent around the
opposite corner, was also served by an axial entrance
corridor leading to a rectangular nuclear court: the axis
was closed by a circular fountain gauged from the mass
separating the two courts; stairs to the left rose to a
loggia serving the main reception room.

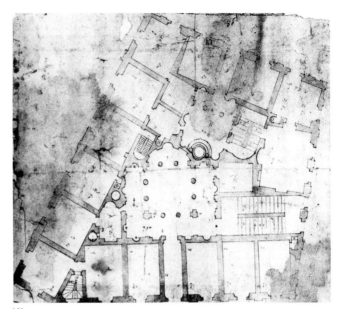

1.2c

with the Via Giulia site which Raphael planned to develop
as his own residence and atelier just before he died (see
AIC4, page 857).[1.2]

Mastery of the rules had licensed the creative mind to
assert supremacy over convention and Raphael's survey of
ancient Rome had introduced him to the operation of
licence in the antique. On the linguistic analogy, it may
well be maintained that if Bramante had mastered the
grammar of antique architecture, Raphael comprehended
its colloquialism but also its refinement. However, his
achievement is difficult to disentangle from the contribution of his most brilliant assistant, Giulio Pippi (1492 or
1499–1546) who asserted his Roman birth – unique among
his main colleagues – by adopting the surname Romano:
ancient Rome was his birthright and working with
Raphael as an archaeologist he may be presumed to have
contributed as much as he gained from the association –
especially if he was twenty years old on entering Raphael's
studio about 1512.

At his death Raphael was on the verge of a seminal architectural career: he had yet to transform S. Pietro but he was building palaces with innovative façades and working on equally innovative villas. Their significance deriving not least from their relationship to their environment, real or feigned, the latter ranged from the dazzling Psyche Loggia at the Villa Farnesina to the small casino commissioned by Baldassare Turini on the Gianicolo and finally to the huge complex commissioned by Pope Leo X on Monte Mario above the Milvian Bridge in the northern outskirts of Rome. The first two of these were completed with the aid of assistants: Giulio Romano is often given the leading role in the production of Turini's work, now called Villa Lante. Leo X's retreat – now known as the Villa Madama – remained incomplete on the death of both principal architect and patron between April 1520 and December the following year but it would be hard to overestimate the significance of the surviving fragment.[1.3, 1.4]

1.3a

At the instigation of his patron, on the Monte Mario site Raphael set himself to recreate an antique Roman country retreat of the type described in somewhat ambiguous detail in the letters of Pliny the Younger. In doing so he went beyond Renaissance practice of honouring Classical precept in the design of modern buildings inspired by ancient remains or even borrowing Classical motifs like the temple front and triumphal arch for their formal or symbolic significance: Classicizing an entire complex in a thoroughgoing revival of antique form, he asserted his equality with the ancients at their most sophisticated.

1.3b

The inception of the Villa Madama

Used to moving between his family's many villas and educated by humanists in them, Giovanni de' Medici inherited an obsession with the writings of Pliny the Younger: as pope he encouraged the proliferation of publications

1.3c

›1.3 ROME, GIANICOLO, CASINO TURINI (later Villa Lante), work begun c. 1518, interrupted following Raphael's death, resumed by Giulio c. 1522: (a) entrance front, (b) loggia front, (c) loggia interior.

The Casino Turini was built as a suburban retreat on the site of the ancient villa of the poet Julius Martialis, who wrote that from it he could appreciate all Rome. Emulating this in the view that modern Rome was no less admirable, Turini and his architect were highly innovative: rather than communicating with the protected terrain of an estate, the loggia of their little building addressed the real world beyond the control of the patron – albeit from a secure height – and may thus be seen as taking the crucial step beyond Peruzzi's Farnesina illusionism (AIC4, page 859).

The loggia opens to the view through a triple serliana (see page 17): its original context, characteristic of Raphael, was of rich materials – indeed simulated antique reliefs in marble. Variations in the weight of the Orders, of their spacing and of their distribution on the four sides of the cubic block have suggested Giulio, rather than Raphael, to modern analysts. These gestures – honouring standard Classical practice in the breach – may be seen as somewhat unrefined but the detailing of the loggia all' antica, especially the stucco grotteschi of the tunnel vault and the contraction of the Ionic architrave/frieze, well accord with Raphael's late refinement. The extrusion of Ionic volutes across the piano nobile windows, cheekily assimilating the latter to the neighbouring pilasters, may be due to either artist – the motif appears elsewhere in their collaborative efforts.[1.4i]

devoted to the ancient author and, above all, pursued his ambition to emulate him as a builder. The project was conceived in 1517 when the pope bought the sloping site, with its magnificent outlook and easy access to the Vatican, 3 kilometres to the south-west, and Rome to the south-east. Work began on Raphael's first project in the middle of the following year ostensibly for the pope's cousin Cardinal Giulio (later Pope Clement VII). Presumably to the latter – perhaps to Castigilione, or to the pope himself – Raphael addressed a description in the manner of Pliny which largely matches the definitive project.[1.4a]

The backing of Monte Mario, the terracing of the site and two main axes of approach were naturally crucial to the general disposition of the complex: revisions were largely internal. The first project incorporated a rectangular court and grand entrance portico served by the Vatican road (which must have been steeply ramped), a cryptoporticus (basement entrance) below a great loggia in the centre of the entrance front served by the Milvian road from Rome (which must have ascended terraces), a central rectangular court with a 'Vitruvian' theatre excavated from the hill beyond it to the south-west and a great loggia to the north-west, addressing a garden raised over a fishpond. The terraced site dictated asymmetry in the disposition of the living rooms to either side of the long main axis – linking the entrance from the Vatican direction with the garden loggia – and therefore of the side elevations. However, even the fenestration of the Milvian front is not matched to either side of the portico opening the short cross-axis which culminated in the theatre.[1.4b]

›1.4 ROME, VILLA OF POPE LEO X ON MONTE MARIO (later known as Villa Madama after its owner from 1536, Margaret of Parma, the illegitimate daughter of Emperor Charles V): (a) ideal overview of completed complex, (b) plan of the first project drawn by

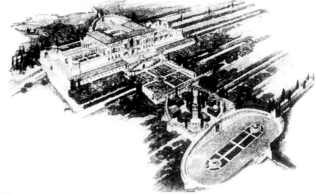

1.4a

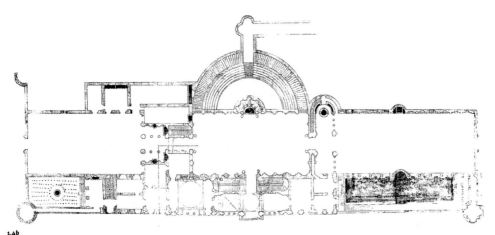

1.4b

By the end of 1518 the landscaping embraced three terraces of different shapes and a hippodrome on the Milvian axis, in addition to the north-west loggia terrace from which a door opened to the world at large – in particular via a link to the Viterbo road.**1.4c,d** In the revised plan, too, steps were introduced to the southern atrium to obviate the steep incline of the approach road, the central court had assumed its definitive circular form at the crossing of the main axes, new rooms appeared in space won from the original quadrangle to redress the imbalance in the size of the two main blocks, the staircases were relocated and the great garden loggia reformed. Asymmetry persisted on the atrium and garden loggia elevations but it was suppressed on the revised Milvian front – apparently even with resort to blind fenestration.**1.4e**

Antonio da Sangallo was responsible for the surviving drawings from late-1518 but the transition from the original scheme to the one with the circular court may be traced in Raphael's *all' antica* description in which the Vitruvian building types and the Laurentine villa of Pliny the Younger are evoked. To the latter's account are such features as the two main approach roads, the 'diaeta' or circular belvedere tower which marked the outer corner of both the 'atrium' and the 'xystus' (formal garden terrace) to the south and north of the main block, thermal baths to the south of the cryptoporticus, the fishpond, the hippodrome and the O-shaped court (perhaps a misreading of 'D' inspired by Bramante's unexecuted context for the Tempietto of S. Pietro in Montorio or even the Roman Pantheon). In general, Pliny

Gianfrancesco da Sangallo, (c–e) plan of terraces, revisions drawn by Antonio da Sangallo, and façade of corresponding modern model, (f) plan of executed work, (g) Raphael's copy of an interior view of the Pantheon which may have inspired the conception of the circular court, (h) surviving segment of central court, (i) *salotto* with 'Ionic' mantelpiece, (j, k) loggia front and interior detail, (l) view over north-west terrace garden to outer portal.

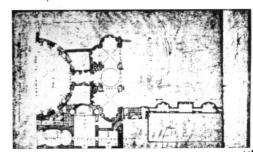

1.4f

1.4g

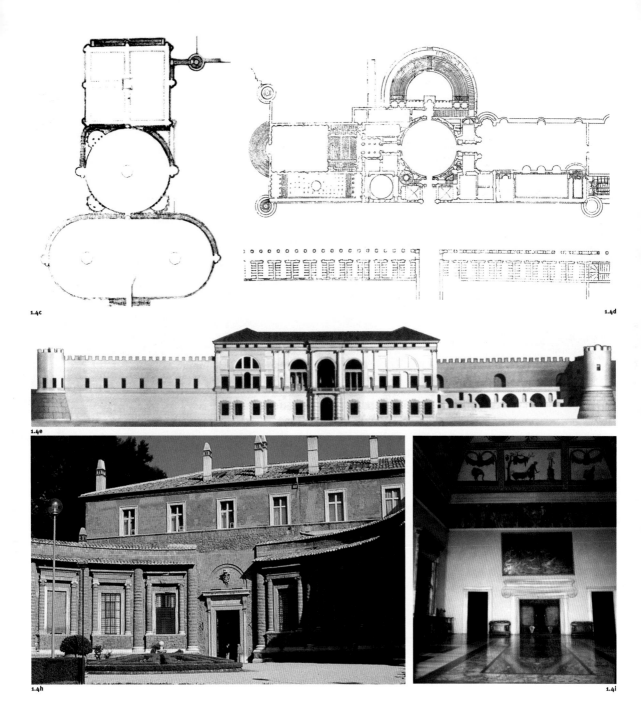

1.4c

1.4d

1.4e

1.4h

1.4i

›ARCHITECTURE IN CONTEXT »FROM THE HIGH RENAISSANCE TO MANNERISM

projected an accumulation of spaces which might be appreciated, not at a glance of the mind's eye, but only with the emotions aroused by passage through and views from them – rather than along them, as in the typically formal imperial thermal complex (AIC1, pages 626f). In all, built to cater both for private retreat and public representation on the grandest scale, like the complex of Emperor Hadrian at Tivoli, this astonishing work is *sui generis* – unidentifiable with the typical Renaissance villa or palace.

Though completed by Giulio Romano and Giovanni da Udine, the Villa Madama's great loggia alone is a measure of Raphael's success in his dedication to Classicizing design: modelled on Bramante's nymphaeum at Genazzano (AIC4, page 856), it emulates an imperial thermal hall in scale and the Domus Aurea or the Baths of Titus and

1.4k

their followers in sumptuousness of ornament (AICI, page 643). Indeed, it was in his revival of imperial embellishment that Raphael implied – in a letter to the pope dating from about the time he was working on the Vatican loggie – that it was the resurrection of antique ornament which took architecture beyond the achievement of Bramante.

1.5b

1.5a

>**1.5 ROME, VILLA FARNESINA (ORIGINALLY CHIGI), PSYCHE LOGGIA,** Raphael and assistants, 1518: (a) general view of vault, (b) detail of simulated tapestry representing the 'Feast of the Gods' – the wedding banquet of Cupid and Psyche, (c) project drawing for 'The Three Graces' (Windsor, Royal Collection).

Facing the garden, the loggia is transformed into a bower whose trelliswork supports vines laden with fruit and flowers (usually attributed to Giovanni da Udine). It was destined to house an antique statue of Psyche acquired by the patron, the eminently rich Sienese banker Agostino Chigi. In accordance with Raphael's programme and drawings, various members of his team – particularly Giulio Romano – assisted in the revelation of the Psyche story beyond the trellis: the sky appears through the triangulated structure of the cove as the realm of the *dramatis personae* but it is mostly obscured by the *velaria* representing the wedding banquet before the court of Zeus. In that quintessentially Classicizing exercise, Classical relief and antique models are translated from sculpture to tapes-

try – with palpable sensuality despite the fiction. The latter presumably recommended itself as preferable to distorting the prodigious company with the foreshortening required if they were to be viewed *di sotto in sù*: that had yet to be achieved on this scale but Correggio was soon to do so in a rather different context (see page 32).

1.5c

Comparison of the Madama's *grotteschi* with the complex illusionism of the Psyche Loggia in the Villa Farnesina is particularly instructive. There, rather than re-evoking the lost world of the antique at its most opulent, Raphael and his team manage to evoke both the real world of the garden and a supernatural paradise. The vine-clad structural frame of a simulated pergola, incurving like a cove as it ascends, reveals patches of sky beyond a canopy stretched across the centre in form: the Classical myth of Cupid and Psyche is developed with simulated corporeality in the evocation of infinite celestial space but its culmination in marriage is recorded for posterity in the ceiling canopy, in the two dimensions of *quadro riportato*, as a simulated tapestry. And all this was barely a generation on from Mantegna.[1.5]

The scale of the Madama loggia departs from the humanist norm towards the colossal: it is impressed on the exterior in the freely interpreted Ionic Order which runs through two storeys separated by a stringcourse and thus, denying support to the second floor contrary to structural logic, denies the measure of man. That, however, is retained in the subsidiary Order of the Milvian front: with an entablature on the line of the first-floor stringcourse, this screens the secondary arches of the central loggia and forms the pair of minor bays which support the great central arch of the side zones: both follow Bramante (AIC4, pages 837, 856 and see above, page 17).

The garden is no less significant. With the integration of house and garden after the introduction of the loggia, as we have seen, the regular chequerboard pattern of the latter was subjected to the central axis extended from the former. The axes projected through the site of the Villa Madama were unprecedented in scale and richness. From the loggia of the main front the principal one linked a descending series of terraced enclosures, varied in design like the rooms inside the house. From the great side loggia, a secondary one ran through a more traditional enclosure on the terrace above the fishpond and out of its gate to an avenue leading off to infinity. Thus, not only were the villa's inhabitants offered a view of the world beyond their control, but the more adventurous among them were enticed beyond the garden wall – despite the discouragement of guardian giants – perhaps for the first time since the descent of the Dark Age and the terror it brought to the world at large.

GIULIO ROMANO: FROM ROME TO MANTUA

Giulio Romano sustained Raphael's Roman practice and developed his idiosyncratic style in his own paintings and buildings. Of the latter, the Palazzo Maccarani is the main survivor but the scheme for the architect's own house was the most influential – especially in its startling treatment of the rustication as an aggressive organism.**1.6**

1.6a

1.6c

›1.6 GIULIO AFTER RAPHAEL IN ROMAN BUILDING: (a, b) Palazzo Maccarani (c. 1522), street front; (c) the architect's own house, project drawing as reproduced by Doso Dossi (1524).

The work for Maccarani, amalgamating several structures addressing the Piazza S.'Eustachio, was commissioned by Cristoforo Stati after the death of Pope Leo X aborted plans for the comprehensive refection of the area. The five-bay scheme recalls Bramante's Palazzo Caprini in extent but subverts the logic of its articulation. The distinction between the world of the street traders and the elevated plane of nobility is still asserted, and even the doubled Order is retained. However, the latter is the reduced Tuscan – with architrave moulding projecting over the pilaster shafts for the capitals – of the Palazzo Alberini (on which Raphael may ultimately have been assisted by Giulio; see AIC4, page 858). As in that work too, there is an upper floor but the panelling is unmoulded.

It will be recalled that the lunettes of the Alberini mezzanine, carried on a continuous stringcourse, ironically asserted the proper role of the voussoir against its wilfully implausible application to the lintels below. On the face of the Maccarani basement relieving arches have ceded to oblong windows supported on exaggerated lintel voussoirs; the latter overwhelm the stringcourse but, unlike their equivalent in Raphael's 'Borgo' palace (see above, page 17), their protean strength is deployed only against void between the piers which sustain the 'Order'.

In contrast, rustication is all-pervasive in Giulio's own house, devouring the Doric Order of the main portal and even the Ionic of the piano nobile aedicule: that was to provide the following generations with an equally pervasive motif.

1.6b

In 1524, after work on the Villa Madama stopped under Pope Adrian VI (1522–23), Giulio was invited to Mantua by the new marquis, Federigo Gonzaga (1500–40) through the agency of Castiglione. Settling his atelier there permanently after the Sack of Rome in 1527, Giulio was ultimately to extend the Gonzaga palace, renovate the cathedral and lay out new quarters of the town but he was first commissioned to transform suburban riding stables into a vast villa – the Palazzo del Te. After the incomplete Villa Madama, this is the prime work of secular Mannerism: fecundity of invention in the confection of architecture and decoration and endless surprise in the breach of convention in the process were the essence of the exercise and the result may still shock the unprepared.**1.7**

Palazzo del Te

The project began as a modest hunting lodge associated with the cele-brated Gonzaga stud but ultimately extended to four long wings – each of one storey with mezzanines – framing a square court inherited from the stable complex. The south side is unarticulated. The west and north fronts, centred on the entrance androne and an arcaded loggia respectively, are vigorously rusticated throughout – stucco masquerading as stone in the Maccarani manner – but overlaid with Doric pilasters in irregular rhythms of increasing intensity from the centres to the sides: structural logic cedes to the visual necessity of strength at the corners but ambiguity attends the assertion of continuity by the rustication below the unbroken entablature and its denial by the caesura in the incidence of the pilasters. The east front, facing a parade court over a fishpond, is centred on an ironically ponderous paraphrase of the central loggia of the Villa Madama, its three arches car-ried on doubled columns and the so-called serliana motif is freely varied to a smaller scale below a miniature gallery to either side – or was before its regrettably academic 18th-century revision.

In witty allusion to Giuliano da Sangallo's engraving of the Arco di Gallo in the process of collapse (AIC4, page 832), the antithetical articulation of the cortile façades demolishes the pretensions of the Order to represent structural stability: blocks from the entablature slip through into voids below. And heavy rustication in the inconsistent intercolumniations, rusti-cated keystones devouring pediments, even undressed columns providing excessive support for the filigree vault in the western vestibule, complete

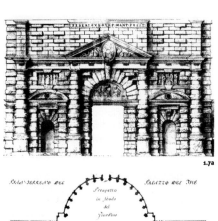

1.7a

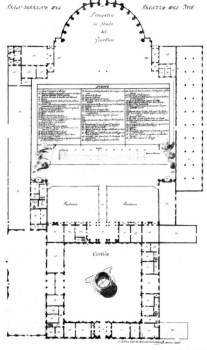

1.7b @ 1:2000

1.7c

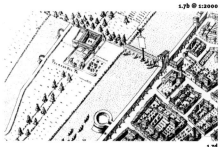

1.7d

1.7e

1.7f

1.7g

›1.7 GIULIO AT MANTUA, SUBURBAN WORK:
(a) Porta del Te project (Vienna, Albertina); (b–s)
Palazzo del Te (from 1525), plan, overview c. 1628 (G.
Bertazzolo; Mantua, City Library), model, original elevations respectively of west, north and east fronts,
detail of court entrance to north range, exterior from
south-west, court façades to north-west, Sala dei Cavalli, Sala di Psiche, Loggia di Davide, Camera degli
Stucchi, Sala dei Giganti, secret garden entrance, loggia and grotto.

the reversal of the first convention of Classical ordonnance: that the Order
is the virile, active agent and the wall passive. Giulio's inspiration is drawn
– ironically, of course – from the reality of ruins rather than the ideality of
their reconstruction.

1.7h

1.7i

1.7j

›ARCHITECTURE IN CONTEXT »FROM THE HIGH RENAISSANCE TO MANNERISM

1.7k

1.7l

Within, a stunning succession of rooms defies the constraint of the quad-rangle: some are frescoed, some stuccoed with exceptional refinement, some stuccoed and frescoed, some extended illusionistically to the sides, some vertically through vaults ostensibly open to the sky and at least one opened entirely to the denial of structural tectonics. The first phase of deco-ration began c. 1527 with the Sala dei Cavalli, in which portraits of select horses from the stud defy the spatial conventions so carefully established by Alberti (AIC4, page 692): it culminated two years later in the resplendent Sala di Psiche, in which the multiple two- and three-dimensional illusionism of Raphael's Farnesina loggia is taken to extreme complexity: walls are treated to individual episodes set in their own extensions of quasi-terrestrial space; the vault is divided by a network of raised mouldings into square and octag-onal compartments revealing the stages of the subject's celestial elevation.

Beyond the *all' antica* gravitas of the great southern loggia, the second phase of embellishment (1530–35) culminated in the Sala dei Giganti. There, in contrast to the elaborate coffering or sumptuous *grotteschi* which respect the normal tectonics of rooms elsewhere, one vast apocalyptic fresco encompasses undefined walls and vault with giants and gigantic architecture collapsing in an astonishing extension of the space below the gods of Olympus presiding in a domed rotunda carried on clouds.

1.7m

1.7o

1.7n

›ARCHITECTURE IN CONTEXT »FROM THE HIGH RENAISSANCE TO MANNERISM

1.7q

1.7r

1.7s

1.7p

Raphael and his circle had given decoration *all'antica* the added dimension of illusionism in the Vatican loggias – under the inspiration of the master's own achievement in the Farnesina loggia. Giulio followed the latter in the Palazzo del Te's Sala di Psiche. However, his most extravagantly comprehensive development of the mode, in the Sala dei Giganti, may best be seen as inverting Mantegna's pioneering exercise in the Camera degli Sposi of the Mantuan ducal palace: solid becomes void and void solid (AIC4, page 698). Mantegna's example was immediate: it had already been developed by Correggio in the cathedral and the church of S. Giovanni Evangelista at Parma into the main mode of dissolving the fabric of a dome to reveal a vision of heaven (see page 17 and AIC4, page 698).

Giulio furthered his games with expectations about load and support in his two surviving Mantuan exercises in façade design: for the Cortile della Cavallerizza in the ducal palace and his own town house. The latter shows him still playing with virile rustication twenty years after his novel Maccarani exercise: it has finally triumphed over any residue of Bramante's ordonnance and even in the window frames the logic of trabeation is denied by the continuity of the interlace moulding through every element. More assertively rusticated – admitting the authority of entablature but denying it to stringcourse and lintel – the Cavallerizza design retains more of Bramante's palace façade formula but impishly traduces it with reference to both Raphael and Michelangelo: the Solomonic Order was contributed by the former; Michelangelo contributed the console supporting the column whose implausible engagement with the wall completes its derision as an articulating agent.**1.8**

Quite contrary to Giulio's derisory attitude to column or pilaster when applied to a wall was his full re-evaluation of the early Christian colonnaded basilica in his

1.8a

1.8b

›1.8 GIULIO IN MANTUA, URBAN WORKS: (a) his own palace, façade (applied from 1540 to a renovated structure, extended in the early 19th century); (b) Palazzo Ducale, Cortile della Cavallerizza (begun with the palace front in 1538, extended to the three outer sides c. 1550).

›1.9 GIULIO, LATE ECCLESIASTICAL WORKS: (a–c) Mantua cathedral, interior and vault details (from 1540); (d) S. Benedetto Po, nave to sanctuary.

1.9a

1.9b

1.9c

1.9d

renovation of Mantua's double-aisled cathedral. However, the proportions of the Corinthian Order which screens nave and aisles are uncanonically heavy – though that was dictated by the inherited fabric – and quite original is the interposition of coffered tunnel vaulting over the inner aisles in contrast to the no-less-richly coffered ceilings of the nave and outer aisles. In his contemporary renovation of the abbey church of S. Benedetto Po, where the 13th-century structure obviated colonnades, Giulio deployed the serliana motif to counter irregular bay widths in the screening of nave from aisles under Bramantesque lunettes: the same problem was denied with the disposition of the 'rhythmic bay' in wilful irregularity outside.[1.9]

Giulio's facility for interior decoration was never to be surpassed in richness and variety but it established the grotesque combination of delicate stuccowork and fresco as the dominant style for much of the 16th century in Italy and its sphere of cultural influence. Limited in specific practice, on the other hand, his influence on the articulation of structure was inspirational in principle. Competing with one another in virtuosity after him, the 16th-century Italian Mannerists loved games of ambiguity and ambivalence, confusing the relationship between appearances and reality in general, overturning convention in articulating structural forces in particular. There were, of course, as many variants as there were courts and erudite – in particular, architecturally literate – courtiers keen to be diverted by the frame, as well as the content, of lives in which the potential for boredom was immense.

STEPS EAST

First to feel the impact of the Palazzo del Te, transmitted from the incomplete Villa Madama, was the Urbino of Duke Francesco Maria della Rovere. In 1530 he – or ostensibly the duchess – commissioned his court architect,

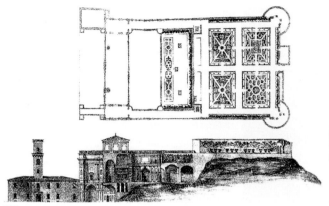

1.10a

1.10b

›1.10 PESARO, VILLA IMPERIALE, from 1530: (a) plan and site section, (b) overview of quadrangle (Francisco de Holanda, c. 1540), (c) ceiling in the Camera dei Semibusti, (d) detail of fresco in the Sala delle Cariatidi.

Girolamo Genga (1476–1551) to amplify the mid-15th-century Sforza Villa Imperiale near Pesaro. The Madama precedent is followed in the terracing of the hillside site, if not in the variety of spatial form. On the other hand, the varied rhythms of the articulation, especially of the court fronts, and the varied approach to internal spatial enclosure – in which Genga was assisted by Dosso Dossi, among others – attempt to follow Giulio's precedent. The former was too personal for a self-respecting follower to imitate and the internal decoration was confined not to the new building, which was devoid of grand apartments, but to the original Sforza house.**1.10**

As early as 1522 Genga asked Castiglione to transmit Raphael's account of his ideas for the Villa Madama and clearly tried to emulate his command of the antique: in the event his strategy at Pesaro recalls rather Bramante's ascending, corridor-framed, Vatican Belvedere courts. Beyond a grotto in the rear wing, below the upper terrace, the main facility is a bathing complex.

1.10c

1.10d

›**1.11 PALAZZO GADDI**, c. 1518: (a, b) street front with loggia and cortile detail.

1.11a

1.11b

TRANSMISSION NORTH

If Giulio's peculiar manipulation of the Orders could be copied by no Mannerist pretending to personal *virtù*, his aggressive approach to rustication, taken to an extreme in the project for the Porta del Te, was often developed. Most influential internationally was Serlio through his engraved publications, as we shall see after visiting the Rome of his master Peruzzi. Most assertive in initial practice were Sansovino and Sanmicheli in the Veneto.

The Florentine Jacopo Sansovino (1486–1570) and the Veronese Michele Sanmicheli (1484–1559) were jointly responsible for the rapid transition from High Renaissance to Mannerism in the north. The former moved from Florence to Rome in 1506 and again in 1518, when his profession was dominated by Raphael and Antonio da Sangallo under the overarching achievement of Bramante (AIC4, pages 857ff) – as his Palazzo Gaddi of c. 1518 clearly acknowledges.**1.11** Quitting Rome in the aftermath of the 1527 Sack, he would have passed through Mantua on his way to establishment in Venice where the restoration of peace after the war of the League of Cambrai (1529) opened an extended period of prosperity favourable to lavish public building – as we shall see in the context of a career which spanned forty years in the Serenissima.

Sanmicheli is first noticed in Orvieto, where he was employed at the cathedral on Bramante's recommendation, and by the mid-1520s he was assisting Antonio da Sangallo – at least as an inspector of papal fortifications. Fully apprised of contemporary developments while pursing putative private practice, he also left Rome about the time of the Sack. He was working on fortifications for the Venetians in 1530. Thereafter he returned to Verona where he was well placed to study Giulio's achievements in Mantua.

Back home, Sanmicheli was commissioned to transform the city gates into triumphal portals: from the early 1530s

1.12c

1.12e

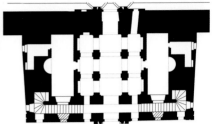

1.12a,b @ 1:1000

›1.12 SANMICHELI, PORTALS OF VENETIAN POWER: (a–c) Porta Nuova (from 1533, remodelled in the 19th century), plan, reconstruction and detail of central arch; (d) Porta Palio (from c. 1555), plan and view from without; (e) Venetian Lagoon, Forte S. Andrea; (f) Zadar, Kopnena vrta (Land Gate, from 1543).

Originally a gun emplacement, the massive bulk of the Porta Nuova – and its selective articulation – was lost to two extra arched carriageways in the 19th century except for the pedimented central portal, with its Doric Order in antis devoured by rustication in the manner of Giulio Romano. The later Porta Palio, with a major central carriageway flanked by a pair of generous passageways from the outset, has fared better: the antique model of the Arco di Gallo, recorded in dilapidation by Giuliano da Sangallo, has been restored to stability for the exterior elevation – unlike Giulio's witty paraphrase in the cortile of the Palazzo del Te in Mantua.

1.12d

1.12f

he did so with bravura variations on rusticated themes in which the exertions of column and wall confront one another in counterpoint. As in the Claudian Porta Maggiore in Rome – and Giulio's Mantuan Porta del Te project – rustication best expressed the protean strength required of a gun emplacement and Vitruvian decorum required the Doric Order for the expression of ceremonial civic dignity in that context. The formula was adapted to the service of Venetian pretension elsewhere in the Republic's domains, for instance, at the mouth of the lagoon and at Zadar on the northern Dalmatian coast.[1.12]

In practice for Veronese nobility, Sanmicheli adapted Bramante's Caprini façade formula on three major occasions: as the basements of each have service rooms rather

1.13c

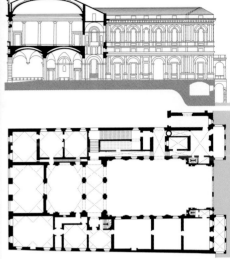

1.13a, b @ 1:1000

›1.13 SANMICHELI, PRIVATE PRACTICE IN VERONA: (a–c) Palazzo Canossa (c. 1530), section, plan, street front; (d) Palazzo Pompei (originally Lavezola; after 1536), street front; (e, f) Palazzo Bevilacqua (mid-1530s), general view and detail of street front.

than shops, the ordonnance may be seen as expressing the order of the household rather than the social hierarchy at large. The fenestration of the basement is varied: so too, in response, is the rhythm of the piano nobile Order and the nature of its base. Above all, the proportions are varied either by concealing the attic or suppressing it in favour of mezzanines in both storeys and countering enhanced elevation with extended horizontals. The median work, the Palazzo Bevilacqua, is distinguished by Mannerist virtuosity in the extreme: Classicizing in its detail, derived from the adjacent Arco Borsari, ingenious in its reconciliation of the horizontals and verticals of a modern building type, it ranks at the top of a brilliant class (AICI, pages 604, 857).**1.13, 1.14**

1.13d

1.13e

1.13f

Sanmicheli: Classicizing modernism

In contrast to the earlier and later works, the complexity of the Bevilacqua façade is intense: the triglyphs of the basement's rusticated Doric are moulded into consoles to support the piano nobile balcony which, with its extended horizontals and intermittent verticals, both separates and connects the two levels to the advantage of adjusting the proportions of whole and part. Above the socles which punctuate the balusters, the Corinthian columns rise from high pedestals through both the piano nobile and a mezzanine without breaching the Vitruvian canon – or, rather, the proportions derived from the Arco Borsari. Then follows an ingenious solution to the problem of proportioning the upper entablature (to the Order of which it is part or to the elevation as a whole): the attic space having been found below the architrave – rather than above it, as in some representations of Bramante's formula – the frieze conforms to the fully enriched Corinthian norm; the cornice exceeds the canon but the doubled columns are reinforced as load bearers by their engagement with 'triumphal arch' piers; rising from the ground to form minor bays on both levels, these are supplemented in the major arcaded bays not only by the keystones but by spandrel 'frames' – ie a richly enhanced entablature is carried on richly enhanced support in which the rusticated Doric base plays its full protean part.

The Canossa façade retains the essentials of Bramante's formula but varies it in several important respects: in place of shops, the arcaded portico – called 'atrio' – recalls Giulio's entrance to the Palazzo del Te; doubled pilasters replace columns; a mezzanine elevates both main storeys and, instead of Bramante's enhanced entablature, a balustrade is added to provide termination for the elevation as a whole.

The latest of Sanmicheli's three Veronese palazzi is more purely Bramantesque than the other two. The Order is regular, rather than doubled, but wider in the central intercolumniation and reinforced by piers at the corners, with a wider central bay. There is no mezzanine but a diminutive attic is lit through slit windows hardly visible above the cornice.

1.14c

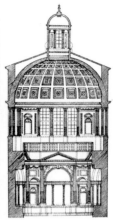

1.14a,b @ 1:1000

1.14d

›1.14 SANMICHELI, ECCLESIASTICAL WORKS IN AND NEAR VERONA: (a–d) S. Bernardino, Pellegrini Chapel (from c. 1527), section, plan and interior details; (e–g) Sanctuary of the Madonna di Campagna (from 1559), section, plan and view of exterior.

Beyond a rectangular vestibule linking it to the church of S. Bernardino, Sanmicheli's Pellegrini Chapel is composed of cylinder and hemisphere like Bramante's Tempietto (in its original form): similarly inspired, ten years earlier he had enlivened the perimeter of a rotunda with the rhythm of a triumphal arch on the minor scale of the Petrucci Chapel in the crypt of S. Domenico in Orvieto – and developed a distinct sanctuary between the access stairs. Considerably larger, the main Pellegrini volume extends through two full storeys: the upper one, carrying the dome, is ringed with columns reinforced with piers in the quadrants – presumably in the light of Antonio da Sangallo's contemporary criticism of Bramante's colonnaded scheme for the dome of S. Pietro (see below, pages 140ff).

A simplified enlargement on an octagonal plan – more heavily reinforced in elevation to the detriment of the exterior in particular – provides the main space in Sanmicheli's last essay of the type, the Sanctuary of the Madonna di Campagna which enshrines a miraculous image of the Virgin: around it is an incongruously low colonnade; beyond it is a semi-detached domed crossing for choir and presbytery.

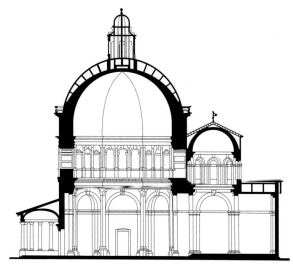

Sanmicheli developed the idea of overlapping triumphal arches, articulated after the style of the Arco Borsari like the piano nobile of the Palazzo Bevilacqua, for the internal perimeter of the Pellegrini Chapel attached to the church of S. Bernardino in Verona c. 1527. Under the inspiration of Bramante's Tempietto, he experimented with centralized form and its augmentation on at least two other occasions, at the beginning and end of his career. The first was on the small scale of a chapel in the crypt of S. Domenico in Orvieto. Much later – and well beyond the definition of a chapter dedicated to inception – is the large-scale pilgrimage Sanctuary of the Madonna di Campagna, outside Verona, which was to prove influential despite its unsatisfactory posthumous realization.[1.14]

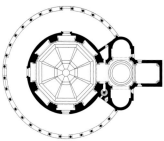

1.14e,f @ 1:1000

1.14g

2 ROMAN REVIVAL

After the Sack of Rome in 1527 and his flight, Pope Clement VII was not in a position to glorify the pontificate – morally or materially. That waited for the election of the Farnese pope Paul III (1534–49). Considerable talent returned to interrupted work and grand new projects. Prominent among the latter was the decoration of the papal apartments in the Castel Sant'Angelo, especially the Sala Paolina: there Raphael's colleague Perino del Vaga translated multifaceted illusionism from vault to wall under the inspiration of Michelangelo and Peruzzi as well as his erstwhile master.**1.15** Foremost among the projects revived for the Farnese clan was their great palace on the Via Giulia. Foremost of all was the basilica of S. Pietro in the Vatican. In collaboration with Peruzzi on the latter, both were entrusted to Antonio da Sangallo.

›1.15 ROME, CASTEL SANT'ANGELO, SALA PAOLINA: end wall (Perino del Vaga from 1545, assisted by Pellegrino Tibaldi).

Imprisoned during the Sack of Rome, Perino went to Genoa on his release in 1528 to work for the Doria. Back in Rome in 1538, his first commission from the Farnese pope Paul III was for dadoes in the Sistine Chapel and the Vatican Stanza della Segnatura (see page 18). The vault of the Sala Regia followed in 1542 but progressed no further than the stuccowork because the claims of the Castel Sant'Angelo suite took precedence from 1545 (see below, page 180). In Genoa and in Rome, Perino seems to have imparted his expertise in the new art of stuccowork to contingents of artisans from Como – a traditional source of workers in the building industry.

Except for the building's patron (Emperor Hadrian), the principals in the cycle are the pope's namesakes: Alexander the Great and S. Paul. S. Michael triumphing over evil – as the new pope would triumph over pontifical adversity and the evil which brought it – follows Raphael's celebrated image and the dado recalls the similar feature in Raphael's Stanza di Eliodoro, for which Perino may well have been responsible. The simulated bronze medallions have their counterparts in the Sistine vault and they are supported by clothed females in place of Michelangelo's nude youths. The simulated ordonnance recalls Peruzzi's in the Villa Farnesina (AIC4, page 859), though rather than Doric it is Ionic as in the Vatican Sala di Costantino's 'Baptism of Constantine'.[0.16b]

Tibaldi completed the work after Perino's death in 1547: apart from an important Alexander panel, he is credited with the winged nudes and the false door with its passengers.

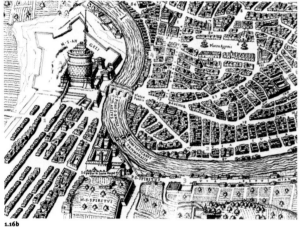

›1.16 SANGALLO AS ENGINEER: (a) Florence, Fortezza da Basso; (b) Rome, street pattern as improved under Leo X with (1) Via Alessandrina, (2) Via Giulia, (3) Via Septiniama in Trastevere, (4) Via di Ripatta.

The Florentine fortress was commissioned by the pope's nephew, Alessandro de' Medici, who was installed as duke in 1532 after the defeat of the republican insurrection of 1529–30. Built on its flat site northwest of the city to a pentagonal plan, the platform is sunk low into a ditch to level the ordonnance at the plane of approach: the oblique-angled triangles of its five spearheaded bastions were recommended as best for flanking fire by Francesco di Giorgio (AIC4, page 765).

Sangallo went on to improve the defences of Rome, particularly at the Porta Ardeatina.

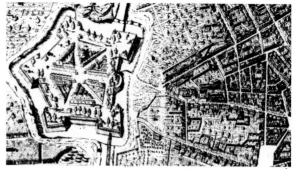

ANTONIO DA SANGALLO AND PERUZZI

Distinguished in both technical capacity and managerial efficacy at S. Pietro, Antonio da Sangallo the Younger (1484–1546) was promoted to the position of principal architect on Raphael's death in April 1520. His expertise recommended him as an assessor of structural stability in the designs of others, most notably Zaccagni for S. Maria della Steccata at Parma and Cola da Caprarola's S. Maria della Consolazione at Todi (AIC4, pages 843, 846). He had first made his name as a military engineer and continued to work on fortification and other utilitarian projects for his pontifical patrons – and their potential successors.[1.16]

Sangallo, engineer in Rome under Leo X, oversaw the improvement of the arteries of communication between the Vatican and the medieval rump of the city. A new urban order had been inaugurated in 1500 by Pope Alexander VI with the opening of the Via Alessandrina to link the Vatican with the Castel Sant'Angelo, though that recalled plans first elaborated for Nicholas V half a century earlier. Under Julius II, next, the Via Giulia was rammed straight through the medieval quarter and doubled on the other side of the River Tiber. After the advent of Sangallo, crucially, Leo X's Via di Ripetta extended the scheme in the opposite direction, somewhat circuitously to link the Ponte Sant'Angelo – and thence the Vatican – to the Piazza del Popolo, the northern entrance to Rome.

Naturally, Sangallo's predominant concern was S. Pietro: assisted there by the Sienese painter and architect Baldassare Peruzzi (1481–1536), he spent a quarter-century elaborating various projects for extending Bramante's scheme: uppermost in his mind were practical considerations ranging from the support of the dome to the integration of the basilica with the papal palace. The culmination followed the elevation of his principal private patron, Alessandro Farnese, to the pontificate as Paul III in 1534.**1.17**

›1.17 ROME, VATICAN, BASILICA OF S. PIETRO AFTER RAPHAEL: (a) extent of construction on the death of Raphael (drawing by Martin van Heemskerck); (b–d) Antonio da Sangallo the Younger's basilican project variations of c. 1519 and contemporary elevation sketches; (e) Peruzzi's derivation of a centralized plan from the crossing of a revised Sangallo basilican scheme c. 1521 (copy published by Sebastiano Serlio in his third book of architecture c. 1540); (f) Peruzzi's bird's-eye perspective of c. 1535 (Florence,

1.17a

The S. Pietro project – second phase

As early as 1519 the younger Sangallo had taken his departure from his uncle Giuliano's penultimate basilican project which preserved Bramante's choir, developed ambulatories around the apsidal transepts and projected free-standing towers: he was also clearly aware of Raphael's 1518 project (AIC4, page 839). However, he introduced domical bays to the nave and a secondary cross-axis through the central one between amplified lateral chapels.**1.17b,c** Like Raphael, he retained Bramante's colossal Order in his west-front experiments but raised the height of the minor Order to effect concordance between the exterior and interior aisle elevation.**1.17d** A synthesis effected with Raphael was approved by the pope in 1519 and work began on the southern transept.

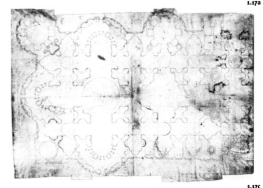

1.17c

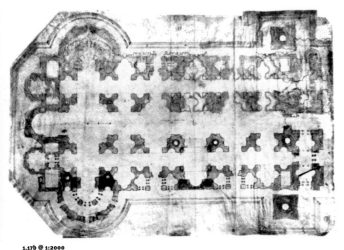

1.17b @ 1:2000

1.17d

Uffizi Gallery); (g, h) Sangallo's bifocal revision of c. 1537 with two overlapping centralized elements; (i–l) Sangallo's definitive scheme (1538–46, engraved later), plan, section, front elevation and Great Model.

1.17e @ 1:2000

After Raphael's death Sangallo presented the pope with a withering criticism of the hybrid exercise in course of construction – its structural inadequacies, inconsistencies of style and spatial infelicities such as the tunnel-like nave and lack of adequate chapels. Leo X, perhaps uncharacteristically concerned by the projected cost, seems to have been convinced by the criticism, confirmed its author as first architect and called for revisions preserving Bramante's executed choir arm. Peruzzi produced a wholly centralized scheme closely following Bramante's ideal (according to the later testimony of his disciple, Sebastiano Serlio).[1.17e] Sangallo pursued the idea of a domed secondary axis across an extended eastern arm of an otherwise centralized crossing developed from the seductive ideal. Models were made but Leo X died before anything came to fruition and work, which had advanced slowly on the southern arm of the transept, was halted altogether by the Sack of Rome in 1527 – not least by the destruction of the papal economy.

Clement VII ordered drastic reductions on his return to Rome in 1533: the pruning of the western end of Sangallo's bifocal scheme is represented in a Peruzzi drawing from this time. On his accession in 1534 Pope Paul III confirmed Sangallo's position but raised Peruzzi to equal collaboration and called for revisions which took account of financial reality – though that was transformed with donations elicited by the wily pope from kings enriched in

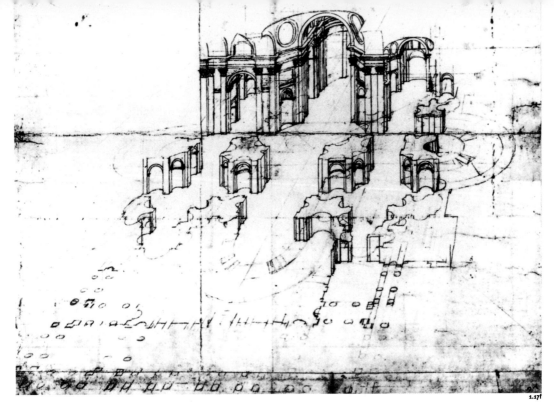

1.17f

their New World. The endless problems of the basilican conception – ranging from extent and cost to reconciliation with a centralized crossing – recommended its abandonment. Thus, apparently in accordance with the new pope's assessment of practicality and his own aesthetic preference, Peruzzi returned to Bramante's centralized ideal in a magnificent bird's-eye perspective drawing of c. 1535, strengthening the structure and projecting a grand narthex which returned along either side of the apsidal eastern entrance.**1.17f** Sangallo persevered with his bifocal ideas.**1.17g,h**

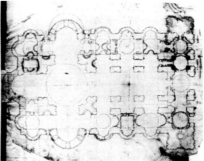

1.17g

In spring 1538, more than two years after Peruzzi's death, Sangallo produced his definitive scheme: it combined a centralized crossing and multiple subsidiary spaces derived from Bramante's 'parchment' plan with a secondary centralized element embracing a great vestibule preceded by a narthex.**1.17i–l** The vestibule was of uncertain liturgical purpose – or cost-effectiveness – but pushed the narthex out towards the existing benediction loggia at the front of the Constantinian complex, the key position for integration with the pontifical palace as it had developed since Nicholas V.

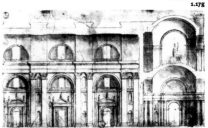

1.17h

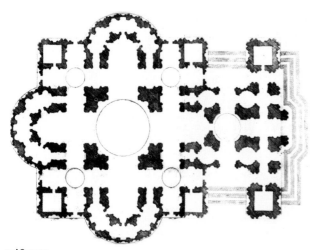

1.17i @ 1:2000

1.17j

1.17k

The projected portico supported a new benediction loggia which communicated through the Pauline Chapel (from early 1538) with the Sala Regia on the piano nobile; from there stairs descended to a lobby at its northern end.

Sangallo's other major practical concern was with the stability of a dome which surpassed that of Florence or Pavia cathedrals in scale and luminosity. He started with his competition project for S. Giovanni dei Fiorentini (AIC4, page 851). At least twenty years of experimenting and of assessing the ideas of others culminated in the series of studies for the Great Model

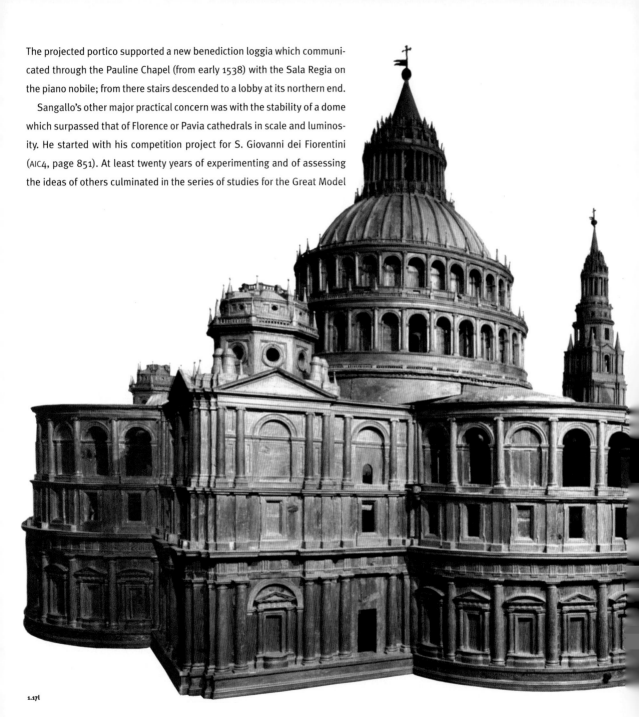

1.17l

scheme. The radial system of buttressing, developed over the cylindrical base of S. Giovanni, is adapted to the entirely different circumstances of a circular structure raised over an octagonal crossing. The two-tier double-skin drum is set firmly on the entire mass of the great crossing piers and, therefore, projects out over the vaults of the cross-arms which would have been reinforced accordingly. The latter, at least, seems to have been foreseen by Bramante and Raphael, but to bear the dead weight of a homogeneous coffered shell – stepped at base like that of the Pantheon – they made do with concentric rings of columns in the single Order of the drum (AIC4, page 840). Sangallo's version is far more tautly braced and stoutly buttressed: the weight of the dome bears primarily on the inner circle of the drum structure, of course, but the lateral thrust is resisted by the upper tier of the external structure and transmitted to the perimeter arcades of the lower tier by the internal system of radial arches which, with tunnel vaulting between them, replace S. Giovanni's volute consoles.

Exhaustively detailed by an obsessively analytical mind, the scheme presented by Sangallo to Paul III in 1538 was accorded the accolade of realization in the grandest, most expensive model of the era. Its very scale must have given the patron pause but, beyond that, the precise – indeed, pedantic – resolution of whole and part was self-defeating: the execution of such a project would long outlast its creator's span but nothing was left to the future's imagination.

Following Bramante's latest ideas for S. Pietro – and the Albertian ideal (AIC4, pages 838f) – Raphael had retained the giant Order inside and out but stamped its triumphal-arch rhythm on the east front under a temple-front pediment and over superimposed colonnades which responded to the internal ordonnance of his ambulatories (AIC4, page 840). At that time, too, Sangallo modulated the theme in his sketch elevations but he abandoned it twenty years later in his Great Model. The floor level was raised by some 3 metres to reduce the pedestals which took Bramante's Order to extravagant height. Outside, a mezzanine was introduced between the Doric Order at ground level and the Ionic which masked the springing of the vaults: the discretion of parts, vertically and horizontally, was assiduously sustained – as in Bramante's original – but the result, intricate in its complexity, was not essentially monumental.

1.18

The scheme for an aisleless volume with multiple chapels followed the basilican alternative for S. Giovanni dei Fiorentini – and Cronaca's Florentine church of S. Salvatore al Monte (AIC4, page 793).

›1.19 ANTONIO DA SANGALLO AND THE ROMAN PALAZZO: (a, b) Palazzo Baldassini (c. 1516–19), ground-floor plan and entrance elevation; (c) the Zecca (the papal mint later occupied by the Banco di S. Spirito): parade front (completed 1525).

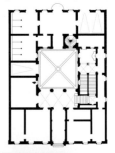

1.19a @ 1:1000

1.19b

The superimposed Orders of the Great Model's exterior articulate the storeys of the narthex and ambulatories but therefore ignore the colossal scale of the main spaces in breach of the Albertian conception of *concinnitas*. In Sangallo's contemporary revision of the post-Albertian Roman church façade formula for S. Spirito in Sassia, again, the superimposition of the two Orders ignores the entity of the main volume but responds to the vertical and horizontal divisions of the typical basilican section and internal elevation: it provided the basis on which all later Roman architects were to work (AIC4, pages 736ff).**1.18**

Sangallo was also exemplary in the genre of the palazzo. The prominent trapezoidal corner site of Raphael's work for Jacopo da Brescia (c. 1515) invited the incorporation of a triumphal-arch motif at the truncated apex. Ten years later, on an even more exposed site, Sangallo developed

The raising of the Zecca's Order through both the upper storeys, over a comparatively low basement, provided a solution to the problem of proportioning the entablature – to the whole or to the pilasters supporting it – which was to prove enduringly convincing. The gesture is bold enough without multiplication of the pilasters – but a further novelty is the slight concavity of the parade front. Sangallo adopted a similar approach on a grander scale for the Porta S. Spirito (begun 1540, unfinished). He had adopted a semi-colossal Order (embracing a mezzanine as well as a ground-level arcade) in his elevations for the basilica of S. Pietro c. 1518. At much the same time Raphael was also developing the motif both in his elevations for S. Pietro and for the Villa Madama.

The alternative system, without Orders, was projected by Raphael for the Florentine Palazzo Pandolfini c. 1518 and, at much the same time, by Sangallo for the Palazzo Baldassini in Rome: he and his uncle Antonio the Elder both preferred it at Montepulciano (AIC4, pages 842f). As we have seen, Sansovino followed the mode in the central three bays of the Palazzo Gaddi's street front where the side bays incorporated variations on the serliana motif: in the cortile, on the other hand, he adopted a colossal Order for the piano nobile and mezzanine.

1.19C

the idea in his precocious revision of Bramante's palazzo formula for the papal mint (Zecca): with his imposition of the motif on the upper two levels, visual integrity was achieved at the expense of structural logic.**1.19c** Ten years earlier he preferred logic in his designs for the street front and court loggias of the Palazzo Baldassini, the latter with superimposed pilasters, the former with no major Order or rusticated basement: that approach, favoured also by Raphael and other members of the Sangallo clan before 1520, was largely to prevail as it suited street or square. (AIC4, page 860).**1.19a,b**

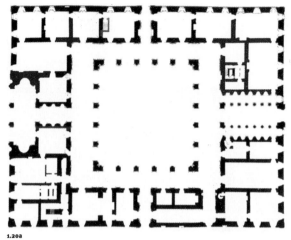

1.20a

›1.20 ROME, PALAZZO FARNESE, 1520s–50s:
(a, b) Sangallo's plan and cortile elevation c. 1541, (c)
androne competed under Sangallo, (d, e) cortile and
piazza front (as completed by Michelangelo, see page
159), (f) extent in 1546 (after Ackerman).

Some time before 1529, Cardinal Alessandro Farnese commissioned Sangallo to transform a palazzo on the site to accommodate his two sons in a pair of apartments: one of the prospective beneficiaries, Ranuccio, died in 1529. The scheme was reviewed on a scale of unprecedented grandeur when the patron became Pope Paul III in 1534. Progress was desultory but early in 1547, shortly after Sangallo's death, the thirteen-bay front range had reached the third level and the apartment occupying the northern half of the piano nobile was nearly habitable. The cortile arcading was advanced but the garden loggias were hardly begun on Sangallo's death: originally to have been inserted between projections to the side wings, which did not materialize, these were completed by Giacomo Vignola from 1568.

Sangallo had originally thought of superimposing Orders on the upper two floors but instead opted to confine them to supporting the alternating triangular and segmental pediments of aedicules, contrary to his earlier Baldassini exercise but as in the Pandolfini manner. As in the latter, moreover, rustication was confined to the main portal and the quoins (AIC4, pages 86of). On the other hand, three superimposed Orders of applied columns – rather than the Baldassini's two

Working for the Farnese clan in Rome, Sangallo was initially responsible for the greatest representative of the palazzo type with multiple unarticulated storeys which he had developed for the Palazzo Baldassini c. 1518. With full Orders confined to the window frames and a cornice emulating that of the Palazzo Strozzi in the grandeur of its proportional relationship to the entire elevation, the stupendous freestanding pile remains unsurpassed in reconciling assertion of the discretion of the parts with concern

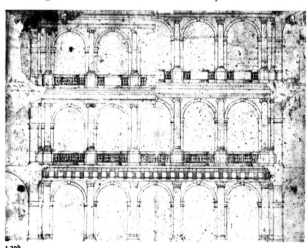

1.20b

1.20c

1.20d

›ARCHITECTURE IN CONTEXT »FROM THE HIGH RENAISSANCE TO MANNERISM

for the integrity of a monumental whole. The Strozzi apart, the great block recalls a grand ancient Roman insula and the triple superimposed Orders of the cortile were inspired by the Theatre of Marcellus. Michelangelo was called in to

levels of pilasters – were retained for the cortile: the Doric arcade dates in part from revisions to the earlier edifice of c. 1519 – and may be likened to the work of Antonio da Sangallo the Elder at Montepulciano – but the heightening of the vaults after 1541 entailed the

1.20e

insertion of a highly unorthodox second impost moulding on each of the arcade piers. Michelangelo, called in to redesign the main cornice about the time of Sangello's passing, imposed his own ideas on both the entrance and the upper level of the cortile.

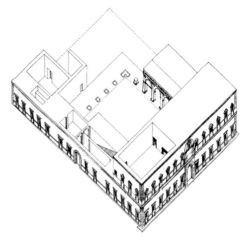

1.20f

complete it from 1546, five years after the contract had been let for the final phase of Sangallo's work (see AIC1, pages 575f, AIC4, page 860).[1.20]

Assuming principal responsibility at S. Pietro and the Villa Madama on Raphael's death, Sangallo seems also to have taken on the latter's mantle as *Commissario delle Antichità* – if he had not already shared it. He had been studying the antique legacy from early in his Roman career, initially at the instigation of his uncle Giuliano, who was the leader of his generation in the recording of the remains (AIC4, page 832). And, of course, the younger Sangallo's antiquarian interest extended to Vitruvius: dismayed – like many others – at the discrepancy between Vitruvian precept and subsequent imperial practice, aware of the problems of interpreting Vitruvian terminology, dissatisfied with previous commentaries and translations, he planned a new Italian edition of *De Architectura* based on the earliest available Latin manuscript sources and comparison with the ancient remains (1531). This did not materialize but his pupil and assistant, Antonio Labacco, published a collection of views and reconstructions of antique Roman buildings – and a modern centralized church plan – which was indebted to the master at least in part.[1.21]

PERUZZI AND SERLIO

Like Sangallo, Peruzzi planned a treatise which he failed to realize but his work provided the basis for publication by his compatriot amd pupil Sebastiano Serlio (1475–c. 1554) – with spectacular success, as we shall see. Like Sangallo too, Peruzzi was an outstanding military engineer. After the Sack of Rome he retured to his native Siena: not without private patrons there, he was principally engaged on fortification works but also produced unrealized projects for remodelling the dome over the eccentric hexagonal crossing of the cathedral and rebuilding S. Domenico with a sequence of canopy-domed compartments inspired by antique thermae. Three-dimensional scenographic exercises of this kind are, of course, matched by the two-dimensional evocation of the visual effect illusionistically: his innovative work in the medium is best represented at the Farnesina; he indulged in stage-set design in response to humanist concern with the revival of antique drama (AIC4, page 859).**1.22**

Back in Rome after the trauma had subsided under Pope Paul III and elevated to the top of his profession, as we have seen, Peruzzi produced his secular masterpiece: the Palazzo Massimi alle Colonne. Existing work, incorporating a loggia, prompted a variation on Raphael's theme

›1.21 ROMAN DORIC TEMPLE RECONSTRUCTION (from *Libro d' Antonio Labacco*, Rome 1552).

Labacco's publication included Sangallo's design for S. Giovanni dei Fiorentini: it seems probable that the records and restorations of antique buildings had the same provenance. Apart from recording Alberti's intentions for S. Sebastiano at Mantua (AIC4, page 746), Labacco's main claim to fame is making the Great Model of Sangallo's definitive scheme for S. Pietro.**1.17l**

›1.22 PERUZZI AS SET DESIGNER: (a) for an unknown tragedy (datable to the era of Leo X; Stockholm, National Museum); (b) for 'The Presentation of the Virgin in the Temple' (1518).

The stage-set design, incorporating the so-called serliana invented by Bramante, is compatible with one known to have been devised for a Medici family celebration under the auspices of Pope Leo X in 1513. The rusticated palace façades to the left in that image and in the 'Presentation' painting could have been known

1.22a

1.22b

to Sansovino before he designed the Venetian Zecca –
to which the latter is most relevant, as we shall see.

›1.23 ROME, PALAZZO MASSIMO ALLE COLONNE, from 1532: (a) street front, (b) vestibule, (c) plan, (d) cortile.

The commission was to replace a palazzo damaged
in the Sack: it was issued by Pietro Massimo whose
brothers had engaged Giovanni Mangone and Antonio
da Sangallo on rebuilding next door and opposite
respectively. Pietro's site, on a bend in the main proces-
sional route through medieval Rome to the Vatican, was
opposite a perpendicular street (now overbuilt): the
axis of that street penetrated the medieval building
through an off-centre loggia imposing eccentricity on
the palace plan. The loggia – which countered the urban
domestic norm everywhere but Venice and survived the
proscription of open porticoes in Rome by Sixtus IV –
was redeveloped by Peruzzi as the principal feature of
the street front: dislocation of the internal axis was
unavoidable, therefore, but the acquisition of a fragment of the adjacent site admitted symmetry to the
façade alone. The Order of pilasters, confined to the
lowest level of the lightly rusticated façade where Bramante would have had shops, progresses to the
columns of the loggia extracted from the garden context
of a villa. The contrast with the academic exercise of
superimposing Orders over a rusticated basement in
Peruzzi's early Roman works – the Villa Farnesina or the
Palazzo Ossoli, for example – is stark, not least in the
variety of architectonic, tectonic and atectonic window
surrounds on the upper storeys.

of inverting the normal progression from solid to void
(page 106). It also prompted a most significant exercise in
what the Postmodernists of the later 20th century would
call 'contextualism': the façade curves in conformity with
the street instead of asserting its own regular geometry –
and the natural intractability of rusticated masonry.[1.23]

Aggressive rustication was foreign to the style of
Peruzzi's main surviving buildings – if not his scenography.[1.22a] However, his legacy of drawings informed the
handbook on architecture published in several volumes
from 1537 by Serlio: that provides straightforward exposition of the reversal of roles as the rusticated wall devours
the Order in the manner of Giulio. The context is a suite
of fashionable 'modern' inventions in the last volume, pub-

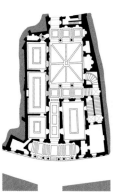

1.23d   1.23c @ 1:1000   1.23b   1.23a

lished as an extra series in 1551. However, fertility of invention was essential from the outset.

After Francesco di Giorgio – also Sienese – Serlio was the first overtly to address not the erudite but the 'needs of architects seeking instruction or guidance in practical building tasks'. Vitruvius is his guide, but not blindly as he is well aware of the discrepancy between Vitruvian precept and antique practice. However, writing in the comprehensible vernacular, he avoided the abstruse in providing limited theory – or even critical evaluation – and has been vilified by savants accordingly. On the other hand, a painter in origin applauding the painterly origins of all great architects, he has been highly valued by practitioners for providing a manual with flexible guidelines and models of great variety which could be adapted to specific requirements. Above all, the key to the success of the venture was comprehensive illustration.

The treatise on the Orders in Book IV – which Serlio deemed 'more necessary than the others' – exceeds Vitruvius by including the Composite as well as the Tuscan, Doric, Ionic and Corinthian: in illustrating them in one comparative diagram, it expanded on the precedent set by Cesare Cesariano in his Italian edition of Vitruvius (1521).**1.24** Dealt with systematically in terms of their ascending base:height ratio, each is to be applied in accordance with Vitruvian decorum adapted to Christian and secular purposes – but not without the informed discretion of the architect or respect for local traditions. Each is illustrated, with exhaustively varied rhythm and motif, in a comprehensive survey of compositional types – not without the admission of licence in the propagation of hybrids. Thus a manifesto of the orthodox managed also to promote Mannerist heterodoxy, especially in the *Extraordinario libro di Architettura* – and therein lay its immense success.**1.25**

›1.24 CESARE CESARIANO, VITRUVIAN ORDERS.

The plate surveying alternative proportions for the three original Orders is the first of its kind: the style reflects Cesariano's training in Milan under Bramante.

›1.25 SERLIO, ARCHITETTURA: (a) the five Orders compared; (b) rusticated portal (IV,5,10); (c) triumphal arch (IV,8,50); (d, e) fireplaces (IV,7,43 and

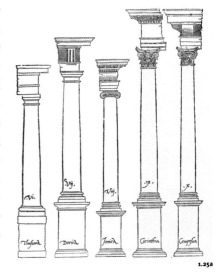

1.25a

1.25b   1.25c

IV,9,61); (f, g) exemplary modern buildings (IV,6,27 and 29); (h) Venetian palazzo type with 'serlianas' (IV,6,31); (i) Bramante's Tempietto in a projected circular court (III,4,19); (j, k) exemplary antique buildings, the Roman Colosseum (III,4,32) and the Veronese Porta Borsari (III,4,73); (l) domed temple (IV,8,55); (m) basilican church façade (IV,8,51); (n–p) variations on centralized church plans (V, 14,2, 4 and 9); (q) domestic hierarchy ranging from the artisan to the merchant (VI, various plates); (r–t) various 'situations' which include exemplary villa designs (VII, various plates); (u) representation of Neapolitan Poggioreale (III,4,72).

The series began with a review of the Orders published as Book IV in 1537. Often republished separately, it initiated the tradition of the treatise on the Orders which guided the development of Classical architecture in Europe – and its colonies. It honoured the Vitruvian conception of propriety – or decorum – in

1.25d,e

1.25f   1.25g

The survey continues (in Book III) in graphic records and not implausible reconstructions of the exemplars of Classical Antiquity, ordered in accordance with the Albertian hierarchy of types. Here Serlio succeeds where even the most eminent of his predecessors had failed – Francesco di Giorgio, Raphael and Antonio da Sangallo in particular – in producing a comprehensive compendium of the legacy of the Romans – and revealing precocious recognition of the primacy of the Greeks. Less than comprehensive, on the other hand, is his record of contemporary achievement. He ignores Bramante's seminal plans for S. Pietro, for example, and his highly influential palazzo façade devised for the Caprini. Yet he provides records of several lost modern masterpieces, as well as the representation of unexecuted or partially realized projects purportedly in accordance with their creator's original intentions – as, for instance, Bramante's Tempietto with its hemispherical dome and circular court and his project for S. Pietro's dome (AIC4, pages 834f).

Serlio's plates in Book V, devoted to the design of churches, include variations on the basilica and its façade type incorporating the triumphal-arch motif. On the other hand, a series of plates canvasses all the varieties of centralized plan from circle to square and Greek cross via various polygons. Like Francesco di Giorgio, Serlio prefers the circle as 'the most perfect form of all' but eccentrically includes an ellipse: this, of course, is a bifocal form with a long axis which may be generated from two circles and with a perimeter which may be treated to a rhythmic variation of the regular sequence of bays natural to the circle. It was espoused – innovatively – by Peruzzi in a scheme devised for the semi-trapezoidal site allotted to the Roman hospital church of S. Giacomo degli Incurabili – and it was ultimately to prevail there, as we shall see. Most significantly, however, it was with the ellipse that the late-Renaissance architect was able to reconcile his own will to maximum coherence of form and the prescriptions for the Counter-Reformation church laid down after the Council of Trent in the 1550s: as we shall see with Vignola.

Canvassing multiple domestic examples – eleven urban and nine rural – Serlio naturally conforms to current ideas of social hierarchy but he is innovative in the degree of attention he pays to the lower orders. Moreover, writing in France, he is also concerned to differentiate between national preoccupations, offering elementary insights into the influence of climate and material resources on the evolution of vernacular traditions.

Demonstrating the versatility and ingenuity of its compiler – not only in the *Extraordinario libro* – Serlio's work is the prime example of the genre of the 'pattern book' – which goes some way to explaining, for example, why the

1.25h

the application of the Orders but was innovative in the degree to which it prescribed the proportions native to each one and the definition of its appropriate use in the hierarchically ordered Christian society of its time: the Doric for Christ and male saints, the Ionic for 'matronly' female saints, the Corinthian for the Virgin Mary and other 'stainless' female saints, etc.; the Tuscan for fortifications, the Doric for the houses of warriors, the Ionic for those of a contemplative disposition, the Corinthian and Composite for the grandest private and public works, etc. (see AIC1, pages 572f).

Book III, published in 1540 and dedicated to the French king François I, is primarily devoted to an account of the antiquities of Rome. Books I and II, which deal with geometry and perspective, appeared in Paris in 1545: asserting the primacy of graphic art in the formation of the architect, they concluded with an

1.25j

1.25k

1.25i

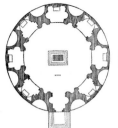

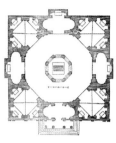

1.25l–p

important appendix on theatrical scenography which doubtless spoke for Peruzzi.

Book V, on church planning, appeared in Paris in 1545. The *Extraordinario libro di Architettura* was published in Lyon in 1551. Book VII (published posthumously in Frankfurt, 1575) is a digression on the 'many accidents which might befall the architect': it draws a distinction between Italian and French traditions, unflattering to the latter. Book VI, which covered urban and rural domestic building for all classes of society, and Book VIII, which mainly deals with urban planning and fortification, were not published until the late-1960s.

The books first appeared in single volumes and were quickly translated into all the major European languages – even Latin. A much cheaper edition, combining Books I–V and the *Extraordinario libro* in a single volume, was published in Venice in 1566. Another single-volume edition, also including Book VII, was published in Venice in 1584. Obviously, the many editions are witness to a need fulfilled.

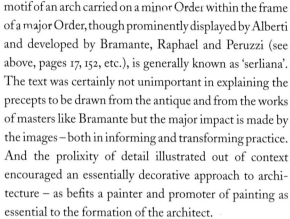

1.25q

motif of an arch carried on a minor Order within the frame of a major Order, though prominently displayed by Alberti and developed by Bramante, Raphael and Peruzzi (see above, pages 17, 152, etc.), is generally known as 'serliana'. The text was certainly not unimportant in explaining the precepts to be drawn from the antique and from the works of masters like Bramante but the major impact is made by the images – both in informing and transforming practice. And the prolixity of detail illustrated out of context encouraged an essentially decorative approach to architecture – as befits a painter and promoter of painting as essential to the formation of the architect.

Decorative elaboration in elevation – even in plan – was characteristic of Mannerist Italy, where wit usually tended to play with logic. It was especially marked abroad where unsophisticated artists and patrons long looked to Italy for the trappings of a fashionable style – and found them in pattern books.

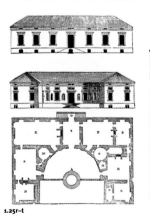
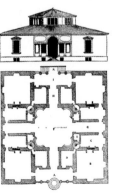
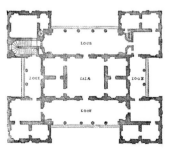

1.25r–t

1.25u

MICHELANGELO

His highly inventive works at S. Lorenzo in Florence incomplete when the Medici pope Clement VII died in 1534 (pages 105ff), Michelangelo was recalled to Rome to oversee the completion of Pope Julius II's tomb – first projected for a central position in the basilica of S. Pietro but realized in the rather more humble church of S. Pietro in Vincoli.**1.26, 0.6** However, the new pope, Paul III, was determined on surpassing Julius II: as we have seen, he reactivated the great Vatican building site and he commissioned Michelangelo to complete the decoration of the Sistine Chapel with the stupendous fresco of the 'Last Judgement'.**0.17** He also expected the eccentric genius to find time to fresco the Pauline Chapel which Sangallo had installed by the papal route to his projected basilica's benediction loggia.

As sculptor/architect, Michelangelo was first called upon by the Farnese pontifical authorities to provide a new plinth for the antique bronze equestrian statue of Emperor Marcus Aurelius: in an assertion of papal authority it was to be moved from the Lateran to the Capitol – the ancient seat of divinity, the medieval seat of municipal government and opposition to the monarchical pretensions of the papacy. That accomplished in 1539, attention turned to ordering the statue's rough environment: the field known as Campidoglio, bounded to the south-west by the Palazzo dei Conservatori (in which the patrician council met) and to the south-east by the Palazzo dei Senatori (which housed the chief communal administrator). Other than an external double staircase to the piano nobile of the latter, little had been done by 1555 and the master's ideas were not fully realized on his death, as we shall see.**1.30**

While his ideas for the Campidoglio were in the early stages of their long gestation, Michelangelo was diverted

1.26

›1.26 MICHELANGELO: TOMB OF JULIUS II, first projected for Julius II's new basilica of S. Pietro, revised c. 1532–42 for S. Pietro in Vincoli, Rome.

›1.27 MICHELANGELO AT THE PALAZZO FARNESE, from 1545: cortile loggie (engraved by Lafreri, 1560).

Michelangelo reordered the façade by elaborating the central bay and adding the monumental cornice surpassing that of the Florentine Palazzo Strozzi (AIC4, page 776, and see above, page 142). He diversified the cortile elevations by effecting a transition from the open to closed arcades: Sangallo's Doric ground-floor loggias were certainly to have been open; both the Doric and Ionic levels in the centre of the garden range are shown as open in the engraving of 1560 but that part of the building post-dates Sangallo's death. The fenestration elsewhere within the blind arcades of the second floor is unexceptional but the treatment of the top floor is entirely different: pilasters, rising in two planes from high plinths as on the blind parapet of the Colosseum, frame the unarcaded mural bays relieved by interpenetrating mouldings of window surrounds

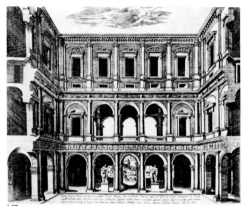

1.27
which, incorporating fragments of Doric detached from context, are highly characteristic of Michelangelo's complex style.

›1.28 MICHELANGELO AT THE BASILICA OF S. PIETRO: (a) presenting the model to Pope Paul IV (Domenico Passignano), (b–d) plan, section and side elevation as engraved by Étienne Dupérac (1569), (e) detail of southern section of the exterior, (f) details of attic fenestration.

1.28a

to the revision of Sangallo's plans for completing the Palazzo Farnese – before their author's death in 1546.**1.27** Then, on that event, he acceded to the highest position in his profession, architect to the fabric of S. Pietro. He proceeded to revise – indeed supersede – Sangallo's definitive Great Model project, which the pope had approved only the year before, and assumed responsibility for the final solution to the immense problem of realizing Julius II's ambition of replacing the Constantinian basilica with the greatest building in Christendom (AIC4, pages 835ff).**1.28**

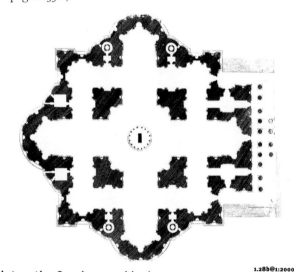

1.28b@1:2000

Achieving S. Pietro: the Greek-cross ideal

The biaxial complexity of Sangallo's scheme is eliminated with the suppression of his imposing narthex in favour of the freestanding portico: Bramante's great Greek cross remains but the subsidiary crosses in the corners – and the scenographic perspectives through them – have been amalgamated into a square ambulatory about the central piers. These are greatly augmented in mass and so too is the perimeter – especially at the junction of ambulatory and arms – in a simplification of structure which fully accords with the radical clarification of the spatial conception.

On the outside the superimposed Orders of the Great Model, elaborated by Sangallo from his predecessors' projects and specifically deplored by Michelangelo, cede to the giant Order which originated with the interior elevation of Bramante's main volume: Albertian *concinnitas* is completely satisfied as protean strength overwhelms the discretion of horizontal strata which had been present only in the eliminated subsidiary spaces. Over his great Order, however, Michelangelo superimposed an attic to mask the coffered vaulting of the cross arms and admit clerestory lighting. The fenestration of the latter was apparently simplified in execution to enhance the effect of the triglyph consoles and scallop shells. In the design of the main window and niche aedicules below, Michelangelo refrains from the complexity of thought which informs his style elsewhere.

The great dome, the largest projected since the Pantheon, sits firmly on the four-square mass enclosing the ambulatory and the canted corners between the latter and the apses upon which the peculiar integrity of the whole depends. It benefits both in scale and integration from the juxtaposition of the minor domes of the junction spaces – though even in Dupérac's image these lack Michelangelo's gravitas. The Pantheon's stepped profile, retained by Bramante to contain thrust and developed into a double drum by Sangallo, has been much reduced in response to the adoption of a double shell: the paired columns of the drum, echoing the rhythm of the giant Order below, articulate radial buttressing piers – as in Sangallo's extended experiments but contrary to the load-bearing role assigned to them by Bramante and Raphael (AIC4, pages 840 and 851).

Michelangelo began work on the north and south arms of the cross in 1550: these were virtually complete on his death in 1564 and so too was the drum but the dome had not been started: the vaulting and the domes over the ambulatory corners were completed by Giacomo da Vignola – who ultimately replaced Michelangelo as superintendent and conceived the first of many papal memorial chapels for Gregory XIII and Clement VIII.

Michelangelo demolished Sangallo's scheme but not his Great Model: his own scheme is represented by building completed under his direction, of course, by a model of the dome – but not by a complete model – and by Étienne Dupérac's engravings of plan, section and elevation. The latter, produced in 1569, are the only sources for the distinction of the east end with a great portico.

1.28e

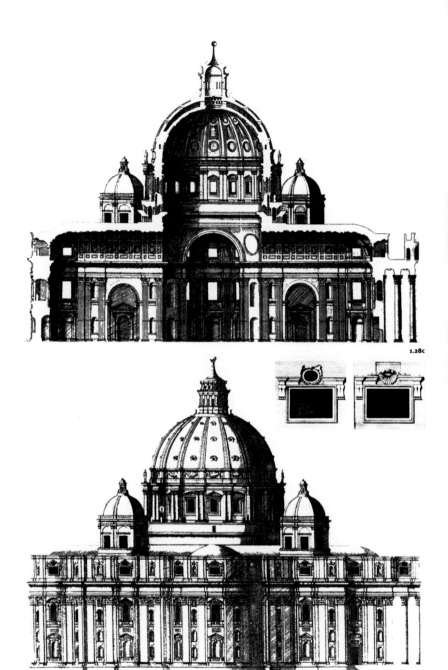

1.28c

1.28d; 1.28f inset

On the accession of the Medici pope Pius IV in 1559, Michelangelo was called on to revise the project for S. Giovanni dei Fiorentini: he devised a rotunda with alternating rectangular and oval projections but it was unrealized.[1.29a] Material indeed, however, was the out-

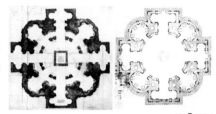

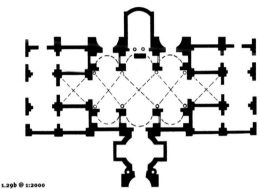

1.29b @ 1:2000

›1.29 MICHELANGELO AND THE ROMAN CHURCH: (a) S. Giovanni dei Fiorentini, plans of 1559 and as revised for final model (after 1560); (b) great hall of the Baths of Diocletian remodeled as S. Maria degli Angeli, plan (after 1561); (c, d) S. Maria Maggiore: Sforza Chapel (1560–73), section, part plan and detail of articulation.

S. Giovanni seems to recall the early 2nd-century entrance pavilion of the Piazza d'Oro at the villa of Emperor Hadrian below Tivoli (c. 130 CE; see AIC1, page 628): moreover, both these exercises were unusual for their eras in the degree of rapport between complex volume and external mass.

come of the pope's slightly later commission to convert the great hall of the Baths of Diocletian into a church to be graced with the papal tomb (AIC1, page 640).[1.29b] Happy too was the outcome at S. Maria Maggiore of Michelangelo's contemporary project for a memorial chapel to the Sforza nephew of the late Pope Paul III: again he alternated elliptical and rectangular forms but this time in extension of a Greek cross: rectangular is the sanctuary beyond the central square on the main axis; semi-elliptical are the walls terminating the cross axis; extraordinary is the obtuse-angled disposition of the Composite columns which emerge from the pilaster Order to support the free-form canopy vault at the crossing.[1.29c,d]

Major exercises in urbanism were initiated in the new pontificate: a new artery – the Via Pia – was extended out from the papal palace on the Quirinale to the north-east; the municipal buildings on the Capitol were to be renovated and a piazza made of the field between them – the Campidoglio. Michelangelo's response when called upon to design a major element of the one and the whole of the

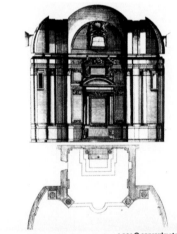

1.29c @ approximately 1:500

1.29d

1.30a

**›1.30 MICHELANGELO AND URBANISM IN
ROME:** (a) Via Pia, (record c. 1590); (b, c) Porta Pia
(1561, attic changed in 19th-century execution), 17th-
century engraving and current view; (d–h) Piazza
Campidoglio, site c. 1555, plan and overview (engraved
by Étienne Duperac, 1569), Palazzo dei Conservatori
detail, general view from the west with Palazzo dei Senatori beyond the statue of Marcus Aurelius (centre) and
Palazzo Nuovo (now Capitoline Museum, left).

1.30c

other was to have a stunning impact – on Rome and on
the history of architecture.

Straddling the Via Pia, the Porta Pia was commissioned
to mark the city limit. It also marks the apogee of its
author's style. Accumulation and interpenetration of
mouldings, denying integrity to self-sufficient forms on
the one hand, giving motifs new identity out of context on
the other, were characteristic of Michelangelo's work from
the outset at S. Lorenzo. It distinguished his fenestration
at the Palazzo Farnese. It was taken to an extreme in the
Porta Pia: under pediment within pediment, carried on
three planes of support, three different ways of sustaining
mass over void are combined – the arch, the lintel and a
synthesis between the two complete with assertive key-
stone. The 'Order' is unorthodox too: guttae are retained
from unchannelled and over-extended triglyph blocks for
redeployment as capital mouldings on indeterminate
fluted pilasters.**1.30a–c**

1.30b

The Via Pia was, of course, of prime practical importance and the gate is a landmark in the history of Mannerism. Of unsurpassed importance is the final realization of Michelangelo's ideas for transforming the Campidoglio: the Palazzo dei Senatori was to be refaced, the Palazzo dei Conservatori was to be rebuilt and its façade copied for a 'palazzo nuovo' on the opposite side of the field – which was to be paved as a piazza. The ingenuity brought to bear on whole and part, on reconciling awkward alignments inherited from the past and on transforming the repertoire of Classical forms would be hard to exaggerate.**1.30d–h**

1.30d @ 1:1000

1.30e

1.30f

Campidoglio

As funds were forthcoming for the project in the new papacy, Michelangelo (then in his eighty-fifth year) proceeded to finalize his plans for the new piazza and its defining buildings. The earliest complete representation of the scheme is an engraving of 1569 – five years after the master's death. However, the key design of the Palazzo dei Conservatori (to the south) had been ready for work to begin in 1563 under the executive architect Guidetto Guidetti: it was finished in 1584 and its copy opposite followed in the first half of the 17th century. The ramp and balustrade to the west were in place in the mid-1580s and work on refacing the Palazzo dei Senatori, begun in the late-1570s, was completed under Giacomo della Porta by the end of the century.

Except for the double-ramp staircase inherited from the recent past – and, of course, the tower and projecting side bays – the Palazzo dei Senatori façade is a revision of Bramante's Caprini formula to encompass two full storeys with one colossal Order rising from a rusticated basement: Antonio da Sangallo had set the secular precedent in his design for the Zecca.[1.19c] Respecting the hierarchy of the buildings expressed in their heights, Michelangelo's Palazzo dei Conservatori ordonnance is similarly colossal but it followed the precedent set by Bramante in his latest scheme for the interior of S. Pietro in rising from high pedestals based on the ground (AIC4, page 840). Neither approach presented problems with the proportioning of the entablature in relation to the pilasters but the scale of the unbroken Conservatori version is overwhelming as a basementless palazzo, perhaps, but not of the broad piazza which it addresses.

In accordance with tradition descended from the antique forum, the Palazzo dei Conservatori and its pendant are open to the piazza with loggias at ground level, as we shall see in Sansovino's earlier great work in Venice. The massive piers to which the colossal Order is attached and the corresponding internal structure, buttressed by stout spur walls defining cubicle spaces, would have been more than adequate to carry the groin-vaulted arcades usual to such loggias: instead Michelangelo chose coffered ceilings and, therefore, daringly to span his great intercolumniations with the entablatures of a minor Order of Ionic columns – two to the front and back of each bay. These support the window aedicules of the piano nobile, with their Composite columns and massive overarching pediments, yet there is no sense of vertical continuity: the mural bays into which these magnificent frames are set have their own distinct identity (except in the centre which departs from the scheme engraved in 1569). Thus, unequivocal respect is retained for the entity of the whole elevation and each of the two storeys which constitute it: never had the Mannerist

1.30g

›ARCHITECTURE IN CONTEXT »FROM THE HIGH RENAISSANCE TO MANNERISM

urge to reconcile contradictory objectives been so convincingly – and simply – realized.

The medieval disposition of the principal buildings bordering the Campidoglio was not rectangular. Briefed to reface the Palazzo dei Senatori and renovate the Palazzo dei Conservatori, Michelangelo's will to symmetry in completing the perimeter with a pendant to the latter produced a trapezium. The paving of the field with a stepped ellipse, recessed on the short quadrants and inset with faceted parabaloids issuing from a star, confuses the eye into seeing rectiliniarity. The longitudinal axis thus fore shortened, moreover, the scale of the chief executive's building seems enhanced and, most significantly, so too does the statue of the emperor. Again the ingenuity of the manoeuvre is supremely Mannerist but the means of conjuring optical illusion are antique (AIC1, page 401, etc.).

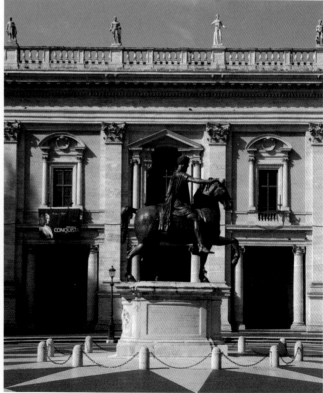

1.30h

1.31a

›**1.31 VIGNOLA IN BOLOGNA:** (a) Palazzo Bocchi, façade project (1545); (b) Portico dei Banchi (1561),
general view from the Piazza Maggiore.

The palazzo was commissioned by Achille Bocchi,
professor of law at Bologna University, to house both
himself and the academy over which he presided: thus
the eclectic exercise provides strength for the academy
in terms quoted from Giulio Romano and Serlio on the
lower level, elegance for the pedagogue on the piano
nobile in the orthodox manner of Sangallo, and again
resorts to Serlio for the balconied attic supported on
bold mezzanine cornice consoles in response to the
perennial problem of crowning whole and part.

The extensive façade of the Portico dei Banchi was
imposed on a late-medieval market arcade over which
the civic authorities commissioned a new storey. As in
Raphael's Palazzo Branconio dell' Aquila, the Order
frames the arcades of the shops. As in the Palazzo
Alberini, the top floor is astylar – the framework of the
bays is unpanelled to enhance the effect of the window
frames and their idiosyncratic convoluted pediments
(AIC4, page 858).

3 VIGNOLA AND HIS CONTEMPORARIES IN THE ORBIT OF ROME

Supervision of the works at S. Pietro was entrusted to
Giacomo da Vignola (1507–73) and Pirro Ligorio
(c. 1510–83) on Michelangelo's death in 1564: Ligorio was
given the leading role but – according to Vasari – he was
ousted within a year for not conforming closely enough
to Michelangelo's plans. In any case, as an antiquarian
his forte was not structure but decoration, indeed *mise-
en-scène* in antique style – as in the villas for which he is
best remembered. Before their elevation to oversight at
S. Pietro both he and Vignola had been extensively
employed by princes of the Church on the design of villas in the suburbs of Rome and further out in Lazio. The
Villa Madama had provided the precedent – and the
challenge.

1.31b

Vignola, from the vicinity of Bologna, worked primarily for the Farnese. He first appears in his native city as architect to S. Petronio from 1543, after two years with the court of François I at Fontainebleau – supervising the casting of copies of antique sculpture, as we shall have occasion to recall. He left little mark on S. Petronio or with his early private commissions, notably the somewhat bizarre Palazzo Bocchi, but he returned to make his major impact on Bologna with the Portico dei Banchi in 1561.[1.31]

The stark difference between the Palazzo Bocchi and the Portico dei Banchi – the transition from rampant eclecticism to relatively restrained regularity – must be viewed in the light of Vignola's emergence over the decades which separate them as the prime orthodox Classical theorist of his age. In the year after he had returned to work in his native city he laid the foundation of his international fame by publishing a treatise on the Orders: the work was long in gestation.

Vignola approached his theoretical œuvre as a member of the Vitruvian academy established in 1542 under the auspices of Cardinal Maffei. The objective, recalling that of Antonio da Sangallo, was defined by the Sienese humanist Claudio Tolomei: the production of annotated and illustrated Latin and vernacular editions of Vitruvius based on manuscripts – rather than post-Albertian work – and checked against antique remains. Like Sangallo's, the academy's objective remained unrealized – though the participation of the French humanist Guillaume Philander had important implications beyond the Alps, as we shall see. However, the work which Vignola drew from it was most successfully realized because it was published in terms which practitioners could readily understand and illustrated with copious examples of application.[1.32]

1.32a–c

Vignola's order

The prime purpose of Vignola's dissertation on the Orders (*Regola delli cinque ordini darchitettura*) was to set a standard for orthodox Classical procedure. Finding rich variety of plan and scale but no consistency in the application or proportions of the Orders in his survey of the antique – like all other would-be Vitruvian students of the imperial legacy – he sought to deduce one from the means between the extremes in the standard Classical manner. By the time of his publication in 1562, he seems to have been bent on obviating the 'pernicious' effects of egocentric licence – as perpetrated by the followers of Michelangelo.

Not conceived on the erudite humanist model of Alberti, but following the precedent set by Serlio's separate publication of his Book IV (see above, page 154), the *Regola* offers a rationalized distillation of the proportions drawn from the author's own measurement of generally applauded antique prototypes for application on the predetermined scale of the individual building project. Unlike those of his predecessors who were concerned with proportion in the ideal, he starts with the whole and its subdivision rather than with the parts and their accretion: not with the modular dimension of the column base diameter but with the measure of the projected elevation to be ordered and that, of course, is determined by the nature of the site, the requirements of the patron and the consequent scale of the entire project – in accordance with normal procedure and common sense.

The immediate relevance of Vignola's *Regola* to the ordinary practitioner – one of 'average intelligence' – is manifest in the self-explanatory plates devoted to each Order, measured in modules, consistently sequential and

›1.32 VIGNOLA: (a–c) Doric, Ionic, Corinthian from *Regola delli cinque ordini d' architettura* (published in Rome, 1583, and probably as early as 1562); (d, e) two plates from *Porte di Michel Angelo* (published Orlandi, 1602).

Vignola's tabulated regulations first set constant ratios for the elementary divisions of the Order as a whole: column and entablature (post and beam, of course) or pedestal, column and entablature, which will respond to the dimensions of each particular building project but must be in the ratios of 4:1 (12:3) or 1:4 and 3:1 (3:12:4), respectively, in any case. With 12 as the common factor of the column, there are 15 and 19 subdivisions (12:3 and 3:12:4) whatever the Order. Progressing to differentiation within these consistent parameters, Vignola derives the mean modular base-to-height ratios of 1:14, 1:16, 1:18 and 1:20 for the Tuscan, Doric, Ionic and Corinthian/Composite column from his analysis of antique remains and produces the module from the division of the projected column height by the number designated for the chosen Order – though he also provides formulae for readier reckoning. The subdivision of the module determines the proportions of the minor elements of the Orders.

annotated to the exclusion of convoluted commentary available elsewhere. Its success was such that his work has provided the main standard
of reference for Classical architects ever since – but not without adventitious rigidity.

Vignola directed the preparation of seven plates representing *Porte di
Michel Angelo*. In addition to details from the Campidoglio and the Porta
Pia, these included two belonging to gardens opening off the Via Pia.

Though evidently introduced to Rome and high office by
Cardinal Alessandro Farnese, grandson of Pope Paul III,
Vignola's first major Roman work was for the latter's successor, Julius III (1550–55). The Villa Giulia is a highly
original variation on the Roman villa *sub-urbana*: unity
cedes to diversity in the axial succession of external rooms
to which the main block of interior space, fronting the
monumental semi-circular loggia, seems merely an
adjunct. The work was executed in collaboration with
the Florentine Bartolomeo Ammannati (1511–92) and
Giorgio Vasari (1511–74).[1.33]

1.33a

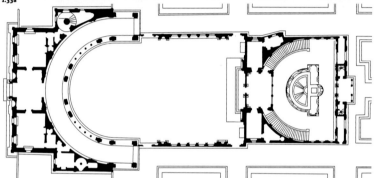

1.33b @ 1:1000

1.33c

Realizing the patron's conception, informed by the Cortile del Belvedere on a relatively intimate scale, the overall scheme is credited to Vignola by some, to Vasari by others. Vignola is generally given the main building. Ammannati is given the dependent enclosures – with undetermined help from Vasari.

The articulation of the entrance front is confined to the corners and the centre where the motif of the 'rhythmic bay', ultimately derived from the antique triumphal arch and echoed throughout the complex, distinguishes the portal on both levels: the vigorous rustication devours the Doric Order of the ground floor, as in the portal of Giulio Romano's Palazzo Maccarani and Vignola's own work for Bocchi in Bologna; the rustication extends into the niched side bays, as in the cortile of the Palazzo del Te, and aggressive keystones invade the pediments of the paired window frames in Giulio's manner and as represented by Serlio. The pediments of the upper windows incorporate antique 'altars' supported by volutes: often reiterated, the motif emerged from a rare excursion into invention for the author of orthodoxy. The curved loggia – and the incompletely resolved juxtaposition of major and minor Orders above – was inherited from a scheme projected for the site a generation earlier by Jacopo Sansovino: there is also a precedent, based on the Belvedere Nicchione, in a plan for a villa in Serlio VII.

Ammannati is credited with the side walls of the first external room – designed to accommodate antique sculpture – and the loggia which, effecting transition to the nymphaeum, provides a belvedere for its overview and serves the twin staircases which curve around its semi-perimeter. Excavated from a deep lower level to receive the waters of an ancient aqueduct, the nymphaeum may also have been decorated to Ammannati's direction with or without the intervention of Vasari – some Michelangelesque detail is contrary to Vignola's taste. Beyond a second logetta, on the main level again, is a rectangular private garden.

1.33d

1.33e

1.33f

1.33g

Apparently superseded by Ammannati at the Villa Giulia, at the end of the 1550s Vignola received his two most important secular commissions from the Farnese. At Piacenza, a vast palace was to be built for Pope Paul III's grandson Ottavio and his wife, Charles V's natural daughter, Margaret of Parma. At Caprarola, strategic to the family's Viterbese domains, the moated pentagonal fortress on its elevated site above the little town was to be converted into an exceptionally palatial villa for Cardinal Alessandro, another of the pope's grandsons.**1.34**

Military severity is sustained at Caprarola in the rusticated portals, which succeed one another on the splendid terraced base, but it is relieved by superimposed pilaster Orders on the two upper levels where the wall is cut back from stucco framework – except, of course, in the Ionic central loggia. The style aimed at orthodoxy in conscious rejection of Michelangelesque novelty – the objective pursued in the treatise on the Orders which Vignola was

Caprarola had been purchased in 1504 by the future Pope Paul III who, in due course, commissioned Antonio da Sangallo to fortify it. A pentagonal scheme with a circular courtyard (now in the Uffizi), unidentified but matching the circumstances of Caprarola, may have been the response: if so, Sangallo, tempering military might with domestic grace to flatter the patron's pretensions, translated the pentagonal form of his Florentine Fortezza da Basso to the commanding site and introduced the courtyard from the Villa Madama with which he had also been heavily involved. Be that as it may, these are the prime features of the executed scheme.

Access to and communication within the building are both efficient and impressive. Beyond an axial route imposed on the medieval village, the pentagonal structure – which appears to be rectangular from the street – is elevated on three terraces. Of the three por-

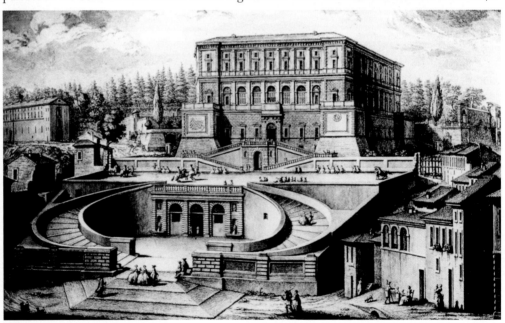

1.34a

tals, the lowest one serves limited stabling facilities, the middle one serves an internal carriageway which curves back on itself below the cortile, the upper one is for visitors on foot: in all three, the rustication asserts itself decisively over the Order – as in the Villa Giulia. The median carriage entrance communicates directly with the superb Doric spiral staircase, in the southern pentagonal corner, which serves the loggia in the centre of the piano nobile, which serves the cortile ambulatory which, in turn, serves the twin apartments of the south-west and north-east ranges. The second floor is similar. The circular court – prefigured by Vignola himself in an unexecuted villa design for Pope Marcellus II before his elevation – recalls Raphael's latest thoughts for the Villa Madama (part executed by Sangallo) but the two-storey articulation is adapted from Bramante's Caprini formula with reference to the rhythmic bay system of the Cortile del Belvedere. The frescoed decoration of the galleries and the rooms they serve, mainly *grotteschi*, set a widely emulated standard.

1.34b

1.34c

1.34d

1.34e

1.34f

1.34g

then compiling – and the planning is truly Classical in the ingenuity with which axial order is imposed on obtuse-angled form. A sequence of regular rooms is fitted into the pentagonal perimeter around the most magnificent of circular courts: indeed the symmetry of the plan hinges on circles in pentagons – repeating the basic form of the whole in relative miniature for circulation – at the outer corners.

1.34h

Caprarola is of unexcelled magnificence but the Piacenza project, with its five-storey façade and vast cortile culminating in the semi-elliptical cavea of a theatre, was never to be fully realized. In so far as the façade is concerned, some compensation is provided by the contemporary Palazzo Borghese in Rome.[1.35, 1.36]

1.35b

>**1.35 PIACENZA, PALAZZO FARNESE,** from 1560: (a) plan, (b) exterior detail, (c) section through cortile showing theatre (Parma, State Archive).

Raphael's Villa Madama – which was assigned to Margaret of Parma and took its name from her courtesy title – provides the obvious precedent for the theatre court. The addition of two mezzanines to supplement three regular storeys – thence a five-storey façade – was not uncommon in the work of Raphael and his circle, but Vignola's alternation of the major and minor forms recalls the courtyard of the Palazzo Maccarani.

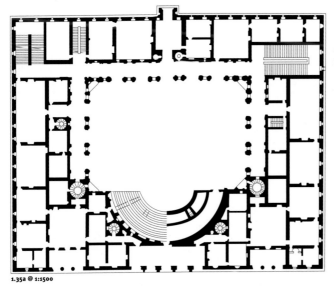

1.35a @ 1:1500

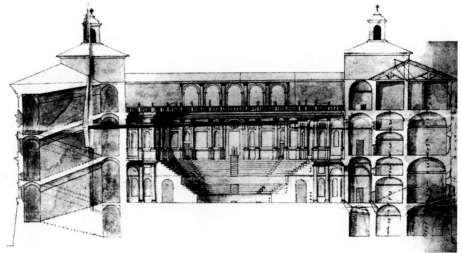

1.35c

›1.36 ROME, PALAZZO BORGHESE, c. 1560: façade.

The design for the façade, expanding the Farnese formula with the insertion of two mezzanines and an attic, is attributed to Vignola in general because he similarly inserted mezzanines in his unfinished Farnese palace at Piacenza, in particular because the portal follows a design reproduced in his treatise on the Orders. However, the execution lacks Vignola's gravitas: it was completed by Martino Longhi the Elder, to whom the cortile is attributed.

1.36

Encrustation of exteriors with stucco relief, in association with Classical statuary salvaged or copied from the antique, enjoyed a brief vogue in mid-century Rome. The ultimate inspiration, of course, was Raphael's Palazzo Branconio dell' Aquila (page 106). The grandest example is the Palazzo Spada: outside and in, the lavish stucco embellishment exceeds most else of the kind in Rome, even the syncopated framing to the fresco panels added to Antonio da Sangallo's Sala Regia in the Vatican – and that was considered the grandest room in Europe at the time.[1.37]

›1.37 STUCCO EMBELLISHMENT IN MID-CENTURY ROME: (a) Vatican palace, Sala Regia detail (framework from c. 1550); (b–d) Palazzo Spada (c. 1549–59), salone detail, cortile and entrance front.

The Sala Regia was installed in 1538 by Antonia da Sangallo for Paul III: the vault was stuccoed by Perino del Varga. Daniele da Volterra's frames were adapted to incorporate the Medici emblem of Pius IV (1559–65), for whom the frescoes were executed by Giuseppe Salviatti and Taddeo Zuccaro. Entities are dissected, but if they are not turned against themselves their meaning is flagrantly ambiguous: the half-pediments consort with one another as echoes of the regular pediment between them over the door but they belong primarily to the frames of the panels.

Palazzo Spada's patron was Cardinal Girolamo Capodiferro, who was elevated by Paul III in 1544 on his return from assignment to the court of François I at Fontainebleau. The palace was begun between his return visits to France in 1547 and 1553: the influence of the Gallery of François I at Fontainebleau (see below, pages 321ff) is detectable in the embellishment.

1.37a

1.37b

1.37c

1.37d

›ARCHITECTURE IN CONTEXT »FROM THE HIGH RENAISSANCE TO MANNERISM

VIGNOLA AND THE CHURCH

The first great architect specifically to meet post-Tridentine requirements for church planning was Giacomo da Vignola. He provided two formulae: one based on the Albertian revision of the basilica, the other on the oval. His work was seminal in the first degree.

It required a Mannerist mind to see both axial and centralizing tendencies in one and the same form, the oval, as Peruzzi and Serlio had done. Vignola first followed Peruzzi's elliptical example in his own unexecuted project for S. Giovanni dei Fiorentini c. 1550. He achieved it the next year in the little church of S. Andrea in Via Flaminia – just to the north of the main entrance to the Eternal City – as a dome over a rectangular volume articulated inside and out with variations on the triumphal arch motif. Finally, in the rectangular enclosure of S. Anna dei Palafrenieri the volume is oval, the entrance-altar axis is extended to form vestibule and sanctuary, the cross-axis is closed by chapels and the point of intersection in the centre is the focus for all the elements of the internal elevation organized in rhythmic sequence around the perimeter. **1.38a–f**

Vignola produced the prototype for the post-Tridentine grand congregational church in 1568 in response to a commission from the Jesuits for their mother foundation,

1.38a

1.38b

1.38c

›1.38 VIGNOLA AND THE ROMAN CHURCH:
(a, b) S. Andrea in Via Flaminia (from 1550), exterior and interior detail; (c–e) S. Anna dei Palafrenieri (from 1565), plan, interior and exterior; (f) S. Maria dell'Orto, façade (1564); (g–k) Il Gesù (constructed from 1568–73 under Vignola, completed for consecration in 1584 by Giacomo della Porta), longitudinal section, plan, lateral section, interior to east, west front project.

Innovative in executing an ellipse to simulate centralized planning on a corner site, Vignola provided the commissioners of S. Anna dei Palafrenieri with distinct major and minor axes respectively for the commissioning body – the confraternity of papal grooms – and the public. The imposition of oval on rectangle at vault level in S. Andrea is carried through to base for the interior perimeter here and the discrepancy in the length of the perpendicular axes is denied by varying the dimensions of the axial bays. Lack of accord between exterior and interior countered the Renaissance ideal but, of course, the insertion of a centralized form into a rectangular one was certainly not uncommon: Bramante's complex ideal for S. Pietro and its permutations apart, Antonio da Sangallo the Elder had enclosed an octagon in a square at S. Maria di Loreto, for instance, but the orthogonal sides of the former were contiguous with the latter (AIC4, page 850). Vignola had first experimented with the disparate disposition of oval in rectangle in c. 1559 for a chapel in the Vatican Belvedere.

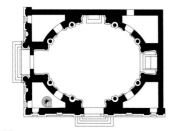

1.38d @ 1:500

1.38e

1.38f

known as Il Gesù. Alberti's substitution of chapels for aisles, asserting the uncompromised dominance of the main volume, was the key to the profound gravitas of S. Andrea at Mantua (AIC4, pages 748f). The clarity of that volume, its uninterrupted sightlines and excellent acoustics, recommended it to Vignola in serving a preaching order. The work was completed by Giacomo della Porta (c. 1533–1602), who also acceded to prime responsibility at S. Pietro on Vignola's death in 1573.**1.38g–k**

The conception of the Church Triumphant

The project for Il Gesù had been at least twenty years in gestation before work started on Vignola's scheme in 1568: a decade earlier Michelangelo had been consulted but debate on whether the plan should be basilican or elliptical, the main volume vaulted or lined in timber, was protracted until Alessandro Farnese pledged the funds in 1562 *ex voto* for recovery from an illness. The patron determined the aisleless basilican form and, opting to be buried in it, insisted on the grandeur of tunnel vaults and domed crossing.

In response to the client's requirements as interpreted by the patron, Vignola produced a theatre: the sanctuary is the stage for the priest to perform the holy mystery of the eucharist viewed by the congregation in the unencumbered auditorium through the proscenium arch beyond the domed crossing. To each side of the nave (18 metres wide) are three arcaded chapels and a cylindrical vestibule beside the crossing, all saucer-domed under grilled galleries and, thus, less assertive than Alberti's great tunnel-vaulted recessions in S. Andrea: the bays are divided by paired pilasters which carry the unbroken entablature, attic and tunnel vault. Beyond the great domed crossing, with its projecting pilaster groups, a repeat of the vestibule bay precedes the sanctuary apse: the fabric enclosing the vestibules reinforces the crossing piers; the thrust of the tunnel vault is resisted by the mass enclosing the chapels. The main volume is well lit from the west front and from the clerestory which penetrates the vault, departing from Alberti's model. All the vaulting and the dome were built under the supervision of Giacomo della Porta: the great illusionist frescoes and the splendid stucco framework were executed in the next century and will be discussed in context. Travertine pilasters ceded to marble in the 19th century.

In executing the vaults, Della Porta heightened the attic above the main cornice. As the overall height of the building had been increased, the façade needed revision. In distinct advance on his recent design for S. Maria dell'Orto, which projects only with the columns of the portico, Vignola's scheme recalls Sangallo's S. Spirito formula and Serlio's version (see pages 138, 149). However, it breaks forward in three clear stages culminating in the transition from pilasters to columns on both levels of the central bay to support the semi-circular pediment of the portal and the corresponding projection of the main pediment.

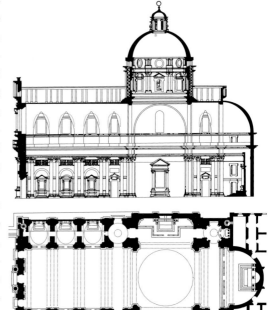

1.38g, h @ 1:1000

1.38i

1.38k

1.38j

1.39b

1.39a @ 1:1000

VIGNOLA AND HIS CONTEMPORARIES IN THE GARDEN

Vignola's colleague, the Neapolitan Pirro Ligorio, was elevated to his prestigious position at the Vatican by the Neapolitan Pope Paul IV (1555–59). In that capacity he completed Bramante's extensive courtyard project, inserting a semi-circular theatre against the main palace front of the lower zone and, on the top level, reducing the great niche of the Belvedere within an enhanced elevation (AIC4, page 855). Also in that capacity he produced his most celebrated Roman work: the Villa Pia (also known as the Casina Pio) in the Vatican gardens to the north of the Belvedere courts. Composed of distinct pavilions which address one another across a colonnaded court, the complex is a discrete entity in a naturalistic context: like the Villa Madama, it is a re-evocation of Pliny's Villa Laurentiana but in miniature and encrusted with reliefs in the antique style – if not actually reused from some antique prototype which the author had unearthed in his enthusiasm for archaeological excavation.**1.39, 1.40**

›1.39 ROME, VATICAN GARDENS: (a–c) Villa Pia (from 1559), plan, general view and detail.

Internal space is insignificant compared to the open-air reception area: it is mainly provided in the triple-height upper building (to the south-west of the court), with its ground-floor loggia effecting transition from interior to exterior. The most agreeable space on hot days must have been the biapsidal double-fronted loggia of the pavilion opposite, which projects into the fish-pond. The columns are marble but the walls were stuccoed: the effect on the main front is overwhelming, with its blind central level and elevated attic far surpassing Raphael in inverting the conventional progression from solid to void. Internal decoration incorporated Classicizing reliefs, like the exterior, but in the context of frescoes of both religious and secular subjects.

1.39c

After his retirement from the Vatican, Ligorio was mainly employed by the d'Este rulers of Ferrara. The most extensive surviving work attributed to him, commissioned by Cardinal Ippolito c. 1560, is the villa at Tivoli. The biaxial garden is replete with the full repertory of elements inherited from remote Antiquity: apart from the regularity of the grid itself, watercourses, fountains and pools for exotic flora and fauna, useful plants regularly planted, topiary and sculpture in durable materials – especially of deities in a context descended from the age-old sacred grove (AICI, pages 142f).**1.40**

1.40a

>**1.40 TIVOLI, VILLA D'ESTE:** (a) engraved overview (Étienne Dupérac, 1573), (b) nymphaeum, engraved view with watered visitors, (c) grotto, (d) water garden with 'Ligurian village', (e) main cross-axis with reflective pools, (f) triumphal fountain.

1.40b

Tivoli, Villa d'Este: sense and sensibility

The villa – undistinguished in its present state, at least – is perpendicular to the view of the Roman Campagna from the clifftop site but addresses the main axis of the garden. The visitor descending from the elevated portico of the house, on its rusticated basement, to the rusticated terraces of the garden below is constantly deflected from the main axis by diagonally disposed steps and paths: these join a secondary cross-axis, enlivened with repetitive waterspouts, which leads right to the water-cooled semi-circular grotto and its collection of antiquities, left to an irregular water garden with the antiquarian author's model of primitive Rome – the Rometta – perched on the edge of the cliff over a nymphaeum. In each of these, concealed springs could be activated to wet the unsuspecting visitor from below.

Diagonal paths rejoin the main axis at a circular fountain court beyond which is an extensive cruciform pergola. Before arriving there, however, the visitor's attention is caught by a series of calm rectangular pools which assert the main cross-axis: beyond these to the left, at last, is a semi-circular platform for the contemplation of the view; at the other extremity is an elevated triumphal arch which the patron could call upon to produce both water and music in abundance. Thus the spirits, having been soothed by reflection in turquoise pools and distant haze, are aroused by the sight and sound of a stupendous cascade. Arranging events of varied types and shapes was the standard approach of the landscape gardener after the Villa Madama but never before had the appreciation of rational geometry been so successfully countered by the psychology of emotion – sense by sensibility.

1.40d

1.40e

1.40c

1.40f

›**1.41 BAGNAIA, VILLA LANTE,** from 1566: (a) overview (fresco, Raffaellino da Reggio c. 1575, in reception pavilion), (b, c) source and spring, (d, e) waterfall and cascade, (f) lowest terrace with 'lake'.

1.41b

1.41c

1.41d

MAN AND WILDERNESS

The visitor to the Villa d'Este at Tivoli enjoys the view from the periphery but is secure in the regulated world of the extended central axis – except for the hazards of the plumbing. Beset by wilderness to all sides beyond the great walls of the Vatican Belvedere, the miniature order of Ligorio's Villa Pia seems to sail like a ship at the mercy of the sea – as did the Villa Giulia but with less exposure and greater size. At Caprarola, beyond twin four-square gardens aligned with the north-western sides of the pentagon, wilderness offers not threat but enticement – via a convoluted cascade – to a secret loggia on the highest point of the hilltop site. Also engaging the wilderness and incorporating a convoluted cascade, the Villa Lante at Bagnaia – on which Vignola advised the local architect – is the summation of the main line of development in 16th-century garden design: others went even further.[1.41, 1.42]

Bagnaia to Bomazzo

The axis of the Lante garden, punctuated by fountains as in the Villa d'Este at Tivoli, descends through a succession of terraces, as on the Milvian side of the Villa Madama (see page 110). However, while the main villa block of the latter is set in the centre of the top terrace, here the accommodation is

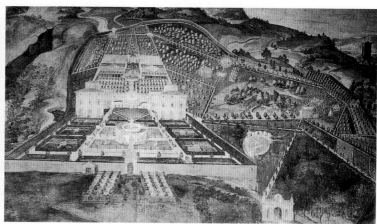

1.41a

divided between two identical pavilions separated by the descending terraces. Further, while the uppermost terrace of the Villa Madama communicates with wilderness through a guarded portal and the Villa Pia floats in contained wilderness, the Villa Lante is set in wilderness at large. Most significantly, moreover, the axis of the watercourses here follows a literary theme stemming from wilderness: the history of a river from its mountain spring, through cascade and waterfall to pool, canal, lake and sea. From the naturalistic source at the top, there is a progressive increase in order to the culmination in the great square fountain at the bottom. And, of course, that is an allegory for the course of the civilization of man from brutality to the triumph of reason – its thin and fragile line imposed upon, but at the mercy of, the wilderness.

The Villa Lante was built for Gianfrancesco Gambara whose crustaceous device asserts itself everywhere. His neighbour at Bomarzo, Prince Orsini, shunned order and abandoned himself to wilderness altogether – except for a Temple to Virtue. The precinct of the latter apart, the Sacro Bosco below his castle is apparently untamed nature – nature, indeed, whose irrational forces are represented by a wide range of bizarre sculptures and collapsing buildings discovered at random in the undergrowth – or were, before the site was tamed for the accommodation of tourists.

1.41e

1.41f

1.42b

›1.42 BOMARZO, SACRO BOSCO: (a) view towards palace with monster in foreground, (b) elephant and castle, (c) Temple of Virtue, honouring the patron's wife, (d) 'Mouth of Hell', (e) leaning pavilion.

1.42c

1.42d

1.42a

1.42e

1.43a

1.43b

›1.43 VASARI: (a) 'Apotheosis of Cosimo I' (1565; Florence, Palazzo Vecchio, Salone dei Cinquecento); (b) 'The Forge of Vulcan' (oil on copper, c. 1567; Florence, Uffizi).

The subject of Vasari's allegory is nominally Vulcan forging armour for Thetis's son Achilles. However, the forge is relegated to the background (top right) and Thetis doubles as Minerva (left) directing Vulcan in the embellishment of a shield with the Medici arms. The allegory extends to the representation of a vaulted artists' studio (top left) in allusion to the Accademia delle Arti del Disegno. A further complication – visually, if not intellectually – is the introduction of the Three Graces to the studio as models representing the Academy's principal fields of study: painting, sculpture and architecture.

4 THE DUCAL ARCHITECTS OF FLORENCE

From 1537 Florence was ruled by Duke Cosimo I de'Medici whose title had been confirmed by Emperor Charles V in return for help against the French. He formed an indirect alliance with Spain, marrying the daughter of the viceroy of Naples, Don Pedro Álvarez de Toledo. He defended himself with Swiss mercenaries, his domains with modern forts and his coast with a navy which later took part in the Battle of Lepanto. He reformed the administration, promoting the development of an initially efficient bureaucracy – certainly in the raising of taxes to pay for his defences and his lavish patronage of the arts.[1.43]

As we have seen, the principal court painter was Agnolo Bronzino: he produced a major fully integrated fresco decoration for Eleanora di Toledo's chapel in the Palazzo Vecchio.[1.44] Giorgio Vasari (1511–74) and Bartolomeo Ammannati (1511–92), Tuscans recalled from Rome at the end of Julius III's pontificate in 1555, were the principal court architects. As usual, architecture was not their original calling: sculptor and painter in origin respectively, both were devotees of Michelangelo – in whose studio Vasari briefly found himself as a teenage student of painting and from whose studio Ammannati reputedly stole drawings as a teenage student of sculpture.

In 1563 Duke Cosimo founded his Accademia delle Arti del Disegno at the instigation of Vasari: initially director under the aged Michelangelo – whose role was honorary – the latter played a prime role at the centre of the Mannerist stage – with Bronzino, Ammannati, Cellini, and Giambologna, the most prominent of his co-founder members active in Florence. The patron's initiative was flattered by the director in 'The Forge of Vulcan': representing art serving dynastic ambition under the aegis of wisdom, the work marks the tendency of Mannerist painting – in the *disegno* mode – towards abstruse erudition promoting

1.44a

>1.44 FLORENCE, PALAZZO VECCHIO RENO-
VATIONS: (a) Bronzino's Chapel of Eleanora di Toledo
(1540–45), (b) Vasari's ceiling of the Sala di Cosimo il
Vecchio (Paris, Louvre), (c) Studiolo di Francesco I,
(d, e) axonometric drawing of ascent from atrium to
Salone dei Cinquecento as devised by Vasari and general view of latter.

Beyond the Cortile di Michelozzo, decorated by
Vasari, is the latter's scenographic, double-flight staircase and the arcaded lightwell around which it returns
in flights to each side. The prime purpose of the latter
is to provide grand access to the huge Salone dei
Cinquecento: a lateral extension serves the Udienza tribune of the great room and the council chamber, known
as the Sala dei Dugento, in the north-west corner of the
old palace block. Diagonally opposite are the Quartiere
di Leone X and, above it, the Quartiere degli Elementi
which Vasari redecorated for Cosimo I with frescoes
relating the history of the Medici and the genealogy of
the gods respectively. Opening from the south-west
corner of the great room – to provide retreat from ceremonial into intimacy – is the Studiolo di Francesco I.
Between the latter and the main piazza front are the
rooms decorated in the first campaign of work under
Cosimo I for his Spanish duchess.

Projected in 1494 by Cronaca for the republic's Consiglio Maggiore and decorated by Pollaiolo, the Salone
dei Cinquecento was the scene of the rivalry between
Leonardo and Michelangelo in their ill-fated attempts to
represent the battles of Anghiari and Cascina.[0.4] Raising its height at the suggestion of Michelangelo, Vasari
was commissioned in 1560 to design the ceiling and
fresco the walls anew: the latter glorify Florence's military exploits, the former its ducal house culminating in
the 'Apotheosis of Cosimo I'. As elsewhere, much of the
execution was left to an extensive team of assistants.

highly refined complexity of form which may elicit a concerted effort of concentration in deciphering allegory but
may not elucidate the ostensible subject.

As ducal architect, Vasari had first been commissioned
to renovate the Palazzo della Signoria – to which Cosimo
I had moved from the Palazzo Medici in 1540. The project extended from a new atrium to an exceptionally large
audience hall via an innovative double-ramped staircase
which ascended around all four sides of a central vestibule:

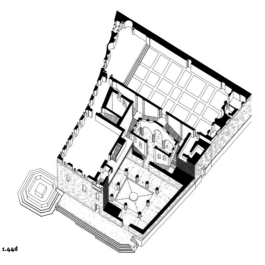

1.44d

1.44b

1.44c

1.44e

›ARCHITECTURE IN CONTEXT »FROM THE HIGH RENAISSANCE TO MANNERISM

1.45a

1.45b

1.45c

›1.45 VASARI AND THE FLORENTINE UFFIZI,
begun c. 1560: (a) view from the enclosed street; (b) the
ducal corridor crossing the Arno over the Ponte Vecchio; (c) detail of Vasari's frescoes on the gallery vault.

Commissioned to house the administrative arm of
government – and also court artists and their best
products – on the extended site between the Palazzo
della Signoria and the river, Vasari responded with parallel buildings flanking a long, narrow concourse. Only
the northern range opens at 'street' level through
colonnaded loggias, distyle in antis: the cortile, rather
than the street front, of Peruzzi's Palazzo Massimo alle
Colonne is recalled even in the clerestory lighting
through the mezzanines separated by Michelangelesque brackets; above the piers, astylar pilaster strips
separate triads of pedimented windows. The top floor
is the colonnaded gallery which takes part in the Pitti
corridor: it bridges the gap between the wings over a
fenestrated piano nobile and a grand serliana loggia
which opens the concourse to the view of the river at
ground level. The corridor had a Roman precedent in
the link between the Vatican palace and the Castel
Sant'Angelo.

The success of the Uffizi scheme as an exercise in
town planning – or, rather, ordered intervention into a
medieval context – recommended its author for extensive employment elsewhere, notably Pisa and Arezzo.
The medieval morphology of central Pisa obviated the
triumph of reason but symmetry was imposed on the
main buildings addressing the irregular Piazza dei Cav-
allieri (from 1562). At Arezzo (from 1570), on the other
hand, Vasari was able to impose strict regularity on the
northern perimeter of the medieval Piazza Grande with
an extensive new shopping loggia surmounted by
offices – as Vignola had just done in Bologna, if rather
more mechanically.

›1.46 AMMANNATI AND THE FLORENCE OF DUKE COSIMO I: (a–e) Palazzo Pitti, garden court (from 1560), overview and detail of Neptune fountain, Cythera zone and Boboli Garden plan; (f) Ponte Santa Trinità (from 1565 after destruction by flood in 1557); (g) S. Giovanino; (h) Palazzo Montalvo; (i, j) Palazzo Griffone.

Michelangelesque windows distinguish the first phase of extension to the Pitti, facing the town. Most notable, however, is the three-sided court facing the garden: basic inspiration may have come from Sangallo's Palazzo Farnese cortile scheme but aggressive rustication engulfs all three Orders in the manner of the Villa Giulia portal – or, perhaps more particularly, of Sansovino's Venetian Zecca (see below, page 219). The scheme is centred on a fountain at the foot of a cascade

the architect provided the drawings for the extensive narrative fresco cycles of the great room and the renovated ducal apartments beyond it. As an adjunct to his new seat, moreover, the duke commissioned the Uffizi to house his reformed bureaucracy – and a corridor to link it across the river to the projected definitive ducal residence in the Palazzo Pitti – which had been acquired at the instigation of the duchess in 1549. In response Vasari produced parallel buildings whose matching façades define the first uniformly ordered street since antiquity and were deployed to regularize piazzas in several of the duchy's major towns.[1.45]

1.46a

1.46b

1.46c

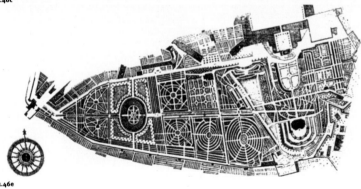

1.46e

1.46f

1.46d

1.46g

1.46h

which had been inserted into the 15th-century chequerboard garden to provide an engaging central axis: it descends from a statue of Ceres and embraces a fountain dedicated to Neptune – thus retaining the services of the deified fertility spirits of earth and water.

Ammannati's return to his native town was first marked by the Palazzo Griffone. The site, at the corner of the Via dei Servi and the Piazza della Santissima Annunziata, invited complementary exercises in eclectic display: the astylar approach to both fronts follows the Palazzo Pandolfini prototype (AIC4, page 860) but the exposed brick, at least, recalls Sangallo's Farnese exercise: window and door frames are variously borrowed from Sangallo, Michelangelo and Serlio. The Palazzo Montalvo site on a narrow street invited Michelangelesque windows at base level but simple rusticated frames in the context of *sgraffito* above.

Michelangelesque articulation in terms of columns in antis, specifically that of the nearby Laurentian Library *ricetto* turned inside out, distinguishes the façade of S. Giovannino (from 1570).

1.46i

1.46j

1.47a

Ammannati was primarily engaged by Cosimo I on the augmentation of the Palazzo Pitti to accommodate a modern monarchical court matching the dignity of the newly elevated grand-duke. He also served the public with the most elegant of Florentine bridges, the elliptically arched Ponte Santa Trinità, and the most spectacular of its fountains – presided over by Neptune in the Piazza della Signoria. He worked, too, for leading courtiers, most notably Ugolino Grifoni, the grand-ducal secretary, and Ramirez da Montalvo – a principal figure in the suite of the duchess, Eleanora di Toledo. He returned to Rome twice in the 1570s to work for the grand-duke's nephew.**1.46, 1.47**

›1.47 AMMANNATI IN ROME FOR CARDINAL FERDINANDO DE' MEDICI: (a) Palazzo Firenze (1572), court front; (b) Villa Medici, garden front (1576).

In both his Roman works of the 1570s, Ammannati further developed his eclectic style. While the clarity of the Palazzo Firenze's court front ordonnance echoes Vignola's central bays of the Villa Giulia's court hemicycle, the multiple mouldings of the mezzanine windows and upper floor niches are distinctly Michelangelesque and the serliana may derive from Sansovino's Palazzo Gaddi if not from the precedent set by Raphael and Bramante – or indeed Serlio.

In enlarging the villa on the Pincio acquired in 1576 by Cardinal Fernando – after whom it was subsequently to be known as Villa Medici – the ever-eclectic Ammannati's major contribution was the loggia front to the garden: the great serliana recalls the Uffizi loggia of his erstwhile colleague Vasari but the *all' antica* context is clearly inspired by Pirro Ligorio's Villa Pia.

1.47b

1.48a

›ARCHITECTURE IN CONTEXT »FROM THE HIGH RENAISSANCE TO MANNERISM

1.48c

1.48b

›1.48 FLORENCE, SCULPTURE IN THE PIAZZA DELLA SIGNORIA: (a) view from Bandinelli's statue of Hercules, past the copy of Michelangelo's David to Ammannati's Neptune and Giambologna's equestrian statue of Cosimo I; (b, c) overview of Ammannati's fountain and detail of the bronze ancillary figures.

As sculptor, Ammannati left his most prominent legacy to Florence with the fountain of Neptune on the Piazza della Signoria. Deferential homage to Michelangelo is most obvious in the virtuoso contortions for the bronze attendants but the marble figure of Neptune looks for inspiration from nearby David – and with disdain at the latter's pendant, the Hercules of Michelangelo's bitter rival Baccio Bandinelli (1493–1560). Power, rather than psychological ambivalence, was required and Ammannati demonstrates that the representation of the male nude in heavy maturity – and colossal scale – need not be stolid.**1.48**

By 1569, when Cosimo I had been elevated to the rank of grand-duke, Vasari and Ammannati had been joined by Bernardo Buontalenti (1531–1608), the Florentine engineer, decorator, *metteur en scène* and inveterate designer of villas for his Medici masters. As a military engineer and urban planner, he ceded nothing to his peers in rationality: a prominent example is the new town of Livorno, though his grid was varied in implementation after his death.**1.49** Of course, too, his architecture conforms to Vitruvian conventions of *firmitas*, *utilitas* and *venustas* – the latter at least in its essential symmetry. However, furthering the more radical elements of Michelangelo's style – and

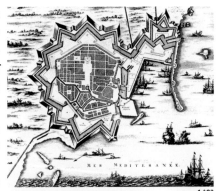

1.49a

1.49b

>**1.49 LIVORNO:** (a) plan of port city and fortifications (c. 1575); (b) Piazza Grande.

>**1.50 BUONTALENTI'S FLORENTINE MANNERISMS:** (a) cathedral façade model (competition entry, 1588); (b) S. Stefano al Ponte, pleated altar steps from Santa Trinità (1576); (c) Casino Mediceo (early 1570s, now Palazzo Corte d'Appello), window; (d) Uffizi, Porta della Suppliche (1576); (e) Palazzo Nonfinito (from 1593), general view from the south-west.

1.50b

1.50a

1.50c

1.50d

not without apparent knowledge of the Vatican Sala Regia[1.37a] – his forte was the countering of convention and the denial of structural logic. Beyond that, he was fecund in the design of bizarre quasi-zoomorphic detail and the real or imagined realm of nature was his peculiar sphere of operation.[1.50, 1.51]

1.50e

Man and the irrational

Buontalenti was the consummate master at exploiting the ambivalent relationship between man and nature. At the Villa di Pratolino the 'naturalistic' elements to either side of the garden's formal axis were as celebrated as the pools and fountains. As we have seen, however, wilderness became a garden elsewhere at that date: unique was Buontalenti's realization of the consequences. These are clearly vexing to Giambologna's giant statue of the 'Appennines' at Pratolino (c. 1580). They had already been even more disturbing to the 'January' which Ammannati was commissioned to sculpt at the apex of the Villa di Castello garden (1563): is he struggling out of the mire or being sucked back – is he victor or victim?

Beyond the elemental struggle of superman and nature, Buontalenti produced the most engrossing dramatization of the relationship between the animate and the inanimate – in any work of the period – in the grotto in the Boboli Gardens (c. 1585): exceeding Raphael's Villa Farnesina Psyche loggia in the combination of the arts, he fused painting, sculpture and architecture in a context of illusion as complete as Giulio's Romano's frescoed Sala dei Giganti in the Palazzo del Te. The real space, defined by fruit-like stalactites clearly transposed from Raphael's floral pergola, is extended in paint to a cavernous wilderness inhabited by wild animals eyeing goats; reversing the process, sheep and shepherdess in turn seek refuge with us as sculptures in the grotto, materializing in its space from

>**1.51 MEDICI WILDERNESS:** (a, b) Pratolino, lunette by Giusto Utens (1599; Florence, Topographical Museum), Giambologna's 'Appennines'; (c, d) Castello, detail of Ammannati's 'January' and grotto; (e, f) Florence, Boboli Gardens, grotto exterior and interior.

Castello was laid out by the sculptor Niccolò Tribolo from 1539: Vasari took over on the latter's death in 1550 and augmented the grotto; the villa was enlarged from

1.51d

1590 by Buontalenti. Ammannati's statue of 'January', commissioned during Vasari's involvement, completed the central axis which Tribolo had enlivened with the rather more orthodox fountains of Hercules and Venus.

Pratolino was laid out between 1569 and 1586 for the future Grand Duke Francesco de' Medici (Cosimo's successor in 1574) in a pine wood which he had purchased the year before. The main interventions were an axial avenue, paths through the woods, naturalistic cascades and numerous fountains of which the sole significant survivor on the devastated site is Giambologna's rustic masterpiece 'Appennino' – a distressed giant emerging from an artificial hillock with grottoes in a small lake (erected c. 1580).

1.51e

the stalactites of its structure. Further confusing the animate with the inanimate, moreover, the figures emerge from the rock as Michelangelo maintained sculpture is released from the block – indeed, they reproduce the slaves destined by Michelangelo for the tomb of Pope Julius II but never completely freed from their blocks. And the final dimension is revealed with the inner fountain from which rises Giambologna's 'Venus Anadyomene': this sinister cave is the birthplace of love.

1.51f

1.52a

5 SANSOVINO, SANMICHELI AND THEIR VENETIAN INHERITANCE

Colour – sensuality, indeed – had always been preferred to strict logic in Venetian design. Before the advent of Mauro Codussi in the late-15th century, rich materials and deep contrasts of light and shade were rarely subjected to strict symmetry in the design of palace façades, for instance, as long narrow sites did not facilitate the organization of plans around regular nuclear courts (AIC4, pages 646, 787f). Pietro Lombardo was the dominant figure and in the first quarter of the new century his legacy – at least as much as that of Codussi – was developed by the Bergamesque Bartolomeo Buon (c. 1450–1509), his probable son Pietro (died 1529) and the Milanese Antonio Abbondi known as Scarpagnino (c. 1470–1549) whose chief assistant was another immigrant from Bergamo, Guglielmo dei Grigi (c. 1485–1550). Representative of their joint efforts in the first quarter of the new century are the Procuratie Vecchie lining the north side of the Piazza S. Marco, the Palazzo dei Camerlenghi beyond the Rialto, the church of S. Sebastiano and, above all, the lavish polychrome front screening the Scuola Grande di S. Rocco with tangential concern for interior reality and limited regard for canonical precept.**1.52**

Furthering the development in the era of renewed prosperity opened in 1529 by the Peace of Bologna, which put

›1.52 VENICE, REPRESENTATIVE WORKS OF THE FIRST 16TH-CENTURY GENERATION: (a) Procuratie Vecchie (from 1512, as recorded by Canaletto c. 1750); (b) Palazzo dei Camerlenghi (from 1523); (c, d) Scuola Grande di S. Rocco (from 1515), plan and entrance front; (e) S. Sebastiano, interior (from c. 1507).

A master from the Buon dynasty, probably Pietro, was appointed chief architect (*proto*) to the procurators (trustees) of S. Marco in 1505: he was charged with completing Codussi's Torre dell'Orologio (from 1510), adding the belfry to the great tower begun by Giorgio Spavento (from 1511), and with the rebuilding of the trustees' apartment block, known as the Procuratie Vecchie, after the fire of 1512. Though the design followed lines laid down by Codussi (and inherited from the Byzantine original), the colouristic style returns from the latter's early High Renaissance achievement to that of Pietro Lombardo (compare AIC4, pages 787f) – the compatriot of both Buon and his chief assistant, Guglielmo dei Grigi.

After the disastrous fire which destroyed most of the market area at the Rialto in 1514, Scarpagnino was entrusted with the rebuilding: he preoccupied himself with the extensive, utilitarian Fabbriche Vecchie, the main market building. He delegated the restoration of the city treasurer's Palazzo dei Camerlenghi which survived the fire in a state of advanced dilapidation: his contribution ran to a new façade in Istrian stone which again recalls the style of Pietro Lombardo.

Guglielmo elaborated homage to Codussi in adding the Cappella Emiliana to the latter's church of S. Michele in Isola after 1527 (AIC4, page 802). He assisted Pietro Buon in the first phase of work on the Scuola Grande di S. Rocco where Pietro's father Bartolomeo had built the church (mainly replaced). The components of the charitable institution's complex – an undercroft for the distribution of alms surmounted by a hall for the assembly of the members served by a grand staircase projecting from the side – the asymmetrical composition, the varicoloured marble revetment and the rich relief recall the Scuola Grande di S. Marco, where Codussi succeeded Pietro Lombardo (AIC4, pages 788f). The ground floor, with its fenestration in the style of Codussi, is due to Pietro Buon. After the latter's fall from grace with the patron in 1524, Scarpagnino took over and completed the upper floor: he is also usually credited with the attached columns, reiterated from the portal of the Scuola Grande di S. Marco, but distributed as on a triumphal arch, and with the grand staircase. With twin flights leading to a landing from which a central flight ascends, the latter is comparable to the so-called imperial type developed in Spain – though, as we shall see, that would be in an open cage rather than parallel tunnels as here.

Early in his career Scarpagnino seems to have been commissioned to build the parish church of S. Sebastiano (begun c. 1507 but long in completion). The plan, with nave flanked by chapels instead of aisles, follows precedents at least as old as S. Francesco at Rimini – for which Alberti designed the façade followed by Codussi for S. Michele in Isola (AIC4, pages 742 and 802). The grid of articulating pilasters recalls Codussi's approach, as does the interior of S. Giovanni Crisostomo – whose centralized plan matches that of S. Giovanni Elemosinario which Scarpagnino restored in conjunction with his work on the Rialto after 1514.

1.52b

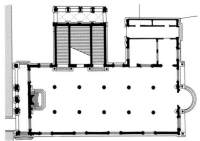

1.52c @ 1:1000

1.52d

paid to the disastrous turn of the Serene Republic's fortunes in the War of the League of Cambrai, Sanmicheli and Sansovino demonstrated conclusively that Roman – or Florentine – discipline and Venetian display were not incompatible. While Sanmicheli was developing his defensive projects, Sansovino received the major civic and ecclesiastical commissions, as we shall see. In the private sector, each is credited with major surviving palazzi: Sansovino was first with his work for Dolfin in the late-1530s, Sanmicheli last with his work for Grimani of twenty years

1.52e

1.53a

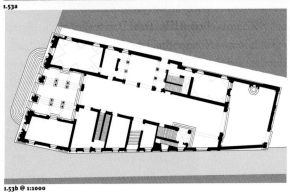

1.53b @ 1:1000

1.53c

>1.53 SANMICHELI IN VENICE: (a–c) Palazzo Grimani (from c. 1556), canal front, plan and hall interior; (d) Palazzo Corner a S. Polo (1545), canal front.

The Palazzo Grimani's awkward corner site obviated strict regularization of the traditional deep Venetian domestic plan: pragmatism disposed successive courts on an off-centre axis which diverges at an acute angle from the axis of the water portal. However, the aisled 'atrium' provides the basis on which the typically Venetian tripartite elevation is sustained. The central three bays on all levels follow the form of the triumphal arch: the major and minor bays are all framed by columns on both upper floors, as in Codussi's Palazzo Loredan (from c. 1500, later known as Palazzo Vendramin-Calergi); rustication is avoided but pilasters respond to the greater mass of the high basement and add strength to the corners at all levels. And at all levels, the arches rise from an inset Order in the manner developed by Bramante into the so-called serliana which was to be extremely popular with architects working in Venice and the Veneto (see AIC4, page 856).

The Cornaro family's secondary residence at S. Polo was destroyed by fire in 1535 – three years after the catastrophe at their S. Maurizio site: as there (as we shall see), rebuilding awaited resolution of the family's contentions towards the middle of the next decade. Like many Venetian domestic complexes, but unlike the one at S. Maurizio, the new building at S. Pietro was to accommodate separate extended families in stacked apartments of comparable grandeur – that of the second Cornaro brother and his tenants. As usual, the rusticated basement accommodates commerce. The twin piani nobili above, each with a mezzanine, provided each family with self-contained accommodation accessible by separate staircases. Thus heightened in elevation, the façade addressed a narrow *rio* which imposed sharply oblique views – though an orthogonal glimpse was offered by an alley perpendicular to the opposite bank. Therefore Sanmicheli dispensed with superimposed Orders, whose proportions would have been gravely distorted, in favour of Ionic and Corinthian aedicules surmounted by plain mezzanine window frames. The accretion of discrete units is substituted for the comprehensive ordonnance of the Grimani or, indeed, of the plate in Serlio's Book IV, which had recently been published in Venice and with which the result has otherwise much in common (see above, page 148).

later: in between they both worked for the vastly rich Cornaro family. By the time these major exercises were nearing completion Venetian prosperity was in steep decline and no comparable commissions were forthcoming until well into the next century – as we shall see.**1.53, 1.54**

Sanmicheli introduced the triumphal arch motif to the uncanonical superimposition of the Corinthian Order on the three full floors of his Palazzo Grimani, dismissing the problem of proportioning part to whole by varying the impact of the entablatures. Sansovino avoided the problem altogether at the beginning of his distinguished career as a palazzo builder for the Gaddi in Rome (see page 127). In Venice, like his Veronese colleague, he was inevitably uncanonical in his solution to the problem and could allow pragmatism to override precept in the distribution of his

1.54a

›1.54 SANSOVINO IN VENICE, PRIVATE PRAC-
TICE: (a) Palazzo Dolfin (from 1538), canal front; (b–d)
Palazzo Corner della Ca' Grande, S. Maurizio (from
1545), section, plan and canal front.

The Dolfin commission was let c. 1536: the site,
bounded by an alley to one side and a *rio* to the other,
was set back from the Grand Canal by a stretch of *fon-
damenta*. Permission was granted to provide an arcade
for the latter and to project the upper two floors out
over it. Sansovino's sense of Vitruvian decorum, prefer-
ring the public domain to the private, countered the
usual incentive to centralize façade composition on a
dominant void: an element in an extended line of
waterside communication, the arcade was given six
regularly repeated bays which set a solid in the centre.
Logic requires solid to support solid: Sansovino com-
plies in the centre but not at the sides of his four-bay
upper loggias. The original disposition of the interior
has been obliterated.

The Cornaro commission, probably let in 1537, was
to replace the progenitor's main seat which had been
destroyed by fire in 1532. The project was to accommodate one branch of the extended family in great magnificence on a prestigious site bordering the Grand Canal:
that involved much wrangling over the division of the
family's assets between the patron and his brothers
which delayed the work for nearly a decade. The site
was broad enough for the redefinition of the traditional
plan with regular geometry: the main entrance from the
canal opens to a vestibule and an elongated 'atrium'
(androne) beyond which is the 'peristyle' (cortile)

Orders. For instance: he was conventional in observing
Albertian – ultimately Vitruvian – decorum in his superimposition of Ionic and Corinthian Orders over Doric for
his Palazzo Dolfin but the upper floors project over a public gallery whose six arcades produce a solid in the centre
and impose regularity on the disposition only of the Doric
Order which frames them. Less than a decade later Bramantesque precedent is honoured in the breach on the
façade of his highly influential Palazzo Corner: Doric
pilasters cede to rusticated Doric piers on the base level but
the largesse of the site lets precept reign in the ordering of

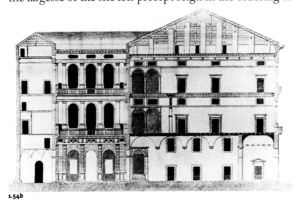

1.54b

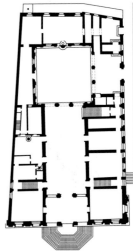

1.54c @ 1:1000

exposed to the side entrance from paved ground; the stairs are no longer in the open court but in tunnels ascending from the androne; the major reception rooms and principal apartments are on the piano nobile, of course, the family rooms on the top storey (AIC4, pages 646, 788). The rusticated Doric is confined to the window frames of the rusticated ground floor, to either side of the triple-arched portal which follows Sanmicheli's homage to Giulio's Palazzo del Te. Full expression is given to the Ionic and Corinthian of the first and second floors – though the Corinthian frieze is uncanonically enlarged to accommodate an attic in the attempt to cap the whole without crushing the part: this exercise in constructive inconsistency, typically Mannerist, involves distancing the cornice from the columns of the Corinthian Order by giving the median frieze an astylar life of its own. Contrary to the norm elsewhere, the canal corner site invited the continuation of the ordonnance in a return bay to the right.

1.54d

1.55

›1.55 CASTELFRANCO, VILLA LA SORANZA,
c. 1540: elevation and plan (engraving).

This is a prime example of Classicizing the traditional estate residence and its flanking barns in accordance with Vitruvian decorum: all three elements are comprehensively rusticated – recalling the origin of that type of masonry in the rustic rural environment; the extended arcades of the barns are condensed to provided the loggia in the centre of the residential block which consists of one storey raised on a semi-basement and surmounted by a reduced attic. On axis with the loggia is the salone and to either side of both are apartment blocks, each of the front ones incorporating a grand antechamber as well as a bedroom and private withdrawing room, each of the others having an extra service room.

solid and void. As the Classical concept of propriety required, Sanmicheli brought astylar rusticity to the development of the villa on the Venetian *terra firma*: his work in the genre is largely lost but the Soranza complex at Castelfranco is well recorded. Sansovino fared better in his sole contribution to the genre, at Pontecasale: there he turned the Doric and Ionic ordonnance of the Farnese cortile inside out for the central loggias in his otherwise sober Villa Garzoni.**1.55, 1.56**

›1.56 PONTECASALE, VILLA GARZONI, after
1537: (a) entrance front, (b) cortile.

Like that of Sanmicheli's La Soranza, Sansovino's residential block for the Garzoni at Pontecasale stands detached from the estate *barchesse*. Unlike Sanmicheli's work, however, it is not rusticated: the unrecessed five-bay arcaded entrance loggia, repeated at first-floor level, is articulated with engaged columns – Doric below, Ionic above, of course – and leads through to a similarly articulated arcaded court.

1.56a

1.56b

1.57a

›1.57 SANSOVINO AND THE TOMB: (a) of Antonio Orso and Cardinal Giovanni Michiel (c. 1520, Rome. S. Marcello al Corso); (b) of Francesco Venier (from 1555, Venice, S. Salvador).

1.57b

1.58a

Sansovino worked on ecclesiastical and funerary as well as secular commissions in Rome and remained faithful to the triumphal arch format of the genre in Venice.**1.57** There he was involved in the fabrication of some six ecclesiastical works, one charitable institution and several tombs. Lost are the monastic church of S. Spirito and the hospital church of S. Salvatore degli Incurabili (from c. 1560 and 1565 respectively), both sited on islands, and the parish church of S. Geminiano, which was rebuilt over medieval foundations at the western end of the Piazza S. Marco (from c. 1540).**1.52a centre** Also renovated over centralized plans, the parish churches of S. Martino and S. Giuliano (both from the 1550s) survive intact but the master's role in the former, at least, was probably only consultative. And he was unable to complete his most important work in the genre, the monastic church of S. Francesco della Vigna, or the Scuola Grande della Misericordia (both from the mid-1530s).

S. Francesco is notable for its aisleless hall, clear in sightlines and acoustics, extended into sanctuary and retro choir along lines traced at the behest of reformed Franciscans in the mid-15th century: the Florentine sobriety of the internal Doric articulation is singularly appropriate to a mendicant establishment. The foundation project had a two-storey façade of the standard basilican type, with volutes effecting transition from aisles to nave, but realization (from 1562) was accorded instead to the greatest architect of the age and the result was to be of great

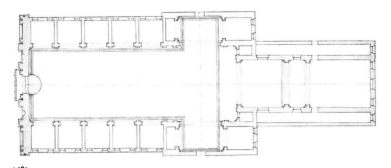

1.58c

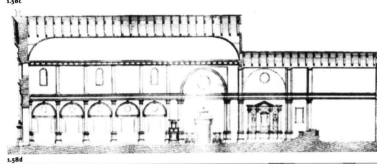

1.58d

1.58e

1.58b

›**1.58 SANSOVINO AND VENETIAN ECCLESIAS-
TICAL WORKS**: (a) Santo Spirito (18th-century
engraving); (b–e) S. Francesco della Vigna (from c.
1530), foundation medal, plan, section and interior; (f)
S. Giuliano, façade project; (g) Scuola Grande della
Misericordi, façade project (devised c. 1531 but here
represented by a drawing dated to c. 1570 and attributed to the office of Palladio); (h) S. Giorgio dei Greci,
façade (Sante Lombardo, from 1539).

The Franciscans of the reformed Observant branch,
dedicated to solitude and sobriety, commissioned
Sansovino to replace a Gothic basilica on their remote
vigna site in clear distinction from the grand, central
Frari of their Conventual brothers. Additions were made
to the site from 1527, papal authorization was granted
in 1533, work began the following year. As in Francesco
di Giorgio's Basilica dell'Osservanza in Siena (from
1467) and its fraternal contemporary S. Giobbe in Venice
– or, indeed, S. Francesco in Rimini even before Alberti's
involvement in the mid-15th century (AIC4, pages 741f) –
the Order's requirements were met with a broad hall
flanked only by side chapels (amplified to suggest a
transept). As usual in Venice, the main space was flat-
roofed but there is a vaulted ceiling over the extension
from the narrower sanctuary to the elongated choir
beyond the elevated high altar retable. The internal
ordonnance recalls that of Cronaca's S. Salvatore al
Monte in Florence (AIC4, page 793), its discipline
imposed on the well-established Venetian approach of
works like Scarpagnino's S. Sebastiano (from 1506; see
above, page 209). The scheme was revised in 1535 by
the friar responsible for executing it, Fra Francesco
Zorzi, whose concern was not to change the plan but to
develop a neo-Platonic Trinitarian harmony from the
consistent application of the ratio 1:3 to the elevation of
the various parts. Building was substantially complete
by the mid-1550s – except for the façade, to which we
shall return.

The Albertian approach to basilican façade design,
standardized in Rome by Antonio da Sangallo and elaborated by Serlio,[1.18, 1.25n] was deployed at least four

times by Sansovino – or at his behest: in the usual two-storey form unexecuted for S. Francisco but realized for S. Martino (from c. 1550); in three-storey variants for Santo Spirito and S. Geminiano – lost but recorded, the former with narthex arcade, the latter interposed between the multistorey buildings terminating the Piazza S. Marco. In contrast, he adopted the triumphal arch motif for the Misericordia and S. Giuliano (from c. 1555). Builders of great churches had never failed to appreciate the relevance of the triumphal arch motif to the conception of the church façade: Alberti led in respect of antique form, Giuliano da Sangallo in reviving the high imperial motif with archaeological exactitude – for S. Lorenzo in Florence, for example, where Raphael and Michelangelo followed. A more immediate precedent for Sansovino's work was the Santa Casa at Loreto, designed by Bramante in 1509 and embellished with relief sculpture by Andrea Sansovino from 1513 (AIC4, pages 841, 849).

The most celebrated antique precedent for syncopation in ordonnance (projection of the entablature of an upper Order over a recession in the entablature of a lower Order) is provided by the Library of Celsus at Ephesos (c. 120 CE). Whether or not that was known to the Greek community in Venice – or its architect – a variant was ready to hand in the Porta Borsari at Verona – and probably elsewhere in Italy (AIC1, pages 602ff).

1.58f

1.58g

1.58h

moment (as we shall see). The exterior of the Misericordia's stacked rectilinear halls also awaited Palladio, but in vain: Sansovino's basic two-storey ordonnance is impressed in the extant brickwork; its embellishment in a splendid Palladian drawing is restrained only by the tectonic logic of the most sumptuous of antique Roman forms, the triumphal arch, to satisfy the native taste for floridity. Clearly related is the façade of S. Giuliano, begun by Sansovino in 1553. A rather more wayward antique mode, Mannerist in the syncopation of its superimposed Orders, was adopted slightly later by Sante Lombardo for the façade of S. Giorgio dei Greci.**1.58**

In the aura of Serenissima's renewed prosperity at the beginning of the century's fourth decade, Sansovino launched his Venetian career with the celebrated scheme for ordering the Piazza S. Marco and the neighbouring Piazzetta, incorporating the Libreria Marciana: his responsibilities as chief architect to Serenissima's principal procurators preoccupied him for much of his long career, and his masterpiece in that capacity was unmatched in richness for several generations – except for its derivatives in painting. In severely appropriate contrast, generously arcaded and fenestrated in the Venetian manner but stoutly rusticated, is the near-contemporary building for the Republic's mint (Zecca) where precious metals were stored, refined and pressed into service as *specie*. Work on these great projects spanned decades and inevitably led to disputes between the builders, the architect and/or the authorities – not to mention recalcitrant shopkeepers squatting in the path of progress. Sansovino lost official favour in the 1550s, soon after he was accorded the commission for a new market building (Fabbriche Nuovo) on the banks of the Grand Canal to the north-west of the Rialto: his project – for the execution of which he was denied full responsibility – was a strictly utilitarian extrusion of the definitive mint scheme, with superimposed Orders but without rustication.**1.59**

Sansovino: colore from disegno on the civic stage

Brilliantly highlighting superimposed columns against arched voids, constantly reiterated to the exclusion of wall, the composition of the Marciana library block is of primary importance as the *scaenae frons* to the extension of the Republic's main urban space. The ground-floor loggia, backed by shops, respects an Italian urban tradition descending from the antique forum porticus, revived with urban commerce in the early Middle Ages (AIC1, page 625, AIC4, page 620) and Classicized in schemes like the one (sometimes attributed to Bramante) at Vigevano: it well represents the base of the city's affluence, humanist learning and rich patronage. Brutally juxtaposed, the mint building is singularly appropriate in its radically contrasting style: rustication lends apparent strength to the original Doric ordonnance and the arcaded basement where security was of the utmost concern. This was suitably moderated for the new Ionic level where simple triangular pediments replaced the extraordinary hoods of the windows below.

Sansovino draws on the portal style of his colleague Sanmicheli and, beyond that, of Giulio Romano but he would also have known Peruzzi's experiments in rusticating façades before he left Rome.**1.22b** While satisfying the city's taste, the Classical detail on both levels of the library is also foreign: the primary Orders are modelled on Antonio da Sangallo the

›1.59 SANSOVINO IN VENICE, PUBLIC WORKS: (a) Piazza S. Marco, plans before and after Sansovino's intervention; (b, c) general view of Piazzetta with Campanile and Zecca as rebuilt from 1536, and again from 1554; (d–f) Libreria Marciana (1537–58 and 1588–91) and Loggetta (Ridotto dei Nobile, 1538), view from the basilica's balcony, reading room (executed from 1556) and staircase.

Twenty years after Buon had rebuilt the Procuratie Vecchie on the north side of the piazza, Sansovino was commissioned to rebuild the south range, which accommodated the procurators themselves, on a revised line terminating to the south of the great campanile. There it would join the matching two-storey return block on the Piazzetta which was to house the state library (Libreria Marciana). The mint, adjacent to the latter, on the return along the lagoon front, was to be rebuilt to Sansovino's plans approved in 1536.

To sustain production, the mint was to be rebuilt in stages on its restricted site – from which inappropriate but revenue-earning shops had to be moved. The first phase quickly supervened but the project was altered in 1539 with the projection of the main floor

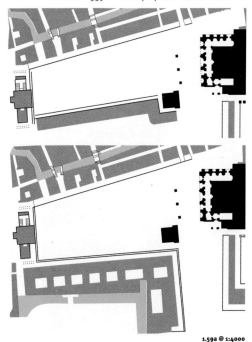

1.59a @ 1:4000

out over vaulting extended to a shopping arcade on the lagoon front. Twenty years later, the clerestory which lit the gold refinery on the piano nobile was replaced with a full second floor: Sansovino was out of official favour at the time and the plans were unattributed.

Work on the library was delayed for reasons unknown – probably difficulty in finding alternative accommodation both for the procurators and for the keepers of the shops at ground level, possibly shame at having hitherto failed to house the priceless collection of Greek and Latin manuscripts bequeathed to the Republic by Cardinal Bessarion in 1468. Be that as it may, work began in 1537 on the three eastern bays which – on cleared land under the lee of the campanile – formed the northern end of the library range. At this time too Sansovino projected the lavish pink and white marble Loggetta from the base of the disengaged campanile, facing S. Marco, for use by the Council of State during public ceremonies.

As the site was gradually reclaimed from shop- and inn-keepers, sixteen bays of the library block's return along the Piazzetta were built by 1556. At first incorporating masonry vaulting over the main spaces, much of the structure collapsed in 1545 and was rebuilt over the following decade with false vaults: the reading room's roundels were allocated to painters from mid-1556: the vestibule (accommodating a school dedicated to humanistic studies under a painting of 'Wisdom' by Titian) and the staircase were decorated from 1559. The last five bays were added under the supervision of Vincenzo Scamozzi from 1588 and the same architect realized Sansovino's scheme to continue the system of his library façades along the south side of the great piazza – but with a third storey.

1.59b

1.59c

1.59d

Younger's original Farnese courtyard, in general, but the Doric proportions specifically recall the primitive strength of Antonio the Elder's Madonna di S. Biagio at Montepulciano; as there, the terminal triglyphs are set back from the corners by half a metope; but to counter apparent structural weakness at these salient points they are here supported not by simple pier-pilasters (or squared columns) but by pilasters applied to the perpendicular faces of piers. This superseded the antique norm, represented in Giuliano da Sangallo's seminal record of the Arco di Gallo (AIC4, page 832). However, such details as the spandrel 'trames' over the inset minor Orders derive from the antique triumphal arch not least through the agency of Giuliano, who also favoured the festooned frieze. The latter, here enlarged to accommodate attic lighting as in Sansovino's own project of 1518 for the Palazzo Gaddi in Rome, is displaced from Raphael's Palazzo Branconio (page 106), and Sansovino had already borrowed the serliana from Bramante for his Roman Palazzo Gaddi.

Probably commissioned at much the same time as the library to replace a simple triple-arched shelter, the Loggetta originally had no end bays to the attic or balustrade at ground level – these were added over two centuries. Its basic ordnance is Bramantesque to the sides but –

1.59e

somewhat incongruously – a close follower of the front of Giuliano da Sangallo's first design for the façade of S. Lorenzo (c. 1516; AIC4, page 849) – the Florentine project to which Sansovino also contributed at the outset of his career and which he adapted for his first Venetian project, the façade of the Scuola Grande della Misericordia (1531). Built of brick, like the latter, but lavishly clothed in varicoloured marble, relieved in Istrian stone and peopled in bronze by Sansovino himself, the conception of the Loggetta was essentially one of extreme opulence – for which, beyond local practice, a precedent is most readily to be found in Raphael's Chigi Chapel (see page 13). Thus, ironically, the Venetian taste for *colore* was satiated by a Florentine in the mode his Florentine predecessors had derived from the Roman antique. Rather than opting to complement the florid late-Gothic of the Doge's Palace opposite, Sansovino challenged it in opulence – inside as well as out.

The Venetian ceiling

The type of ceiling (*soffitto*) with richly framed compartments of different shapes and sizes, varied by Sansovino in both ecclesiastical and public works, was developed to accommodate the illusionistic oil paintings on canvas with which the Venetians had largely displaced fresco by the second quarter of the 16th century.**1.60, 1.61** Tectonic coffering in timber, extending between the structural beams, was the Renaissance norm – at least for grand spaces. Coved rather than planar and divided into zones for frescoed imagery by a network of frames, the most proximate precedents for its Venetian development are Mantuan: they range from Mantegna's Camera degli Sposi in the Palazzo Ducale (1474), with its seminal central illusionism, to Giulio Romano's various works in the Palazzo del Te (after 1528) (AIC4, page 698, and see above, page 127). The former anticipates, the latter follows, Raphael's work in the Vatican *stanze* – and its Roman and Florentine tectonic lineage.

For the vault of his library staircase late in the 1550s, Sansovino drew on the Florentine tradition represented by Giuliano da Sangallo's Santo Spirito sacristy vestibule. Earlier in the decade Sangallo's regular repetition of circles in squares was translated to the vault of Sansovino's reading room. At the same time variety was introduced to the compartments of the nave and

1.59f

1.60a

1.60b

›1.60 VENICE, S. SEBASTIANO: (a, b) details of nave and sacristy ceilings with paintings by Paolo Veronese (1555).

1.61a

›1.61 VENICE, PALAZZO DUCALE: (a) Sala del Consiglio dei Dieci, ceiling (from c. 1553); (b) Sala del Collegio, ceiling (from 1575), (c, d) Sala del Maggior Consiglio, general view of ceiling (from 1578) and detail

sacristy vaults at S. Sebastiano. Slightly earlier still is the rich framework of circles and rectangles in the ceiling of the Palazzo Ducale's Sala del Consiglio dei Dieci. The stages of Venetian development to these splendid alternatives are largely lost. The varied type was represented by the early 1540s in Sansovino's lost church of Santo Spirito in Isola and Sanmicheli's Palazzo Corner a S. Polo from which, respectively, the varishaped canvases of Titian and Vasari survive: the composition of the latter was similar to that of S. Sebastiano's sacristy but all the compartments were rectangular; in the Santo Spirito composition, there were circles as well as rectangles – as at S. Sebastiano again. Ironically, thus, a key role in the evolution of the mature Venetian form may fairly be credited to the city's most industrious Florentine immigrant, if not to his equally eminent colleague from Verona.

The coved ceiling of Sansovino's reading room is divided with framed *grotteschi* – generally of Raphaelite inspiration – into compartments for allegories commissioned from several painters, Veronese above all. That

1.61b

supreme master contributed to the exercise for the Sala Consiglio dei Dieci and was naturally employed at his parish church of S. Sebastiano: in the former the spaces between the iconic panels are filled with allegorical figures; in S. Sebastiano's sacristy those areas are given to grotesque masks entwined in 'strapwork' which was probably inspired by Rosso Fiorentino – who is credited with inventing the motif at Fontainebleau, as we shall see, but had passed through Venice on his way there in the early 1530s. Strapwork scrolls play their subsidiary part in the free-ranging reliefs which fill the interstices of the Sala del Collegio ceiling in the Palazzo Ducale, installed by Antonio da Ponte after the fire of 1574. However, nowhere is this eclectic opulence lavished on Venice with greater relevance than on the ceiling of the new Sala del Maggior Consiglio installed after the fire of 1577: there, where Sansovino had been succeeded by Cristoforo Sorte among others, the *grotteschi* achieve three dimensions as the context for paintings by Tintoretto, Palma Giovane and Veronese's resplendent 'Apotheosis of Venice.'

of compartment inhabited by Veronese's 'Apotheosis of Venice'.

The suite of rooms used by the Consiglio dei Dieci was part of the last campaign of building in the complex before the fire of 1574: the structure was begun in 1546 and the framework of the main room was complete by 1553; the paintings of Veronese and his colleagues had been installed by the end of 1555.

Unlike the suite of the Dieci, the chambers of the Collegio did not survive the fire of 1574: Antonio da Ponte was immediately commissioned to design the framework for paintings by Veronese in the replacement ceiling and the work survived the fire of 1577.

The Sala del Maggior Consiglio was lost in 1577: the commission for the framework of the replacement ceiling was given to Cristoforo Sorte – an engineer and cartographer from Verona – in the middle of the following year; the paintings of the principal artists involved – Veronese, Tintoretto, Bassano and Palma Giovane – were installed in 1582.

1.61d

1.62

As we have seen, Veronese was a supreme master in the sumptuous display of decorum. The *virtù* of his *mise-en-scène* accords sublimely with the ethos of its age. Staging the clemency of Alexander to the family of Darius against an architectural screen clearly inspired by Sansovino, he distills the essence of the courtly ideal of *maniera* with gorgeous facility: the 'Apotheosis of Venice', in the centre of the ceiling of the Sala del Maggior Consiglio is more than merely proto-Baroque.**1.62, 1.61d** Elsewhere, the architecture of Veronese's most sumptuous tableaux distinctly recalls the most masterful exercise in urban scenography contributed by Sansovino.

›**1.62 VERONESE:** 'The Family of Darius before Alexander' (1565–67; London, National Gallery).

1.63a

1.63b @ approximately 1:1000

›**1.63 CRICOLI, VILLA TRISSINO,** mid-1530s?:
(a) loggia front, (b) plan.

Giangiorgio Trissino was an amateur architect and apologist for Vitruvius with an advanced bent towards convenience in domestic design – like his friend Alvise Cornaro, also an amateur architect, whose common sense specifically commended an astylar aesthetic. Working with Falconetto, the latter had introduced the High Renaissance villa to the north-east at Luvigliano – with a Bramantesque ordonnance – but the simpler style favoured by Trissino owes more to the Odeon built in the courtyard of his Padua residence: it owes even more to Peruzzi's Villa Farnesina in Rome but corrects the asymmetry of the latter's plan. Beyond that, indeed, it is a Classicizing contraction of the late-Gothic type represented by the Palazzo Porto Colleoni at Thiene: in contrast to the homogeneity preferred by Florentines, it followed the additive – usually tripartite – approach to massing which the Venetians retained from their colourful medieval traditions.

One of Trissino's main purposes at Cricoli was the convocation of a putative academy of the liberal arts: Palladio attended at the outset of his relationship with the patron. The euphonious allusion to Pallas (conferred on Andrea c. 1540) had been introduced in Trissino's *L' Italia Liberata da' Gotti* – an epic poem on the expulsion of the Goths by the forces of the Byzantine Emperor Justinian under Belisarius – for the angel was sent to guide the conqueror through the palace of the conquered.

6 PALLADIO

The second half of the 16th century in the Veneto was dominated by the career of Andrea di Pietro della Gondola, known as Palladio (1508–80) – perhaps the greatest, certainly the most influential, of all Renaissance architects. Born in Padua, he was first active there as a stonecarver in the aura of Giovanni Maria Falconetto and his great humanist patron Alvise Cornaro (AIC4, page 862). In 1524 he took his masonry talents to Vicenza where he was discovered by the humanist nobleman Giangiorgio Trissino (1478–1550) at work on a villa the latter had designed for himself at Cricoli.**1.63** Thereafter Trissino, grooming his master of building, gave him his erudition, his patronage and the euphonious name derived from Pallas Athena which certainly did not inhibit the acquisition of fame.

To advance his education, Palladio would have gained access through his patron to the upper echelons of patronage in vital centres of architectural excellence within easy reach: the Padua and Luvigliano of Cornaro and Falconetto, which he already knew; the Mantua of Giulio Romano; the Verona of Sanmicheli; the Venice where Sansovino was still working on his great library and where Serlio published his first two volumes between 1537 and 1540. After a sojourn in Padua, Trissino took him to Rome in 1541 to study the masters, ancient and modern – which he would previously have studied as selected by Serlio. He was back there between 1545 and 1547 and in 1554 with Daniele Barbaro, his most fervent admirer after Trissino. His studies in Rome and his contacts with colleagues who had long been involved in surveying the ruins, particularly Antonio da Sangallo the Younger, naturally deepened his appreciation of the rich diversity of the antique legacy – as well as providing him with the pre-eminent model of the modern palace.**1.64–1.66**

1.64a

›1.64 PALLADIO'S SKETCHBOOK: (a) Bramante's Palazzo Caprini; (b) Temple at the Springs of Clitumnus, elevation and section in perspective (possibly after Pirro Ligorio c. 1541); (c) Mausoleum of Romulus on the Via Appia, Rome, plans and elevations (late-1560s); (d) Temple of Fortuna at Palestrina, ideal reconstruction (1560s – Palestrina is ancient Praeneste; see AIC1, pages 522f); (e–h) Baths of Agrippa, plan, restored elevation and sections (1554).

The drawings after Bramante and antique thermae admirably demonstrate the range of Palladio's interests. In his record of the baths, he clearly appreciated the Roman taste for varied spaces and rich visual effect

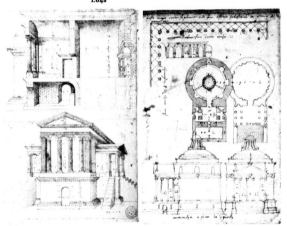
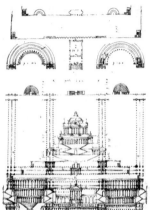
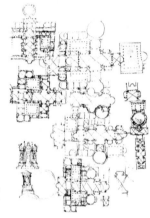

1.64b–e

drawn from views through them. Further, the axial planning and hierarchical massing are interpreted to enhance climax in the calidarium at the expense of the frigidarium – though in fact it was the other way round. These lessons were applied to his interpretation of domestic planning from antiquity.

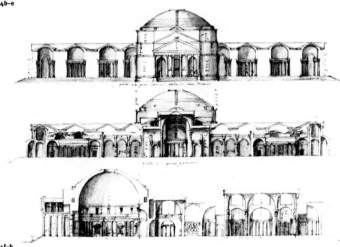

1.64f–h

›1.65 RECONSTRUCTION OF THE ROMAN HOUSE: (a) elevation with portico, (b) plan.

The plan belongs to a suite provided by Palladio to illustrate Daniele Barbaro's commentary on Vitruvius (1556). It is clearly ideal in its wholly regular geometry producing absolute symmetry (approximated, but rarely realized, in the Graeco-Roman world; AIC1, pages 483, 492, 540ff). The illustration of its façade with pedimented portico – bequeathed by antiquity solely with durable religious architecture – represents the ideal response to the pragmatic view that the dwelling of man was perfected for the dwelling of God rather than that the former was the inferior follower of the latter· Vitruvius implies this at the outset of his Book II (and in fact true even for the Hellenic world at the foundation of its architectural tradition – though Palladio and his contemporaries would not have commanded all the evidence (see AIC1, pages 11ff, 158f, and 371).

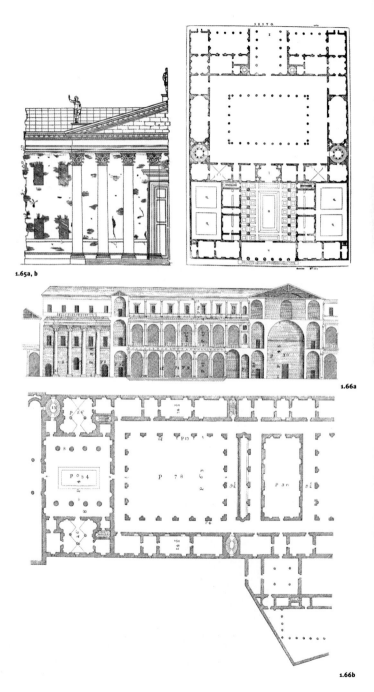

1.65a, b

›1.66 VENICE, S. MARIA DELLA CARITÀ (now Accademia di Belle Arti), 1564: (a, b) section and plan (as published by the author in 1570 in *I Quattro Libri* – hereafter referred to as *QL*).

Eight years after Palladio had produced his ideal reconstruction of a grand Roman house he applied the formula to his Carità project. The elevation ran to three storeys (for which there was no evidence from antiquity): superimposed Orders were applied to the peristyle arcades. The project was never to be fully realized.

1.66a

1.66b

Well before his first visit to Rome, immediately on graduating from the site of Trissino's villa at Cricoli, Palladio had been set to work on designing houses for several of his patron's compatriots. The urban commissions were for an ubiquitous type well represented by contemporary work in the Roman High Renaissance style at nearby Verona. The rural commissions were of the rarer type of the estate house – as distinct from the suburban retreat – which provided practical but dignified accommodation and offices for gentry dedicated to improving their landholdings.

The earliest Palladian estate house, built for the Godi at Lonedo in the early days of the Venetian agricultural revolution, stands with Sanmicheli's Villa La Soranza and Sansovino's Villa Garzoni at the head of a long line of development from a late-medieval prototype: in contrast to the homogeneous type of mass promoted by the Florentines and their Roman colleagues, it varies the tripartite form of Trissino's work at Cricoli and prefers

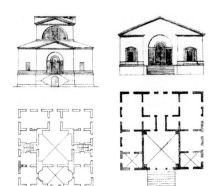

1.67a, b

›1.67 EARLY VILLAS, c. 1540: (a, b) projects possibly associated with the evolution of the Villa Valmarana at Vigardolo; (c, d) Lonedo, Villa Godi, plan (from *QL*), and overview.

The site at Lonedo is elevated for the view and there is a defendable compound. The forecourt of the house is closed to the farmyards: except for subservient three-bay wings, the stabling and storage dependencies are remote from the house at the edge of these yards – unlike La Soranza, for example, or the Villa Tiretta Agostini at Cusignana, north of Treviso. Not unique, the late-Gothic Villa dal Verme at Agugliaro (to the south of Vicenza) provides a freestanding precedent: an arcaded basement loggia met the purpose of dependencies, at least in part. The villa of Caterina Cornaro (sometime Queen of Cyprus) was a much grander example with detached dependencies in an extensive compound.

Like the massing, of course, the plan of the house varies the tripartite division of Cricoli: symmetry is absolute, private 'apartments' flanking the central spine of representational space which is dislocated in depth to provide an entrance terrace. As Rudolf Wittkower demonstrates (exhaustively in his *Architectural Principles in the Age of Humanism*, 1949), this tripartite-plan formula, responding to the basic need for gradations of space from public to intimate, was sustained with infinite variation throughout Palladio's career as a villa designer. Giuliano da Sangallo set the precedent at Poggio a Caiano (AIC4, pages 778f).

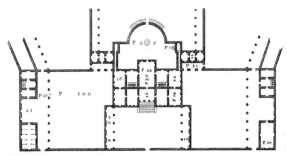

1.67c

1.67d

1.68a

›1.68 EARLY VICENTINE PALACES: (a) Civena (c. 1540), projected elevation; (b–d) Thiene (1542), plan (from *QL*), cortile, façade detail.

The Civena design is based on Serlio's interpretation of Bramante's Caprini formula – rather than on Sanmicheli's recent work in Verona (Serlio VII.25,63; see also above, pages 155f). Shops at base level in the Caprini prototype are here sheltered by an arcade, as Palladio was later to recommend with Padua in mind.

The Thiene cortile design still responds directly to Sanmicheli's Veronese variations on the Caprini formula – though simplification is furthered with the adoption of a regular Order of single Corinthian pilasters for the unusually elevated proportions of the piano nobile. The dominant influence on the exterior was Giulio Romano's partially executed project for his own Roman house.[1.6c] The plan (as later published by Palladio) of a square court framed by four ranges of rooms in single file recalls the Palazzo del Te – indeed it has been suggested that Giulio might have produced the initial design when he visited Vicenza in 1542 to advise on the unsound structure of the Palazzo della Ragione (see below, page 235).

unrelieved austerity to High Renaissance articulation – like La Soranza rather than Sansovino's exceptional work.[1.67] On the other hand, the early forays into the genre of the ubiquitous urban palazzo are immature confections in the manner of Serlio or pale reflections of Sanmicheli's variations on Bramante's Caprini formula.[1.68]

Immediately after his return from Rome Palladio invigorated both the Palazzo Caprini façade formula and the villa loggia in the manner of Giulio Romano – derived directly, rather than via Serlio, and not of lasting impact on his style. However, by the end of the decade – mid-century – exercises in emulating the antique and in assimilating the Roman High Renaissance – specifically the Bramantesque motif of a major arch framing a minor one supported on columns – had propelled him towards mastery on his own highly distinctive terms.[1.69,1.70] That mastery was ultimately deployed for the reduction of both urban and rural domestic design to flexible formulae of immense influence and he would provide models of ecclesiastical architecture never surpassed for their clarity and wholly architectonic gravitas. However, his fame was first established in the public sphere.

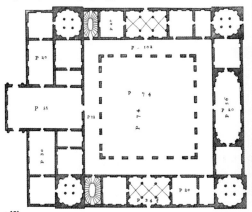

1.68b

1.68c

1.68d

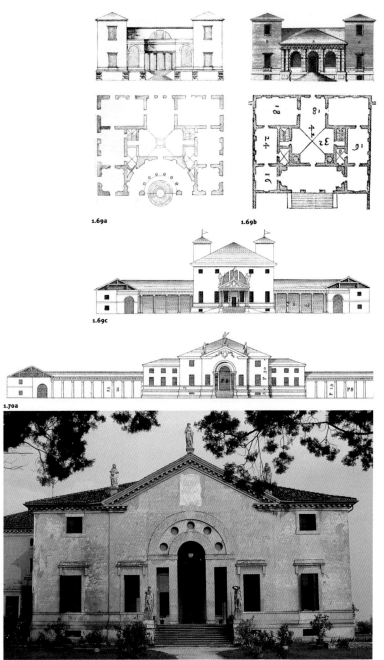

1.69a

1.69b

1.69c

1.70a

1.70b

›ARCHITECTURE IN CONTEXT »FROM THE HIGH RENAISSANCE TO MANNERISM

›**1.69 BAGNOLO DI LONIGO, VILLA PISANI,** from 1542: (a, b) plan and loggia front, project drawings and as represented in *QL*, (c) court front from *QL*.

The commission from the wealthy Venetian Pisani family marked a major turning point in Palladio's fortunes. Revising the informal distribution of the residential and service buildings of the agricultural estate in the manner previously adopted most prominently by Sanmicheli, the scheme was to embrace house, stables and agricultural dependencies in a unified, hierarchically ordered complex. Work on the house was complete by 1545. It incorporates antique and modern motifs. The loggia, flanked by towers as at Cricoli but confined to the raised ground floor, was first to reflect the semi-circular scheme which Serlio derived from Bramante and Raphael: in execution it was rusticated in the manner Sanmicheli derived from Giulio Romano and crowned with a pediment.

The T-shaped vaulted salone is lit by a thermal window from the court side where a portico in the form of a temple front, incorporated in Palladio's published project, was never executed. These were the dominant motifs in the contemporary design of a villa for the Thiene at Quinto Vicentino but the project proved to be too ambitious for more than fragmentary realization. Palladio seems first to have applied a temple front as portico at Bertesina for the Villa Marcello c. 1541. He would have known that Giulio Romano incorporated the motif in the garden front of the Palazzo del Te in Mantua.[1.7P] Undated, but possibly due to a late Lombardi, it appeared in the Veneto as a two-storey loggia on the entrance front of the Villa Giustinian at Roncarde.

›**1.70 POIANA MAGGIORE, VILLA POIANA,** from c. 1548: (a) part elevation (from *QL*), (b) view of extant asymmetrical complex, (c) rear loggia, (d–f) antechamber, chamber, cabinet.

The patron was the Vicentine Bonifacio Poiana, whose family had long supported Venice on the basis of their extensive land holdings. Building work on the dependencies was incomplete after some fifteen years when the interior decoration of the main block was completed. The scheme published in *QL* is symmetrical but only the range to the left of the villa conforms to it: work on the other side was undertaken in the 17th century.

1.70c

Over a service basement, the principal accommodation consists of a tunnel-vaulted hall flanked by twin apartments of vaulted rooms: the variety of the latter suggests transposition of scenographic planning from the great public context of the antique thermal complex to the minor setting of the country house. The inclination of the cornice mouldings to form a pediment gable also has thermal precedents – specifically the perimeter of the Baths of Diocletian – but the double arch with oculii is Bramantesque except for the astylar abstraction.

1.70d

1.70e

1.70f

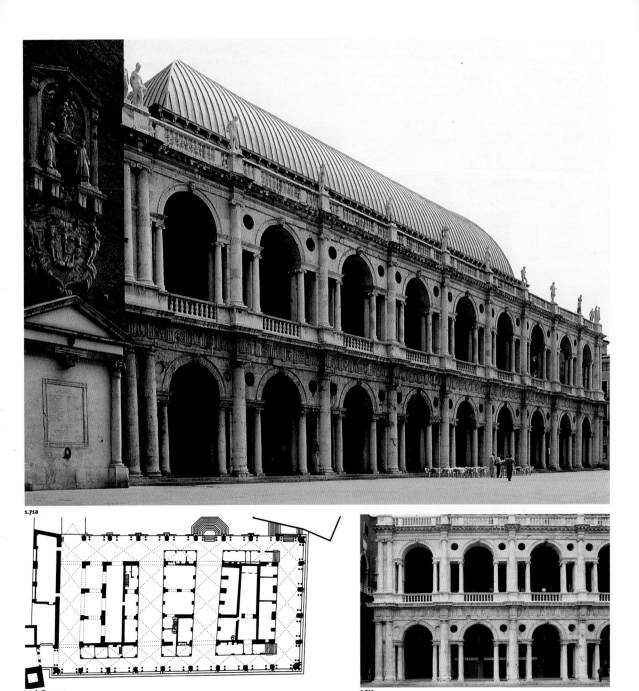

1.71a

1.71b @ 1:1000

1.71c

›ARCHITECTURE IN CONTEXT »FROM THE HIGH RENAISSANCE TO MANNERISM

‣**1.71 VICENZA:** (a–c) Palazzo della Ragione ('Basil-ica', projected in 1546, under construction from 1549), exterior, plan and detail; (d) Loggia del Capitaniato (from 1571), exterior.

The medieval meeting hall of the governing council was traditionally built over a shopping arcade in a commercial piazza. The mid-15th-century one at Vicenza, built with a huge timber vault over three ranges of shops separated by two corridors of different widths, was surrounded by loggias which proved unsound: Giulio Romano and his great Veronese contemporaries were consulted but Palladio was preferred by his influential patrons. The perimeter was distorted from rectangle to parallelogram: naturally, the humanist incentive was to regularize it but, of course, Classical will was constrained by medieval dimensions and structure. Major Doric and Ionic Orders, with recessed entablatures between the attached columns, are imposed on the ground and first floors respectively: the bays they define, narrower at the corners and subtly differentiated elsewhere (inevitably at the expense of regularity in the Doric frieze), are screened with doubled serlianas of the same Orders: the ingenuity in relating the latter to the intermediate corridors as well as to the end galleries is not to be underestimated. Throughout, the screen is of stone.

Commissioned to rehouse the military representative of the Venetian government in Vicenza, the Loggia del Capitaniato was only partially executed: it was devised to replace a medieval structure destroyed by imperial troops in 1521, but the new grandeur of Palladian Vicenza most probably called for the extension of the original project to five bays (1565). Palladio was absent in Venice when work began and when, six years later, the design for the side façade was altered to celebrate the Venetian contribution to Christian victory over the Turks at Lepanto (October 1571): it has a regular Corinthian Order defining the rhythmic bays of a triumphal arch; the outer columns support statues in the context of rich stucco relief; the inner columns support the balcony of appearance which is served by a serliana. The front façade fragment is entirely different: as befits political authority – as distinct from bourgeois activity – Palladio adopts an overbearing colossal Order of Composite columns engaged to minimal piers between which the ground-floor loggia and the piano-nobile fenestration seem squeezed – indeed the window frames burst up into the order's architrave. The stability asserted by the triglyph consoles in support of the balconies and the trophies of war piled into interpolated relief may well be seen as representing the benefits of the Serenissima's rule.

PUBLIC WORKS

In 1550 Palladio was awarded the commission to Classicize the irregular medieval basilica in Vicenza. Clearly inspired by Sansovino's most public work in Venice, he encapsulated the hall on the first floor and the market galleries below in loggias but Sansovino's richness of ornament gives way to complexity of motif: the Palladian motif or serliana. The combination of arcade and colonnade was essentially flexible and varying the intercolumniations both masked the irregularity of the original building and expressed greater strength at the corners – as antique Classicists had always properly done.[1.71]

1.71d

1.72a

1.72b

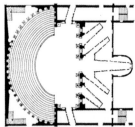

1.72c @ 1:1000

›1.72 VICENZA, TEATRO OLIMPICO, commissioned 1579, begun before Palladio's death in August 1580, finished by Vincenzo Scamozzi in 1585: (a) view of cavea and part of *scaenae frons*, (b) section, (c) plan.

Peruzzi and Serlio prefigured the *scaenae frons* in their illusionistic stage-set designs. Vignola provided the immediate precedent for the cavea in his incompletely realized project for the Palazzo Farnese at Piacenza: that, in turn, was inspired by the cortile theatre of Raphael's Villa Madama which also inspired Pirro Ligorio's scheme for the lower Belvedere cortile in the Vatican. Perhaps under the influence of the Colosseum, Palladio gave his cavea an ovoid perimeter – like contemporary reconstructions of the Theatre of Marcellus which are the obvious inspiration for Palladio's scheme as a whole.

The junction of stage and auditorium was awkward in the re-evocation of the antique prototype and the *scaenae frons* inhibited flexibility of production: the way ahead for theatre design – in the context of the princely court rather than the humanist society – was the rectangular hall with a deep stage beyond a proscenium arch.

About the time he was engaged on projecting the Loggia del Capitaniato, Palladio was commissioned to design a theatre for the Accademia Olimpica in Vicenza: he was a founding member of the learned confraternity in 1556 and subsequently assisted with its theatrical productions in temporary structures. For a quasi-public building type not yet familiar to the Renaissance, he turned to the antique and, aided by Vitruvius, reproduced the Roman formula of elliptical cavea addressing an elevated stage backed by a *scaenae frons* representing a palace façade (AICI, pages 576f): wholly of timber, his work miraculously still stands as a supreme example of the Classical ideal of emulation.[1.72]

Palladio entered the civic list in Venice, unsuccessfully, with the project for the Rialto bridge: the commission went elsewhere but the published image was to inspire 'palladian' bridges all over Europe.[1.73] He was not to build palazzi in Venice either but was called on for works of a secular type by religious communities.

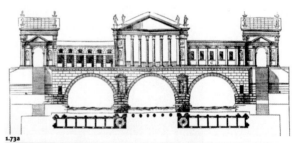

1.73a

1.73b

›1.73 VENICE, THE RIALTO BRIDGE: (a) Palladio's unexecuted project; (b) the extant work of Antonio da Ponte, chosen because a single arch was deemed preferable to three and executed from 1588.

ECCLESIASTICAL WORKS

Early in the 1560s, Palladio was engaged by the Bene-dictines of S. Giorgio Maggiore to provide them with a refectory. Well pleased with their exceptionally grand hall and cloister, the Benedictines returned to Palladio in the middle of the decade for their church. He responded with an unsurpassed masterpiece. And that prompted the state to commission the great votive church of Il Redentore after the passing of the plague in the mid-1570s.

Like all his humanist predecessors, Palladio's aesthetic preference in planning the discrete entity of a 'temple' was for the circle which 'mirrors God's unity, infinity, homo-geneity and justice' (Book IV of his treatise). Towards the end of his career he was able to build a circular church at Maser – on the Barbaro domain of his most faithful

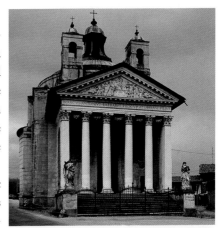

1.74a

1.74b

1.75a

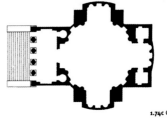

1.74c @ 1:500

›1.74 MASER, CHAPEL OF THE VILLA BAR-BARO: (a) exterior, (b) interior, (c) plan.

The interior articulation, in terms of triumphal arches framing the chapels in the cross arms, recalls Sanmicheli's work for the Pellegrini at S. Bernardino in Verona, but Palladio projects the arms of his cross beyond the circular perimeter. Otherwise, the exterior is clearly a much reduced revision of the Pantheon – like the so-called Mausoleum of Romulus on the Via Appia out of Rome (see above, page 228).

›1.75 VENICE, ECCLESIASTICAL WORKS: (a)
S. Francesco della Vigna, façade (1562); (b–f) S. Giorgio
Maggiore (1566 to c. 1600), plan with portico and cloisters (c. 1565), side view from first cloister, exterior from
west, half project elevation with portico, interior to
sanctuary; (g–k) Il Redentore (from 1577), north front,
interior to sanctuary, section and plan, view from west.

Of S. Giorgio's two cloisters, the second was added
to a design by Palladio which clearly respected the
style of the first with its ground-floor arcades carried on
columns and its upper-floor windows crowned with
alternating triangular and segmental pediments – all
inherited from the Quattrocento. The incomplete S.
Maria della Carità cloister, on the other hand, takes the
Ancient Roman peristyle to heights of grandeur
inspired by the Theatre of Marcellus but unprecedented in the domestic field except by Antonio da Sangallo for the Farnese (pages 140f and AIC1, pages 575f).
The superhuman scale of the whole Carità scheme is
asserted at the outset in the giant Order of the 'atrium'
– in the unrealized section illustrated in QL.

private client.[1.74] On the grand scale of the Venetian commissions, however, he recognized that the practical
requirements of Church liturgy – and Christian symbolism – were best met by the Latin cross: for the great Benedictine monastery of S. Giorgio Maggiore, on its
prominent island in the middle of the Venetian lagoon, he
conformed to the antique tradition of the basilica; for Il
Redentore, founded ex voto on its prominent Giudecca
site, he acknowledged the theatrical example of Vignola's
aisleless hall – no doubt in awe of the Albertian precedent.
Unlike Alberti in his great Mantuan exercise (AIC4, pages
748f), but like Bramante and his followers, he chose not to
ignore physical reality in reviewing the problem endemic
to the basilican section of effecting Classical *concinnitas* –
ideal unity – between exterior and interior.[1.75]

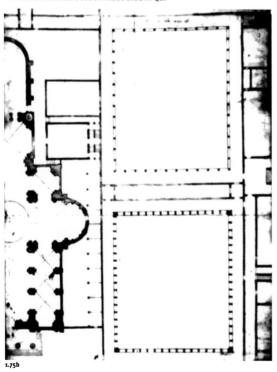

1.75b

1.75c

1.75d

1.75e

Scenographic churches

S. Giorgio is a basilica with groin-vaulted aisles and tunnel-vaulted nave lit through windows of the antique type found in the Baths of Diocletian – and hence known as 'thermal' (AIC1, pages 639f). The domed crossing of a broad apsidal transept – reinforced with pier pilasters at the corners, like Sansovino's Libreria Marciana – is inserted one bay short of the un-aisled, rectangular groin-vaulted sanctuary and its apsidal choir. The ultimate inspiration for the plan was probably Bramante's early revision of Rossellino's project for extending S. Pietro's basilica (AIC4, page 835). Palladio's simple square aisle bays are neither doubled nor domed as in Bramante's complex original – which the master himself is reputed to have reduced to the basic elements of a quincunx in the plan sent to Roccaverano for S. Maria Annunziata (AIC4, page 842). Perhaps aware of Bramante's intentions, doubtless familiar with Raphael's S. Eligio degli Orefici, Palladio's grey stone arcades and their unfluted Orders reign supreme in a white environment – unchallenged by

1.75f

illusionist frescoes or sculptural embellishment – but the bright vistas through the dual Orders of his arcades and choir screen are unrivalled.

The nave of Il Redentore may follow Vignola in homage to Alberti but the trilobed sanctuary, constituted by the domed crossing of a contracted apsidal transept and the apsidal screen of the monks' choir, does not. Multifoil sanctuaries derived from pagan prototypes are far from uncommon throughout the history of the Church: S. Lorenzo in Milan is the major early Christian example in northern Italy (AIC1, page 723); Sanmicheli's Madonna di Campagna provides an immediate – if partial – precedent (see above, page 137). However, reviewing the post-Rossellino projects for S. Pietro and Vignola's plans for the Gesù, Palladio seems to have reverted directly to the antique and eliminated the rectilinear arms of the crossing under the inspiration of the tepidarium at the centre of the quintessentially scenographic alignment of distinct spaces in the Baths of Diocletian or Caracalla. Be this as it may, the Redentore's stunning sequence of rectangular and circular spaces, provided in revision of the Roman domed cruciform model, established a standard for Venetian scenographic design which was of seminal import – not least for its introduction of a proscenium arch at the threshold of the sanctuary and a colonnaded screen between sanctuary and choir.

As he began with Bramante in evolving a formula for the palazzo façade, so Palladio resorted to the same source at the outset of his exercises in solving the façade problem presented by the composite form of the basilica and its aisleless derivative. Preceded by his work on Sansovino's S. Francesco della Vigna, the extremely exposed fronts of his two great churches vary the theme of overlaying temple fronts which Bramante seems first to have orchestrated in response to the obscure commission for the church of S. Maria Annunziata at Roccaverano. As in the designs for the exterior of S. Pietro bequeathed by the master and his followers, the hierarchical distinction of space is accepted, the volume represented by the nave is distinguished from the lower more extensive volume projected by the aisles (or side chapels) and a temple front is provided for each in whole or part (see above, page 140).

At S. Francesco a tetrastyle front of Composite columns, associated with piers to either side of the wider entrance bay, is flanked by the partially

1.75g

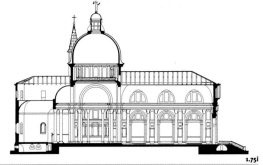

1.75i

1.75k

1.75h

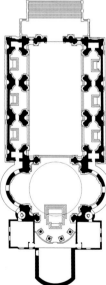

1.75j @ 1:1000

pedimented outer bays of a Corinthian composition: a temple front by implication only, the latter rises to half the height of the former from a common plinth. At S. Giorgio – altered in execution after Palladio's death – the imposition of the major freestanding tetrastyle temple-front motif leaves the entablature and more than half the pilasters of a hexastyle front unmasked. Doubled at the ends, the latter rises from the same base level as the pedestals of the major Order which matches the interior but not Palladio's projected temple front. At Il Redentore, the tetrastyle motif is relatively lower than in the earlier compositions, without pedestals and *in antis* like the minor temple-front bays of S. Francesco. It is again associated with piers which mask the continuity of the lower Order's entablature. However, the latter reappears in the central bay on the forward plane of the entrance portal which introduces its Corinthian Order to the principal role in the articulation of the interior. The pediment fragments of the lower front are echoed as flying buttresses on the level of the attic to which the main pediment is applied in the manner of the Pantheon.

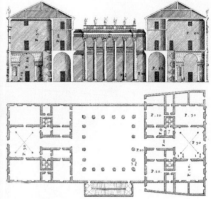

1.76b

PALAZZI

Palladio's formula for the design of the palazzo depended on antique precedent but current practice in Vicenza rarely admitted it. Indeed his Vicentine patrons were military or civil officers whose profits from the conflict between France and the Empire in Italy hardly matched their pretensions and few of their urban schemes were fully realized behind their façades.

The theoretical – and, in the absence of concrete evidence, grandiose – reconstruction of an ancient Roman house correctly incorporates both atrium and peristyle, surrounded by rooms of varied size and various degrees of privacy.**1.65** Adapting this approach to modern purposes – and relatively narrow-fronted urban sites contiguous with their neighbours – Palladio reduced the atrium to a vestibule and developed the peristyle as the nuclear court of family and service rooms if the extent of the site allowed. Only the ground-floor plan is delineated in his published projects: it is likely that a piano nobile accommodated private apartments to either side of a communal salon over the vestibule.

Bramante's Caprini formula – and its expression of the

1.76a

›1.76 PALLADIO AND THE PALAZZO: (a, b) Iseppo Porto (1549), plan and section (from QL), street front with late-medieval precedent next door; (c, d) Chiericati (1550), plan and 'forum' front; (e) Barbarano da Porto (1570) street front; (f, g) Valmarana (from 1565), plan with executed part superimposed (from QL after Ackerman), street front; (h) Porto in Castello (late-1570s?), unfinished façade; (i) unidentified project for a palazzo façade (c. 1570 for a Venetian client?).

Presenting its long side to open space – contrary to the Vicentine norm – the Chiericati site dictated lateral distribution behind a tripartite façade and permitted only a truncated court – actually little more than a light-well. To compensate, the patron secured permission to project his piano nobile out beyond the site line on condition that he provided the public 'forum' with a gallery: Palladio responded with an antique colonnaded porticus supporting the major reception room and its flanking colonnaded loggias – and a sequence of generously broad axial entrance spaces. At the intersection of narrow streets, the situation of the Palazzo Barbarano was quite different but Palladio reprised the theme of superimposed Orders for the perpendicular façades and for the court.

The Palazzo Iseppo Porto, for which Palladio produced his final revision of the Caprini façade formula, had a typically Vicentine long narrow site. It was supposed to have matching blocks for the patron and his guests facing one another over a square central 'peristyle' defined by a colossal Corinthian Order: the ambition was not realized. Projected over fifteen years later

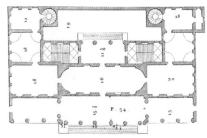

1.76c

for a similar site, the Valmarana was even more ambitious: the ideal, more original than Porto's variations on the antique, projected doubled apartments and a vast gallery beyond the nuclear court but resources ran only to the front range which was cut at an awkward angle by the street.

Palladio first applied a colossal Order to a façade for the Valmarana: Raphael had provided the precedent in the house he designed for himself at the end of his career and Palladio's work is hardly less rich in

1.76d

1.76e

prevailing social hierarchy – informed the early maturity of Palladio's palace designs in principle but not in practice. For Iseppo da Porto c. 1550 he provided family accommodation and service rooms on the ground floor, after the antique example, but not shops. The piano nobile is not described in plan but its distinction is sustained with an Order of single attached columns – unlike the earlier essays for Civena and Thiene but like Sanmicheli's work for the Pompei in Verona – and there is considerable sculptural enrichment.

The abandonment of social imagery is manifest in the articulation of both main storeys with an Order of columns in contemporary and later works: the Palazzo Chiericati, on its shallow site flanking the open space of a putative 'forum' c. 1550, and the Palazzo Barbarano da Porto of twenty years later. A master of restraint, avoiding self-indulgent complexity and ambiguity, Palladio also enjoyed overtly Mannerist games: for the Valmarana, for instance, he seems to betray some knowledge of the interlocking major and minor Orders of Michelangelo's contemporary Campidoglio palaces but wilfully weakens the ends by having the minor one prevail there in support of atlantes.**1.76**

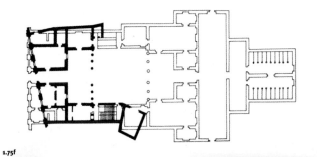

1.75f

1.76g

embellishment than late-Raphael – though the 'colouristic' approach may be seen as characteristic of the Venetians. For the Palazzo Porto in Castello he progressed from flat plane to bold relief, setting semi-colossal columns on high pedestals, thrusting balconies out beyond them and draping heavy swags between the Corinthian capitals – like Raphael in the Chigi Chapel of S. Maria del Popolo. Only two bays were completed (by Scamozzi). The scheme is analogous to that of S. Giorgio Maggiore's façade and another variant on the theme may be Palladio's only known Venetian palazzo design (c. 1570).

1.76h

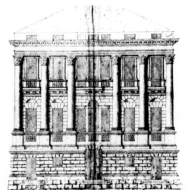

1.76i

1.77a

> **1.77 MATURE VILLAS, VARIATIONS IN PLAN AND ELEVATION (FROM QL) AND/OR AS EXECUTED:** (a) for the Pisani at Montagnana (from c. 1553), street front, and (b, c) for the Cornaro at Piombino Dese (from c. 1560), garden front; (d) for Sarego at S. Sofia di Piedmont (from c. 1560?), open court front; (e–g) for the Badoer at Fratta Polesine

1.77b

(from 1554), plan, elevation and entrance front; (h, i) for the Barbaro at Maser, plan and entrance front, and (j, k) for the Emo at Fanzolo (from c. 1560), plan and entrance front; (l–q) for the Foscari at Mira on the Brenta (c. 1560), plan, river front and side with and without dependencies, garden front and salone; (r–t) for Canon Paolo Almerico at Vicenza (from 1566, bought by the Capra brothers in 1591), plan, section, exterior; (u) for Trissino at Meledo, project plan and elevation (*QL*).

The freestanding two-storey houses of the Pisani at Montagnana and Cornaro at Piombino Dese represent the typological sub-species of the urban villa – or freestanding palazzo – of which there was another built for the Antonini at Udine and several unexecuted projects for Vicenza. On their restricted urban sites, the projects extended to minimal dependencies: the business of

VILLAS

Palladio's formula for the planning of villas had perhaps the most enduring influence. In particular, it appealed to the well-educated British landed gentleman who preferred rural life to urban society and acquired the taste for its unostentatious dignity from his peers in the Veneto – by personal acquaintance but more usually by acquiring Palladio's graphic publications (on which see below). Defined in essentially modest terms, in general it admitted of variation for both suburban and rural sites responding to different degrees of affluence and their requirements. There were, of course, exceptional works which seem to respond to distinct local traditions – or personal tastes – inimical to a generic formula.**1.77**

1.77c

The Palladian villa

The estate house will usually be on a flat site, easy of access to estate workers and their vehicles but ideally the suburban villa will crown an elevated site – as Alberti recommends and Falconetto demonstrated (AIC4, page 863). The suburban villa is ideally a discrete entity in contrast to the agricultural estate house: the centre of a complex, the latter will usually – but not always – have the major storage facilities attached to it as wings in the symmetrical manner of Sanmicheli's Villa La Soranza (see page 214). In any case, the composition is hierarchical: solid and void progress through gradations of scale to culmination in the pedimented portico with its enhanced central intercolumniation opening the main axis – and in the loggia or thermal window through which that axis penetrates into the garden.

At the top of a flight of podium steps, the four-square structure of both species will respond to a highly systematized design formula. It will invariably have the open centre and relatively closed side blocks of the tripartite tradition – as at Cricoli and Godi. There will sometimes be only one main storey, sometimes two, always an attic. Beyond portico and vestibule, a large central space for communal representation – the salone typical of the grand Venetian domestic tradition – is invariably flanked symmetrically by apartments consisting, essentially, of antechamber, bedroom and cabinet: decreasing in size in inverse relationship to privacy, there is usually room for a mezzanine over the cabinet. The upper storeys – destined for minors and servants or storage – are served by minimal internal staircases, like the service rooms in the basement.

Palladio's many subtle variations on his villa-plan formula (drawn from a basic 'tartan grid' of alternating broad and narrow divisions of a potentially infinite field on both perpendicular axes) have been comprehensively traced by Wittkower (in his *Architectural Principles in the Age of Humanism*). The process begins with a rectangle subdivided into a central square (salone) flanked on all sides by oblong communication and private zones as in the Villa Thiene at Cicogna. It achieves perfection with the similarly subdivided square of the Villa Capra. In between it redefines the shapes and sizes of the subdivisions of various rectangles (exhaustively) but always preserves the hierarchy.

The elementary ratio is, of course, the length of a room to its breadth: Palladio recommends the square and its development (by a third, a half and the double). To integrate the plan of an entire storey, one of these dimensions will be repeated in the neighbouring room and so on to the

1.77d

running the estate was conducted on the ground floor which, of course, was unusual for a villa but not for a town house. Unusually for a town house but not for a villa, on the other hand, the site invited the opening of loggias on both main levels: Chiericati provides a precedent but for the first time the temple-front motif was adopted here on both main fronts at Montagnana – the entrance portico projecting through bracing arcades, the garden loggias recessed behind their screens of columns *in antis*. The scheme was elaborated on a larger scale for the Cornaro at Piombino Dese.

The incomplete Villa Sarego, north-east of Verona, is an example of a unique response to special circumstances. The extraordinary rusticated colossal Ionic Order of the open forecourt – hardly matched in the œuvre even of Giulio Romano – supposedly responds to the patron's military prowess.

The villas Badoer at Fratta Polesine, Barbaro at Maser and Emo at Fanzolo, each of one main storey integrated with dependencies, well represent more-or-less elaborate variations on the estate complex.

Badoer's high base recalls Falconetto's work at

1.77e

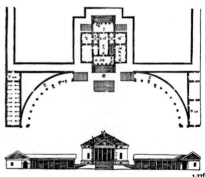

1.77f

Luvigliano and, beyond that Giuliano da Sangallo's Poggio a Caiano. As at the last, too, the entrance portico is recessed behind the columns *in antis* of a grand hexastyle Ionic temple front – but it rises to the full height. Quadrant colonnades of a minor Doric Order screen the estate dependencies: Palladio projected the motif on several occasions – notably for the Foscari at Mira on the Brenta ('La Malcontenta') and for Trissino at Meledo – but this is the sole executed example.

Barbaro's central block, with its Ionic temple front, is filled by the main representational space: unusually, therefore, the private apartments are found on the

1.76g

upper level of the lateral arcaded wings; the estate offices and services are provided in the end pavilions whose elevation extends to dovecots behind sundials. Other than Veronese's splendid frescoes in the salone, nothing better illustrates the determination of Venetian aristocrats to have the best of two worlds – agrarian and antiquarian – than the provision of accommodation for the Olympian deities in a nymphaeum behind the house and its utilitarian extensions.

The lateral disposition at Maser was repeated for Emo at Fanzolo: in accordance with Palladio's usual formula for villa planning, however, the salone is flanked by the main apartments in the central block. As at Fratta Polesine, the high podium accommodates service rooms and the recessed portico, with its Doric temple-front *in antis*, is served by a grand external stair ramp.

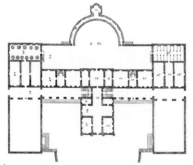

1.77h

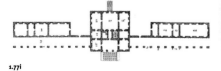

1.77i

next. Beyond that, as he evolved his formula Palladio applied 'proportionality' to determine a triad of ratios embracing the height as well and, thus, integrated the section and elevation. Geometric progression was the easiest to calculate but harmonic progression was preferred because it was believed to effect the visual equivalent of aural harmony – and through that to mirror the order manifest in divine creation (AIC4, pages 736ff). That was the ideal but Palladio, like Vitruvius (AIC1, page 572), was a pragmatist: practicality won when it clashed with the projection of the precise 'proportionality' in a triad – for instance, if it would send the vault of a room too high up into the space above.

Essential to the formula in plan, section and elevation, a fully integrated system of proportions governs the disposition of the masses and the distribution of the rooms within them, horizontally and vertically: though there is usually the Order of a portico, the integrity of the whole is achieved in the abstract terms of pure mathematics. Thus it may be said that Palladio graduated intellectually to the Albertian ideal of *concinnitas* – of course Alberti aspired to do so too but, working with composite rectangles, even at S. Andrea he applied mathematics with a motif of order repeated inside and out against physical reality (AIC4, pages 748f). In addition to his mathematical method, however, Palladio drew visual integration of sequential spaces from the antique – from his interpretation of the Roman thermal complex in particular (see above, page 228).

1.77j

1.77k

1.77l

1.77m

1.77n
Instead of curved Doric colonnades, the straight arcades of Maser are retained to shelter the estate offices and storage facilities which, as at Maser again, terminate in dovecots. As usual in the earlier works – but not the Villa Barbaro – the fenestration is frameless.

1.77o
'La Malcontenta', on the banks of the River Brenta, easily accessible from town but commanding rich agricultural land whose produce is well served by informal estate buildings, is a suburban-rural hybrid exercise of a freestanding block with one main storey raised over a high basement. Unconstrained by the practicalities of daily living, the suburban type receives its supreme expression in the square and circular geometry of 'La Rotonda', ideal on its eminence in all its four aspects.

'La Malcontenta' stands alone but the scheme published in *QL* incorporates side courts with estate offices and service facilities which would have masked the unprepossessing side façades. The gravitas appropriate to the accommodation of the ducal Foscari family is, of course, derived from the antique – specifically Palladio's reconstruction of the Temple by the Springs of

1.77p

Palladio enjoyed much variation in elevation, of course, but most characteristically he incorporated a loggia to invite entrance and/or provide a link between internal space and a garden. Postulating that the Ancients derived their temple architecture from their houses – as Alberti implied – he usually expressed the loggia as a temple front, as he had already done for the Marcello at Bertesina but with columns *in antis* or projected prostyle instead of pilasters. He provided relief otherwise only with the frames of doors and windows in the way traditionally associated with the Greeks – or, rather, the Hellenistic style of the early Roman temple (AIC1, page 520). Such economy of Classical articulation was deemed appropriate to a brick-built, stucco-rendered rural building type with minimal stone detailing – even by the grandest patrons.

1.779

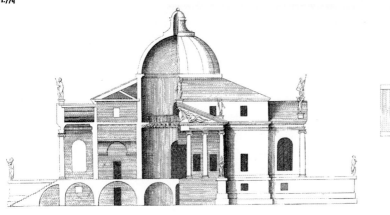

1.778

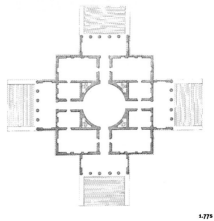

1.775

Clitumnus (see above, page 228) – but it is moderated for the holiday purpose by the elegant Ionic of the unbraced portico: it faces the river from the unusually high basement designed to raise the living rooms above the humidity of the site. The main hall of an antique thermal complex is recalled for the salone – in vaulting and fenestration at least – via Raphael at the Villa Madama.

'La Rotonda' is unique in the perfection of its geometry but, beyond the four identical porticoes, there is a discrepancy in the width of the axial vestibules because two provide access to the reception rooms of the identical corner apartments while the other two serve cabinets. The building was completed after Palladio's death by Scamozzi who substituted a saucer dome for the purely hemispherical form illustrated by Palladio in *QL*: the dome was unusual in domestic architecture but its secular credentials were presented to Palladio by the antique bath buildings. In any case, it was the nucleus of an outward-looking hill-top belvedere built for a retired ecclesiastical grandee.

Though Capra went to his villa to entertain rather than oversee the administration of an agricultural estate, agricultural dependencies are provided on a sunken lower level. The integration of a similar house on such a site with Classicized dependencies, through symmetrical quadrant colonnades, was projected for Trissino at Meledo: only a fragment materialized but the publication of the scheme in *QL* launched it on an inspiring career. The original inspiration is revealed by Palladio's imaginative reconstruction of the Temple of Fortuna at Palestrina (see above, page 228).

1.77t

1.77u

(a) Lonigo, Rocca Pisana (1576); (b) Mandria, Molin (1597).

Scamozzi's relationship to Palladio is well demonstrated by the Pisani scheme which was to be prototypical in his œuvre: similar centralized designs are illustrated in his treatise *L' idea dell' architettura universale* for both villas and chapels. Even more advantageously elevated – in accordance with both Alberti and Palladio – than the Villa Valmarana at Vicenza, Scamozzi's villa is clearly a reduced revision of Palladio's masterpiece but one which was to prove no less influential. Apart from asymmetry within the square plan, the most obvious similarity is the purely architectonic articulation – the restriction of 'ornament' to the Orders and the frames of doors and windows. Apart from the scale, the most obvious divergence is the elimination of the four prostyle porticoes in favour of a screened loggia in the entrance and serliana-lit halls on the other three sides. Scamozzi's indebtedness to Serlio is not to be discounted but, as we have seen, the so-called serliana – also often called the 'Palladian motif' – is most fairly attributed to Bramante.

The symmetrical ideal of the Villa Capra ('La Rotonda') has excited endless fascination. Vincenzo Scamozzi (1552–1616), who trained in the Vicenza of Palladio and followed the latter's example in several urban and rural commissions, was the first of many to adapt it for various sites.[1.78] He had overseen the completion of the Teatro Olimpico – among other Palladian schemes – after the master's death in 1580 and was soon to emulate that stunning work, on a small scale, at Sabbioneta.[1.79] In Venice – where he settled in 1580 after a sojourn in Rome – he followed Sansovino in providing the Piazza S. Marco with its southern range in the style of the adjacent library – except for the additional storey. He took the rare opportunity presented by a greenfield site at Palmanova to propose the full implementation of the Vitruvian urban ideal realized, graphically, by Pietro Cataneo in particular: the gridded scheme published in his treatise was revised along radial lines to meet military requirements.[1.80]

›1.79 SABBIONETA, COURT THEATRE OF DUKE VESPASIANO GONZAGA, 1588: interior.

At Vicenza, Scamozzi provided the illusion of streets leading back from the portals of Palladio's palatial *scaenae frons*: at Sabbioneta he deleted the latter in favour of the former. At Vicenza, the commodious *cavea* accommodated the members of the Olympian Society in no specifically hierarchical order – except, no doubt, for the committee in the front row: the crowning colonnade screened circulation space. At Sabbioneta the colonnade distinguished the ducal seating: the entourage was relegated to the curved benches below. Apart from opening the stage to the auditorium, the scheme was innovative in the purpose-built structure with its own façade.

›1.80 IDEAL URBANISM AND ITS REALIZATION: (a) project of Pietro Cataneo (Book I of *I Quattro Primi Libri di Architettura di Pietro Cataneo Senese*, Venice 1554/67); (b) Palmanova, aerial view.

The Vitruvian essence is filtered through the grid of Cataneo who, in turn, was heavily dependent on Francesco di Giorgio and Peruzzi for his projection of stellar fortifications for ideal polygonal towns: this constitutes the most significant addition to the genre of the treatise on civil and military building in mid-16th-century Italy.

Palmanova was built to defend the Veneto's eastern frontier from possible Turkish attacks. The military engineers preferred linking all nine bastions diametrically through a central piazza but their pretension was countered by humanism: ultimately only six arteries connected three major with three minor bastions and the other radial streets – six leading through square piazzas – terminated in a nonagonal ringroad around the central hexagonal piazza.

1.79

1.80a

1.80b

THEORY

Palladio's extraordinary influence is undoubtedly due to the clarity and lucidity of his *Quattro Libri*. Scamozzi sought to cap it with his erudite, eclectic, rigidly rationalist exercise but that was never to enjoy much popularity. Unique in its constitution – partly because the project was never fully realized – Palladio's work acknowledged a theoretical tradition stretching back to Alberti but also emulated Serlio. Thus it combined a humanist treatise written by an architect for practitioners – rather than by an Albertian scholar for his peers – with an immediately accessible pattern book in which formulae for the main genres of architecture were drawn from the author's own work – especially where antique procedure was obscure. The model was Serlio but the designs were infinitely better and their presentation was far more ordered: the book's success is due not least to its beautiful production both in the typeface and in the woodblock illustrations which consistently comprise plan and strictly orthogonal section and elevation.**1.81**

Like most of his predecessors over the century since Alberti, Palladio prefers antique example yet acknowledges that he always found Vitruvius indispensable, notwithstanding the textual obscurities of the *Ten Books on Architecture* and the disparity between their precepts and antique practice as it had developed in the post-Augustan era. In much of this – and particularly in seeing *firmitas* as subservient to *utilitas* and *utilitas* (*commodità*) as integral to *venustas* – he followed his mentor Trissino and Trissino's friend and fellow amateur architect, Alvise Cornaro. But he is Albertian in combining all three to effect an harmonious whole greater than the sum of the parts: *concinnitas*, 'congruity, that is to say the principal law of Nature' (Alberti, *De re aedificatoria* IX.5; AIC4, page 737).

Trissino was followed (c. 1550) in Palladio's counsels by the Paduan humanist Daniele Barbaro. He was working

1.81a

›1.81 PALLADIAN PRACTICE AND PRECEPT:
(a) *I Quattro Libri dell' architettura* (Venice, 1570 and often subsequently in all the major European languages), title page, (b) the four Orders: Doric, Ionic, Corinthian and Composite, (c, d) Corinthian and Egyptian halls, plan and section.

A draft manuscript was reputedly in hand by 1555. Vasari claims to have seen a text in 1566, four years before the publication of the *Quattro Libri* in separate pairs, the first *dell' architettura*, the second *dell' antichità*: it is thought that ten books were projected (and the missing ones drafted) in emulation of Vitruvius and Alberti, as the prospectus outlined in the preface to the first book was not fully realized (basilicas apart, antique public building types and fortifications were not covered).

Book I deals with materials, construction techniques and an account of five Orders. Palladio adds the Composite to the Vitruvian list, like Serlio, but in revising the latter's system of regulating the relative modular proportions of the five styles, the relationship between their individual constituent elements and the correct measure of their intercolumniations, he is con-

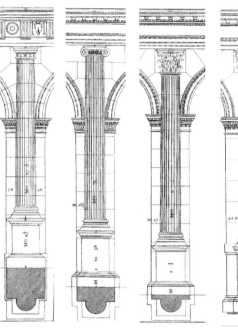
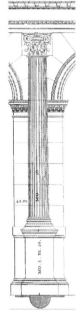

1.81b

sistent with Vignola. Regular geometry and the proportional systems enshrined in the Orders of architecture are the most graphic manifestation of the rational order of Nature, axiomatic to the humanist: Palladio and his Renaissance predecessors subscribed to this in defining the five Classical styles, of course, but the macrocosmic principle was most clearly articulated by Scamozzi who found nothing in his comprehensive survey of humanist architectural theory to counter his reduction of all sound design practice to applied mathematics.

Book II is devoted to the reconstruction of Vitruvian house types, variously incorporating atrium, tablinum and peristyle (AIC1, pages 537, 572). Transposing the ideal, uncategorically and largely on the lines of his work for Barbaro, Palladio develops modern practice with a conception of convenience (Trissinian *commodità*) which comprehends Vitruvian decorum – that is, he amplifies Vitruvian *utilitas* to embrace décor, the facet of Vitruvian *venustas* representing appropriateness of style. The houses illustrated in plan and elevation are Palladio's own Vicentine works but the medieval urban morphology and the circumstances of

on a new translation of Vitruvius with a formalist commentary which Palladio was commissioned to illustrate. This was the first edition of Vitruvius illustrated with such authority: idealism and practicality variously informed the plates. Much was drawn from Palladio's studies in Rome, begun with Trissino in 1541 and continued with Barbaro in 1554. At that time, Palladio was also producing a guide to the ancient city (*L'Antichità di Roma*).

His work with Barbaro on Vitruvius and the antiquities of Rome – prompted Palladio to provide his own elucidation of Classical precept for the modern practitioner. Like Barbaro, he stressed the fundamental importance of proportion as the manifestation of reason in the designs of man and Nature. Nature is moved by an intelligence like that of man: reason effects Order, the Good – the Platonic Truth. Aspiring to this absolute Truth in the application of reason to projected form, Barbaro elevates the ethical aspect of architecture over the practical. Palladio agrees that architecture imitates Nature in effecting order through regulation and respect for the logic of physics: for him the natural is the rational but also the practical – like the symmetrical, well-proportioned organism of the human body.

The influence of Barbaro's idealism on Palladio's practice is manifest most graphically in the fully integrated system of proportions governing the distribution of villa rooms horizontally and vertically – especially, of course, at Maser (see page 249). However, Palladio knows that in practice the patron – like Trissino and Cornaro – will first want convenience. Rather than unequivocally rationalist, thus, his aesthetic is essentially functionalist: *venustas* is inherent in *utilitas* and *firmitas* and in equation with the ideal order of untrammelled 'truth' it effects simplicity – the simplicity of a purely rational, strictly architectonic ordonnance derived from a commodious portico, the 'noble simplicity' of the future academic Classical ideal.

Published in 1570, *I Quattro Libri dell' archittetura* were evolved over the decades when 'strange abuses and barbaric inventions' – identified with Michelangelesque Mannerism not least by Vignola – were perceived as threatening to subvert the development of the Classical tradition: likewise, Scamozzi saw the need for a polemic against the new style of his time which would later be called 'Baroque'. The eccentricity of licentious genius would entice its follower to perdition. The only sure bases for progress were the emulation of the antique example, the most exemplary of modern masters – Bramante above all – and the laws of physics. Palladio respects the idealism of Barbaro and he is preoccupied with antique example but the practicality of his early mentors is not forgotten: indeed, minimizing abstract theory in teaching through example, his approach is essentially empirical in the bold equation of the legacy of his own practice with the inheritance from antiquity. And, ruefully, he concedes that in practice 'it is often necessary for the architect to comply with the wishes of those responsible for the expense, rather than with that which ought to be observed'.

Abstracted from the specific and clearly delineated, Palladio's formulae were intended for universal application – at least in the climatic conditions known to their author. However, public or private, prototypical or unique, the quality of the buildings themselves is inescapable. Above all, the purity of geometry, the thoroughly integrated proportions and the economy of articulation of the villa ideal are ineluctable – and of special appeal to unostentatious taste in the Protestant lands of the north and their colonies from America to India and Australia. Yet Palladio's Venetian church façades and his late Vicentine palazzi delight in colouristic contrasts of light and shade produced as much by the manipulation of articulation in three dimensions as by sculptural enrichment: to that extent it is sen-

patronage in Vicenza obviated full realization of his conception of the antique ideal. The villas are his too, of course: he does not differentiate between the seat of agricultural activity and the resort of contemplation – between the estate house and the suburban retreat – but in general recommends siting on an imposing hill by a convenient river – or one or the other to which, naturally, differentiation in design will respond. Satisfying the requirements of both *décor* and *commodità*, their porticoes express the nobility of the patron while serving his convenience in sheltering the entrance. That, he believed, was antique practice developed after man first domesticated himself in society but before he turned to public building (Book I, Preface; and see above, page 229).

Book III, on public building, opens with the assertion that the measuring of prototypes, though arduous, is the sure route to sound instruction. Of course he recognizes that modern needs will demand the transformation of ancient types: plagiarism obviated, thus, emulation will test native genius. The basilica is the outstanding case in point. He defines the type in Vitruvian terms as a place of judgement but he contrasts Vitruvian example with his own Vicentine work: the medieval original which he was called on to Classicize,

1.81c

1.81d

raised over a shopping arcade, had external loggias whereas both main Vitruvian varieties, with no comparable substructure, had internal colonnades – the Corinthian on one level, the Egyptian on two. His response to the commission, he believed, had produced 'one of the most beautiful buildings that have been erected since antiquity' (Book III, page 42).

Except for Bramante's Tempietto, his catalogue of temples in Book IV is wholly antique: he illustrated no ecclesiastical project of his own. He asserted his preference for centralized forms, especially the simple, uniform circle which represents the 'Oneness, the Infinity, the Uniformity and the Justice of God' – hence his admiration for the Tempietto – but he makes no reference to his church at Maser. Nor does he refer to the experiments with incorporating the temple-front motif in a basilican façade which he had begun nearly a decade before he published his treatise. However, he endorses the cruciform plan as praiseworthy, noting his adoption of it for S. Giorgio Maggiore in Venice. And, as there, he promotes unfrescoed plaster surfaces in case 'the meaning (of pictures) alienated the soul from the contemplation of Divine things' – presumably not least those manifest in rational geometry.

sual as well as intellectual. To those who have complemented study of the book with experience of the actual buildings, this is the true dimension of Palladio's greatness.

The hybrid form of the *Quattro Libri* was new but the two constituent elements had their immediate precedents: Vignola's *Regola delle Cinque Ordini* (1562) and Serlio's *I sette libri dell'Architettura* (published from 1537). Vignola accompanied Francesco Primaticcio to the French court at Fontainebleau after having assisted him in taking casts of antique sculptures for François I: he stayed for two years. Serlio entered the service of the French king and dedicated Book III to him in 1540. Thus to their first-hand experience of Neoclassicism gained on campaign in Italy, the French acquired guidance in their transition to maturity from Italians in France.

The needs of French Classicists, ordering their medieval inheritance of diversified mass, were more immediately served by Vignola's abstract of the Orders than by Palladio's concrete formulae which rarely matched the pretensions of an absolute monarchy and its principal retainers – at least until the era of so-called Neoclassicism (as we shall see). On the other hand the British, who first followed the French example in Classicizing medieval forms, imbibed Palladianism directly from the source – before and after the abrogation of absolutist monarchy but during the construction of their worldwide empire.

1.82a

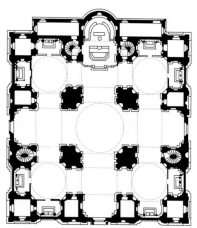

1.82c @ 1:1000

7 ALESSI AND HIS COLLEAGUES IN LOMBARDY

1.82b

›1.82 GENOA, S. MARIA ASSUNTA IN CAR-IGNANO, contract 1549, construction from 1552, dome after 1567: (a) exterior, (b) interior, (c) plan.

The plan, finalized before Michelangelo's definitive revisions to his predecessors' centralized schemes for the basilica of S. Pietro, retains a simplified variant of the subsidiary Greek cross which fills each corner of Bramante's ideal scheme but the great cross projects beyond the perimeter only in the apse of the sanctuary arm: the master had shown the way to simplification in his plan for SS. Celso e Giuliano which was realized by Sangallo. Like schemes for S. Pietro descending from Bramante's latest thoughts, the articulation inside and out depends on a colossal Corinthian Order of fluted pilasters – reinforced beside the base of the towers and projected in support of unusually steep pediments on all three entrance fronts: in contrast to the Neoclassical purity of this ordonnance, the interpolated basement and mezzanine window frames are Michelangelesque in their complexity. The ideal of a tower at each corner was only half-realized and the saucer domes of the subsidiary crosses are designed not to compete with the great dome of the central crossing: that was begun a decade after Alessi had provided the cathedral with its crowning element.

The dominant architect in mid-16th-century Genoa was Galeazzo Alessi (1512–72) who was born and first active in Perugia where he had trained in humanist circles. He moved to Rome in 1536 to witness developments under Paul III – particularly Antonio da Sangallo's work on the Palazzo Farnese and the Vatican. Back at Perugia, he is reputed to have fitted out Sangallo's Rocca Paolina, built several Doric loggias and designed S. Maria del Popolo along the lines of Sangallo's Vatican Capella Paolina (1547).

GENOA

Alessi had returned to Perugia in 1543 in the train of the papal legate whose administration drew on Genoese talent. Treasurers to the legation, the Sauli brothers called on Alessi to rebuild their Genoese family church, S. Maria Assunta in Carignano: the influential result is based on a simplified revision of Bramante's ideal plan for the basilica of S. Pietro but with marked clarity of articulation throughout.[1.82] The patronage of the Sauli and their peers extended to several secular works, most notably for the Grimaldi, the Pallavicini and, first, the Giustiniani.[1.83]

1.83a

1.83b

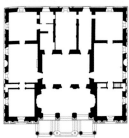

1.83c @ 1:1000

›**1.83 GENOA, VILLA GIUSTINIANI (NOW VILLA GIUSTINIANI-CAMBIASO),** from 1548: (a) entrance front, (b) grand loggia addressing the garden, (c) plan.

Alessi's first Genoese commission, the villa is a reduction of the Farnesina type – with loggia between slightly projecting wings. Sanmicheli is recalled – in general mode rather than precise model – by the lavishness of the articulation, with Composite pilasters over

Doric half-columns, but the semi-colossal Order ultimately derives from Antonio da Sangallo (or Raphael). A further Roman allusion is to be found in the detail of the internal embellishment of the garden-front loggia: the caryatids/herms, which raise the splendidly coffered tunnel vault over the arcades, follow those executed by Raphael's assistants on the dadoes of the Stanze di Eliodoro and della Segnatura. As we have noted, Perino dell Vaga introduced the style to Genoa and there – as later in Rome – seems to have informed contingents of artisans from Como in his *all' antica* techniques of interior decoration.

While Alessi was active in Genoa, the civic authorities conceived a scheme for a monumental new residential district on rising ground above the insalubrious medieval urban area. As ultimately realized over several generations, its spine was the Strada Nuova (now Via Garibaldi). There are streets lined with grand palaces in most seats of Italian courtly government but – except for the special case of the Florentine Uffizi's extended cortile – they never attained the consistency of the Genoese venture.[1.84]

1.84a

Arterial grandeur in Genoa

The consistent development of a salubrious height above the unhealthy portside quarter where even the patricians lived was projected in 1550 but it was eight years before the site was cleared for construction to commence along an artery 225 metres long and 7.5 metres wide. Over the following decade grand and commodious detached palaces were constructed in conformity to the masterplan on most of the fifteen designated plots – all of which are separated by alleys.

The master architect was Bernardino da Cantone, who had worked under Alessi on S. Maria di Carignano: executive architects – of some obscurity

›1.84 GENOA, THOROUGHFARE AND PALATIAL ARCHITECTURE: (a, b) Strada Nuova from the east with Palazzo Pallavicino-Cambiaso (Bernardino da Cantone, from 1558) and west with Palazzo Rosso (Pietro Antonio Corradi, from 1671) right; (c, d) Palazzo Doria Tursi, plan and section (Domenico and Giovanni Ponsello, from 1565); (e–g) Via Balbi, Palazzo dell'Università (ex-Jesuit College; Bartolomeo Bianco, from 1630) plan, section and staircase from atrium to court.

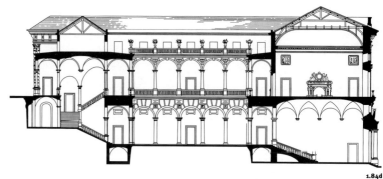
1.84d

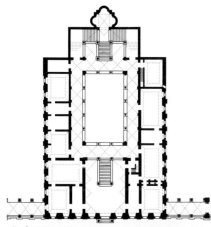
1.84c @ 1:2000

1.84g

otherwise – include Giovanni and Domenico Ponsello, who had also worked on Alessi's great church; much of the stucco embellishment was due to the Bergamasque master Giovanni Battista Castello. The strict prescription of dimensions determined façades of two storeys and a mezzanine over a basement but a certain amount of latitude was allowed in their articulation and embellishment without detriment to overall consistency of style. On the other hand, internal distribution was largely unregulated where it had no bearing on the appearance of the street. The steep site through which the course was cut presented a challenge to the individual designers: to the south it fell away and required substructure; to the north it rose steeply and required excavation. On the terraces of the latter, the problem was dramatically resolved by the Ponselli in the scenographic arrangement of the stairs beyond the colonnaded court of their Palazzo Doria Tursi.

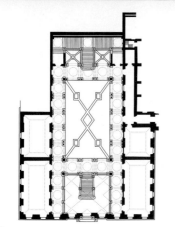
1.84e @ 1:1000

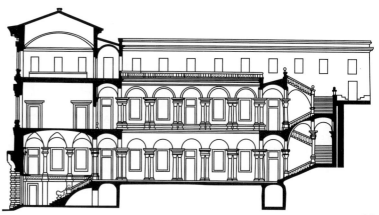
1.82f

1.85a

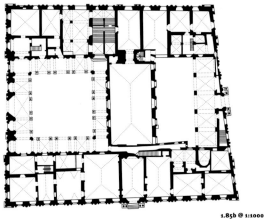

1.85b @ 1:1000

All levels are rusticated behind regular Orders. These are Doric and Ionic on the first two floors, but Corinthian cedes to a tapering herm-like abstraction thrust up into three-sided rectangular mouldings which assert an interest in Michelangelo: Ionic ground-floor aedicules, devoured by rustication in the now-familiar Mannerist manner, prepare for the piano nobile, and the latter's aedicules, with downward tapering shafts, prepare for the irregular 'Order' of the top floor. Assisted by a high balustrade – in the manner of Sanmichele – the full entablature relates to the whole elevation without crushing the top floor and its monumentality is moderated by brackets springing from the caps of the irregular upper 'Order'.

Rather than a regular sequence of arcades on columns, the broad intercolumniations of the ground-floor cortile loggia suggest syncopation of the serliana motif – the outer columns of each become the inner columns of its neighbour. In the piers of the piano nobile – corresponding to the intercolumniations in width, of course, but contrary in weight – a major artic-

1.85c

MILAN

After establishing himself as the leading architect in Genoa, Alessi moved on in the late-1550s to major practice in Milan – for both secular and ecclesiastical clients.

ulatory role is given to the herm-like caryatids which played a relatively minor part in the spandrels of the Genoese Villa Cambiasco. As on the exterior, even the subsidiary detail has an architectonic role: the masks in the broken pediments of the piano nobile exterior aedicules support the frames of the mezzanine, for example, and the three-sided capital mouldings of the irregular 'Order' are borrowed to provide intermediate support over the pier niches of the piano nobile loggia in the cortile.

1.86

›1.86 MILAN, PALAZZO LEONE LIONI (or Casa degli Omenoni), from 1565: street front.

The atlante ('telamoni' or 'omenoni' after which the house is named) were carved by Antonio Abondio (known as l'Ascona, died 1578). The house was the residence of the sculptor Leone Leoni (1509–90) who presumably determined the design.

›1.87 MILAN, VILLA SIMONETTA, from 1547: loggia façade.

The patron was Ferrante Gonzaga who had acquired the site on the outskirts of town in 1547. Domenico Giunti was commissioned to enlarge an existing villa. Apart from the three-storey loggia applied to the outer façade, the new work ran to ground-floor loggias and wings flanking a terrace overlooking twin ponds and a garden.

He was called to the Lombard capital by the scion of another Genoese banking family, Tommaso Marino, to build the enormous palace which perpetuates his name. Two extended ranges of public and private rooms are separated by two courts and a huge hall: in elevation, the lavish sculptural relief of late-Raphael – and Giulio Romano – served the Milanese taste for opulence in general. In particular, detail derived from Michelangelo and his radical followers invades the classic armature of superimposed Orders which had characterized his villa style in Genoa and the Ionic cedes to herms over contracted serlianas in the cortile. While that was being realized in the mid-1560s, the herm motif received its boldest expression to date as the major articulating agent of the façade of the Palazzo Leone Leoni.[1.85, 1.86]

In stark contrast to Alessi's opulence is the elementary Classicism of his leading predecessor in Milan, the Tuscan Domenico Giunti (1506–60) who was brought from Sicily by the king-emperor's viceroy, Ferrante Gonzaga. The most celebrated secular example of his work is the three-storey loggia façade of the Villa Simonetta with its completely unadorned colonnades.[1.87]

1.87

Giunti's patron was Emperor Charles V's Gonzaga viceroy of Lombardy. The regime's extensive refortification of Milan had removed several churches, notably S. Angelo

1.88a

›1.88 GIUNTI AND THE MILANESE CHURCH: (a, b) Sant'Angelo (from 1552), façade and interior toward sanctuary.

The tunnel-vaulted aisleless structure ultimately descends from the traditional Franciscan – indeed mendicant – type represented by S. Francesco at Rimini which, as we have seen, was where Alberti began his seminal work in church design. As we know, that is where Vignola began the definitive Counter-Reformation reform of the traditional basilica. Here, however, Giunti provides a proscenium screen before a barrel-vaulted transept and sanctuary. The façade, with its colonnade applied to the full width of nave and aisles at base level, is also a novel reinterpretation of the traditional basilican formula.

1.88b

›1.89 **ALESSI AND THE MILANESE CHURCH:**
(a–c) SS. Paolo e Barnaba (from 1561), plan, façade
and interior; (d, e) S. Vittore al Corpo (from c. 1560),
exterior, interior; (f) S. Maria presso S. Celso (from c.
1570): façade.

Separation of monks and lay worshippers had usually involved a screen across the nave in the medieval
church: Giunti, Alessi and their colleagues opened the
choir to view beyond the high altar – and a domed
crossing in the grander schemes – but distinguished it
by raising it on a podium above the level of the nave:
fully in accord with Trentine reform, this was certainly
in the brief of Counter-Refomation orders like the Barnabites for whom Alessi, with spectacular theatricality,
telescoped the arches on the stage of the crossing to
concentrate attention on the mystic performance of the
eucharist in the sanctuary.

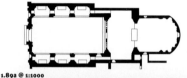

1.89a @ 1:1000

of the Franciscans which Giunti was commissioned to
rebuild within the new perimeter. He went back to the
Albertian source at Mantua – a decade before Vignola
evolved his Gesù formula – and produced a huge hall with
arcaded side chapels framed by an Ionic Order of pilasters
and lit through oculii in a novel clerestory.[1.88]

Giunti and his followers built several grand churches on
the Mantuan model in response to the patronage of
Counter-Reformation orders; Vicenzo Seregni and/or
Alessi at S. Vittore al Corpo even including the domed
crossing which Alberti may have projected – and which was
to play a crucial role in Vignola's formula. Alessi at SS.
Paolo e Barnaba conforms to Giunti's domeless type on a
much-reduced scale but, rather than in planning, his most
impressive contribution to the Milanese church was in the
extraordinary articulation of the high façade of S. Maria
presso S. Celso.[1.89]

1.89b

1.89c

1.89d

1.89e

›ARCHITECTURE IN CONTEXT »FROM THE HIGH RENAISSANCE TO MANNERISM

S. Maria presso S. Celso was a medieval foundation enlarged by Cristoforo Lombardini – one of the leading Milanese architects of the generation after Amadeo and the departure of Bramante for Rome. His extraordinary Neoclassical scheme for the façade of c. 1550 – with superimposed temple fronts oversailing a continuation of the existing atrium arcades – was unrealized when Alessi was appointed to the superintendence of work on the site in 1565. The aim of achieving medieval heights in temple-front terms was foreign to him: instead, as the framework for statuary and the rich relief beloved of Lombards, he superimposed three variously proportioned 'Orders' and a mezzanine below a massive pediment: the existing atrium arcades imposed Corinthian on the base level, contrary to Vitruvian norm, and that prompted Composite at the top; in between Alessi inserted an irregular attic Order in which the 'capitals' are extruded from the architrave moulding (in the manner popular with late Raphael and Giulio Romano). Martino Bassi, executing the scheme after Alessi had left Milan c. 1570, preserved the ordonnance in all essentials but changed the proportions of the niches, substituted relief panels for windows and greatly enriched the pediment.

1.89f

In 1564 Cardinal Carlo Borromeo, nephew of Pope Pius IV and a leading Trentine reformer, was elevated to the archbishopric of Milan: his extremely important instructions on the design of churches, issued in 1577, reveal appreciation of the work carried out by Giunti, Alessi and their colleagues before his advent. However, his patronage went elsewhere – particularly to Pellegrino Tibaldi (1527–96).

After assisting Perino del Vaga in the Castel Sant'Angelo,[1.15] Pellegrino returned to his native Bologna in 1550 where he first distinguished himself in the Sala di Ulisse of the Palazzo Poggi with his authoritative confrontation of *quadratura* with *quadri riportati* in homage to both Raphael and Michelangelo. His patron, Cardinal Giovanni Poggi, gave him his first architectural exercise – the Poggi Chapel (1556) in S. Giacomo Maggiore – and probably introduced him to Cardinal Borromeo who chose to

›1.90 PELLEGRINO AT THE BOLOGNESE PALAZZO POGGI: the vault of the Sala di Ulisse (usually dated to c. 1555 but as probably to 1550–51 because the patron's arms are not surmounted by the cardinal's hat awarded in 1551).

The patron was the papal diplomat and financier Cardinal Giovanni Poggi who had served popes Clement VII and Paul III. The young Tibaldi, who had worked at the Villa Poggi in Rome, was allotted two rooms on the ground floor for his mythological cycle. Ulysses's saga perhaps recommended itself as allegorical of the vicissitudes of the patron's peripatetic life and is not irrelevant to a painter named Pellegrino.

To the simulated colonnades of Raphael's Vatican loggie, open to the sky, Tibaldi adds *ignudi* who rival Michelangelo's Sistine boys in contortion of pose seen from below. 'Rectilinear' frames, richly stuccoed, cede to more convoluted forms in the smaller room: there the fantastically coloured 'colonnades' in the corners flank herm-borne aedicules and heaven is visible in the centre (where Perino del Vaga was the inspiration).

▸1.91 PAVIA, COLLEGIO BORROMEO, 1564:
(a) entrance front, (b) court.

Courts with superimposed serliana were to proliferate in late-16th- and early 17th-century Milan and it is probable that a Milanese architect introduced the form to Rome. The courtyard of the Palazzo Borghese in Rome was provided with Doric and Ionic loggias of the type in extensions begun from 1586 by the otherwise undistinguished Lombard architect Martino Lunghi: the ordonnance of the court side of the original front wing is unknown but the style followed by Lunghi was not hitherto characteristic of Rome.

prepare him to be the executive of his architectural ideals: by 1564 the two were in Rome together studying the latest developments in Counter-Reformation church planning.**1.90**

Pellegrino's eclecticism at the outset of his career as an architect in Borromeo's archdiocese is well demonstrated by the vast Collegio Borromeo in Pavia and the extensions to the archiepiscopal palace in Milan. The main court of the latter suggests familiarity with Ammannati's recent work on the garden court of the Palazzo Pitti. The cortile of the Pavia complex retains the serliana motif of Alessi's Palazzo Marino on both levels, without the rich embellishment: it had its Roman affiliate in the cortile of the Palazzo Borghese (see page 282) which was probably Milanese in its derivation, but the exterior rivals Serlio in its complexity.**1.91**

1.91b

1.91a

1.92a

1.92d

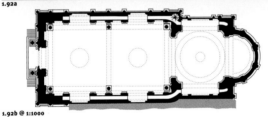

1.92b @ 1:1000

1.92c

Borromeo's prescription of cruciform planning in principle is not followed by Pellegrino's two most important surviving Milanese churches. S. Sebastiano (1577) is cylindrical in the manner of the Pantheon: it was founded ex voto after the passing of the plague of 1576 and was not, therefore, destined to meet conventional parochial needs. S. Fedele (1569) at the Jesuit headquarters, on the other hand, is a vast assembly hall composed of two commensurate squares with a smaller square and semi-circular apse for the raised sanctuary: later in execution, the latter are

**›1.92 PELLEGRINO AND THE MILANESE
CHURCH:** (a–d) S. Fedele (1569), interior to sanctuary,
plan, west front and detail of side-altar aedicule; (e) S.
Sebastiano (1577), exterior.

The cruciform ideal may not be met by S. Fedele
though the requisite clarity of the nave's volume –
uncomplicated and well lit – has rarely been surpassed.
As on the façade, where the aedicule dominates but the
pediment denies the activity of the general ordonnance,
there is Mannerist ambiguity within: the columns seem
to allow the wall only a screening role, yet each section
is a 'rhythmic bay' with a chapel recession in the high
central arch revealing considerable mass. Within the
latter is an altogether different, wittier, game with the
Roman conventions of articulating load and support:
the anthropomorphic origins of the 'Order' are taken to
apotheosis by the winged angels who relieve the
columns of their structural role in the altarpieces.

**›1.93 MILAN, EXERCISES IN CENTRALIZED
PLANNING:** (a, b) S. Alessandro, plan and view
towards sanctuary (Lorenzo Binago, from c. 1600);

1.92e

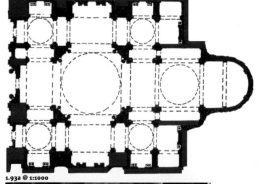

1.93a @ 1:1000

1.93b

domical but the vaulting of the nave bays springs from freestanding columns, as in the great hall of the Baths of Diocletian whose conversion to Christianity by Michelangelo
had been witnessed by Pellegrino.**1.92**

The most important ecclesiastical commission in Milan
during Borromeo's period as archbishop was for the
rebuilding of the ancient basilica of S. Lorenzo: it went to
Alessi's successor at S. Maria presso S. Celso, Martino
Bassi (1542–91). The original building was a rare double-
skin quatrefoil and the cardinal archbishop ordered that it
be reconstructed on the same plan (AICI, pages 722f). The
wide span of the octagonal dome had been the problem,
of course, though it had stood for a millennium: obscuring
the original subtly lit conception, Bassi ensured stability
with massive masonry whose overbearing gravitas derives
from the retention of a drumless dome – or, rather, from
the suppression of the drum to the zone of the bold Doric
entablature supported on huge panelled blocks corbelled
out over the canted corners between the four great
arches.**1.93**

1.93d

(c, d) S. Lorenzo (reconstructed on early Christian foundations by Martino Bassi after 1573), exterior, interior.

A reduction of Bramante's centralized scheme for S. Pietro, S. Alessandro belongs to a widespread type developed from Alessi's S. Maria di Carignano, Genoa, primarily by Giuseppe Valeriano in Genoa and Naples – S. Ambrogio (1587) and the Gesù Nuovo (1593) respectively. The important Roman example of the type, S. Carlo ai Catinari, built from 1611 by Binago's fellow Barnabite Rosato Rosati, will be reviewed in due course.

The quadrant arcades are reinforced in stone to buttress the massive masonry of the four great Doric piers: the outer walls are further reinforced with buttresses between the ungenerous fenestration and the original towers survived to receive the residual thrust of the suspended central mass. On the exterior, most of the dome is obscured behind a drum, quite contrary to the interior arrangement but fully in accord with the traditional Lombard way of resisting splay by elevating masonry bands into an articulated façade (*tiburio*): the immediate – and most impressive – precedent was Cristoforo Lombardino's double-storey *tiburio* on S. Maria della Passione but the form may be traced back beyond Bramante's S. Maria della Grazie at least to the mid-15th-century Portinari Chapel at S. Eustorgio.

8 ROME AT THE TURN OF A NEW ERA

1.94a

1.94b

A new confidence in Rome, awakened at the Council of
Trent, was manifest in the opposition of the reforming
Pope Paul IV to Spanish domination in Italy. That confidence proved premature and Roman opposition to the
Catholic world's greatest champion somewhat bizarre in
the era of advancing Protestantism. With the drawing of
the Council to its determined conclusion, however, there
was room for real satisfaction as the revived Church –
invigorated by the zealous new missionary orders – began
to regain ground north of the Alps. The containment of
'heresy' – at least – was anticipated well before the end of
the century and to celebrate it Rome was on the threshold of a new era in its art and architecture. Meanwhile the
topography of the Eternal City itself was being transformed by a vigorous elderly pope and his formidable
engineer.

SISTINE AMBITION

After the Sack, the Via Pia was the prime example of an
axial thoroughfare to new development in Rome but the
most ambitious programme, designed both for the amelioration of the old and expansion into the new, was instituted by Pope Sixtus V (1585–90). The scheme of the papal
engineer-architect, the Ticinesi Domenico Fontana
(1543–1607), is illustrated in a lunette framed by the vaulting of the great library inserted at the elderly, erudite and
energetic pope's behest over the stairs which led from the
lower to the upper Belvedere court. At the terminus of the
scheme and along the way, Fontana was required to expand
the Laterano and Quirinale palaces, refashioning their
huge parade fronts, and to the north of S. Maria Maggiore,
in the vast papal *vigna*, he built the Villa Peretti. Rising to
the challenge as urban engineer, as palatine architect he fell
somewhat short.[1.94]

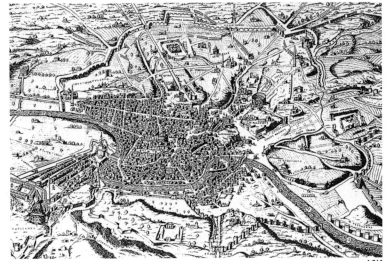

Served by the Acqua Felice – the restored ancient aqueduct – the Moses fountain is given the appropriate, but elementary, form of the triumphal arch inscribed with a eulogy of the pope's beneficence. From 1610 Paul V's favoured architect, Flaminio Ponzio (c. 1560–1613), expanded the triumphal-arch formula at the outlet of the Acqua Paola on the Gianicolo but his five bays lack the Michelangelesque sculptural relief which ameliorated the academicism of its model.

1.94c

Dogmatism and pragmatism in planning

The prime objective of the Sistine regime was to provide pilgrims with an integrated network of routes to their destinations in the capital. As these were seven major basilicas distributed at random throughout the site and served at disparate angles by arteries which could not be eradicated, a regular network – let alone a single dominant axis – was elusive. Yet so pervasive was thought along axial lines that the succession of roads linking the Vatican to the pope's seat as bishop of Rome at the Lateran is projected in the Sistine image as an unbroken spine: though slighting geography, this honours topography in representing the route – the Via Sistina no less – as rising to its apogee at S. Maria Maggiore where the pope was to be interred.

Limited as it inevitably was in the context of an existing town, even when designed in part to encourage expansion into unpopulated areas, the development of urban order in Sistine Rome still depended on the piazza. Off or on the arteries, some squares already existed or could be formed from the residue of antique space. The greatest of these, hardly rivalled anywhere, is the Piazza Campidoglio, on which work continued. The prime example on a larger scale, surrounded by diverse buildings, is the Piazza Navona formed from the ancient Campus Martius – which we shall visit in a later context. Foremost – at least from the visitor's point of view – was the Piazza del Popolo, from which radiated a triad of streets: Leo X's Via di

1.94e

Ripetta, which joined another triad at the Ponte Sant'Angelo, the ancient Corso which terminated in the Piazza Venezia beside the antique centre and Paul III's Via Paolina Trionfario (later del Babuino). The last was prevented from progressing to underdeveloped areas beyond the Piazza di Spagna by rising ground but the Via Sistina was determined to pursue its course at the upper level.

At each junction or terminus great possibilities were opened for the future but most were initially endowed with an obelisk as a landmark or a fountain: the latter celebrate the ancillary triumph of bringing water to the people; the triumph of Christianity over paganism – and of Fontana's engineering – is marked by the former. In addition, the restoration of the columns of Trajan and Marcus Aurelius, with S. Peter and S. Paul in place of these respective emperors at the top, asserted the renewed triumph of the Roman Church – or, at least, its new virility – after the Protestants had been countered at Trent and the Muslims defeated at Lepanto in the previous two pontificates.

1.94d

1.94f

1.95a

S. MARIA MAGGIORE AFTER FONTANA

The obelisk set up in the piazza of S. Maria Maggiore, at the bend in the Via Sistina and on axis with the approach to the old pope's Villa Peretti, is inscribed in commemoration of Christ's birth under Emperor Augustus – who had it brought to Rome – and surmounted by the cross of the Church Triumphant. The Sistine Chapel within the venerable basilica centres on the deceased pope adoring the ancient tabernacle supposedly enshrining the holy crib from Bethlehem. The programme embracing urbanism and mausoleum is thus simple and direct but that cannot be said of the overwrought design of the chapel itself. The witty countering of expectation in the juxtaposition of complex motifs, essential to high Mannerism, is lost to complicated accumulation in honour of the patron – and his patron, Pius V – and to the lavish marble revetment innovative in extent. Paul V followed the example on the other side of the basilica for himself and Clement VIII.[1.95]

›1.95 ROME, S. MARIA MAGGIORE: (a) Sistine Chapel (from 1585), (b) Pauline Chapel.

If Sixtus V's ambition for Rome was not matched by the distinction of his engineer as architect, his aspiration for his own memorial chapel also far exceeded the talents of the artists entrusted with its embellishment. In the context of Fontana's lapse from the pedestrian austerity of his palace exteriors, most prominent is the mediocrity of the statues of the popes and the reliefs of episodes from their lives by the Flemings Gillis van Vliet and Mostaert. Paul V employed Flaminio Ponzio (c. 1560–1613) to emulate Fontana in the design of his chapel and replaced mediocre Flemings largely with mediocre Lombards for the embellishment.

1.95b

Fontana's brilliance as an engineer is in complementary relationship to his dullness as an architect: the qualities of systematic organization and procedure essential to the efficiency of the one may well be inimical to the vivacity of invention essential to the excellence of the other. However, a fastidious individualist – unwilling to be commemorated on a grand scale as wholly derivative in style – is unlikely to have achieved the enormous Palazzo Laterano on schedule in the lifetime of the impetuous old pope. And the latter does not seem to have had much of an eye for art.

Vanished (from the site of the modern Termini below the Esquilino, above S. Maria Maggiore), the Villa Peretti was built on land acquired by Cardinal Felice from 1570 and greatly augmented on his accession to the pontificate: the tripartite arrangement of avenues serves the villa and the entrances to the enclosed gardens on either side. The arrangement has its macro-urban precedent in the triad of streets radiating from the Piazza del Popolo.

The Quirinale complex was begun c. 1583 by Ottaviano Mascarino with a casino for Pope Gregory XIII: the garden grid is contemporary. Sixtus V acquired the site in 1587 and commissioned Fontana to build the range facing west over the piazza (incorporating the casino to its north) and its return south on the Via Pia (now Via del Quirinale). The east wing, returning from the south to enclose a vast court, was begun for Paul V by Flaminio Ponzio in 1608 and completed from 1613 by Maderno – who installed the Pauline Chapel in the south wing and transformed the main entrance from the piazza. Gian Lorenzo Bernini devised the benediction loggia over the latter for Urban VIII in 1638: twenty years later he began the protracted extension of the south range for Alexander VII.

By 1600 Fontana had taken his palatial style to serve the Spanish viceroy in Naples. Seventeenth-century developments there, opening with that work, will be reviewed in due course.

1.96a

PALACE AND VILLA AT THE END OF THE CENTURY

The orchestration of the axis was the key to expansion of an urban order from the nucleus of the piazza: this, of course, was the role of the palazzo and expansive popes expected the prominent figures in their entourage to build

1.96b

1.96c

1.97a

1.97b

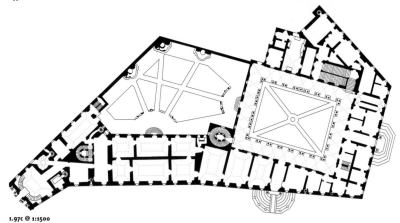

1.97c @ 1:1500

them – as Pius II had required, with incomplete success, at Pienza. The Farnese formula, with the Orders confined to the window aedicules, was most common: there were somewhat tired mechanical revisions, inevitably, like Ottaviano Mascarino's outer façades of the Cortile di S. Damaso in the Vatican or Fontana's work on the Palazzi del Quirinale and Laterano – apart from his several lesser efforts.[1.96, 1.94f] And there were variations, of course, as in the supple modulation of rhythm in the fenestration of Porta's work for Serlupi and Aldobrandini. This follows the incorporation of two mezzanines and an attic in the Borghese façade attributed to Vignola: the major development to that great work, however, is the courtyard and the extension of the complex towards the river.[1.97]

>1.97 ROME, PROTRACTED PALAZZI: (a–c) Borghese (expanded from the original Giglio block after 1586 for Cardinal Pedro de Deza and again after 1605 for the family of Paul V), cortile, river front with loggia, plan; (d) Aldobrandini (from c. 1590, expanded from 1618 and, further, from 1659 on acquisition by the Chigi).

Within Tommaso del Giglio's palazzo, attributed to Vignola (see above), the cortile was projected for Cardinal Deza by Martino Longhi and furthered on the latter's demise in 1591 by Flaminio Ponzio: it was incomplete on the patron's death in 1600. Cardinal Camillo Borghese bought the property in 1604 and consigned it to his nephews on his election to the papacy the following year: by 1614 they had completed the cortile and extended the garden wing to the Via di Ripetta. After the death of the pope in 1621, his nephew Scipione added the riverside loggia and suspended garden under the direction of Maderno and Vasanzio.

1.97d

Begun by Porta, the work for Aldobrandini was furthered by Maderno. Apart from the main portal, the latter's personal contribution is difficult to determine, especially after the extensive work carried out by Felice della Greca for Alexander VII from 1659 – including the major façade on the Piazza Colonna.

›1.98 GRID AND AXIS IN THE GARDEN: (a) for Mattei (by Giacomo del Duca, from 1583), engraved overview (Giovanni Falda, c. 1690); (b) for Ludovisi (from 1621 in a late-16th-century context).

The Mattei villa was originally built by Giacomo del Duca in an existing *vigna* (acquired by the family in 1553) but both it and the estate had been transformed in enlargement over the century before Falda recorded their situation. The Ludovisi also worked in the context of an old *vigna* with a casino of the late-16th century: the latter was reformed in 1621 on cruciform lines as the context for Guercino's astonishing illusionistic vault fresco of Aurora; the main building, addressing the axial transformation of the original grid, is traditionally attributed to Domenichino but was probably actually built by Maderno. The regular radial pattern of avenues in the Mattei extension contrasts markedly with the dominant and subsidiary cruciform axes of Ludovisi's lateral zone.

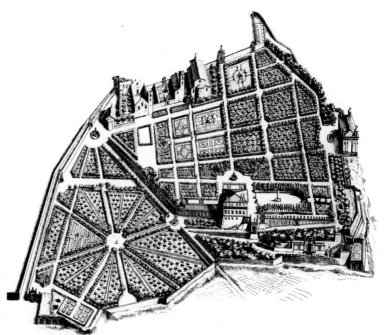

1.98a

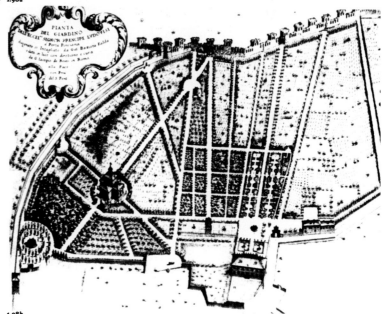

1.98b

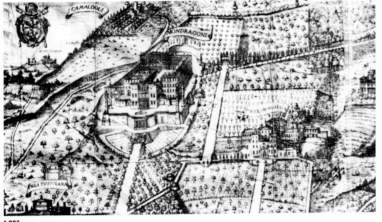

1.99a

1.99b

(a, b) Villa Mondragone, Frascati, overview (engraved by Greuter, 1620) and loggia; (c, d) Villa Borghese, Pincio, overview (engraved by Falda, c. 1690) and garden front.

The Mondragone complex was begun in 1573 by Martino Longhi the Elder with a casino for Cardinal Markus Altemps: a wing was extended to the south from 1577. The site was acquired in 1613 by Cardinal Scipione Borghese, Pope Paul V's nephew. Vasanzio (Jan van Santen from the Netherlands) was commissioned to extend the villa: the new work included the U-shaped block framing the celebrated two-storey loggia. Giovanni Fontana, the era's leading hydraulic engineer, equipped the garden with its water features.

Cardinal Scipione had begun acquiring land on the Pincio soon after the elevation of his uncle in 1605 and commissioned Flaminio Ponzio to build him a casino there: the Farnesina formula was adapted to a higher block without projections to the loggia front but with lateral projections beside towers on the other side. Vasanzio completed and embellished the building after Ponzio's death in 1613, two years before he was active at Mondragone: the incorporation of antique sculpture (now mainly gone) followed the fashion set by Pirro Ligorio in the Vatican Casino of Pius V and continued by Ammannati at the Villa Medici.[1.47b]

In the later 16th century too, popes or their nephews took to the hills, Roman suburban and Alban in particular, and built villas or casinos in extensive gardens. For the latter, the conservative grid survived into the penultimate decade of the 16th century, at least, but axiality was asserted by the second decade of the new century.[1.98, 1.99a,b] The U-shaped Farnesina villa type, with framed loggia, also proved enduringly popular – especially with the Borghese clan of Pope Paul V on Rome's Pincio and at Frascati.[1.99c,d]

The nephew of the Aldobrandini Pope Clement VIII

1.99c

1.99d

called for something novel from Giacomo della Porta: in response to his steeply sloping site at Frascati, the extraordinarily elevated structure raises the loggia as a belvedere to command a comprehensive view of the domain.[1.100] The extended axis of the garden, charged with the current of the cascade coursing from a rustic grotto to a semicircular nymphaeum, was realized after Porta's death by Carlo Maderno (1556–1629), Domenico Fontana's Ticinesi nephew and pupil, who was soon to demonstrate his superior talent at the summit of his profession.

1.100b

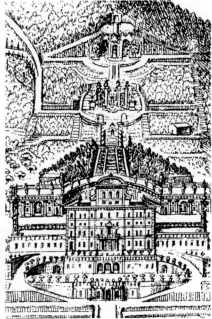

1.100a

1.100c

›1.100 FRASCATI, VILLA ALDOBRANDINI, from c. 1599 incorporating earlier work: (a) overview (engraved by Matteus Greuter, c. 1620), (b) loggia front, (c) detail of hemicycle and cascade.

Like the family's palazzo, the villa was begun by Porta and furthered by Maderno (to completion in 1603). The latter produced the scheme for the cascade and nymphaeum (or 'water-theatre') in 1600 and executed it in collaboration with Giovanni Fontana: the axis, conceived primarily for the coup d'œil, is clearly to be distinguished from the axis of event and exploration typical of the High Mannerist approach.

1.101a

THE CHURCH AFTER VIGNOLA

Giacomo della Porta, who completed S. Pietro with a variant on Michelangelo's dome, revised Vignola's Gesù façade. He adopted the basilican type of that seminal work with chapels in place of aisles on the reduced scale of his S. Maria ai Monti (1580) and on a large scale for the Theatines at S. Andrea della Valle (1591).[1.101] The façade of the former, at least, asserted a conservative standard in the untroubled consistency of its pilaster ordonnance: clearer, the work was dryer than its author's response to Vignola's Gesù exercise (see pages 176f). However, as Vignola may

>1.101 GIACOMO DELLA PORTA AND THE ROMAN CHURCH AFTER VIGNOLA: (a) S. Pietro, dome (from 1588), model; (b) Il Gesù, façade (as completed by Porta c. 1584); (c–e) S. Maria ai Monti (1580), section, plan and exterior; (f) S. Andrea della Valle (1591), interior.

Porta, architect-in-chief at S. Pietro since Vignola's death in 1573, was commissioned by Pope Sixtus V – with that venerable pontif's characteristic drive – to press ahead with the construction of the chancel arm to the west and the dome. In doing so from 1588–91 he honoured the double-skin conception of Michelangelo's great dome model – and Dupérac's engraved section – but drew the hemisphere into a slightly pointed, more aspiring form in accordance with the master's initial response to his study of Brunelleschi's great dome.

The complication introduced into the design of the Gesù façade, stressing the verticals, is again apparent in the breaking of the entablature forward over the single pilasters separating the nave bays – rather than maintaining a single dominant horizontal to assert the unity of the main volume, as Vignola had done.[1.38k]

The Theatine order clearly sought to emulate the Jesuits in commissioning a mother church of compara-

1.101b

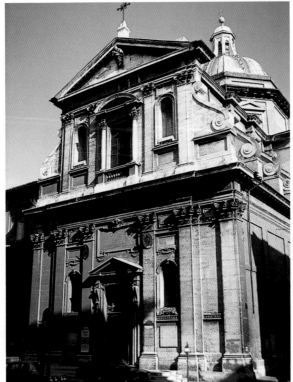

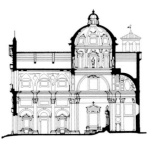

1.101c, d @ 1:1000

ble size and conception: they engaged Porta as consultative architect on S. Andrea in association with their own Fra Francesco Grimaldi. The vertical emphasis in Porta's revisions of Vignola elsewhere is furthered here: the chapel arcades rise to the full height of their bays, the divisions are strengthened with pilaster groups, the entablature is again projected out over these and the vertical momentum is now directed through the vault by transverse arches.

be seen to have had his reservations about the effect of Michelangelesque licence, so Porta was reacting to the Mannerisms of Michelangelo's followers – such as his sometime colleague Giacomo del Duca.[1.102]

The Gesù formula was naturally foremost in meeting the needs of all the Counter-Reformation orders. Well within a decade, Martino Longhi the Elder adapted it for the Oratorians at S. Maria in Vallicella (the Chiesa Nuova, 1575) and before the century was out it was followed by many others elsewhere in Italy – as we have seen, notably in Milan where there was experimentation with other traditional types too. The ellipse was developed on several occasions by Ottaviano Mascarino (1536–1606) and more notably by Francesco da Volterra (1530–94) in

1.102

S. Mari ai Monti is based on a contracted variant of the Gesù plan. In the internal elevation, however, verticality is stressed by the projection of the entablature over single pilasters as supports of the springing of the vaults. Again, the façade is an elementary reiteration of the Gesù formula with minimum complexity.

›1.102 ROME, S. MARIA IN TRIVIO: Giacomo del Duca's façade (from 1573).

In designing the Trivio portal, Michelangelo's late assistant starts from the portal of the Porta Pia: the broken segmental pediment is extracted from within the triangular one and draped on the exterior of the diagonals in a manner worthy of Buontalenti. In a manner worthy of Alessi, moreover, support for the pediment is disputed between a fragmentary Ionic Order and volute consoles: the former wins though it seems rather to be distanced than connected to the load by the even more fragmentary frieze.

Del Duca's most prominent contribution to the Roman skyline is the ribbed dome of Sangallo's S. Maria di Loreto: particularly notable is the lantern in the form of a tempietto buttressed by spur walls terminating in an attached Order (AIC4, page 850).

1.101f

the final realization of the church of S. Giacomo degli Incurabili (1592).[1.103]

A scheme related in plan to Volterra's Roman work was begun on a large scale at the end of the century as a mausoleum for the Dukes of Savoy at Vicoforte di Mondovi (from 1596).[1.104] The original architect was Ascanio Vitozzi (1539–1615) whose work for the Duke in beginning the transformation of Turin will be reviewed in due course. His previous activities at Orvieto would certainly not have prevented him from studying S. Giacomo – especially as his patron actively sought advice from Rome.

Both Vignola's approaches, as interpreted by Porta and Volterra, were adopted by the greatest builders dedicated to celebrating the Church Triumphant in the following century, the age of High Baroque: succeeding Porta, Maderno led the way but the old guard was still in charge at the turn of the century – at least, appropriately enough, in funerary architecture.

1.103a @ 1:500

›1.103 VOLTERRA AND S. GIACOMO DEGLI INCURABILI, from 1590: (a, b) interior and plan.

The plan is clearly an elliptical revision of Michelangelo's unexecuted scheme for the Florentines:[1.29] as there, but contrary to Vignola, the complexity of the composite volume is expressed by the exterior mass. However, the oval of the main volume is defined by the unbroken entablature of a regular pilaster Order except to extend the axis of entrance and sanctuary: there, appropriately, the narrowing of the intercolumniations recalls the rhythm of a triumphal arch which is echoed on a more expansive but less elevated scale by the treatment of the side chapels. Clarifying, Volterra dropped his original idea of doubling the pilasters throughout the interior as at the salient points of the exterior.

›1.104 VICOFORTE DI MONDOVI, SANTU-ARIO DI S. MARIA, from 1596: (a) exterior, (b) interior, (c) plan,

Vitozzi met Duke Carlo Emanuele I's objective of establishing a dynastic necropolis in a pilgrimage sanctuary of a miraculous image with an ellipse in which the burial chapels radiated from the central sacred image.

1.103b

1.104a

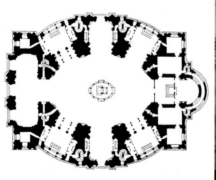

1.104c @ 1:1000

1.104b

FIN-DE-SIÈCLE REFORM

Instead of concealing artifice as Castiglione required, court art of the late-Mannerist era – after Bronzino in particular – was artifice, virtuoso performance not for its own sake but for approbation, self-consciously contrived to demonstrate the clever facility of the artist. Beyond his own native ingenuity, his fantasy, his *virtù*, in the elaboration of elegant line for sensual effect – not necessarily without intellectual rigour – the Mannerist sought inspiration beyond nature, often in witty allusion to the antique, in wilful breach of expectation conditioned by command of antique precept and precedent. Abstruse, allegoric, enigmatic, ironic, Mannerism was pre-eminently calculated to appeal to the sophisticated courtier with insatiable appetite for enjoyment – and endless opportunity for boredom.

With court artists bent on satisfying an insatiable appetite for the perfection of beauty, the improvement on nature implicit in idealization tended towards over-refinement and abstraction, and their obsession with abundance and variety recommended caprice in the sense of conceit and fantastical invention – particularly of ways to further self-indulgent excursions into *difficoltà*.[1.43] Thereafter the descent was from Mannerist to mannered: to stylistic convention and egotistical affectation creditable mainly in terms of synthetic adroitness and technical expertise – unless substance subsisted in wilfully abstruse allegory, comprehensible only to the intimately initiated. The facile work of Federico Zuccaro in the Sistine library, avoiding the latter if not the former, is perhaps principally memorable for its unsubtle idealization of topography.[1.94a]

Classical in inspiration and in ambition to excel, the 'stylish style' had turned un-Classical in its reversal of the usual relationship between form and content, in its contradiction of the Aristotelian definition of good design in terms of equilibrium between motive and motif, of mor-

1.105a

>**1.105 TOWARDS THE AESTHETIC OF REFORM:** (a) Cecchino Salviati, 'Deposition' (c. 1547; Florence, Museum of S. Croce); (b) Federico Barocci, 'Deposition' (c. 1568, Perugia cathedral).

Indecorous nudity is avoided by Salviati's figures in their dispersed business and eclectic lineage. Avoided thus too, is the concentrated passion natural to this subject – in stark contrast to Barocci's dramatically lit, chromatically fused, iconographically focussed, intensely emotional exercise.

1.105b

phology sensitively moulded to fitness of purpose and ornament sagely constrained – of indefinable 'good taste' – which few later commentators have found in the Sistine or Pauline chapels of S. Maria Maggiore.[1.95] However, the paintings and sculptures in those chapels – perfunctory though they may be as decoration – may not fairly be described as indecorous in the sense of Carlo Borromeo's prescriptions. Indeed decorum would generally rule again after Borromeo's codicil to Trent and with it the direct communication of moral consequence in sacred art, cleared of the wilfully abstruse and untrammelled by whimsy. Stages on the way to the realization of Borromeo's ideal may be marked in the work of Cecchino Salviati and Federico Barocci.[1.105]

By the end of the century, two supremely important artists were exploring entirely different means of meeting Counter-Reformation objectives in sacred art. Michelangelo Merisi da Caravaggio (1571–1610) took his departure primarily from Leonardo da Vinci and preferred to be guided by his observation of life rather than the conventions of Classical art. Annibale Carracci (1560–1609) was bent on effecting a synthesis drawn from the achievements of all the High Renaissance masters – Florentine, Roman, Parmesan and Venetian – in accordance with venerable Classical procedure. Caravaggio produced his most penetrating work within the first decade of the new century. The achievements of these masters will be assessed in an introduction to a new volume devoted to the new style then being developed in all the arts.

DV
LOVVRE

LA FACE
OPPOSITE
DV TRIBV
NAL

2.27n

DV
LOVVRE

FACIES
TRIBVNALI
OPPOSITA

PART 2 SEMINAL FRENCH

1 FROM MISUNDERSTANDING TO MANNERISM UNDER FRANÇOIS I

The French Renaissance in architecture, whose brilliant course began about the turn of the 16th century, was inevitably hybrid – and that would be the norm elsewhere north of the Alps. Essential to the native Flamboyant stock were diversified masses of enhanced verticality and exuberant decoration (AIC4, pages 810f). Essential to the Italian Neoclassical graft, on the other hand, was the homogeneity of form first extracted from the late-medieval Florentine environment for rational revision in terms of the Orders of antique architecture (AIC4, pages 728f, 751f). Aspiring to the imported ideal of unity in the context of indigenous traditional diversity – after forsaking Flamboyant floridity for the fashionable foreign repertory of antique ornament – the French developed an alternative to the Italian Renaissance which would be of seminal importance in the north.

SUMMARY BACKGROUND

The impact of the Italian Renaissance was first felt in France in painting. Apart from tapestry design, the major media of late-medieval French graphic art had not been large-scale painting but illumination in both senses of the word: of manuscripts on vellum in miniature and in stained glass at large (AIC4, pages 262, 214, 294, etc.). The French Gothic structural system, essentially skeletal – unlike the Italian – left great voids to be filled with glass but few plane surfaces for paint. Faced with unwonted mass in their churches, the 14th- and 15th-century Italians devoted their major endeavours in fresco to developing the means of projecting the illusion of spatial extension on to their walls as the theatre for naturalistic actors, though their engagement was sacred mystery (AIC4, pages 266, 219, 687, etc.).

The French, illuminating their interiors through the evocation of those same sacred mysteries in vast tracts of stained glass, exploited the ethereal qualities natural to their medium.**2.1a** The paradoxical corollary was that while the one masked the reality of building, the other remained subservient to it despite its extraterrestrial motive.

Obsession with the increasingly realistic observation of nature – characteristic of the so-called International Style which luxuriated in the central generations of the 15th-century – was particularly marked in tapestry design and Franco-Burgundian illumination of missals and books of hours (AIC4, pages 242f, 478f, 482f, 580f).**2.1b** It was reinforced by the achievements of Jan van Eyck and his Flemish school in evoking atmosphere while charting the physiognomy, penetrating the psychology and luxuriating in the panoply of portraiture (AIC4, pages 243, 704f). The greatest French painter of the era, Jean Fouquet (c. 1420–81), took these skills to the service of Pope Eugene IV in Rome in 1446: while in Italy he acquired a taste for Neoclassical ornament in its uncanonical, pre-Albertian, mode; he also comprehended the scientific means of

›2.1 MAJOR MANIFESTATIONS OF FRENCH GRAPHIC DESIGN IN THE SECOND HALF OF THE 15TH CENTURY: (a) the Annunciation Window (anon., c. 1450; Bourges, cathedral of S. Étienne, Chapel of Jacques Cœur); (b) 'La Dame à la licorne À mon seul désir' (from the tapestry cycle, after c. 1480; Paris, Cluny Museum).

Monumentality of figure was assisted by the development of glazing technology, especially the cutting of larger tracts of glass, by the mid-15th century (compare AIC4, page 214 of two centuries earlier). However, despite the implication of an octagonal vault, the figures stand on an insubstantial ledge.

2.2a, b

constructing the illusion of space on a plane surface. Refining his late-medieval inheritance in the light of Florentine rationalism rather than rejecting it for the rigours of single-vanishing-point perspective, he preferred a more empirical approach not far remote from that which Leonardo da Vinci would later establish as of cardinal importance (AIC4, pages 241, 700ff).**2.2**

2.2c

>**2.2 JEAN FOUQUET:** (a) 'Lit de Justice of Charles VII' (1458, from *Des cas des nobles hommes et femmes malheureses*); (b) 'S. Martin' (late-1450s, from *Les Heures d' Étienne Chevalier*); (c) Guillaume Jouvenal des Ursins (c. 1460).

Panel painting, particularly portraiture, proliferated in France after Fouquet. Prints widened French knowledge of developments in Renaissance Italy, of course, but large religious works were atypical. Indeed, the prime generator of the French Renaissance was not to be painting or even sculpture: it was to be architecture and, unlike most of their Italian colleagues, the progenitors emerged from the mason's yard rather than the artist's studio.

After the triumph of the French over the English at the end of the Hundred Years' War – the assertion of putative French 'nationalism' over English 'imperialism' – and the consolidation of the power of the central monarchy under the late-15th-century Valois, the defensive character of the French château was relaxed: the military mentality was retained only for prestige in the context of the courtyard house. Derived from the old enceinte of walls punctuated with bastion, the ranges (corps de logis) which framed the court met in massive towers (pavillons): the former normally had rooms aligned in single file (enfilade); the pavillons had rooms grouped into putative apartments on several levels. The juxtaposed masses retained the traditional high and flamboyant roofline, open and elaborate staircases, large windows, elegant tracery and naturalistic decorative detail (AIC4, page 572f).

Diminished by the centralizing policies of Louis XI (1461–83), in particular, the feudal magnates were upstaged in the transformation of the château by the new nobility emerging from the corps of the royal administrators and their suppliers. In the previous reign of Charles VII the highly successful merchant and financier Jacques Cœur built in town with unrivalled magnificence but his very success terminated his career there. His contemporaries Étienne Chevalier and Guillaume Jouvenal des Ursins,[2.2c] treasurer and chancellor of France respectively, principal councillors to the king, are best known as patrons of Jean Fouquet rather than for building and they survived into the next reign. In the following generation, however, financiers would lead the transition of their new class from town to lavish country residence and from late-medieval Flamboyance to putative Renaissance Classicism.

Meanwhile, the new leaders to prominence in patronage included scions of the lesser gentry promoted by Charles VII. One such was Pierre de Brézé who, having distinguished himself in the Valois army, rose rapidly to be grand chamberlain and seneschal of Normandy – and the defunct title of Comte d'Évreux with its several entailed seigneuries, including Anet. Another was Antoine de Bueil whose career followed a similar course, who married the natural daughter of the king but who bankrupted himself in the extremely picturesque reconstruction of his seigneurial seat at Ussé – where the work was continued by Jacques d'Espinay, chamberlain to Louis XII. Yet another was Pierre d'Amboise whose military ser-

2.3

vice also earned him multiple senior offices under Charles VII but dispossession when the latter's rebellious son succeeded as Louis XI: his family was restored to royal favour and his heirs Charles I and II furthered the rebuilding of his seigneurial seats at Chaumont and Meillant with great *éclat* – not least in the display of redundant defensive features (AIC4, pages 578f).

Well before great Flamboyant works like Meillant were completed early in the new century, well before the end of the 1490s indeed, French soldiers and statesmen were assiduous in acquiring the taste for antique decorative motifs through the importation of Italian books and engravings and the exportation of dynastic ambition to Naples and Milan. Predisposed towards the fecund, they were seduced in particular by the Neapolitan incorporation of the antique triumphal arch with the medieval twin-towered portal and in general by the brick and terracotta style of Lombardy – especially as translated into marble for the façade of the Certosa di Pavia (AIC4, pages 773, 806). Only gradually were they to understand and assimilate the intellectual essence of Florentine Classicism – order and unity based on symmetry, the harmony of proportions enshrined in the Orders.

›2.3 TOMB OF LOUIS XII, begun 1515: Abbey of Saint-Denis.

Attribution is to the Italian Giusti brothers but acknowledges the precedent set for Louis XI at Cléry and Charles VIII at Saint-Denis in showing the living king in prayer. It also conforms to earlier 15th-century Burgundian practice in representing the deceased recumbent (*gisant*) underneath – as in the mausoleum of Philibert of Savoy at Brou (AIC4, page 433). Novel to France in form and scale, the arcaded enclosure recalls the late-15th-century tabernacle tomb of Gian Galeazzo Visconti – whose wife Isabelle de Valois provided the French king with his claim to Milan – but the attendant Virtues derive from the Angevin tombs in Naples. The latter, like the Apostles, have usually been attributed to the Giusti as lame followers of Andrea Sansovino. On the other hand, something of the expressiveness of the French late-medieval sculptural tradition has been detected in the royal figures – especially the *gisants*.

›2.4 BURY, CHÂTEAU, from 1511, destroyed: bird's-eye perspective from the garden side (J.A. du Cerceau, *Les Plus Excellents Bastiments de France* 2, 1759 – henceforward referred to as *PEBF*).

The patron was Florimond Robertet, issue of a line of jurists, treasurer and notary to Charles VIII, Louis XII and François I. Classical regularity is brought to the late-medieval quadrangle, as at Plessis-Bourré (c. 1470) and more recently at Le Verger (from c. 1499) but not on the basis of existing work as at Gaillon. Novel symmetry is pervasive in the fenestration of Bury, as recorded by du Cerceau. In general, prestige claimed the retention of the once-defensive moat, twin-towered gatehouse and cylindrical bastions: the court framed by an entrance screen and three ranges of living accommodation (corps de logis) with towers (pavillons) at least at all four corners, was to remain standard for well over a century. Novel in its axial relationship to the house – at least in France – the garden belongs to the type, splendidly represented by du Cerceau at Amboise, Blois, Gaillon and elsewhere, imported with Pacello da Mercogliano: he was a Neapolitan priest whose expertise seems to have been horticultural and it may be doubted whether the planting of the individual beds was patterned in the manner of du Cerceau's later plate.

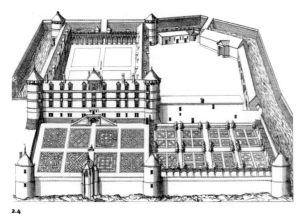

2.4

Robertet's town house in Blois of c. 1508 – called Hôtel d'Alluye after the barony conferred on him by Louis XII before he was accorded that of Bury – is still essentially Flamboyant in the verticality and asymmetry of its fenestration – despite the tentative intrusion of minor 'Classical' motifs into the gables.

›2.5 TOMB OF THE AMBOISE CARDINAL-ARCHBISHOPS, Roullant Le Roux, from c. 1515 (Rouen, Notre-Dame Cathedral).

2.5

The first phase of the French Renaissance may be considered, for convenience, to have begun with the Italian war of Charles VIII and continued until towards the end of the reign of François I (1515–47). Its principal characteristic is the skilful, if naïve, adaptation of imperfectly understood Classical detail to essentially un-Classical Flamboyant forms – the prime examples are Charles VIII's Amboise and Louis XII's entrance wing at Blois (AIC4, page 819). On the other hand, Louis's tomb was modelled on that of Gian Galeazzo Visconti and his French wife in the Pavia Certosa (AIC4, page 807).**2·3**

At the end of the first decade of the new century a prophetic regularization of the medieval courtyard was realized in the château of Bury and symmetry was imposed on elevations in which the vertically aligned windows were framed by a network of thin pilasters:**2·4** in plan, if not strictly in elevation, the precedent had been set some forty years earlier at Plessis-Bourré for the treasurer Jean Bourré, from the new class promoted by Louis XI. The lead was followed at Azay-le-Rideau and Chenonceau, by financiers enriched in the Italian war of Louis XII, and above all by François I at Blois and Chambord. The chequerboard garden was a legacy of the Italian war of Charles VIII at the end of the previous century: it was invariably set in a walled enclosure which sometimes retained the moats of a defended enceinte but was not necessarily related to the château – as at Bury (AIC4, pages 871ff).

Meanwhile, Pierre d'Amboise's son Georges, cardinal-archbishop of Rouen and Louis XII's principal officer of state in France and Lombardy, employed French and Italian craftsmen on his tomb in Rouen cathedral and on the augmentation of the archiepiscopal summer residence at Gaillon with lavishness beyond the dreams even of his brother and nephew at Meillant (AIC4, page 872).**2·5** The tomb apart, most prominent among the remains of his legacy is the precocious attempt at unifying the disparate elements of the symbolic twin-towered château postern by subjecting it to the elements of an Order, recalling the pattern of the Roman triumphal arch. Many others followed this lead too, including the king in the transformation of Louis IX's château at Fontainebleau: attributed to the master-mason Gilles le Breton, the slightly asymmetrical Porte Dorée (1528) clearly recalls Luciano Laurana's superimposed loggias of Urbino (AIC4, page 769).**2.6a**

2.6a

›**2.6 FONTAINEBLEAU, DEVELOPMENT OF THE MEDIEVAL CHÂTEAU,** from 1528: (a) outer gatehouse known as the Porte Dorée, (b) inner portico on the Cour Ovale, reconstruction.

The Porte Dorée provided a new entrance to the old enceinte at the head of an avenue flanking a lake: fed by the eponymous spring to its west, that would provide the central motif for the future development not only of the park but of the château itself. The Italian origin of the portal motif, with superimposed triumphal arches between towers as at Urbino or Naples (AIC4, pages 768, 773), is obscured by the typically French stress on the verticals which culminates in the high and elaborately diversified roofs. The latter are characteristic of the Flamboyant late-medieval château in the design of which – as here – symmetry was not a fundamental principle and decorative detail was unconcerned with the articulation of structure. All this had changed three years later, when Le Breton is credited with the construction of the inner portal and its external staircase probably under Italian guidance. Incidentally, the greater width of the central intercolumniation in both structures predisposed the retention of flattened arches.

Magnificently Flamboyant in its embellishment, the open-cage staircase had been a major feature of the late-medieval château court and the enclosed spiral form had been taken to its apogee for François I at Blois – with 'Classical' motifs substituted for the naturalistic Flamboyant ones (AIC4, pages 575, 876). Liberation and roughly rectilinear geometry had supervened, probably under Charles VI c. 1400, at Montargis where the prece-

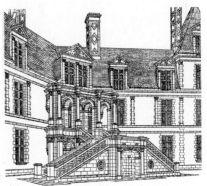

2.6b

dent for the new work at Fontainebleau was approximated by triple flights leading to a landing and a bridge to the arcaded grande salle on the upper level of the main corps de logis. In the generation before Le Breton, the form of the external staircase with twin flights was adopted for the garden front of the Château of Bury.**2.3**

Other members of the Le Breton dynasty (Guillaume and Jacques) are sometimes credited with work on the (much altered) château at Villers-Cotterêts – initially a hunting lodge built in the Forêt de Retz (Aisne).

›2.7 VILLANDRY, INDRE-ET-LOIRE, from 1532: (a) court, (b) garden.

At Villandry, Jean le Breton (secretary of state to François I) added an open court to a great rectangular keep inherited from the 14th century. Arcaded galleries, with pilasters, address the court on two sides: the original ordonnance, defaced in the 18th century, was restored in the early 20th century. At that time, too, the early 16th-century chequerboard garden – of the type attributed to Pacello de Mercogliano (c. 1455–1534) and planted largely with vegetables – was restored along lines revealed by the contraction of the ground in a dry summer and backed by original documents.

EMERGENCE OF FRENCH ARCHITECTURAL PERSONALITIES

In the first half of François I's period, composition in terms of agglomeration betrayed an obsession with the parts rather than the whole and late-medieval virtuosity often went untamed. Moreover, the ubiquitous thin pilaster was essentially decorative, interpolated ornament usually denying it any virility (AIC4, pages 874ff). A more austere ordonnance, consistently applied to rectangular masses, was preferred by Gilles le Breton at Fontainebleau. There too, in the lost staircase of the Cour Ovale, he introduced detached columns as well as flat pilasters, carefully spaced and proportioned with proper entablatures of architrave, frieze and cornice.**2.6b**

The integrity of Le Breton's pilasters and the regularity of their disposition soon recur in several works by the Loire: for example, Valencay or Villandry where a 16th-century chequerboard garden has been re-evoked.**2.7**

2.7a

2.7b

›2.8 TOULOUSE, HÔTEL DE BERNUY, 1530: detail of court.

The complex is of the medieval type with a corps de logis overlooking a court and linked by the flanking wings to an entrance screen: here the right wing has a gallery carried on an extended ovoid arch and open arcades raise the entrance screen to full height.

›2.9 NORMAN DEVELOPMENT: (a) Caen, Hôtel d'Escoville (from c. 1535); (b) Fontaine-Henri: château (begun late-15th century on 13th-century foundations).

The château was built on the site of Henri de Tilly's 13th-century fortress. The first campaign, from the late-

2.8

2.9a

15th century, produced the corps de logis with staircase tower (right). The second staircase tower was built under Louis XII and the central corps de logis was begun early in the reign of François I. The articulation of the latter was carried over to the adjacent side of the tower-block (left) but the pilasters ceded to attached columns on the outer face from c. 1537. The work is attributed to the master-mason Blaise Le Prestre who effected similar vertical unity with selectively applied columns in the Hôtel d'Escoville. Like the Hôtel de Bernuy in Toulouse, the latter perpetuated the medieval town house type.

Examples further south include Bussy-Rabutin, Assier or Montal and the Hôtel de Bernuy in Toulouse – though rectangular massing has yet generally to prevail over the cylindrical.[2.8] However, it is not until the fourth decade of the century that a fuller understanding of the correct form of the Orders is widely apparent. Boldly juxtaposed, the three main blocks of the château of Fontaine-Henri (1537) represent the three clearly defined phases of French late-medieval and early Renaissance provincial architecture: the later phase is also well represented in Caen.[2.9]

2.9b

The verticality in the disposition of these blocks and their articulation, as of the Porte Dorée of Fontainebleau, was hardly less relevant to the problem of 'Classicizing' medieval ecclesiastical forms – as on the west fronts of Angers cathedral and S.-Michel in Dijon, and generally in the Parisian church of S.-Eustache.**2.10, 2.11**

S.-Eustache was one of three major early 16th-century metropolitan ecclesiastical exercises not completed until well after the wars of religion had subsided: the others, re-founded a generation earlier, were S.-Étienne-du-Mont

›2.10 ROMANESQUE TO RENAISSANCE IN CHURCH ARCHITECTURE: (a) Angers, cathedral of S. Maurice, west front with 15th-century spires framing superimposed square and octagonal tempietti inserted by Jean de l'Espine from c. 1540; (b) Dijon, S. Michel (late-15th century), west front added from 1529 in neo-Romanesque style with Renaissance articulation extending to octagonal cupolas on the twin towers and a circular tempietto over the central portal.

Italian forms, pure in their geometry, were occasionally imported direct by patrons with Italian experience like Jean Daniello for his circular chapel at Vannes cathedral (1537).

2.10a

2.10b

2.11a

›2.11 GOTHIC TO RENAISSANCE IN CHURCH ARCHITECTURE: (a) Bourges, cathedral of S.-Éti- enne, Tullier Chapel window (anon., 1532); (b) Paris, S.- Gervais-et-S.-Protais, detail of chancel; (c–e) Paris, S.-Eustache (begun 1532), plan, general view, interior.

In the Tullier window at Bourges, contemporary with the foundation of S.-Eustache, the influence of the Renaissance is to be seen not only in motif but in spa- tial concept. In contrast with the work commissioned for the same cathedral three generations earlier by Jacques Cœur, in which the Virgin of the Annunciation and her attendants are covered by an octagonal canopy but stand on a depthless sill,**2.1a** the Tullier family kneel on a receding pavement before apostles inhabiting deep antique tabernacles.

The plan of S.-Eustache approximates that of the Parisian Notre-Dame, including transepts contained within the perimeter of the doubled aisles and their outer chapels; the section and corresponding eleva- tion, with double-tiered flying buttresses, are mature Gothic in proportions and structure (see AIC4, page 286). However, pointed arches cede to semi-circular ones (except in the apse) and the shafts from which the vaulting springs are transformed into pseudo-Classical engaged columns over pilasters.

and S.-Gervais-et-S.-Protais. S.-Eustache recalls the most Classical of France's High Gothic churches in the coherence of its lucid form but all three mark the persist- ence of the Gallic high medieval structural tradition, despite the intrusion of 'Classical' detail, and that in turn entailed the persistent predominance of stained glass in the graphic art of France. However, if the imported detail was adventitious in the first phase of embellishing the structure in each case, it was certainly not so in the filling of the voids.**2.11d**

2.11b

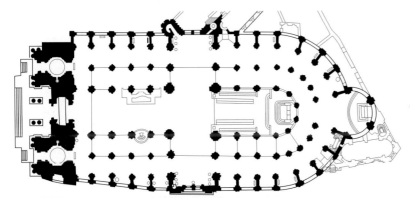

2.11c @ 1:1000

2.11d

›ARCHITECTURE IN CONTEXT »FROM THE HIGH RENAISSANCE TO MANNERISM

2.11e

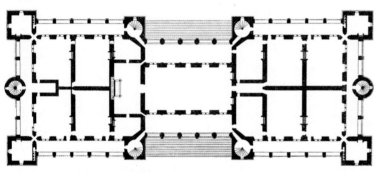

2.12a,b

Girolamo della Robbia's name is associated with the loggias of the Château de Madrid: he seems to have been responsible at least for the rather more canonical disposition of the terracotta ornament than had been common in France. However, the conception of the whole – with its corner pavillons, projecting staicase towers and plethora of tall roofs – is likely due to the French masons named in early records as Pierre Gadier and Gatien François and it seems improbable that Domenico da Cortona, the architect involved with Chambord, was not accorded at least a consultative role.

The door from the grande salle to the *salette* (secondary reception room) and the extraordinary chimneypiece in the latter are supported by caryatids – actually truncated in the manner of the herm. Even in Italy the precedents for anthropomorphic supports are rare and recent: Michelangelo's atlante on the Sistine vault; the caryatids of Raphael's school on the dadoes of the Stanze di Eliodoro, della Segnatura and Sala di Costantino as well as the herms in the border of the Sistine tapestries. Perino del Vaga developed the latter motif when a refugee in Genoa from the Sack of Rome and applied it on a grand scale on his return to Rome. Girolamo della Robbia, recorded as sculptor at the Bois de Boulogne hunting lodge for three decades after work began on the site, could have encountered Perino en route to France but would have known of the latter's work for Paul III in Rome only by repute. By then, in any case, herms were playing a strong supporting role at Fontainebleau.

Old attitudes – and medieval foundations, of course – ensured the persistence of the cylindrical pavillon beyond mid-century but Le Breton's rectangular geometry presaged a more coherent approach to the planning and mass-

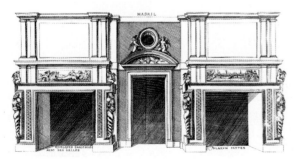

2.12c

2.12d

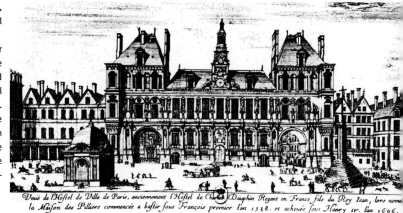

›2.13 PARIS, HÔTEL DE VILLE, begun 1529, completed 1628, destroyed 1871 (engraving by Israël Silvestre).

The site found for the Hôtel de Ville was an irregular trapezium with the long side facing the Place de Grève to the west: even that needed extension across a road to the south and the masking of access to the Hôpital du S.-Esprit with a matching bridging arch to the north. Only the ground floor and the southern pavilion were completed when work stopped in 1551: it is not known whether it was originally intended correctly to leave the upper floor unarticulated with an Order and confine relief to the statue-filled niches which Henri IV's architects contributed from about 1606.

ing of secular building than had hitherto been traditional in France. A radical example, contemporary with the Porte Dorée at Fontainebleau, is François I's Château de Madrid near Paris with twin square blocks of self-contained apartments surrounded by loggias and separated by grand salons. The high French roofs survive, their base line broken by the dormers which complete the vertical alignment of voids as usual, but the loggias are notable for their Italianate regularity. The latter reappear – with free-standing Corinthian columns – on the raised ground floor of the Hôtel de Ville commissioned in 1529 for the *échevins* of Paris by the king from his Italian architect Domenico da Cortona: it was unfinished for nearly a century but even then was not remotely Italian with its tall pavillons, turrets and highly differentiated roofs.**2.12, 2.13**

The first campaign of building at the Hôtel de Ville was directed by the master-mason Pierre Chambiges (active c. 1509–44) to whom transformation of the courts at Chantilly (from 1527) and Saint-Germain-en-Laye (1539) are usually credited. He and several of his French contemporaries were aware of the importance in Roman High Renaissance design of three-dimensional relief, of the contrast between solid and void, light and shade, of the

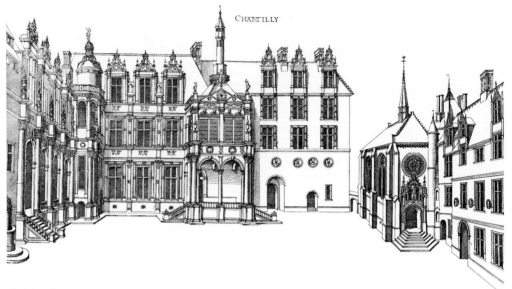

CHANTILLY

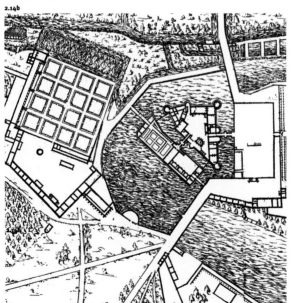

2.14b

expression of the weight of the enclosing fabric, even of homogeneous masses with concealed roofs – though the work at Saint-Germain is rare in that last respect.**2.14, 2.15**

›2.14 CHANTILLY, 'GRAND CHÂTEAU', founded late-14th century: (a, b) plan and court as transformed by Pierre Chambiges (from 1527, destroyed; du Cerceau, *PEBF*, 1607).

The island site, in a lake by the north-eastern approach to Paris, had been fortified from the 10th century. By the end of the 14th century it supported the massive triangular château of Pierre d'Orgemont (chancellor of France) which passed by marriage to the Montmorency in 1450. Modernizing it from 1527 for Anne de Montmorency, Chambiges closely followed developments at Fontainebleau in effecting the transition from an etched Order of insubstantial pilasters (centre left) to arcades with attached columns (left and centre).

›2.15 SAINT-GERMAIN-EN-LAYE, CHÂTEAU, from 1639: court fronts.

The work is punctuated with superimposed arcades framing deep-set fenestration in the manner of the town front at Blois (AIC4, page 877) – rather than screened with Italianate loggias in the manner of the Château de Madrid. However, the roofs of the latter are thoroughly French whereas here they are concealed behind balustrades in the style known to the French as Italian. Pierre Chambiges also worked on the lost hunting lodge of La Muette near Saint-Germain.

2.15

ITALIAN ASCENDANCY

By the end of the reign of François I, Vitruvius and Italian theorists and commentators on him, especially Alberti, were being assiduously studied in France. Italian theorists and practitioners had come to work in France, notably Rosso Fiorentino, Francesco Primaticcio, Giacomo da Vignola and Sebastiano Serlio. The contribution of the first two would be of international importance, as we shall see. Vignola, called to Fontainebleau to supervise the reproduction of antique sculptures from the Vatican collection for the royal gardens, stayed too briefly for much impact. Serlio's invitation was prompted by the introductory volume of his treatise on architecture – published in Venice in 1537 where Georges d'Armagnac was François I's ambassador. At large his fame would always rest primarily on his books but Serlio's projects for the 'Grand Ferrare' in Fontainebleau and the château of Ancy-le-Franc (c. 1546) provided the French with exemplary exercises in the Classicizing of traditional forms.**2.16**

The scheme for Ancy, recorded by du Cerceau, is notable for its complete integration – long characteristic of the Italian garden, as we have seen (pages 186ff). The old chequerboard subsists; so do the moats – as much for *venustas* as *utilitas*. However, the latter hardly disclaim the former as an early example of the parterre: the terrace, axially related to the house and patterned with low-growing plants, was to be the central essential element in the French

2.16a

2.16b @ approximately 1:1000

›2.16 SERLIO AND THE CLASSICIZING OF FRENCH DESIGN: (a, b) Fontainebleau, Grand Ferrare (c. 1542), entrance screen and reconstructed plan; (c–g) Ancy-le-Franc (begun c. 1546) plan and reconstructed elevation of first project, general view and court fronts, plan and overview with parterre and bosquet (du Cerceau, *PEBF* 1576); (h) bosquet and 'green room' (Antoine Caron, tapestry design, 1560s).

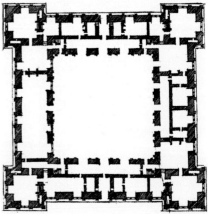

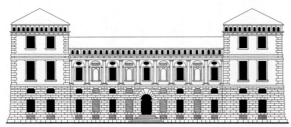

2.16d

2.16c @ 1:1000

2.16e

The Grand Ferrare is lost except for the typically Serlian portal and early graphic records; the château survives intact. The quadrangular plan of both represents
the regularization of the late-medieval French types –
as at Bury. The low entrance screen of the town house is
characteristic, though pavillons were evidently lacking
at the junction of the wings and the corps de logis – all
three of which had a single range of rooms. With its
symmetrical street front and square court, the ideal
was not to be realizable on the normal urban site.

The pavillons at the four corners of the château
acknowledge the French tradition but rather in the
manner of an early 16th-century Vicentine villa: more
particularly, the plan as a whole is an expansion of the
author's own ideal scheme for a country house, III.72,
with the court instead of the unlit central salone and
enfilades in place of the loggias. In a project at variance
with the executed scheme, the corps de logis are Bramantesque but in a manner related to Sanmicheli's
works of the previous decade in Verona or the more
recent ideas for the Palazzo Thiene at Vicenza (see
above, page 231). A miniature arcade was inserted

2.16f

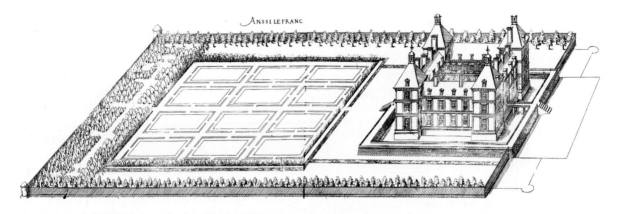

the French formal garden. Also essential to the latter – if peripherally – is the bosquet (a zone of higher-growing plants or 'wood') and that too appears here with paths and 'rooms' cut into it. Of no mere incidental significance, the 'green room' is second only to the grotto for those seeking to immerse themselves in nature: indeed, it stands for the reductivist idea of the origin of architecture in nature.**2.16h**

below the eaves at the patron's instigation but it was eliminated in execution when an attic was added in high French roofs; presumably at the same time, pilasters were applied to both storeys (in the manner of Peruzzi's Roman Farnesina; AIC4, page 859) and the niches projected for alternate bays were eliminated from the exterior but introduced to the court façades in the context of Bramantesque 'rhythmic bays'.

'Green room' and grotto were designated as retreats in the garden in particular, by Bernard Palissy in *Le Dessein d' un Jardin Délectable* which he dedicated to Catherine de' Medici in 1564. At about the same time Antoine Caron was employed by the queen mother on the design of a series of 'Valois Tapestries': a green room dominates the site of 'Le jeune roi apprenant les beaux-arts'. Palissy and Caron must have known the other – and neither is likely to have been ignorant of Ancy, whether or not du Cerceau had added it to his portfolio in the mid-1560s when he is known to have been drawing for his *PEBF*.

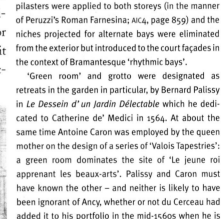

2.16h

 2.17a

 2.17b

›**2.17 TANLAY, YONNE, PETIT CHÂTEAU,** begun before 1569: (a) entrance front, (b) 'The Olympians' (fresco in the south-east tower of the main château, from the original phase of construction).

Accorded in 1559 to the Protestant François d'Andelot by his mother, Louise de Montmorency (sister of the constable, Anne), the medieval château was progressively rebuilt from the 1560s on its quadrangular foundations. The complex was not finally to be realized until the mid-17th century (as we shall see).

The patron was forced out by his Catholic opponents and died in 1569, having completed only the rusticated ground floor of the Petit Château and at least one of the round towers which flank the court of the main château. The domical vault of the 'Tour de la Ligue', in which the chief Huguenots met to discuss resistance to oppression, is embellished with an allegorical representation of the contentious forces in Classical guise: Charles IX, shown in the centre as two-faced Janus overawed by his father as Mars and his mother as Juno, is flanked to the right by Catholics forging weapons of war, to his left by the Protestants led by Coligny as Neptune.

A prominent example of Serlio's influence on building, in close proximity to Ancy, is the Petit Château of Tanlay (early 1560s).²·¹⁷ At the centre, however, Serlio was eclipsed by Primaticcio. The latter would recall Bramante for his Aile de la Belle Cheminée at Fontainebleau (1568)

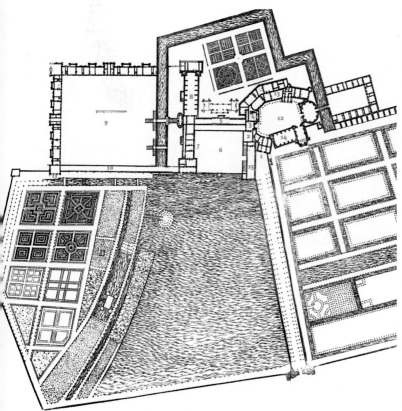

2.18c

›2.18 FONTAINEBLEAU AND ITS SCHOOL:
(a) Rosso, 'Pietà' (oil on canvas, executed c. 1535 for
Constable Anne de Montmorency; Paris); (b, c) overview of château and plan (*PEBF*, after 1568 but corresponding to gardening carried out by Claude de Creuil
in accordance with a contract of spring 1538), (1) Porte
Dorée, (2, 3, 4) king's guard room, great chamber and
bedroom, (5) Galerie de François I, (6) Cour de la
Fontaine, (7) queen mother's apartment, (8) Trinity
Chapel, (9) Cour du Cheval Blanc, (10) Galerie d'Ulysse,
(11) Grotte des Pins; (12) Cour Ovale (with external staircase removed), (13) queen's apartment, (14) Salle de
Bal, (15) Aile de la Belle Cheminée; (d) east façade facing the Cour du Cheval Blanc with semi-circular staircase as projected by the end of the 16th century;
(e) Escalier du Roi, upper well preserving embellishment from the former bedroom of the Duchess d'Étampes (c. 1541, adapted mid-18th century); (f) queen's
bedroom overmantel; (g, h) Galerie de François I (begun
c. 1533); (i, j) Salle de Bal (constructed 1540s, decorated from c. 1552); (k) king's bedroom ceiling detail;
(l, m) Galerie d'Ulysse, part engraving of decorative
scheme (*PEBF*), 'Ulysses and Penelope' (oil on canvas
after one of the murals, attributed to Primaticcio c.
1545; Ohio, Toledo Museum of Art), 'Olympia', study for
vault scene by Primaticcio/Niccolò dell'Abbate (after
1552?), (n) Grotto des Pins (c. 1543).

When the king first settled on Fontainebleau in
1527, after his return from captivity in Madrid, he was

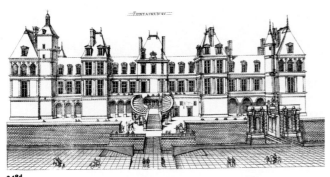

2.18d

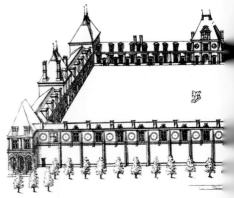

2.18b

but, with outstanding virtuosity, he and Fiorentino Rosso
had already shown the French the way beyond the High
Renaissance to Mannerism in the fecund diversity of

2.18a

media and motifs with which they decorated the Galerie de François I in the same château. That addressed the lake over a new fountain court flanked to the west by the queen's apartments and to the east, in due course, by the Salle de la Belle Cheminée: gardens developed to the east and west of the lake from 1538 show little advance over the form of the previous generation except for the introduction of a 'wilderness' of pines to the latter and a canal to the former. However, beyond an extensive pergola parallel to the king's gallery, the queen's garden to the north seems to have been welded into biaxial unity.**2.18**

housed temporarily in the main range of the Trinitarian monastery to the west of the medieval château while work was carried out on the transformation of the latter. The monastic building was to be replaced somewhat haphazardly between 1535–40 by a palace range accommodating the Trinity Chapel, a new entrance and the queen mother's apartment: meanwhile it was linked to the modernized château with the great gallery (conceived c. 1528, decorated from c. 1535) which took the king's name. Built over baths, that led directly from the new western vestibule to the king's bedroom (where it had always been in the castle keep) and acted as the main reception space. The bedroom (redecorated by Primaticcio from 1531) doubled as the main audience space and, indeed, as an anteroom to the pri-

Fontainebleau and its School

In the late years of François I and the relatively short reign of his son, Henri II, embellishment of the extended château at Fontainebleau was entrusted primarily to the Florentine Il Rosso (1494–1540) and the Bolognese Francesco Primaticcio (c. 1504–70) – and their School. Rosso was active in his native town from 1517–23, moved to Rome – where Raphael and Michelangelo were active – but fled the Sack four years later, failed to settle elsewhere until he was called to France in 1530 where he died ten years later having circumvented a High Renaissance in the sparse local school of religious painting by importing the starkly mannered pathos of his Florentine 'Pietà'.**2.18a**

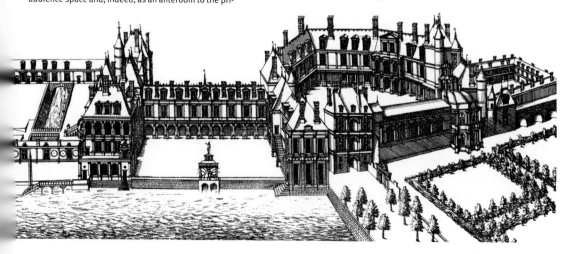

Primaticcio was in the studio of Giulio Romano at Mantua from 1526 until he left for France in 1532, taking with him experience of Mannerist developments in other north Italian towns – especially the Parma of Parmigianino: he returned to the source on his progress to Rome early in the next decade. In 1552 the School was joined and its style developed by the Modenese Niccolò dell'Abbate (c. 1512–71) after the latest Italian fashion – particularly in illusionist painting inspired by Correggio's great achievements in Parma.

Essentially characteristic of Giulio's work at Mantua – in the Palazzo del Te in particular – is the mixture of stuccowork and fresco in the context of richly varied tectonic or architectonic framework and coffering. Primaticcio had assisted in the elaboration of this formula and brought it to France. From the year after his arrival at Fontainebleau, he applied it to the decoration of the royal bedrooms and, in collaboration with Rosso, developed it in the ingenious scheme for François I's great gallery: the room is the first important example of a major northern European type and the precise determination of responsibility in the realization of its embellishment – indeed in the evolution of the style identified with the School of Renaissance Fontainebleau – is elusive.

A frieze of stucco and fresco over panelling is not uncommon in Italy but the two zones of François I's gallery approximate a novel equality of depth. Scibec de Carpi was imported by his compatriots to execute the coffered ceiling and the wood panelling of the dado, with its bold cartouches. Above the latter, and originally between windows on both sides, the frescoed fields are variously framed in highly complex abstract and/or figurative stuccowork. From Mantua, Primaticcio brought swags of fruit and zoomorphic figures like sphinxes, prominent in the sole surviving element of his work in the queen's bedroom too. Rosso is credited with inventing the imitation of leather strapwork in stucco and with introducing the dominant figures in high relief. The former may have been transposed from engraved borders representing cut and curled paper. The nudes have no Mantuan lineage but it has been suggested (by Blunt, 1953/1970) that they may have been inspired by the reliefs supporting frescoed panels on the mezzanine storey of Raphael's Palazzo Branconio dell'Aquila in Rome, with which Rosso would have been familiar; beyond that, of course, they are related – in motive, if not motif – to the young

vate closet in which the business of government was transacted in relative privacy: initially the king had occupied the bedroom traditionally assigned to the queen – to which the external staircase and portico of 1531 provided direct access.**2.6b** The original royal apartment extended to the south of the keep through a great chamber ('Salle'), where the king ate in public, only to a guard room entered from the Porte Dorée.

2.18f

2.18g

2.18h

men variously deployed by Michelangelo (AIC4, pages 822, 829). The herms emerged from Raphael's studio – particularly at the behest of Perino del Vaga – and played their supporting role at Mantua (see above, pages 18f, 122f).

Primaticcio's development after the death of his colleague is marked by the decoration of the former bedroom of the duchess d'Étampes: strap-work and swags of fruit still play the parts allotted to them by Rosso. Roman robustness was not denied when the iconography called for it but the emotive virility which may charge his figures is rarely preferred to a somewhat brittle permutation of Parmigianinesque elegance: willowy elongation of anatomy, carefully contrived if not contorted by the pose of the players, is furthered in the fresco schemes evolved for the Salle de Bal and the Galerie d'Ulysse – in so far as the limited legacy testifies.**2.18g**

The structure of the Salle de Bal is attributed to Serlio: the thick walls were originally intended to carry vaults but a sumptuous coffered ceiling was installed instead by Scibec de Carpi to the design either of Philibert

2.18i

2.18j

2.18k

de l'Orme or Primaticcio: the latter designed the frescoes executed on the perimeter wall surfaces largely by Niccolò dell' Abbate, who had been called in from Modena in 1552. The Galerie d'Ulysse, begun under Primaticcio in 1541, is a tragic loss (to dilapidation by the 1730s and the need to provide more accommodation for the royal suite): the scheme is grotesque, in the manner developed by the followers of Raphael, with painted panels relating the saga of the dedicatee. A tendency towards enhanced illusionism in the second half of the series may be explained by the intervention of Niccolò dell'Abbate under the influence of Correggio.

The sole survivor of the Aile d'Ulysse is the Grotte des Pins (addressing the pine-planted western sector of the park) with which Serlio or Primaticcio relieved the basement of its south-western end pavilion. Giulio Romano provides no precise precedent for the atlante which emerge from – or, rather, are devoured by – its rusticated masonry: however, they are but the anthropomorphic equivalents of columns undergoing the same fate while pretending to provide extramural support at Giulio's frequent behest.

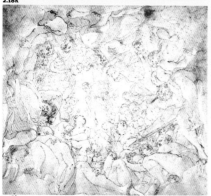
2.18l

2.18n

2.18m

Primaticcio's mannered elegance, rather than Rosso's more rebarbative drama, was generally to be preferred as a basis for development on the relatively rare occasions during the rest of the century when French painters turned their attention from excellent portraiture to religious or mythological subjects – though the 'Lamentation' attributed to Charles Dorigny is an exception in its filtering of late-medieval expressionism through Rosso's lens.

Engravings of the Italian duo's decorative work disseminated its influence as widely as anything produced in their native land and certainly ensured that 'strapwork', in particular, would ramp through all the lands of the northern Renaissance. It frames the major surviving religious images of the age, from the S. Mammès cycle characteristically designed for tapestry, in which the figures and even the Neoclassical architecture seem to derive largely from the school of Raphael and Giulio Romano – though not without the elongation favoured at Fontainebleau.**2.19**

›2.19 EARLY IMPACT OF FONTAINEBLEAU'S SCHOOL: (a) S. Mammes tapestry cycle: 'S. Mammès at the Cappadocian Tribunal' (after Jean Cousin, c. 1544; Paris, Louvre); (b) page from Andrea Alciato's *Emblemata* (1548).

No longer heraldic or flattened in plane, the tapestry still relishes naturalistic detail within the border of stylized strapwork as the setting for architecture which ranges in recollection from Bramante's Tempietto to the genetically Serlian triumphal arch.

In addition to the relatively fluid curve of simulated curled leather in Alciato's woodblock, there is flatter angular strapwork more natural to woodwork.

2.19b

2.19a

›2.20 THE TRIUMPHAL ARCH AND VALOIS

›2.20 THE TRIUMPHAL ARCH AND VALOIS HIGH RENAISSANCE CEREMONIAL ARCHITECTURE: (a) Saint-Denis, Tomb of François I, begun 1547; (b, c) at Saint-Jacques-de-l'Hôpital and and on the Rue Saint-Denis, two of the provisional triumphal arches for Henri II's entry into Paris (1549) to the designs of Jean Goujon.

The pavilion formula, derived from the Visconti tomb in the Certosa di Pavia for Louis XII, is revised by de l'Orme for François I in terms of a High Classical triumphal arch.

The manifestation of sovereignty on the one hand, fealty on the other, the ceremonial entry of a ruler into his capital – or other important towns of his realm – progressed along an artery punctuated with temporary architectural set pieces – usually, but not invariably, in the form of a triumphal arch – provided by the court architects in accordance with the eulogistic programme provided by the court savants. Increasingly elaborate from the late Middle Ages, its the origin was the acclamation of Roman emperors on their triumphal adventus – and that provided the humanist scholars of the Renaissance era with ideal themes for the programme. For a Classical Italian model of the ephemeral made permanent and for that objective unrealized in the genre see respectively AIC4, pages 773, 832.

2.20a

2 MANNERISM VERSUS CLASSICISM UNDER THE LATE VALOIS

2.20b,c

Though prefigured in graphics and promoted by Serlio, French achievement in architecture comparable to the Italian High Renaissance followed the founding of the School of Fontainebleau only after a decade and a half. In the event it was marked by an ability to subject the parts to the whole, to co-ordinate horizontals and verticals, to think in terms of mass and volume, and to comprehend the importance of rational forms, of proportion and the symbolic meaning and compositional value of the Orders. The development was promoted primarily by Pierre Lescot (c. 1510–78) and Philibert de l'Orme (c. 1514–70).**2.20**

THE HIGH RENAISSANCE OF DE L'ORME AND LESCOT

De l'Orme was born in Lyon, the son of a master-mason, and inherited Gothic France's great skill at stereotomy. Like most great Classical architects, he also studied the antique and the modern masters in Rome (c. 1533–36). There, in the circle of the French Cardinal du Bellay and his secretary François Rabelais, he can hardly have escaped a thoroughly humanist education to supplement the practical one imbibed in his father's workshop: he was to be the first French architectural theorist of note.

De l'Orme was back in Lyon c. 1536.**2.21** His practice burgeoned but he had abandoned it for Paris by the end of the decade: this was probably at the instigation of Cardinal du Bellay who engaged him to design a château at Saint-Maur-des-Fossés.**2.22** Through du Bellay, he was introduced to the service of the Dauphin just before his accession as Henri II in 1547 and was commissioned to build a château at Anet for the royal mistress, Diane de Poitiers. Descent from Bury, awareness of Ancy, are apparent in the axial ensemble but, referring to his work for the cardinal, the author claimed primacy among his compa-

›2.21 LYON, HÔTEL BULLIOUD, c. 1536: court.

De l'Orme's earliest surviving work, for Cardinal du Bellay's friend the financial administrator Antoine Bullioud, admirably combines a scrupulously observed Ionic Order and virtuoso masonry.

›2.22 SAINT-MAUR-DES-FOSSÉS, VAL-DE-MARNE, begun c. 1541: (a, b) plan and detail of principal court front (as published by de l'Orme).

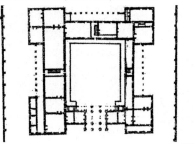

2.22a

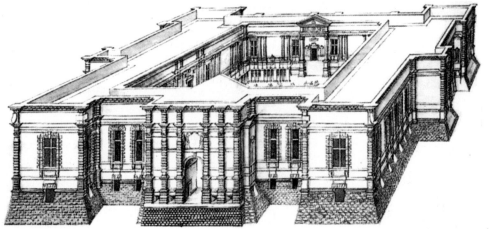

2.22b

Only the main range of a projected quadrangle was completed on the death of the cardinal. The widowed queen Catherine de' Medici bought it in 1563 for her son, King Charles IX, and sought its completion to an augmented plan: this incorporated galleries on both fronts of the main corps de logis and substantial projections for twin royal apartments to either side. The perspective drawing of the entrance range published by its author shows pediments to the attic on the side wings: the corresponding drawing of the main block has a similar pediment on the central frontispiece; pitched roofs are nowhere shown.

›**2.23 ANET:** (a) entrance pavilion, (b) central frontispiece, (c) overview (*PEBF* 1607), (d) Fountain of Diana from the stable court, (e–h) chapel, plan and section (*PEBF* 1607), exterior and interior.

Mme de Poitiers inherited the estate from her husband, Louis de Brézé, on his death in 1531. An unknown architect seems to have begun building a new

triots for his comprehension of Classical proportion. For Mme de Poitiers he went further and established the formula for the disposition of the Orders to bind all the traditional parts of the château along horizontal lines and cope with the stressed verticals of the pavillons.**2.23**

From Saint-Maur to Anet

Conceived before Serlio's advent to France, the work at Saint-Maur was directly informed by de l'Orme's Italian experience: the closest precedent for a rectangular court framed by single-storey flat-roofed wings of rooms *en enfilade* is the Palazzo del Te at Mantua. However, projections to the front and sides acknowledge the French tradition of diversified massing – even if, unlike pavillons, they are not distinguished from the corps de logis in height. More significantly, unprecedented in France was the consistency of the ordonnance – especially on the court fronts where the 'rhythmic bay'

2.23a

derives through Bramante – and Giulio at Mantua – from the antique triumphal arch.

Each of the main elements at Anet represents a variation on the theme of the triumphal arch. The most powerful of these, the last composed but the first encountered, distinguishes the entrance pavilion: the motif, applied to full height in the centre below an uncanonical attic and in association with sarcophagus-shaped chimneys, is truncated to either side to expose unarticulated D-shaped blocks which – except for their filigree balustrades – are reminiscent of medieval bastions in refined tribute to the military basis of the Brézé fortunes. The radical composition, merely screened by the Order, anticipates the dislocation and juxtaposition of abstract masses popular in the late-18th century.

At its last encounter, the triumphal-arch motif is stated at its most literal in the main frontispiece. This emulates Francesco Laurana's work at Naples – rather than the superimposed loggias between the towers of Urbino – and is in direct line of descent through Fontainebleau's Porte Dorée from the medieval tradition culminating in Louis XII's Blois (AIC4, pages 773, 768, 819). However, the combination of strength and florid grace in its regular Orders, unprecedented in France, is not unworthy of a Venetian High Renaissance master.

At Anet, as at Saint-Maur, the Order of the court fronts progresses from pilasters to columns with the projection of the central frontispiece on the axis of the entrance: this was not the first time the French had sought to Classicize their medieval inheritance in this way but it was innovative in the consistency of its hierarchical disposition and in the later work – with its strictly canonical superimposition of Doric, Ionic and Corinthian columns – the gravitas was unprecedented in France.

A Classical screen and abstract massing also distinguish the exterior of the chapel. Preceded in France only by de l'Orme's own trefoil project for a chapel at Villers-Cotterêts (where he worked extensively on the king's northern outpost), the plan is an exercise in complex formal geometry: the arms of a Greek cross are inscribed in concentric circles, the inner one providing the domed rotunda. Over a freely interpreted Corinthian Order, defining, as it were, the semi-circular façades of four overlapping triumphal arches whose soffits curve through three dimensions – necessar-

2.23b

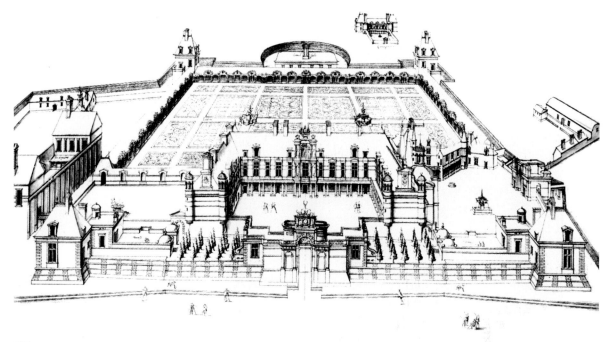

2.23c

corps de logis before the proprietress's fortunes changed with the accession of Henri II in March 1547: thereafter the project was revised – presumably to an enhanced scale – by de l'Orme. The work in hand on the main block was completed accordingly, with the

2.23d

ily but skilfully: the virtuoso coffering of the dome spins the spiral pattern of the floor into more than three dimensions.

Overlooked by a terrace, the garden was still divided into squares but a eulogistic poem by Olivier de Magny (c. 1529–61) refers to monogrammatic planting. Du Cerceau records a variety of patterns – if not monograms. Primacy in welding the enlarged together into the greater whole of the axial *parterre de broderie* is accorded to Jacques Mollet and Étienne Dupérac, gardener and architect respectively to Diane's son-in-law, the Duc d'Aumale at Anet – Dupérac having taken up his post on return from Italy in 1582 with extensive knowledge of current developments there. The claim was entered by Jacques's son Claude, gardener to Henri IV, in *Théâtre des plans et jardinages* (published posthumously in 1652 but written much earlier): the analogy with *broderie* was meant to convey continuity of design but not necessarily convoluted patterning. Elaborated from the emblematic or monogrammatic 'knot' (*entrelac*), the motifs were usually formed of cut box and turf over coloured sands.

2.23e

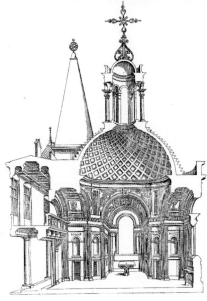

2.23f

2.23g

celebrated frontispiece probably responding to a new general ordonnance. The side wings, the chapel and the entrance range probably followed in that order.

The estate was passed to Louise de Brizé, daughter of Louis and Diane, and her husband Claude, Duc d'Aumale (1526–73). Confiscated by the Crown from Claude's rebellious son Charles, it was accorded to César de Vendôme, natural son of Henri IV, and passed by descent to the duc de Penthièvre – and the ravages

2.23h

of the French Revolution. The entrance pavilion and screen, the adjoining left wing and the chapel, but not the right wing on which it was dependent, survive on site; the frontispiece, detached from the main corps de logis c. 1810, is preserved at the École des Beaux-Arts in Paris.

›2.24 PARIS, S.-ÉTIENNE-DU-MONT: bridge between nave and choir (from c. 1545).

›2.25 SAINT-GERMAIN-EN-LAYE, CHÂTEAU-NEUF: (a) elevation, (b) plan (conjectural restoration after Blunt of 1557 contract scheme, left; as published by du Cerceau in 1576, right).

The single-storey main block with its four corner pavilions stood as a discrete entity, unencumbered by wings, and the forecourt, square with a semi-circular recession to each side, was bordered only by low walls. The quadrilobe plan of the court may derive from the 'triclinium' of Emperor Hadrian's villa at Tivoli which had been uncovered – but not fully understood – by the time de l'Orme was involved in antique Roman archaeology (AIC1, page 632). According to the record of du Cerceau, this court was framed by rooms of various sizes in two one-storey blocks and their dependencies: according to the contract of 1557 there was to be only one corps de logis with four corner pavillons.

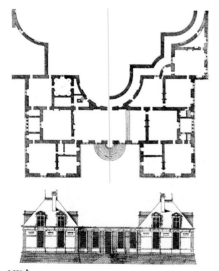

2.25a, b

2.24

Boldness of conception and similarity in detail with his entrance pavilion at Anet have prompted the attribution to de l'Orme of the bridge between nave and choir in S.-Étienne-du-Mont, Paris.**2.24** If so it has little – other than the fames in the spandrels – in common with his near-contemporary tomb of François I at Saint-Denis. However, as we have seen, de l'Orme is generally renowned for structural virtuosity no less than for Classical discipline.

With his first major royal commission, the tomb of François I, de l'Orme assumed responsibility for all the royal works except the Louvre. At Fontainebleau he is credited with the influential horseshoe-shaped staircase in the centre of the main front on the Cour du Cheval Blanc and, as we have noted, with the definitive form of the ball-room.**2.18d,j** With that controversial exception, all his work for Henri II has disappeared. The major loss is the last of these, the Château-Neuf at Saint-Germain-en-Laye; begun in 1557, it would ultimately overlook an Italianate garden, as we shall see.**2.25**

The demolition of Charles V's Louvre and the construction of a Classical palace, ordered towards the end of his life by François I, was the occasion for the most prominent expression of French High Renaissance maturity. Serlio apparently sought the job but it was given to Pierre Lescot who was the first official French architect to emerge from the study of the gentleman *savant* rather than from the *chantier* of the master-mason. The earliest work inconclusively associated with him is the Brézé tomb in Rouen cathedral: the sculpture is attributed to Jean Goujon and the latter at least is credited with the superb doors and organ case of S. Maclou in the same city.**2.26** Similarly, the

2.26 ROUEN, WORKS ASSOCIATED WITH LESCOT AND GOUJON: (a) Tomb of Louis de Brézé, Seigneur d'Anet (died 1531) in the cathedral; (b, c) organ case and western portal exterior detail of the church of S. Maclou (1540s).

The patron of the tomb was the widow of the deceased, later Henri II's mistress Diane de Poitiers. The work, which seems to have progressed slowly as the High Renaissance style developed, is attributed in part at least to the sculptor-architect Jean Goujon who is known to have been working in Rouen by 1540 – indeed that is where he first appears, at S.-Maclou. The equestrian statue may be due to an earlier hand but the caryatids are clearly affiliated to those Goujon produced in collaboration with Lescot at the Louvre and the Corinthian Order below them bears comparison with its Parisian successors.

2.26b

2.26c

2.27a–c

›2.27 PARIS, CIVIC AND DOMESTIC WORKS ATTRIBUTED TO PIERRE LESCOT AND JEAN GOUJON: (a–c) Fontaine des Innocents, c. 1548, (originally Fontaine des Nymphes at the junction of the Rue Saint-Denis and Rue Bergers, where it had only three embellished sides; it was re-erected in the centre of its eponymous square with a matching fourth side by the Neoclassical sculptor Augustin Pajou in 1788), general view and details; (d–g) Hôtel Carnavalet (des Ligneris, much altered before and after its conversion into a museum), plan, inner and outer elevations of original entrance front with Serlian rusticated portal (after J. Marot), court front with the reliefs in the style of Goujon;

2.27g

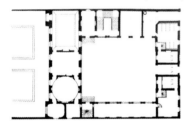

2.27d

2.27e

2.27f

mid-century Parisian works traditionally credited to him are outstanding for the consistent application of canonical Orders, as in the triumphal Fontaine des Innocents, and rich sculptural detail executed by Jean Goujon, as in the court of the Hôtel des Ligneris (now the Hôtel Carnavalet) which may be seen as the refinement of early Renaissance practice in Lescot's native Normandy after the example of Serlio's 'Grand Ferrare'. The Louvre project is resplendent in both respects, but the sculpture is always subordinate to the architecture.**2.27**

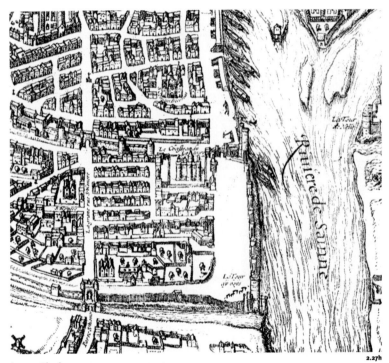

2.27h

Lescot's Louvre

On his return from captivity in Spain in 1526, François I installed himself at Saint-Germain-en-Laye. Relocating the centre of royal gravity from the central Loire to the Seine at Paris, he determined to replace the keep of Charles V's Louvre château with a modern palace. Demolition of the great circular mass was begun early in 1527. Nearly twenty years passed before Pierre

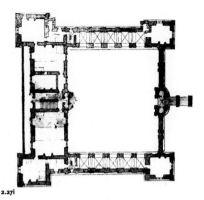

2.27i

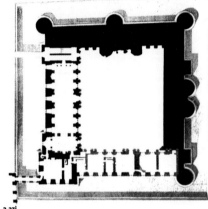

2.27j

(h–p) Louvre, plans of 1546 (identified by L. Hautecœur, *Histoire du Louvre*, as commensurate with the quadrangle of Charles V and corresponding to subsisting foundations of the unrealized central staircase) and of 1549 (reconstructed by Adolph Berty, *Topographie historique de vieux Paris*, 1866), façade on the Cour Carée, Salle des Caryatids to north and south, south front (as recorded by Israël Silvestre in the mid-17th century), Pavillon du Roi and Chambre du Roi ceiling.

Lescot was commissioned to build on the site of the old west range (August 1546) and construction began on the site of the medieval great chamber, in the west wing of the court, before the king died in March 1547. The plan associated with this initial project has paired pilasters on the entrance screen and side galleries but not on the main block: there, single pilasters frame the central portico in which the main entrance, leading directly to the major internal staircase, is recessed behind a minor open staircase with twin curved flights.

Henri II called for a new start in mid-1549. He wanted more accommodation on a grander scale. Beyond that, however, he was presumably impressed by Philibert de l'Orme's contemporary ideas for articulating the main court façade at Anet. Beyond that, again, it is difficult to discount determination to perpetuate the triumph accorded to his majesty on his entry to his capital through a series of variations on the theme of the triumphal arch.[2.20] Certainly the theme of the new scheme, with its antique trophies and fames, its Classical allegories of war and peace, would be elaborated in festive counterpoint played over the base motif of the triumphal arch.

In Lescot's revision, an attic with an unbroken corps-de-logis roofline instead of dormers was to be added to the original two floors, the lowest one distinguished with arcades in the manner of the Hôtel de Ville. Two new end pavilions matched a revision of the one in the centre. Instead of dividing the reception rooms, the staircase was to be displaced to the northern pavilion and one grand ceremonial hall inserted between it and a vestibule in the southern pavilion: the main entrance stayed in the centre. Beyond the southern vestibule – the colonnaded 'Tribunal' – the principal royal apartment occupied the three-storey Pavillon du Roi: the queen was accommodated in the adjoining riverside wing which replaced the southern range of the old keep.

The Pavillon du Roi was distinguished by an extra storey and that was distinguished in its embellishment: its lower levels were relieved only by the frames of the windows, like the wings perpendicular to it. On the other hand, the perpendicular court fronts were unprecedented in France for the opulence of their Classical articulation and sculptural relief. Not least for practical reasons, the traditional expression of pavillons and corps de

2.27k

2.27l

2.27m

logis continued to provide the variety of forms which the French preferred in contrast to the homogeneous blocks of the Florentines or Romans. In their richly diversified context, however, Lescot's superimposed Corinthian and Composite Orders – scrupulous in their proportions and detail – were used in a way of crucial importance for the future: as in de l'Orme's Saint-Maur and Anet, the progression from pilaster to column with the projection of the mass of the pavilions from the body of the building, binding these disparate elements together but asserting the verticals of the former, provided the basic means for the idiosyncratic French tradition to effect Classical unity in the context of medieval variety.

Jean Goujon's embellishment of the exterior extended to the celebrated caryatids – betraying unaccountable knowledge of the Athenian Erechtheion – which give the ground-floor ceremonial hall its name. Doric columns articulate the piers between the windows for the first time in France and are extended to screen the 'Tribunal' opposite the caryatids. Elsewhere the decorations devised by Lescot were executed in wood by Scibec de Carpi: the most splendid surviving elements are the ceiling and doors of the Chambre de Parade du Roi which was commissioned by Henri II in 1556 (originally the main room of the Pavillon du Roi but moved by Charles X to the east wing in the late-1820s): coffering, which cedes little to contemporary Italy in its sumptuous framework, marks a radical departure from the lightly embellished joists and beams of the traditional French ceiling though, unlike the ceiling of the Salle de Bal at Fontainebleau, it is not based on the expression of structure.

That Lescot foresaw the quadrupling of the Louvre scheme is suggested by those ultimately responsible for the definition of the 'Cour Carrée' – and for the inclusion of a commensurate plan in Serlio's lately published Book VI. On the other hand, Catherine de' Medici – now queen mother – began a much vaster development to the west c. 1565: the 'Petite Galerie', projected by Lescot towards the river to the south-west of the Pavillon du Roi, was to join a 'Grande Galerie' linking the Louvre with the new garden palace then being built at the Tuileries.

2.27n

2.27o

2.27p

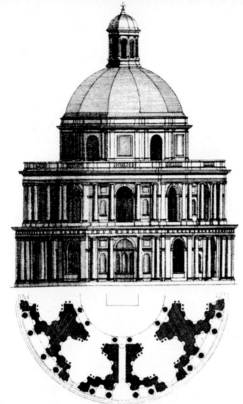

2.28c, d

Corinthian columns canted across the corners provide admirable backing for the Virtues, raised from their seated positions at the corners of Louis XII's arcade to stand on diagonally disposed plinths: the conception responded to the central position the monument was to take in a centralized space. However, more even than in de l'Orme's ampler – essentially orthogonal – format, the breaking of the entablature forward over the austerely robust columns of Primaticcio's compact scheme stresses verticals unresolved by the disposition of the sculpture above. Monumental beyond the reach of its predecessors, kneeling or recumbent, clothed or naked, Pilon's works are nevertheless replete with intricate detail and still infused with the natural vitality – or its stark absence – of the late-medieval tradition so movingly transmitted by Louis XII's master to de l'Orme's collaborator on the tomb of François I.[2.20]

2.28a

France lost Jean Goujon – with other Huguenot artists – to religious discord by 1562 but Lescot continued to work under the patronage of the crown until his death in 1578. De l'Orme met reverse: due in part to his association with the circle of Diane de Poitiers, he was eclipsed at the court of the widowed Queen Catherine in the early 1560s. She had commissioned him to build her a château at Montceaux near Meaux but work had not progressed beyond part of the foundations by the death of the king and then it stopped altogether.

Despite the splendid tomb de l'Orme had devised for François I, the queen mother commissioned Primaticcio to produce a freestanding variant on the same theme for the monument she was to share with her late husband at Saint-Denis: as for the earlier work, the sculptor was Germain

2.28b

2.28e

Construction of the enveloping chapel was begun by Primaticcio but little had been achieved by his death in 1570. Reference was most plausibly made to Antonio da Sangallo the Younger's centralized exercise for S. Giovanni dei Fiorentini but perhaps not without knowledge of Michalengelo's contemporary experiments for the same project.[1.29] Furthered, haltingly, during the troubled latest Valois reigns, the structure had reached the upper entablature by the accession of Henri IV but his Bourbon dynasty had no interest in its final achievement.

A rusticated Order – rather in the manner of Vignola than Giulio Romano – was introduced to enliven the basement of the Aile de la Belle Cheminée: on his last visit to Italy in 1563 Primaticcio may well have been inspired by his masterly compatriot's work for the Farnese on Caprarola (commissioned in 1556, see pages 174f). Notable for the central recession accommodating the twin flights of its external staircase – both prominent features at Caprarola, though not fused – otherwise the scheme distantly recalls Bramante's Palazzo Caprini formula with a rather dry, if irregular, Order of pilasters in place of doubled columns on the piano nobile.

Pilon, whose ancillary masterpiece contains the king's heart. The tomb was to be the centrepiece of a centralized mortuary chapel projected, but unrealized, as an attachment to the basilica. In the last decade of his long involvement with the augmentation of Fontainebleau, however, the elderly Italian decorator did realize the transformation of the Cour de la Fontaine with the Aile de la Belle Cheminée and new apartments for the queen mother on either side of the great gallery which had made his name.[2.28]

While out of royal favour in the early 1560s, de l'Orme devoted himself largely to writing. His *Nouvelles Inventions pour bien bastir et à petit frais* was ready for publication in 1561. The first part of his *Architecture* – the first comprehensive French treatise on the subject, indeed the first to originate outside Italy – appeared in 1567, the second part was unrealized on his death in 1570. Together, they articulate the dual nature of his expertise, practical and theoretical.[2.29]

›2.29 PHILIBERT DE L'ORME, LE PREMIER
TOME DE L'ARCHITECTURE:** (a) the 'French'
Orders; (b, c) allegories of the bad and good architect.

Blind and deaf, the bad architect stumbles through
the wilderness context of redundant building types.
The good architect, clothed in the robes of academe,
has eyes for the past, present and future, the doubled
hands of theory and practice, the winged feet of inspiration: his context is the fecund garden of modern
building types disciplined by ancient precept.

French Classical theory of architecture: inception

Nouvelles Inventions pour bien bastir et à petit frais is a manual mainly
devoted to the construction of vaults and such virtuoso features as *trompes*
(corbelled projections, usually through various arcs, to support a turret or
oriel). De l'Orme's grounding in the medieval masonry tradition is at base
here. Medieval too is his resort to allegory in the woodcuts representing the
good and bad architect in *Le premier tome de l' Architecture*. Otherwise, the
exhaustive illustration of its author's projects well serves the purpose of a
treatise in nine volumes primarily concerned to convey the lessons of his
own practical experience and the relationship of his works to the humanist
theoretical tradition. That, and the insistence that the architect must have a
comprehensive education – especially embracing the sciences – distance
him from the craft-based tradition of his predecessors.

L' Architecture is impressed with the permutations of the Sienese tradition from Francesco di Giorgio to Serlio – without constituting an illustrated catalogue of formulae. Alberti and Vitruvius are, of course, the
ultimate models – despite one less book: crucially, however, de l'Orme
explicitly prefers *utilitas* or *commoditas* to *venustas* – in so far as he inter-
prets the last rather narrowly as 'the richness of houses made only to
please the eye and not for any benefit to the health and life of man'. Rich-

ness may be appropriate for palaces but in principle ornament is to be applied rationally – to elucidate, rather than to mask, structure. Rather more important than the builder's mastery of ornament, however, is his ability to assess the practicalities of a commission, resolve all aspects of the scheme in advance and assert his authority in its execution. Most important is the command of regular geometry for that is the key to convenience: the essential aesthetic emerges from the logic of a building's plan, not the embellishment of its structure.

The first two books are devoted to the architect, his rounded education, and his relationship to his patrons: essentially, close collaboration to determine the budget and define the project before beginning to build and complete independence in the execution of the approved drawings and models thereafter. Books III and IV deal with practical issues: with basic design technology and with the mathematics of planning and structure; with environment and the site, preferably unencumbered by existing work as that is likely to obviate regular geometry and, therefore, inhibit convenience. The mathematics of *venustas*, in the broader Vitruvian sense, comes next: Books V–VII deal with the Orders – with specific reference to the Theatre of Marcellus, after Vignola, but no specific canon of proportions (failing the promised second part of the treatise to which the Bible was to be fundamental). Ornament is last: Books VIII and IX deal with the detailing of doors, windows, chimneypieces, etc.

Propriety admits richness of ornament and materials for public building, especially royal palaces, but de l'Orme advises against the use of Italian marbles in lieu of the wide variety of excellent French stones. Indeed, he is disparaging of those who ape Italian models, not least because they are ill-suited to the northern French climate: reason, not fashion, should be the French architect's guide. And his Gallicism went as far as adding a French strain to the Graeco-Roman canon of the Orders: the ringing of the column shaft with bands of ornament. Characteristically the chauvinism – and the apparent contradiction of anti-ornamental bias – was rationalized (on largely spurious grounds): the Ancients, beginning with the tree trunk, worked in marble from which columns could be cut in single shafts; working in stone which did not run to such lengths, the French needed to disguise multiple joints.

2.30a,b

›2.30 FANTASY AND REALITY IN THE LATE PARISIAN WORKS OF DE L'ORME: (a, b) Hôtel des Tournelles, festive portal (1559) and S.-Nicolas-des-Champs: south portal (anon., c. 1576); (c–e) Tuileries, detail of court and garden façade and central pavillon as built by de l'Orme (*PEBF* 1607); (f) overview of ideal project (elaborated by du Cerceau).

Not long out of favour, de l'Orme was called back into the service of the queen mother in 1564 to provide a garden palace on the site of a tileworks outside the west walls of Paris. The garden conformed to the traditional chequerboard approach, but for the ordonnance of the palace – known from its site as the Tuileries – de l'Orme developed a sumptuous new style which foreshadowed the decorative 'Mannerism' of later 16th-century French practice and pattern book. Beyond that, however, festooned with garlands and drapery threaded through triglyph consoles in thrall to physics, the attic of the Tuileries was to provide

The 'rhythmic bay' of the Tournelles triumphal-arch scheme was defined by a perfect square, as its author insisted and its emulator acknowledged at S.-Nicolas.

The ground floor of the Tuileries central pavilion, with its triumphal 'rhythmic bay', and twin seven-bay corps de logis with attic had been constructed by the time of de l'Orme's death in 1570. As published by du Cerceau, the Ionic Order progressed from pilaster to columns for the central pavilion on both fronts but every fifth bay of the corps de logis (including each end) was also articulated with columns on the garden front.

Departing from the executed scheme (in detail) and providing little useful internal space, the vast scheme elaborated by du Cerceau is best treated as a pattern-book fantasy. It is inconsistent in plan and elevation but it is likely to be correct in representing the completion of the central pavilion with a truncated pyramidal roof to the three-bay first floor – without the doubled Order shown in the elevation but not on the plan. The latter, faithful to de l'Orme's work, may well represent the original intention of closing the extended enfilade with

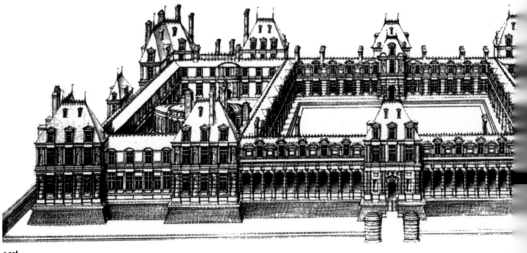

2.30f

2.30c–e
apartments in square pavillons. Du Cerceau's repetition of the latter (beyond subsidiary corps de logis) achieved the length needed to join a riverside gallery linking the complex to the new Louvre: Queen Catherine may have conceived that idea but it was not developed until 1595.

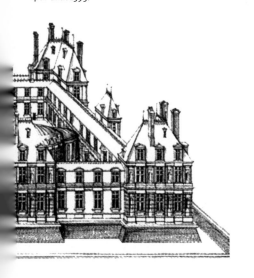

an essential ingredient of the architectonic repertory of decorative detail with which French Classical architecture was to be reformed in the age of the Enlightenment.**2.31**

The invention of de l'Orme's Tuileries style responded to the queen's specific demand for richness of both ornament and material – as the author makes clear in his treatise. It was drawn from her architect's own exercises in the *mise-en-scène* of festivities whose transitory nature allowed fantasy to deny structural reality – most notably, in general, the triumphal entries of the monarch into his capital and, in particular, the festive entry into the Hôtel des Tournelles for the fateful tournament of 1559. Even before it was deployed for apotheosis at the Louvre, the motif had recommended itself for decorative elaboration in the iconography of furnishing for the grandest buildings, secular and religious. Further, in the generation of de l'Orme's followers, the portal attached to the south flank of S.-Nicolas-des-Champs in Paris demonstrates how literally the master's fantasy could be realized.**2.30b**

2.31

›**2.31 DIJON, MAISON MILSAND,** 1561: street front.

The astylar scheme which Lescot and/or Goujon adopted for the court front of the Hôtel Carnavalet, dominated by reliefs, has its provincial equivalent in the main work associated with the Burgundian sculptor/architect Hughes Sambin (c. 1520–1601).

›**2.32 VALLERY, CHÂTEAU,** from 1548: exterior with corner pavillon inserted after the model of the Pavillon du Roi at the Louvre to receive Henri II in 1550 (*PEBF* 1607).

The work, for the Maréchal de Saint André, is attributed to Pierre Lescot.

›**2.33 SERRANT, MAINE-ET-LOIRE, CHÂTEAU,** founded 14th century, rebuilt from mid-16th century: view from the south-east.

Replacing his ancestors' medieval structure, Charles de Brie kept the quadrangular form defined by the moat: funds were exhausted on his death in 1593 with only half the corps de logis completed – including the central pavillon with its staircase and its somewhat old-fashioned pilaster Orders. The property was acquired by Guillaume de Bautru, a founder member of the Académie Française, who completed the corps de logis from 1638 according to the original project. Half-wings were added to each side of the court in the next generation.

An essentially decorative Mannerism was not foreign to the provinces. Astylar, the embellishment of the Maison Milsand at Dijon is the outstanding representative of one mode.**2.31** Another manifestation is the 'keep' of Vallery in Burgundy, modelled on the Pavillon du Roi of the Louvre and built to receive Henri II in 1550.**2.32** In contrast, scrupulousness in the expression of the Orders, if not always sophistication in their handling, is apparent in disparate provincial works – especially in the south where, in addition to developments by the High Renaissance masters in

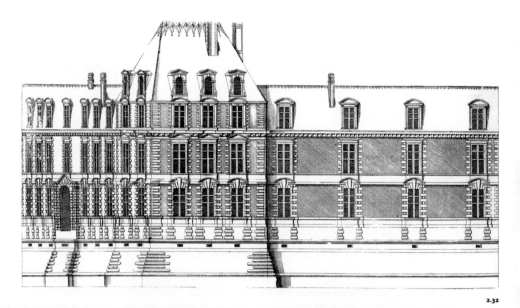

2.32

2.33

›ARCHITECTURE IN CONTEXT »FROM THE HIGH RENAISSANCE TO MANNERISM

Paris, antique remains and contiguous Italy provided more or less direct inspiration. Anthropomorphic style distinguishes contemporay work at Toulouse.

The canonical superimposition of Doric, Ionic and Corinthian Orders in the manner of de l'Orme – but framing arcades in the Serlian manner – is nowhere better represented than on the court fronts of the Hôtel d'Assézat at Toulouse (1552). Other three-storey examples include the somewhat coarser court fronts of the château at Suze-la-Rousse (Drôme), the less assertive – Le Bretonesque as much as Serlian – pilastered frontispiece at Serrant and

2.34a

›2.34 TOULOUSE: (a) Hôtel de Béringuier Maynier (popularly known as du Vieux-Raisin, from the mid-1540s), court façade detail (1530); (b) Hôtel d'Assézat, court façades (from 1552).

The Hôtel de Béringuier Maynier is one of several in the town attributed to Nicolas Bachelier (1487–1556). He was a sculptor from Arras and brought with him a taste for anthropomorphic sculptural detail: exceeding the norm, as on the window frames here, his first and boldest exercise of the kind, the portal of the Hôtel de Bagis, dates from 1533. The School of Fontainebleau (the Galerie de François I in particular), the prime source for such motifs in France, may be too late for Bachelier's Bagis portal but he could have met the protagonists on his transition from the north to the south and he would have seen works like the great chimney-pieces in the Château de Madrid (later illustrated by du Cerceau):**2.12c, d** anthropomorphic motifs were popular with 16th-century French furniture-makers – and with Serlio for chimneypieces (Book IV, folios 43, 58) .

The consistent application of superimposed Orders – correct in their vertical disposition if irregular in their spacing – in the Assézat court may well be contrasted with the selective emphasis of the earlier Renaissance work.

2.34b

›2.35 UZÈS, GARD, CHÂTEAU: court front of principal corps de logis (c. 1565).

The main elements of the feudal castle, the square Tour Bermonde (the keep) and the cylindrical Tour Fenestrelle, date from c. 1200. The south side of a court and the chapel in its north-west corner were built more than a century later, when the rank of the Uzès proprietor was elevated, but the domain passed with the marriage of the heiress to the Crussol of Vivarais in 1486. Further elevated to the rank of duke in 1565 – to secure him to the Catholic faith – Antoine de Crussol was responsible for the principal corps de logis which is traditionally attributed to Philibert de l'Orme without documentary evidence. The severity of the Classicism is certainly unusual in the provinces at that date: the three Orders, canonically superimposed, frame window bays with alternate triangular and segmental pediments: the alternating rhythm is enriched by the interpolation of panels with low-relief sculpture in the antique manner.

›2.36 MAULNES, YONNE, CHÂTEAU, c. 1570: (a) plan (*PEBF* 1576), (b) as recorded by Israël Silvestre c. 1650.

Antoine de Crussol of Uzès began building in 1570 to designs from the circle of Serlio, who had worked for his brother-in-law at neighbouring Ancy: the architect of the main corps de logis at Uzès is an obvious candidate for attribution. Rising from a circular moat in a rectangular compound, the exceptional pentagonal main block suggests knowledge of Caprarola but it is centred on a Doric spiral staircase rather than a court.

2.35

the unusually severe exercise traditionally – but unverifiably – attributed to de l'Orme on the court at Uzès. The patron there, Antoine de Crussol, was the brother-in-law of Antoine de Clermont, who had employed Serlio at Ancy: de Crussol went on to implement a Serlian pentagonal scheme at Maulnes.**2.33-2.36**

2.36b

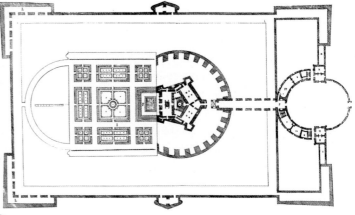

2.36a

Derivative exercises range from the secular to the ecclesiastical fields. A quaint example of the latter is the miniature Roman church front which implausibly provides the gable above the west façade of Rodez cathedral (1562). The more spectacular secular examples include the two-storey arcaded screen to the east of the court of the château of Bournazel (c. 1550) and the triumphal-entrance arch of the château of La Tour d'Aigues (1571), where the principal corps de logis (c. 1560) follows Lescot's Louvre.**2.37–2.39**

›2.37 LA TOUR D'AIGUES, VAUCLUSE, CHÂTEAU: entrance arch (1571).

The eclectic exercise – ancient and modern in its references – was built on medieval foundations for the seigneurs de Bouliers: the main corps de logis was badly damaged by fire in 1780 and the site pillaged for its masonry during the French Revolution.

›2.38 RODEZ CATHEDRAL: west front gable (1562).

An accomplished essay in Roman church façade design, wildly out of context, the work is attributed to Guillaume Philander, the humanist scholar attached to the embassy of Georges d'Armagnac, Bishop of Rodez, to Venice in 1536. Having been inspired by Serlio to produce a critical French edition of Vitruvius, Philander was appointed architect to the cathedral of Rodez in 1544 – presumably after having visited Rome.

›2.39 BOURNAZEL, AVEYRON, CHÂTEAU: arcaded screen (from c. 1545).

Only two sides of a projected quadrangle were built for Jean du Buisson, Seigneur de Mirabel. First came the north wing which enclosed the main apartments behind a façade with pedimented windows in bays defined by regular Orders of Doric and Ionic columns. The entablatures continue across the open arcades of the east wing where they are supported by columns defining 'rhythmic bays': the robustness is Roman High Renaissance, the inconsistent entablature line is not.

2.38

2.39

2.40a,b

›2.40 FÈRE-EN-TARDENOIS, CHÂTEAU: (a, b) bridge over ravine and entrance to its gallery (from 1560).

A long-fortified motte, rising from a deep ravine, was crowned with a stone castle in the early 13th century by the counts of Dreux: it passed to the duchy of Orléans at the end of the 14th century and then to François I who accorded the fiefdom to his constable in 1528. The latter modernized and augmented the château from 1540 and, after his rehabilitation, commissioned Bullant to link it with modern dependencies by bridging the ravine. A vast arcade, recalling an antique Roman aqueduct – in scale and sobriety if not extent – supports a now-ruined gallery entered through a triumphal arch: as in the Arch of Tiberius at Orange in Provence (AIC1, page 602), the colossal columns support an entablature interrupted by the penetration of a window into the tympanum.

Before the end of the 1550s – well before de l'Orme had evolved his scheme for the Tuileries – the end of the short-lived period of French High Renaissance maturity was announced by Jean Bullant (c. 1515–78) in the service of the constable Anne de Montmorency at Écouen, Fère-en-Tardenois and Chantilly. Each of these châteaux was

›2.41 CHANTILLY, PETIT CHÂTEAU, from 1560: general view.

After his rehabilitation Montmorency called Bullant from Écouen and Fère-en-Tardenois to augment Chantilly with a building for the controller of his household on a separate 'island' in the broad moat which contributes so much to the site: a huge platform for enjoying the view of the putative water garden setting of the whole complex had been constructed to the east of the old château in the 1530s. The Order of the new detached building is semi-colossal: on both the external and court façades the uppermost windows in the vertical alignment no longer merely punctuate the base line of the roof but slip below it as they had often done in the Flamboyant context – before there was a Classical entablature to interrupt. The central motif of the façade facing the entrance is derived from the portico of Écouen via the frontispiece at Fère. The medieval mode of Pierre Chambiges's first campaign of work on 'Classicizing' the court of the château is perpetuated in the vertical continuity of the fenestration across the line of the eaves into high dormers.[2.14] However, the misunderstanding of Classical rule has ceded to the Mannerism of their conscious flouting.

2.41

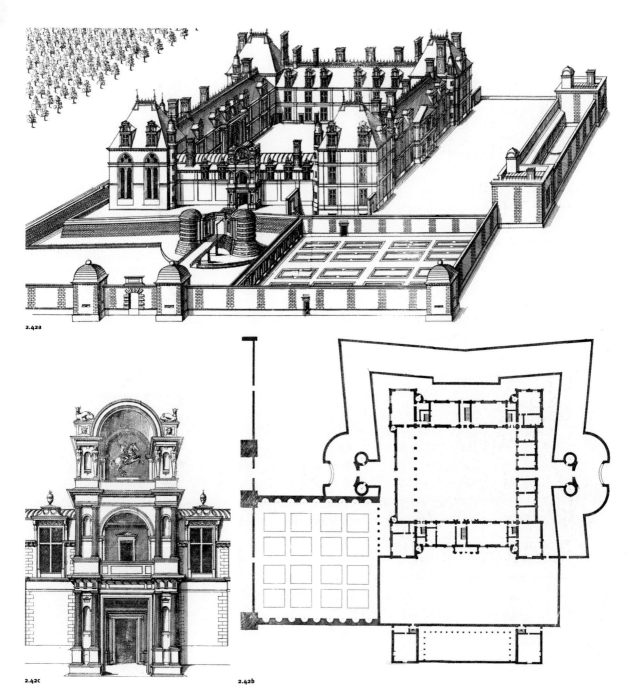

2.42a

2.42c

2.42b

›ARCHITECTURE IN CONTEXT »FROM THE HIGH RENAISSANCE TO MANNERISM

2.42d

›**2.42 ÉCOUEN, CHÂTEAU:** (a–c) overview, plan and entrance portal (after du Cerceau), (d) model, (e, f) court front and external frontispiece of north wing, (g) court frontispiece of south wing, (h–k) chimneypieces.

The constable, Anne de Montmorency, achieved his highest rank of military service fighting for François I against the Emperor but fell from favour in 1540: rehabilitated by Henri II, he was elevated to the highest rank of nobility as Duc de Montmorency.

At Écouen the construction of a modern house was begun c. 1538 under the direction of the master-mason Pierre Tâchcron: still prestigiously moated, it had the regular quadrangle of Bury and the rectangular pavillons of Le Breton. Only the west and south wings had been built before work was halted by the patron's disgrace. Jean Bullant appeared on the site soon after the death of François I: he probably began on the north wing (which bears Henri II's monogram) before completing the scheme with the lower entrance wing to the east. Apart from the Doric dormers, his major contribu-

2.42e

tion was the imposition of frontispieces to relieve the abstract grid which Tâcheron had extended over his façades with scant regard to the fenestration – in the early Renaissance manner.

The influence of de l'Orme is apparent in the superimposed Orders of the court frontispiece of the north wing. Familiarity with Anet and the Brézé tomb at Rouen, as well as the Porte Dorée of Fontainebleau, is apparent in the entrance arch of the lost east wing as recorded by du Cerceau. In the superbly detailed court frontispiece of the south wing, certainly, Bullant quotes the portico of the Pantheon out of context.

provided with frontispieces incorporating colossal Orders. The culmination of a series, disparate in derivation, the one at Écouen is the first executed in France: in it, typically, Bullant proved himself to be Classical in attention to detail – not least in the dormers – but not in scale and less interested in integration than in incident. These different characteristics may well derive from his use of his detailed studies of antique buildings, made while in Rome in the mid-1540s, which informed *La Règle générale d'architecture sur les cinq manières de colonnes* (published in 1564 and 1568). His knowledge of current developments in Rome also informed the development of his Mannerist style.**2.40–2.42**

2.42f

2.42g

2.42h

2.42i

2.42j

2.42k

›2.43 ANCY-LE-FRANC: Chambre des Arts, from c. 1565.

›2.44 CHENONCEAU, CHÂTEAU: (a, b) bridge (c. 1558), gallery interior and exterior (from 1576), (c) ideal project for forecourt extensions (*PEBF*).

De l'Orme's bridge (begun 1556) initiated a vast scheme of landscaping embracing both banks of the river: a record of 1565 refers to gardens on the south bank as newly made and at about that time du Cerceau drew the site with two four-square parterres, variously planted, in that location; the gallery followed after Bullant's appointment as architect to the queen mother in 1570. Grandiose additional building, unrealized, is illustrated, and was probably invented, by du Cerceau.

Roman developments of the previous generation, particularly the decoration of the Vatican Sala Regia by Daniele da Volterra (c. 1547; see page 180), are observed in the Mannerist division of responsibility for supporting the pediments between the windows and the intermediate panels: syncopated rhythm of this kind was deployed in antiquity (AIC1, page 603). Inside, the mantelpieces are Michelangelesque in their complexity.

Interior suites are, naturally, rare survivals from the mid-16th century. The Galerie de François I at Fontainebleau and its adjuncts or Henri II's bedroom at the Louvre apart, the most impressive are those of Écouen but the superb Chambre des Arts at Ancy-le-Franc may also be singled out: both perpetuate the style of the Fontainebleau School.**2.42g,h, 2.43** The Ancy chamber, like the most sumptuous rooms elsewhere, has coffering to its ceiling but the panels are inset between beams – the repetition of which in parallel ranges was the norm, as in the medieval tradition. This was the case at Écouen. Panelled wainscoting provided the base for tapestries or, rarely, murals, in the most sumptuous apartments: at Écouen it is modest in height; at Ancy it rises to nearly half the elevation – as in the Fontainebleau gallery – to support the painted frieze with its splendid cartouches encapsulating the arts between a plethora of arabesque motifs. The fireplace is always the dominant element – nowhere more so than at Écouen where the range embraces the architectonic and the sculptural in both three and two dimensions.

Mannerism was very much to the taste of the Florentine queen mother. She employed Bullant at Saint-Maur with vast pretension but no lasting result, and at Chenonceau where he built her a gallery on de l'Orme's bridge and was

2.44a

2.44b

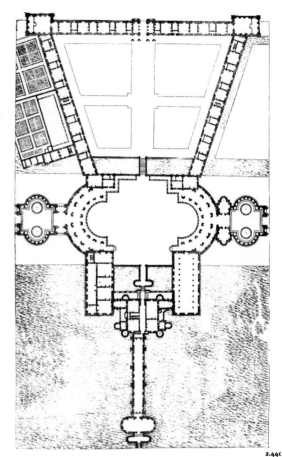

2.44c

perhaps responsible for a grandiose 'pattern-book' fore-court project. According to de l'Orme, as we have seen, she prompted his festive style at the Tuileries and she employed Bullant to apply it, as de l'Orme's successor from 1570, to the continuation of that project. However, fearing for her future at the Tuileries in the light of astrological progno-sis, in 1572 she commissioned Bullant to build her a house – the Hôtel de la Reine (later de Soissons) – on an expan-sive site near Sainte-Eustache as a retreat: plans were final-ized only after 1576 and the main body of the building was completed after Bullant's death in 1578.**2.44, 2.45**

2.45

›2.45 PARIS, TUILERIES: Bullant's pavilion, garden front (as recorded by Marot).

De l'Orme's ground-floor Ionic Order of columns (in the centre and every fifth bay) is the basis of the three-storey design: banding and florid detail deleted, the unfluted columns frame alternating windows and niches on both main floors; the attic, with its alternation of blind panels with convoluted pediments (over the niches) and dormer windows, also derives from de l'Orme but the architectonic essence has disappeared from the panels. The articulation of the east front seems to have taken its departure from de l'Orme's prevalent pilasters.

French architects in the later 16th century, inspired by the virtuosity of the Italian Mannerists but lacking their sophisticated grasp of licence in the antique, reverted to an essentially decorative approach to articulation. Unlike the work of the earlier Renaissance, but like Bullant's, this was not the result of misunderstanding. In contrast to Bullant's subtle dependence on the comprehension of Classicism, however, their conscious return to prolixity led to a flagrant anti-Classicism involving the wilful misuse of the Orders as elements in a pattern of detail, masking rather than elucidating the structural realities of the building. Partly surviving but well recorded, the Hôtel du Faur is a rare example of the former.[2.47a] The more flagrant tendency may best be represented by the grandest châteaux projects of the progenitor of the du Cerceau architectural dynasty – and in the collection of architectural props which constitute the *mise-en-scène*

2.47a

›2.46 ANTOINE CARON, 'AUGUSTUS AND THE SIBYL' (oil on canvas, c. 1580; Paris, Louvre).

for Antoine Caron's fantastic allegories of late-Valois festivities.**2.46–2.48**

Jacques I Androuet du Cerceau (c. 1510–85) had studied in Rome in the 1540s and was subsequently particularly prominent as the editor of various suites of fantasies on Classical architectural themes, decorative detail and furniture. Decorative patterning is at its most extreme, naturally, in the plates devoted to his own projects in his major publication, *Les plus excellents Bastiments de France* (1576–79) which celebrates the achievements of French

2.47b

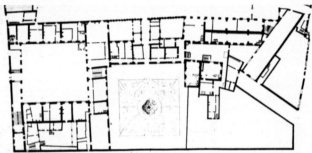

2.47c

›2.47 THE PARISIAN TOWN HOUSE: (a) Hôtel du Faur (after 1565, façade as recorded in *Statistique monumentale du vieux Paris*, 1867); (b, c) Hôtel de la Reine (begun by Jean Bullant after 1576, extended in the early 17th century for the Comte de Soissons), garden front (Israël Silvestre, c . 1650) and plan (c. 1700); (d–f) designs XIII (front), XIIII (front and plan), XXI (front, plan and back) and XXXVIII (overview) for ascending classes of residence from J.-A. du Cerceau the Elder's *Livre d'architecture* (1559); (h) Hôtel de Nevers, garden front as projected c. 1572 (F. Poinsart); (i, j) Hôtel d'Angoulême (built from 1584), garden front (mid-17th-century view by Israël Silvestre), detail of court front; (k) Philibert de l'Orme, house project (*L'Architecture*, 1567, folio V, 252).

architects since the Renaissance with the clear objective of asserting parity with Italy – at least. On the other hand, variety of plan rather than ornament characterizes his *Livre d'architecture* (1559): this is devoted to domestic building for all classes of society after Serlio's example but in resolutely French, totally un-Italian, form: it establishes the unostentatious combination of stone quoins with brick infill as the dominant mode.

Du Cerceau built several houses in Paris which reflected the practical contribution of his *Livre d'architecture* to the improvement of domestic planning, particularly through the provision of apartments of two or three rooms according to the means of the patron. None sur-

Bullant approximated the square court of the 'Grand Ferrare' for the queen mother's new house: it was centred on a monumental unfluted Doric column which may have served as an observatory. Contrary to Serlio's approach, but as in the original plan for the Louvre, the staircase is on axis with the entrance (from the south) in a corps de logis mainly occupied by a reception hall (to the west). The royal apartments were accommodated in a triad of pavilions ranged to the north of the hall, backing a garden court to the east and overlooking the expansive garden to the west from a first-floor terrace framed by projecting cabinets. Subsidiary accommodation was provided in the wings flanking the entrance court.

FACIES INTERIOR IN AREAM SPECTANS *Littera Notata M*

FACIES ANTERIOR ÆDIVM QVA PATET ADITVS *Littera Notata M*

2.47d

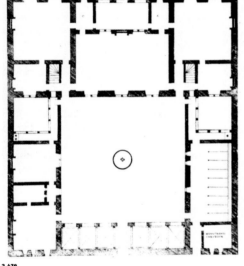

2.47e

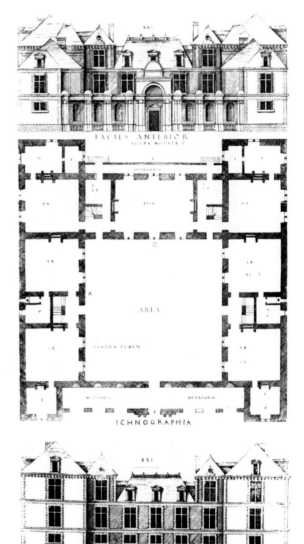

FACIES ANTERIOR
Littera Notata P

ICHNOGRAPHIA

FACIES POSTERIOR AD HORTVM SPECTANS

2.47f

The grandest of the elder du Cerceau's houses, like the Hôtel de Nevers or Plate XXXVIII of his *Livre d'architecture*, are virtually urban châteaux but the lesser norm develops the medieval formula represented in Paris by the Hôtel de Cluny in the manner of Serlio's 'Grand Ferrare' (AIC4, page 626).**2.16a** As in XIIII, a commodious court is framed by an entrance screen, higher side wings and a dominant corps de logis: open 'areas' separate its twin corner staircases from the service wings – with their smells of cooking and horses.

vives intact and, naturally, only the grandest are recorded – notably the Hôtel de Nevers which resembled the *Livre*'s most ambitious designs (c. 1572) and, like them, is devoid of pattern-book ornament.**2.47h** Other members

2.47g

Unlike the flagrant extravagance of his main château designs – or the Hôtel du Faur's apparent concession to the taste of the Tolosane jurist who commissioned it – most of the elder du Cerceau's house projects are restrained in ornament: indeed, the grand project XXXVIII – which seems to have been most closely followed for Nevers – is astylar and only the windows of the entrance wing have rusticated frames, like the lesser project XIIII. The Hôtel de Nevers was commissioned by Louis de Gonzague, duc de Nevers – ally of Henri III, then of Henri IV – but only the riverside pavilion, the central pavillon and the range between them had been completed on his death in 1595. Attribution to du Cerceau is speculative but highly plausible. Brick and stone structure, first taken to four storeys here, had long been familiar in town and country: a particularly prominent grand example is the royal château of Saint-Germain-en-Laye where the bricks form the quoins and the infill is plastered rubble; the norm may be represented by work carried out in the mid-1550s at Fleury-en-Bière.

2.47h

of the dynasty were also prominent as builders of Parisian houses well into the next century: in the 16th century their depleted legacy is most prominently represented by the hôtel which Louis Métezeau (1559–1615) is now credited with having built from 1584 for Diane de France, duchesse d'Angoulême.**2.47i,j**

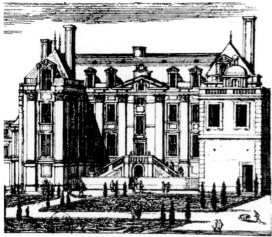

2.47i

Like the Hôtel du Faur, the Hôtel d'Angoulême departs from the courtyard norm. The former's main body ran perpendicular to the street in a semi-urban setting. The later work had an H-shaped plan: this and the mismatch between the similarly articulated court and garden fronts – both providing entrance to the house – suggest that existing building compromised the project's ideal symmetry. Louis Métezeau was clearly impressed with Bullant in adopting the colossal Order on his two fronts here but he was obviously also aware of Philibert de l'Orme's unique exercise in aggrandizing the Parisian hôtel in his *L' architecture*.

Like the Hôtel de Nevers, the Hôtel d'Angoulême was altered in the mid-17th century.

2.4j

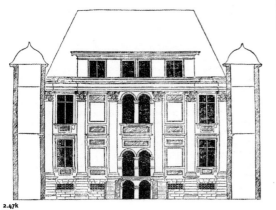

2.47k

Providing an invaluable – if not always accurate – record of many masterpieces now lost, *Les plus excellents Bastiments* was to constitute a 'pattern book' for contemporary patrons and practitioners. The reproduction of plan, elevation and perspective exceeds even Palladio – or any other of his contemporaries – in presenting models of modern design and its media. However, the production of a pattern book and the elaboration of a decorative mannerism are hardly unrelated.

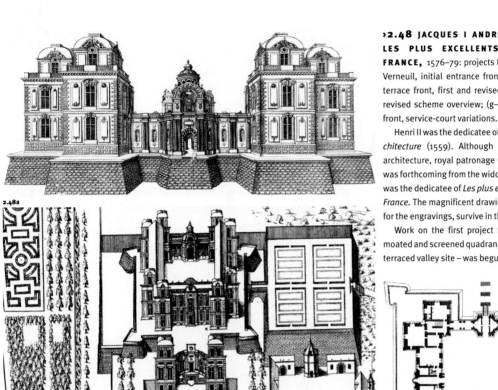

2.48a

2.48b

1576–79: projects for the châteaux of (a–f) Verneuil, initial entrance front, overview and garden terrace front, first and revised second project plans, revised scheme overview; (g–i) Charleval, plan, court front, service-court variations.

Henri II was the dedicatee of du Cerceau's *Livre d' architecture* (1559). Although that covered domestic architecture, royal patronage was the objective and it was forthcoming from the widowed queen who, in turn, was the dedicatee of *Les plus excellents Bastiments du France*. The magnificent drawings on vellum, prepared for the engravings, survive in the British Museum.

Work on the first project for Verneuil – a single-moated and screened quadrangle at the head of a richly terraced valley site – was begun in 1568 for Philippe de

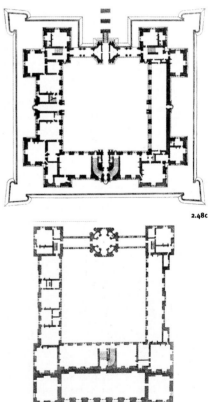

2.48c

2.48d

Boulainvilliers but he exhausted his resources in pursuing it and sold it in 1575 – with only the north wing nearly complete – to the duc de Nemours, son-in-law of Renée de France, who was the daughter of Louis XII and wife of Ercole d'Este, Duke of Ferrara. Work began again to a reduced plan without the projections to the sides but still with apartments in two of the surviving corner pavilions and retaining the ordonnance of the internal façades to accord with the executed work. The duke died ten years later and work stopped again. At the beginning of the new century, Henri IV bought the site for his mistress Henriette d'Entragues who finished the building between 1608 and 1616.

The terracing of the parterres on the grand axis of Verneuil, and the emphasis on square geometry in the main ones, were extraordinary in France at the time, though perhaps anticipated in unrealized plans for Saint-Germain-en-Laye associated with de l'Orme's Château-Neuf. Precedents were, of course, to be found in Italy at the Villa Madama near Rome, the Villa Lante at Bagnaia and above all the d'Este family villa at Tivoli which Étienne Dupérac had drawn and published in 1573. However, the last two sites, at least, were much more expansive than Verneuil's valley and therefore must be accounted as of only inspirational value.

The vast project for Charleval was commissioned in 1570 for her son, Charles IX, but his troubled reign saw little of it realized: a richly patterned, wholly integrated complex of multiple courts and gardens on a flat site. Patterning is as apparent in elevation as in plan. In the articulation of the quadrangular château the voiding of the entablature counters structural logic – contrary to de l'Orme's procedure at the Tuileries if not always to Bullant's – and in the embellishment of which fecundity sleights proportion. The incentive to patterning is nowhere more clearly manifest than in the putative *broderie* of the parterre beds – biaxially organized in whole and in part between bosquets within a cadre of canals. The unity of the two main four-square zones is greater than formerly due to the extrusion of major and minor axes and the cutting of the corners of the constituent squares to form subsidiary geometrical units: moreover, there is new unity in limited diversity of pattern within each compartment. Perhaps the manoeuvres of du Cerceau's burin in the garden squares of plates like this inspired Dupérac to his innovative implantation of broderie at Anet after his return from Italy in 1582.

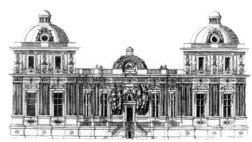

2.48e

Needless to say, the more flagrant flights of the du Cerceau imagination – lacking a sophisticated grasp of licence in the antique, perhaps, and the will to constrain the pencil – rarely rose to reality in building. The elder du Cerceau's work in the field, furthered by his sons Jean Baptiste (c. 1545–90) and Jacques II (1550–1614), was dominated by the châteaux of Verneuil (begun 1568) and Charleval (1570). Both these are amply represented among the most excellent buildings of France and amply represent the bizarre extremes to which the author took his anti-Classical tendencies: modified, only the earlier work was realized and its formal combination of the enfilade and the *appartement* set a highly beneficial example.**2.48**

The ostensible patron of Charleval, Charles IX, died before much had been done on the site. His brother Henri III, the last of the Valois, was far too preoccupied with the Wars of Religion for lavish building. A new beginning awaited until a measure of stability had been regained under a new dynasty at the beginning of the new century.

2.48f

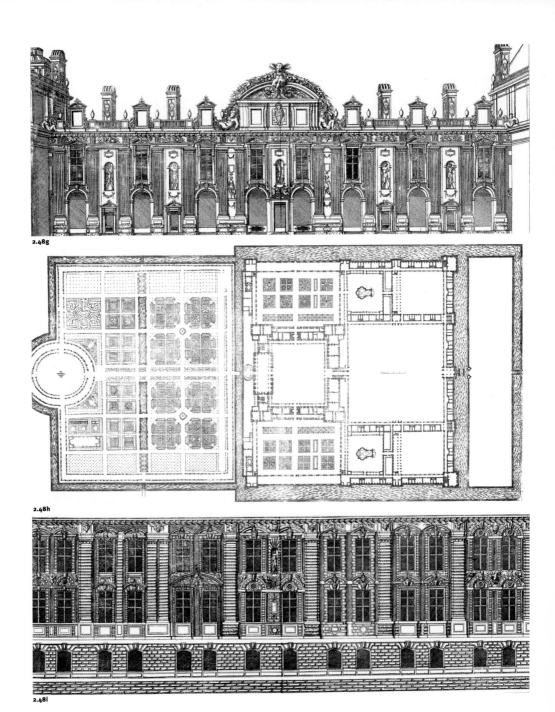

2.48g

2.48h

2.48i

›ARCHITECTURE IN CONTEXT »FROM THE HIGH RENAISSANCE TO MANNERISM

›2.49 FONTAINEBLEAU, AILE DE LA BELLE CHEMINÉE: overmantel relief of King Henri IV (Mathieu Jacquet, 1599).

3 CLASSICISM VERSUS BAROQUE UNDER THE EARLY BOURBONS

The succession of the Bourbons to the Valois in the final phase of the Wars of Religion did not, of course, mean a sudden change in architectural style in the palatial royal works – all of which were predisposed anyway. New direction was needed in painting and sculpture, but it would take time to find. Meanwhile, French painting was at a particularly low ebb: few had challenged even the allegories and narratives of Antoine Caron at the nadir of the late era and as François Clouet was followed by none comparable in portraiture the new era relied on Frans Pourbus and other Flemings. French sculpture fared better with Mathieu Jacquet, a follower of Germain Pilon, but his forte was the traditional one of the high relief, especially for application to portals or chimneypieces – as in the exercise which gives its name to the Aile de la Belle Cheminée at Fontainebleau.**2.49** To commemorate the new king with an equestrian statue for prominent display in Paris, the

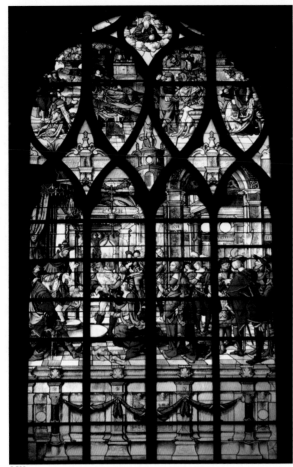

2.50a

2.50b

›2.50 PARISIAN CHURCH IMAGERY: from illumination to etching and oil painting at the turn of the Valois/Bourbon eras: (a) 'The Judgement of Solomon' (attributed to Nicolas Pinaigriers, painted glass. c. 1600, S.-Gervais-et-S.-Protais); (b) 'The Annunciation' (Jacques Bellange, c. 1610); (c) 'The Marriage at Cana' (Quentin Varin, oil on canvas, c. 1618, from S.-Gervais-et-S.-Protais, now in the Fine Art Museum, Rennes); (d, e) 'The Two Pantaloons' and the Louvre-Tuileries complex from the Tour de Nesle (Jacques Callot, c. 1730).

regime had to look to Italy. As we shall soon see, that was to provide the culmination of an exercise in urban order inherited from the past but symbolizing the renewed ordering of the kingdom.

A new start in the patronage of the fine arts was initiated in the practical way typical of the new regime: the most industrial medium, tapestry weaving, was favoured with the appointment to the 15th-century Gobelins factory of two Flemish masters commissioned in 1609 to produce a pastoral cycle. In contrast, the other media of graphic art

2.50c

2.50d

at which the medieval Franco-Flemish had excelled, illumination through stained glass and on vellum, were in eclipse. Printing was promoting engraving instead of the latter and developments beyond the Rhine were transmitted to Henri IV's seat through Lorraine, in particular by Jacques Bellange (1575–1616) and Jacques Callot (1592–1635) of Nancy who found that their burin could readily serve Church or state – and, in Callot's case, satire. For its part figurative glazing, stained or painted, had been in decline from its early Renaissance high at least since the work of Nicolas Pinaigrier in S.-Étienne-du-Mont and S.-Gervais-et-S.-Protais at the end of the old regime: it is hardly surprising that it ceded predominance in French religious graphic art to oil painting just when these last great Parisian Gothic churches were completed and new Classical ones were conceived (see page 309).**2.50**

2.50e

The shift of emphasis from stained glass to painted canvas in the religious field is apparent in the title of the treatise published in 1600 by Antoine de Laval: *Des peintures convenables aux Basiliques et Palais du Roi*. Beyond the decoration of secular spaces, especially festive ones, figurative painting must be subjected to the concept of propriety: the gravitas appropriate to the new regime prefers the examples of biblical and secular histories to the mythological fantasies elaborated by the followers of the School of Fontainebleau for the late Valois. Naturally, however, the regime of Henri IV – dubbed 'Vert Galant' - understandably remained committed to the idea that appropriateness of subject matter was relative to context: so too did numerous of his subjects who were decorating the galleries or salons of their châteaux at the time.

2.51a

›2.51 ECLECTICISM OF STYLE AND SUBJECT MATTER IN EARLY BOURBON FONTAINE-BLEAU: (a) Galerie de Diane (from c. 1601, record by Charles Percier, 1793, a decade or so before its destruction); (b) 'The Battle Between Tancred and Clorinda' (Ambroise Dubois, from the lost Cabinet de Clorinda, c. 1605).

2.51b

The taste for mythology was sustained by the crown in the first decade of the Bourbon century for the decoration of Fontainebleau's latest gallery, dedicated to Diane, together with rooms dedicated to Tasso's Clorinda and the rather more obscure Heliodorus's Theagenes. This was by the Fleming Ambroise Dubois (c. 1542–1614): the gallery ensemble is lost but his work on the Clorinda cabinet reveals a wide-ranging eclecticism informed by the wealth

2.52a

2.52b

›2.52 FONTAINEBLEAU, TRINITY CHAPEL,
1608–19: (a) altar wall, (b) vault.

Martin Fréminet, who designed the scheme and executed the paintings, spent a protracted period in Rome
where he associated himself with the circle of the Cava-
liere d'Arpino but is bolder in his architectural illusionism. Barthélemy Tremblay executed the plasterwork,
the design of which is rather more reminiscent of late
Buontalentesque Florence than early Baroque Rome.

of international engravings available in his native
Antwerp. In the same decade in the same château, the Trinity Chapel received the first great cycle of religious vault
paintings. This was by a home-grown artist, Martin
Fréminet (1567–1619), whose eclectic style evolved over the
last decade of the Mannerist century in Rome, Venice and
Turin. In the next generation, the promotion of French
painting to new eminence – furthered by the proliferation
of galleries in town and country houses – was largely due
to Flemings, above all to Rubens who commemorated
Henri IV and his queen for the gallery of her Luxembourg
Palace on unmatched scale, as those who persevere with
this exercise will ultimately see. **2.51, 2.52**

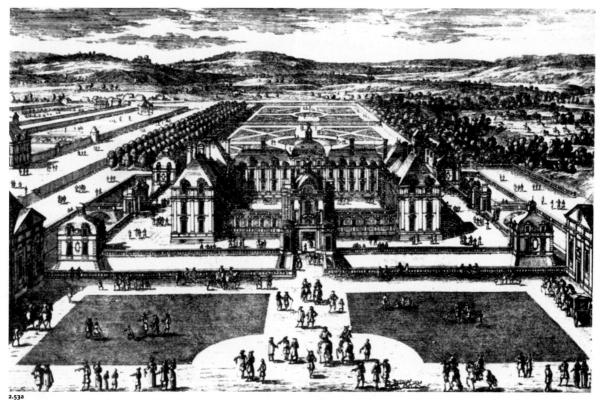

2.53a

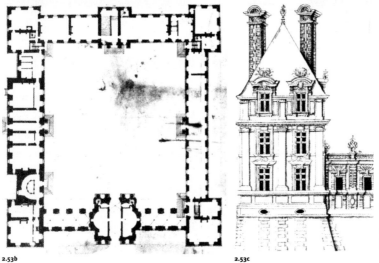

2.53b

2.53c

›**2.53 MONTCEAUX-EN-BRIE, CHÂTEAU:** (a) overview from the east, (b) plan, (c) detail of south-east pavillon and adjoining entrance screen bays.

Henri IV acquired the site in 1596 and destined the completed château for his mistress Gabrielle d'Estrées: she died in 1599 but work continued. Stylistic considerations – especially comparison with his work on the Tuileries – suggest that Jacques II Androuet du Cerceau was the architect. The articulation in general has something of the adventitious denseness of his father's pattern book – in particular, the rusticated Order of the entrance screen bears close comparison with variants for Charleval and the pavillon derives from Verneuil. The apartments are not as commodious as there but the foundations laid by de l'Orme probably inhibited the development of modern planning. The square parterres of Verneuil recur on the main axis here, terraced on less dramatically falling ground.

overview (engraved by Abraham Bosse after
Alessandro Francini, 1614).

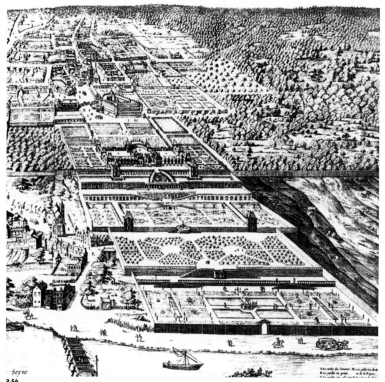

It is not known how far terracing had proceeded
after the construction of Philibert de l'Orme's Château-
Neuf. The perfection of the terraced garden in the Italian style, represented by Francini and Bosse, was
doubtless the responsibility of Étienne Dupérac who
knew the most modern gardens of Italy – as we have
noted – and had been appointed *architecte du roi* in
1595: translated from Anet, he collaborated with his old
colleague Mollet's son, Claude, who was by then 'premier jardinier de France'. The latter's reports imply that
work was underway well before the end of the century.
In 1600 Alessandro Francini (died 1648) came with the
new queen from Medici Florence to join his brother
Tomasso (1571–1651) who had arrived two years earlier: from a family of hydraulic engineers, their remit
seems to have run beyond advising on waterworks to
the devising of automata and the creation of grottoes.

There is no evidence that the scheme was ever completed as represented by the younger Francini (and
Bosse), with the lower fountain terrace copied from
that of the Villa Lante at Bagnaia: a mid-17th-century
plan matching a view engraved by Israël Silvestre
(1655) shows no such detail – and different planting on
the intermediate terraces. It will be noted that the early
17th-century conception incorporates *parterres de
broderie* in Mollet's sense of unities resulting from the
subdivision of large squares in place of the chequerboard accretion of small ones.

Henri IV may live on in a prolixity of paint but that was
at the behest of his widow, Marie de' Medici – and it takes
us beyond his era. Of the arts, the king himself preferred
architecture. As a palace builder he was preoccupied with
realizing the ambitions of his predecessors. He commissioned the revision of Philibert de l'Orme's abortive project for Catherine de' Medici's château at Montceaux-
en-Brie. He implemented a revised scheme for a great terraced garden before Philibert de l'Orme's Château-Neuf
at Saint-Germain-en-Laye – at least in main part. At
Fontainebleau, in addition to the decoration of the Trinity Chapel, he oversaw the development of an imposing
service court to the east of the Cour Ovale, before a new
triumphal entrance arch, and the modernization of the

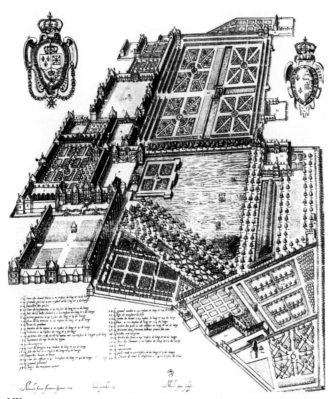

2.55a

2.55b

2.55c

›2.55 FONTAINEBLEAU, CHÂTEAU: (a) overview (Alessandro Francini, 1614, engraved by Israël Silvestre); (b) Cour Ovale, entrance arch (1602), (c) Cour des Offices, entrance arch (Rémy Collin, 1606).

The modernization of the gardens extended to imposing unity on the parterres. This emerges from Francini's somewhat exaggerated perspective in the two pairs of the eastern garden (at the top of the image) and the new island terrace garden projected in 1595 from the Cour de la Fontaine into the lake. The queen's garden (to the left) conforms less clearly to Mollet's definition of *parterre de broderie* than in a plan of 1600 where it is represented as a near square subdivided along major and minor axial lines – as in du Cerceau's Charleval.**2.48e**

The brick and stone mode, promoted by du Cerceau's *Livre d' architecture* for most of his domestic buildings (see pages 368f), is taken to an extreme by Collin in the new service court: the portal has been seen as a translation into those French terms of Bramante's Vatican Belvedere niche (Blunt, *Art and Architeture in France*); less remotely it may be seen as an astylar revision of du Cerceau's first Verneuil project portal. In contrast, the portal to the Cour Ovale, incorporating an arch of Primaticcio removed from the Cour du Cheval Blanc, is a sumptuous variation on its equivalent at Écouen.

2.56b

gardens. Above all he continued the schemes of the late queen mother at the Louvre, the Tuileries and the great gallery between them. Still prolix, if less bizarre, are the diverse ranges of that gallery and the smaller ones at right angles to each end of it, with which the names of Jacques II Androuet du Cerceau and Louis Métezeau are generally associated: the work at Montceaux is clearly related to the former.**2.53–2.56**

›**2.56 PARIS, LOUVRE-TUILERIES COM-PLEX:** (a) Grande Galerie, eastern bays attributed to Louis Métezeau (1560–1615); (b) Petite Galerie of the Louvre (from 1565 and 1595, as recorded in the mid-17th century by Israël Silvestre); (c) Petite Galerie of the Tuileries (Jacques II Androuet du Cerceau, 1608–10, as recorded in the mid-17th century by Jean Marot).

Identification of the architects of the Grande Galerie is obscure: Jacques II Androuet de Cerceau (son of the elder Jacques, brother of Jean Baptiste) is credited with the western half because he was working on the Petite Galerie extension to the Tuileries; Louis Métezeau is credited with the rest because he was working on an adjunct to the Petite Galerie of the Louvre.

The articulation of the Petite Galerie, attributed to Pierre Lescot, was taken over to the first five bays of the Grande Galerie (discrepancies may reflect changes subsequently made to the eastern façade of the former during its completion under Henri IV). Thereafter some twenty-nine bays extended west along the river to a

2.56c

2.56a

2.57a

The Grande Galerie amounted to an unprecedented exercise in urbanism: some 500 metres long, it was an extravagantly extended adjunct to a palace but, more than double the Strada Nuova in Genoa, it also defined the longest ordered promenade since the height of Roman antiquity. And the new regime undertook three other crucial exercises in urban development, at least two conceived by the late Valois. The 'square' or *place* – and open air – was introduced to Paris as the nucleus of order in urban

five-bay block and pavillon matching the Petite Galerie and its lateral extension. The long intermediate elevation incorporated a rusticated basement and panelled mezzanine, which together reached the same height as Lescot's arcades from a lower level, and a main floor of the same height as that of his upper gallery level. The Composite Order of pilasters, framing the windows between niches and supporting alternate triangular and segmental pediments, derive from the southern end of the Petite Galerie and define rhythmic bays translated from Lescot's Louvre court facades.

Beyond the central pavillon, the gallery continued at slightly greater length to the bizarre, four-storey Pavillon de Flore: the colossal Order applied throughout was carried over from Jacques II Androuet's Petite Galerie of the Tuileries – which, ironically, was adjacent to Jean Bullant's two-storey pavillon but seems to derive from the latter's northern court frontispiece at Écouen through Métezeau's work at the Hôtel d'Angoulême (Lamoignon).[2.47h] This western range was refaced to match the eastern one in the second half of the 19th century.

2.57b

> **2.57 PARIS, THE INCEPTION OF ORDERED DEVELOPMENT:** (a) the Seine upstream with the Grande Galerie du Louvre (left), the Pont Neuf and

development along the lines drawn in Flanders and several parts of Italy. However, the aggregation of similar houses, characteristic of the former, was revised without reference either to Italy or the antique in imposing uniformity of style – the simple brick and stone style promoted by the elder du Cerceau in his practical domestic designs. Like the salutary development of the Hôpital S.-Louis to isolate contagious diseases beyond the city walls, all were apparently directed by the king himself – as he directed the restitution of order throughout the fractured kingdom. The example was quickly followed by the founders of new towns in the provinces: first the duc de Nevers who called Clément Métezeau (1581–1652), brother of the architect of the Parisian model, to work for him at Charleville.**2.57, 2.58**

2.57c

Place Dauphine right centre (engraved by Israël Silvestre, 1650); (b) overview with the Tuileries foreground from the 'Plan Hoiamis' (1619); (c) overview from the 'Plan Turgot' (1739) with (1) the Pont Neuf and Place Dauphine, (2, 3) Rue Saint-Denis and Rue Saint-Martin leading south to the overbuilt Ponts au Change and Notre-Dame, (4) Place Royale (des Vosges); (d) Pont-Neuf and Place Dauphine, exterior and interior (1607); (e, f) Place Royale (from 1605), overview (1612, engraved by C. Chastillon) and detail of north range; (g) Place de France, overview (engraved by Chastillon).

Beside the work on the Île de la Cité, the Île Saint-Louis (Notre Dame) was subjected to regular development at the instigation of the entrepreneur of Christophe Marie whose name attaches to the new bridge providing access to it. Similarly, development spread to the Faubourg Saint-Germain as well as the Marais.

In his ideal scheme for the Tuileries (*PEBF*, 1579), du Cerceau presents the garden as an irregular grid (of parterres and *bosquets*) aligned with the salient parts of the palace but separated from it by a road and a wall: that is repeated in the topographical map of Quesnel, 1609 – with the central axis newly emphasized – but Hoiamis in 1619 improbably dislocates the axes. How far Catherine de' Medici had progressed in implementing the plans before she abandoned the site is indetermi-

Bourbon inception: urbanism and landscape

First, to relieve pressure on the twin north–south axial arteries – the Rue Saint-Martin and the Rue Saint-Denis – and link the Faubourg Saint-Germain with the north bank, a regular new thoroughfare – the Rue Dauphine – was projected to join a new bridge over the Seine – the Pont Neuf – and prompt development on the left bank. The bridge had been projected in 1578, with houses and shops flanking the carriageway in accordance with the medieval norm represented further upstream, but left incomplete during the civil strife of Henri III's unfortunate reign. Begun in 1598 on a revised project without marginal building, the bridge cut through the western tip of

2.57d

the Île de la Cité whose configuration invited the development of the triangular Place Dauphine with a statue of Henri IV at the apex. The latter (destroyed in 1794) was commissioned in 1604 from the studio of Giambologna in Florence: the master's partner, the Fleming Pierre Francqueville (Pietro Francavilla), was called to France to produce the attendant figures and supervise the erection of the monument – which was completed only in 1614.

The square Place Royale, in the eastern sector of the city, was originally conceived by Catherine de' Medici to displace the royal residence and tournament ground, the Hôtel des Tournelles, where her husband had been killed: it was designed to govern the development of drained marshland to its south – the Marais to which the affluent were encouraged to resort. The third scheme, designed as the focus of radial development to the northeast but largely unrealized, was the semi-circular Place de France (150 metres in diameter). The civic buildings projected to define it were turreted like the corps de logis of an earlier Renaissance château and they had covered shopping galleries to the ground floor, as in the various medieval and Renaissance Italian precedents derived from the antique Classical forum. This was a feature of the Place Royale too: the perimeter was designed by

nate: planting, underway from 1566, accelerated early in the next decade with numerous fruit trees; Bernard Palissy had forged a grotto from terracotta in an equally indeterminate place. A gardener named Pierre Le Nôtre, already present in the 1570s, was retained by Henri IV in 1594 to restore the parterres nearest the palace (his son Jean appears in the records from 1618 and his son André from 1637). A garden was projected for the eastern side of the palace in 1598 and consigned to Claude Mollet: he was responsible for the development of *parterres de broderies* there and in the zones adjacent to the palace

2.57e

2.57f

2.57g

on the western side from 1608 (his sons André and Claude II appear in 1630 and 1634). At the king's behest, a terrace was constructed along the northern edge of the garden and planted with white mulberries to feed the silk industry.

›**2.58 CHARLEVILLE,** from 1606: (a) overview (as recorded by Caspar Merian, *Topographia Galliae*, 1655); (b) Grand Place, northern range.

Old towns were necessarily slow to follow the metropolitan lead: not so the founders of new towns. Before his untimely death, Henri IV was commemorated by his great minister Sully in the foundation of Henrichemont (1608) and even that was preceded by Charleville which was named for Charles de Gonzague, duc de Nevers, who conceived it as the capital of his sovereign principality of Arches.

the royal architects led by Louis Métezeau, with four-bay houses of two main storeys supported by arcades and surmounted by attics in high roofs. Only the higher central Pavillons du Roi and de la Reine on the main east–west axis were constructed at official expense: the other plots were let on condition that their private proprietors built to the common standard. This conformed to the modest prescriptions of du Cerceau's *Livre d' architecture*: the articulation of the two storeys over the stone arcading, like those of the Place Dauphine which closely resembles a scheme published in *PEBF*, was restricted to stone quoins at the salient points of their structures and the frames of large windows offset from rendered or unrendered brick infill. And these opened the inhabitants to advantages of light and air previously accorded only to those grand enough to enjoy a commodious forecourt.

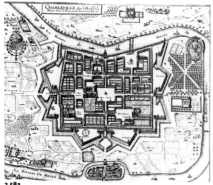

2.58a

2.58b

To achieve the height of the Gothic nave (conceived in the 13th century but reaching its definitive form in the late-15th century), the unknown architect superimposed the rhythmic bays with which Louis Métezeau had attempted to vary his long gallery at the Louvre – after Lescot but with alternate triangular and semicircular pediments. The tenuous relationship between this richly embellished frontispiece and the rest of the relatively plain façade is not assisted by the minor Italianate scrolls nor the medieval pitch of the gable.

The example set by Henri IV's regime in the revived Valois urban projects moderated all but the grandest domestic practice. Decorative exuberance persisted in the public sphere but the degree to which ornament overwhelmed architecture can be overstated in reference to actual building – as distinct from projects produced for engraving or

>2.60 VERSAILLES, HUNTING LODGE OF
LOUIS XIII: overview with later garden (modest
house of 1624 replaced from 1631).

The considerable estate of the Gondi family, including Trianon, had been added to the king's modest original acquisition by 1631: this permitted the laying out of
an extensive park and prompted the replacement of the
original shooting box. Designed by Philibert Le Roy, the
form of the new house was traditional: a square court
entered through a low screen opposite the principal
corps de logis. The style was modest: apart from the
stone quoins, the brick walls are relieved only with
medallions framing busts of emperors.

the wilder excesses of provincial masons. The major
Parisian ecclesiastical exercise of Henri's reign for
instance, the façade of S.-Étienne-du-Mont, is far from
austere but its superimposed Orders are not quite eclipsed
by the reliefs.**2.59**

The reclusive Louis XIII was not a great builder on his
own account. The vast expansion of the Louvre was undertaken in his name, as we shall see, but he preferred to live
at Saint-Germain-en-Laye. He had been a minor for most
of the first decade of his reign but after he attained
his majority he was personally responsible only for the
hunting lodge at Versailles which he began c. 1624.**2.60**

However, the stability of his regime – largely unshaken even by the shocking assassination of the progenitor in 1610 – encouraged extensive building throughout France to make up for time lost in the troubles of the late-Valois era. Naturally the magnates of his father's preference were at the forefront of patronage but, new or old, the nobility built with *éclat* in styles old, new and mixed.

The restrained articulation of Henri IV's squares – and the more modest prescriptions of du Cerceau's *Livre d'architecture* – were appreciated by both hôtel and château builders. Inevitably, however, they covered the whole range of approaches from astylar rustication or supercharged sculptural relief to Mannerist variants on High Renaissance themes drawn from de l'Orme or Lescot – via Métezeau – and Mannerist ones drawn from Bullant or the older du Cerceau. In the main, of course, the objective was to discipline medieval diversity, in particular to Classicize the motifs of feudal fortitude. The former was not always fully realized – or even understood – but many châteaux were well endowed with variants of the triumphal arch – usually taking their departure from Serlio's rusticated models – as the major occasion for architectural display in place of the twin-towered symbol of past power.

2.61

›**2.61 TOULOUSE, HÔTEL DE CLARY** (or 'de Pierre' due to its unusual construction of stone in a largely brick environment), c. 1615.

›**2.62 ROSNY (YVELINES), CHÂTEAU,** from 1595: entrance front.

The *domaine*, with the remains of its feudal castle destroyed in the Hundred Years' War, was acquired in 1529 by the progenitors of Henri IV's great minister, Maximilien de Béthune, duc de Sully. His new work followed the quadrangular plan of the old but it ceased on the death of Henri IV: the principal corps de logis, with its twin pavillons, was complete but not the projected wings. The style is that associated with the urban exercises executed by Sully for Henri IV: stone quoins, *chaînes* and window frames in contrast to pink rendered brick walls; slate roofs, steeply pitched to different degrees over the two types of mass.

›**2.63 GROSBOIS (VAL-DE-MARNE), CHÂTEAU,** late-16th–early 17th century: entrance front.

Begun c. 1580 by Raoul Moreau (a state treasurer) and continued by his son-in-law Nicolas de Harlay: the main corps de logis, with the unusual semi-circular

2.62

2.63

recession in its façade, seems to date from early in the 17th century – possibly after Rémy Collin had built the great niched portico to his service court at Fontaine-bleau. Bought by Charles de Valois, duc d'Angoulême (natural son of Charles IX), it was amplified with corner pavillons and the arcaded wings of the open court from 1615. Each mass has its distinct roof and variety of elevation relies solely on the contrast between brick and stone: stone for the quoins, brick for the window frames and plastered brick infill – instead of the revealed brick infill and white quoins of Rosny.

›2.64 SAINT-LOUP-SUR-THOUET, CHÂTEAU, begun before 1610: entrance front.

The work was begun by Gilbert Gouffier, duc de Roannais, under Henri IV and completed early in the next reign by his son, Louis XIII. Brick cedes to plastered rubble but stone is retained for the quoins, string-courses and window frames. The novelty for a château of this scale remote from the metropolis was the 'H' plan which – inevitably – is supposed to pay homage to the king. The narrow central pavillon, housing the staircase, is richly embellished with a Mannerist variety of pediments but is less charged on the other side.

Still essentially quadrangular in form, representative examples of the colouristic use of materials in a largely astylar context include the châteaux of Rosny (from 1595) and Grosbois with its incurved façade (1616).**2.62, 2.63** Saint-Loup-sur-Thouet (c. 1610, Deux-Sèvres) is similarly conservative in its brick and stone articulation, except for the centre, but it is innovative in dispensing with wings.**2.64**

2.64

2.65a

2.65b

›**2.65 VIZILLE, CHÂTEAU,** from 1611: (a) general view from the park, (b) main portal with the equestrian statue of the proprietor, Constable François de Bonne, duc de Lesdiguières (Jacob Richier de Saint-Mihiel).

A feudal stronghold commanding a route through the Alps, founded in the 9th century, Vizille was later a seat of the rulers of Dauphine whose *domaine* passed to France on the extinction of their line in 1349. Of perennial strategic importance, it was much contested in the Wars of Religion, ending in Catholic hands. However, as part of his settlement on his accession, Henri IV ceded it in 1593 to one of his principal Protestant supporters in arms, François de Bonne, with the office of lieutenant general in Dauphine and the title of duc de Lesdiguières. Except for one tower protecting the entrance, he replaced the feudal castle from 1611–20. Of the main court, with its entrance screen and triumphal arch, only the right wing survived a fire in the 19th century.

›**2.66 EFFIAT (PUY-DE-DÔME), CHÂTEAU,** c. 1625: garden front.

Gilbert Cöffier (treasurer of France) acquired the estate in 1557 and commissioned the moated quadrilat-

2.66

Vizille (Isère), entered through a triumphal arch, offers variation on the comprehensively rusticated theme favoured by warriors.[2.65] The colossal Order is deployed variously for the Château d'Effiat (Puy-de-Dôme) and, exceptionally, the Hôtel de Clary in Toulouse.[2.66, 2.61] On the other hand, Classicizing the medieval, through the interpolation of superimposed Order in the context of superficial ornament, was rife but nowhere more bizarre than at Brissac.[2.67]

eral château. His grandson Antoine (superintendant of finances, governor of the Auvergne, marshall of France, etc. under Louis XIII) completed the wings, added the triumphal entrance arch and embellished the principal corps de logis in a manner befitting his conception of his state from 1625, particularly with the colossal Order of doubled Doric pilasters.

›2.67 BRISSAC (MAINE-ET-LOIRE), CHÂTEAU: corps de logis and pavillon (incompletely inserted into a medieval complex from 1606).

The cylindrical corner towers survive from the château-fort built for Pierre de Brézé, who held a superior position in the administration under both Charles VIII and Louis XI in the second half of the 15th century – their relationship with those of the royal castle at Langeais is close (AIC4, page 576). The estate was acquired in 1502 by René de Cossé, one of the ministers of Charles VIII and Louis XII, and descended to Charles de Cossé, governor of Paris, who surrendered the city to Henri IV and was subsequently elevated to the rank of duke. He initiated the Classicizing transformation of the medieval quadrangular structure in 1606 but completed little more than half of the projected corps de logis: the central pavillon, clashing with the neighbouring cylindrical tower, encloses the principal staircase, but the parallel ramps arrive at landings lit by single great arched windows under a variety of broken pediments and the side bays are doubled. The next generation added a rectangular pavillon on the other side of the projected court but did not succeed in uniting it with the earlier work.

2.67

SALOMON DE BROSSE

Out of the melée of competing styles – but on the ground laid by Henri IV's sensible regime – one great architect emerged with a crucial revision of the High Renaissance past. In the second decade of the century – a decade before Louis XIII began his retreat at Versailles – Salomon de Brosse (early 1570s–1626) reasserted Classical values though he was the grandson of Jacques Androuet I du Cerceau with whom the promotion of French decorative Mannerism is usually associated. He started with the château disposition of his teachers and emulated their planning. However, progressive coherence in massing, clarity of volume, purity of line, control of detail and coordination of articulation may be traced through his series of monumental works including the near-contemporary châteaux of Blérancourt and Coulommiers (from c. 1612/13), the Luxembourg Palace in Paris (1615) and the Palace of Justice at Rennes (1618). The major contemporary Parisian ecclesiastical exercise, the face of S.-Gervais-et-S.-Protais, is comparable in the latter respect.**2.68–2.73**

2.68a

›**2.68 COULOMMIERS, CHÂTEAU** (from 1613): (a) plan, (b) *guérite* (sentry box), (c) entrance front (engraved by Marot), (d, e) section through court showing façade of principal corps de logis and perspective view from the south (anonymous 17th-century drawings; Paris, National Library).

De Brosse was commissioned by Catherine de Gonzague, widow of Henri d'Orléans, duc de Longueville, who had died in 1599. The plan is related to the first scheme for the château of Verneuil with its curved central staircase and projecting side pavilions – though here they are less assertive, especially on the south side where the gallery is doubled with rooms *en enfilade*. The roof elevation is varied in response to the diversity of the massing in the usual French manner: its base line, sustained throughout all three main wings, is punctuated with dormers and the curved pediments of central pavilions inspired by those of the Louvre. The building was of brick and stone. The outer façades and entrance rotunda were to have been rusticated on each level: compared with earlier-17th-century records, Marot seems to have refined these under the influence of the later Luxembourg Palace and left little impression of brickwork. The court fronts, with quadrant arcades linking the central block to the side wings and columns superimposed throughout rather than deployed for selective emphasis in the manner of Lescot, were to have been embellished with sculpture in excess of de Brosse's practice elsewhere. The sculptural programme was not fully realized and the

2.68b

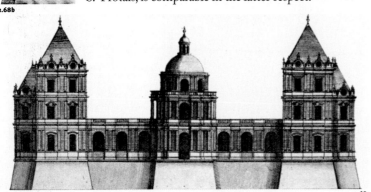

2.68c

Classicism reasserted

De Brosse's debt to his grandfather, Jacques Androuet du Cerceau the elder, is apparent in his initial approach to massing at Coulommiers and in his internal planning, with the staircase in the centre of the principal corps de logis, on axis with the entrance pavilion, separating the principal reception

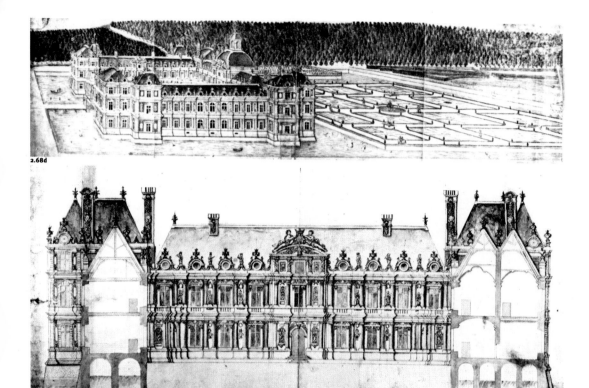

2.68d

2.68e

entrance pavillon had not been built on the death of the
patroness in 1629. Finished with modifications by
François Mansart, including a balustrade closing the
court between sentry boxes, the château passed
through the female line to the duc de Luynes who had it
demolished in 1737.

rooms and an apartment on each floor of the pavillons which invariably project from the corners. The square domes of Verneuil reappear at Blérancourt but, more consistent in height, de Brosse's roofs avoid asserting the
parts at the expense of the coherence of the whole. The discretion of the
main block, complete at Blérancourt in the suppression of extended side
wings, is indebted to Serlio and de l'Orme – the latter's Château-Neuf at
Saint-Germain-en-Laye providing the most immediate precedent. At
Rennes even greater coherence is indebted to Serlio and Primaticcio – the
latter's Aile de la Belle Cheminée at Fontainebleau offering instructive comparison.

Uncharacteristic of his subsequent development, de Brosse's debt to
his grandfather is even apparent in the rich embellishment of Coulommiers: the more bizarre reaches of detail are avoided and the High Renaissance superimposition of the Orders prevails but, significantly, Lescot's

sage gradation of the ordonnance from pilaster to columns in response to the projection of the mass is not respected. This was not the case at Blérancourt or the Luxembourg Palace. Opposing the anti-architectonic obsession with surface detail, moreover, the lucidity of his progressive ordonnance is, of course, enhanced by his restrained use of sculpture: contrary to the wilder excesses of his grandfather's burin, typically he tended to draw his effects solely from the Orders as articulating agents and the frames of doors and windows.

2.69a

2.69b

›**2.69 BLÉRANCOURT, CHÂTEAU** (from 1512): (a) outer entrance arch, (b) inner entrance arch, screen and pavillons from the south-east (with roofs as replaced after 1652), (c) reconstruction (after P. Smith), (d) north front (simplified mid-17th-century record engraved by Israël Silvestre), (e) central frontispiece details (anonymous 17th-century drawings; Paris, National Library).

Louis Potier, who rose from the bourgeoisie to be secretary of state under both Henri III and Henri IV, bought the estate in 1595 and gave it to his second son Bernard in 1600 on his marriage to Charlotte de Vieux-Pont, confidante of Marie de' Medici. Early in 1612 work was commissioned on the château from the master-mason Charles du Ry, de Brosse's principal collaborator in his major works, but the site seems already to have been active.

A late site plan but no floor plan survives. The free-standing H-shaped block occupied the centre of a moated rectangular terrace reached across a bridge from a square outer court: triumphal arches celebrated entrance to both zones. The corner pavillons of the great platform, if not the triumphal entrance arch, recall those of the Montceaux scheme associated with the du Cerceau circle.

2.69c

The French precedents for dispensing with wings – or, rather, drawing them into the main body of the building as massive pavillons – are inexact: François I's Château de Madrid is the earliest, and most remote, Henri II's Château-Neuf at Saint-Germain-en-Laye the nearest. The latter is of particular relevance in so far as it seems to follows an exercise of Serlio's inspired by the reconstruction of the remains of the antique villa at Poggio Reale (Book III, folio 72, Peake ed. 1611): de Brosse would have known de l'Orme's work, of course, but probably returned to the Serlian source which, as we have noted, possibly also informed the design of Ancy (see pages 316f). Du Cerceau's *Livre d'architecture* also offers various relevant ideas on the design of compact country houses.

2.69d

The material was stone throughout. Apart from the surviving fagments of the ground floor, guidance in ameliorating Silvestre is provided by anonymous drawings detailing the superimposed Orders articulating the central pavillon: Lescot's Louvre is the model but the standard sequence of Doric and Ionic is preferred to the more sumptuous Corinthian and Composite favoured for the expression or royal apotheosis. Beyond du Cerceau, a source of inspiration for the entrance arches – close indeed for the inner one – is to be found in Vignola's Porte di Michell Angelo and the windows of the flanking pavillons may also be seen as Michelangelesque.[1.32d,e]

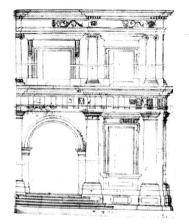 

2.69e

2.70a

2.70b

›2.70 PARIS, LUXEMBOURG PALACE, from 1615: (a) entrance screen and pavillon, (b) court, (c–e) sections and plan, (f) garden front, (g, h) garden plan and view of Medici fountain.

The widowed queen seems to have conceived the idea of building herself a palace: she bought the Hôtel Luxembourg in the Rue de Vaugirard in 1611 and later that year told her aunt, the grand duchess of Tuscany, that she wished to build on the model of the Pitti palace. She sent Louis Métezeau to Florence to study the latter but began building to de Brosse's plans, not modelled on the Pitti, in 1615. Work slowed during her exile in Blois from 1617–20 (when she was in revolt against her son) but accelerated from 1623. When the queen left France definitively in 1631, work was substantially complete: the interiors on the west side of the building were finished, including the Rubens gallery (1625) and the royal apartment in the south-west pavillon: these have been changed and much of the rest was never completed. The original garden front, with arcaded terrace flanking the central chapel pavillon, was lost when the building was doubled on that side to accommodate the Senate in the 19th century. Unfortunately too, the late addition of dormers breaks the base line of roofs.

To form her garden, the patroness continued to

The difference between decorative whimsy and architectural imagination is nowhere better illustrated than in the comparison between the entrance pavillons of Verneuil and the Luxembourg. Nevertheless, the massing of the latter complex as a whole still derives from the French tradition of the screened quadrangle as amplified by its author's grandfather: only the pervasive rustication of wall and Order responded to the queen-mother's desire to emulate the Pitti – but with rather more moderation than Ammannati is celebrated for displaying in the strong Florentine light. Rather than decorative virtuosity, any Mannerism in de Brosse's work elsewhere tends to promote an Italianate reversal of the conventions of articulation, as in the triumphal arches at Blérancourt and their variant, the so-called Medici fountain in the Luxembourg garden.

2.70c

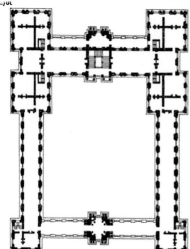

2.70d

2.70e

expand her holdings until 1627: longitudinal extension had been blocked by a Carthusian monastery to the south but there was considerable scope for lateral extension. Coincidentally, thus, the configuration of the site was not unlike that of the Boboli gardens of her Florentine home which she wished to emulate. She had the royal gardener, Jacques Boyceau, reproduce the main lines of its gardens – notably the amphitheatrical parterre in front of the palace and the extended axis to Cythera but not the evocation of that island or, indeed, the rest of the Boboli's Olympian denizens. And the planting is specifically French. The parterres, no longer subdivided on geometrical lines, are treated to wholly

2.70f

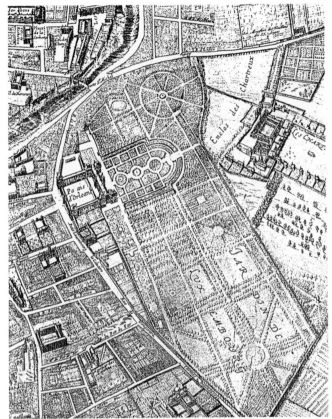

2.70g

2.70h

unified, lacelike patterns for the first time – lending a new dimension to the term broderie. That development is sometimes credited to Boyceau: he was the first to illustrate such designs in his important *Traité du Jardinage* (1638) but the illustrations may have been prepared by Claude II Mollet – whose father is credited with the original conception of the parterre de broderie, as we have seen. Tommaso Francini was responsible for the waterworks but not for the so-called Medici fountain which, converted only in the 19th century, was conceived as a grotto. Distantly indebted to Buontalenti's Boboli masterpiece, the latter was built from 1623 probably in collaboration between de Brosse and Alessandro Francini who published similar designs in his *Livre d'architecture* (1631).

›2.71 RENNES, PALAIS DE JUSTICE (formerly Palais du Parlement), 1618: (a) general view, (b) original state with external staircase.

De Brosse was called to Rennes in August 1618 to review the plans of the local architect Germain Gaultier who had been retained for the job the previous year: a description, but not the drawings, of Gaultier's approved scheme survives with copies of de Brosse's definitive plan. The general layout of the latter is consistent with the former except that the perimeter is square rather than oblong: the revisions, effected in little more than a week, were principally to the design of the main south front and the ordonnance of the great hall. De Brosse returned to Paris before the end of the month. The approved plans were consigned to Gaultier for execution: he occasionally went to Paris to consult the oracle until he was killed on site early in 1624. Having reached first-floor level in the main by then, construction was not complete until 1655: in general, it followed the 1618 plan but the roofs of the north-east and north-west corner pavillons were raised. The external staircase and platform were removed after 1726 and the height of the basement unfortunately enhanced.

The galleried court seems to have been Gaultier's idea. The square perimeter with inset terrace seems to have resulted from de Brosse's attention to the main façade: in general, the inspiration may have been one of several plans by Serlio with a portico in antis; in particular, an external staircase serving a terrace between projecting pavillons may be seen as a variation on the

2.71a

scheme of Primaticcio's Aile de la Belle Cheminée at
Fontainebleau. This part of the building was the last to
be completed above first-floor level: it was to follow the
original scheme in accordance with a directive of 1647
and in framing the central portal with columns, where
the 1618 plan continues the austere Order of coupled
pilasters, it conforms to earlier descriptions of the project which, in turn, match de Brosse's practice elsewhere. The main hall as built differs substantially in
plan, and therefore elevation of course, from the project of 1618.

2.71b

›2.72 PARIS, PALAIS DE JUSTICE: Salle des
Pas Perdu (early 19th-century engraving).

In 1618 the great hall of the Palais de Justice on the
Île de la Cité in Paris – the Salle des Pas Perdu – was
destroyed by fire: de Brosse was awarded the rebuilding contract while on his way to Rennes. Work was
finally completed in 1624. De Brosse's walls survived
the fires of 1776 and 1871 in the main and his grave
Doric ordonnance – with a central arcade in the typical
medieval manner – may be taken as admirable compensation for the absence of its equivalent at Rennes.

2.72

›2.73 PARIS, S.-GERVAIS-ET-S.-PROTAIS: façade (founded 1616, constructed from 1621).

›2.74 VERNEUIL: parish church, north porch (undated, attributed to Salomon de Brosse).

2.73

2.74

2.75a

**›2.75 PARIS, HÔTELS OF THE EARLY BOUR-
BON ERA:** (a) Soissons, porte-cochère (drawing
attributed to de Brosse's colaborator Charles du Ry
associated with a project of Salomon de Brosse c.
1606); (b–d) Sully (from 1624, originally Gallet) plan,
street and court elevations, orangery; (e) Alméras, portal (from c. 1611); (f) Chalôns-Luxembourg, portal (from
c. 1625); (g) Duret de Chevry, detail of court façade
(from 1618, much expanded).

The portal of the Hôtel de Soissons was described
by a near contemporary (H. Sauval, *Histoire et
recherches des antiquités de la ville de Paris*) as the
first of its grandeur – the veritable prototype for a
henceforth indispensable feature – derived from that of
the Farnese palace at Caprarola. The identification of
the drawing with the Soissons project is confirmed by
the ciphers on the jambs. Variations on the theme of
the rusticated portal recurred in work associated with
de Brosse on the Hôtel Bénigne Bernard (lost but
recorded by Le Muet, *Le Vignole de France*, plate
XXXVII) and in the parish church at Verneuil.

The anonymous Hôtel d'Alméras, built on the proceeds of controlling the Post, is essentially conserva-

The main ecclesiastical work traditionally attributed to de
Brosse, the façade of S.-Gervais-et-S.-Protais in Paris, is
associated in the accounts only with Clément Métezeau –
but not necessarily beyond an executive role. Clearly
indebted to de l'Orme's Anet frontispiece, it stands as the
consummate illustration of the application of uncompromising French High Renaissance principles to the solution of the problem of providing a Classical front to an
essentially Gothic form of church.[2.74]

De Brosse's contribution to the development of the
Parisian hôtel is limited, at least in so far as the accidents
of survival testify. It must have been significant at a time
of vigorous demand for the renovation of old houses and
for new houses in the newly developing districts, especially
by patrons newly emergent from the *haute bourgeoisie*. He
is known to have extended existing houses for several
members of the *noblesse de robe*. An early commission came
from Pierre Forget de Fresnes, one of Henri IV's secre-
taries of state and *intendant des bâtiments du roi*: work,
beginning in 1608, incorporated an early example of a
porte-cochère – a portal large enough for coaches to enter
the courtyard – but the complex has disappeared. The
motif was developed for the Comte de Soissons, who had
bought Catherine de' Medici's Hôtel de la Reine and
called on de Brosse for its modification: the superb drawing of the portal is all that survives of the scheme.[2.75a]
There are also records of his work on the Hôtel de Bouil-
lon (formerly Dauphin), but most of it disappeared later
in the century at the behest of another new owner, the duc
de Liancourt – as we shall see.

Towards the end of his life, de Brosse's career was
under judicial review and the younger du Cerceaux were
still leaders of their profession: Jean Baptiste's son Jean
(c. 1585–1649), in particular, responded spectacularly in
1624 to the commission from the financier Mesme Gallet

2.75b

2.75c

tive in its retention of brick and stone but its portal – the definitive example of the 'tabernacle' type – is a close follower of de Brosse's innovation in its breadth. The Hôtel de Chalôns-Luxembourg (dating from the mid-1620s but obscured behind a later multi-storey building) is a variant whose porte-cochère well represents the latest phase of contained ornamentalism: as on the pavillon of Coulommiers and, indeed, around the cartouche of the Soissons portal, stylized floral ornament or the curled leather of strapwork have ceded to flayed hide – rather than to the fleshy abstraction of the Florentine arch-Mannerist Buontalenti.

Jacques I Androuet du Cerceau's formula for the noble town house is admirably represented by his grandson Jean's work for Gallet (then duc de Sully), the finest surviving representative of his dynasty's achievement. Like Jacques II's earlier Hôtel de Mayenne (1605), and the much earlier Hôtel de Ligneris (Carnavalet), the form is conservative: ultimately descending from Serlio's Grande Ferrare at Fontainebleau, the quadrangle is defined by an entrance screen between pavillons linked by side wings to the main corps de logis – which retains a central staircase like Lescot's original project for the Louvre. Beyond a garden, the almost equally splendid orangery (with subsidiary access from the Place Royale) is also attributed to Jean du Cerceau.

2.75d

2.75e

2.75f

2.75g

for a hôtel in the Rue Saint-Antoine which was bought by Henri IV's great minister, the duc de Sully, ten years later. The exuberant sculptural detail is bold but it hardly represents licentiousness in either case despite the enhanced stone revetment: the portal, a natural feature of display, is a Classical exercise of marked restraint in comparison with those of the anonymous Hôtels d'Alméras (1611) or Chalôns-Luxembourg (from the mid-1620s) – for example.**2.75b–f**

Louis Savot (c. 1579–1640) and Pierre Le Muet (1591–1669), near contemporaries respectively of de Brosse and Jean du Cerceau, both furthered the genre. Savot's main contribution was a practical building manual, his *L'Architecture Françoise des bastimens particuliers* (1624). Le Muet was active as theorist and practitioner. In his *Maniere de bien bastir pour toutes sortes de personnes* (1623 and 1647), reprising the format of du Cerceau's *Livre d'architecture*, he takes categorization in terms of social status even further, offering guidance to lowly proprietors whose resources did not run to retaining an architect. In his practices he may have had a broad range but he illustrates the grander houses in the expanded edition of his work which appeared in 1647. By then he had tamed exuberance in works like the Hôtel de l'Aigle but in his earlier hôtels d'Avaux and d'Assy he showed himself to be far less fastidious than de Brosse – like most of his contemporaries in the wealth of town houses they constructed in the Marais. Jean Thiriot's assertively rusticated, trophy-embellished Hôtel Duret de Chevry (1635) is a particularly prominent example owing to its later expansion for Cardinal Mazarin and incorporation in the complex of the Bibliothèque Nationale.**2.75g**

The tide of French ornament had turned in all but the grandest ranks of urban housing but the florid style was perennially popular for civic works – whose bourgeois

›**2.76 LA ROCHELLE, HÔTEL DE VILLE:** façade of 1606 to a medieval and early Renaissance complex.

›**2.77 RHEIMS, HÔTEL DE VILLE:** entrance pavillon (1636, attributed to Jean Bonhomme, comprehensively reconstructed after damage in World War I).

The Halle Échevinale of 1593 was the victim of 19th-century urban development. Like the early 17th-century buildings on the great squares of Antwerp or Brussels, the opulent embellishment of the Bourse – which incorporates twenty-four houses around a court – belongs to the conservative world of the Spanish Netherlands: the city was not annexed by France until 1668.

builders were always in assertive competition with their lords spiritual and temporal. In stark contrast with de Brosse's building for the Parliament of Brittany at Rennes (later the Palais de Justice), the hôtels de villes at La Rochelle and Rheims are prominent examples from a decade earlier and later respectively.**2.76, 2.77** In the north, the florid style was particularly popular in the orbit of Flanders: Lille offers – or offered – outstanding examples ranging from the late-16th to the mid-17th century but the region was not yet France.**2.78**

2.78

3.21

3 ORBIT OF EMPIRE

Bella gerant alii, tu felix Austria nube!

3.1a–e

1 SEMINAL NETHERLANDERS

The Renaissance was announced in the north through the medium of the triumphal arch, in particular the temporary sets erected in 1515 to mark the ceremonial entry route of Duke Charles of Habsburg – soon to be Emperor Charles V – into the major towns of his Burgundian domain. However, most of these were diffident in the application of Classical decorative detail to essentially medieval forms. Other such exercises followed with increasing sophistication motivated by the importation of engravings after the works of the Italian High Renaissance masters, Raphael and his circle in particular, by itinerant Italians and especially, as usual, by the advent of Serlio's books. The most spectacular manifestation was the mid-century ceremonial entry into Antwerp of the Habsburg heir, the future Philip II for whom the north-western pole of the Empire had been detached and ceded to Spain's extensive imperium.**3.1**

›3.1 IMPERIAL ENTRIES TO FLEMISH DOMAINS: (a–e) Charles, duke of Burgundy and king of Spain, into Bruges (1515), reception at the bridge and the city's main monuments, arches in transition from medieval to proto-Renaissance; (f–k) Philip of Spain and his father, Emperor Charles V, into Antwerp (1549), title and end pages, variations on commemorative, presentational and triumphal arches including those of the English and the Spanish (Pieter Coecke van Aelst, *Le Triomphe d' Anvers faict en la susception du Prince Philips, Prince d' Espaigne*).

Doubt subsists about the allocation of credit to the various artists involved in creating the ephemeral, but highly influential, structures for the 1549 entry: Coecke himself presumably produced the title page for his publication but Cornelis Floris is usually thought to have played the major role, assisted by Hans Vredeman de Vries. On these publicists and their works, see below.

3.1f–k

3.2

>**3.2 BRUGES, HEILIG-BLOEDKAPEL** (Chapel of the Holy Blood): façade.

The two-storey chapel enshrines a phial believed to contain a drop of Christ's blood (retrieved from Palestine by the crusader Dietrich of Alsace in 1149). The Romanesque lower chapel survives from the original scheme: the upper chapel is a late-Gothic exercise of 1480. The hybrid Flamboyant façade, with its proto-Renaissance columns, was completed between 1529 and 1534.

>**3.3 LIÈGE, PALACE OF THE PRINCE-BISHOPS,** medieval foundation rebuilt from 1526, extended with southern range from 1734 (now the seat of Walloon administration and law courts): (a) 17th-century overview of the original double-courtyard scheme, (b) first court, north-east corner.

The patron of the rebuilding exercise was Erard de la Marck (prince-bishop 1508–38); the architect was Arnold van Mulckens (1472–1538). The double-court scheme, with corner towers and steeply pitched slate roofs, is typical of medieval institutional and grand secular buildings – though not invariably with the regular geometry of Classical order. Transition from Gothic to Renaissance in style is apparent in the first court only in the ground-floor colonnade – but the baluster columns are entirely uncanonical.

In permanent building, as in ephemeral sets, the Renaissance arrived in Flanders, as in France, as ornament applied to Flamboyant structures. The most flagrant ecclesiastical example is the façade of the Chapel of the Holy Blood in Bruges from the beginning of the process.**3.2** More restrained, the most prominent early secular examples include the Hof van Busleyden, the Hof van Savoye of Margaret of Austria (1507, now the Gerechtshof) in Mechelen, and the Palace of the Prince-Bishops of Liège, in all of which the familiar late-

3.3a

3.3b

›3.4 MECHELEN: (a, b) Hof van Savoye (1507–30, now Gerechtshof), detail of street front and elevation to forecourt; (c) Hof van Busleyden (1503–08, now Stadsmuseum), court front.

The ovoid arches and high dormers of both complexes are typically late-Gothic: the loggia motif, but not the colonettes, may be seen as Italianate. The gables on the courts retain the familiar late-medieval multiple stepped form without transitional scroll mouldings. However, those on the external elevations of the later work for Margaret of Austria, duchess of Savoy, seem to follow *Quattrocento* Italian experiments with easing transition from low aisles to high nave in the elevation of the basilican church type: Alberti led, of course, but works like the Roman church of S. Agostino seem most relevant here (AIC4, page 799). By the time work stopped on the Hof van Savoye, with the death of the patroness in 1530, the Orders were in pseudo-canonical vogue but their intrusion into the zone of the pediment did not affect the profile.

3.4a

3.4b

3.4c

medieval arcaded court is dressed in 'Classical' fashion to various degrees: as in the vernacular, stone is reserved for detail in a predominantly brick context.**3.3, 3.4** Well into the century, indeed until internecine strife inhibited grand building, seats of nobility in the countryside perpetuate medieval forms varied in their massing and vertical profile: as usual, advance is marked by the incorporation of fashionable Italianate decorative detail, especially in colonnades, and the will to symmetry.**3.5–3.8**

3.5

3.6

›3.5 GHENT, KASTEEL VAN OOIDONK, from the early 16th century, expanded in the 19th century: general view.

An early medieval fortified farmhouse was developed into a moated castle in the 14th century. Damaged by fire in 1491, its rebuilding was completed on a grander scale, but still in a transitional Flamboyant-Renaissance style, after another fire in 1579 and again after it changed ownership in 1864.

›3.6 WESTERLO, CASTLE, mainly 16th century.

The early medieval castle was acquired by the lords of Mérode in 1482. Over the next century the island complex was developed from the nucleus of the 14th-century keep with perpendicular ranges flanking a regular rectangular court. By the opening of the next century, symmetry began with the entrance pavilion joined to a canted block that matched the termination of the main accommodation range on the opposite side of the court.

›3.7 TURNHOUT, CASTLE OF THE DUKES OF BRABANT, after 1531 on medieval foundations: aerial view.

The medieval hunting lodge was transformed from 1369 into a suburban residence by Maria of Brabant (sister of Duchess Joanna, 1322–1406). Mary of Hungary (1505–58), widow of Louis II of Hungary, sister of Emperor Charles V, for whom she was regent in the Netherlands from 1531, was responsible for the reformation of the enlarged building on the formal lines of regular geometry.

›3.8 CASTLE AND GARDEN C. 1550 (Lucas Gassel, 1490–1568; oil on panel, private collection).

By mid-century the great garden was still additive in composition, the chequerboard still informed the proximate zone, and there was no axial relationship with the house. However, the maze – or topiary – was dominant and there were spectacular water features elsewhere in northern Europe.

3·7

3.8

3.9a

›3.9 BRUGES, CIVIELE OR OUDE GRIFFIE
(Old Civic Registry), from 1534: (a) façade (see also
AIC4, page 632); (b) chimneypiece of 1529 in the neigh-
bouring Schepenzaal (lay magistrates' court).

Beside the Stadhuis to its north-east, the early
Renaissance articulation of the Civiele Griffie's two
main storeys marks the striking advance of Classical
order in the five years since the inception of the last
phase of work on the Heilig-Bloedkapel (on the opposite side of the Stadhuis) – but symmetry is approximate and the gable retains Flamboyance.

The conception of the Schepenzaal chimneypiece is
attributed to the painter Lanceloot Blondeel; execution
in oak over black marble and alabaster was under the
direction of Guyot de Beaugrant. The statues in the
florid and armorial upper register are of Duke Charles
(Emperor Charles V), his parents (Philip and Joanna of
Castile) and both sets of grandparents (Emperor Maximilian I and Mary of Burgundy; Ferdinand of Aragon
and Isabella of Castile).

3.9b

APPREHENSION OF ORDER

At about the time Italians were prompting the French to superimpose freestanding Orders in the loggias of the Château de Madrid and in the Cour Ovale at Fontainebleau, they also appeared at Bruges on the Oude Civiele Griffie and slightly earlier at Mechelen on the Huis De Zalm.**3·9, 3·10** More advanced than the latter, the former ranges Doric, Ionic and Corinthian in the correct ascending sequence across the façade but not with canonical proportions or entablatures. Next, as in France, varia-

3.11

›3.11 LIÈGE, S.-JACQUES: engraved view from the north with portals varying the triumphal-arch motif.

Construction of the Gothic church – on Romanesque foundations – was completed in 1538. The triumphal north portals were added in 1558 by the local painter-architect-polymath Lambert Lombard (1505–66), whose name suggests Italian parentage and who was in Rome in 1537.

›3.12 ADVENT OF CLASSICISM TO THE NORTHERN NETHERLANDS: (a) IJsselstein (Utrecht), Protestant church, tower (c. 1535); (b) Buren, castle court with serlian gable (from c. 1540,

tions on the triumphal-arch motif distinguish two generations of additions to the church of S.-Jacques in Liège.**3.11**

Further north, columns carried arches around the castle court at Breda, in additions by Tommaso di Andrea Vincidor from 1529, and pilasters were superimposed in

3.12b

3.12a

3.12c destroyed); (c) Breda, castle court front with external stairs (from 1536, remodelled).

The new Classicism was imported by Count Hendrik of Nassau-Breda, the duke-emperor Charles's deputy in the province, with the Bolognese Alessandro Pasqualini (1485–1559), a military engineer, and Tommaso di Andrea Vincidor (1493–1536), a draftsman sent to Flanders by Pope Leo X to supervise the weaving of the Sistine tapestries to Raphael's cartoons. The latter was entrusted with the reformation of the court. The former was initially engaged on fortifications which extended to the outworks of Breda castle: he was subsequently retained by Floris van Egmond, count of Buren, on his castle and the church at IJsselstein, and by Duke Wilhelm of Jülich-Kleve-Berg (as we shall see).

›3.13 BRUSSELS, PALACE OF CARDINAL GRANVELLE, from 1549, destroyed): loggia front (as recorded in *Choix des monuments, edifices et maisons les plus remarquables du Royaume des Pays-Bas* by Pierre Jacques Goetghebuer, 1827).

The patron was Antoine Perrenot de Granvelle (1517–86) from the imperial free city of Besançon: his father, Nicholas, was the chancellor of the duke-emperor Charles V. Bishop of Arras from 1540, he represented the Emperor at Trent, led the peace negotiations after the imperial victory at Mühlberg, conducted the negotiations for the marriage of Queen Mary Tudor and Prince Philip, whom he continued to serve as statesman. His career culminated in his appointment in 1559 as chief minister to Margaret of Parma, viceroy of the Netherlands, his promotion to the archbishopric of Mechelen in 1560 and in the following year to the college of cardinals.

the rhythm of a triumphal arch on the tower added to the late-medieval church at IJsselstein by Alessandro Pasqualini from 1532: that Italian was primarily involved with renovating the castle of the Count of Buren.**3.12** By then the importation of architectural ideas from Italy – in print or by travellers across the Alps in both directions – had proliferated and at the end of the decade Serlio was published in Flemish by Pieter Coecke van Aelst who is credited with the principal role in devising the arches through which Philip of Habsburg passed on his entry into Antwerp in 1549.**3.1**

Just when Pierre Lescot was launching his specifically French High Renaissance at the Louvre in Paris, an exceptional building in Brussels returned to the Roman source and quoted the canonical ordonnance of Antonio da Sangallo's Palazzo Farnese cortile loggias: that was the palace of Cardinal Granvelle built from 1549 by Sebastiaan van Noye, who was the leading native practitioner with direct experience of Italy.**3.13** However, the medieval legacy of Flanders would ensure that the French Renaissance proved of more enduring influence there than the Italian, though a synthesis of the two distinguishes the grandest buildings.

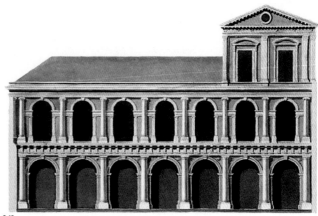

3.13

FLORIDITY AND CONVOLUTION IN CLASSICAL GUISE

The son of a mason who specialized in funerary memorials in Antwerp, Cornelis Floris II (c. 1513–75) studied sculpture and architecture in Rome in the late-1530s but did not emerge from sustaining his father's practice until ten years after he returned home. He published his suite of Vases in 1548 and the next year he seems to have played a significant part in the team of craftsmen assisting Pieter Coecke van Aelst to elaborate the temporary arches erected for Philip II's ceremonial entry into Antwerp.**3.14** From then too dates his work on tombs for the Danish royal family at Roskilde which culminated with that of Christian III (1568).**3.15** His influential suite of related

3.14a

›3.14 CORNELIS FLORIS, ENGRAVED DESIGNS PUBLISHED BY HIERONYMUS COCK: (a) the Antwerp entry viewing platform for the prince and its adjunct for the entourage (from Coecke, *op. cit.*, 1550); (b, c) plates from the suite of ornamental designs (*Veelderley veranderinghe van grotissen ende compartimenten*, and *Veelderley niewe inventien van antycksche sepulturen, etc.*, 1556–57).

3.14b,c

›3.15 ROSKILDE CATHEDRAL, TOMB OF KING CHRISTIAN III, from 1568.

Enshrining the recumbent defunct and surmounted by the latter in prayer, the black and white marble monument is of the canopy or pavilion type developed from Lombard precedents by the Valois kings of France from Louis XII to Henri II.**2.3, 2.20**

›3.16 ZOUTLEEUW, S.-LEONARDUSKERK: tabernacle (from 1550).

The church is rare among its peers of the former Spanish Netherlands in the degree to which its furnishings survived both Protestant iconoclasm and French revolutionary vandalism: Cornelis Floris II's stone tabernacle is the prime example of the specifically Flemish type of reliquary structure with its accumulation of Old and New Testament icons in seven tiers.

3.16 **3.15**

›3.17 COLOGNE, RATHAUS (town hall), founded mid-14th century: (a–c) portico (from 1557).

The project was designed to mask the antiquated medieval façade with room for fifty-one councillors to appear before the populace in the square below: the five-bay design, originally incorporating a staircase, may be seen as an amplification of the three-bay arcaded portico to the open staircase in the Cour Ovale at Fontainebleau which also masked an older façade.**2.6b** Wholly trabeated and partially arcuate alternative project drawings (from 1557) are initialled CF (which is taken to stand for Cornelis Floris) but the executive architect for the richer alternative was Wilhelm Vernukken from the vicinity of Cleves – whom we shall encounter working in a very different mode at Horst.

As it stands, the building is somewhat heterodox in the pointed arches of its upper floor but that has been rebuilt. Ornament is still subjected to ordonnance: that was not generally the case with Floris's ephemeral works for the Antwerp entry of 1549 – appropriately – but the objective was admirably reconciled with the city's requirements for permanent display on the façade of its Stadhuis.

3.18a

›3.18 ANTWERP, STADHUIS (town hall), from 1561: (a, b) main front on the Grote Markt.

Floris had at least a dominant advisory role in the design of the extensive main front: in contrast to the vertical norm even of civic buildings in Flanders, the lateral extension of the design is more typical of France. High Renaissance French, too, is the deployment of Orders progressing under assertive cornices from pilaster to column with the advance of the frontispiece from the plane of the side walls – though the rusticated basement is Italianate. The upper gallery has a precedent in the château of Blois but may equally be

tomb designs and ornamental motifs was published in 1557 as his 'new inventions'. At home, meanwhile, he took the characteristically Flemish stone tabernacle to its apogee in the S.-Leonarduskerk, Zoutleeuw (finished in 1552).**3.16**

Floris's first important work of architecture was the portico of the Cologne Rathaus (1557) in which, unexpectedly

3.17a, b

3.17c

3.18b

perhaps, architecture prevails over sculpture.**3.17** The greatest work attributed to him, unexcelled in 16th-century Flanders or its neighbours, was the Stadhuis of his native Antwerp on which he collaborated with Willem van den Broeck (from 1561).**3.18** Memories of High

seen to derive from Floris's fertile imagination, encouraged to novelty by the medium of drawing for engraving, as does the substitution of sculpture groups for volute consoles. The obelisk finials are reiterated from his ephemeral works for the Antwerp entry of 1549 – and from Serlio.

Renaissance Italy may be detected in the articulation of the main body of the building but the incorporation of the spectacular frontispiece adapts Philibert de l'Orme's formula for the disposition of the Orders to bind diverse masses along horizontal lines and cope with the stressed verticals inherited from Gothic towers: at least for its strapwork, the lavish ornament is indebted to the School of Fontainebleau. Highly and widely influential, the work's major followers include the additions to the Flamboyant Stadhuis of Ghent around the end of the century and, more immediately, the façade of the Hague's Oude Stadhuis.**3.19**

›**3.19 THE HAGUE, OUDE STADHUIS,** from 1564, extended to the rear from 1733 by the French architect Daniël Marot: street front (by an unidentified follower of Floris).

3.19

3.20a

3.20d,e

3.20b,c

3.20f

The publication of Cornelis Floris's suite of ornamental motifs and sepulchral designs informed patronage and inspired other ornamentalists. The most important of these was the Dutch painter and designer Hans Vredeman de Vries (1527–1606). Later acknowledging the use of Serlio in his *métier* as a cabinet-maker, he first emerged from his studies as an assistant to Coecke van Aelst in embellishing the Antwerp entry of 1549: twenty-one years later he designed the major set piece for the entry of Philip II's queen Anna of Austria into the great port city.

Throughout his career, Vredeman was busily engaged on producing ideal architectural and fantastic ornamental designs for publication in pattern books inspired by both Serlio and J.-A. du Cerceau. This extended phase of his endeavours embraced cenotaphs, fountains, gardens, grotesques, caryatids, perspective drawing, scenography and variations on the Vitruvian Orders (1560s and 1570s): it culminated in the publication of *Perspective* (1604) and of *Architectura*, in collaboration with his son Paul (1606).

3.20g

›**3.20 HANS VREDEMAN DE VRIES, FANTASY AND ARCHITECTURE:** (a–g) plates from the suite of variations on aedicular, pavilion and sepulchral tomb

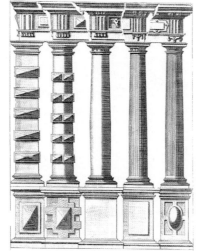

3.20h–j

types (from the collation of *Pictores, Statuarii, Architecti*, 1600); (h–l) plates from the suite of variations on the Tuscan, Doric, Ionic, Corinthian and Composite Orders; (m–p) plates from the suite of variations on Ionic, Corinthian and Composite secular façade design with incidental internal detail and variations on gable design (all from *Architectura* 1577/1581); (q, r) plates from the Granvelle series of architectural perspectives (published by Hieronymus Cock, Antwerp, 1562).

3.20k,l

3.20m

More than his limited output of actual buildings, his plates disseminated a style of architecture which, for all its rational ordering under concealed roofs and incorporation of Italianate loggias, dissolves into convoluted scroll mouldings and strapwork fretted out of the planar context which they were usually designed to relieve by the followers of the School of Fontainebleau.**3.20, 3.21**

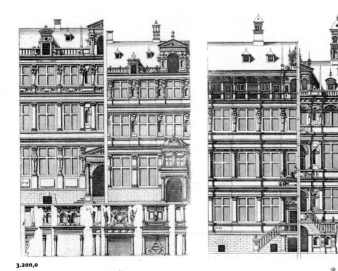

3.20n,o

Vredeman's influence, particularly his strapwork embellishment, was overwhelmingly transmitted through his publications (first in 1563) – and his contribution to the design of the ephemeral works erected for the 1549 Antwerp entry. One of the few tangible remains of his activity as a builder in Antwerp is the gable of the House of the Four Winds (1578) in the Gildenkamerstraat.

3.20q

3.20r

›**3.21 SCENES FROM OVID'S STORY OF VER-TUMNUS AND POMONA,** early 17th-century Brussels tapestries from the workshop of Geubels and Raes (pages 404–405).

Vredeman's publication of architectural perspectives, dedicated to Granvelle in 1562, had its impact on the fine arts and on gardening: the two come together in tapestry, the art form in which Flanders was preeminent. Here the garden drawn from Vredeman **3.20q** retains the enclosure divided rigorously into rectangles but it is crossed by an artery on axis with the house. Moreover, Italian Mannerism and its elaborators at Fontainebleau had had their impact on the proliferation of the typical garden structures – loggias and pergolas in particular.

3.20p

3.21

›ARCHITECTURE IN CONTEXT »FROM THE HIGH RENAISSANCE TO MANNERISM

3.22a

THE HYBRID GABLE

Virtually everywhere in northern Europe, except England, the deep but narrow plots within walled towns were invariably developed with the main axis of building perpendicular to the street under a roof ridge running back from a steep gable. Combining palace and basilican façade types, this promoted individual assertiveness – not least in the Mannerist mode devised by Vredeman. Thus tall, narrow, lavishly ornamented guild and residential buildings, of brick or stone or both, are characteristic of the most affluent Flemish towns – and their chief glory after their unrivalled Flamboyant civic halls (AIC4, pages 631f). The lineage may be traced from the largely medieval examples on the Graslei embankment at Ghent to those rebuilt in Antwerp after the fire of 1576 (AIC4, page 625).**3.22** Of the latter, the Guild Hall of the Archers (Huis van de Schutters) asserts the predominance of the volute console – extracted from the Roman basilican church façade – as the support for the several levels of the tiered gable and their favourite obelisk finials: relief was provided to perimeters by scrollwork or strapwork and similar mouldings framed cartouches or occuli at the apexes. Inevitably, Mannerism matched mercantile assertiveness no less than it conjured courtly diversion but the northern and southern modes were hardly comparable in wit – in *sprezzatura*.

3.22b

›3.22 ANTWERP, GROTE MARKT: (a, b) north range including the Gildehuis der Kuipers (coopers at No. 5, early 17th century), and detail of the dominant Huis van de Schutters (archers at No. 7, from 1580, crowning statue of S. George replaced in the late-19th century).

›3.23 **ALBRECHT DÜRER:** fantasy project for a triumphal arch celebrating Emperor Maximilian I (1515).

3.23

2 ECLECTIC GERMANS AND THEIR EASTERN NEIGHBOURS

As in France, the Renaissance of architecture in the Empire and its neighbours was essentially synthetic: imported Classical style was grafted on to indigenous medieval form following the widespread fashion for prestigious Italian modes. As in France, traditional building throughout north-central Europe was diversified in its massing and predominantly vertical in aspiration in stark contrast to the homogeneity revived by the Italians from their antique heritage (AIC4, pages 624ff). And as in France, the initial attempt to clothe un-Classical form in a repertory of mouldings derived via modern Italians from antique Orders and artefacts betrayed misunderstanding of Classical purpose.**3.23** As we have seen in the French context, Gothic verticality did indeed set a problem for the would-be Classicist, striving for a harmonious relationship between all the parts of his building, and France would provide Germany with the most pervasive solution for both secular and religious building.

Long after the advent of the Renaissance, the virile late-medieval Gothic tradition persisted in all genres of building, but particularly in the elevation and vaulting of churches: the choir of S. Ulrich in Augsburg (completed 1603) is a splendid example (AIC4, page 442). Roofing over those vaults was inevitably steep. Beyond that, of course, all genres of building in areas of high precipitation need steeply pitched roofs to shed copious amounts of water. In the urban context, moreover, the domestic norm in Germany and its eastern neighbours, as to its north-west in the Netherlands, was a deep plot with a narrow street front from which a triangular truss carried the roof ridge back on the perpendicular, a steep pitch providing for secondary accommodation as well as storage space. Thus the gable is the most characteristic feature of building throughout the area: usually, but not invariably, stepped in profile, its Gothic elaboration flourished well into the 16th century but, beyond that, abstract ordonnance was as much neo-Romanesque as neo-Renaissance (AIC4, page 628).

After the loss of the Berlin Joachimsbau to vandalism post-World War II, the first phase of grafting imported style on to indigenous stock is nowhere better represented than in the Saxon elector Johann Friedrich's Schloss Hartenfels at Torgau on the Elbe – except for the incompletely restored Residenzschloss of Dresden and apart from the imperial or royal castles at Vienna, Prague and Krakow, to which we shall return. Typical is the irregular courtyard plan incorporating a great tower descended from the early medieval *Burgfried* and lesser vertical elements, of which at least one rises from the ground with a staircase, but most are gables punctuating the roofline. At Berlin, as at Dresden, the gables were at their most profuse: at Torgau, as formerly in Berlin, the open-cage staircase tower is at its most spectacular (AIC4, pages 884f).**3.24**

3.24a

›3.24 TORGAU, SCHLOSS HARTENFELS, from c. 1535: (a) view from north-western approach, (b) main-floor plan with (1) Serlian entrance portal, (2) Albrechtsbau (from 1470), (3) Johann-Friedrichs-Bau with great hall and external staircase, (4) Schöner Erker and (5) chapel; (c) Schöner Erker (chapel vestibule oriel, from 1544), (d, e) chapel portal interior, (from 1543).

Torgau was the birthplace of Luther's protector, the Saxon elector Ernestine Friedrich (the Wise) and principal residence of his brother and successor, the elector Johann – the Albertine branch retained Meissen. After a catastrophic fire in 1482, rebuilding was begun in the partially preserved south-west sector. The great Renaissance work, the south-east range with its enormous hall and spectacular open staircase, was begun soon after the accession of the elector Johann Friedrich in 1532: the master-mason was Konrad Krebs. On the latter's death in 1540, after a new range to the north-east had been projected, he was succeeded by Nickel Gromann to whom the chapel is due.

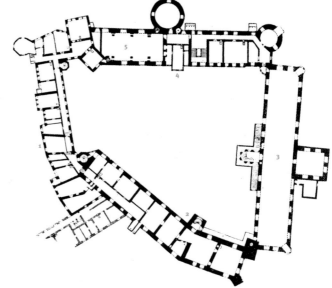

3.24b @ 1:1500

3.24c,d

Apart from the enormous hall served by its great stair-case, Torgau has a special claim to significance in its chapel. Except for castle chapels, ecclesiastical building was not to the fore in the first three-quarters of the 16th-century Empire, apart from conversion of Catholic churches to Protestantism and, often, their subsequent reconversion. Prompted by the specific requirements of the Reformers, especially uninhibited focus on the declaimer from the Biblical lectern and the preacher in the pulpit, innovation began in the princely court chapel.**3.24e** The lead was taken in the late-1530s at Neuburg by the Bavarian Duke Ludwig's cousin, Ottheinrich of the palatinate. However, the prototype was developed at Wittenberg for the Saxon elector Friedrich the Wise – Luther's protector – and for his heir, Johann Friedrich, at Torgau. Deprived of aisles, the Gothic hall-church type provided a single-volume with clear sightlines to the pastor augmented by raising a considerable amount of congregational accommodation to surrounding galleries: the latter originated in continuation of the tribune reserved for the patron and his family at the level of the private apartments.

3.24e

The gable, the oriel and the portal were inevitably first to feature fashionable Renaissance decorative detail, as we shall see. Beyond superficial apparel, however, the importation of substantial Classical forms – particularly the loggia, with or without superimposed galleries, and the triumphal arch – was earlier practice in the Empire and its neighbours than in France. Indeed, the mature Renaissance was announced in Germany with an entirely imported Italian building. That was in the late-1530s, as we shall see, long after the first manifestation of the Renaissance beyond the Alps and across the Rhine in substantial Italianate structures.

Primacy in patronage of Italian artists – and military engineers – in East-Central Europe may justly be claimed by Matthias Corvinus of Hungary (from 1464–90) who married an Aragonese-Neapolitan princess in 1476. Renaissance style was brought to the transformation of the royal castle at Buda and the construction of a new palace at Visegrad: beyond the (restored) arcaded nuclear court of the latter, little of their original work has survived the depredations of the Ottoman Turks. In the next generation, however, a dynastic alliance between Poland and Milan has proved more lastingly productive of building.

3.25a

3.25b

3.25c

›ARCHITECTURE IN CONTEXT »FROM THE HIGH RENAISSANCE TO MANNERISM

›3.25 RENAISSANCE KRAKÓW: (a–c) Wawel Zamek (Royal Castle), general view, great court exterior and interior (c. 1502–35); (d) Cloth Hall (Sukiennice, late-14th century, transformed from 1555, much restored from 1870).

Working in collaboration with the Sienese sculptor Giovanni Cini (died 1565) on King Sigismund's burial chapel in Wavel cathedral (AIC4, page 886), the Florentine-trained Tuscan architect Bartolommeo Berrecci (c. 1480–1537) replaced one Franciscus Florentinus who died in 1516. The latter was commissioned in c. 1502 to modernize the late-15th-century royal residential block in the castle and the project was well under way by 1507. The arcaded galleries in the great court were probably conceived before Franciscus's death but they were not completed until the mid-1530s, well into the period of Bartolommeo's responsibility.

By the middle of the century, at Brzeg (near Wroclaw on the Oder), the arcuate and the trabeated were correctly distinguished on the partially realized triumphal-arch motif of the gatehouse: ornament remained profuse in the early Renaissance style.

POLISH INITIATIVE

Far off in Poland, King Sigismund I (1506–48) had married Princess Bona Sforza in 1518: her compatriots were immediately commissioned to introduce Renaissance style to the great dynastic complex embracing the medieval castle and cathedral which overlooked the city of Kraków, the capital until superseded by Warsaw in 1609.**3.25** Work began in 1519 with the dynastic funerary chapel attached to the cathedral under Florentine direction (AIC4, page 886). The palace, renovated over medieval foundations – as usual north of the Alps – is centred on an arcaded court as usual in Italy – but with the arches rising from columns in the early Renaissance manner. However, the Italian architects doubtless quailed at the stark contrast between the Romanesque gravitas of the arches below and the extraordinary spindly doubling of the upper posts in response to the elevation of the great senatorial assembly room located there. The Italians also served the burghers in the forum below the castle with the design for the Cloth Hall and its arcaded gallery: the attic storey was added from 1560 – and there were further changes in the 19th century.**3.25d**

3.25d

IMPERIAL EXAMPLE

A generation after the Polish initiative, in Vienna the new emperor Ferdinand marked his accession in 1549 with a Serlian triumphal entrance to his Hofburg palace, the Schweizertor: like the triumphal-arch motifs then being incorporated in his nephew Philip II's gate at Toledo and soon to be built into Henri II's new Louvre in Paris, it effected the transition from the ephemeral to the permanent.**3·27** Inevitably, however, there was no such clean break in the transition from Gothic to Renaissance: as in France and elsewhere in northern Europe, the type of Classical mouldings popular with late-15th-century Venetians or Lombards were applied to medieval forms – in stone and in woodcuts – without comprehension of the order essential to Classicism (AIC4, pages 882f).

›3.26 INNSBRUCK, HOFKAPELLE, 1553–63: interior detail.

Emperor Maximilian (1459–1519) had wished to be buried in the court chapel at Wiener Neustadt but that building could not accommodate the grandiose memorial projected for him (AIC4, page 881). The interment followed the emperor's will but his grandson (the executor of his will) decreed that the memorial would be housed as a cenotaph in a new court chapel at Innsbruck. The commission for the latter was let to Andrea Crivelli from nearby Trento but he was instructed to conform to the Germanic type appropriate to the late Habsburg patriarch: late-Gothic form was duly 'Classicized' with extremely attenuated columns of a Corinthian Order separating the nave from the similarly high, galleried aisles. The gallery preserves its original rib vaulting but the nave was revaulted after an earthquake in the 17th century.

›**3.27 VIENNA, CROWN AND PALACE:** (a) crown of Rudolf II (1602; in the apostolic form incorporating a mitre, created in Prague by Jan Vermeyen of Antwerp); (b) Viennese overview; (c) Hofburg plan with (1) Schweizertrakt, (2) Stallburg, (3) Amalienburg; (d, e) Schweizertrakt (Swiss wing, from 1552), portal (Schweizertor) and court; (f) Stallburg court arcades (from 1558); (g) Amalienburg (begun 1575, elevation extended above basement from 1582, completed 1611) as depicted by Samuel van Hoogstraten in 1652 (before early 18th-century alteration); (h) Neuegebäude (from 1569).

Even Dürer produced flagrantly un-Classical confections from Classical components in cross-fertilizing the medieval and the antique – most notably in the triumphal arch he devised in ideal for an entry of Emperor Maximilian into Nuremberg (1515).**3.23** Usually from the infertile Como region – which, as we have noted, was the traditional source of itinerant workers in the building trade – even these could be flagrantly eclectic when translated over the Alps: the prime example is their response to the future emperor Ferdinand's commission for the design of the Hofkapelle at Innsbruck to enshrine his grandfather's cenotaph. Working at the same time on the palace in the imperial capital, they led the way from canonical Classicism to elementary Mannerism.**3.26**

Renaissance Vienna

Within the decade of his advent to power in Vienna, Emperor Ferdinand I faced catastrophe from the besieging forces of the Ottoman sultan Suleiman the Magnificent: the Turks turned back but left much of the

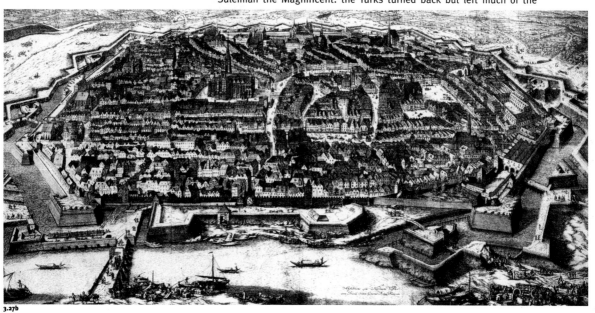

3.27b

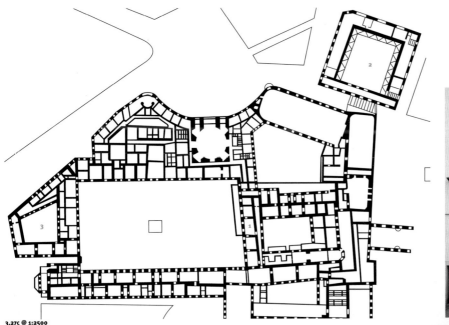

3.27c @ 1:2500

3.27d

3.27e

imperial seat derelict. The suburbs had been cleared to form a *glacis* – an unobstructed field of fire – and this was retained as the precinct for a new circuit of ramparts designed along modern Italian lines with stellar barbicans and bastions. Built over their predecessors, these left the city no less constricted than it had been as a medieval organism. A second wave of Ottoman aggression was repelled in 1533, the final wave in 1685.

Within the southern ramparts, the emperor was provided with an Italianate palace on the basis of a medieval court in the centre of the Hofburg (from 1552). Well before that, Serlio was in vogue in Spain (as we shall see): he was certainly familiar to the archduke's chancellor, Gabriel von Salamanca-Ortenburg, who promoted him as inspiration for improving Ferdinand's lodging. The work is due to Serlio's compatriot, the master-builder Pietro Ferrabosco: the dominant motif of the internal ordnance is an arcade carried on colossal Tuscan pilasters (like Serlio IV.6.28). Fenestrated in the latter's manner too, the façade is relieved only by the portal, the latest element in the complex and the most assertively Serlian (IV.7.46).

The arches in the Schweizertrakt (Swiss wing) were to be walled and fenestrated but intact are the splendid series of arcades in the so-called

Much of the early Italianate work at the Hofburg is associated with the Comesque fortification designer and scenographic painter Pietro Ferrabosco (1512–96) who entered the service of Emperor Ferdinand to reform the imperial capital's defences before his probable deployment to modernize the accommodation within – where he is first recorded as an interior decorator (in 1549). Contemporary with the Schweizertrakt is his work on the castle at Bratislava. Thereafter he went on to improve the fortification of Slovakian and Hungarian towns in the Ottoman firing line. He was still working on the Amalienburg in the 1580s in association with

Stallburg court: correctly framed by Tuscan pilasters on three levels for the first time in central Europe, they provide access to the single enfilade of rooms in each range. The complex was built (from 1562) for the imperial heir, Archduke Maximilian, on his return from his education and service with his cousins in Spain in 1558. On his accession as emperor six years later, he moved to the Schweizertrakt and the ground floor of his transitory residence was converted for the stabling of the horses from Spain with which the celebrated riding school would soon be established. The exterior is plain but the façade of the Amalienburg, begun in the mid-1570s for

3.27f

3.278

the future Rudolf II and his oldest brother Archduke Ernest, was vigorously rusticated in a Mannerist mode: Florentine at base, this extended over the protracted building history to pilaster piers cut by stringcourses in the manner of Sanmicheli but without the Giulian Mannerist purpose of devouring an Order.

Meanwhile (from 1569), Emperor Maximilian ventured beyond the city defences to a suburban palace at Neugebäude. Distantly recalling one of the wings of Giulio Romano's Palazzo del Te, like that work it was designed for receptions and the display of art rather than regular habitation: the architect is unrecorded but the scheme was probably devised under the direction of the Mantuan polymath Jacopo Strada (1507–88). Backed by a

the Fleming Antonis Muys (Antonio de Moys) who had trained in Italy as a furniture designer and was perhaps first employed in the imperial service as a model maker before acting as master-mason to Ferrabosco's direction. Construction of the Amalienburg (renamed after a later empress) was protracted because Rudolf II's attention was focused on Prague.

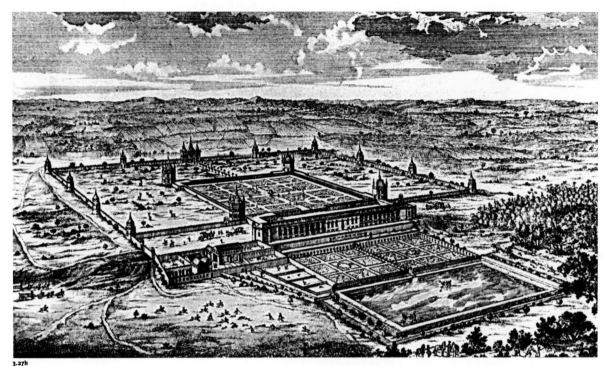

3.27h

rectangular compound, punctuated with towers and centred on a four-square garden; lost, it commanded a view of the countryside over a lower garden terrace and a rectangular tank in the mid-century Italian manner.

Apart from grafts on to medieval fabric, especially the Classical portals introduced to the castle's Vladislav Hall by Benedict Reid c. 1500 (AIC4, page 605), the Renaissance reached Prague at much the same time as it made its initial impact on the court at Vienna at the instigation of the same patron, Archduke Ferdinand, king-consort of Bohemia. During the crisis of the Turkish siege the future emperor retreated to Prague. The work on accommodating him in the great castle there has largely been obliterated by later development: there is, however, one spectacular survival: the summer garden palace pavilion built for the queen-empress Anna with whom he had

acquired the crown of Bohemia. He imported the Italian sculptor Paolo della Stella from the studio of Andrea Sansovino at Padua to advise on the design. The executive architect, masons and decorators were Comesque: elsewhere in the imperial-royal heartlands thereafter, stucco and fresco embellishment would usually be provided by integrated and notoriously clannish Comesque teams of mobile building workers whose masters aspired to architecture. However, the work was completed by the German court architect Bonifaz Wolmut who went on to produce the other major Renaissance survivor, the ball-game hall.**3.28**

›**3.28 PRAGUE CASTLE, ROYAL GARDEN STRUCTURES:** (a) belvedere (*letohrádek*, from 1534) exterior from south and detail of arcade; (b, c) ball-game hall (*micovna*, from 1569), exterior and detail of *sgraffito* embellishment.

Paolo della Stella's inspiration came somewhat randomly from the civic basilica of the Paduan type (AIC4, page 620) but the peripteral arcade was Classicized with semi-circular segments of architrave carried on columns in the early Renaissance manner rather than the contemporary High Renaissance work of Jacopo Sansovino. The executive architect was Giovanni Spazio from the prominent clan of Comesque building workers, the master-mason was the Ticinese Giovanni Maria Aostalli (died 1567). The building was damaged by fire in 1541: thereafter Serlio was available in print to

influence the design of detail. The work was finished in 1563 – only a year before the emperor's death – under the direction of the Viennese-trained German master-mason Bonifaz Wolmut: the clerestory and roof date from after he assumed charge as imperial architect in 1558. The following year, Wolmut was strictly canonical in the external articulation of the ball-game hall with post-Albertian High Renaissance logic.

3.28a

3.28c

3.28b

3.29a

3.29b

›**3.29 SPITTAL AN DER DRAU, SCHLOSS PORCIA,** begun c. 1535: (a, b) court galleries.

The patron had accompanied Archduke Ferdinand from Spain as his secretary; the architect seems most likely to have been a Comesque Italian but his name is not recorded. The work was completed c. 1550, more than a decade after the patron's death. The four-square quadrangular format with corner towers and galleried court – derived from the late-medieval Italian *castello* type and its early Renaissance followers (AIC4, pages 587f, 770, 781) – was to be enduringly popular in Austria. The current name derives from Hannibal Alphons von Porcia who occupied the complex for forty years from 1698.

›**3.30 SCHALLABURG, SCHLOSS:** court (from 1573).

Adjoining an early 12th-century keep, the Renaissance block was built for the Protestant Hans Wilhelm von Losenstein (1540–1601) by an unidentified architect. It follows Schloss Porcia's Italianate precedent with its perpendicular wings and corner towers: the upper registers of the court incorporate terracotta herms, masks and heraldic devices in the earlier Lombard manner of works like the Certosa of Pavia (AIC4, page 806).

Following the emperor's lead, the imperial nobility inserted Renaissance courts into the castles on their Austrian or Bohemian estates and redecorated their halls sometimes even behind fashionably painted façades. In the south, examples range from Schloss Porcia at Spittal an der Drau in Carinthia, built for the imperial chancellor Gabriel von Salamanca-Ortenburg (died 1539) who had promoted the authority of Serlio at court, to Schloss Schallaburg in Lower Austria from 1572. Even that late, the Stallburg court model with superimposed galleries was not always faithfully followed with canonical distinction between the arcuate and trabeated elements yet a generation earlier the Graz Landhaus exceeded the imperial court in sophistication – except for its inconsistent Tuscan proportions.**3.29-3.31**

3.30

›3.31 GRAZ, LANDHAUS, from 1557: (a) plan, (b) street front, (c) court,

The genre of the Landhaus, the seat of the assembly of provincial nobility, was of particular importance in Austria. The one at Graz was built to the plans of Domenico dell'Allio I (1515–63), a Comesque military engineer who had been reforming the fortifications of Graz – and other towns potentially vulnerable to the Turks – on modern Italian stellar lines since 1543. Completed after Domenico's death by his assistants, the masons Benedikt de la Porta and Peter Tadai, it is outstanding in the degree to which it rivalled the seats of imperial authority.

3.31b

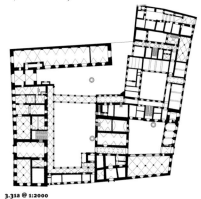
3.31a @ 1:2000

3.31c

In the west, at Innsbruck, Schloss Ambras was modernized for Emperor Ferdinand's son, Ferdinand, archduke of Austria: the architects were probably Italians borrowed from the current project to enshrine Emperor Maximilian in the new Hofkirche. Beyond the usual court loggias, the interior is particularly notable for its Spanische Saal (1570). In accordance with the Austrian vernacular tradition of building on this scale, well represented earlier at Kufstein or Raabs an der Thaya and comparable with works like Schloss Hartenfels elsewhere in central Europe, the exterior is of barely relieved severity: now regular in its fenestration, the block-like mass extends only into stair turrets, except for the residue of a *Burgfried*, under pitched roofs rising to pyramids with tiered lanterns over the projections.**3.32, 3.33** Intimate politically, the relationship between Habsburg Austria and Spain in architectural form will be noted in due course.

3.32

›3.32 RAABS AN DER THAYA, BURG, 12th-century construction over early 10th-century foundations, comprehensive enlargements from late-14th century to early 16th century: general view.

›3.33 INNSBRUCK, SCHLOSS AMBRAS, from 1563: (a) general view with forecourt framed by museum buildings, banqueting house and formal garden below the Hochschloss (middle-ground left and right respectively in the mid-17th-century engraving of Matthäus Merian), (b) court (*sgraffito* embellishment

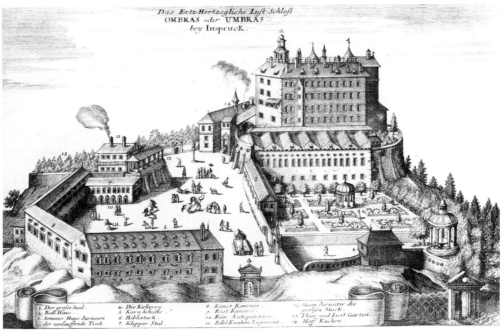

3.33a

from 1566, restored), (c) Spanische Saal (from 1570).

The patron, the second son of Emperor Ferdinand I, was regent of Tyrol from 1563 and proceeded forthwith to convert the medieval castle into an Italianate palace: much is attributed to Giovanni Lucchese. Typical of such exercises after the precedent set at Spittal an der Drau for Ferdinand's treasurer Gabriel von Salamanca-Ortenburg, it is roughly quadrangular about a court; the autonomous block containing the banqueting hall – the first of its kind north of the Alps – is no less essentially Italian, though called Spanische Saal in honour of the patron's dynastic connections: nevertheless, while the conception may be due to Giovanni Battista Fontana (c. 1524–87), author of the ancestral portraits, the coffered ceiling is due to one Conrad Gottlieb and the stuccowork to Antonis van Brackh.

The schloss was initially the residence of the archduke's morganatic wife Philippine Welser of Augsburg. Two years after her death in 1580, she was succeeded by Anna Caterina Gonzaga of Mantua, and the castle was extended to house the patron's eclectic collections of art and artefacts. Rudolf II bought the complex from Ferdinand's heir Margave Karl in 1606.

3.33b

3.33c

ITALIANATE COURTS IN GERMANY

Italian publications on architecture and design supported itinerant Italians in the dissemination of Classical detail – and fashion – to several of the imperial estates. At the issue of the Brenner Pass through the central Alps from the Comesque region, which traditionally sent masons abroad with knowledge of the latest developments in Lombardy, Bavaria was uniquely well placed for the introduction of fundamental principles from High Renaissance Italy. And, indeed, that was instigated by the Bavarian duke Ludwig X in 1537 with the commission of the Italianische Bau for his Landshut seat, which he had begun with the Deutsche Bau the year before – just three years after the projection of the empress's Belvedere at Prague. Purer than that, the scheme derives from the Mantua of Giulio Romano: the patron, who was at the Gonzaga court in 1536, records having imported masters from there but their identities are obscure. Their work was exceptional in Germany, far more sophisticated than anything then being built by Italians in the Netherlands – or, indeed, much else in northern Europe for at least another century.**3.34**

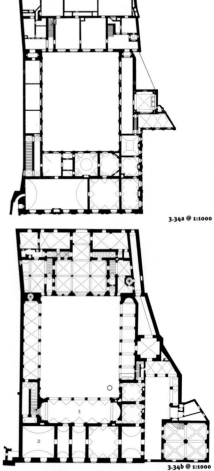

3.34a @ 1:1000

3.34b @ 1:1000

›3.34 LANDSHUT, STADTRESIDENZ: (a, b) basement and first-floor plans of Deutsche Bau and Italienische Bau respectively with *sala terrena* (1) and Italienische Saal (2); (c) engraved overview from the east with original Deutsche Bau front (c. 1710), (d–k) Italienische Bau, west façade, south side detail, court elevation and interior details.

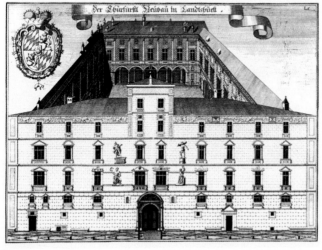

3.34c

3.34d

The identity of the Italian immigrants primarily responsible for the Italienische Bau is obscure. The duke records Meister Sigismund and his assistant Anthoni as having been engaged in Mantua at the beginning of 1537: they were soon followed by one Bernard (surnamed Walch) at the head of a team of twelve artisans.

3.34e

3.34f

Italianate Landshut

The Wittelsbach duke Ludwig X was joint ruler of Bavaria with his brother Wilhelm IV. The seat of the latter was at Munich. The seat of the former was the medieval Burg Trausnitz on the peak above Landshut where he welcomed Italian humanists and from which he descended on Mantua about the time Giulio Romano was completing the internal decoration of the Palazzo del Te. Underemployed there, many of Giulio's assistants were ready to enter the service of the enlightened Bavarian ruler – Primaticcio, one of their principals, having embarked for Fontainebleau.

The Italienische Bau extended beyond the Deutsche Bau which addressed the main street of the Landshut Altstadt. Above the expansive cross-vaulted entrance hall, the latter housed the private apartments in a doubled range: begun early in 1536 by Augsburger master-builders in distant echo of various late-15th-century north-Italian styles, the front was altered in the 18th century. In contrast, the surviving western elevation of the Italienische Bau – in stuccoed brick like the rest of the complex – follows the High Renaissance Roman approach to façade design, defined by Bramante but extended with a colossal Order by Raphael and his circle: the basement is rusticated in the manner of Giulio Romano and the irregular rhythm of the Tuscan pilasters, which extend up through blind panels to a perforated entablature, clearly derives from the north front of the Palazzo del Te (pages 122f). The rustication is carried through to the arcading of the strictly rectangular court. There it was out of context and there

3.34g, h

was no place for strident keystones: the anachronistic confusion of the trabeated and the arcuate was common in the unsophisticated first phase of the Renaissance in Germany but here, between the minor terms of incomplete rhythmic bays, the mockery of mural pretensions sustained by columns is worthy of Giulio himself. Above this the over-extended Tuscan of the exterior cedes to the correctly proportioned, regularly spaced colossal Corinthian Order supporting the revealed roof and defining the bays in which the Roman type of pedimented window is repeated without consoles.

The court is framed by shallow wings, the one to the south containing the first-floor corridor which serves the chapel: cubical, the latter is extended into cross-arms by the disposition of the elegant Corinthian Order. Opposite the entrance, the western range of court arcades screens the apsidal *sala terrena*: here and in the main rooms of the piano nobile the designs of the vault compartments are reminiscent of the variations produced by Giulio's school in Mantua. In particular, the scheme of the Palazzo del Te's great loggia is recalled for the main reception room (the Italienische Saal): the walls here were redecorated in the 18th century but the door frames, the chimneypiece and the richly varied stuccoed framework of the vault are the work of the early Mannerists imported from Mantua. Comesques may have been involved in the execution but, unlike Austria, or Bohemia, Bavaria would usually draw its craftsmen from the eastern Swiss canton of Graubunden.

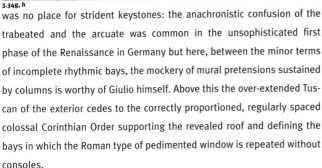

3.34i

3.34j

3.34k

Punctuated with towers, the quadrangle was the norm as the nucleus of the castle throughout northern Europe at the end of the medieval era, as we have seen (pages 401f and see AIC4, pages 572, 588, etc.). As Ludwig's successors would ultimately do in their ancestral Burg Trausnitz above the town, Classicizing reformers pursued regularity in the geometry of planning. Usually the medieval foundations inhibited the ideal: sometimes they approximated it. The partly pragmatic, partly rational norm may well be represented by examples ranging from the Hartenfels complex at Torgau or the great electoral castle at Heidelberg to the semi-regular Residenzschloss at Dresden (see pages 427f, 476ff and 449ff). Examples of near-complete rectangularity range widely in place and style from the imperial Viennese Hofburg to, say, provincial Weilburg on the Lahn in western Germany.**3.35**

›3.35 WEILBURG, SCHLOSS: engraved overview (after c. 1545).

The south and west ranges, which framed the quadrangle from the late-1540s, differ in the near-symmetrical disposition of solids and voids from the other two wings, the founding of which spans the era of transition from the medieval to the proto-Renaissance. Modernization ran to Italianate gables but the gate-house tower retains the medieval form. The end result may instructively be compared with the achievement of the French early Renaissance a generation earlier in works like the château of Azay-le-Rideau (AIC4, pages 873, 875).

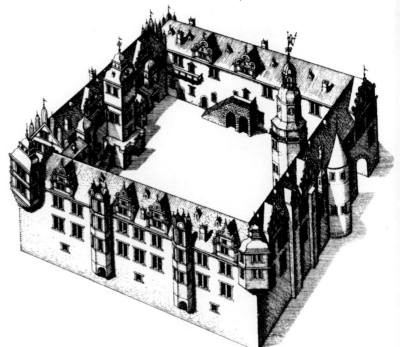

3·35

The devastation of the Thirty Years' War savagely depleted the legacy of the early Renaissance in the imperial domains – indeed of anything central European from the 16th and early 17th centuries. Yet much is left for selective review which, as elsewhere in the north, shows that the pace of Renaissance development was rapid but irregular in both morphology and motif. Beyond the gratuitous application of mere elements like pilaster shafts or candelabra, widespread – but not numerous – works carried out in the median decades of the century demonstrate that, in concert with regular planning, halting advance towards the comprehension of Classicism ran to symmetry in fenestration and the placing of portals in bays defined by more-or-less correctly superimposed Orders. Naturally, it extended to following the imperial precedent in the application of triumphal arches for portals and the insertion of loggia arcades around courts.

›3.36 STUTTGART, ALTES SCHLOSS, from 1553: court.

The medieval palace at Stuttgart was largely rebuilt over a plan distorted from the rectangular to a near-parallelogram: the patron was Duke Christoph of Württemberg who acceded in 1550. The ducal architect Alberlin Tretsch lined the court with galleries on the three reconstructed sides – to an extent unprecedented in Germany but approximated in the Wawel Zamek at Kraków. In contrast to the main ranges of the latter, moreover, the proportions of the superimposed Corinthian and Composite Orders and the flattened arches which they carry are uncanonical.

The Stuttgart court was followed by the one in the Munich complex now known as the Mint but built as an art gallery over stables by the court architect Wilhelm Egkl (died 1588): the patron was Duke Albrecht (acceded in 1550). Less sophisticated – surprisingly in the light of Landshut – the work is uncanonical in its proportions, in the superimposition of Tuscan over a debased Corinthian Order and in still springing flattened arches from columns.

3.36

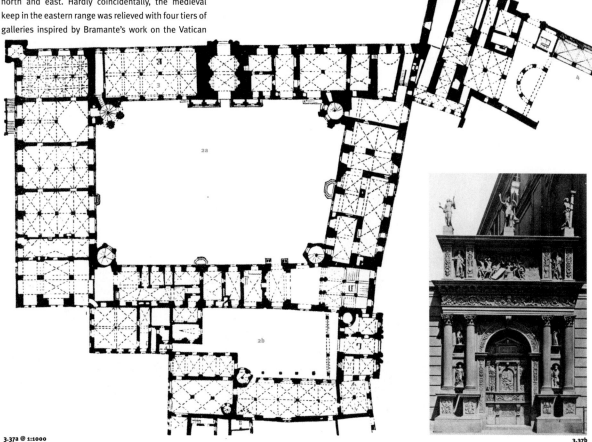

›3.37 DRESDEN, RESIDENZSCHLOSS: (a) plan with (1) Georgenbau, (2a, 2b Moritzbau, Grosser and Kleiner Schlosshof, (3) chapel, (4) Langer Gang; (b) chapel portal (dated 1555; pre-War image), (c, d) model of Grosser Schlosshof from south-east and west front of Moritzbau (from the mid-1540s, revised 1899, restored), (e) Kleiner Schlosshof and great court interior, (f, g) Grosser Schlosshof (restored), (h) Langer Gang (from 1586).

The work of the 1530s was commissioned by Duke Georg der Bärtige (died 1539). Duke Moritz, who acceded in 1541, was awarded the Electorate on his conversion to Catholicism in 1547 and celebrated his elevation by reforming the great court beyond the Georgenbau along rectilinear lines – at least to the north and east. Hardly coincidentally, the medieval keep in the eastern range was relieved with four tiers of galleries inspired by Bramante's work on the Vatican

Contemporary with the evolution of the emperor's Schweizertrakt, the arcaded court of the Altes Schloss in Stuttgart (from c. 1550) may be taken as representing the early Renaissance norm.**3.36** In Dresden, where the medieval complex was extended at the instigation of the Albertine elector Moritz (1547–53), the arcading was confined to superimposed loggias below the tower of the Grosser Schlosshof and reiterated in the contiguous Kleiner Schlosshof towards the end of the century.**3.37** These were destroyed in the horrendous bombing of the

3.37a @ 1:1000

3.37b

Cortile di S. Damaso: the upper level is trabeated, the lower ones arcuate but the proportions of the superimposed Orders and the profile of the arches depart from the model. The tiered gables flanking the loggia block, like the one over the centre of the north wing are buttressed with scroll volutes and capped with pediments in the manner of the Roman basilican church façade:

3.37c

3.37e

3.37d

beyond Antonio da Sangallo, Serlio was doubtless the source.

The chapel was completed with its portal under Moritz's successor, the elector Augustus: moved to the Judenhof, only the portal survived remodelling of the chapel in the 1660s. The triumphal-arch motif, deployed here by an Italian identified as Johann Maria, was repeated with sculptural flourish for the Wettin dynastic tombs at Freiberg thirty years later by the far-less obscure Italian Giovanni Maria Nosseni (1544–1620) – as we shall see. The latter's High Renaissance style was not preferred to the less-sophisticated local master-masons, Paul Buchner and Hans Irmisch, for the contemporary additions to the schloss – notably the Langer Gang.

city in 1945: much has been rebuilt, including the central block of the Moritzbau and the arcaded range of the Langer Gang (long corridor) which connects the palace with its stable court. That was built two generations later than the court loggias but the style shows little advance towards comprehension of the logical distinction between arcuate and trabeated structure.

3.37f

3.37g

3.37h

3.38

›3.38 JÜLICH, ZITADELLE PORTAL, c. 1555.

Duke Wilhelm V of Jülich-Cleves-Berg ordered the comprehensive reconstruction of the town after its destruction by fire in 1547: Pasqualini was entrusted with the design of the citadel and its quadrangular palace. After Alessandro died in 1558, the fortifications were extended and the palace was completed (c. 1570) by his sons Maximilian and Johann.

›3.39 WISMAR, FÜRSTENHOF: (a, b) main portal and court front (from 1555).

The patron was Duke Johann Albrecht I of Mecklenburg: in Lombard style, the terracotta ornament is Lombard in derivation but the Italianate profile of the building's front resulted from the suppression of the original gables (in 1574). The craftsmen came from the great trading town of Lübeck where the brick tradition ran to elaborate moulding – including some Renaissance motifs as early as the late-15th century.

Arresting is the advance from the portal of the Dresden Residenzschloss Georgenbau to that of the chapel over the twenty years from c. 1535 (AIC4, page 883):**3.36e** Renaissance-Romanesque quickly cedes to Serlio for re-evocation of the antique triumphal arch to represent the threshold of heaven in the time-honoured way (see Serlio, Book III, 4.57). At mid-century, the High Renaissance was turning to Mannerism in Vienna with the aid of the Serlian follower who provided the emperor with his Hofburg portal.**3.27d** Five years further on, similar maturity was taken across the Rhine from Holland, to Jülich, by Alessandro Pasqualini whom we have encountered at Buren and IJsselstein: the banded rustication of his Zitadelle portal and chapel is clearly inspired by Giulio's Porta del Te at Mantua.**1.7a, 3.38** The mode was sustained in the latest phase of work on the portal range of Schloss Hartenfels, at Torgau. On the other hand, pre-Serlian Lombardy – or France – seems to have guided those taking less than certain steps towards Mannerism: beyond adopting that mode for their fenestration, however, the builders of the Fürstenhof at Wismar had acquired a taste for Serlian anthropomorphism when they came to devise the outer portal.**3.39**

3.39a

3.39b

3.40b

3.40a

3.40a

›3.40 KULMBACH, SCHLOSS PLASSEN-BURG: (a) model with Schoner Hof right, later barracks and arsenal buildings left, (b, c) Schoner Hof, south face of north range and east face of west range (early 1550s and late-1560s respectively).

Work on modernizing the castle for Margrave Albrecht Alcibiades of Brandenburg-Kulmbach in the early 1550s extended from the north to the east wing. The latter was masked with its exceptional arcades in a campaign initiated in 1557 by Albrecht's successor, Georg Friedrich, to further restoration work after severe damage was inflicted by troops from Nuremberg hostile to his pretensions to suzerainty over their city. Much of both campaigns extended to fortification but from 1561 the amelioration of the accommodation was the responsibility of the master-mason Caspar Vischer (died 1581) who witnessed the later stages of construction at Heidelberg, but advice was sought from Alberlin Tretsch who was working on the court of Stuttgart's Altes Schloss. Given the disparity between the Stuttgart and Plassenburg styles, it may be assumed that Tretsch's role was rather more technical than aesthetic. Whatever the extent of Vischer's responsibility, the armorial, allegorical and astrological embellishment is credited to the sculptor Daniel Engelhardt.

At Kulmbach the portal in the west range would have seemed old-fashioned in comparison with the Serlian exercises we have just reviewed: work on the expanded court to which it provides entrance began c. 1561. Forty years later, the author of Margrave Christian Heinrich of Brandenburg-Kulmbach's massive Mannerist barracks portal went far beyond Serlio, in his awareness of the latest craze for Mannerist accumulation of bombastic motifs – as we shall see. On the other hand, the celebrated arcades which give the court its name represent considerable advance on the adjacent work of the previous decade and, indeed, on many of the galleries we have so far encountered elsewhere: the arches are framed by pilaster strips – rather than carried on columns – but the profusion of Classical mouldings does not run to the elements of a canonical High Renaissance Order.**3.40** A decade behind the comparable development at Silesian Brzeg, that work was contemporary with Cornelis Floris's design for the portico of the Cologne Rathaus which introduced the canonical relationship between arch and framing column – but the model was French rather than Italian, as we have seen.

3.41a

3.41b

›ARCHITECTURE IN CONTEXT »FROM THE HIGH RENAISSANCE TO MANNERISM

>3.41 NELAHOZEVES, CASTLE, from 1553: (a) exterior from the south, (b) court front.

The original patron was the Bavarian nobleman Florian Griespek von Griespach who died in 1588 in the entourage of Emperor Rudolf II; the property was acquired by the Lobkowicz in 1623. The original design – incompletely realized on Griespek's death – is attributed to the court architect Bonifaz Wolmut who was then active in Prague but the open quadrangular form is ultimately Italian. The *sgraffito* embellishment of the external façades – simulating rustication and figurative – is not uncommon in Bohemia: on the court fronts, however, its combination with an applied Order framing window bays over the substantially rusticated arcades of the basement was advanced for its date in Bohemia.

>3.42 ČESKÝ KRUMLOV: (a) general view of castle with 13th-century tower's galleried superstructure (1580s), (b) *sgraffito* decoration of third court (c. 1575).

The castle, first mentioned in the middle of the 13th century, was acquired by the powerful lords of Rožmberk (from whom the Hradecs were descended) in 1302 and extended as their headquarters instead of nearby Rožmberk nad Vltavou. Modernized from c. 1575, it was acquired in 1602 by Emperor Rudolf II from Petr Vokz Rožmberk, who had no male heir.

3.42a

3.42b

ITALIANATE BOHEMIA

There are few better examples of the contracted, even confused, course of Renaissance developments in the imperial domains in the third quarter of the 16th century than several of the great houses of Bohemia and Moravia: in particular Nelahozeves (1550s), Telč, (from the late-1550s),

Bučovice (from the mid-1560s) and Český Krumlov (from mid-1570s).**3.41–3.45** Outside or in, transformation in the Italianate mode was first effected superficially in *sgraffito* as at Nelahozeves, Český Krumlov or Telč. As in the log-

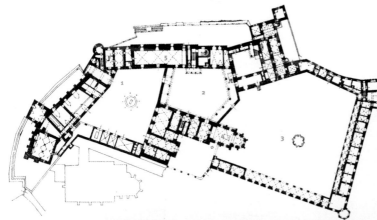

3.43a @ 1:2000

3.43b

3.43d

3.43e

›**3.43 TELČ, CASTLE,** from the early 14th century, extended from the 1550s; see also page 467): (a) plan with medieval range (1), Renaissance courts (2, 3), chapel with Marble Hall over (4), undercroft of Golden Hall (5); (b) arcaded loggia and trabeated gallery (1560s), (c) treasury, *sgraffito* in perspective (1550s), (d) Marble Hall, coffered ceiling detail (finished c. 1570), (e) Golden Hall, ceiling detail (early 1570s).

3.43c

The patron was Zachariáš of Hradec, governor of Moravia (died 1589), whose ancestors acquired the early 14th-century complex in 1339. The *sgraffito* perspectives of the treasury, the earliest of their kind to survive in the kingdom, were commissioned on his return from Genoa in 1552; then, in the 1560s, the Luganese architect Baldassare Maggi was imported to project new ranges of grand rooms linked by trabeated galleries over arcaded loggias and with spectacular coffered ceilings (from c. 1570). Maggi also worked for Zachariáš's nephew Adam II of Hradec, chancellor of Bohemia, at nearby Jindřichův Hradec.

›3.44 JINDŘICHŮV HRADEC, CASTLE, from the mid-16th century, extended in the late-17th century and later: (a) overview with Rondel left, (b) court with *sgraffito* embellishment and superimposed loggias, (c) Rondel interior.

Founded c. 1220, the castle was transformed in the mid-16th century for Adam II of Hradec by Baldassare Maggi. His most outstanding contribution is the Rondel music pavilion of 1591.

3.44a

3.44c

3.44b

3.45a

gia of the latter's central pentagonal court, the arcades superimposed on the court fronts of Bučovice represent the earlier phase of the Renaissance when arch and column were still uncanonically combined – as at Breda and even François I's Parisian Château de Madrid. However, the contemporary interiors are hardly surpassed in the virtuosity of their stuccowork by anything at Fontainebleau.

›**3.45 BUČOVICE:** (a) court (from 1566), (b, c) details of antechamber and chapel vaults, (d) Hall of the Hares (Zaječí sál), (e) Emperors' Room (Cisarského sálu).

Built for Jan Sembera Cernohorski, the Renaissance palace is attributed to Jacopo Strada – the Mantuan polymath who was working for the emperors Ferdinand I and Maximilian II within the Viennese Hofburg – and executed with extensions to the court by Pietro Gabri

3.45b

3.45c

3.45d

3.45e

who was active as a master-builder in Brno. The quadrangular block with corner towers is another derivative of the Italian *castello* type popular with early Renaissance patrons across the border in Austria. The particularly sumptuous stuccowork in the Emperors' Room is ascribed to Hans Mont, one of Rudolf II's court sculptors who had trained with Giambologna and worked with Bartholomäus Spranger at Neugebäude – probably under Strada's direction – for Maximilian II.

›**3.46 BARANÓW SANDOMIERSKI ZÁMEK,** from 1591: (a, b) west and south fronts, (c) court.

The patrons were Rafał and Andrzej Leszczyłskl: authorship is attributed to Santi Gucci, the court artist of King Stephen Báthory. The first phase of interior decoration (from c. 1625) is due to a team of stuccadors led by Giovanni Battista Falconi. A second phase (from later in the century) was commissioned by new owners, the Lubomirski, from the Dutch-Polish architect Tylman Gamerski, who was also engaged on construction of the western gallery wing.

›**3.47 WARSAW, ROYAL PALACE,** 16th- and early 17th-century extensions of an early 15th-century structure, astonishingly rebuilt in its entirety from the late-1970s: (a) overview with pre-Trevano ranges centre right (aerial photograph c. 1926), (b) entrance front of Giovanni Trevano's quadrangle (from c. 1600) from the south-east.

Masonry construction was introduced to the site in the early 14th-century but the Gothic brick castle was built for the Warsaw ruler Janusz I from 1407. A royal residence from 1526 – after the passing of the last local ruler – it was assigned to the widow of Sigismund I, Bona Sforza (died 1557). The Gothic range, extended at an oblique angle for Sigismund II Augustus, provided the basis for Trevano's rectilinear expansion into a pentagonal complex accommodating the royal family and the principal offices of state. Severely damaged by Swedish troops in the mid-17th century, the complex was comprehensively restored: it was entirely rebuilt after near-complete destruction by the Nazis during World War II.

EXCURSION TO POLAND

The perseverance of Italian activity and Italianate form into the last quarter of the 16th century was certainly not unique to Bohemia. The Polish castles of the era are spectacular in their native eclecticism, especially at parapet level, but Italianate Classicism is predominant both in the application of Orders – canonical or otherwise – and in the adoption of abstract ordinance in the mode descending from Raphael's school. The great king Sigismund II Augustus (1548–72), author of the Polish-Lithuanian confederation, entrusted the extension of the castle in Warsaw to the Luganese Giovanni Battista di Quadro (died

3.47a

462c. 1590), who first appeared in Poznań where his most prominent work is the town hall.**3.48** For his works at Kraków, King Sigismund preferred Santi Gucci (c. 1530–1600), possibly a Florentine who came to Poland c. 1550: he was retained by the next king, Stephen Báthory (1576–86), and his nobles.**3.46** On Gucci's demise, Sigismund III Vasa (1587–1632) imported the Lombard Giovanni Trevano (died 1644) to modernize the royal apartments in Kraków's castle and further to enlarge the palace in Warsaw, to which he had moved the administration in 1596. Like Gucci's lower storeys at Baranów Sandomierski, the façades of Trevano's extensions to the Warsaw complex are extremely plain in style though pilasters provide minimal relief to the lower storeys of the tower over the Serlian entrance portal.**3.47** Further down the social scale the distinctive parapet of the typical town

3.47b

3.48

The late-13th-century quadrangular building was destroyed in the great civic fire of 1536: repairs proving unsound, replacement was commissioned from di Quadro in 1550: the two main storeys of his loggias, distantly reflecting knowledge of the superimposed arcades of Antonio da Sangallo's Palazzo Farnese cortile, introduce the High Renaissance to East-Central Europe about the same time as its first manifestation in imperial Vienna. Di Quadro's work was completed c. 1560: the tower was rebuilt in the late-17th century and the roof profile transformed in the early 20th century.

›3.49 ZAMOŚĆ (LUBLIN): (a) aerial view; (b) market square; (c) Morando house; (d) Lviv Gate.

The town was conceived to aggrandize the birthplace of Jan Zamoyski (1542–1605), *generalissmo* and chancellor to the Polish kings Sigismund II and Stephen Báthory. The site was traditionally vulnerable to attack from the Tartars and more immediately from the rising power of Muscovy – against which the Polish-Lithuanian Commonwealth was formed on the basis of a defensive alliance. Bernardo Morando was imported primarily to devise the ring of defensive walls projecting into arrow-head bastions in the latest Italian manner and punctuated with typically rusticated gates. Within, the Vitruvian ideal runs to a grid of streets framing a square forum crossed by the axial

house is wide-ranging in its eclectic mix of abstract, anthropomorphic and elementary Tuscan ordonnance in a highly Florid context – especially in early 17th-century Kazimierz and Zamość.**3.49, 3.50**

CIVIC HYBRIDS

Even in town planning, Italianate order extended to the far east of Poland, uniquely at Zamość: a defensive outpost at the crossroads of trade, the new town was projected by the Paduan architect Bernardo Morando after 1580 but the eclectic local builders were no more immune to vernacular influence than their compatriots at Baranów.

3.49b

avenue which culminates in the residence and a grid: the site permitted near symmetry in the semi-pentagonal eastern half but not in the western sector where the river system was drawn upon for the moat – now reduced to a reservoir lake beside the contracted ramparts which protect the residence. The fortifications and the original grid survived invasion, influx of itinerants and considerable development in the 17th century: the single- or double-storey houses over arcades derive from Morando's High Renaissance translation of his native Paduan vernacular.

›3.50 KAZIMIERZ, HOUSES OF MIKOŁAJ AND KRZYSZTOF PRZYBYŁA, c. 1615: façades on the market square.

3.49a

3.50

3.49c

3.49d

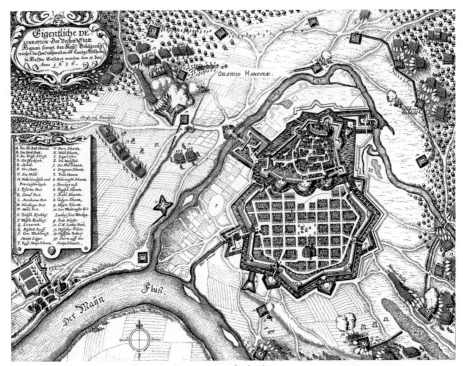

›3.51 HANAU NEUSTADT, from 1597. engraved overview of 1636.

Built to the south of the medieval fortified town and protected with its own stellar ramparts, the new town is centred on a commercial forum with matching ecclesiastical precinct to the south.

Outstanding among the rare instances of ideal town planning in Germany is Hanau Neustadt (from 1597) which realized Italian ideals stretching back from Scamozzi to Vitruvius – at least in main part (see page 255).**3.51** In contrast, traditional urban development organically from the nucleus of a forum may well be represented by Moravian Telč on its peninsula site – though the alternatives are many and various despite the ravages of war across four centuries. The clothing of the medieval townscape in Renaissance guise was, of course, ubiquitous. Largely reclothed in later fashions, the market squares of Kraków or Prague or Leipzig are prominent examples of the epicentre of such development: Rothenburg ob der Tauber may be quoted as typical of its depleted legacy in Germany.

In addition to the insertion of Italianate galleries into buildings new and old, the halting advance towards the

›3.52 TELČ (MORAVIA): (a) overview of town from north-west with castle in the foreground; (b) north side of market square.

The settlement followed Moravian victory over the Czechs c. 1200. It was in Hradec hands by the mid-14th century when a major phase of development was furthered in dependency on the enlarged castle: housing was extended along the enlarged rectangular marketplace where annual markets were held under charter granted by Emperor Charles IV after 1354. The western half of the forum was destroyed by fire in 1386 and further damage was inflicted during the Hussite rebellion forty years later. Full recovery awaited the advent of Zachariáš of Hradec and his Renaissance projects in the mid-16th century: the Italian – or Italianate – craftsmen working for him on the castle were also busy working for the burghers on modernizing the houses. Much restoration was needed, and considerable expansion furthered, after severe damage from Swedish occupation in the Thirty Years' War – but the original morphology subsisted except in so far as it was modified by a new phase of church building following the arrival of the Jesuits in the early 1650s.

3.52a

3.52b

comprehension of Classicism ran to the incorporation in civic and domestic buildings of loggia arcades opened on to public squares – as they had often done in the medieval urban context. Beyond the attractive suite at Telč and the Paduan progeny at Zamość, prominent examples range from Leipzig's great Altes Rathaus (from 1566), to Rothenburg ob der Tauber (a century after the main phase of construction from 1570).**3.53, 3.54**

The tiered gable with scroll brackets and triangular pediment – derived from the Roman church front via Serlio – long survived in the towns of the Empire's orbit. Orders or abstract pilaster strips were often superimposed in the tiers in the manner which we first encountered at the Hof van Savoye at Mechelen or the later, less-sophisticated

3.53a

›3.53 ROTHENBURG OB DER TAUBER: (a) view from the Rathaus tower towards the junction of the market square and the Obere Schmiedgasse with the Baumeisterhaus of the local master-mason Weidmann (1596) right; (b) Rathaus from the market square showing 17th-century arcade.

3.53b

3.54a

›3.54 LEIPZIG, ALTES RATHAUS, from 1556,
reroofed in the 18th century, renovated from c. 1906
and largely rebuilt post-World War II. (a) engraved elevation, (b) detail of west front, (c) south end.

The prominence of the Rathaus in the saga of German Renaissance architecture matches the sustained
significance of the free city in post-medieval imperial
Germany: in general, of course, the scale varied with
the size of the town but concordance was not invariable. Matched only by Kraków's Cloth Hall among its
contemporaries, the grandest is the one in Leipzig
formed to the designs of the mayor, Hieronymus Lotter
(c. 1497–1580), from two late-medieval civic buildings:
the clock tower at the junction – octagonal on a square
base – is off-centre due to the disparity in the extent of
the constituent parts; unequal in disposition thus too,
the tiered gables are of the Serlian type. These strident
vertical accents are effectively countered by the sustained horizontals of the cornice and the terrace above
the repetitive arcading which replaced the timber original early in the 20th century.

3.54b

3.54c

3.55a

3.55b

›**3.55 ORDERED GABLES:** (a) Erfurt, Haus zum
breiten Herd (1584); (b) Minden, Hagemeyerhaus
(1592).

›**3.56 RENAISSANCE PRAGUE, SCHWARZEN-
BERG PALACE,** from 1543: front.

The original patron was Jan Lobkowicz, his contract-
or was Agostino Galli (Czech Augustin Vlach). The
palace passed to the Schwarzenbergs in 1719. At this
stage of the Renaissance in Bohemia, the tiered gable
is articulated with an abstract Attic 'Order' over *sgraffito* simulated rustication and a florid cornice.

›**3.57 GDAŃSK:** (a) Dom Angielski (from 1568); (b)
Green Gate (Brama Zielona, from 1564), from the south.

The so-called English House was built by the local
German military engineer/architect Hans Kramer (died
1577): it acquired its name from its use in the 17th century by the English merchant community.

In place of the medieval Koga Gate at the head of the
royal route through the Long Market, the so-called
Green Gate was to accommodate the itinerant Polish
king. The architect Reiner van Amsterdam had clearly
left home before the floridity of Cornelis Floris overwhelmed Classical order. The arches bear the emblems
of Poland, Prussia and Gdańsk.

Georgenbau at Dresden (from c. 1535; see AIC4, page 883).
In addition to the ones encountered in passing so far, examples range geographically and in obsessiveness from
Lübeck (in mid-century) to Alsfeld to Münster and Minden (in the 1590s), on to Rottenburg and beyond. Further
east, examples come from early Renaissance Prague or
later provincial Telč in Bohemia to Kraków in Silesia and
Gdańsk in the far north of Poland.**3.55–3.57**

After works like the Bamberg Alte Hofhaltung portal,
herms or caryatids were widely in vogue for ordonnance
by the last decade of the century, as on the court galleries
of Schloss Isenburg at Offenbach (c. 1575), the gables of the
Brunswick Gewandhaus (1590) or the Haus zum breiten
Herd at Erfurt.**3.55a, 3.58** Not un-Serlian, of course, the

3.56

3.57a

3.57b

3.58

›3.58 BAMBERG, ALTE HOFHALTUNG, 1570: Ratsstube with adjacent portal.

The modernization of the medieval bishop's palace was commissioned by the prince-bishop Friedrich van Wirsberg in 1570 from Caspar Vischer who had been working for the Protestant margrave of Brandenburg-Kulmbach on his Schloss Plassenburg. In a markedly different style to that of the latter's arcades, both the oriel of the Ratsstube and the semi-triumphal-arch motif of the portal are richly relieved: herms stand in for an Order on the latter but the oriel retains columns as uncanonical in their proportions as Vischer's earlier work on the court of the Stuttgart Altes Schloss. The sculptor Pankraz Wagner may have been responsible for the divergence of style in the two parts of the scheme.

›3.59 CONVOLUTION OF THE GERMAN CIVIC GABLE: (a) Celle, Rathaus, north side (ascribed to local master-mason Jakob Riess, from 1577); (b) Lübeck, Rathaus, screen façade (attributed to Netherlandish masons Hans Fleminck and Herkules Midow, from 1570); (c) Lemgo, Rathaus, oriel (ascribed to local master-masons Hermann and Johann Rolff, from 1612).

›3.60 GDAŃSK, ARSENAL (Wielka Zbrojownia), from c. 1600: street front.

Like the city's old town hall (from 1587), this building is due to the Flemish military engineer/architect Anthonis van Obbergen (1543–1611) in collaboration with the local mason Jan Strakowski. We shall encounter Anthonis again at Kronborg in Denmark.

motif was particularly popular with the Flemish Mannerist engravers. And in Germany, as widely in the north, from c. 1570 anthropomorphic or abstract Orders were often to be overwritten with strapwork in the manner of Cornelis Floris or Vredeman de Vries.

THE FRANCO-FLEMISH CONTRIBUTION

Not incompatible with the retention of Orders, naturally, fashionable convolution was never more spectacular than when deployed to distinguish the seat of urban authority. Of legion examples, those of the most opulent of civic buildings include the town halls of Lübeck (from 1570), Celle (from 1577), and Lemgo (from 1612). Among Polish cities, Gdańsk is as rich as any in Germany or the progenerative Netherlands.**3.59, 3.60**

3.59a

3.59b

3.59c

3.60

All the Flamboyant resources of a Floris or a Vredeman were deployed on the gables of the rural magnate too. However, German builders rarely adopted the French High Renaissance means of integrating elevated vertical and extended horizontal masses with superimposed Orders progressing from pilaster to column – even in Floris's more relevant variation for the Antwerp Stadhuis (see above, pages 415f). For the unification of the distinct elements instead, for example, the architect of Schloss Güstrow relied on varied rustication and doubled stringcourses – or, rather, disembodied entablatures – to bind his expansive central pavilion and octagonal corner towers to the main body (from 1558).**3.61**

The promotion of unity through continuity of motif, void and solid, resorted to increasing elaboration as the 16th century progressed and the German Renaissance

›3.61 GÜSTROW, SCHLOSS, from 1558, partially destroyed: entrance front.

The patron was Duke Ulrich III of Mecklenburg-Güstrow: work began in 1558 under the direction of Franz Parr, whose Milanese father Giacomo had followed his compatriots to Silesia and worked on the town hall of Brzeg. The massing of the main (western) front may have its French equivalents but it is unbalanced by the disparate size of the end pavilions – the northern one is in fact a stair turret – and the ordonnance owes little even to Serlio: inconsistent, it runs to the novel superimposition of miniscule columns and abstract pilasters in the otherwise typically German tiered gable on the southern pavilion.

turned to Mannerism: the Mannerism of the virtuoso decorator which the contemporary French were developing in response to de l'Orme's Tuileries. This is notable in works of the late-1550s and early 1560s like the castles at Horst, Horrem or Hovestadt. However, the most spectacular surviving example of the transition from early Renaissance to Mannerism, via an incomplete grasp of the essence of Classicism, is the schloss at Heidelberg as it was developed in several phases between the mid-1540s and the beginning of the 17th century.**3.62–3.66**

3.62a

›3.62 HEIDELBERG, SCHLOSS, rebuilding begun c. 1545 over medieval foundations, damaged in the Thirty Years' War, ruined from 1689 in the War of the League of Augsburg: (a) general view from north (engraved c. 1620), (b) Elector Otto Heinrich of the Palatinate (Barthel Beham, oil on panel, c. 1535), (c) detail of sculptural surveyors (from the Gläserner Saalbau), (d) plan showing phases of reconstruction,

Eclectic Heidelberg

The earliest manifestation of the Renaissance in the castle compound is the arcaded front of the Gläserner Saalbau built for Friedrich II c. 1550: the uncanonical Corinthian Order supporting the flattened arches of the portico is not unrelated to the near-contemporary work in the court of the Altes Schloss at Stuttgart but on the upper two levels sturdy Tuscan

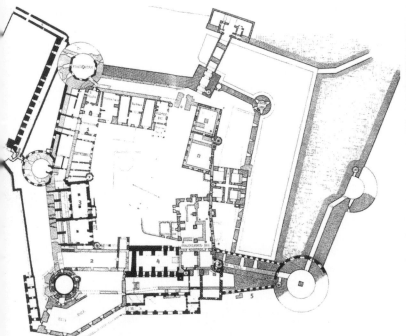

3.62d @ 1:2000

3.62b

(1) Ludwigbau, from c. 1535, (2) Gläserner Saalbau, from c. 1550, (3) Ottheinrichsbau, from 1557, (4) Friedrichsbau, from 1601, (5) Englische Bau, from 1613; (e, f) Ottheinrichsbau, court front and portal, (g, h) Friedrichsbau, court front and detail, (i) Englische Bau, ruins with Elisabethentor (Arch of Elizabeth, 1615, at entrance to Stückgarten named after the artillery terrace), (j) from the east with the garden of Salomon de Caus (after *Hortus Palatinus*, 1620).

Fortifications on the site were probably founded in the mid-12th century by Conrad of Hohenstaufen, who was elevated to the county palatinate by Emperor Friedrich I Barbarossa in 1155. A castle on the site was

3.62c

columns support semi-circular arches of Romanesque, rather than Roman Renaissance, gravitas. The contrast with the next work on the site is stark – though that was not the adjacent building which belongs to yet another stylistic era.

Heavily involved with building projects and art collecting elsewhere before he succeeded his uncle late in life, the elector Otto Heinrich (1502–59) was devoted to the Italian High Renaissance but followed the fashion for Serlio rather than his contemporary Landshut cousin's example of returning to the fountainhead. Rather than employing Italians, moreover, he seems to have drawn on his own studies in collaboration with Netherlandish sculptors – notably Alexander Colyn from Mechelen. The hand of the enthusiastic amateur shows in the eclectic result: much of it displaying misunderstanding – or misdeploying – of Serlian motifs rather than Mannerism *avant la lettre* of du Cerceau or Vredeman.

Unadorned in its surviving state, the outer façade of the Ottoheinrichsbau depends for its impact on the regular repetition of graded windows on the upper two levels: the larger, lower ones are asymmetrically granted to Count Palatine Ludwig I by Friedrich II: it remained the seat of the Count and then of the Elector Palatine. Rupert I was confirmed in that title by the Golden Bull of 1356. The major surviving (though ruined) palace buildings are the Ludwigsbau of Ludwig IV (1436–49) extended by Ludwig V (1508–44), the Gläserner Saalbau of Friedrich II (1544–56), the Ottheinrichsbau of Otto Heinrich (1556–59), begun before 1558 but completed under Friedrich III (1559–76), the Friedrichsbau of Friedrich IV (1583–1610), built between 1601 and 1607, and the Englische Bau of Friedrich V (1610–23).

3.62f

3.62e

disposed. In stark contrast, except for the high podium, the court front is prolix in its unprincipled symmetry. In general, ornament tends to master, rather than to serve, architecture – as it had done in the earliest phase of supplanting late-Gothic Flamboyant with fashionable Classical motifs. In particular, as the storeys are graded with decreasing height, the variously embellished Corinthian and Composite Orders superimposed over the rusticated Ionic (and its Doric frieze) are uncanonically diminished in scale, if not proportion: on the other hand, similar height is maintained for the niches which displace pilasters in the doubled bays of each level at the expense of congestion. The statues naturally provide the major sculptural relief though all the windows are divided into twin lights by herms: comparable height is sustained for all these, too, by dividing those of the taller Ionic level into aedicules set on slender rusticated piers. However, scale is changed spectacularly in the elaboration of the triumphal-arch motif for the portal. Supported by Serlian caryatids and surmounted by the statue in the elevated central niche, this interpolation manages to upstage all else: prophetically, it exceeds Serlio in the manner of Cornelis Floris, whose leathery membrane makes a precocious appearance in association with the attic.

Otto Heinrich's self-assertive addition to the complex of disparate buildings was restored mid-century after suffering heavily from shelling in the Thirty Years' War, and again after shelling by the French towards the end of the 17th century but was gutted by fire in 1764: the accidents of survival have left the horizontals uncomplemented by the verticals originally asserted by gables. The new century's Friedrichsbau suffered a similar fate but preserved its traditional German form with its gables after comprehen-

3.62h

3.62g

3.62i

The garden, begun by Salomon de Caus in 1614, was not complete with its projected waterworks when the patron left for Prague in 1619 but the author immediately published his project as *Hortus Palatinus* (Frankfurt 1620). The terracing, the biaxiality, several of the planted zones and the complex waterworks reflect the inspiration of the Villa d'Este at Tivoli and the Villa Lante at Bagnaia – to name the most obvious examples which he would have studied while travelling through Italy in the late-1590s: however, the additive approach to composition, unvivified along a dominant aqueous axis, had been outmoded there at least since the completion of work at Bagnaia a half-century earlier (see pages 187ff).

sive restoration in the late-19th century. Its patron engaged the Strasbourg architect Johannes Schoch whose work respected the basic ordonnance of its predecessor but opted for more consistency of architectural detail and revised the proportions of the superimposed Orders. Nevertheless, crowded with statuary in voids in place of supportive solids, the result may be seen as approaching the culmination of Flamenco-German decorative Mannerism. That style was rejected in the next generation, that of the so-called Englische Bau of a decade later.

The Englische Bau was built for the elector Friedrich V and his wife Elizabeth, the daughter of the British king James I and his queen, Anne of Denmark: in stark contrast to the pattern-book Mannerist complexity favoured in the complex hitherto, the style accords with the current Palladian tastes of the English court – as we shall see. Dynastic, that English influence was specific to Heidelberg. Contemporary with its manifestation there, however, and in clear contrast to the approach at Horst and Hovestadt,

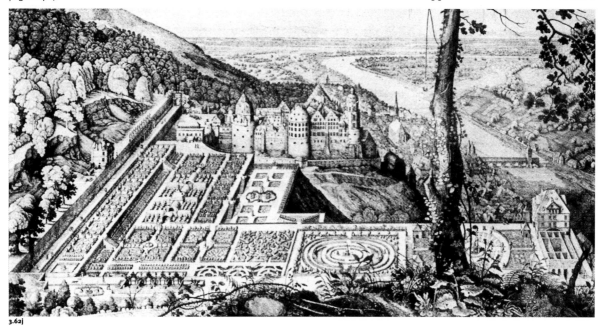

3.62j

3.63a

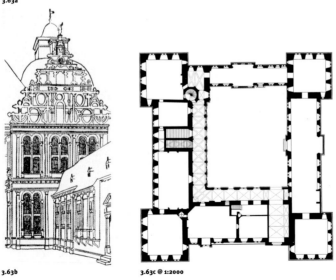

3.63b

3.63c @ 1:2000

›**3.63 HORST, SCHLOSS,** from 1558: (a, b) north-east wing, external elevation and inner frontispiece of south-east pavilion (late-1560s?, drawn in the early 19th century), (c) plan (south and west wings lost).

The patron was Rütger von der Horst from the new class of bureaucrat: he served the elector of Cologne as court marshal. The architect was Arndt Johannsen of Arnheim who employed the French sculptor Joist de la Court. Except for the tower roofs – only one of which recalls the square 'dome' invented by the du Cerceaux in a similar context at Verneuil, symmetry is preserved in the elementary ordonnance recorded for the north-east front but is lost to the front. The lavish embellishment of the latter by Heinrich Vernukken of Cleve (from 1559) incorporates herms, attenuated columns with figuration to the base drums in the manner of Vrede-man and much strapwork. A strapwork web covered the gable of the south-east corner pavilion which must follow the completion of the east wing in the early 1560s.

›3.64 HORREM, SCHLOSS FRENS: north front (undated, late-1560s?, frontispiece c. 1840).

In the style of the lost south-east gable recorded at Horst, the north-eastern one here was erected in the 1560s by Adolf Raitz von Frenz: the north-western one was built to match in the late-17th century.

›3.65 SCHLOSS HOVESTADT, from 1563: north front (engraved record).

Laurenz von Brachum's design was derived from the French quadrangle, at least in the distinction between corps de logis and four-square corner pavillons. Most of the northern and eastern ranges survive but only one of the pavillons (reroofed in the French manner). Other than the geometric patterning in raised brick, which recalls the strapwork web of Horst without the details, the articulation is distinguished by the banding of the paired pilasters in Vredeman's Tuscan or Doric manner. The rustication of the Order in this way was certainly not unique to Hovestadt: for example, it was applied to the abstract pilaster-piers of the Rathaus at Emden.

3.64

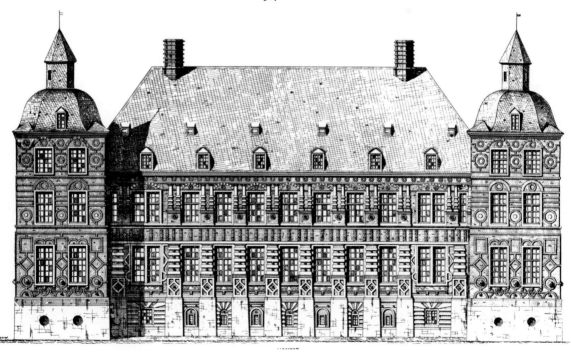

3.65

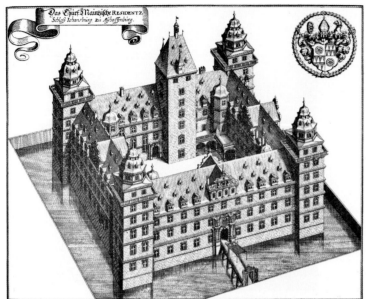

3.66b

3.66a

3.66c

**›3.66 ASCHAFFENBURG, SCHLOSS JOHAN-
NISBURG,** 1605: (a) from south, (b) overview
(engraved by Matthäus Merian, 1646), (c) court front of
north-west range, (d) entrance front.

The patron was Johann Schweickhardt von Kron-
berg, elector-archbishop of Mainz: conservative (or
directed to be so), the architect was the Strasbourger
Georg Ridinger (born 1568). Conservatism ran to the
incorporation of the ancient *Burgfried* even though it
was the sole disruptive element of the rigorous quadrangular symmetry: centrality was denied it by the
chapel to its east but the latter, and its rusticated portal, seem constrained.

The austerity of the form, Classical in all but style,
was not conservative in the early 17th century: the
rejection of Mannerist complexity in favour of the regular repetition of rectilinear elements was current. However, as the detailing of the window frames and the
convolution of the gables reverted to the Netherlandish mode of nearly half a century earlier, it may be seen
as reactionary – though so too were many Rathaus
commissioners and builders.

3.66d

the archbishop-elector of Mainz was reclaiming basic
sobriety – at least – within the native tradition at Aschaffenburg (1614): apart from the portals, the walls are unarticulated; as usual, the main relief is provided in the
Netherlandish manner by the repetitive gables. As at this
late stage even in France, the four ranges framing the court
were generally one room deep: contrary to modern French
practice, however, here there were no apartments in the
corner pavillons.**3.66**

France exerted considerable influence in planning and massing. The punctuation, or framing, of the body of a building with towers was the norm throughout post-medieval northern Europe – especially, of course, for castles (AIC4, pages 532f, 564f). As the 16th century progressed, the plan was regularized about a rectilinear court as in Serlio's Ancy, Philibert de l'Orme's Anet, Jean Bullant's Écouen or du Cerceau's Verneuil. The haphazard process may be traced from the late-medieval irregularity of Hei-

3.67a

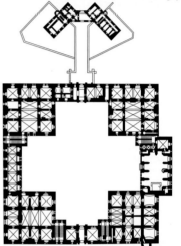

3.67b @ 1:1000

3.67c

3.67f

3.67d

>**3.67 AUGUSTUSBURG, SCHLOSS,** from 1567: (a, b) overview and plan, (c–e) portals, (f) court, (g) chapel.

The patron was the Albertine elector Moritz of Saxony's brother and successor Augustus (1553–86). Hieronymus Lotter, author of the Leipzig Rathaus, seems to have been employed to realize the patron's own conception (perhaps drafted by the court architect Hans Irmscher). The master-builder was Erhard van der Meer: probably a Netherlander, he superseded the laggardly Lotter in 1572 and completed the chapel under the supervision of Count Rochus zu Lynar (1525–96) who had trained in Italy and served François I at Fontainebleau in 1542.

On its elevated site, Augustus's hunting lodge replaced the fire-damaged medieval Schnellenberg but the design was unconstricted by remains. Generally symmetrical in fenestration, under bold continuous cornices, the external and internal façades are astylar in articulation except for a variety of axial portals. The chapel follows the Hartenfels form but was the first Protestant work to be articulated in accordance with High Renaissance principles: the two-storey elevation required superimposed Orders and the tunnel vault has a web of flattened northern strapwork, of the kind deployed by Johannsen at Horst, rather than late-Gothic ribbing or Italianate coffering.

3.67e

delberg, with the oblique junction of its several ranges about its court, to Güstrow and Horst (late-1550s) to Hovestadt (mid-1560s) to Wolfegg (1580s) and on to Aschaffenburg (1605) where there are square corner towers but no change of plane under the central gables, the unifying purpose of the stringcourse is supported only by repetitive fenestration. In the middle of the cycle (c. 1565), the designer of Schloss Augustusburg varied the Gallic formula by setting his four square corner pavilions wholly within the square perimeter to produce a cruciform court: twenty years later the towers were reduced to turrets in rectangular Schmalkalden schloss. In both cases, only the highly important chapel or its adjunct breaks from the strict symmetry (see also pages 316f, 329f, 355f and 368f).**3.63–3.68**

3.67g

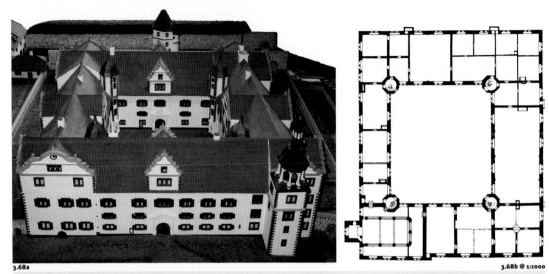

3.68a

3.68b @ 1:1000

3.68c

With increasing regularity of plan went increasing sobriety of ordinance. Except for the portals, the exteriors of the Schmalkalden schloss are astylar – as at Augustusburg. On the other hand, the interior frames of doors and windows are often painted with elaborate anthropomor-

›3.68 SCHMALKALDEN, SCHLOSS WILHELMSBURG, from 1585: (a) model (entrance and chapel tower foreground), (b) plan, (c) court (with patron over portal left), (d, e) chapel (dated 1588), (f) Weissersaal, (g) Reisensaal (late-1580s).

The patron was the Lutheran William IV, landgrave of

Hesse, who acquired unencumbered control of the Schmalkalden domain in 1583. Two years later he embarked on the replacement of the medieval castle. The master-builders were the Saxon Christoph and Hans Müller who also worked for the patron's principal seat at Kassel in the same role. Wilhelm Vernukken (whom we have encountered at the Cologne Rathaus and Schloss Horst) was responsible for the embellishment of the most important interiors: the splendid chapel and its adjunct the Weissersaal. These are unexcelled in their period for the lavishness of their Netherlandish stuccowork: the Weissersaal provided the patron with an antespace to his chapel, the latter follows the form of Augustusburg (ultimately Torgau) but carries the arcades around three sides to include the

3.68d

3.68f

family tribune opposite which the pulpit is centred above the altar, below the organ. The great hall (Reisensaal) has a no-less-florid chimneypiece and painted figural motifs which are varied throughout the rooms of the main floor.

3.68e

3.68g

3.69a

3.69b

3.69d

**›3.69 FROM HIGH RENAISSANCE TO MAN-
NERISM IN INTERIORS:** (a, b) Halle, Moritzburg,
Ialamt Festzimmer, portal with interpolated strapwork
and ceiling with varied rectilinear compartments (c.
1616); (c) Marburg, Schloss, Furstensaal, grand portal
with Serlian architectonic order supplemented by Mannerist volutes (1573); (d) Jever, Schloss, Audienzsaal,
detail of rectilinear coffered ceiling with High Renaissance Classical mouldings (c. 1560); (e) Heiligenberg
Schloss, Rittersaal, ceiling detail (c. 1580); (f) Kirchheim an de Mindel, Fuggerschloss, Cedernsaal ceiling
with convoluted mouldings (c. 1585, attributed to the
Augsburg woodworker Wendel Dietrich).

3.69e

3.69f

3.69c

phic and strapwork motifs. The application of that mode
to interior decoration in stucco is outstanding in the chapel
and its adjunct there: we shall view another lavish scheme
of the late-1580s in the Franciscan church at Hechingen,
near Tübingen in due course.**3.86** Comparable to the
elaboration of the gable under the influence of the Netherlandish Mannerists, developments in interior design elsewhere may be represented by details of timber ceilings and
panelling from Halle, Marburg, Jever, Heiligenberg,
Kirchheim or Halle.**3.69, 3.33c, 3.74f**

3.70g–j

3.70k–o

3.70p–r

3.70b–f

3.70a

>3.70 THE FANTASIES OF WENDEL DIETTER-
LIN AND THEIR IMPACT ON PRACTICE: (a–r)
plates from *Architectura* (1598), Doric, Ionic and
Corinthian Orders and their ideal application; (s) Kulm-
bach, Plassenburg, barracks bastion with equestrian
statue of margrave Christian Heinrich of Brandenburg-
Kulmbach (from c. 1606, attributed to Hans Werner);
(t) Tübingen Schloss, portal (1606); (u–w) Bückeburg,
Schloss portal and Goldener Saal (both from 1604),
Stadtkirche façade (from 1610); (x) Coburg, Fortress,
Hunting Room (Jagdzimmer of 1632).

THE IMPACT OF DIETTERLIN

The promotion of extreme complexity in decorative
design – and the provocation of reaction against it – are
ultimately attributable to the native German painter,
engraver and architectural fantasist, Wendel Dietterlin (c.
1550–99) who spent most of his life in Strasbourg. Departing from the prolix mode interwoven half a century earlier through the celebratory ephemera of Floris's Antwerp
Entry, he took the northern Mannerist style to a delirious
extreme with its epicentre in his adoptive city. For its widespread dissemination, by far the most important of his
works is his *Architectura* (published in Nuremberg, 1598):
the theor-etical content of the text was minimal but the
burin ramped with unbridled invention over the disposition of the five Orders. The many variants in the elaboration of style in the masculine or feminine terms native to
each – the former for the Tuscan and Doric, of course, the
latter for the other three – were seen by architects as applicable on rare occasions to the portal of a castle or the façade
of a church, more readily by cabinetmakers working with
the most fecund of interior decorators and by sculptors as
admirable for funerary monuments or altarpieces.**3.70, 3.71**

3.70s

3.70t

3.70u

3.70V

3.70X

3.70W

3.71a

3.71b

3.71d

3.71c

3.71e

The excesses of northern Mannerism in the funerary genre may well be contrasted with the *éclat* of the memorial scheme effected for the Saxon electoral Wettin dynasty not a generation earlier in the choir of the Freiburg Münster. That is due to the Italian Giovanni Maria Nosseni (1544–1620) who combined the gravitas of High Renaissance ordonnance with exuberant sculpture and a semi-

›3.71 THE CLERICAL FUNERARY MONUMENT, from Vredeman to Dietterlin, c. 1600: (a) Mainz cathedral, south transept; (b, c) Magdeburg cathedral, north aisle (Canon Johann von Bothmar, died 1592, and Ludwig von Lochow, died 1616; sculptors Sebastian Ertle and Hans Klintzsch respectively); (d) Freiberg Dom (Saxony), narthex; (e) Bamberg, S. Michael, north aisle.

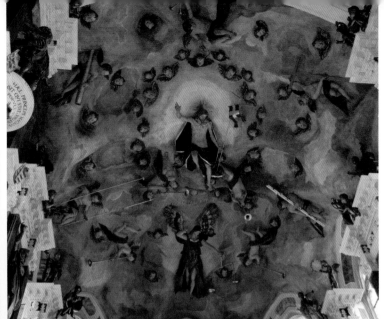

3.72a

›3.72 FREIBURG (UPPER SAXONY), MÜNSTER, CHOIR: (a) Cenotaph of elector Moritz (died 1563), (b, c) choir with Wettin funerary monuments.

The Münster had been chosen for his interment by Duke Heinrich der Fromme in 1541. Thereafter its development as the dynastic necropolis was initiated by the Elector Augustus's insertion of a cenotaph – multitiered over a Doric base – for his brother Moritz in 1563. Twenty years later Augustus furthered the development by employing the Luganese sculptor-architect Giovanni Maria Nosseni to line the Gothic choir with a series of aedicular monuments reiterating the triumphal-arch motif in coloured marble as frames for statues below armorial reliefs: those on the right are dedicated to Augustus himself, his predecessor Duke Moritz and his successor Christian I (1560–91) who completed the scheme; those on the left are dedicated to their wives. The empyrean is viewed in illusionistic *quadratura* over an upper storey of aedicules inhabited by prophets, but Archangel Michael the Judge and Christ the Redeemer, together with an angelic host, are depicted in three-dimensional *quadro riportata*.

3.72c

illusionistic view of heaven in the painted vault: in the combination the work approximates the confection soon recognized as Baroque in the author's homeland.**3.72**

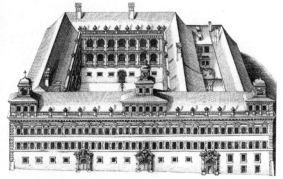

3.73c

3.73a

›**3.73 NUREMBERG, RATHAUS,** from 1616, comprehensively restored after World War II: (a) overview, (b, c) western range from the south and portal detail.

Jakob Wolff was commissioned to extend the Rathaus behind a new west range with a 'modern' façade: his project, fronting much of the original Gothic building (from 1332 enlarged with new council chamber c. 1520), was executed between 1616 and 1622. Major decorative effect is drawn from reproductions of the imperial crown, scepter and orb which were kept in Nuremberg from 1424 to 1796 (in the Holy Ghost Hospital). The new building addressed a relatively narrow street, unlike its celebrated contemporary counterpart at Augsburg.

HIGH RENAISSANCE AND MANNERISM IN BAVARIA: SECULAR WORKS

The influence of Vredeman had reached north-west Bavaria at Aschaffenburg and penetrated into Franconia at Würzburg, where it met with the masculinity of Dietterlin. However, the major Bavarian cities on the roads from Italy proved less susceptible to the anti-architectural fashion unleashed by Netherlandish or native fantasists. As we shall see, the Munich court was not immune to the pattern-book virus propagated by du Cerceau. Elsewhere, Roman High Renaissance logic was preferred for the most important civic commissions but there were occasional excursions into the Mannerism of Alessi's Milanese type.

In the elaboration of its gable, Jakob I Wolff's Nuremberg Pellerhaus (from 1602) betrayed some predilection for Netherlandish elaboration, before its destruction in World War II. Quite to the contrary, in line with the dominant trend, his son Jakob II's Nuremberg Rathaus (from 1616) may be seen as transalpine in its superstructural massing but it is resolutely High Renaissance Italian: the regular repetition of its pedimented and unpedimented windows between the extremely extended horizontal lines of stringcourse and cornice: only the portal aedicules fight a losing battle with sculpture in the provision of relief.**3.73**

3.73b

3.74b,c

3.74a

›3.74 ELIAS HOLL IN AUGSBURG: (a–c) project drawings for the Zeughaus (1602), the Siegelhaus (1605) and the Stadtmetz (1609); (d–f) Rathaus (from 1616, restored after World War II), exterior from the north-west, section, Goldener Saal (from c. 1420, reconstructed after World War II).

At the beginning of the 17th century the town council decided on the renovation of the Gothic Rathaus (1385) to accommodate the imperial Diet. Elias Holl was commissioned to undertake the exercise in 1609: his projects deemed inadequate, full replacement was decreed in 1616. Holl was retained and work began on his innovative new project of six storeys – greater than any building of comparable type in Europe at the time – before the end of the year: construction was virtually complete early in 1620, and the interior well advanced in 1624. The style of the exterior was presented as Florentine: Augsburghers compared themselves to Florentines because of their perceived financial and cultural pre-eminence. However, the dominant motif is the Holy Roman imperial eagle, the badge of the free city's charter.

The interior ascended through ground- and first-

Augsburghers commissioned monuments and altarpieces of extreme Mannerist complexity, as in S. Ulrich's church (AIC4, page 442) but the local master Elias Holl developed his style in the opposite direction. Early in his career he imposed a brutal Mannerism on the Zeughaus but moderation may be traced in two of the master's other Italianate exercises, the Siegel Haus (1605) and the Stadtmetz (1609), the first with superimposed colossal Orders in lieu of the earlier variety of console brackets, the latter with rusticated pilaster strips throughout, both with portals of which Serlio might have been increasingly proud. Further, he essayed translation of the basic Italianate palazzo fenestration to castle design, notably for the quadrangular Willibaldsburg on its spur at Eichstatt (also 1609). His sober Augsburg Rathaus is his masterpiece in its combination of an Italianate body, without Orders in the manner of the Palazzo Farnese, and a central pavilion articulated with pilaster strips in support of a gable derived from the post-Sangallan Roman church front (from 1615): inside Roman sobriety cedes to a measure of Venetian exuberance, especially in the ceiling of the Goldener Saal.**3.74**

3.74d

3.74e

floor halls (*Fletz*) to its culmination in the Goldener Saal and the adjacent Fürstenzimmer, (Prince's Rooms): the former, attributed to Johann Matthias Kager, was completed in 1643.

3.74f

The dominant architect at the Munich court in the last decades of the 16th century was Friedrich Sustris (1540–99), a painter of Dutch descent born in Venice but trained in Rome and active in Florence with Vasari before being imported to Augsburg in 1569 by the Fuggers. His work for the latter – a library and gallery attached to their town house which largely disappeared in World War II – recommended him and his team of Italian assistants to

Wilhelm V of Bavaria (1579–97): he was primarily employed on the transformation of the ducal residence at Burg
Trausnitz with court loggias in the Roman High Renaissance style and sumptuously decorated reception rooms
(from 1573).**3·75** On inheriting the other half of the divided

>3.75 **LANDSHUT, BURG TRAUSNITZ,** from 1573: (a) open court with loggias, (b, c) reception room vault details, (d, e) staircase details.

Duke Ludwig of Bavaria died in 1545, less than a decade after beginning work on his Landshut Stadtresidenz and importing Italian Mannerists to work on most of it. His ultimate successor, Wilhelm V, preferred Burg Trausnitz, but not as a medieval anachronism.

3.75b

3.75c

3.75d

3.75e

duchy in 1578, the duke moved to its Munich seat and took Sustris with him to extend the development of a Renaissance palace beyond the walls of the Gothic fortress. After their deaths at the century's end, they were succeeded by Duke Maximilian (1597–51, elector from 1623) and his Bavarian-born sculptor-architect Hans Krumper (c. 1570–1634) who continued the exercise on a grand scale.[3.76]

Ducal eclecticism in Munich

In 1385 burgher rebellion against ducal control prompted the regime to move its seat from a central urban palace (Alte Hof) to a new fortress (Neuveste) in the north-east corner of extended ramparts: typical of the era, it was a moated quadrangle with accommodation in the four wings, accessible only over a bridge from an extensive forecourt (1). Wilhelm V's predecessor, Duke Albrecht V (1550–79) installed a great hall dedicated to S.

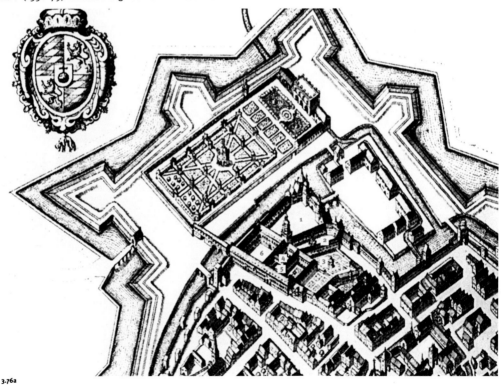

3.76a

Krumper is credited with working beside Hubert Gerhard: it takes its name from the fountain first formed c. 1613 with statues cast in bronze by Gerhard c. 1592 and earlier (it was altered later in the century). Hans Reiffenstuel and Heinrich Schön collaborated with Krumper in the work on the long new street front (from 1612) which extends from the Kaiserhof. Within that complex, the imperial staircase does not follow the eponymous form developed in Spain earlier in the century: with three flights returning at right-angles around a solid core past ducal statues in complex aedicular niches to a colonnade supporting boldly embellished groin vaults, it was the most sumptuous of contemporary transalpine exercises in the Genoese groin-vaulted mode. The Kaisersaal has been reconstructed post-war with *scagliola* fireplace and portal frames and its coffered ceiling, Venetian in the varied shapes of its painted panels, in stucco rather than the original wood.

George in 1559 but as there was no further scope for Renaissance expansion within the enceinte, the future development of the residence lay beyond the jousting ground to the south-west of the keep, on the city side of the complex (2). That development culminated in the destruction of the remaining medieval wings in the 19th century when the regular rectangular Apothekenhof was extended over the site.

Duke Albrecht begun the most important phase of transformation from the medieval to the modern with the Antiquarium (1569). Projected as a freestanding structure on the north-west–south-east diagonal parallel to the south-western side of the elongated jousting ground (3), it was designed to house his library over an immense tunnel-vaulted repository of antique sculpture. The duke's brother-in-law, Emperor Maximilian II, recommended the services of his antiquarian architect-painter-inventor Jacopo Strada: his designs were followed by the ducal architect Wilhelm

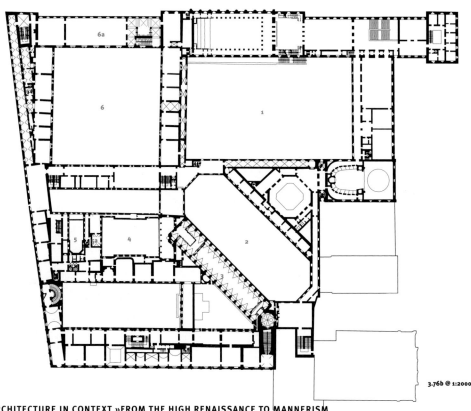

3.76b @ 1:2000

3.76c

3.76d

3.76e

3.76f

3.76g

Egkl under the direction of the Augsburg brothers Bernhard and Simon Zwitzel who had been recommended by the duke's principal antiquarian advisor, the extremely wealthy humanist collector Hans Jacob Fugger.

After a fire in 1580, Duke Wilhelm knew little restraint in furthering the modernization of the complex, particularly in transforming the Antiquarium by lowering its floor, raising tunnel vaulting at the expense of the library accommodation above and decorating it in *quadratura, quadrata riportata* and grotesque painting which cedes nothing to contemporary Rome in the sumptuousness appropriate to a palatial gallery – or banqueting hall as it was now to be. Beyond that, the new elements contributed by Sustris included accommodation for the dowager duchess (lost to later building), a major reception room to the east of the Antiquarium (called the Schwarzer Saal after its marble door surrounds) and the partially surviving Grottenhof, with its red marble arcading and crustaceous revetment appropriate to a simulated grotto, to the west of the Antiquarium: it launched the fashion for the grotto-like Sala Terrena incorporated in the base level of the house rather than isolated in the garden – as in Italy and even France.

The first campaign of Maximilian's era, conducted by Hans Krumper on the west flank of the Grottenhof (from 1601), was devoted principally to the Hofkapelle and its adjunct, the private ducal oratory known as the Reiche Kapelle (from 1601 and c. 1605 respectively): achromatic, the former is

3.76i

articulated with an Order of Corinthian pilasters raised over a basement to support a clerestory attic and richly stuccoed tunnel vault; the oratory is a sumptuous confection of multi-coloured marble inlay, *scagliola* imitation of the same, precious metal or its imitation in gilded stucco iconic panels dependent on arabesques, and stained glass. The next campaign (begun in 1611) transformed the jousting ground into the Brunnenhof and began the Kaiserhof in the north-west quarter. For the former, Krumper superimposed elementary Orders in light relief over simulated rustication: slightly enhanced relief distinguishes the Serlian portals in the canted corners below voluted gables which provide the only departure from sobriety. No such excess troubles the Kaiserhof's façades but nor does Classical rule:

3.76j

3.76h

the articulation in terms of paired pilasters – elongated Corinthian over truncated Tuscan – define rhythmic bays of varied fenestration as entirely in *sgraffito*. The complex takes its name from the Kaisersaal, the great hall provided in the north range to receive an imperial visitor but primarily provided new suites of ducal apartments in the eastern and western range: the quadrangular plan probably derived from J.-A. du Cerceau's *Livre d'architecture*; the long new west front, extended to the south along the Residenzstrasse, cedes little to du Cerceau in Mannerist detail short of rupturing the extended entablature in the manner of Charleval (see pages 368ff).

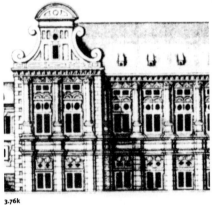

3.76k

LATE RENAISSANCE IN THE IMPERIAL HEARTLANDS: SECULAR WORKS

In Austria, as in the orbit of Munich, Italians rather than Netherlanders were predominant in building grand houses and civic buildings. As in the examples already encountered in Vienna, Graz and elsewhere, Italianate loggias and galleries were common within but austerity, even severity, was characteristic of exteriors throughout the 16th century. Indeed the medieval tradition of siting and massing was widely sustained for the post-feudal seat: one of the most spectacular examples, even in its early 17th-century transformation, is the castle of Hochosterwitz with its ascend-

›3.77 HOCHOSTERWITZ, BURG, from 1570: (a) general view, (b) main accommodation range, (c) Italianate gallery.

The site was granted to the archdiocese of Salzburg in the mid-9th century but an 11th-century archbishop ceded it to the duke of Carinthia in return for support in the Investiture Dispute with Emperor Heinrich IV (AIC4, page 59). The duke bestowed it on his cupbearer whose Osterwitz descendants held it until the last of the line was captured by the Turks in 1476: it then reverted to Emperor Friedrich III. Much damaged in subsequent conflict with the Turks, restoration was begun under Maximilian I who had given it to the bishopric of Gurk. By 1541 it had passed to the governor of Carinthia: his descendant, Baron Georg Khevenhüller, was responsible for the comprehensive refortification works and modern palatial accommodation from 1571.

3.77b

3.77c

3.78

›3.78 LINZ, SCHLOSS: exterior with Rudolfstor, from 1604.

The site, fortified from the late-8th century, underwent major phases of development in the late-12th and late-15th centuries. Reconstruction under Rudolf II, attributed to Alfonso Ferobosco's collaborator, Antonis Muys, resulted in unvaried, unarticulated four-storey ranges around two courtyards: the only relief is provided by the Serlian Rudolfstor, the main gateway to the city.

›3.79 PRAGUE CASTLE: western range with Matthias Gate (1616).

The triumphal arch framing the main passage from the forecourt to the precinct of the cathedral and the palace, commemorating Emperor Matthias, is attributed to the Ticinese architect Giovanni Maria Filippi (c. 1560–1630) who worked for Rudolf II on the new northern range of the palace which contained the sculpture gallery and Spanish Hall (the latter from 1604, much altered). Originally freestanding, however, the arch was the culmination of the series of ephemeral structure erected for the ceremonial entry of the emperor into Prague in 1616: some, at least, of these were contributed by brothers from the Comesque Spezza (Spatz) clan of architects/masons/decorators – one of whom was soon to work for Wallenstein on his palace below the castle.

ing series of fourteen gates, its massive towers punctuating sparsely fenestrated ranges in careful symmetry and a colonnaded, arcaded gallery for the enjoyment of the view from the ramparts.**3·77**

More typical of Austria's late early Renaissance era than reordered medievalism is a measure of High Renaissance architectonic sobriety of articulation and even Italianate homogeneity of mass. As in Bavarian exercises like the Nuremberg town hall, fenestration might follow the Roman example of Sangallo or there might be no aedicular detailing and the only relief would be provided by a Serlian portal: preceded by the 'modernization' of Bratislava castle (begun for Emperor Ferdinand I c. 1552), prominent examples range from the rectilinear block of the Linz schloss, as rebuilt for Emperor Rudolf II (from 1606), to the west range of Prague Castle completed under the late emperor's brother and successor Matthias (c. 1616).**3·78, 3·79**

3·79

3.80a

3.80b

›3.80 PRAGUE, VALDŠTEJN PALÁC (WAL-LENSTEIN PALACE), from 1623: (a) main front on Valdštejnske namesti, (b) main court, (c, d) Wenceslas Chapel, vault detail and general view, (e, f) general view of garden to grand loggia with avenue of statues reproduced from the originals by Adriaen de Vries (removed to Stockholm by Swedish invaders at the end of the Thirty Years' War) and loggia interior.

Architectural initiative is now credited to the Florentine military engineer Giovanni de Galliano Pieroni (1586–1654), son of a an architect in the service of the Medici, who himself studied under Buontalenti: the loggia has its obvious Florentine precedents. However, the detailing of the entrance and court fronts is Lombard or Genoese in elaboration rather than Florentine and overall responsibility for the execution of the scheme is attributed to the Comesque Andrea Spezza (1580–1628), who may have shared responsibility for the Matthias portal of Prague Castle and whose relative Jacopo worked on the Dominican church in Vienna. On Spezza's demise his role was assumed by his compatriot Niccolò Sebregondi. The stucco embellishment of

3.80c
the *sala terrena* and Knight's Hall vaults is attributed to Santino Galli, the namesake of the Comesque Domenico Canevalle, father or uncle of Carlo Canevale (builder of Vienna's Servite church, died 1690) and namesake of the architect who was active in Prague early in the next century: the frescoes in the hall, the chapel and the Ovidian Mythological Corridor are due to Pieroni's compatriot and protégé, Baccio del Bianco (1604–57), who also contributed the frescoes in the great hall, the chapel and the Mythological Corridor.

Begun less than a decade after Emperor Matthias's triumphal entrance to Prague Castle, the last great building in the Bohemian capital before the terrible generation of war supervened to stifle patronage was the palace of the initial hero of Emperor Ferdinand II's Catholic cause, Albrecht von Wallenstein, duke of Mecklenburg, victor over the kingdom's Protestants: fallen from a height which disturbed his imperial client, the patron was assassinated in 1634 – just a year after moving into his grandiose new seat. Italians had begun the history of Renaissance architecture in Prague with the belvedere in the castle garden: Italians closed it on the expansive site amassed by Wallenstein below.**3.80** Much of that was laid out as a garden addressed by the complex's single most impressive element, the *sala terrena*, and peopled by the statues of Adrian de Vries – until they were looted by the Swedes in 1648, at the end of the war which had turned against the imperial cause after the dispatch of its most brilliant general.

3.80d

3.80e

3.80f

The characteristically northern tiered gable was foreign to Wallenstein's Comesque workers. In general, it was uncommon in Austria where Italians – Comesque, Ticinese, Graubundeners – were predominant in the post-Renaissance building industry. The homogeneous astylar Italianate approach to the provision of a façade for relaxed suburban retreat, and the backdrop to the tricky intricacy of a Mannerist garden, is nowhere better represented than by the villa built by the Ticinese Santino Solari for the Archbishop of Salzburg at Hellbrunn.**3.81** Adopted when homogeneity was disrupted by vertical projection and circular form ceded to rectilinear, the gable is treated to minimal architectonic relief rather than to the contortions of strapwork in the manner of Floris and Vredeman or the frenetic fragmentation of architectural elements in the manner of Dietterlin.

As in Flanders and contemporary Habsburg Spain (as we shall see), the square projection – tower or 'pavilion' – with pyramidal roof and prominent cupola is ubiquitous

›**3.81 SALZBURG (MORZG), SCHLOSS HELL-BRUNN,** from 1613: (a) entrance front, (b, c) water garden.

The architect Santino Solari (1576–1646) – who worked on Salzburg cathedral for the same patron, as we shall see – was from the Ticinese canton of Switzerland which, like the neighbouring Graubunden canton and the adjacent Austrian Voralberg (somewhat later in the century) provided itinerant bands of masons/stuccadors employed widely in Bavaria and Austria.

The commission was for a *villa suburbana* which did not require extensive bedroom suites. The water garden is fed from the 'clear spring' which recommended the site: the repertory of al fresco diversions – including grottoes, concealed waterspouts, a theatre and dining facilities – had, of course, been familiar to Solari's compatriots at least since Pirro Ligorio's work for the Villa d'Este at Tivoli and Vignola's for Villa Lante at Bagnaia (see pages 187ff).

In addition to the al fresco dining facilities associated with the water garden and its *scaenae frons*, there was a sala terrena treated like a grotto on the base level of the building itself.

›3.82 KLAGENFURT, LANDHAUS, from 1574:
entrance front.

The building is attributed to Johann Anton Verda: his
seven-storey towers with their bulbous-domed lantern
cupolas were conceived to compete with imperial pretensions to supreme authority. The arms of the
province's estate members are displayed in their first-
floor assembly hall (Grosser Wappensaal).

in Austria's permutation of medieval Renaissance hybrid
form. In the important urban genre of the *Landhaus* that
is well represented at Klagenfurt.**3.82** Following many
early 16th-century works in the genre of the country seat,
it is nowhere better represented than by early 17th-
century Eggenberg near Graz. Giovanni Pietro de Pomis
(died 1633), the Lombard author of that exercise, exceeded
himself in the mode for the façade of the mausoleum of
Ferdinand II associated with Graz cathedral.**3.83**

3.83a

3.83b

3.83c

(a–c) Schloss Eggenberg (from 1625, modified in the mid-18th century, restored after World War II), from the south-west, entrance front and court; (d) Mausoleum of Emperor Ferdinand II (from 1614).

The Protestant Eggenbergs, merchants, acquired the property in 1460 and had built a residence there within a decade. This late-medieval work was transformed by court architect Pietro de Pomis for Hans Ulrich von Eggenberg (1568–1634), who had converted to Catholicism, became a close confidant of Emperor Ferdinand II, was promoted to the upper echelons of the nobility and appointed governor of Lower Austria in 1625. His architect, borrowed from the imperial court, was the Lodi-born Lombard painter-architect-military engineer Giovanni Pietro de Pomis (c. 1565–1633) who knew Rome and had visited Spain in the train of the dowager empress where he studied at the royal palace of El Escorial. The latter may have inspired the work for Eggenberg – though the scale is vastly different, as we shall see – but the triangular block with corner towers and arcaded court follows the form established for Gabriel von Salamanca-Ortenburg at Schloss Porcia at Spittal an der Drau and many times repeated – most recently in Upper Austria at Schloss Greinburg (from 1621). After de Pomis, construction work was taken to completion by the Italian master-builders Antonio Pozzo and Pietro Valnegro. The interior was initially decorated between 1641 and 1646 but the main rooms on the piano nobile were sumptuously redecorated from 1673 – and again, to a limited extent, in the mid-18th century.

The imperial mausoleum, commissioned in 1614 by Archduke Ferdinand of Styria, was built in connection with the church of S. Catherine of Alexandria on the site of a cemetery dating from Roman times. De Pomis's scheme introduced the oval dome to Austria: Rome's S. Anna dei Palafrenieri, if not S. Giacomo degli Incurabili, was doubtless the inspiration but the Michelangelesque multiplication of pediments on the entrance fronts follows Giacomo della Porta's complex revision of Vignola's Gesù scheme. Work slowed after the patron's election as emperor in 1619 and was incomplete on Pomis's death in 1633: as at Eggenberg, Pietro Valnegro and Antonio Pozzo completed the project which was ready for the emperor's interment in 1637.

3.83d

ECCLESIASTICAL CODA

Due to religious contention in the Germanic lands – and the conversion of existing stock – church building was not vigorous in the decades immediately following the Reformation but revival advanced from the tentative as the 16th century progressed. Familiar late-medieval forms – basilican, or the hall type with or without internal supports – prevailed in both Protestant and Catholic domains: exceptional, the most prestigious example of the latter is the Innsbruck Hofkapelle built over the decade from 1553.[3.25] In contrast, there were variations on central planning, especially for court chapels: few rivalled the great cubical

3.84

›**3.84 WOLFENBÜTTEL SCHLOSS, CHAPEL,** from 1558, as engraved by Merian in *Schönsten Schlösser*, 1653.

The extraordinary centralized building (now lost) with its polygonal cupola, is attributed to the Bergamese Francesco Chiaramella who later worked for the duke of Brandenburg as a military engineer.

exercise at Wolfenbüttel (from 1558).**3.84** However, Protestant patrons usually commissioned amplifications of the Hartenfels palatine prototype both for court and parish purposes – as we have seen at Augustusburg and at Schmalkalden.

Beyond the confines of the castle walls, the premier Protestant example was the S. Marienkirche at Marienberg in the south of electoral Saxony but the hall-church interior of c. 1560, with attenuated columns defining the aisles, was gutted by fire fifty years later. Contemporary Catholic activity may be represented by the abbey church at the Tyrolese town of Hall (from 1567). A hall without internal supports, that work was redecorated a century later. The similar form of S. Luzen at Hechingen (from 1586), is outstanding for its stucco revetment in the Netherlandish Mannerist manner of the contemporary Schmalkalden schlosskapelle.**3.85** On a larger scale, the Dreieinigkeitskirche in Klagenfurt (from 1582) is among the most prominent of tunnel-vaulted 'wall-pillar' halls:

›**3.85 HECHINGEN, FRANCISCAN MONAS-
TERY CHURCH OF S. LUZEN,** from 1586: (a)
interior to sanctuary, (b) detail of north nave wall
embellishment.

The Tübingen area was ruled by Hohenzollern
counts who did not follow their more powerful Bran-
denburger relatives in promoting the Protestant cause.
Under their auspices Catholic churches proliferated
but S. Luzen is exceptional, not in the special simplicity
of its rectangular hall but in the prolixity of its ornament. The authors were Württembergers, Wendelin
Nufer and Hans Amann, who had obviously equipped
themselves with the pattern books of Floris and Vredeman: the result, with its foliated Doric Order entwined
in strapwork beside shell-headed niches, may instructively be compared with contemporary Italian stuccowork in both the secular and ecclesiastical context –
within Schloss Trausnitz and S. Michael, Munich, for
example. The high altar dates from 1743.

3.85a

3.85b

originally devised for the Protestants, it was soon converted to Catholicism, raised to cathedral status and transformed in the mid-18th century.

By the turn of the century style had transmogrified eclectically under the impact of the pattern book and fugitives from persecution in France, Flanders or even Spain, where the Renaissance was more advanced: the influence of the Netherlandish Mannerists is still apparent in far-off Lvov's Bernardine church at the turn of the century but had been supplemented, indeed supplanted, in northern Germany by that of Dietterlin – as we have seen at Protestant Bückeburg.**3.86**, **3.70w** An alternative is presented by the Hofkirche at Neuburg an der Donau (from 1607). Realized by a Swiss master who had studied in Italy and gravitated to Augsburg, it is Italianate in the Mannerism of its stucco vault embellishment – rather than Florid – and in its arcading but not in the attenuated proto-Tuscan of its main piers or in the Gothic hall-church plan.**3.88** Similarly, the contemporary modernization of the medieval 'wall-pillar' hall type – with chapel bays rising to full height between spur-wall butresses – has a prominent western representative in the Jesuit church at Dillingen (1610).**3.87** The author was Johann Alberthal (1575–1657) from the Graubunden can-

›**3.86 LVOV, BERNARDINE CHURCH,** c. 1600: entrance front.

The Observantist order of Franciscans, distinguished from the Conventualists as Barnabites, were present in Lvov from c. 1460. Their church was destroyed in 1506, reconstructed and rebuilt again a century later. The conception of the work is attributed to a brother known as Avelid: construction was completed c. 1630 under the direction of a mason known as Behmer.

3.87

›**3.87 DILLINGEN, STUDIENKIRCHE MARIÄ HIMMELFAHRT,** from 1610: interior.

The patron was Heinrich von Knoringen, prince-bishop of Augsburg (1599–1646), whose see extended to Dilligen: the Jesuit college there had been founded in 1564 by Otto Steward von Waldburg-Trauching (bishop of Augsburg 1543–73). Alberthal had worked for the Augsburg court and his plans were revised by the leading Augsburg master, Elias Holl – to whom we shall return. The Rococo transformation was effected by a team of stuccadors and painters directed by Johann Michael Fischer from c. 1750.

3.88b 3.88a

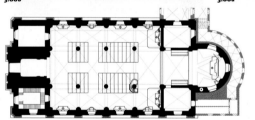

3.88c @ 1:1000

**›3.88 NEUBURG AN DER DONAU, HOF-
KIRCHE,** from 1606: (a) exterior, (b) interior, (c) plan.

Commissioned by Protestant Count Philipp Ludwig von Pfalz-Neuburg, the Neuburg court church was converted to Catholicism by his son Wolfgang Wilhelm on his accession in 1614: the architect (from 1603) was Joseph Heintz (1564–1609), a Bernese who studied painting in Rome and was active in Augsburg (from where he had been called to design the Neuburg Rathaus). After catastrophic failure of construction work begun by a German team, the contract was re-let to Giulio Valentini (Gilg Vältin), a Swiss-Italian from Grigioni, who started work at the beginning of 1607. Albertian *concinitas* is respected – in inspiration, at least – by the articulation of the exterior with Tuscan pilasters though they are more canonical in detail, if not proportions, than the main interior members.

ton of eastern Switzerland which, as noted above, provided itinerant bands of building workers employed widely in south-west Germany: they preferred the German 'wall-pillar' tradition.

Recall of the hall-church tradition introduces the most pervasive alternative: south and north, Protestant or Catholic, churches were still often Gothic in plan, profile, even vaulting, and the pediment ceded to the gable. The retrospective early 17th-century German style is known as *Nachgotik*. Prominent examples of the persistence of Gothic planning include the Wolfenbüttel Marienkirche (from 1608), the Bückeburg Stadtkirche (from 1610) and S. Mariä Himmelfahrt in Cologne (from 1618): all these are covered by Gothic vaulting carried on octagonal or cylindrical pier-columns with hybrid Romanesque-Renaissance capitals and the Wolfenbüttel church offers excellent examples of gable elaboration in the Netherlandish mode to compare with the impact of Dietterlin on Bückeburg.**3.89, 3.90**

3.89a

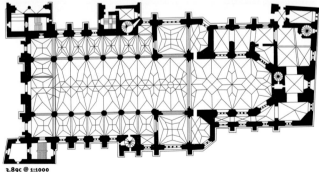

3.89b

3.89c @ 1:1000

> **3.89 COLOGNE, S. MARIÄ HIMMELFAHRT,**
from 1618: (a) west front, (b) interior, (c) plan.

The scheme, attributed to the Jesuit Father Heinrich Scheren, is Gothic in plan, skeletal structure of pointed arches and, therefore, internal elevation. However, the arcaded bays of the aisles and the full gallery storey are defined by attenuated columns which recall the cylindrical piers of an earlier medieval epoch rather than the clustered shafts which might have supported the primary ribs of the vaulting . There is little of Classicism in the capitals – even of the lower, more regular columns supporting the transverse gallery at the west end. The west front, in contrast, rises with superimposed quasi-Tuscan rectangular piers through two tiers of convex and concave volutes of distantly Roman inspiration between essentially Romanesque towers.

> **3.90 WOLFENBÜTTEL, MARIENKIRCHE,**
from 1607: (a) exterior detail, (b) interior to sanctuary, (c) plan.

The city's main Lutheran parish church is dedicated to the Virgin Mary, like the 14th-century chapel which it replaced at the instigation of the Protestant duke Heinrich Julius of Brunswick-Wolfenbüttel: the scheme was

3.90a

devised by the court architect Paul Francke (c. 1538–
1615) and he supervised construction until his death;
completion was protracted thereafter but much had
been achieved by 1618. Like the Neuburg Hofkirche, the
hall of four bays (defined by octagonal rather than
faceted piers) is preceded by a central tower (completed only in 1715) and succeeded by an extended
apsidal sanctuary (polygonal rather than semi-circular). Contrary to the Neuburg style, but like S. Mariä

3.90b

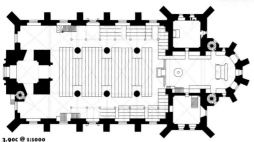

3.90c @ 1:1000

Himmelfahrt in Cologne, the fenestration is resolutely
Gothic. Whereas a late permutation of that style prevails in the Cologne vaulting, here – as at Bückeburg –
the ribs are mainly semi-circular in profile, as in the earliest Gothic quadripartite systems (AIC4, pages 276ff).
On the other hand, the portal and gables (executed
after Francke's death) are Classical in articulation, if
Florid in detail, and the prominent external buttresses
are treated as attenuated Classical plinths supporting
statues of Biblical figures.

After the Council of Trent the Counter-Reformation
Catholic establishment had launched a major campaign
to challenge the proliferation of Protestant works: the
Jesuits were to the fore, of course, founding many orthodox colleges ranging from the Italianate complex dependent on S. Michael's in Munich to the prince-bishop of
Würzburg's Julius-Maximilians-Universität, with its
Renaissance-Romanesque church (from 1583), and on to
the still-essentially Gothic Petrikirche of Münster. With
the latter the campaign extended to the Rhineland (c. 1590)
where the *Nachgotik* style of its galleried elevation was
often to be sustained in preference to the proto-Baroque
of the Roman Gesù or even the Classical ordering of the
traditional German types – though both were attuned to
the preaching of an essentially didactic Order.

3.91a

3.91b

›3.91 KRAKÓW, JESUIT CHURCH OF S. PETER AND S. PAUL, from 1597: (a) west front, (b) interior to sanctuary.

The patron on behalf of the Jesuits was King Sigismund III Vasa: the master-mason was Józef Britius working to the plans of the immigrant Lombards Giovanni de Rossi and, later, Giovanni Maria Bernardoni – who replaced the first generation of their compatriots employed primarily on renovation of the castle. The façade and dome were completed by Giovanni Battista Trevano from 1605.

›3.92 PRAGUE: (a) Jesuit Church of the Holy Saviour, Clemintinum (from 1593); (b) Church of our Lady Victorious (Kostel Panny Marie Vítůzné; from 1611).

The Clemintinum complex was originally developed by the Dominicans from 1232 after they acquired the site and its 11th-century chapel dedicated to S. Clement. It was ceded to the Jesuits in 1556 under the auspices of Emperor Ferdinand I. Most of the complex dates from the mid-17th century; the Church of the Holy Saviour was redecorated in the 17th and 18th centuries but the Roman High Renaissance façade survived behind the triumphal arch which forms its portico in variance of the model as transmitted by Serlio.

Attributed to Giovanni Maria Fillipi, the Church of our Lady Victorious was built for the Lutherans on the site of a chapel dedicated to the Holy Trinity. It was converted to Catholicism after the Battle of the White Mountain and was assigned to the Carmelites.

›3.93 VIENNA, DOMINIKANERKIRCHE, from 1631: façade.

Authorship is inconclusively attributed to Jacopo Tencala: construction was supervised by Antonio Canevale and Jacopo Spezza (Spatz), perhaps a cousin of Andrea Spezza, who was currently working for Wallenstein in Prague. Plan and interior are close to the model, though the tribunes are more generous and the ornament in light relief stucco is quite different. Though dispensing with an upper Order, the entrance front is closer to Giacomo della Poeta's original designs – such as S. Maria ai Monte (1580) – than to his revision of Vignola's Gesù scheme.

Close approximation to the Gesù model (see pages 184f) is to be found in the Jesuit church of S. Peter and S. Paul at Kraków – somewhat less so for the order's church of the same dedication further east at Lvov – but variations on the post-Sangallan Roman basilican façade type were ubiquitous.**3·91–3·93** Active on the Society's prime project

3.92a

3.92b

3.93

in Munich, Friedrich Sustris had been in Rome when Vignola's great work was underway and conformed to it in the definitive plan of the collegiate church of S. Michael (from 1582, revised ten years later). However, the incorporation of a gallery over the chapels, producing the quasi-Gothic interior elevation of the several Protestant works we have already encountered, dictated a façade of two full storeys – plus attic and gable: devised after Sustris's demise in 1599, it has its counterpart wherever Gothic verticality survived to be Classicized.**3.94**

›3.94 MUNICH, JESUIT COLLEGE AND CHURCH OF S. MICHAEL, from 1583: (a–c) church, interior to sanctuary (north), plan (as revised from 1592), south-facing entrance front, (d) former collegiate buildings (from 1583).

Work began on a transeptless hall flanked by apsidal chapels and extending into an apsidal sanctuary beside a tower in the north-east corner – the orientation of the building was roughly north–south. The collapse of the tower ruined the newly built sanctuary and prompted rebuilding to a revised design from 1593 – a decade after the original foundation. Friedrich Sustris was responsible at least for the revised design – preoccu-

3.94a

pied with the extensive work on the Residenz, he may have provided remote – too remote – control over master-masons executing the original design. The triads of apsidal chapels flanking the nave were reformed and a transept was projected to the same width – as in the Roman model – before a still deeper sanctuary. A dome was intended for the crossing, as in the Gesù, but not realized. In the nave – but not the sanctuary – the Gesù's clerestory cedes to a galleried second storey with its own Order supporting the uninterrupted tunnel vault – richly embellished in stucco by Sustris's band of Italian craftsmen. The double-height internal elevation has precedents from the German medieval tradition but the more prominent ones are Protestant: the palatine chapels at Torgau and Augustusburg; more recently, if more remotely, Klagenfurt cathedral, but that was originally articulated with colossal pilasters rather than superimposed Orders.

The façade is an awkward confection apparently designed only at base by Krumper (after the demise of his mentor and father-in-law). The full two-storey interior elevation prompted the stacking of two coterminus storeys below an attic and a convoluted gable – rather than the Roman basilican type developed from Alberti by Sangallo and Vignola. Only the lower one is articulated with an Order but there is no proto-Baroque progression from pilaster to column in concert with the graduated projection of planes from side to centre: on the contrary, the scheme is bifurcated about S. Michael in a niche between twin doors of Mannerist complexity (probably due to Sustris, like the restored high altar). As on the ground floor, Hubert Gerhard's sculpted inhabitants of niches dominate both upper tiers: the sculptor seems to have eclipsed the architect. In stark contrast, the Italianate gravitas of the Jesuit college (Alte Akademie) joined to the west flank is due to Sustris.

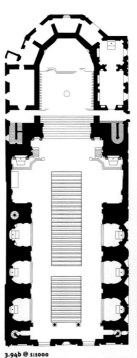

3.94b @ 1:1000

3.94c

3.94d

Built on the site of a primitive chapel by an architect from the Comesque Carlone family, the church served an extensive college later joined to Vienna University. Andrea Pozzo, the Jesuit master of illusionism in the Roman church of S. Ignazio, redecorated the interior and added the superstructure to the towers (from 1703).

The Jesuits of Vienna – and Innsbruck to Trnava in Slovakia – also rejected their order's Roman model in favour of a relatively sophisticated Italian essay in the twin-towered medieval manner to cope with northern elevation.**3·95** They followed the prestigious precedent set in Austria by the authors of the new cathedral commissioned for Salzburg at the beginning of the new century. The Gesù type is respected in plan and internal elevation, with balconied

**›3.96 INNSBRUCK, DREIFALTIGKEITS-
KIRCHE (JESUIT CHURCH OF THE TRINITY),**
from 1627: interior.

The plan is of the Gesù type but the façade is of the
two-storey, twin-towered palace type followed by the
Order's confraternity in Vienna – and those responsible
for Salzburg cathedral – but with only two arcades to
the narthex. As there, the internal elevation incorporates higher galleries than the Roman model, but they
are arcaded and support a clerestory which breaks into
groin vaults. The work replaced a structure begun in
1619 by the Jesuit Father Christophe Scheiner, an
astronomer and mathematician called in from Ingol-
stadt to collaborate with the local architect Matthias
Kager and Father Karl Fontaner: total demolition followed collapse of part of the choir. With some reserva-
tion, attribution of the replacement is to Fontaner who
is known to have consulted Santino Solari in Salzburg
and to have been assisted by Christoph Gump the
Younger.

3.96

tribunes over the chapel arcades between twinned colossal Corinthian pilasters. However, like the greatest of the
churches we shall encounter in contemporary Habsburg
Iberia, it has a narthex over which rises a two-storey 'palace'
façade as the base for the towers. Marking the culmination
of the first phase of Tridentine assertion on a grand scale,
it is the greatest monument of the Austrian age of transition from Mannerism to Baroque.**3.96, 3.97**

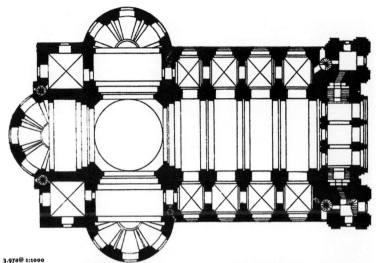

3.97a@ 1:1000

Following the destruction of the Romanesque cathedral by fire at the end of the 16th century, the prince-archbishop Wolf Dietrich von Raitenau called on Vincenzo Scamozzi for a greater modern project and a scheme for rebuilding the Residenz. The latter was begun forthwith but little of the former eventuated before a new start was made by Dietrich's successor Markus Sittikus von Hohenems on the slightly reduced scale of plans by the Milanese Santino Solari (1576–1646): beyond the Vignolan nave, the triapsidal crossing may recall Palladio's Redentore through Scamozzi, or it may follow Milanese precedents descending from the great early Christian church of S. Lorenzo[1.93d] (see also AIC1, page 723). The crossing is lit by a great dome, as in the Gesù model but on an octagonal plan and the tunnel vault of the nave is unpenetrated by clerestory windows: below it the tribunes are more elevated than those of Vignola's work but do not amount to a full second storey as in Klagenfurt's cathedral or Munich's S. Michael. The basic structure was complete on consecration in 1628 but the towers were not fully realized until 1655: they flank a gable which recalls High Renaissance articulation in lieu of homage to contemporary Roman developments.

3.97b

3.97c

3 NETHERLANDISH REVIVAL

The town halls of Antwerp, Ghent and the Hague were the last great civic works undertaken before the revolt of 1568: thereafter the resources of Church and state were diverted to meeting – and mounting – the Protestant challenge. However, the hiatus in patronage ended with the 'Twelve Years' Truce' (1609–21) brokered by the regime of the conciliatory archducal couple Albert and Isabella. Much building promoted much diversity of style. Naturally, there was divergence of development in the two parts of the former Burgundian domain after the Protestant northern provinces asserted their independence from the Catholic south and its Spanish Habsburg rulers in 1581.

›3.97 ANTWERP, GOTHIC SURVIVAL: (a) S.-Jacobskerk (from 1506 to mid-17th century), nave to sanctuary; (b) S.-Pauluskerk (from 1571 to mid-17th century), nave to sanctuary.

The lavish panoply of 17th-century stalls, confessionals, pulpit, altars and monuments in S. Jacobskerk includes the tomb of Rubens and his family (1640) behind the high altar.

The Dominican monastery church of S. Paul was built from 1517 in place of a chapel dating from 1276: from 1571 it was the seat of the Confraternity of the Rosary, founded at the instigation of the Dominican Pope Pius V who attributed the recent Christian victory at Lepanto to Rosarian devotion.

3.97a

3.97b

‹**3.99** S'HERTOGENBOSCH, SINT-JANS-
KATHEDRAAL: marble and alabaster choir screen
(1600–13, now in the Victoria and Albert Museum, London).

The design is attributed to Conrad von Norenberch
(active 1595–1629). The sculpture, particularly the figure of S. John the Evangelist, is by the Protest Flemish
sculptor-architect Hendrick de Keyser (1565–1621) – of
whom we shall see a good deal more below.

3·99

COUNTER-REFORMATION
FLANDERS

Gothic was sustained in the completion of late-medieval
foundations, such as S.-Jakobskerk in Antwerp as late as
c. 1550.**3·98** The furnishings belong to another stylistic
world, as we shall see, but their exuberance was anticipated
in the screen inserted (from 1600) in the Catholic cathedral of s'Hertogenbosch to replace the Gothic original
destroyed by Protestant iconoclasts.**3·99** The impact of
such a feature in situ may be gauged from its relatively
restrained counterparts in S.-Jakobskerk, and the Onze-
Lieve-Vrouwekerk in Scherpenheuvel. Marble screens of
the type, essentially architectural whether or not laden
with iconic sculpture, are – or were – a characteristic feature of the greater Catholic churches in the Spanish
Netherlands.

In the main, late-16th-century Roman Counter-Reformation practice informed architecture in the Spanish
Netherlands, as in Spain. As there too, the Vignolan –
Albertian – Latin cross was preferred to the Serlian repertory of spatial novelties and, as the 17th century advanced,
conservatism was masked by the increasingly elaborate

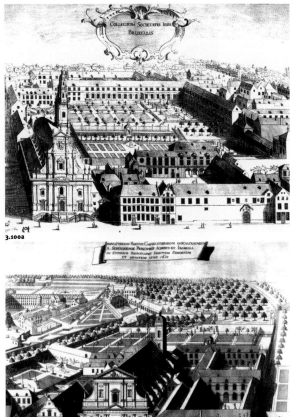

3.100a

3.100b

ornamentation of façades. Coinciding with the ceasefire which led to the truce, the prime ecclesiastical exercises include the lost Jesuit and Carmelite churches in Brussels (1606 and 1607 respectively). The former was revised (from 1616) by Jacob Francart (1583–1651), who had studied in Rome but coped with Gothic elevation by extending the Gesù type of basilican façade to three storeys in the manner soon to be adopted by the Jesuits for their church of S.-Paul-S.-Louis in Paris following the near-contemporary precedent set nearby for S.-Gervaise-et-S.-Protais – in the stricter French High Renaissance mode (see page 399). The Carmelite church by the court architect Wenceslas Coebergher (1561–1634) – Francart's brother-in-law – relates to the conservative mode of Giacomo della Porta's S. Maria ai Monti (see page 290).**3.100**

Coebergher produced a major exception to the Latin-cross rule: the octagonal Onze-Lieve-Vrouwekerk at Scherpenheuvel built (from 1609) for pilgrimage under the distant inspiration of Roman works like S. Maria di Loreto (AIC4, page 850). He varied the Roman type of basilican façade only with a still-moderate amount of local ornament: compared with his Carmelite exercise, the triumphal-arch motif is more assertive and it supports an interrupted pediment.**3.101** In contrast, the façade of the

›3.101 SCHERPENHEUVEL, ONZE-LIEVE-VROU-WEKERK (Church of Our Lady), from 1609: (a, b) exterior and interior detail.

3.101b

3.101a

same architect's Augustinian church in Antwerp (from 1615) has as much to do with the secular vernacular as any imported ecclesiastical style – especially in the inlaid double-height arch and the convoluted gable which spans the whole width of the building though the section is basilican and the aisle arcades are carried on columns.[3.102]

Francart, an architect and painter who returned from studies in Italy in 1608, retained the traditional basilican aisled form and the multi-storey variant of the basilican façade formula on several occasions in Mechelen and Brussels where he was employed by the archducal court. He wrote a treatise which, while Vitruvian in its treatment of the Orders and Vignolan in its prescriptions on proportion, purveys a Michangelesque appreciation of the sculptural qualities of ornament. However, the latter remains subject to the former in his major surviving works which advance slightly on Porta's conservatism. The façade planes of his Brussels Jesuit church advance, as they did in Vignola's seminal Roman Gesù,[1.38k] but the Order does not gain in plasticity to climactic effect in concert – as it was doing in contemporary Rome where Carlo Maderno had asserted the principles of the Baroque style soon after the turn of the century. On the other hand, the plane of Francart's Brussels Augustinian façade does not advance and columns are applied to both the sides and the centre: the result is forceful enough to master the sub-Michangelesque detail of portal and window frames (if not the Buontalentesque cartouche in the attic), but it is not Baroque in the Roman terms essential to that dynamic style's definition.[3.103] Francart's Mechelen Begijnhofkerk façade (from 1629), ascending from five bays through three to an attic, revives planar progression: however, as pilaster progresses to column only in the central three storeys, it may still be analysed in the terms stated by Philibert de l'Orme at Anet, if not those of Vignola suppressed by della Porta.[3.104]

3.102

›3.102 ANTWERP, AUGUSTINIAN CHURCH, from 1615: façade.

3.103

3.104a

>**3.103 BRUSSELS, AUGUSTINIAN CHURCH:**
façade (from 1620, preserved from the demolished
church and re-erected for the Church of the Holy Trinity).

>**3.104 MECHELEN, BEGIJNHOFKERK,** from
1629: (a) façade detail, (b) interior.

The basilican aisled formula is extended in height
on the entrance front to cope with the generous elevation of the clerestory and the high pitched roof. The
assertion of the verticals by breaking the cornice out
over the pilasters and at attic level to support the
springing of the vault admits knowledge of Porta's variation on Vignola's approach to the internal articulation
of the Gesù.

3.104b

3.105a

›3.105 ANTWERP, S. CARLO BORROMEO, from c. 1620 in revision of earlier plans, originally dedicated to S. Ignatius: (a) entrance front, (b) interior to sanctuary, (c) high altar project (attributed to Rubens).

The early Christian basilican form of church with apsidal nave separated from aisles by colonnades was popular in Flanders after Wenceslas Coebergher revived it for the Augustinians of Antwerp (1615). Assuming control of his order's project, Huyssens conforms but introduces an upper gallery with columns of equal height to the those of the lower arcade. Between recessed belfries, the layered space is expressed on the façade in three storeys, two of five bays embracing aisles and nave with the third over the latter though, of course, it is a single vertical volume. If Huyssens dictated the ordonnance, he deployed columns and pilasters to enrich it but showed no interest in the sophistication of French High Renaissance or Roman Baroque methods of effecting unity in diversity: with columns at the sides and in the centre, in neither the French nor Italian sense – that of Pierre Lescot or Carlo Maderno – is coherence enforced by centrifugal progression in the plasticity of the Orders. Moreover, his multiple bays on multiple levels provided ample opportunity for the inventive intervention of Rubens – if tradition is correct in allotting responsibility to the great painter for external decorative detail as well as for the major altarpieces and their settings inside. Lagely destroyed in a fire of 1737, two side chapels were spared. These and the unexecuted project for the high altar may be seen as proto-Baroque – the Solomonic columns presumably derived from Raphael, the broken pediment extracted from Michelangelo (see above, pages 15 and 163).

3.105c

The hall or palace type of façade – which we have already encountered in Munich and Salzburg and which we shall encounter in Habsburg Portugal – is most spectacularly represented on the church of S. Carlo Borromeo in Antwerp.**3.105** A centralized scheme was initiated in 1515, rejected in homage to the Roman Gesù c. 1617 and definitively revised c. 1620: that exercise, sustaining the local preference for internal colonnaded arcades which Francart had respected in his lost Jesuit church but not in the Mechelen Begijnhofkerk, is attributed to the Jesuit Father Peter Huyssens but the decorative detail of the polychrome front is ascribed to Rubens: like the great

3.105b

3.106a

3.106c

3.106b

›**3.106 RUBENS AND ARCHITECTURE:** (a, b) wing and portico of his Antwerp residence; (c) Archducal entry arch (Antwerp, 1635); (d–g) *I Palazzi di Genova* (engravings published in 1622 after the artist's surveys).

Rubens built lavishly in paint and devised temporary ceremonial structures – notably for the entry of the Cardinal-Infante Ferdinand into Antwerp in 1635 – but actually realized his architectural ideas in masonry only in the extension to his own house in Antwerp from 1618. Like the rusticated arcuate architecture in several of the episodes from the cycle of paintings he was currently producing for the French queen Marie de' Medici's Parisian palace (which will be reviewed in due course in the context of the great Baroque painter's stylistic development), the screen between the house's court and garden is inspired by Giulio Romano, either directly

3.106d

from Mantua or via Serlio. However, the form of the central portal, with its canted jambs, comes from Michelangelo and so too do the multiple pediments. The encrustation of the main façades may best be related to the artist's record – and interpretation – of Genoese domestic architecture as it developed on the grand scale by the followers of Galeazzo Alessi (see above).

Rubens drew his main inspiration for *I Palazzi di Genova* from the post-Alessian development of the Strada Nuova (pages 263f): eleven of its palaces are included (some more recognizable today than others) with houses and churches from elsewhere in the maritime city. The book was addressed to noble northern patrons (and had some success there and elsewhere) with the declaration: 'Little by little we see in these parts that the style of architecture which we call Barbaric or Gothic is becoming old and extinct, and that a few very beautiful talents are introducing to the country the true symmetry of that which conforms to the rules of the ancient Greeks and Romans with very great splendour and ornament.'

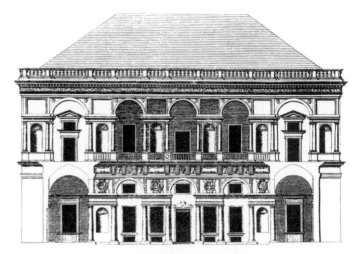

3.106e

Facciata del Palazzo del Sig.^r Luigi Centurione Marchese de Monsascho.

3.106f

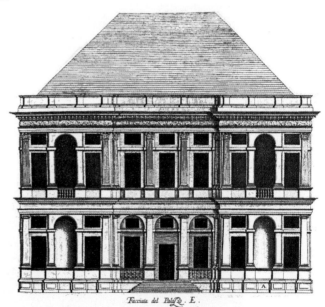

Facciata del Palazzo. E.

3.106g

painter's own house, which follows the publication of his Genoese experience, the result may be categorized as Mannerist rather than Baroque in the nature and profusion of its relief.**3.106** Yet Huyssens, who usually expressed the traditional basilican form in section and elevation like Francart, may be credited with effecting the Flemish transition from the former to the latter style in the light of Roman experience which he acquired in Rome c. 1626.

Mannerist complexity was still favoured over Baroque dynamics beyond the mid-century, by the unidentified author of the Brussels Begijnhofkerk for prominent example.**3.107** Meanwhile, Huyssens had advanced haltingly from the one towards the other. Still hardly more Baroque in the Italian sense than S. Carlo Borromeo, his S.-Walburgakerk in Bruges (under construction from

›3.107 BRUSSELS, BEGIJNHOF, S.-JAN-BAPTIST TEN BEGIJNHOFHERK, from 1657: façade.

The work is attributed to Lucas Faydherbe (1617–97), a Flemish sculptor-architect who emerged from Rubens's studio after the master's death in 1640 to begin independent practice in Mechelen – which had extended to Antwerp and Brussels within a decade.

1628) applies columns to the central elevation, as Francart was doing at much the same time in Mechelen, but they are extraneous to the minimal planar progression.**3.108** Even this is lost to conservatism in his later work on the S.-Pieterskerk for the Benedictines of Ghent (from 1629) with its reiterated doubled pilasters. However, he had been far more progressive in his work for the Jesuits of Namur and by mid-century his followers, particularly Willem Hesius, had not foresworn floridity but fully comprehended the Roman mode – in whose light it will be assessed.

›3.108 BRUGES, S.-WALBURGAKERK, from 1628: (a) façade, (b) interior.

3.108a

3.108b

3.109

›ARCHITECTURE IN CONTEXT »FROM THE HIGH RENAISSANCE TO MANNERISM

›**3.109 LEIDEN, STADHUIS,** from 1593, extended 1604: façade.

The architect Lieven de Key – a Flemish Protestant refugee in London from 1580 who returned to the secessionist north in 1590 and settled in Haarlem – was commissioned to add a new façade to Leiden's town hall (in collaboration with the local builder Claes Cornelisz and the Bremen mason Luder van Benthem). The influence of Cornelis Floris, transmitted via The Hague, is manifest. The eastern extension of 1604 followed Key's design, but not the tower of 1599. Key's career culminated in his extension of the town hall of Haarlem (from 1620).

›**3.110 THE SWEDISH ROYAL FLAGSHIP 'VASA',** built 1626–28: view forward from the stern castle (Stockholm, Vasa Museum).

Along with three others, the ship was commissioned by King Gustavus II Adolphus (whose spectacular military career will be reviewed in due course) from the Dutch shipwright Henrik Hybertsson de Groote (died 1627) who had assumed control of the royal shipyards in 1625. Henrik, or his successor, reluctantly followed orders to increase the new flagship in height for extra firepower – the navy having been seriously depleted by storm – but the result was top-heavy and the ship foundered on her maiden departure from the dock. She was preserved intact in deep silt.

3.110

PROTESTANT DUTCH

The absence of Catholic Church and vice-regal court patronage in the seven secessionist provinces of the northern Netherlands left merchants as the main patrons of architecture – for their own domestic purposes and as dignitaries on civic councils. The major works were town halls: the Stadhuis of Leiden is a prominent example from the first phase of such building, after the standard had been set at The Hague.**3.109, 3.19** The next phase was dominated by Amsterdam.**3.111**

Amsterdam

The Hague was the seat of government but Amsterdam had emerged as the dominant commercial centre in the late Middle Ages. The city developed from the 12th century when the Amstel was dammed and dykes constructed on the estuary banks: the nucleus remains the forum called Dam beside the

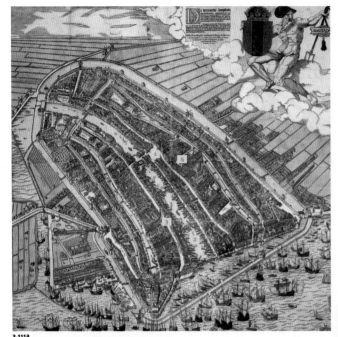

3.111a

›3.111 AMSTERDAM, URBAN DEVELOPMENT AND HOUSING: (a, b) overviews of town and port in 1544 and 1649 with (1) Dam, (2) Damrak, (3) Oude Kerk, (4) Nieuwe Kerk, (5) Groenburgwal and (5a) Zuiderkerk, (6) Oost-Indisch Huis; (c) Dam and Damrak from overview of 1633); (d) Oost-Indisch Huis (East India Company Building, from 1603), court front;

3.111d

estuary port called Damrak: the Stadhuis was sited there. To the east of the latter, the oldest surviving building of note is the S.-Nicolasskerk (the Oude Kerk) of c. 1300: the S.-Catharinakerk (the Nieuwe Kerk) followed a century later to the harbour's west; meanwhile port facilities had been built to accommodate commerce on land reclaimed and embanked around Damrak within defence walls. The destruction of much of the timber-built city within the walls by fire in the late-15th century prompted the decree that restoration and new building must be of masonry – at least for outer cladding. Two further rings of walls had been built by 1500, the outer one contiguous with the Singel.

After the revolt of 1568 and the accession of Protestants to power in place of the former Catholic oligarchy, the former regent's policy of inhibiting expansion was reversed to cater for a population exceeding 60,000: the area to the east of the Oude Kerk was the first to be developed with the Groenburgwal as its spine: this was followed around the circlet of new canals, the Keizersgracht and Prinsengracht, to the west and south (from 1615). The period also saw the conversion of Catholic churches to Protest-

AMSTELODAMI CELEBERRIMI HOLLANDIÆ EMPORII DELINEATIO NOVA

3.111b

't Stadthuys
IJsselbanck

DAM

Wage

DAMRACK

3.111c

ant use and the outbreak of Calvinist iconoclasm. The city's Protestant church-building campaign opened with the Zuiderkerk at the head of the Groenburgwal just after the turn of the century. By then the city on the Amstel had replaced Antwerp, the city on the silted Schelde, as the commercial hub of northern Europe. Its status was marked by the founding of the Exchange building in 1608 and, five years earlier, the Oost-Indisch Huis (VOC, United East India Company Building) to promote shipbuilding, provision fleets for far-flung mercantile activity – much of it at the expense of Habsburg-dominated Portugal – and trade their cargoes. Civic, guild and domestic building naturally proliferated – even the most lavish of the merchant houses usually on narrow plots.

As the dominant commercial centre in the thriving Protestant Netherlands, Amsterdam was naturally prominent in the development of the urban house type but the decorative elaboration of the gable, especially the combination of scrolls and pediments under the influence of the pattern books of Hans Vrederman de Vries, was widespread throughout the Netherlands by 1600. Whether or not a network of architectural elements was imposed on the bays of the main storeys – as in the Leiden Stadhuis – vitality was conjured above from florid and animate sculpture – especially of herms, atlante or caryatids. As on the stern of a contemporary ship, the ornament provided a semblance of coherence to composite form.[3.110] Though supplanted in that role, it survived the subjection of domestic façade design to the discipline of mathematical proportions as a grid of Orders came to the fore in the overt restoration of Classical principle.

The architectonic mode was introduced to Haarlem by Lieven de Key (1560–1627) – whom we have already encountered at Leiden – and to Amsterdam by Hendrick de Keyser (1565–1621).[3.111] City architect of Amsterdam and director of its building company (*Stadsfabryck*), de Keyser had an extensive public and private practice in the first decades of the 17th century. His early work, the Huis de Dolfijn on the Singel for example, is still florid in the Vredeman manner and he sustained the style as late as 1618 for the Stadhuis of Delft. However, leading the development on Amsterdam's new canalized arteries – not least the Keizersgracht – he provided prime examples of the new discipline in façade design with works ranging from the Exchange (1608, demolished in the 19th century) to the Huis met de Hoofden (1622, attributed to Hendrick's son Pieter). The style is anticipated in the Oost-Indisch Huis (from 1603), which is also attributed to the city's chief architect.

3.111e

(e) Huis de Dolfijn (1605) on the Singel; (f) Huis met de Hoofden (House of the Heads, from 1622) on the Keizersgracht; (g) Groenburgwal to Zuiderkerk.

3.111f

3.111g

›ARCHITECTURE IN CONTEXT »FROM THE HIGH RENAISSANCE TO MANNERISM

›**3.112 DELFT, NIEUWE KERK:** tomb of William the Silent, Prince of Orange and first *Stadtholder* of the northern Netherlands (Hendrick de Keyser, from 1614 in black and white marble and bronze).

The commission was let by the Estates-States in 1614. Exceeding the French Valois models, under the inspiration of Vredeman but following the precedent set by Floris for Christian of Denmark in the cathedral at Roskilde,[2.20, 3.15] de Keyser responded with a pavilion of Mannerist complexity sheltering the seated and recumbent effigies of the deceased prince guarded by large-scale Virtues whose formidable presence matches that of his S. John the Evangelist at s'Hertogenbosch.

3.112

3.113b

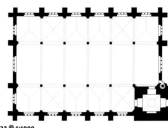

3.113a @ 1:1000

›**3.113 AMSTERDAM, HENDRICK DE KEYSER AND PROTESTANT DESIGN:** (a, b) Zuiderkerk (from 1603), plan and view from south; (c) Noorderkerk (from 1620), plan; (d, e) Westerkerk (1620, tower 1638 to revised design), interior and exterior.

The Zuiderkerk is a simple hall church, its outer perimeter unbroken by transepts though the second and fifth bays are given transverse gables: the style is hybrid, a Tuscan Order supports a keel vault of venerable lineage; the tower is the prime Protestant example of the medieval spire Classicized in receding square and octagonal stages.

The Westerkerk of 1620 followed a similar formula: the tower was completed two decades after de Keyser's death to revised designs attributed to Cornelis Danckerts de Rij. In contrast to these two landmark churches, which may be seen as based on double Greek crosses, the smaller Noorderkerk of 1620 rises over a single Greek cross in an octagon: the plan was drawn by de Keyser just before his death.

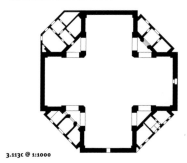

3.113c @ 1:1000

A sculptor by initial training in his father's Utrecht cabinet-making workshop, Hendrick de Keyser did not deny sculptural embellishment to his ordered façades. As the most prominent early 17th-century Dutch artist schooled in the medium, moreover, he won such prestigious commissions as the tomb of *Stadtholder* William the Silent: he responded with the exuberance he had recently displayed in the choir screen of s'Hertogenbosch.**3.112, 3.100** Yet he was essentially severe in devoting himself to developing a specifically Protestant type of church – rationally planned, centralized and rectangular, galleried, focused on the pulpit – in the west, south and northern sectors of the late-16th-century addition to the concentric rings of Amsterdam.**3.113** The style of these pioneering works is in stark contrast with the current Flemish mode and set the tone for a major strand of anti-Baroque architectural development in northern Europe – not least Britain.

3.113d

3.113e

‹**3.114** 'ARRIVAL OF A DUTCH THREE-MASTER AT KRONBORG'** (Hendrick Cornelisz. Vroom, 1614).

‹**3.115 DUTCH DESIGN IN DENMARK:** (a) Helsingør, Kronborg Castle (from 1574); (b–g) Hillerød, Frederiksborg Castle (from 1560), aerial view, general view, detail of gate, courtyard, chapel interior and detail of ballroom ceiling.

Kronborg was founded by Erick of Pomerania in 1420 to control shipping in the Oresund – the strait connecting the Baltic with the North Sea – and paid for with the dues. The outer defences protected three main elements: a ceremonial hall detached from the residential block and a chapel. Rebuilding without the defences, but encapsulating the original elements, began in 1558 but the scheme was superseded in 1564 at the instigation of Frederick II. Under the latter and his successor, Christian IV, the extended campaigns of building and restoration were conducted principally by the Netherlandish masters Anthonis van Obbergen and Hans van Steenwinckel. Restoration after a fire in 1629 and again after damage inflicted by Swedish troops in 1658 appears to have respected the scheme developed by

3.114

TO DENMARK

With trade from Antwerp and the burgeoning Dutch maritime cities went culture, of course.**3.114** Netherlandish architects were in much demand across the Rhine and their compatriots played a leading role in Scandinavia, first for the Danish court. We have already met Cornelis Floris in the employ of King Frederick II (1559–88) as a designer of tombs in the cathedral at Roskilde.**3.15** For his extensive

3.115a

3.115b

3.115c

3.115d

building campaigns at Hillerød and Helsingør – on the castles of Frederiksborg and Kronborg – Frederick imported several Dutch architects.**3.115** Hans von Diskow was involved initially at Kronborg but on his death in 1653 a new start was made under the direction of Hans van Paeschen. Frederick or his successor, Christian IV (1588–1648), also employed Hans van Steenwinckel from Floris's circle. As in the Netherlands, fashionable Italianate mouldings were introduced to the vernacular brick mass and stone framework to articulate order in central portals and symmetrically placed gables, the latter

van Obbergen from 1577 except for the superstructure of the towers and interior fittings: of the interiors, however, the main survivor is the chapel as built from 1582 and restored by Christian IV in the 1630s.

Frederiksborg, the hunting lodge of Frederick II at Hillerød, also originally consisted of three elements – but they were on three small islands in an artificial lake. Flanking the forecourt on extended reclaimed land, the service wings largely survived the rebuilding of the main residential block for King Frederick from 1575 and the transformation of the whole on a grand scale for King Christian between c. 1602 and 1611. The scheme with forecourt has its French equivalents but the style is Netherlandish: apart from the elaboration of the

3.115e

gables, the masking of the court galleries' broad pier arcades – disciplined in the rhythm of the triumphal arch – with aedicules framing statues is particularly noteworthy in this connection (see page 406). The author is unknown: Christian's architect of Kronborg, Hans I van Steenwinckel, probably preceded his son Hans II who is known to have been in charge of a new building campaign. That contained the ballroom and chapel in the west wing: the most splendid interiors of the reign, the former was restored after a fire in 1859 but the latter survives intact.

inevitably susceptible to convoluted scrollwork as well: Serlio was a prime source of inspiration for portals, of course, but the Netherlanders naturally brought the pattern books of their fecund compatriots. Even as late as the first decade of the new century, the splendid chapel installed during the comprehensive transformation of Frederiksborg by King Christian is a hybrid exercise: Classical in the articulation of the galleried bays, Gothic in the elaborate rib vaulting, it stands at the apogee of Protestant *Schlosskapelle* development from Torgau to Schmalkalden and Augustusburg.**3.25d, 3.64c, 3.85**

3.115f

3.115g

Giles Fields

Piazza in Coventgarden

Bedford house

4.45c

›ARCHITECTURE IN CONTEXT »FROM THE HIGH RENAISSANCE TO MANNERISM

4 ACROSS THE CHANNEL

4.1a

1 ELIZABETHAN AND JACOBEAN ECLECTICISM

In France, as we have seen, the early Renaissance followed the Italian at least three generations later: a decade or so later still it first appeared in Britain with the tomb of Henry VII in Westminster Abbey and in the reliefs grafted on to the towers of Hampton Court Palace to the order of its grandiloquent patron, Henry VIII's chief minister Cardinal Wolsey (AIC4, pages 554f and 880f). In the form of medallions commemorating Roman emperors, these embellishments are attributed to Giovanni da Maiano who came from Florence in the wake of Pietro Torrigiani to work on the king's tomb. That was in the second and third decades of the new century: Maiano was paid by the cardinal for his medallions in 1521. After the royal Reformation in the fourth decade, no further Italians translated Renaissance ideals directly to England and the Tudor kingdom was cut off from the flow of the Italian fountainhead – except as it was channelled through France.

If Henry VII's tomb is intrinsically Classical – in the current High Renaissance mode of its author's compatriots –

by definition the embellishment of the Hampton Court gatehouse towers is superficial. As we have seen, such was the far richer approach adopted by the contemporary French to the Classicization of medieval forms in preference to the importation of a generically Classical style from Italy. And the French approach prevailed in England not only because the English Reformation inhibited cultural commerce with Italy but, as elsewhere in trans-Alpine Europe, mainly because of the affiliation between the northern post-Gothic traditions of building – particularly the dominance of verticality in their morphologies.

PRELUDE

The hall with screened entrance to one end, with which England led in the development of domestic architecture, long subsisted as the nucleus of the seat of the landed magnate. By the end of the 13th century diversified needs were already being met with the addition of perpendicular wings to each side: the one beyond the screened passage to accommodate services; the other, opposite, to provide the proprietor and his wife with private space for withdrawal from the rude communal life of the hall itself. At Penshurst Place (Kent) or Haddon Hall (Derbyshire), to name but two of many possible examples, this nucleus is still clearly discernible but diversification and provision for expanded families had led to the proliferation of rooms around courts. With the main portal opening into a corner of the main space and the wings unbalanced, pragmatism was yet to be regulated even with elementary symmetry (AIC4, pages 532ff).

The courtyard plan of the great house perpetuated the medieval monastic and collegiate tradition. The greatest example, begun in the first decade of the new century at the beginning of the first self-consciously Renaissance reign, was Cardinal Wolsey's Hampton Court. The com-

›4.1 HAMPTON COURT, begun by Cardinal Wosley in 1515, augmented by King Henry VIII from 1531: (a) royal armorial panel, (b) court front of inner portal, (c, d) great hall exterior and interior.

4.1b

4.1c

The collegiate tradition upon which Hampton Court was founded was sustained in the elevation of the complex to a royal palace. The king's major addition, planned by Wolsey fully in accordance with that tradition, was the great hammerbeam-roofed hall (AIC4, pages 554f); he also extended wings to provide a symmetrical frame for the open entrance court and inserted an innovative gallery in the range facing south over the privy garden to the river.

The great hall was the principal early Tudor ceremonial room – corresponding to the Salle des Caryatides at the Louvre – but much more overtly medieval in morphology. It was supplemented – soon supplanted – by the 'great chamber' on the floor above in royal usage for ceremony, court feasts and audience: beyond it was the strictly restricted 'privy chamber', where much of the king's life was spent between his dressing and dining in private; then came the sleeping closet accessible only to the king's personal servants. Under Queen Elizabeth – at the earliest and first at Whitehall where the court was principally based – an essentially exclusive withdrawing room was interposed between the Privy Chamber and the bedroom against the encroachment of an expanding court. The English ruler seems to have demanded a greater degree of privacy than the king of France and sought to keep the courtiers – let alone the people – at bay through the proliferation of rooms in the royal suite and gradations of rank in admission to them: the process surely gained special impetus under the Tudor queens regnant.

4.1d

›4.2 LONDON, TUDOR PORTALS: (a, b) White-hall Palace, Holbein and King Street (1532 and c. 1540 respectively); (c) S. James's Palace (early 1530s).

York Place, the London residence of the Archbishop of York beside the Thames to the east of Westminster Abbey, was seized from Cardinal Wolsey in 1529 and was known as Whitehall from the following year. Again, the collegiate tradition underlay the cardinal's plans for reforming the medieval agglomeration of buildings into a relatively ordered two-courtyard complex entered through an axially placed twin-towered portal and dominated from one side by the great hall. The king furthered the project, as at Hampton Court, and built two gates (destroyed): one was of the traditional type with prominent oriel deployed at much the same time – but with less-coloristic masonry – for S. James's Palace; the later one represented an attempt to Classicize the medieval form in a manner tentatively applied to the portal of the palace pavilion at the Field of the Cloth of Gold (1520; see page 44) – and not without affinity with the early Renaissance style evolved for François I.

plex as a whole is still asymmetrical, with the dominant bulk of the great hall to the left of the inner court, but there is new order in the centrality and axial alignment of the gatehouses. The precedent for that form of gate had been set 150 years earlier in monastic foundations like Thornton Abbey in Lincolnshire but, as we have seen, the symmetrical massing at Wolsey's court is relieved with Giovanni da Maiano's fashionable Renaissance medallions (AIC4, pages 543, 548f and 554).**4.1**

In 1529 Wolsey found it politic to cede his palace to the king who, of course, proceeded to amplify its major element – especially the great hall. A decade further on, Henry had taken over the cardinal's seat at York Place near Westminster (by present-day Whitehall), expanded it and endowed it with gates which compare and contrast with the late-medieval type perfected at Hampton Court – or at S. James's Palace in London (after 1532).**4.2**

4.2c   4.2a   4.2b

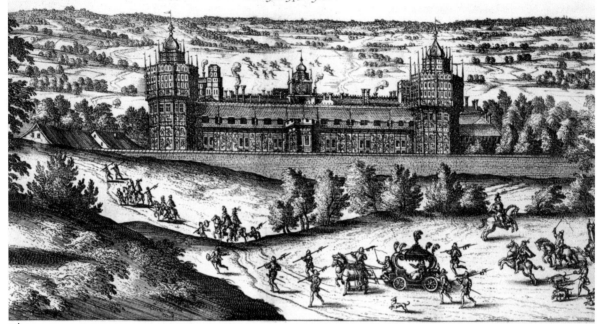

Hoc est nusquam simile.

4.3b

4.3c

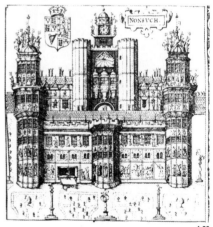

4.3a

›4.3 NONSUCH PALACE, SURREY, from 1538: (a, b) engraved record of entrance front and main residential block addressing the landscape from the far side of the inner court (Joris Hoefnagel, 1568), (c) record of mural embellishment incorporating Tudor heraldry (Paris, Louvre).

The two-courtyard plan furthered by Cardinal Wolsey at Hampton Court and Whitehall subsists: over a masonry base, the superstructure was timber-framed – as is clear from the representation of the front with the projecting gallery between fantastic octagonal towers. If the decoration of the main chamber is to be related to the work of Rosso Fiorentino and Francesco Primaticcio in founding the School of Fontainebleau, it must date from a decade after building began: describing the building in the 1660s, John Evelyn postulates that the life-sized plaster figures and accompanying stuccowork were due to 'some celebrated Italian' (who could have come from or through Fontainebleau). The principal among these has been identified as Nicholas Bellin of Modena, a versatile painter and sculptor who fled to England c. 1535 after attempting to defraud his French royal patron: he appears at Nonsuch five years later.

>4.4 CHIMNEYPIECES IN THE NONSUCH STYLE: (a) Broughton Castle (Oxfordshire, c. 1555); (b) Reigate Priory (Surrey, before 1559).

Broughton's stucco overmantel, with large-scale nude figures supporting the richly moulded frame of an oval cartouche, clearly recalls those of Fontainebleau – particularly in the former bedroom of the Duchesse d'Étampes. Leathery strapwork, an essential ingredient in School of Fontainebleau framework, plays no major role here. On the other hand, a reputedly contemporary timber chimneypiece at Reigate Priory does have a considerable amount of strapwork in its central armorial panel and the niche seats to either side of the grate: like the borders of contemporary Franco-Italian bookplates,**2.19b** the material here prompts largely flat and geometrical motifs, curling like cut leather only at the edges. This work came from the house at Bletchingley of Sir Thomas Cawarden (died 1559) who was Keeper of Nonsuch and Master of Revels at court: Bellin worked under his direction in that capacity, not least on the accession of Edward VI in 1547; so too did the carpenter-joiner Robert Trunquet (probably from Arras), who is most plausibly credited with the work now at Reigate (by Girouard, *Elizabethan Architecture*, 2009). With various similarities to these two works, two chimney-pieces at Lyme Park (Cheshire) may be later as their inspiration seems to have come from Fontainebleau via Vredeman de Vries.

4.4a

4.4b

Determined that no subject would ever again eclipse him in housing, the king's ambition was to outshine François I of France. Having established the Office of the King's Works as a department of state, he embarked on a totally new courtyard scheme, bizarre Nonsuch in Surrey (from 1538): emulation of the royal château of Chambord is likely and the only surviving record of interior decoration associated with the building closely resembles the contemporary work of the School of Fontainebleau. That style is certainly the mode a decade or so later at Broughton Castle (Oxfordshire), for example.**4.3, 4.4**

4.5a

4.5b

THE TUDOR GARDEN

The medieval tradition of the enclosed plot (*hortus con-clusus*), subdivided into roughly rectangular beds by paths, was the basis for the first significant venture into garden design by the servants of Henry VIII at Hampton Court

4.5c

>**4.5 THE TUDOR GARDEN:** (a–c) Hampton Court, re-evocation of a court garden and overviews of the king's great privy garden as recorded by Antonis van der Wyngaerde (c. 1555) and as 'restored' in the 20th century; (d, e) labyrinth plan and overview of replanted Tudor maze at Hever Castle (Kent); (f, g) heraldic and knot patterns of planting; (h) the knot garden at Helmingham Hall (Suffolk).

Nothing but the perimeter survives on Tudor palace sites, of course. The reconstruction of the court garden within the palace complex at Hampton Court follows contemporary accounts of the plots with timber railings painted with white and green chevrons and punctuated with posts supporting the royal 'beasties'. The latter appear in the engraving of Nonsuch's entrance elevation where there were also obelisks and fountains.**4.3a** Thomas Platter, a Swiss visitor to both palaces in 1599, describes the inner court garden at Hampton Court as like a chessboard with alternating squares of lawn and white sand (and also red brick dust); at Nonsuch he described the maze and was charmed by the terraces with 'all kinds of animals ... overgrown with plants'.

Beyond the enclosures within the complex at Hampton Court, between the new gallery and the river to the south was the king's privy garden: it emulated Blois, if not exactly contemporary Fontainebleau, in scale unprecedented in England. It was bordered by raised earthworks providing overviews, beyond which to the south-east, beside the river, was a mound built on a brick base in 1533. Borrowed from the Norman motte-and-bailey castle, the mound had been introduced to the late-medieval gardens of several Oxford colleges.

4.5d

4.5e

4.5f, g

and Nonsuch. As with much other planning in the early years of the reign, Cardinal Wolsey provided the basis both at Hampton Court and at York Place but inspiration was transmitted from Burgundy and the gardens of François I presented a challenge in scale, if not novelty (see above, pages 320f; AIC4, pages 580f).

In the typical Tudor garden an emblematic programme was superimposed on to the ubiquitous garden grid in the patterns of the planting, in topiary and in sculpture. Pillars supported heraldic beasts at regular intervals to enhance the third dimension of design in the enclosed courtyard gardens of Hampton Court and around the perimeter of Nonsuch. Heraldic devices were traced in the planting of the beds, especially the Tudor rose: the dominant colours were the dynastic white and green. Heraldry apart, the peculiar contribution of the English under Henry VIII was the knot garden, the plot within the enclosure in which the pattern of hedging defining the zones for colourful planting was that of the double knot pressed into service for the braiding and buttoning of the doublet: this recommended itself at once for its regularity and symmetrical intricacy. On the larger scale, the indispensable feature was the labyrinth or maze which may perpetuate the medieval symbolism of the journey through the wilderness to the Grace of Salvation which was taken to its abstruse exteme in Francesco Colonna's 1499 romantic quest *Hypnerotomachia Poliphili* (AIC4, pages 581, 732, 763).**4·5**

4.5h

ORDERS OF ARTICULATION

In the extent and style of his building, Henry VIII was no equal to François I: the latter's wing at Blois and the Parisian Château de Madrid apart, the rolling programme for Fontainebleau and the inception of the new Louvre were more than a match for the expansion of Whitehall or Hampton Court: above all Chambord totally eclipsed Nonsuch (and see AIC4, pages 876f). And, as we have seen, François promoted the intervention of Italians to forge a French Classical hybrid as his building works progressed: by the end of the reign near mid-century his architects had gained mature comprehension of the essence of Italian Renaissance Classicism in the application of canonical Orders, rather than their disembodied detail, and were developing their own distinctive High Renaissance means of unifying the disparate masses inherited from their medieval building tradition. England lagged behind: the first glimmer of maturity, reflected from the France of François I's successor, Henri II (1547–59), came a generation later in the reign of Elizabeth I (1558–1603).

4.6a

Following the extended civil war in which the feudal system was finally extinguished with many of the former Plantagenet magnates, non-defensive building was encouraged by the stability provided by the Tudor regime in England – as in Valois France. The modernization of land tenure on a fluid – if still highly stratified – basis was furthered by the extinction of the monastic system and the expropriation of its property. Endowed with the latter, a new civil aristocracy – or those who aspired to it from the ranks of bureaucrats and merchants – had the exceptional means for lavish display which, in the relatively peaceful conditions of the early Elizabethan decades, was increasingly informed by familiarity with advanced developments abroad.

The new mode of architecture, transcending mere embellishment, accelerated as the English ventured south

4.6b @ 1:1000

›**4.6 BARRINGTON COURT, SOMERSET,**
c. 1530: (a) entrance front, (b) plan.

Devised for Henry Daubeney, one of Henry VIII's retinue at the Field of the Cloth of Gold, the symmetry of
Barrington's open courtyard plan is novel – though in
disposition, if not in style, it may seem to have had a
grand precedent in the open entrance court framed by
the king's new wings at Hampton Court. As in the hall
there, a corner bay projects to trap additional light: the
opposite corner is also projected to contain a staircase
but the practical requirements obviated precise symmetry.

again and Protestant craftsmen fled across the Channel
from persecution in the Netherlands or France. And
Antwerp, a major centre of the printing trade, flooded the
market with religious and secular literature and engraved
images of the latest developments in the arts – often
framed with grotesque and/or strapwork motifs developed
under the influence of the School of Fontainebleau.
Among the plethora, the English received the work of Serlio as the indispensable aid to architectural design – until
they grasped the significance of Vignola and succumbed
to Palladio. Meanwhile de L'Orme was peculiarly relevant
to their needs and du Cerceau emerged as a principal agent
of mannered 'modernism'. That was soon supplemented
by the fantasies of Vredeman de Vries in which, as we have
seen, stiffened leathery fretwork played a role at least as
prominent as that taken by the grotesque in earlier works.

'Modernism' in motif was, of course, applicable to the
fabric of building over all types of plan – ancient and modern. Focus on an enclosed court was traditional, extroversion modern. As the century progressed from Henry VIII's
work to the front of Hampton Court, an H-shaped
perimeter resulted from the augmentation of the wings to
either side of open courts separated by the range containing the great hall. An E-shaped variant had confined the
process to the entrance side and projected the portico: that,
of course, was soon seen as flattering to the queen whose
initial it reproduced. With the portico in the centre of
the complex as a whole and the wings assimilated in form,
not least through the agency of articulating Orders, symmetry was the over-riding principle of design in the high
Elizabethan age (from c. 1570). The H-shaped plan is
implicit in the 14th-century nuclei of houses which developed organically like Penshurst or Haddon (AIC4, pages
536ff). Barrington Court (Somerset, from c. 1530) is an
early example of extroverted E-shaped regularity.**4.6**

As extroversion asserted itself, the enclosed courtyard remained in favour throughout the Tudor era and the twin-towered gatehouse had no less appeal in England than in France as the symbol of feudal power – though even residual claim to that eluded most Tudor patrons. However, solid ceded to void on the exteriors even of town houses. From the decades before the High Elizabethan age, splendid examples range from the palace of Lord Protector Edward Seymour, first duke of Somerset, on the London Strand back to Hengrave Hall in Suffolk and forward to Deene Park in Northamptonshire.**4.7, 4.8**

Built more than forty years apart, Hengrave and Deene are equally conservative in the retention of an off-centre

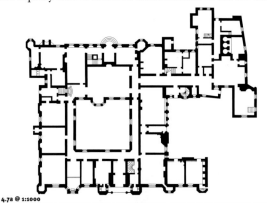

4.7a @ 1:1000

4.7b

›4.7 HENGRAVE HALL, SUFFOLK, from c. 1525: (a) plan, (b) entrance front and gatehouse (dated 1538).

The work for the merchant Sir Thomas Kytson sustains the early Tudor tradition except for the increasingly fashionable Classical embellishment of the oriel which is credited (in contemporary documents) to one John Sparke.

›4.8 DEENE PARK, NORTHAMPTONSHIRE: (a) overview of court with great hall top left (from c. 1572), (b) east front with blind frontispiece (c. 1560), (c) chimneypiece (dated 1571).

The property of Westminster Abbey, leased variously from 1215, was acquired in 1514 by the legal luminary Sir Robert Brudenell (1461–1531). His grandson, Sir Edmund (1521–85), began the comprehensive rebuilding of a largely 14th-century house, recording the founding of the hall in 1572 (the chimney-piece, dated to the previous year, was moved to its present position from a great room in the east wing on the assumption that it was originally destined for the hall). The east range incorporates medieval and early Tudor work (including a bedroom reputedly occupied by Henry VII) but was refenestrated in the 18th century and later: four bays of its great room and undercroft project to an enigmatic blind frontispiece, with engaged columns of a primitive Ionic Order flanking former windows surmounted by panels of strapwork, the upper ones framing the initials of Sir Edmund and his first wife (Agnes, died 1583). Now backed in part by a chimney, this may originally have belonged to a solar (and its undercroft) on axis with the great hall or the vestibules serving the chambers in the east wing and their staircase: if so, it was moved c. 1625 during augmentation of that wing by Sir Edmund's nephew, the future first earl of Cardigan.

The hall chimneypiece is articulated in a relatively straightforward way with superimposed pilasters, those of the upper level framing armorial panels in the manner of the attic of a triumphal arch. The Order is abstracted from the Tuscan, with the architrave moulding projecting where capitals are required. A more canonical approach was adopted for the similar, but simpler, system of the portico.

4.8a

4.8c

4.8b

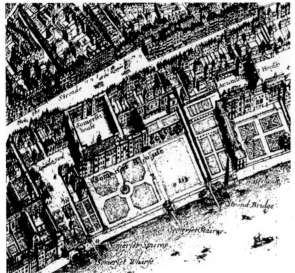

4.9a

4.9c

›4.9 LONDON, OLD SOMERSET HOUSE, c. 1547: (a) overview (from Wenceslaus Hollar's London, 1658), (b) Strand front, (as recorded by John Thorpe), (c) court front with loggia.

The college format is modernized in distant echo of French practice: the portal based on the triumphal-arch motif – henceforth to be the norm in one way or another in England, as in France – and the windows of the projecting 'pavilions' are paired under pediments; the roof is concealed behind a balustrade in the manner called Italian by the French; the court was given an Italianate arcaded loggia, the arches rising from columns in early Franco-Italian Renaissance style except in the centre where the portal was framed by paired columns. The author is unknown but similarities with his work elsewhere suggest the involvement of Sir John Thynne of Longleat (J. Summerson, *Architecture in Britain, 1530–1830*, 1969 and 1993; see below, pages 576ff).

hall entered at the corner: the earlier one retains a twin-towered portal with splendid oriel; the later one dispenses with a gatehouse altogether. Halfway between these works (c. 1547), Somerset House's architect advances beyond Hampton Court in its symmetry about aligned central entrances, the one on the street revising the twin-towered gate in Classical terms: it has long gone but was happily recorded in the 17th century both by the royal surveyor John Thorpe (c. 1565–1654) – perhaps for inclusion in a com-

4.9b

pendium emulating du Cerceau's homage to the best buildings of France – and by Wenceslaus Hollar (1607–77) in his invaluable topographical map of London (1658).**4.9**

Commissioned in the minority of Henry VIII's successor, Edward VI (1547–53), Lord Protector Somerset's London house stood as a prelude to the Elizabethan Renaissance: though its frontispiece rises over a somewhat expansive triumphal-arch motif on axis with the main portal centred on the court loggia, neither in whole nor in part does it parallel the maturity reached at that time by Philibert de l'Orme and Pierre Lescot in France – or, indeed, the arches erected to celebrate the entry of Henri II into his capital in 1547. As might be expected of a work more than twenty years younger, Deene's pilastered portico is much less uncertainly fashionable for all its relative modesty. A similar, if rather more elaborate, system of articulation was favoured for the hall chimneypiece there over the contemporary mode of overtly Serlian elaboration.**4.10**

Before his house was complete, Somerset had fallen. His successor, John Dudley, first earl of Northumberland, cut across the prevailing grain and sent his servant, John Shute, back to the fountainhead in Italy (in 1550): the result was not another house but the prime English architectural treatise, *The First and Chief Groundes of Architecture* (1563) – and, perhaps, some tombs.**4.11** Yet Shute was influenced

›4.10 SERLIO AND THE CHIMNEYPIECE, c. 1580: (a) Whittington Court (Gloucestershire); (b) Baddesley Clinton (Warwickshire).

In contrast with the pragmatic adaptation of the ubiquitous triumphal-arch motif to serve the purpose of a fireplace at Deene, several near contemporaries are overtly Serlian, especially in the wayward contortion of structural elements and the intrusion of one form of support into the context of another – the console bracket or baluster for the shaft of a pilaster, for example. (We shall encounter other examples in context but for this selection I am indebted – as in so much else – to Mark Girouard's excellent survey, *Elizabethan Architecture: Its Rise and Fall, 1540–1640,* and, ultimately, to the generous proprietors of these houses.)

4.10a, b

as much by the pattern book of Serlio and the treatise of Vignola as by anything he observed in their homeland – and his publication did little immediately to counter the influence of the French even on the circle of the late Lord Protector.

4.11a

›4.11 MID-16TH CENTURY TUDOR TOMBS: (a) Fawsley (Northamptonshire), S. Mary's, Sir Richard Knightley (died 1542) and his wife; (b) Sherborne Abbey (Dorset), Wykeham Chapel, pavilion tomb of Sir John Horsey and his son (died 1546); (c) Wing (Buckingham), All Saints, tomb of Sir Robert Dormer (died 1552).

In the reign of Edward VI the 'pavilion' and 'altar' types of tomb remained popular. The former was adopted in an unexecuted project for the boy-king himself on the Lombard model adapted for the Valois kings of France. The alternative – with effigies of the deceased recumbent on a sarcophagus – was adopted for his father and grandfather on the model popular with ducal Burgundy and elsewhere (AIC4, page 453). Each type was often repeated for noble patrons: Sir John Horsey rests in a provincial adaptation of the pavilion tomb type, of which the Dormer tomb is an aedicular adaptation associated with John Shute – at least in inspiration.

4.11b, c

HIGH RENAISSANCE TO MANNERISM IN THE ELIZABETHAN ERA

The progress of the Elizabethan Renaissance, prompted by the realization that the Orders were not merely decorative but the key to coherence in Classical design, may be traced from complexes like Deene through the group of houses dubbed 'prodigy' for that reason. Built to receive the still-peripatetic monarch in suitably grand apartments, these include Longleat, Wollaton, Hardwick, Burghley and Kirby. With singular appropriateness, they were preceded by an extraordinary series of gates commissioned for his college of Gonville by the Cambridge don Dr John Keys who adopted the Latin style of his name after graduating from the University of Padua.**4.12**

Caius's Gates of Virtue and Honour (1565 and 1572 respectively) are correct in the detailing of their Orders and much more adventurous, indeed mannered if not quite

›4.12 CAMBRIDGE, GONVILLE AND CAIUS COLLEGE: (a, b) Gates of Virtue and Honour.

Dr John Caius (or Keys, 1510–73), a highly distinguished Catholic physician, graduated from divinity studies at Gonville College in 1533, and from Padua in 1541. Physician to Edward VI, Queen Mary and Queen Elizabeth, he refounded his Cambridge college in 1557, was its master from the following year, richly endowed it and began his comprehensive rebuilding works there in 1565.

The progression of the student through the largely

undistinguished quadrangular buildings is marked symbolically by the three extraordinary gates devised by the patron possibly with different architectural advisers: the first one dedicated to Humility, the third to Honour, the intermediate one to Virtue on the side of the first court and Wisdom on the reverse. The design of the second gate, taking its departure from the portico of Somerset House with the aid of the Antwerp Entry's English Gate, erected for the entry of Philip II to Antwerp in 1549, is as canonical in the Ionic ordonnance of the basic triumphal-arch motif as the work of Philibert de l'Orme or Pierre Lescot in the previous decade. The Gate of Honour (completed after the patron's death but reputedly to his programme) is far more adventurous in the Serlian agglomeration of forms transmitted via the Spanish at Antwerp: over the triumphal arch is England's first temple-front motif, obelisks and a tempietto – the latter hexagonal rather than cylindrical, as in both precedents.

Mannerist, in the incorporation of prototypical Classical motifs like the triumphal arch and temple front. The inspiration was Serlio (IV.8.55) but, rather than through Shute, it was transmitted via the publication of the series of temporary arches erected for the ceremonial entry of the future Philip II of Spain to Antwerp in 1549, specifically those dedicated to the English and the Spaniards – unsurprisingly at first, when Philip's cousin was still courting Elizabeth.**3.1j,k** Flanders, particularly the work of Vredeman de Vries (published in the same year as Shute's treatise), was to exert prime influence on the embellishment of English architecture throughout the reigns of Elizabeth and her Stuart successors: this was supplemented by Wendel Dietterlin's fantastic *Architectura* at the turn of the century.

4.12a

4.12b

With Caius, the prodigious patrons of the 'prodigy houses' represent a cross-section of the upper strata of Tudor society. Burghley and Longleat were built respectively by Lord Protector Somerset's secretary, William Cecil (1521–98), and steward John Thynne (1515–80). Bess of Hardwick was united with the Earl of Shrewsbury, the queen's lieutenant entrusted with guardianship of the captive Mary Queen of Scots. On the other hand, Sir Humphrey Stafford of Blatherwycke and Sir Francis Willoughby of Wollaton were landed gentry, the latter turned entrepreneur of commerce and industry. Other than the patron, the authorship of Burghley is obscure and Kirby is loosely connected with the master-mason Thomas Thorpe but the invention of Longleat, Wollaton and probably Hardwick is credited primarily to Robert Smythson (c. 1535–1614), the first English builder after Henry Yveley to emerge with a distinct architectural personality (AIC4, pages 554f).**4.13–4.17**

4.13b

›4.13 LONGLEAT, WILTSHIRE, 1559–80: (a) ground-floor plan, (b, c) great hall screen and chimney-piece, (d) façade detail, (e) general view.

Sir John Thynne, whom we have speculatively encountered at Somerset House, began building a modern house on his Wiltshire estate in 1554 but the work was lost to fire in 1567: it is not clear how much was incorporated in rebuilding in accordance with a model prepared the following year. Robert Smythson is thought to have been recommended to Thynne as a mason capable of translating his ideas into stone by

Prodigy houses

Longleat (from 1553 and 1572) retains the double-courtyard scheme of Haddon in a strictly rectangular configuration with an innovative set of four

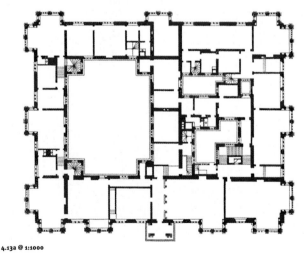

4.13a @ 1:1000

4.13c

vice-chamberlain Sir Francis Knollys who employed him at his Berkshire seat (now lost). The French sculptor Alan Maynard was probably responsible for the refined detailing, but not the disposition, of the Orders. Maynard, who must have known du Cerceau, is also credited with several of the original chimneypieces, including the one in the hall whose mermaids with twisted tails have affiliates in François I's Château de Madrid (as illustrated in *PEBF*; see above, page 312).

The courtyard plan is traditional, but turned inside out. The symmetry and much of the Classicizing detail were novel two decades earlier at Somerset House: the latter may be seen as the English precedent for concealing the roof but Saint-Germain is recalled even in the relief provided by the chimneys and the turrets of the staircases in the corners of the court.

Of the immediate followers, Holdenby House (Northamptonshire, from c. 1578) was the closest with three out of four symmetrical fronts to two courts (at least in plan) but entrance was from the centre of the short east end, rather than the long south side. Toddington Manor (Bedfordshire, from c. 1575) had one court entered from the long south side and three symmetrical façades.

symmetrical façades surmounted by balustrades bordering a virtually flat roof terrace: the projection of twin bays from the regular succession of great windows in each front – centre and sides to the north, east and west, doubled to each side of the southern entrance portico – may be seen as the English equivalent of the French pavillon, with the distinction of pilasters but not of high roofs. In the main, however, the exercise had no clear precedent – or follower. In the great hall here, as elsewhere, Serlio has emerged from among his colleagues in Fontainebleau as the principal influence on the design of the major internal features, the screen and the chimneypiece. The staircase is yet to emerge from the tower as another of these features: however, instead of the traditional spiral, it follows the development of the open cage in Spain to a restricted extent.

4.13d

4.13e

4.14a

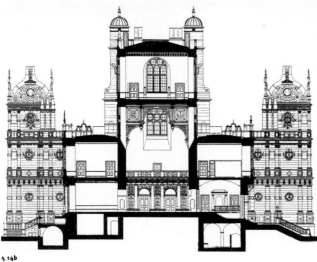

4.14b

4.14c

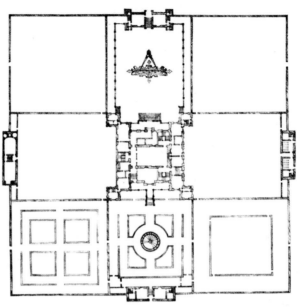

4.14d @ 1:1000

> **4.14 WOLLATON HALL, NOTTINGHAM,**
c. 1580–88: (a) view from the south-east, (b) section, (c) hall vault detail, (d) site plan, (e) late-17th-century overview (Jan Siberechts, 1697).

The patron was Sir Francis Willoughby, Sheriff of Nottingham, who anticipated welcoming the queen. Robert Smythson's extroverted manner was taken to an extreme hitherto unprecedented in England with the hall filling the residue of a court and the environment addressed from the symmetrical façades. Serlio inspired the planning but, beyond his château of Ancy-le-Franc, Longleat is recalled in the basic ordonnance. However, the windows of the extraordinary, uncomfortably accessible upper hall in the 'keep' are Venetian or even Lombard (AIC4, pages 788, 806) – and stylistically incoherent with the decorative detail borrowed from Vredeman de Vries. The hall screen is articulated with greater gravitas than at Longleat: Doric columns supplant Ionic pilasters and the frieze surmounts the panelling of the other walls.

There are minor variations between the plan of the house as recorded by Smythson in 1609 and the present arrangement. The main southern parterre of Smythson's garden survives in the late-17th-century overview and the eastern one is extended with semicircular terracing.

The plan of Wollaton Hall is developed from an H-shaped nucleus with near symmetry in a near-square perimeter. Between the four corner towers, the two pairs of symmetrical façades are distinguished in depth of recession but are articulated with superimposed Orders throughout in an attempt to bind the towers and intermediate projections into a coherent whole: there is no developed attempt to match projection with progression from pilaster to column in the current French manner. Serlio (III.4.72, ostensibly recording Neapolitan Poggio Reale) provided the inspiration for the plan centred on the hall but Robert Smythson follows English tradition in expanding it from square to oblong (parallel to the entrance front) and raises it to a clerestory below an upper chamber: still clearly inspired by the keep of a medieval castle, the form had long been redundant in military architecture but retained prestige as a symbol of feudal power, like the moat, machicolation and the twin-towered postern of early Renaissance France. The parapets of the corner towers are embellished in the manner of Vredeman de Vries. As recorded by Smythson (c. 1609), the site plan projects the integration of house and garden on biaxial lines for the first time in England – in so far as the accidents of survival testify.

Like Wollaton, Hardwick Hall (from 1590) is endowed with towers and the massing is symmetrical about both axes but the compactness of the plan is new – though Smythson produced at least one compact exercise in an ideal square perimeter. The H-shaped plan is atypically English in setting the great hall and its screened vestibule/service passage on the perpendicular axis between colonnaded loggias, as in Palladio's record of the Vicentine Villa Valmarana (*QL* II, plate 42), rather than parallel to the central entrance. Both Longleat and Wollaton – indeed all previous great houses – are exceeded in the predominance of void over solid and repetitive order is derived solely from plane geometry rather than imposed with Orders. The house may have been innovative – even by Continental stand-

›4.15 SMYTHSON IN DERBYSHIRE: (a–g) Hardwick Hall (c. 1590–97), gatehouse, plans of first and second floors with (1) hall, (2) patroness's suite of antechamber (2a) and bedroom (2b), (3a) second apartment of antechamber, (later dining room) and bedroom (3b), (4) high great chamber, (5) withdrawing room, (6) cabinets, (7) gallery; entrance front, chamber, gallery; (h) Haddon Hall, gallery (c. 1589).

A precedent for the compression of the plan at the expense of the court has been found (by Summerson) at Worksop Manor (at least a decade earlier) but the house there disappeared in the 18th century and is recorded only in engraved elevation. The turning of the hall on to the perpendicular axis of the building's entrance seems to have been Smythson's innovation

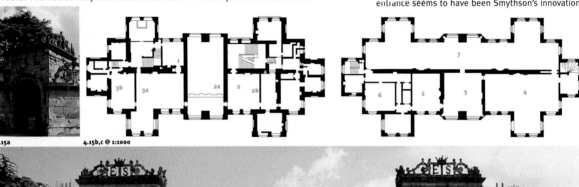

4.15a   4.15b,c @ 1:1000

4.15d

at Hardwick (after Palladio?). The Tuscan colonnaded loggias on both long sides mark a further advance in extroversion but the columns are banded: in this the taste for Vredeman is apparent as in the fretted strapwork of gatehouse, towers and interior plasterwork.

Extroversion of course, is implicit in the huge windows of the top floor Long Gallery and High Great Chamber. The latter, where the patron received and dined in state before withdrawing to the increasingly private rooms beyond, was supplemented by the gallery for great entertainments after Henry VIII set the precedent at Hampton Court: they are prime representatives of the major domestic spaces of the day, after the hall had passed its apogee – and to the servants. However, Hardwick was unique amongst the English aristocratic houses of the day in the scale of these rooms and the extent of the Great Chamber's embellishment. Above the original tapestries, the latter's frieze is inspired by work of the Fontainebleau school but draws on Flemish engravings for sylvan scenes evoked solely in colourful plaster: Philip Galle after Johannes Stradanus produced those of Diana and the hunt, appropriate to the scene of public dining; Abraham Smith is identified as the chief plasterer.

4.15e

ards – in catering for dining in a chamber distinct from the hall but it followed well-established practice in incorporating a long gallery on the first floor – though with greater grandeur than its predecessors, such as Smythson's own exercise at Haddon (c. 1589).

4.15f

4.15g

4.15h

The architects of Kirby Hall and Burghley House (from 1572 and 1577) imposed symmetry on their courtyard plans though they retained great halls off-axis: indeed, this is disguised by assimilating the fenestration of the disparate spaces at Kirby. They were far more overt than Smythson in following current French fashion, with their great courts and three-storey central portal pavilions articulated with superimposed Orders: in the latter respect both represent variants on the work of Philibert de l'Orme at Anet or Jean Bullant at Écouen (see pages 330f, 355f). William Cecil acquired de l'Orme's treatise and presumably knew the plates of Anet and Écouen published by J.-A. du Cerceau in *PEBF* (volume 2, 1579): by then, work was well under way at Burghley but when it had progressed from its variant of the

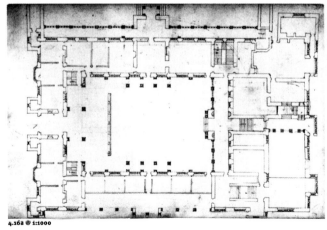

4.16a @ 1:1000

4.16b

4.16c

4.16e

›4.16 BURGHLEY HOUSE, LINCOLNSHIRE, rebuilt c. 1575–87: (a) plan, (b) general view from the north-west, (c, d) court fronts west and east, (e) detail of staircase vault.

William Cecil, first Baron Burghley, heavily involved with building another courtyard house at Theobalds nearer to London, claims to have limited his work at his eponymous seat to rebuilding over existing foundations: the scheme was nevertheless vast. The architect is unknown. Plan and entrance pavilion continue the tradition of Hampton Court – but with greater symmetry, with the new aspect of extroversion in the elevations and with semi-sophisticated awareness of recent developments in France. There is much Flemish strapwork. Juxtaposed Doric columns replace the typical Tudor chimneys with their groups of varied polygonal, cylindrical and spiral brickwork.

4.16d

›4.17 KIRBY HALL, NORTHAMPTONSHIRE, from c. 1570: (a) court frontispiece of southern range, (b) court façade of north range, (c) west range extending into the twin semi-circular bays (probably added for the accommodation of James I c. 1605).

The starting date is derived from the later account of the surveyor John Thorpe who claims to have laid the foundation stone when he would have been seven years old – possibly at the behest of his father, the master-mason: otherwise there are no details of responsibility for the exercise.

4.17a

4.17c

4.17b

English type of twin-turreted gatehouse to the tower at the opposite end of the central court, patron and architect must have been familiar with the pyramidal spires of Anet's chapel and the superimposed triumphal-arch motifs of Écouen's entrance pavilion.

The Kirby scheme is English in the retention of the hall to the side of the central entrance, probably because it was built over medieval foundations, but otherwise it is French – particularly in the closing of the court with an arcaded screen range opposite the main corps de logis and the superimposed Orders of the porch. The builder must have had access to du Cerceau's compilation. The colossal Order, disrupted by pedimented windows over arcades, may have been inspired by the plates of the château of Verneuil's terrace façade (in volume 1, published in 1576): the plates of Charleval are a closer match though they were prepared for the publication of volume 2 after work was advanced at Kirby (see above, pages 368ff).

The interior fittings of grand Elizabethan buildings, religious and secular, admitted decorative detail derived in particular from the engraved fantasies of Cornelis Floris

4.18a

4.18b

4.18c

4.18d

and Vredeman de Vries. Screen and chimneypiece, the major features of the hall, were the most obvious objects of this development in the domestic field. Similarly embellished screens dominated church interiors too and Elizabethan England was particularly rich in all permutations of the funerary monument – the freestanding colonnaded pavilion sheltering sarcophagus and effigy, its contraction into a deeply niched aedicule attached to a wall, and its further contraction to a wall-mounted plaque with an image or epitaph in an architectural frame. And for all these Vredeman provided copious inspiration (see page 420).**4.18**

›4.18 ELIZABETHAN FUNERARY MONU-MENTS: (a) Church Charwelton (Northamptonshire), Holy Trinity, mural monument erected by Thomas Andrews (1590) in memory of his two wives, Frances (died 1567) and Mary (died 1589); (b) Fawsley (Northamptonshire), S. Mary the Virgin, altar and sarcophagus tomb of Sir Valentine Knightley (died 1566) and other members of his family; (c) Bottesford (Leicestershire), S. Mary, 'table' tomb of Henry Manners, (second earl of Rutland, died 1563) and his wife Margaret, with double-arched aedicular tomb of John Manners (fourth earl, died 1588) and his wife Elizabeth (left); (d) Snarford (Lincolnshire), S. Lawrence, pavilion monument to Sir Thomas and Lady S. Pol (c. 1583); (e) Stamford (Lincolnshire), S. Martin, William Cecil, first Baron Burghley (died 1598).

The masterly variation on the aedicular tomb type at Fawsley relates to several of Vredeman's designs with raised and banded sarcophagus: it amplifies the format adopted for the Denton tomb at All Saints in Hillesden (Buckinghamshire) which, in turn, is related to the screen at Holdenby in Northamptonshire attributed to Garret Hollemans. The English norm for varying the aedicular type with an interpolated arch is splendidly represented by several of the Rutland tombs at Bottesford – to either side of the second earl's 'table' variant on both the pavilion and altar types . The most impressive pavilion type is represented in relief at Church Charwelton, in full three dimensions at Snarford and Stamford – the latter following the precedent set in a project for King Edward VI.

4.18e

The greatest hall of the Elizabethan era was not in the grandest of houses but in London's Middle Temple: professional and collegiate building revived after religious conflict had moderated. **4.19** The two registers of the splendid screen belong to sequential stylistic phases: the lower one, with its Doric Order, is still High Renaissance despite some anomalies; the upper one, with its herms and richly

›4.19 **4.19 LONDON, MIDDLE TEMPLE HALL:** (a, b) general view towards and detail of screen (1570s?).

Financing was being arranged in the mid-1570s but the contrast between the lower and upper levels suggest several phases of design and construction: the basement is essentially architectonic but the canonical Doric Order is disrupted by an alien additional frieze which seems to have been interpolated in some confusion over the height of the columns relative to the arches; the Ionic-hatted herms and richly relieved panels of the upper level belong to a different realm of design, probably introduced by Flemish Mannerists a generation after the initial campaign.

4.19a

4.19b

4.20C

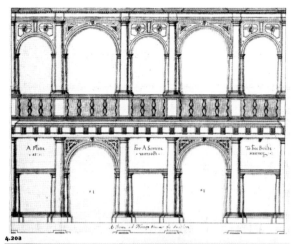

4.20a

4.20b

›4.20 THE RANGE OF HALL SCREEN DESIGN FROM HIGH ELIZABETHAN TO EARLY JACOBEAN: (a) Smythson's design for Worksop Manor (1580); (b) London, Charterhouse, great hall screen (1571); (c) Knole (c. 1605).

Robert Smythson's design for Worksop, in which a Doric Order framed the lower arches and the upper level was Tuscan, is strictly architectonic but uncanonical in its superimposition and elongation. Colonnaded screens of various Orders were not uncommon in the era: of two London examples, the one in Gray's Inn is Ionic, that of the Charterhouse is Corinthian and both have herms in the upper register.

The Worksop project is clearly recalled at Wollaton: of many screens of similar gravitas, the one in Holdenby church (which probably derives from the chapel of the lost great house) is attributed to the Netherlandish sculptor Garret Hollemans who worked extensively on chimneypieces and tombs. The Netherlandish Mannerism of the Knole screen, in contrast, is elaborated in numerous early Jacobean works – like the screens at Hatfield House or Audley End.

relieved panels, is Mannerist in the Flemish mode. The late decades of Elizabeth and the first of James produced notable examples of one or other or both approaches: the poles may be represented by Robert Smythson's essentially architectonic project for Worksop Manor (c. 1580) to the semi-anthropomorphic exercise devised by an unidentified craftsman for Knole in Kent (c. 1605).**4.20**

4.21a

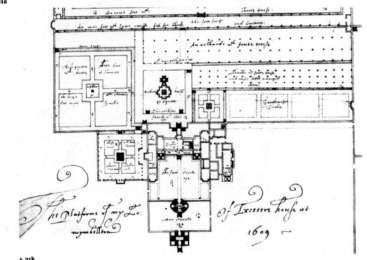

4.21b

›4.21 WIMBLEDON, from 1588: (a) engraved perspective view (17th century), (b) site plan in 1609
(drawn by Robert Smythson).

The plan is neither E- nor quite H-shaped: the wings
are strictly curtailed on the entrance front, but they are
extended to frame a terrace on the southern garden
side: this is preceded by two outer terraces and succeeded at the level of the balustraded roof. The
unknown architect retained an asymmetrically placed
hall and central entrance but projected twin staircase
towers symmetrically from the inner corners of the
upper terrace: thus Barrington Court is recalled except
for the twin staircases – which are still of the restricted
open-cage type. In contrast to the Italianate terracing –
recently adapted at Saint-Germain – the façades further the astylar austerity of Hardwick without the lightness achieved there in the ratio of solid to void – but
also without the heaviness of Barrington. A mean
between these extremes was set at several works
related to Wimbledon, notably Doddington Hall (Lincolnshire, from 1595) and Montacute House (Somerset,
from 1599).

As surveyed by Robert Smythson in 1609, Wimbledon's celebrated garden reveals a haphazard attitude
to axial symmetry in marked contrast to the single-
mindedness of Wollaton. The dislocated disposition of
the northern alignment of zones, particularly that of
the 'Banketin House' (off-axis to the left), ill accords
with the strictly axial relationship between the house,
the privy garden to the left and the terraces to the front.
The latter seems more Smythsonian than the former in
the light of Wollaton.

Many late-Elizabethan and early Jacobean houses sustained tradition in placing the hall to the side of the main
entrance from an open or closed court but some sought
formal satisfaction at the expense of comfort by placing it
on the central axis. Wimbledon (c. 1590) is a lost example
of the former, though the entrance was central – and

›4.22 AUDLEY END, ESSEX, from 1603–16: (a, b)
overview and plan (17th-century engraving by Henry
Winstanley showing the lost entrance court), (c, d) general views of entrance and garden fronts, (e) detail of
porch, (f) great hall.

4.12a

The patron was Thomas Howard, first earl of Suffolk: guidance in the design seems to have been provided by his uncle and mentor, the Earl of Northampton: contemporary tradition accords executive responsibility to the Flemish master-mason Bernard Janssen. The hall is set centrally to close the inner court like a French low entrance range: its great oriel, once on axis with the outer portal in its own low entrance range, is flanked by twin two-storey porches: the southern one serves the screen passage; with no such function, the other asserts symmetry. The central axis is finally closed by a blind bay supporting a tower: that is the highest element in the hierarchy of gables, pinnacles and pavilions rising from concealed roofs in furtherance of the manner introduced on a grand scale at Longleat. With the exception of the central oriel and projecting side bays, the fenestration counters the preceding generation's trend towards lightness. The gables still follow Vederman in their strapwork mouldings and the same reference is apparent in the brackets supporting the ceiling of the hall: the screen is typical of the era in omitting an Order in favour of the semi-anthropomorphic approach to articulation of the Middle Temple's Flemish Mannerist upper register.

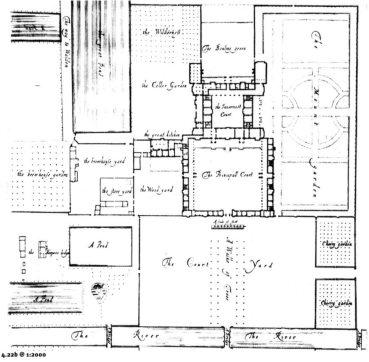

4.22b @ 1:2000

4.22C

schizophrenia extended to the garden.**4.21** Audley End in Essex (from c. 1603) has a spectacular example of a hall placed centrally between two courts but the entrance is still to one side.**4.22** Contemporary with the latter, Ham House (Surrey) retains the off-centre hall but its H-shaped perimeter was symmetrical about both axes in a simplified revision of Hardwick before substantial alter-

4.22d

4.22e

4.22f

4.23a

ation after 1670 (see page 582). Also H-shaped, Charlton House (Greenwich) and Holland House (London) were planned with central halls entered on axes perpendicular to their fronts, as at Hardwick.**4.23, 4.24**

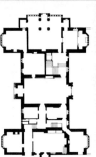

4.23b @ 1:1000   4.23c

›**4.23 CHARLTON HOUSE, GREENWICH,** from 1607: (a) entrance front, (b) plan, (c) great chamber chimneypiece.

The patron, Sir Adam Newton, was tutor to James I's heir, Henry Prince of Wales. The symmetry of the perimeter does not run to a pair of towers in the corners of the entrance front, as at Ham, for example: instead the south and north flanks are varied with one and two towers respectively.

›**4.24 HOLLAND HOUSE, LONDON,** from 1606, destroyed in World War II: plan (after John Thorpe).

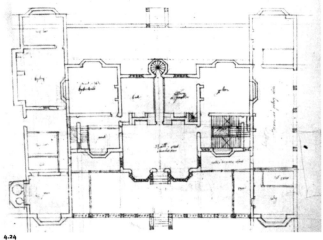

4.24

The patron was Edward, Lord Zouche of Harring-
worth, who built in part over existing foundations: the
elongation of the court is unusual and so too is the lateral projection from the front range of the corner pavilions. The frontispiece, at least, is attributed to the
sculptor Gerard Christmas (1576–1634) on stylistic
grounds – in particular its similarity with its later counterpart at Northumberland House which is traditionally
– but not certainly – associated with Christmas.

4.25

JACOBEAN MANNERISMS

Naturally there was no break between the Elizabethan and
Jacobean reigns in the development of architecture: the
conservative continued in tandem with the innovative. For
example, Audley End is modern in its extroverted aspect
and traditional in its quadrangular plan, like the greatest of
its Elizabethan predecessors, but incorporated a variation
of the contemporary French forecourt with low entrance
screen. Bramshill House (Hampshire) lacks the latter but
its quadrangle was unusually elongated behind an entrance
front with massive pavilions framing a frontispiece in the
latest mode drawn from Dietterlin.[4.25] The architect of
Charlton was also aware of Dietterlin and his H-shaped
plan was modern in its compactness. In lost Holland
House, the hall descended from Hardwick but it was truncated in the manner which led to its dwindling into a lobby
and its eclipse by a great chamber in the continued diversification of space. Along with the first-floor gallery, the
great chamber was supplemented by withdrawing rooms
for the principal inhabitants and one such room was soon
to be designated for dining – as perhaps at Hardwick.

Before and after the turn of the century – and the change
of dynasty – brick was the preferred material for the main
fabric of domestic building even on a grand scale. As in the
'prodigy' generation, however, there were prominent stone
frontispieces: these were echoed, inevitably on a smaller
scale, by elaborate chimneypieces but Vredeman or even
Dietterlin now supplement or supplant Serlio as the source
of inspiration in their design. Large windows leave little
room for articulating Orders but these are out of favour
even when the fenestration is less than generous. Concealed roofs bordered by balustrades endure in notional
homage to Italianate Classicism, echoed from France no
less vigorously than hitherto; moreover, their line is broken by Netherlandish gables and a variety of pavilions in a

forest of chimneys which few Italians would claim as part of their native heritage. Indeed, the architects – or, rather, the master-builders working with apprised patrons – were mainly Netherlandish when they were not English.

Aspiration to modernity in rectilinear symmetry and compactness occasionally prompted resort to pure geometry – in perimeter if not profile. This was not necessarily inconsistent with practicality but convenience usually tends to be in inverse relationship to rationality in planning.**4.26** Beyond that, mundane considerations occasionally ceded to aberrant novelty with symbolic intent in squares, crosses and triangles – for lodges or follies but occasionally even for castles.**4.27–4.29**

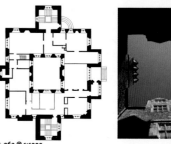

4.26a @ 1:1000   4.26b

›**4.26 CHASTLETON HOUSE, OXFORDSHIRE,** from 1603: (a) plan, (b) court.

The geometry is hardly symbolic but neither is it entirely pragmatic. Within the square perimeter, the circuit of rooms around the oblong central court admits of a degree of privacy only at the expense of a considerable amount of awkward corridor.

4.27b

4.27a

4.28a

4.28b

**›4.27 RATIONAL FOLLY IN NORTHAMPTON-
SHIRE,** 1594: (a) Rushton, Triangular (or Warrener's)
Lodge; (b) Lyveden New Bield.

The elementary Christian symbolism of the garden
centrepiece at Lyveden, the Greek-cross plan, is elaborated in roundel reliefs representing the instruments of
the Passion: the patron, Sir Thomas Tresham, was a
devout Catholic. In his other emblematic work, the Triangular Lodge ar Rushton, Trinitarian symbolism is
taken to an extreme in elevation and fenestration as
well as in the plan.

›4.28 LONGFORD CASTLE, WILTSHIRE, c.
1591: (a) aerial view, (b) detail drawing of apex tower
and part of loggia façade (John Thorpe)

According to Thorpe, the Trinitarian symbolism is
overt in the naming of the towers after its three Persons
and the identification of the linking wings with the conjunction ('est'). On a more mundane plane, the house
was one of the first in England with an open loggia in its
Vredemanesque garden façade.

›4.29 BOLSOVER CASTLE, DERBYSHIRE,
from 1612: (a, b) general view and model of the 'keep'
with its earliest adjuncts, (c–e) interiors.

Sir Charles Cavendish's building, based on the
remains of a feudal keep, is a prime example of the
medieval archaism which would play a prominent part
in English architecture a century hence – and which had
played a prominent supporting role at Wollaton. The
master-mason responsible was John Smythson
(Robert's son). The interiors, especially the sumptuous
chimneypieces devised by patron and mason, are best
described as eclectic Franco-Flemish/Serlian.

4.29b

4.29c

4.29d

4.29a

4.29e

4.30a, b

›4.30 BRISTOL, RED LODGE, from c. 1580: (a) garden front (renovated in the mid-19th century), (b) chimneypiece in great chamber.

The house was built over its roughly square plan for the Collector of Customs, Sir John Young. Serlio (Book IV, 6,28) may have been the basis for the design of the three-bay rectilinear block with its arcaded ground floor. The chimneypiece in the great chamber is attributed to William Collins: the strapwork in the armorial panel is directly derived from a cartouche design of Vredeman de Vries.[3.20a]

›4.31 LONDON, NORTHUMBERLAND HOUSE, from c. 1608: street front (as recorded before mid-18th-century alterations).

The patron was the earl of Northampton who advised his nephew on the design of Audley End: unlike the latter – or a major French house – there is no low entrance screen and Dietterlin's style – unrepresented in the earlier work – is impressed on the prominent central frontispiece. The deciphering of the monogram at the top has led to the attribution of this element to the sculptor Gerard Christmas.

›4.32 LONDON: (a) advent of James I (coronation entry arch (1604); (b) project for a New Exchange in the Strand (c. 1608).

Compact and relatively modest houses, built for clients lower down the social scale than the ones we have so far encountered, were legion, but few survive unaltered, especially in towns: though by no means entirely original, a prominent example is Red Lodge in Bristol (from the 1580s). On the other hand, Northumberland House in London represented the aristocratic urban residence at its grandest.[4.30, 4.31]

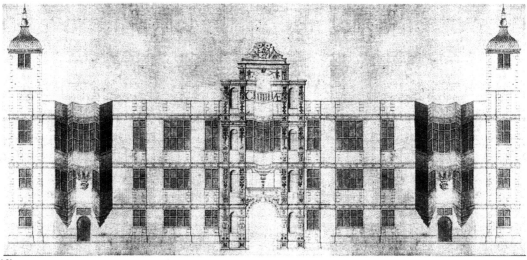

4.31

The royal entry decorations were designed by Stephen Harrison under the direction of Ben Jonson. The Exchange project has been associated with Inigo Jones who was playing a leading role in the design of court spectacles. If that future great architect was involved, it may have been in revising a scheme by Simon Basil who was then surveyor to the king's buildings: the convoluted roof profile ill-accords with Jones's innovative work a decade hence but may not be inconsistent with his decorative sets for the staging of masques.

In the main, reduction in the complexity of H-shaped perimeters began with pruning the wings from the garden front: many Jacobean patrons still resorted to the E-shape even after honour to the late queen was politically obsolete. One of the most prominent examples was begun in the fourth year of the new reign by Lord Burghley's son Robert Cecil, first earl of Salisbury, at Hatfield House (Hertfordshire) – beside the old hall where the late queen had spent much of her precarious childhood. The building is unusual even in this complicated era for its split architectural personality: the unarticulated brick entrance front carries austerity beyond the late-Elizabethan standard; the central block facing the garden, on the contrary, is revetted in stone and articulated in the High Renaissance French manner over a ground-floor loggia. Based on a similar arcaded loggia, an unexecuted project for a new Exchange in the London Strand has been identified as the first known architectural work of Inigo Jones. Thus conjecture has associated that future master with Hatfield.**4.32, 4.33**

4.32b

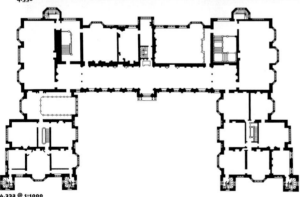

4.33b

4.33a @ 1:1000

›4.33 HATFIELD HOUSE, HERTFORDSHIRE, from c. 1610: (a) plan, (b–d) south, north and east fronts, (e) north entrance, (f) staircase.

A lavish builder in London and at Cranbourne in Dorset, Robert Cecil – second Lord Burghley, first earl of Salisbury – surrendered his father's Theobalds to the king in return for the old royal and ecclesiatical domain of Hatfield. His new house was begun there in 1607 to an E-shaped plan – the slight projection of the entrance-front's end bays hardly constitutes an H. Coherence is not the overriding characteristic of a scheme which runs to stark contrast between the entrance and garden fronts: the former is rectilinear in its massing and austere in unarticulated brickwork penetrated by windows of varied size. The open court facing the main garden zone is addressed by the loggia and gallery of a stone central block articulated with pilasters progressing to columns on the towering pavil-

The main feature of the garden at Hatfield was a pair of terraces, as at Wimbledon: there they were on the main axis of the house; here they descended from the east side,

4.33c

4.33d

ion in the manner of Philibert de l'Orme at Anet: an elevation for the frontis-piece was drawn by Robert Lyminge (died 1628), who had trained as a carpenter. The wings rise higher than the stone face of the central block but are less elevated – and more consistently fenestrated – than the pavilions flanking the entrance range: the coherence which might be expected from one dominant designer is not furthered in the side elevations.

The double-height hall is to the left of the central entrance passage. The latter is, of course, perpendicular to the loggia which runs throughout the lower storey of the central block to a colonnaded lobby at each end. With its lobby, the generous open-cage staircase occupies slightly less than half of the eastern pavilion. Like the secondary staircase at the west end, it serves a great chamber through which access is gained to one of the era's most splendid galleries.

4.33e

4.33f

4.34

›4.34 LLANERCH, DENBIGHSHIRE, MAS-
SEY'S COURT: overview (anonymous, 1662).

The patron was Sir Peter Mutton, H.M. attorney in
Wales from c. 1609 and later chief justice, who inherited the Llanerch estate from his mother's family in
1601 and died there in 1637.

›4.35 JACOBEAN INTERIOR DETAILS: (a)
Prideaux Place (Cornwall), plastered ceiling (c. 1630);
(b) Canons Ashby (Northamptonshire), plastered vault
and chimneypiece (c. 1620); (c) Sherborne Castle
(Dorset, from 1594), dining room with internal porches;
(d) London Charterhouse, hall chimneypiece (1614);
(e, f) Hartwell House (Buckinghamshire, c. 1610),
entrance front and staircase.

While frontispieces and hall screens revelled in rich
relief in a semi-anthropomorphic context indebted to
Vredeman or Dietterlin, the chimneypiece is often in
accord and even from the same hand: to the outstanding examples of both already observed in the work
attributed to Nicholas Stone at Charlton or William
Collins at the Red Lodge in Bristol may be added the
cannon-topped chimneypiece attributed to Edmund
Kinsman in the great hall of the London Charterhouse,
influenced by Dietterlin.[3.70p] Yet architectonic motive
persisted: instead of herms or caryatids, many individual craftsmen retained their allegiance to more-or-less

as at Wollaton.[4.14] A mid-17th-century overview of
Massey's Court, Llanerch (Denbighshire), records a more
extended, more varied series of terraces descending from
the forecourt but on the perpendicular axis: transition was
on staircases no less elaborate than those of Wimbledon
but the internal treatment of the lowest zone clearly
derives from the Villa Lante at Bagnaia or Saint-Germain
(see page 377).[4.34]

One of the main features of the interior at Hatfield is
the open-cage staircase which, with the contemporary one
at Hartwell House (Buckinghamshire), may well represent the type which appeared at Knole in latter-day recognition of developments initiated in Spain to obviate the
Franco-Italian tunnel (see AIC4, pages 729, 789, 874, and
above, pages 222, 586). As we have already seen, Knole also
offers unexcelled early Jacobean elaboration of the hall
screen: Netherlandish craftsmen follow Vredeman and
now also Dietterlin in the complex fragmentation of structural elements, semi-anthropomorphic forms, grotesque
motifs and strapwork in frontispieces too – as at Charlton
and Bramshill.[4.23, 4.25]

4.35b

4.35a
canonical Orders even if they often superimposed them with little concern for structural logic – as at Canons Ashby, for example, in contrast to the more plausible ordonnance of the pair of chimneypieces in the great gallery at Hatfield.

4.35c

4.35d

4.35e, f

After the frontispiece and screen, the chimneypiece continued to be the great glory of the era's domestic architecture: apart from those encountered in context, the main types of post-Serlio may be represented here by the one articulated with superimposed freestanding Orders at Canons Ashby House in Northamptonshire and those incorporating caryatids, atlante or herms like the ones at Charlton – or, indeed, at Longleat.**4.13c** Above all this, the virtuoso plasterwork of the ribbed ceiling, with its inset heraldry and pendant bosses, may be seen as a particularly English domestic derivation from the late-medieval elaboration of the ecclesiastical fan vault – despite the occasional reference to Serlian patterns of coffering or the incorporation of strapwork (see AIC4, pages 424f and above, for example, pages 582f).**4.35**

At Hatfield the influence of Philibert de l'Orme is manifest and seemed to indicate equivalence to the High Renaissance achieved in France at the Louvre and Anet more than half a century earlier. However, the French Mannerism of du Cerceau had already echoed through the façades of Kirby – to name the most spectacular instance.

4.36a

4.36d

JACOBEAN ERA: (a) Oxford, Bodleian Library, Old Schools Quadrangle frontispiece (from 1613); (b–d) Oxford, Wadham College (from 1610), frontispiece, engraved overview, chapel screen; (e) Cambridge, Peterhouse, forecourt and chapel (from 1623); (f) Oxford, S. John's College (c. 1632) .

The main new foundations at Oxford accord with the strong late-medieval quadrangular tradition but subject it to varying degrees of symmetry and fashionable articulation. The Schools, founded by Sir Thomas Bodley, were built between 1613 and 1636 largely by masons imported from Yorkshire with little knowledge of recent developments in the south. The college, founded with a bequest from Nicholas Wadham, was built under the direction of the master-mason William Arnold from the patron's native Somerset where he was

4.36b

And in the detail of early Jacobean works like the frontispieces of Charlton or Bramshill, the influence of Vredeman de Vries and his Flemish Mannerism was supplemented by the convoluted designs of Dietterlin to further complicate the issue. As in Germany, indeed, the development of Classicism in England follows no clear line. The frontispieces of early 17th-century Oxford colleges, rising through four and five storeys, are still overextended in height, not strictly canonical in detail and unrelated to their late-medieval context. This was not the case at contemporary Hatfield House where Vitruvius was not quite lost to translation by de l'Orme: it was not the case later in Oxford either. **4.36, 4.33b**

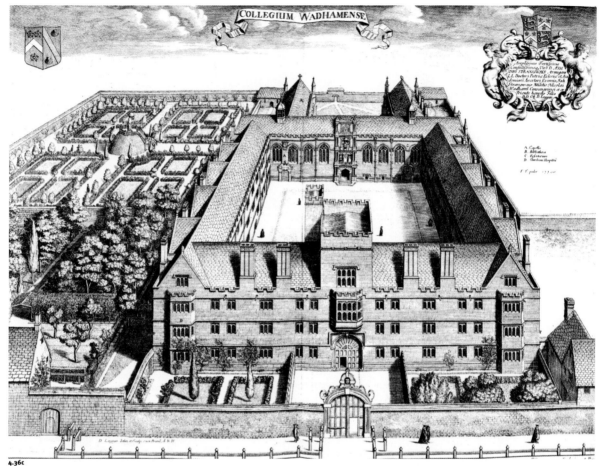

COLLEGIUM WADHAMENSE

4.36c

associated with Montacute: the chapel screen, with its filigree strapwork variations on a Vredeman gable motif, was carved to designs of Arnold related to those of the Montacute House hall screen. The Canterbury Quad of S. John's College in Oxford, founded by Archbishop Laud in 1634, retains superimposed Orders of more canonical form and no longer of medieval elevation.

The unknown late-Jacobean architect of Peterhouse Chapel still worked in the Gothic style but carved out the gable in a latterday Netherlandish Mannerist manner. The original Gothic windows of the side wings were replaced with rectangular ones in 1689.

4.36e

4.36f

The country house is overwhelmingly dominant in the legacy of the Elizabethan and Jacobean reigns, sharing the glory to a limited extent with the collegiate, civic or professional hall and charitable building. This is partly because of the extent of patronage to a self-assertive new class, ambitious to emulate the old landed aristocracy, partly because time has removed most of the lesser domestic buildings from burgeoning – and fire-prone – cities. **4.37**

›4.37 JACOBEAN LONDON HOUSES: (a, b) Holborn street fronts as recorded by John Smythson (c. 1619) with that of Sir Fulke Greville (right) and a project for the latter attributed to Inigo Jones (c. 1617); (c, d) Bishopsgate, Sir Paul Pindar's street front (c. 1624).

At the outset of his career, Jones was mainly interested in picturesque northern Mannerist forms: on return from his trip to Italy in 1615 this persisted but in controlled reference to the urban buildings he would have encountered in northern France, Flanders or even

4.37c

4.37d

Germany *en route*. As we shall see, however, after his return he was to revolutionize the architecture of his homeland under Italian inspiration – mainly that of Palladio and Scamozzi.

4.38a,b

4.38c

›4.38 EARLY CAROLINE CHURCHES: (a–c) Little Gidding, Ferrar Chapel (from 1626); (d, e) Shrivenham, S. Andrew , from c. 1638: exteriors, nave to sanctuary.

Nicholas Ferrar, who built the Little Gidding chapel, was a city merchant whose piety prompted him to retire to a newly acquired estate in Huntingdonshire and found a High Anglican commune which observed its conservative ritual in the rebuilt chapel.

The medieval church at Shrivenham was rebuilt with stylistic schizophrenia to the order of Lord Craven (the soldier son of a lord-mayor of London): the enclosing fabric has Perpendicular windows (and a single low-pitched roof over the basilican volume) but Tuscan columns carrying semi-circular arches between nave and aisles.

4.38d

4.38e

It is also partly because ecclesiastical endeavour, complicated in a century of Reformation turbulence, had largely completed the conversion of England's exceptional range of parish and cathedral churches to Protestant use – with emphasis as much on the pulpit as the altar. There are rare examples of augmenting the stock, of course. However, the glory of the age in church building is its wealth of tombs – again due in no inconsiderable part to the broadening of the patronage spectrum: that wealth is too great for more than cursory accountancy here.**4.38, 4.39**

4.39b

4.39a

›**4.39 JACOBEAN FUNERARY MONUMENTS:** (a) Bottesford (Leicestershire), S. Mary, double-height aedicular tomb of Frances Manners, (sixth earl of Rutland, died 1632) and his wives; (b, c) Hatfield, S. Etheldreda, bier tomb of Robert Cecil, first earl of Salisbury (died 1612) and wall-mounted monument to Dame Elizabeth Brocket (died 1612, above) and her mother Dame Agnes Sanders (died 1588); (d) London, Charterhouse, memorial to John Law (by Nicholas Stone, 1614); (e) Stanford-on-Avon, aedicular tomb of Sir Thomas Cave and his wife (dated 1613) and adjacent memorial to their son Richard (died in Italy in 1606); (f, g) Exton, aedicular tombs of James and Lucy Harrington (died 1592 and 1597) and of Robert Kelway (died 1580, father-in-law of James Harrington's son John, guardian to James I's daughter Elizabeth from 1603, who kneels in witness with his wife); (h) Stratford-upon-Avon, Holy Trinity, George Carew, first earl of Totnes (died 1629) and his wife.

By the end of Elizabeth's reign English craftsmen were proving themselves fecund in the variation of the main types of French and Netherlandish monumental tomb types, certainly not unaided by Vredeman de Vries: the bier with recumbent effigy on a base of the so-called altar type or raised over an undercroft with a *gisant*, with or without supporting Virtues; the free-standing pavilion also with or without accommodation for the *gisant* below the image taken from – or just after – life; the aedicular canopy covering the image of the deceased and supporting his or her arms; the wall-mounted tabernacle or plaque (AIC4, pages 870, 880, and see above, page 590).

4.39c–e

4.39f–h

4.40a

4.40b

The timber-panelled walls – or screens – and plaster ceilings of Jacobean great rooms competed with one another in the intricacy of their carving, the ingeniousness of their motifs. Together with more fashionable Dietterlin, Vredeman and Serlio continued to provide inspiration for the main showpieces of both domestic and ecclesiastical interiors throughout the first Jacobean reign. Of course various manifestations of this eclecticism, and the astylar austerity of work like the north front of Hatfield, continued to inform exteriors too: Blickling (Norfolk), by Robert Lyminge whom we encountered at Hatfield, is a prominent example and so too is the new stone-fronted range at Apethorpe which was undertaken to accommodate the king not long before his demise.**4.40, 4.41**

›4.40 BLICKLING HALL, NORFOLK, from 1618, renovated sympathetically from 1765: (a) entrance front, (b) west flank, (c) great gallery.

The patron was chief justice Sir Henry Hobart; Robert Lyminge is credited as 'architect and builder' in the local burial register (1628). Rejecting the open-court H or E formulae, he returned to the quadrangular tradition as revised for extroverted aspect at Longleat or Burghley but he reduced the courts and limited projection to generous oriels and four corner towers: the detached service ranges were built from 1623. The astylar elevations are more consistent than at Hatfield in the symmetrical disposition of their Anglo-Dutch gabled bays: the pure geometry of the gables – innocent of Flemish prolixity – may not implausibly be related to current rationalist developments in Dutch architecture (see pages 548ff).

4.40C

4.41a

4.41b

4.41c

The patron, Sir Francis Fane, was called on by the king to extend his house to provide suitable accommodation for the royal party on its frequent visits for hunting in the Grafton Forest: the west range was the result but the king was dead within three years of its foundation. Though communicating with the renovated gallery, the king's lodging was self-contained within its own entrances from court and garden.

4.42a

2 INCEPTION OF PALLADIANISM

English stylistic confusion was suddenly dispelled towards the end of the second Jacobean decade: the renewed influence of Italy in effecting a new, alternative, High Renaissance was immediate and direct. The agent was Inigo Jones (1573–1652). A draftsman skilled in surveying surface and space, a designer of court entertainments, he had travelled through Italy perhaps to the Medici court in Florence, certainly to Venice (c. 1600), probably primarily to study painting and scenographic perspective at its source.**4.42** He brought back with him an admiration for Palladio backed by first-hand knowledge of the works of the master, as of his antique and modern mentors in practice and theory. He had also acquired a collection of Palladian drawings to supplement a copy of *I Quattro Libri dell'architettura* as a resource of rationalism beyond the visual stimulus of the Serlian pattern book. He returned to Italy at least twice (in 1605 and 1613), ultimately penetrating as far as Rome with the connoisseur and collector Thomas Howard, Earl of Arundel.

He had, of course, visited France *en route* and as an end in itself (1609). His first official appointment to court circles was as surveyor to Henry Prince of Wales (1611): he was surveyor general of the king's works from 1615.

4.42c

The French-derived Renaissance style of Burghley or Hatfield – let alone French, Netherlandish or German Mannerism – was eclipsed by a thoroughgoing Classicism which admitted no extraneous ornament on exteriors: a note of 1615 in Jones's Roman sketchbook specifically deplores the influence of Michelangelo. The new surveyor general of royal buildings initiated his reform in 1616 with the villa at Greenwich built for James I's queen, Anne of Denmark: he furthered it three years later with the king's Banqueting Hall at Whitehall and (from 1623) with the chapel at S. James's Palace built for Charles I's future queen, Henrietta Maria. Demonstrating the correct use of the Orders, the correct repertory of detail, an integrated set of proportions, basic simplicity and restraint, the understanding that Classicism was not about decoration but about order, these buildings are clearly Palladian – but in emulation of the principles set out in the master's book, not in slavish plagiarism of any of his executed works.

4.42b

>**4.42 INIGO JONES, SET DESIGNS FOR COURT MASQUES:** (a) eclectic palace backdrop design for the masque *Oberon, The Faery Prince* (c. 1611); (b) Classical palace backdrop, 'Cupid's Palace', for an unidentified production (after c. 1619, derived from Scamozzi's Vicentine Palazzo Trissino al Corso of 1588); (c) 'A Roman Atrium' backdrop for *Albion's Triumph* (1632).

The impact of Jones on the post-medieval *métier* of architecture was stunning: emulating the great 16th-century Italians (and de l'Orme or Lescot) in intellect and erudition, he moved motive force from the patron to the professional with determination beyond his Elizabethan predecessors – notwithstanding the individuality of a Smythson. Even more manifestly stunning was the particular impact of the Queen's Chapel on the English ecclesiastical tradition and the Banqueting House on the jumble of medieval buildings which constituted the royal palace of Whitehall – as on the English architectural scene as a whole.**4·43**

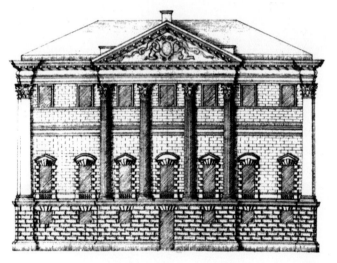

4·43a

The advent of English Palladian rationalism

Inevitably Jones's two most significant surviving buildings represent the two most exportable of Palladio's genres – the town and country house and the formulae evolved by the Vicentine master for their perfection. However, neither has a precise precedent in the Veneto.

The Queen's House at Greenwich was exceptional in its design to span a main road – from Deptford to Woolwich south-east of London – a peculiar behest of the queen who wanted agreeable access from the old Tudor

4.43b

palace by the River Thames to the elevated parkland to its south: work stopped on her death in 1618 but was resumed for her successor, Queen Henrietta Maria, from 1630 to 1635. Jones's scheme was originally H-shaped with parallel wings like Giuliano da Sangallo's Medici villa at

4.43f

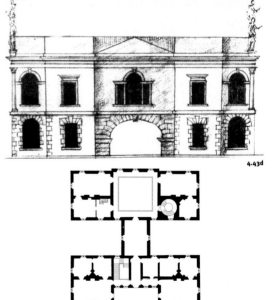

4.43d

4.43e @ 1:1000

4.43C

›4.43 INIGO JONES, WORKS FOR THE STUART COURT: (a) Whitehall, unexecuted project for a basilica to house the Privy Council's Star Chamber (1617), elevation (as revised by John Webb); (b–g) Greenwich, Queen's House (from 1616–18 and from 1630), general views from south-west and north (as revised in the later 17th and 18th centuries), initial project for side elevations, plan of main floor, great hall and spiral staircase details;

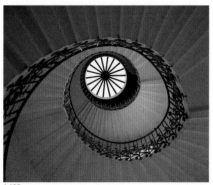

4.43B

Poggio a Caiano but with a side elevation derived from Scamozzi (AIC4, page 778, and above, page 254): the recessions above the road were filled with extra bridging rooms after the restoration of the monarchy in 1660, when the building was renovated for the then queen mother under the direction of Jones's pupil John Webb. Rather than the principal reception room, however, the link was originally the road-bridge room at first-floor level which departed from the gallery of the great hall after the completion of the initial project for the building in the 1630s. In the centre of the northern range, the latter is a single cube room with the gallery at half height to counter perceived divergence from the ideal proportions. The division is carried over to the exterior, articulated in the manner of the Italian High Renaissance town house rather than the typical Palladian villa, with the Ionic Order of the piano nobile rising over a rusticated basement: here, however, the Order is confined to a central loggia on the south front – but not on both levels as in a Palladian hybrid town-villa such as the one devised for the Pisani at Montagnana.[1.77a] The project of c. 1618 for the Prince's Lodging at Newmarket is a closer approximation to that hybrid, without the basement Order.

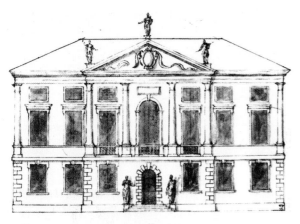

4.43h

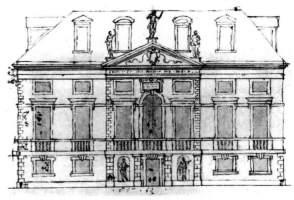

4.43i

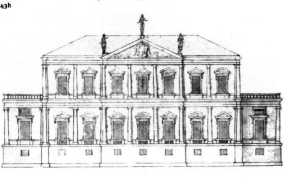

4.43j

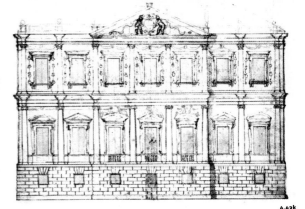

4.43k

(h, i) Newmarket, project for Prince's Lodging; (j–n) Whitehall Palace, Banqueting House (from 1619), plan and elevation of initial scheme and elevation as revised with central projection, exterior and interior; (o–r) S. James's Palace, Queen's Chapel (from 1623), longitudinal section (as measured by Henry Flitcroft for Lord Burlington a century after construction), exteriors and interiors; (s) royal palace project for S. James's Park (conceived 1638, revised 1647 for the Whitehall site), plan and bird's-eye perspective (attributed to John Webb after Jones); (t) Somerset House, project for Strand front (1638, attributed to Webb after Jones).

The relationship between the surviving drawings for the Newmarket lodging – stylar and astylar – and the building as realized in the royal riding establishment

The Banqueting House encloses a double-cube room (33.5 x 16.75 metres): as at the S. James's Palace Queen's Chapel, the adoption of elementary harmonic proportions in accord with Palladio's fundamental precept distinguishes Jones's rationalism from the intuitive – or purely pragmatic – work of his predecessors. The scheme is an interpretation of the antique basilica in the two-storey mode of Vitruvius's Egyptian hall (QL II.10.28, see above, page 259): the horizontal division is expressed outside

4.43l

there eludes determination: not conforming to the former in contemporary descriptions, the latter was
demolished in 1650. However, Jones's drawings were
known to disciples like Sir Roger Townshend of Raynham, Norfolk (on whom, see below).

By the beginning of the 17th century a freestanding
'banqueting house' supplemented the Tudor Great
Chamber for the grandest ceremonial as well as court
theatrical entertainments, as the Great Chamber had
eclipsed the Great Hall: the latter was now largely – if
not exclusively – at the disposal of the vast retinue of
palace servants. On the site of a timber structure (of
1581), Jones's Banqueting House replaced Robert

by the superimposed Orders (doubled for strength at the corners) and differentiated window frames; inside it is stressed by the projection of the
gallery from the lower (Ionic) Order's cornice instead of its recession over
aisles as in the model. Inaccessible, the gallery was interpolated again to
counter optical illusion: as the true nature of the form was the single volume of Vitruvius's Corinthian hall alternative, a precise precedent has
proved elusive. Correspondingly, Palladian Vicentine projects are referred
to for the design of the exterior, specifically to Scamozzi's one for Trissino
after the master's Barbaran da Porto and Chiericati palaces (*QL* II.5.16 and
II.8.54; see above, page 245). On the other hand, the Star Chamber basilica

4.43m

4.43n

Smythson's work (of 1606) which succumbed to fire in 1619: two surviving autograph drawings trace the evolution of the scheme from an expansive one with central pedimented projection to the executed scheme without pediment via contraction and lavish embellishment to the articulated bays over the rusticated basement. Without Orders, the gallery motif was applied to the hall of the Queen's House during the campaign for Henrietta Maria in the 1630s.

The queen was housed in the eastern sector of S. James's Palace which disappeared in a fire of 1809. That connected with the Catholic chapel projected for the proposed betrothal of the Prince of Wales to a Spanish Infanta but completed after his marriage to Henrietta Maria: the coffering derives from Palladio's record of the Roman 'Temple of the Sun and Moon' (actually Venus and Rome, QL IV.10.23); the west-end gallery and east-end serliana date from the 1660s (and later) in their present form but the latter frames the window of Jones's original work. That was the earliest of its kind to have been executed in England – though the motif was introduced to the scheme for the Royal Exchange (referred to above in connection with Hatfield) and to the preliminary bridgeside elevation of the Queen's House at Greenwich which was derived from the side elevation of Scamozzi's Villa Morin (near Padua, 1597) where Jones stayed with Arundel in 1614 – when he met the architect then dominant in the Veneto.

was to have had a gallery but the two internal Orders ceded outside to a colossal engaged Corinthian Order which may derive from, but exceed, those of Palladio's Villa Mocenigo's portico (see page 250). As we have seen, Palladio's publication was extraordinarily successful because it was both theoretical treatise and pattern book.

During the design process, Whitehall Palace hall was elevated from a theatre for masques into a major audience chamber – possibly conceived as the nucleus of the extensive new palace which the king seems first to have called for in 1638. Be that as it may, in that year it was dignified with the great ceiling paintings of 'The Apotheosis of James I' executed from c. 1622 by the foremost artist of the day, Peter-Paul Rubens (and his studio).

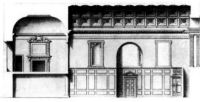

4.43o

4.43p

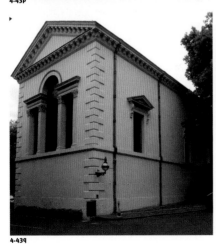

4.43q

4.43r

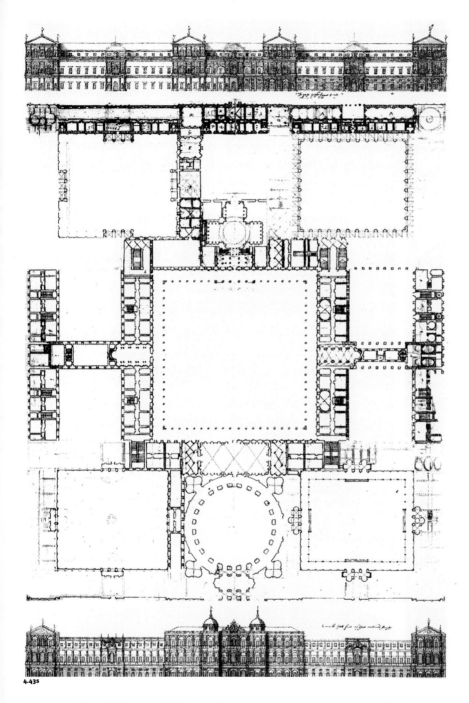

4.435

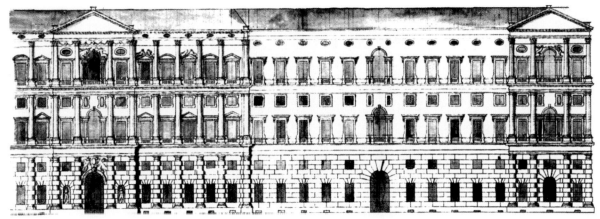

4.43t

Somerset House was assigned to Queen Anne of Denmark in 1617, the year before she died. It was assigned to Queen Henrietta Maria in 1625: protracted work there prompted Jones ultimately to address the problem of the street frontage crammed between undistinguished private buildings: his conception derives from Scamozzi's three-storey variant of his Palazzo Trissino scheme for the Strozzi which was itself indebted to Palladio's project for rebuilding the Doge's palace (1577).

Jones's pupil and assistant, John Webb (1611–72) was responsible for drawing up grand schemes for royal palaces. The one extending from Whitehall into S. James's Park was possibly conceived by the master as early as 1638 in response to a directive of Charles I dated to that year: a scheme for the Strand front of Somerset House is contemporary. Another set of drawings, incorporating the Banqueting House and its double on the Whitehall site, imposed unprecedented integrity on a large tract of Westminster: possibly resulting from a revised directive issued by the king as late as 1647, it was fantasy and the unruly medieval organism was removed only by fire towards the end of the century.

Jones masked the medieval organism of old S. Paul's cathedral with a grand Classical portico (from 1633) but the whole complex succumbed in 1666 to the conflagration fuelled by the warrens of timber houses which were the fabric of medieval London.**4·44** More enduringly, he imposed a Classical order on town planning in developing the Earl of Bedford's estate at Covent Garden (from 1636), initiating the reform of the conditions which produced the fire. The garden of a defunct convent, acquired for development to the north of the earl's house on the Strand,

4.44a

›4.44 LONDON, S. PAUL'S CATHEDRAL:
(a) project with superimposed Orders (1633; (b)
engraved view as executed (Wenceslas Hollar, *The History of St Paul's Cathedral*, 1658).

Commissions for renovating the dilapidated medieval structure were constituted in 1608 and 1620: the earliest surviving project in Jones's hand, centred on a frontispiece of superimposed paired columns, is comparable to the one for the New Exchange produced in 1608[4.32b] – except for the portals which are hardly less sophisticated than the main window frames of the penultimate project for the Whitehall Banqueting House of c. 1620. A new commission, constituted by Bishop Laud in 1631, called for the comprehensive Classicization of the Norman and Gothic fabric: work began at the east end in 1633 and culminated in the great west portico after 1640: the largest work of its kind north of the Alps, modelled on Palladio's unpedimented record of the Temple of Venus and Rome (*QL* IV.10.22), the exceptional grandeur was due to a work paid for personally by the king.

4.44b

became the first formal square in England. Italy again provided Jones with his model for a commercial and residential forum addressed by a church – in particular the Piazza

4.45b

4.45a

›4.45 LONDON, COVENT GARDEN, from 1631: (a) elevations of church and piazza fronts (*Vitruvius Britannicus*, London 1715); (b, c; see pages 558–559) aerial view (Wenceslaus Hollar, 1658); (d) S. Paul's, east front.

The Earl of Bedford's commercial development to the north of his garden was a market forum surrounded on three sides by arcaded loggias – significantly called 'piazzas' by Londoners – with axial streets leading out from the corners and S. Paul's church dominating it from the centre of its western side. This first formal intervention in the non-royal fabric of London demonstrated Jones's grasp of Vitruvian decorum, the unrefined Tuscan Order of the church in particular responding to its commercial context: the earl called for a building 'not much better than a barn'; Jones answered with 'the handsomest barn in England' based on the reconstruction of an Etruscan temple in Daniele Barbaro's edition of Vitruvius, drawn by Palladio. The Order was extended to the 'piazzas' via the rusticated portals to either side of the church. John Evelyn refers to Leghorn (Livorno) as the specific source of inspiration – though the general idea was certainly Parisian. The executive architect was Isaac de Caus whose involvement probably extended from his native *métier* as the designer of gardens.

4.45c

Grande at Livorno, a port linked to London by trade.[1.49] For the shopping arcades and housing which defined the market space to the north and east, however, Jones's collaborator Isaac de Caus referred to a more immediately obvious precedent: the recently completed Place Royale (Place des Vosges) in Paris.[2.57e] Indebted to neither of these models, the church conceived in Tuscan style for its lowly context is an exemplary exercise in Vitruvian decorum.[4.45-4.47]

4.46e

4.46g

4.46f

4.46a–d

›4.46 THE PORTAL IN THE JONESIAN ERA:
(a–d) the master's designs for the London houses of
Arundel (1618), Beaufort (1621) and Hatton (1622) and
for the Vineyard at Oatlands Palace (Surrey, c. 1617); (e)
London, York Water Gate (1626); (f) Oxford, University
Church of S. Mary the Virgin (1637); (g) unidentified
masque design (1608).

Jones was no less impressed than Serlio – or Dietterlin – by the potential of portal design to express the
peculiar characteristics of each Order in exemplary
compression: Serlio and Giulio Romano apart, Vignola
was his preferred source of inspiration. However, compare the scheme for Oatlands Palace with the west
portal of Giulio's Palazzo del Te (see pages 123f). Moreover, the opposing style of Michelangelo's Porta Pia
pediment is recalled in the 'Italian' design for Arundel
over rustication invading the columns and frieze of the
Tuscan Order in the mode descended from Giulio (via
Galeazzo Alessi's Porta del Molo in Genoa, if not Serlio
IV.10.46, and Vignola, *Porte di Michel Angelo*).[1.32d,e]
The Beaufort gate survives at Chiswick House: the most
prominent surviving representative of the rusticated
type is the York Water Gate attributed to the Huguenot
immigrant from the Netherlands, the amateur architect
Sir Balthazar Gerbier.

In an undated scenographic drawing for a masque at Arundel House – as on an unidentified occasion as early as 1608 – Jones (or an assistant) strayed into the Solomonic under influences which descend at least from Raphael. That mode was adopted by Nicholas Stone – the master's master-mason at Whitehall – for his extraordinary work on S. Mary the Virgin at Oxford.

›4.47 LONDON, GRAND TERRACE HOUS-ING: (a) Great Queen's Street (c. 1637); (b) Lincoln's Inn Fields: Conyngham (later Lindsey) House (1640).

The centrepiece in the range of thirty-two houses

4.47a

4.47b

built for the developer William Newton was destined for Sir David Conyngham: the design is credited by association with Nicholas Stone who had worked for Conyngham elsewhere. The colossal Ionic Order over a rusticated basement, probably introduced to England by Jones in the Star Chamber project, had previously been applied to housing in Great Queen Street.

›4.48 LEES COURT, KENT: garden front (c. 1640).

The patron was Sir George Sondes, the architect is unknown but the capitals of the colossal Ionic Order are similar to those of Lindsey House. The pilasters rise from pedestals at ground level rather than a rusticated basement.

4.48

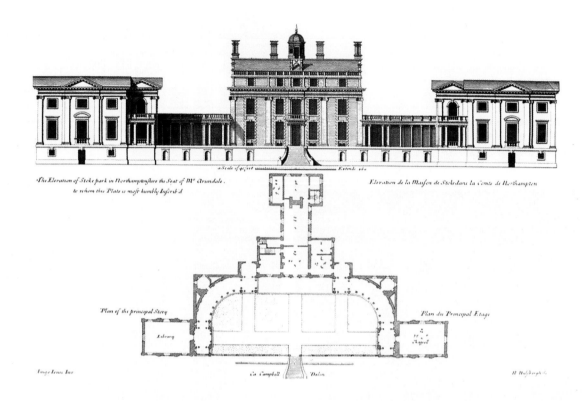

The Elevation of Stoke park in Northamptonshire the Seat of M.ʳ Arundale. to whom this Plate is most humbly Inscrib'd

Elevation de la Maison de Stoke dans la Comte de Northampton

Plan of the principal Story

Plan du Principal Etage

Library

Chappel

Inigo Jones Inv.

Ca. Campbell Delin.

H. Hulsbergh sc.

4.49

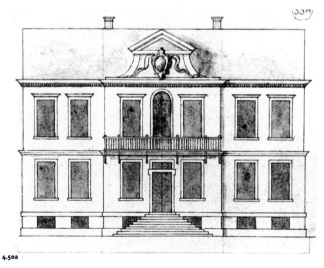

4.50a

>**4.49 STOKE BRUERNE,** from c. 1630, entrance front and plan (engraved for *Vitruvius Britannicus*, 1717).

Stoke Bruerne was built by Sir Francis Crane from 1635: unsubstantiated tradition relates that the patron 'brought the design out of Italy and in the execution therof received the assistance of Inigo Jones'. Be that as it may, the Italian style – or, rather, the eclectic mix of Michelangelesque and Palladian motifs – was probably of the patron's own derivation and its subjection to a conventional Jacobean roof is not unfairly seen as peculiarly amateurish.

>**4.50 INIGO JONES, UNEXECUTED VILLA PROJECTS,** c. 1638: (a) astylar; (b) with portico and belvedere.

4.50b

›4.51 CASTLE ASHBY, NORTHAMPTON-
SHIRE: entrance screen (from c. 1636).
The screen added to Elizabethan Castle Ashby for
the 2nd Earl of Northampton is attributed to Edward
Carter, the London 'surveyor' who worked with Jones
on the Earl of Bedford's Covent Garden – on S. Paul's
church in particular.

There is no evidence that Jones had an extensive private practice in town or country, though drawings even for modest houses may be attributed to him. However, almost every consistent Order, especially colossal, and certainly any temple-front motif applied to a country-house façade in the second Stuart reign has been taken as evidence of Jones's involvement: London squares, Lees Court (Kent), Stoke Bruerne and Castle Ashby (Northamptonshire) are examples.[4.48, 4.49, 4.51] The last may be compared with Jones's unexecuted project for a porticoed villa and contrasted informatively, with his contemporary project for an astylar villa (c. 1638).[4.50] Others followed the latter too, for example, the author of the north front of Kirby.

Of course, Jones's devotees, familiar with his executed work and project drawings, were certainly able to consult him and act on his advice with the aid of their local

4.51

4·52

4·53

›ARCHITECTURE IN CONTEXT »FROM THE HIGH RENAISSANCE TO MANNERISM

›4.52 RAYNHAM HALL, NORFOLK: east front (from c. 1630).

The patron, Sir Roger Townshend, began work on his house in 1622 and evolved the design over nearly a decade as he extended his experience of the latest developments in Jonesian architecture: the hybrid east front emerged at the end of the process – and so too did wooden glazing bars instead of stone mullions.

›4.53 BROOME PARK, KENT, 1635, interiors from late-18th and early 20th century: entrance front.

The patron was Sir Basil Dixwell, a landowner from Warwickshire who inherited the east Kentish estate on which he settled. Whether or not he had access to Jonesian drawings, he presumably knew Nicholas Stone. The style of his work follows closely from Swakeleys in Middlesex (1629) and Kew Palace (1631).

›4.54 KIRBY HALL, NORTHAMPTONSHIRE: north front (from c. 1638).

The great Elizabethan complex was extended for Sir Christopher Hatton under the direction of Nicholas Stone. The austere approach, related to Jonesian schemes like the one for the astylar villa of c. 1638, extends to diversified fenestration after the example of the lost Chelsea house of Sir John Danvers (from c. 1622) – but not without problems of proportion.

master-masons. In so far as the quality of response is concerned, the most creditable of these was Sir Roger Townshend of Raynham Hall in Norfolk. **4.52** He passed through Newmarket on his regular route to London where he is known to have examined Jones's drawings in the Office of Works: into the brick context of convoluted gables in the so-called Artisan – or Dutch – style of his seat, he inserted a stone temple-front motif like that which distinguished Jones's design for the Prince's Lodging at Newmarket – but which has no surviving predecessor. The contrast with its peers striking only in part, the result may well be deemed incoherent but it pointed the way ahead. In the meantime, however, the Artisan style of the side pavilions largely prevailed: distinguished by the form of gable with scrolls supporting a triangular pediment, that was developed for patrons from the lesser rural gentry or the urban merchant class and may derive from Jones's revision of the Netherlandish style in works like Sir Fulke Greville's house (see page 610) or from Nicholas Stone's experience of Amsterdam where he studied until 1613. **4.53, 4.54**

4.54

4.55a

Jones seems to have been consulted on the projection of a new south wing at Wilton before the existing range was destroyed by fire in 1647: in the surviving overview, however, the awkward adoption of a Palladian temple front to mask the junction of two semi-centralized wings, unmatched elsewhere in Jones's work, is most convincingly attributed to Isaac de Caus – the son or nephew of Solomon – who was retained as architect by the Earl of Pembroke in 1636. That scheme was happily reduced to one of its constituent parts, without the portico, in a project (perhaps partially executed from c. 1636) on which Jones may have advised de Caus and which provided Webb with the basis for

4.55b

the work he carried out after the fire between revamped existing towers: these, countering the original weakness of the sides, were to be highly influential.

Jones's preferred double cube, without horizontal division against its nature but with a coved cornice accommodated in the elevation, is finally adopted for the main interior here. The sumptuous embellishment with swags and pendants, supplementing the frames of the splendid Van Dyck family portraits which the rooms were designed to display, is of stylized fruit and flowers in lush contrast to the Vitruvian detail surviving in the halls of the Queen's House in Greenwich and the Banqueting House Whitehall.

The scheme for the garden was evolved by de Caus (died 1655), whose French origins had recommended him to the court of Charles I and his French queen from the outset of their reign. Working at Wilton 'in the Italian manner' (as it was categorized by contemporaries), he followed the prescriptions of Scamozzi in its rectangular enclosure on axis and contiguous with the house and drew elementary variety from unity on a flat site. Overviewed from the latter in the manner of a French parterre, it was divided into several zones, the inner pair of four-squared *compartements de broderies*, the middle pair informal bosquets crossed by a stream, and the outermost ovoid one treated to mirror-image concentricity. A rusticated grotto closed the central axial alley opposite the house.

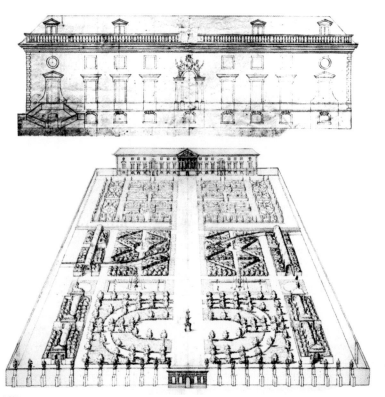

4.54c

Jones was indeed called in to collaborate on the project for rebuilding the southern range of Wilton House (Wiltshire) after a fire had gutted it in 1647: the façade lacks the master's control but, behind it, the Double Cube Room remains one of the kingdom's most splendid domestic interiors. John Webb was a principal in that collaboration and in imposing his own personality on the development of his master's style before the fall of the monarchy in 1649, he prepared the way for bold achievement after the restoration in 1660.**4.55**

5.68c

5 BEYOND THE PYRENEES

5.1a

5.1b

›**5.1 VALLADOLID, COLEGIO DE SANTA CRUZ,** from 1486, as revised from 1488: (a) entrance front, (b) detail of portal.

Work, begun in 1487 on plans finalized the previous year, did not please the patron – in town on a royal visit. At first bent on starting again, the cardinal settled for keeping the groundwork and revising the project to incorporate fashionable Renaissance motifs – hence the Gothic detail on the buttresses flanking the portal as a base for the superimposed pseudo-Classical pilaster groups. The change *a la romana* coincides with the advent of Lorenzo Vázquez but seems to have been prompted by the cardinal's nephew Don Iñigo López de Mendoza who had recently returned from serving as ambassador in Rome. Work was currently also in train on a residence for the cardinal's son Don Rodrigo at Cogolludo, the first of Spain's Renaissance palaces which is also attributed to Vázquez (AIC4, page 865). Like that of the latter, the college portal itself – with the medieval legacy of the emblematic or narrative tympanum – is Classicized in the Florentine aedicular mode of Alberti and Bernardo Rossellino writ large (AIC4, pages 724, 742, 757). In addition to an extensive library, the eclectic taste of the cardinal was informed by his important collection of Italian medals. The first-floor window aedicule was inserted in the 18th century.

1 IBERIA AT THE TURN OF THE RENAISSANCE CENTURY

In the Iberian kingdoms, as in France and elsewhere outside Italy, the first phase of Renaissance was invariably characterized by the grafting of Classical motifs on to medieval forms. In addition to their exceptionally florid Gothic legacy, however, the Catholic Monarchs who completed the unification of Spain with the expulsion of the last Moorish sultan from Granada in 1492 were heirs to an equally lavish Muslim tradition: so too were the Lusitanian kings, whose reconquest and consolidation of independent power had been completed 250 years earlier. Not surprisingly, the application of imported Italian motifs to these hybrid legacies effected styles noted for prolixity largely insubordinate to structure but differing across the peninsula both in the nature of the native hybrid and the effect of the foreign import.

Mid-17th-century critics characterized the approach of the Arcarrena school, which fostered Spanish Renaissance architecture largely under Flemish and French masters, as Plateresque after stone-carving of such elaborate intricacy that it resembles beaten metalwork. Of many examples, the portal to the Hospicio de los Reyes Católicos – the pilgrim hostel built in 1501 beside the great cathedral enshrining S. James at Santiago de Compostela – is unsurpassed in this respect by anything in France – except perhaps the chevet of S.-Pierre at Caen (A1C4, pages 806, 866, 871).

Pseudo-Classical Orders, superimposed to achieve Gothic height, had appeared in the secular field early in Spain's first Renaissance century: the prime example distinguishes the façade of the otherwise Gothic Colegio de Santa Cruz at Valladolid: the patron was Grand Cardinal Don Pedro González de Mendoza, archbishop of Toledo and primate of Spain from 1482; execution is attributed to the master-mason Lorenzo Vázquez.**5.1** The potential of the portal as the context for experimentation in fashionable 'modern' design was quickly realized, not least by Francisco de Colonia (c. 1470–1552), Juan de Álava (c. 1480–1537) and above all, perhaps, Alonso de Covarrubias (1488–1570). And the motif of the triumphal arch, introduced to funerary architecture at the end of the old century, took its appropriate position to the fore.

5.2

The young sculptor Alonso de Covarrubias began working in Salamanca in 1510 under the brothers Enrique and Antón Egas – the former his father-in-law. He had moved on to Toledo with them by 1513 where they collaborated on the hospital project from 1517 to 1524. Late-Gothic masters, the Egas brothers are credited with the hospital's innovative open-cage staircase, but not with responsibility for the introduction of Renaissance detail to the works on which they collaborated with the young Covarrubias.

›5.3 BURGOS, CATHEDRAL OF OUR LADY:
Puerta de la Pellejería (1516).

A hybrid Flamboyant-Renaissance exercise, commissioned by Bishop Don Juan Rodríguez de Fonseca, Francisco de Colonia's eastern portal to the north transept is essentially of the retable type.

5.3

Covarrubias's career opens with the portal of the Hospital of Santa Cruz at Toledo (c. 1520, AIC4, page 867): the semi-circular tympanum containing the relief of the Holy Cross is surmounted by a miniature pavilion articulated in the rhythm of the triumphal arch.**5.2** That rhythm is varied for the contemporary portal of the Convent of S. Marcos at León: heraldic embellishment predominates in a manner far from foreign to Spain though, in place of the semi-circular tympanum, the equestrian image of Santiago the Moor-slayer echoes contemporary developments at Louis XII's château of Blois (see AIC4, pages 876f).**5.4** At the same time, again, triumphal arch and semi-circular tympanum constitute the Puerta de la Pellejería of Francisco de Colonia on the north transept of Burgos cathedral.**5.3** Similar elements are embedded in the Plateresque plethora of attenuated pilasters which relieve Juan de Álava's S. Esteban in Salamanca in the following decade.**5.5d–f**

>5.4 LEÓN, CONVENT OF S. MARCOS, founded mid-12th century: portal (from 1515).

The sumptuous rebuilding was commissioned by the Catholic Monarchs: the architects included Juan de Orozco for the chapel, Juan de Badajoz for the sacristy and cloister and Martín de Villareal for the façade.

Behind a Plateresque screen of pilasters and candelabra, the late-Gothic tradition persisted well into the 16th century at many of the great ecclesiastical buildings – naturally where work was already in train, as at Burgos or Palencia, for example, but also on new ones, such as the cathedrals of Salamanca and Segovia begun by Juan Gil de Hontañón (c. 1480–1526) and continued by his son Rodrigo (1500–77). In contrast to the basilican profile of Salamanca cathedral, the hall type with aisles rising to the height of the nave was taken to its apogee at Segovia: Juan de Álava's S. Esteban at Salamanca is another important example. The aisleless form frequently served as the collegiate, monastic and/or funerary chapel: Juan de Orozco's work for the convent of S. Marcos at León or Álava's for the Colegio de Fonseca at Salamanca are typical but the supreme example is Enrique Egas's shrine for the Catholic Monarchs at Granada (AIC4, pages 459f, 864).**5·5**

5.5a

›5.5 CONSERVATISM AND INNOVATION IN
THE GREAT CHURCH ON THE EVE OF RENAIS-
SANCE: (a, b) Salamanca, Catedral Nueva, view from
south and nave to sanctuary across the trascoro; (c)
Segovia, Catedral de Nuestra Señora (begun by Juan Gil
de Hontañón in 1522, four years before his death), nave
detail; (d–f) Salamanca, S. Esteban (begun 1524 by
Juan de Álava), west front, nave east to sanctuary, west
to choir.

In a wide-ranging treatise, highly eclectic, the science of architecture was identified with Gothic structure
by Rodrigo Gil de Hontañón who collaborated with his
father on the planning of the last of Spain's great Gothic
cathedrals, at Salamanca and Segovia, and pursued
their construction throughout his life. The Segovia nave
was vaulted by 1562; the revised crossing and apsidal
sanctuary were unvaulted when Rodrigo died in 1577
but had been completed by 1591; the dome and tower
were added in the early 17th century. The Salamanca
vaulting was complete c. 1550; the dome and tower
were achieved definitively in the early 18th century – the
former by the Churriguera brothers, the latter in recognition of Rodrigo Gil de Hontañón's homage to Toledo.

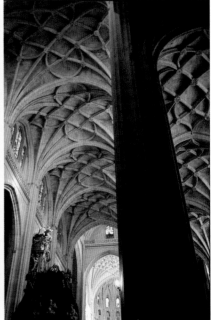

5.5b

5.5c

5.5d

5.5e

5.5f

Flamboyant ornament, which had ramped through the penultimate generation of Spain's great churches, may still infiltrate vaulting well into the 16th century but semi-circular arches prevail and Gothic shafts may cede to attenuated pilasters, superimposed as in France, or even single great columns. Early examples range from S. María la Mayor at Antequera (Málaga) to the Church of the Assumption, Moratalla (Murcia) and on, more prominently, to Covarrubias's Nuestra Señora de la Piedad in Guadalajara (1526) or Álava's S. Esteban in Salamanca in the mid-1520s.

Exemplary, the S. Esteban façade is of the retable type: naturally, the Flamboyant-Classical hybrid found its most fertile field of propagation in the retable itself. And that, in turn, took its departure from the Neoclassical transformation of the wall tomb at the end of the 15th century – specifically for Grand Cardinal de Mendoza in the presbyterium of his cathedral at Toledo. Cross-fertilization is nowhere better illustrated at this early stage than in Covarrubias's contiguous monuments in the north transept of Sigüenza cathedral: the altar retable dedicated to S. Librada, the see's patron saint, and the tomb of Don Fadrique of Portugal, its bishop until 1532. Both adhere to the Mendoza sepulchral type but, paradoxically, the bishop's

›5.6 THE NEOCLASSICAL TOMB AND RETABLE: (a, b) of Grand Cardinal Mendoza (died 1495) and Alonso Carrillo de Albornoz, Bishop of Ávila (died 1514) in the cathedral of S. María of Toledo; (c, d) tombs of the Vázquez brothers and retables of S. Librada and Bishop Don Fadrique of Portugal (1514–18 in the main) in Sigüenza cathedral.

Mendoza, bishop of Sigüenza from 1468, archbishop of Seville and chancellor of Castile from 1473, was promoted to the primacy at Toledo in 1482. At his insistence his tomb was located in the presbyterium – hitherto reserved for royalty – to the dismay of the chapter but with the approbation of Queen Isabella in recognition of his support in her struggle for the throne. The first Castilian exercise in the guise of a Classical triumphal arch – but displaying the sepulchre in the central arch in the manner of the neighbouring medieval royal tombs – it is attributed to the Florentine sculptor Jacopo Sansovino (or one of his associates) due to its stylistic similarity to his later work in Portugal. In the central ambulatory chapel of S. Ildefonso, the Ávila tomb (sculpted by Vasco de la Zarza c. 1515) is a derivative of prime importance.

5.6a

5.6b

5.6c

The transition from the Flamboyant to the early Renaissance form of wall tomb (via the Ávila example) is admirably represented by those of the brothers Martín and Fernando Vázquez de Arce (bishop of the Canaries), of 1486 and 1523 respectively, in the Chapel of S. Catalina which opens off the south transept of Sigüenza cathedral. The north transept monuments are both credited in conception to Covarrubias: execution, directed by Francisco de Baeza, was furthered by Sebastián de Almonacid and Juan de Talavera who were probably also responsible for Fernando Vázquez de Arce's tomb.

5.6d

funerary monument reverts from the overtly sepulchral to retable typology – though the rhythm of the triumphal arch is sustained in the central zone with its great niche accommodating the cardinal and his attendants.**5.6**

5.7b

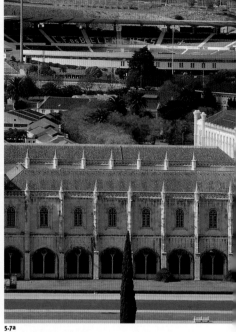

5.7a

The addition of Mudéjar ingredients to the mixture of Gothic and Lombard motifs effected the so-called 'Cisneros' style of Pedro de Gumiel, Enrique Egas and their more colourful contemporaries: the former's theatre in the University of Alcalá and Egas's contribution to the Toledo Hospital de Santa Cruz are prominent examples – though the medieval Christian component triumphs in combination with early Italian motifs in Covarrubias's elaboration on Vázquez's theme for the aedicular portal to the latter.**5.2**

Meanwhile, across the border to the west the peculiarly Portuguese Manueline style, named after the reign of King Manuel I (1495–1521) in which it flourished, was an even more extravagant exercise in eclecticism than the 'Cisneros' style of contemporary Spain: to Flamboyant and Mudéjar patterns in rib-vaulting, in particular, and Plateresque accumulation of Lombard decorative detail, were added maritime, marine and exotic Indian motifs

›5.7 FROM MANUELINE TO RENAISSANCE IN PORTUGAL: (a–c) Belém, church of the Jerónimos Monastery (1502–19), exterior general view, detail of west portal with image of Manuel I and Queen Maria of Aragon and interior detail; (d, e) Tomar, church of the Convent of Christ (1510–14), interior and exterior details; (f) Setúbal, church of the Monastery of Jesus (Diégo Boytac, c. 1498); (g) the Chanterene retable of c. 1529 (Sintra, Palácio Nacional da Pena, chapel); (h–l) Sintra, Palácio Nacional da Pena, Manueline wing (1515–18), exterior, reception rooms, chapel and Sala dos Brasões (the armoury).

5.7c

5.7f

5.7d

5.7e

borrowed from the caravels and their voyages of discovery which so enriched the kingdom in the early 16th century. The prosperity and the style continued well beyond the eponymous reign (AIC4, pages 473ff).**5·7**

No monument better illustrates Manueline eclecticism than the great Jeronomite monastery founded by the king himself at Belém, west of Lisbon – other than the churches of the Convent of Christ at Tomar and of the Monastery of Jesus at Setúbal. Beyond the style, these churches display the several characteristics which were to remain typical of Portuguese ecclesiastical building long after the triumph of a more rational approach to articulation: large volumes in massive blocks with storeyed elevations and concealed roofs, with or without the internal supports of the typical hall church. Not of lasting effect, however, were the essentially late-medieval filigree pinnacles, balustrades and framing motifs which deny the intrinsic solidity of the massing and establish continuity of decorative detail from the layered sides to the ends: these were the first and obvious victims of the triumph of the Italianate – and the rational. And that waited on the instigation of King Manuel's successor King João III, the initiative of the French immigrants Nicolau Chanterene and Jean de Rouen and the conversion of Juan de Castillo who, born in Santander but trained in Naples, was the foremost Manueline master until the new king succumbed to the new fashion.

5.78

5·7h

5·7k

5·7i

5·7j

5.71

2 ADVENT OF CLASSICISM IN PORTUGAL AND ESTILO CHÃO

After the charming excesses of the Manueline response to the maritime kingdom's new world of material and cultural enrichment, rationalism is first displayed in Portugal under Manuel the Fortunate's less happy heir, João III (1521–57). Beginning with anti-sumptuary laws, the long reign was one of retrenchment: its first two decades admitted greatly reduced architectural activity – usually in furthering Manueline exercises. Renewed initiative in the second decade was left primarily to military engineers – of whom Diogo de Arruda and his nephews Francisco and Miguel (died 1531, 1547 and after 1549 respectively), Alfonso Álvarez (died 1575), Diogo de Torralva (c. 1500–66) and

5.8b

5.8a

›5.8 LUSITANIAN TRANSITION TO THE ESTILO CHÃO: (a) Ponta Delgada, S. Sebastião (begun 1533), west front (completed 1545); (b–f) Coimbra, Santa Cruz, church portal (c. 1527), cloister fountain (c. 1533), section, plan, elevation and overview; (g) Viseu cathedral, cloister (completed 1532).

Originally the centrepiece of Coimbra's Augustinian cloister, the so-called Manga Fountain was probably devised by Fra Brás de Barros, the Jeronimite reformer of the Santa Cruz community from 1527 at the instigation of the king: the architect is unknown. The cruciform composition of four-quartered geometry pivoting on a circle responds, of course, to the basic symbolism of the faith of its patrons: it is also a permutation of the paradise garden, the image of Eden not only in Persia but also in the medieval European monastic cloister (AIC3, pages 433f, AIC4, pages 580f). The cylindrical cell, providing hermetical retreat from the impurities of the world, is not unprecedented but the connection of a quartet with a colonnaded central rotunda is bizarre in its novelty. (The attribution reiterated here is derived from George Kubler, *Portuguese Plain Architecture*, 1980 – as is much else in the two chapters of my coverage of the *estilo chão*.)

At Viseu the same patron, Bishop Dom Miguel de Silva, under the same royal auspices, oversaw the vaulting of the choir tribune in the Manueline style and the construction of the cloister in an early Italianate Renaissance style – with arches rising from uncanonically Classical columns, as in contemporary Spain.

5.8c–e @ 1:500

5.8f

Manuel Pires (died 1569) were the most important: Torralva was the son-in-law of Francisco de Arruda who built the iconic fort at Belém (AIC4, page 591).

Frugality and functionalism combined to promote austerity: the *estilo chão* which, in so far as the accidents of survival testify, had emerged to challenge Manueline eclecticism by c. 1530. That was not much later than the first High Renaissance works in Spain – as we shall see – but the subsequent formulation of relatively unembellished, clearly ordered architecture in Portugal anticipated the Spanish assertion of austerity in the *estilo desornamentado* by at least a decade. As in Spain at the outset, however, it was naturally far from rare for the new style to confront the old within the same complex: examples range from the renovation of thr Augustinian Santa Cruz monastery at Coimbra, to the last phase of work on the cathedral at Viseu and on in the opposite direction to S. Sebastião in far-off Ponta Delgada of the Azores.**5.8**

The Viseu cathedral cloister ranks among the first Portuguese exercises wholly in a permutation of Italianate Renaissance style. However, the aspiration to rationalism, through elementary geometry in planning and canonically Classical order, is first manifest in a fountain in the

5.8g

cloister of the Santa Cruz monastery at Coimbra. Dated to the early 1530s, it is attributed to Nicholau Chanterene whose contemporary work in the medium of the retable marked the first triumph of Classical discipline over eclectic licence at the advent of Renaissance to Portugal.

By the 1540s – hardly later than the Spanish or even the French – the Portuguese were beginning to understand that the essence of Classicism was order, not ornament. However, their initial exercises in rationalism were strictly limited in number and scale, as in mastery of the Classical repertory of mouldings, and it would be another generation before they produced a masterpiece of modern Italian inspiration which matched the achievements of their neighbours in sophistication.

Italian influence extends decisively to various later centralized exercises: the very variety suggests the inspiration of Serlio and the serliana is recurrent. The most elemen-

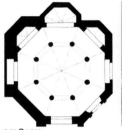

5.9a @ 1:500   5.9b

›**5.9 CENTRALIZED CHURCHES FROM THE CIRCLE OF DIOGO DE TORRALVA:** (a, b) Elvas, Dominican church, plan and interior (1543); (c–f) Lisbon, S. Amaro, plan, exterior from west and east, narthex (1549); (g, h) Salvaterra de Magos, palatine chapel of the Infante Dom Luís, interior to and from sanctuary (c. 1555); (i, j) Mitra, Bom Jesus de Valverde, chapel of the convent founded by the infante Dom Henrique, plan and section (c. 1550); (k, l) Estremoz, S. Maria do Castello, plan and interior (1559).

The octagonal building for the Dominicans at Elvas replaced a Templar church of similar plan. The incompletely resolved centralizing exercise devised for the

5.9d, e

5.9c @ 1:500

pilgrimage church of S. Amaro in Alcántara, Lisbon, is inconclusively attributed to Diogo de Torralva. The unorthodox geometry apart, the Tuscan serlianas at

5.9f

5.9g,h

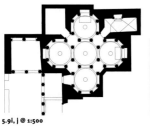

5.9i, j @ 1:500

Salvaterra de Magros anticipate the great cloister of Tomar (see below) by a couple of years and have therefore prompted Kubler to attribute it to the latter's principal architect, Torralva. The same stylistic considerations associate Torralva with the miniature exercise in juxtaposed rotundas at the Convent of Bom Jesus de Valverde. The patron of the latter was the cardinal-infante Dom Henrique (later king) who was also responsible for the work based on the extended quincunx at Estremoz: that has prompted the plausible alternative attribution of the latter, at least, to Manuel Pires whom we are about to see operating in a similar style on an even larger scale at nearby Évora – where the infante was archbishop.

5.9l

tary is the Dominican convent church of Nossa Senhora da Consolação at Elvas (1543): opening from the simple octagon, the series of radiating chapels is incomplete and there is nothing Classical about the colonettes which support its dome.**5.9a, b** The most accomplished, S. Amaro in Lisbon (1549), is attributed to Diogo de Torralva: the domical rotunda of the cella is ringed with an arcaded portico except where it opens into the smaller domical rotunda of the sanctuary.**5.9c–f** Unusually, the palatine chapel of the infante Dom Luís at Salvaterra de Magos combined an aisled sanctuary with a hexagonal cella (1555) to the unverified credit of Miguel de Arruda.**5.9g, h** Domical octagons form a Greek cross in the monastic Chapel of Bom Jesus de Valverde at Mitra (1550) which is convincingly attributed to Torralva.**5.9i, j** S. Maria do Castello at Estremoz (1559), attributed to Manuel Pires, is based on a Greek cross inscribed in a square with groin vaults over all nine com-

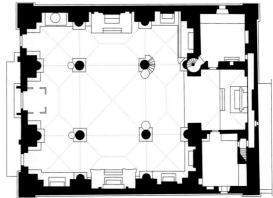

5.9k @ 1:500

partments.**5.9k–l** Over all these varied plans, columns support internal vaulting to a degree unusual in contemporary Italy but prophetic of later Neoclassical practice in France.

Experiments in centralized planning may have been the most engaging, but the main form of church architecture in mid-century Portugal, as in Spain, was the single-volume hall with or without internal support. In the Nossa

5.10a, b

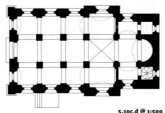

5.10c,d @ 1:500

›5.10 EARLY BASILICAN MANIFESTATIONS OF THE ESTILO CHÃO: (a–d) Tomar, Chapel of Nossa Senhora da Conceição, exterior, interior, section and plan (1530s); (e, f) Évora, S. Antão (from 1527), exterior and interior; (g–i) Leiria cathedral (1550–74) exterior, interior and plan.

Juan de Castillo was active in Tomar until his death in 1552: the coffering and the filigree relief of his dormitory corridor pilasters are echoed in the Conceição chapel. The Leiria plan, with cloister enveloping the sanctuary, has its most important Portuguese precedent in the old Sé at Lisbon: the rationalist approach, based on the consistent development of 3:2 (*sesquialter*) ratios from the module of the pier pilaster, is characteristic of the current age of Juan de Herrera at El Escorial – where the projecting rectangular sanctuary was similarly framed by a cloister. Consistent rectilinearity extends to the vaulting ribs. The ribs of S. Antão in Évora are similarly square in section but, rather than rectangular, the supports are cylindrical like those of Pires's work in Estremoz.

Senhora da Conceição Chapel at the important dynastic site of Tomar, an early Italian Renaissance permutation of the Corinthian Order supports tunnel vaults of near-

5.10f

5.10e

5.10g

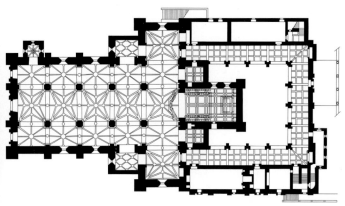

5.10i @ 1:1000

5.10h

Albertian gravitas in a traditional basilican scheme attributed to Juan de Castillo. On a much larger scale, basilican planning and order of Classical derivation – if not Classical proportion – marked the revival of monumental activity near the end of the reign for the cathedrals at Leiria, Miranda do Douro and Portalegre (begun 1550, 1552 and 1556 respectively) and the substantial church of S. Antão at Évora (begun 1557): whether of columns or attenuated pilasters applied to piers, the colossal Order within was anticipated in the rectilinear grid applied to the articulation of the enclosing walls and Classical aspiration prompted the elimination of continuous filigree balustrades to reveal a low-pitched roof with pedimented gables.**5.10**

The great churches of Miranda, do Douro Portalegre, Leiria and Évora are all attributed to military engineers: Diogo de Torralva, Miguel de Arruda, Manuel Pires and Alfonso Álvares. Working for the Jesuits of S. Roque in Lisbon in 1667, Álvares produced the prototype of Portugal's unvaulted hall churches without internal supports but with interconnecting side chapels in the manner associated with Alberti's S. Andrea at Mantua – and the contemporary Roman Gesù. Working for the Jesuits back in Évora the year before, Pires provided his compatriots with a prototype for a tunnel-vaulted hall in his project for the church

5.11b

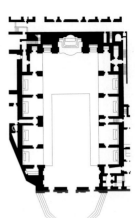

5.11a @ 1:1000

›5.11 PROTOTYPICAL HALL CHURCHES IN THE ESTILO CHÃO: (a, b) Lisbon, S. Roque (from 1567), plan and interior (as restored after the earthquake of 1755); (c) Évora, Nossa Senhora da Graça (c. 1570), entrance front; (d) Évora, S. Mamede (14th century, renovated in the mid-16th century), entrance front (c. 1566?); (e–h) Évora, Espírito Santo (from 1566), plan, section, interior and exterior.

Manuel Pires began work for the Jesuits of Évora on their college of the Espírito Santo in 1559, progressing in 1566 to the church which was to cater for the female congregation excluded from the college chapel. On his death three years later he was succeeded by Afonso Álvarez who completed the work in 1574. A local precedent for the plan was provided by the late-15th-century reworking of the 13th-century church of the Franciscans – and that distantly recalled S. Francesco in Rimini (AIC4, page 741).

The royal commission for the Lisbon work may be seen as a response to the impact made by Pires in Évora, monitored by the king's brother Dom Henrique. Half as wide again as the Espírito Santo, the span of S. Roque's nave seems to have inhibited tunnel vaulting: that had been the original intention but execution was delayed by the disastrous crusade in which the young King Sebastião died and the new Habsburg regime commissioned its architect (Filippo Terzi, see below, pages 76off) to finish the work hastily – and economically – with a timber ceiling suspended from triangular trusses. Like many others,

of the Espírito Santo (1566): unlike either of the Italian precedents, the arcaded chapels support continuous galleries along each side and an arcaded screen carries a platform for the choir across the end; the exterior is relieved only with pilaster strips above and beside the projecting arcaded portico. Probably at much the same time, Évora's S. Mamede – a hall church rib-vaulted in the late-Gothic style and devoid of interconnecting perimeter chapels – was distinguished with a choir projecting out over a Serlian narthex portico built of marble. In the same town, Nossa Senhora da Graça also has a narthex sotocoro but the façade is quite exceptional for the possible date (c. 1570) in its florid eclecticism which may be seen to incorporate the motif of interlocking temple fronts invented by Bramante and recently evolved by Palladio (see pages 238ff).**5.11**

5.11c

the much more modest monastery of S. Salvador at Grijó managed vaulting in faithful homage to the model.

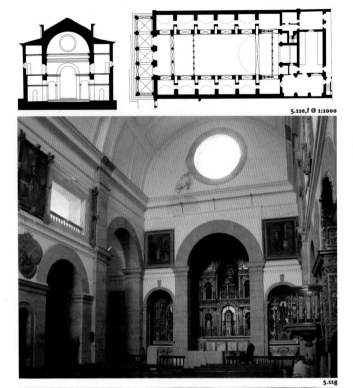

5.11e,f @ 1:1000

5.11g

5.11d

5.11h

5.12

The primary example of a tunnel-vaulted sanctuary, the work reiterates motifs found in Torralva's work at Tomar, the external cornice and the internal panelling in particular.

>5.13 TOMAR, CONVENT OF CHRIST, MAIN CLOISTER, from 1558: (a) overview with Manueline church in background, (b) plan, (c) upper gallery.

The conventual complex of the Templars at Tomar was greatly expanded with a grid of cloisters when it was reassigned to the Benedictines in the wake of the reforms instituted by João III (from 1523). Juan de Castillo was responsible for the expanded scheme which was influenced by the Milanese Ospedale Maggiore. On Castillo's death, the main cloister had yet to be roofed over superimposed repetitive arcades which seem not to have been well founded: Torralva took – or created – the opportunity for its demolition and comprehensive reworking in collaboration with the architecturally literate king. Approved in spring 1558, the revised scheme achieved enhanced strength – and greatly enhanced visual richness – by incorporating piers with engaged columns between the arcades of both storeys, convex in the corners where there were stair turrets: Bramante's rhythmic-bay system, revised for greater breadth of intercolumniation and depth of pier, was varied with serliana in the main bays of the upper level over the single great arches below. On Torralva's death, as on that of his predecessor, the upper cloister remained to be completed with vaults instead of timber ceilings, as originally planned. Only after twenty years – and the Habsburg succession following the untimely death of King Sebastião and the brief reign of his uncle, King Henrique – was work resumed under Filippo Terzi who completed it to Torralva's plans.

Kubler (op. cit.) postulates that Torralva knew of the Villa Imperiale at Pesaro through a drawing of c. 1540 by Francisco de Hollanda:[1.10b] certainly corner turrets

Severe rationalism was to triumph even in the greatest of all Manueline monuments, the monastic church of the Jerónimos at Belém itself: beyond the amazing juxtaposition of hall churches on both the main and cross axes – with their rib vaults of Mudéjar and Flamboyant style respectively (see page 651) – the cavernous tunnel-vaulted sanctuary was added in a style as austere as anything conceived in metropolitan Spain: the work was executed over little more than the year to March 1572 by Jerónimo de Ruão but he seems to have been following the intentions of Diogo de Torralva.[5.12] Operating near the top of the hierarchy of royal architects from at least 1545, the latter reached the apex on the death of Juan de Castillo in 1553. His principal concern immediately thereafter was with the revision of the late master's scheme for the Convent of Christ at Tomar. This extended to reconstruction of the

5.13a

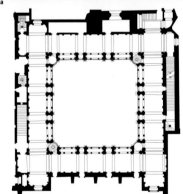

5.13b @ 1:1000

and rhythmic bays are shared but the relationship between solid and void is much less complex in Genga's work where, in particular, the serliana plays a much less decisive role. For that, Torralva built on the inspiration derived from Serlio perhaps with distant knowledge of Palladio's achievement at Vicenza.[1.25f,g, 1.71a]

5.13c

main cloister to a new design. Acknowledging Serlio, that was unsurpassed in its High Renaissance Classicism by anything yet built in Spain – in now turning to which we must return in time.[5.13]

The gate in the southern sector of the city wall, dating from the 11th century, was renovated in the 15th century: the embellishment was commissioned to commemorate the reconciliation of the city with the king-emperor Charles V after the unsuccessful revolt of the 'commons' in 1521. Francisco de Colonia was assisted by Juan de Vallejo. The city's patroness, the Virgin, is in the upper niche; below, the monarch is accompanied by prominent figures from the city's history, El Cid in particular.

5.14

3 SPAIN IN TRANSITION: CAROLINE RENAISSANCE; PHILIPPINE MANNERISM

The somewhat confused eclecticism of the so-called Cisneros strain was the cause of disquiet in Spain by the third decade of the century – the first of the reign of the young king-emperor Charles I and V – and a polemic against it was published by Diego de Sagredo. He had been in Italy, was familiar with the circle of Raphael and inspired by the Vitruvius of Fra Giacondo, but inevitably also drew on Alberti and Francesco di Giorgio in his *Medidas del Romano* of 1526: reiterating the classification of five

Orders, this is an exegesis on the subject asserting the primacy of proportion and its derivation from the human figure. The royal architects immediately began emulating Italian High Renaissance Classicism: even the high-Plateresque master Francisco de Colonia tried to change for his intervention in Burgos's Arco de S. María to proclaim the fealty of the city fathers to the king-emperor (from 1534).**5.14**

MACHUCA AND SILOÉ

The first of the High Renaissance generation to emerge with *éclat* were Pedro Machuca (c. 1490–1550) and Diego de Siloé (c. 1495–1563). The latter began his career in and near Burgos,**5.15, 5.16** Machuca appears in Granada. Both began as sculptors, both worked in Italy in the second half of the second decade of the century. Machuca's early style suggests close association with the studio of Raphael. probably as an assistant. Siloé was in Naples working on sculptural embellishment in the recently completed

›5.15 BURGOS CATHEDRAL, ESCALERA DORADA IN NORTH TRANSEPT, 1520–22: (a, b) general view and detail.

Diego de Siloé capitalized on the Spanish invention of the staircase which turns through at least one right angle as it rises through an open well – as in the Hospital of Santa Cruz in Toledo. More specifically, however, the model here is Bramante's intermediate staircase in the Cortile del Belvedere (AIC4, page 854). Raphael's rediscovery of the grotesque is translated to the rich sculptural embellishment.

5.15b

5.15a

Diego de Siloé's portal incorporates the triumphal-arch motif in canonical form for the first time in Spain. The model is the Arch of Alfonso of Aragon at the Castel Nuovo in Naples but the rhythm is also that of the Caracciolo de Sole Chapel's ordonnance (AIC4, pages 773, 848).

5.16

Caracciolo del Sole Chapel of S. Giovanni a Carbonara (AIC4, page 848). Traits in his style also suggest familiarity with the contemporary work of Raphael: that and his Neapolitan experience may be traced in his first architectural exercises in the north. Both informed his greatest achievement when he moved on to Granada where Machuca was already working on his masterpiece in the Alhambra.**5.17, 5.18**

Grenadine Renaissance

Pedro Machuca began work on building his palace for the king-emperor Charles in the Alhambra in 1527: nowhere is the contrast between the native and the imported more spectacular than in that extraordinary context. Only the central part of a vast project was realized. The Orders reign, adventitious embellishment is largely banished, yet the High Renaissance is already eclipsed: pure Classicism is confined to the circular court and is encapsulated in Mannerism. The effect of the latter depended on the

5.17b

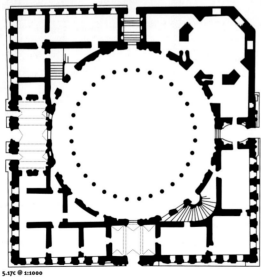

5.17c @ 1:1000

›5.17 GRANADA, ALHAMBRA PALACE OF CHARLES I, begun in 1527, construction ceased in 1568 when funding was cut following internecine strife in Granada: (a) south front, (b) western frontispiece, (c) plan, (d) court.

Like Siloé, Machuca is thought to have been associated with Raphael's workshop while in Rome from the middle of his second decade. His circular court, with superimposed Doric and Ionic Orders of canonical purity, may well reflect Bramante's unexecuted project for the environment of the Tempietto at S. Pietro in Montorio, Rome: he may have left for home before Raphael evolved his project for the court of the Villa Madama (see pages 114f).

5.17d

articulation of conflict between the active and passive forces in the wall in terms of applied trabeation which respected the conventions of structural realism in the breach: this was novel even in Italy among the heirs of Raphael (see pages 122ff).

The Orders rise uncanonically through more than one storey, as on the façade of the Villa Madama in Rome except for the exaggerated pedestals, and the ground floor exceeds even Giulio Romano in the virility of its rustication. In that context, the projection of the southern and western frontispieces may be seen as intrusive: however, they respond to a medieval tradition of varied masses – like that of the French – and though generally foreign to Italian homogeneity, they assert familiarity with Raphael's design of 1516 for the façade of S. Lorenzo in Florence – which itself draws on themes of Bramante (AIC4, page 849).

Shortly after the inception of the intrusive work in the Alhambra, Diego de Siloé began his great cathedral in the centre of the city below. The colossal scale of its internal ordonnance may have been drawn from the work of Bramante or even Raphael: indeed, Siloé's combination of basilican and centralized elements suggests knowledge of developments at S. Pietro in Rome (AIC4, pages 835ff). The double-aisled, double-ambulatory basilican plan, with a choir occupying the inner bays of the nave, owes more to Spanish tradition than to developments elsewhere – as does the

›5.18 GRANADA, METROPOLITAN CATH-EDRAL OF THE INCARNATION, from 1528: (a) interior from south aisle, (b) plan, (c) rotunda, (d) Puerta del Perdón.

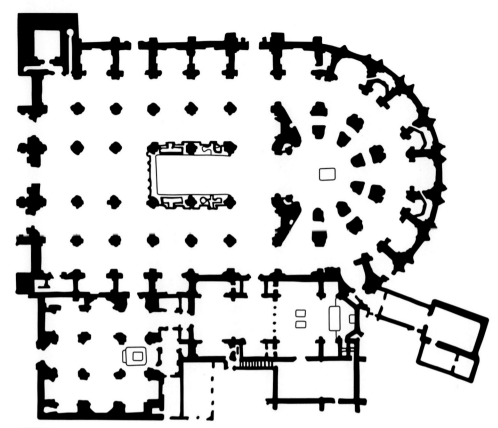

5.18b @ 1:1000

decorative web vaulting, despite the consistent application of semi-
circular arches to define the domical bays. However, the integration of a
circular sanctuary has early Italian Renaissance precedents: primacy is
claimed by Michelozzo Michelozzi's Santissima Annunziata in Florence;
Alberti may well have developed the idea for S. Francesco at Rimini and is
credited with a miniature reduction of the venerable Jerusalem shrine for
his Florentine patron Giovanni Rucellai at S. Pancrazio (AIC4, pages
726,742ff). Developed by Bramante on the small scale of S. Biagio in
Rome, the formula is implicit in the schemes for S. Pietro which would have
been current when Siloé could easily have made the trip from Naples in
1518. As that great work was originally intended to enshrine Pope Julius II
in the centre, so Siloé's rotunda here was originally intended for the tomb
of the king-emperor Charles.

Santissima Annunziata would certainly have been familiar to the Italian immigrants known as Francesco and Jacopo Florentino who are credited with primacy in furthering awareness of Vitruvian principles in southern Spain – and influencing Siloé accordingly. Early in the 1520s Francesco was

5.18c

5.18d

5.19

›5.19 GRANADA, CHURCH OF THE MONASTERY OF S. JERÓNIMO: ribbed crossing dome (of Mudéjar inspiration; see AIC3, pages 204f) and vaults (Francesco Florentino and Diego de Siloé, from 1528).

engaged on the Jerónimos church in Granada: in 1528 Siloé began work on the domed octagonal crossing of the choir there – as a mausoleum for the Duke of Sessa – while occupied with the cathedral.**5.19**

The triumphal-arch ordonnance of the S. María del Campo tower portal is revised with greater gravitas for the Puerta del Perdón which serves the Metropolitan Cathedral of the Incarnation's northern transept: the only element of the exterior impressed with his intentions, just the base level was completed in Siloé's lifetime. A preliminary variation on the theme, S. Jerónimos's new south portal was designed to respond to the Puerta del Perdón: the lower storey was completed in 1532; like its predecessors and followers, it was to be finished above with further variation on the theme. The related work on the Sacra Capilla del Salvador at Úbeda gives some indication of the degree to which the design of the upper levels is likely to have been inspired by the Arch of Alfonso of Aragon at the Castel Nuovo in Naples (AIC4, page 773).

The verticality of Siloé's Grenadine masterpiece was, of course, medieval in derivation. So too was the taste for rich relief which he displayed from the outset with enhanced plasticity but the motifs were neo-Antique *grottesche* as revived by Raphael and his circle, rather than Flamboyant or Lombard. The embellishment of the innovative Escalera Dorada in Burgos cathedral – Siloé's first important work, reputedly designed in collaboration with the Burgundian Philippe Vigarny – is still somewhat Plateresque though architectonic principle begins to emerge. That is more fully developed in the tower of S. Maria del Campo, which may be seen as a preliminary exercise for the Puerta del Perdón in particular, in general for ordering medieval verticality with superimposed variants of the triumphal-arch motif. Yet more opulently Classical, his Grenadine style marks the sophistication of the Plateresque mentality: beyond awareness of Roman High Renaissance strictures, it anticipated the development of an essentially decorative Mannerism like that of later-16th-century France.

5.20a

5.20b

5.20c

>5.20 ÚBEDA, SACRA CAPILLA DEL SAL-
VADOR, planned 1536; executed from 1540: (a) general view in context with the Palacio del Deán Ortega
left, (b, c) west front portal and detail, (d) plan, (e, f)
sacristy and its portal, (g, h) interior from nave and
detail of rotunda.

Siloé left the work to his assistant on his return to the
north. Andrés de Vandelvira's Plateresque background –
shared by Siloé, as we have seen – is apparent in the
richness of relief extending to the shafts of the lower
Order, if not in the uncanonical proportions of the upper
one. The articulation of the sacristy is notable not only
for the correct respect for the distinction between the
arcuate and the trabeate but above all for the deployment of caryatids in the zone of the spandrels.

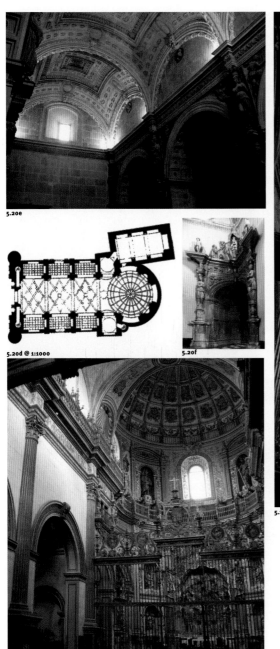

5.20e

5.20d @ 1:1000

5.20f

5.20h

5.20g

Apart from the choir crossing of S. Jerónimo in Granada, Siloé's main work in the south was the Sacra Capilla del Salvador at Úbeda: his plans, again combining basilica and rotunda, were executed from 1536 by his associate Andrés de Vandelvira (1509–75).**5.20** The latter took over his master's mantle in the orbit of Jaén where he was called on to revise the reconstruction of the cathedral in 1534 and the cathedral at Baeza in 1567 – as we shall see.

5.21a

5.21b

(a, b) the cathedral's Sacristía Mayor (from 1534); (c) Ayuntamiento (from 1527), detail of exterior.

In Seville from 1523, the master-mason Riaño was active both there and in Valladolid by 1527, collaborating on the latter's collegiate church (later absorbed into the cathedral) with Álava and the Gil Hontañón brothers. The year after beginning the Ayuntamiento in Seville, he was appointed master of works to the cathedral where his eclectic work ranged from the Gothic to the Plateresque and beyond to some comprehension of the gravitas of Siloé.

In Seville Riaño was assisted and succeeded by Martín de Gaenza (active c. 1527–56). The latter finished the Sacristía de los Cálices, largely due to Juan Gil de Hontañón but furthered by Riaño, and the latter's Sacristía Mayor (1544). Among several other interventions, Gaínza was responsible for the design

5.21c
and partial construction of the Capilla Real (from 1551, see below).

Meanwhile Neoclassical centralized form – super-charged with relief sculpture – was introduced to Seville for the vast aisled cathedral's Sacristía Mayor (from 1530): Siloé is credited with the cupola but the main body is claimed for Diago de Riaño (died 1534) to whom the highly elaborate but not uncanonical Ayuntamiento (town hall) is also attributed (AIC4, page 869).**5.21** There is comparable work at Murcia too, in the Capilla de Junterones which Jerónimo Quijano (c. 1500–63) inserted into the cathedral in the late-1530s.**5.22**

Extensively elsewhere, the new Classicism was introduced to existing buildings in portal frontispieces, sacristies, chapels and particularly in the great retables which distinguish most Spanish churches following the plethora of Flamboyant precedents: examples of the latter from before Siloé's intervention, such as Covarrubias's spectacular exercises in the transept of Sigüenza cathedral, may instructively be compared with the portal of the Sacra Capilla del Salvador at Úbeda and the translation of its double-height triumphal-arch motif for the articulation of the rotunda there.**5.20h** Whatever he intended for

›5.22 JERÓNIMO QUIJANO AT MURCIA CATHEDRAL: (a, b) Capilla de Junterones (1530–41).

A sculptor probably trained at Burgos, Quijano's influence on developments at Murcia was rich. He succeeded Jacopo Florentino as master-mason at Murcia c. 1525: among the first of his several interventions in the cathedral was the revision of his predecessor's plans for the chapel founded by Gil Rodríguez de Junterón, a prominent cleric who had been posted to the Roman curia during the pontificate of Julius II. The executed project is notable for the elaborate coffering of its shell vaults but mainly for its precocious elliptical plan.

Quijano's influence extended to work on the church of S. Martín and the cathedral of Valencia undertaken respectively from the late-1540s and the mid-1550s.

5.22a

5.22b

5.23a

5.23b

›5.23 SALAMANCA, COLEGIO FONSECA (later de los Irlandeses), founded 1521, begun 1528: (a) portal, (b) court.

Granada, the master here amplified the intermediate zone of Alfonso of Aragon's Neapolitan arch – with its image of triumph in relief – into a full storey. This might be seen as according with the Plateresque tradition in the emphasis placed on the iconographically relevant narrative or heraldic emblem in the superstructure – as in Francisco de Colonia's Puerta de la Pellejería of Burgos cathedral or the aedicular exercises of Vazques and Covarrubias respectively for the Colegio de Santa Cruz at Valadolid and the Hospital of Santa Cruz at Toledo. **5.1, 5.2**

The college was founded by Alonso de Fonseca, then archbishop of Santiago de Compostela where he founded a similar institution. The Gil de Hontañón (father and son) and Alonso de Covarrubias may have been consulted on the plan but Juan de Álava and Diego de Siloé were called in. Work began in 1528 on Siloé's revision of court and portal with Álava as executive architect: the chapel is attributed to the latter, the retable to Alonso Berruguete who also produced the medallions in the court. The lower arcade of the court

was the first in Spain effectively to respect the distinction between the arcuate and the trabeate in accord with Albertian stricture, derived from Antique practice most prominently represented by the Colosseum in Rome – and represented there most prominently in early modern practice by the cortile of the Palazzo Venezia on which Giuliano da Sangallo is thought to have worked (AIC4, page 782). Similarities in the complex at Santiago, especially the portal, have been explained in terms of Siloé's intervention there too.

Siloé's approach is represented across the country at Salamanca, in the Colegio Fonseca, where the master himself was associated with an exercise to which Juan de Álava, Alonso de Covarrubias, Rodrigo Gil de Hontañón and the native-born, Florentine-trained sculptor Alonso Berruguete (1488–1561) contributed.**5.23** Revising Álava's original project, his contribution may be gauged by comparing the portal and patio arcades with the extraneous efforts of his contemporaries who had not been to Italy: such as Covarrubias.

RODRIGO GIL DE HONTAÑÓN

Rodrigo Gil de Hontañón was master of the great cathedral works at Salamanca, Segovia, Palencia, Plasencia and Astorga at various stages of his career and active at numerous lesser sites, notably Medina de Rioseco. The last is Gothic up to the vaulting: there ribbed groins survive over

5.24a

>**5.24 RODRIGO GIL DE HONTAÑÓN AND THE HYBRID ECCLESIASTICAL STYLE:** (a) Santiago, Medina da Rioseco (from 1533); (b) Astorga cathedral, general view of exterior from south transept to nave (1530–59); (c) Salamanca, Chapel of Las Bernardas de Jesús, interior detail (1552).

5.24b

5.24c

the aisles but over the nave pendentives support saucer domes – some with bizarre coffering. The situation is reversed twenty years later in the convent chapel of Las Bernardas de Jesús at Salamanca: attenuated pilasters support semi-circular arches over shell vaults in the apse below a network of Gothic ribs. Across the period, work on Astorga cathedral continued in the late-Gothic style pursued by Rodrigo in his other major cathedral projects but, as at Salamanca, the fenestration of the transepts in semi-circular arches is clearly Italianate.**5.24, 5.25**

5.25a

Outstanding secular examples of Rodrigo's foray into Renaissance Neoclassicism are the façades of the University of Alcalá de Henares and the Monterrey Palace in Salamanca begun in 1537 and 1539 respectively: in the former, his most prominent such exercise, elements imported from High Renaissance Italy – such as aedicular pediments and scroll brackets – are applied out of context in a cinquepartite scheme defined by uncanonically proportioned Orders superimposed in the manner of the previous generation to form a prominent frontispiece – as in France. In Salamanca's Monterrey elevation, begun the year after Rodrigo took charge of work on the cathedral,

5.25b

›5.25 RODRIGO GIL DE HONTAÑÓN AND THE SECULAR FAÇADE: (a, b) Alcalá de Henares, University (1537–53), entrance front and detail of gallery; (c) Salamanca, Monterrey Palace (from 1539); (d) Santi-

5.25c

ago de Compostela, cathedral treasury and south
entrance; (e) León, Guzmán Palace (1559).

Hontañón's work completed the 'Cisneros' complex
attributed to Pedro de Gumiel at Alcalá. At Salamanca
he achieved only one wing of a vast four-square project.
The late-medieval – ultimately Moorish, quite un-Italian
– tradition is still acknowledged in both works by the
contrast between the largely solid lower storeys and the
arcaded gallery: in the earlier work it is furthered by the
flattened arch-and-rope moulding of the portal. Though
there is still inconsistency in the proportioning of the
Orders, Italian rationalism disciplines the morphology
of the Alcalá work in general: the whole is defined by
two squares which overlap to accommodate the central
frontispiece; likewise the residual façades are defined
by two squares which overlap for the middle storey.

5.25d

5.25e

the tripartite layering is repeated but not the cinque-partite vertical division: indeed centrality is obviated as, apart from the characteristic central attic gallery, ornament is confined to the vast corner towers of the medieval tradition. Twenty years on (again), in stark contrast, clarity is achieved for the Guzmáns of León with concentration on the portal: tradition is sustained in the attic gallery but for the main, Plateresque exuberance cedes to the mannered Classicism of the late royal style of Alonso de Covarrubias (as we are about to see). A similar synthesis was sustained in the next generation by the architect of the palace of the counts of Gómara in Soria.**5.26**

The same traditional type of quadrangular palace with corner towers and attic gallery – ultimately Moorish – is retained for the Guzmán Palace at León but the portal in the main (west) front must be seen against the development of Alonso de Covarrubias's style at the alcázars of Madrid and Toledo (see below).

5.26a

5.26b

›5.26 **SORIA, GÓMARA PALACE,** from 1577: (a, b) entrance façade and portal detail, (c) patio arcades.

Begun in 1577 but unfinished when work effectively ceased in 1592, the building was projected for Francisco López de Río y Salcedo whose heirs were counts of Gómara from 1592. Right and left wings were presumably originally conceived to match in the arcaded style reminiscent of Roderigo Gil de Hontañón's earlier work but the portal and the bays to its left follow his development away from the Plateresque already marked in the lower storeys of the Guzmán Palace at León – and in the late work of Covarrubias.

5.26c

5.27a

5.27b

5.27c

ALONSO DA COVARRUBIAS:
TOWARDS MATURITY

In his intervention in the Capilla de los Reyes Nuevos in
Toledo cathedral, to frame the sepulchres of several late-
medieval Trastámara kings (1529), Covarrubias observed
the logical distinction between the arcuate and the trabeate in accordance with the canonical practice of Diego
de Siloé – and Vitruvius (AIC1, page 576). In the next year,
in the sacristy of the cathedral of Sigüenza, the distinction
is observed with enhanced gravitas which may be seen as
Albertian despite flattened arches and rich relief (AIC4,
page 742).**5.27**

In his widespread work elsewhere in the early 1530s, on
the other hand, Covarrubias is inconsistently canonical.

5.27d

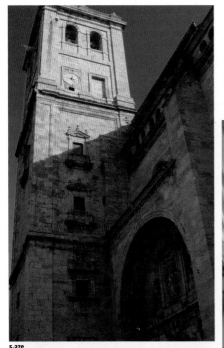

5.27e

For example, his splendid church of S. Benito Abad at Yepes (1534) is fully Renaissance in clear advance over his first independent ecclesiastical essay, the essentially Gothic royal monastery of Nuestra Señora de Guadalupe at Cáceres, but arch still rises from uncanonical pilaster in reformation of the typical Gothic hall-church skeleton.

5.27f

5.27g

5.27h

Again, neither in this respect nor in embellishment is the arcading of S. Bartolomeo's cloister at Lupiana or even the more accomplished façade and patio galleries of the Archbishop's Palace at Alcalá de Henares (both datable to the mid-1530s) comparable in sophistication to Siloé's Colegio Fonseca scheme. And that, of course, is true of the general run of arcading in the first half of the 16th century: the

(h) Lupiana, Monastery of S. Bartolomeo, patio galleries (c. 1535); (i, j) Alcalá de Henares, Archbishop's Palace (from c. 1535, restored after extensive damage in the Civil War), main façade and detail of cloister (prewar photograph of subsequently damaged work).

Bracket capitals, as on the upper level at Lupiana, were sustained well into the 16th century as a native response to Classicizing trabeation. They do not recur in Covarrubias's works for metropolitan patrons, such

5.27j

à5.27i

as the galleries of the upper level of the Alcalá palace where the system was repeated around the patio but with lavish sculptural ornamentation.

›5.28 OPENING THE AYUNTAMIENTO: (a) Sigüenza (Juan de Garay, from 1512); (b) Ciudad Rodrigo (architect unknown, early 16th century).

civic authority buildings (ayuntamiento) of Sigüenza and Ciudad Rodrigo might be taken at random as exemplary not least because they are early Renaissance representatives of the late-medieval trend to open the façades of civic authority to a public plaza.**5.28**

5.28a

5.28b

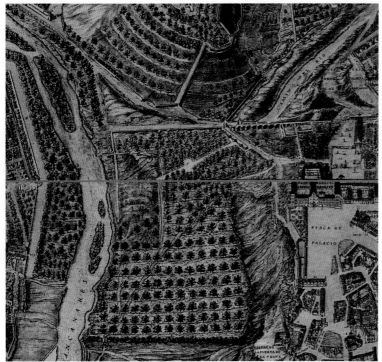

5.29a

after revisions from 1537 and before destruction two hundred years later: (a) overview of site with the escarpment at Madrid's western extremity (detail from Pedro Teixeira's plan of 1656), (b) reconstructed model, (c) plan with the royal apartments as revised for Philip III after 1606.

The near symmetry of the extended façade is echoed in the distribution of the two courts about the spine, off axis with the entrance but occupied by the chapel and, beyond it, the ceremonial staircase. The latter is the premier example of the H-form resulting from the doubling of the side flights of the square open-cage U-type introduced by Lorenzo Vázquez and possibly by Covarrubias's father-in-law Enrique Egas – early in the century

As we are about to see at Toledo, the next move was to double the U to form an E rather than an H. From the outset the process seems to have been pragmatic, responding to the staircase's open central position between two ranges of apartments – primarily those of the king and queen. Initiated by the king-emperor Charles, however, it coincided with the latter's extension of Burgundian court etiquette to Spain: formally, that was first to Prince Philip's court at Valadolid in 1548 but actually it was recorded earlier in the decade as already operating wherever the venerable ruler held court. Apart from its issue to twin royal suites, the type of staircase which emerged from the process admirably provided the king with the various levels to which it was appropriate for him to descend if there receiving foreign potentates or their high plenipotentiaries, in accordance with the Burgundian rule, and it well served to process distinct entourages of multiple courtiers for entry to the several antechambers of the royal suites – earlier, but more extensive than the ones at the Louvre – in accordance with a hierarchy of rank matching that of Burgundy in its intricacy and exclusiveness.

LATE COVARRUBIAS AND BUSTAMANTE

Toward the end of an illustrious career, Alonso de Covarrubias remained adaptable to new developments in architectural theory and practice. The protégé of Cardinal Juan Pardo de Tavera, who ascended to the primacy of Spain as archbishop of Toledo in 1534, he was entrusted with responsibility for the fabric of the cathedral and for the cardinal's works elsewhere. Three years later, the king-emperor Charles appointed Covarrubias as surveyor to the fabric of the alcázars of Madrid, Toledo and Seville: he began at Madrid.**5.29** His work there, destroyed in 1734, was innovative in its degree of axial formality and in the form of the ceremonial staircase: these were to be furthered with great significance in the major works of Toledo.**5.30**

5.29b

5.29c

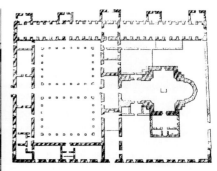

5.30a

>5.30 TOLEDO, MID-CENTURY ECCLESIAS-
TICAL AND ROYAL WORKS: (a–d) Hospital de
Tavera (1541–50), Covarrubias's initial plan of 1541,
plan implemented from 1542 (after the advent of Bartolomé Bustamante), façade and court detail; (e) Archbishop's Palace (from 1541), portal; (f–h) Alcázar
(transformation 1543–69, much rebuilt in the second

5.30c

5.30d

half of the 20th century after severe damage in the Spanish Civil War), plan (presented by Covarrubias in 1552, modified with the extension of the staircase to the full width of the court in 1553), entrance front, court (as finished by Francisco de Villalpando).

These projects evolved together but the portal of the Archbishop's Palace was probably the first of the surviving series to have been resolved (c. 1543): the portal of the hospital is an 18th-century variant of insufficient substance. The armature of Order, stripped of decorative elaboration, is that of the miniature pavilion which surmounts the portal of the Hospital de Santa Cruz at Toledo and the window frames flanking it – if not the altar of the Capilla de S. Librada at Sigüenza cathedral – but Siloé's Colegio Fonseca portal at Salamanca has clearly been observed in effecting the transition of scale. The portal of the Alcázar is less closely related to its equivalent at Madrid than to the Archbishop's portal but conforms to the royal heraldic tradition: Serlian influence need not be postulated and would probably

5.30b

5.30e

The Archbishop's Palace at Alcalá de Henares was the first of Cardinal Tavera's projects: his palace in Toledo followed in 1540. The Hospital of S. Juan Bautista, outside that city's walls, was next. On that project Covarrubias was joined by the Jesuit priest Bartolomé Bustamante (1501–70), the cardinal's secretary, chaplain and diplomatic envoy who had recently returned from Italy. The patron died in 1545 and his two architects abandoned the project six years later when it was only partially realized: revised from a still more formal variation of the scheme Covarrubias was imposing on the Madrid Alcázar, that included the lower storeys of the entrance front and the double courtyard. The architraves of the latter's galleries still curve into arches rising from columns and the upper range is still flattened but the columns are doubled in the corners and their proportions are canonical: doubtless due to Bustamante, the effect is Florentine in the mode of Brunelleschi as developed by Lorenzo Laurana (AIC4, pages 716, 771). However, the exterior is impressed with the impact of Giulio Romano, probably also transmitted by Bustamante –

though extreme austerity informs the latter's independent production of numerous colleges for his order.

Across his career, Covarrubias's trajectory from the opulence of the Plateresque followed the extraction of the Classical armature of coherence from its exotic context under influences ranging from Siloé to Bustamante. The main field was the portal frontispiece, characteristic of Spain as of France and the rest of Europe where accentuated verticals were essential to the medieval legacy. After the Toledo Archbishop's Palace and the Madrid Alcázar, the key examples are the Toledo Alcázar and Puerta de Bisagra (1546 and 1559 respectively).

Beyond the portals and courts, sober in their articulation, Covarrubias's schemes for the two alcázars are most significant for their advance towards axiality and their staircases. The square open-cage type of the latter, which

be anachronistic anyway. This is also the case with the rustication of the window frames on the two main storeys of the hospital's west front: the lower ones were completed in 1545. Bustamante could have seen Serlio in Italy but is more likely to have shared a common source with him.

Rustication makes a bizarre appearance on the top storey of the Alcázar, in Mannerist disdain of structural logic, as the context for an arcaded gallery articulated with a minor Order: otherwise the entrance façade is astylar but the side one, overlooking the town, has an Order of Doric pilasters superimposed on rusticated piers, each embracing a full floor and a mezzanine, over an arcaded base. The quadrangular plan and corner towers are inherited from the Moors, of course (AIC4, page 150). However, Covarrubias projected a court articulated after the style he and Bustamante had developed for the Hospital de Tavera and, as the younger man had insisted there, with Italianate groin vaulting in place of Spanish beamed ceilings: instead of Doric and Ionic, superimposed with displaced

5·308

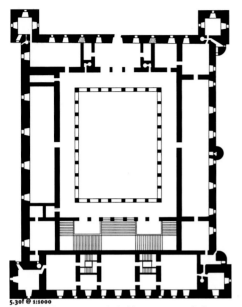

5.30f @ 1:1000

friezes, both ranges are Corinthian as executed after 1550 by Francisco de Villalpando.

The great innovation of the hospital plan was the absolute symmetry of the double court separated by a double-height arcaded gallery. Covarrubias had originally planned to site an H-shaped staircase and the chapel on the central axis, as in the Madrid Alcázar, but revision set a greatly enlarged chapel back beyond the courts and reduced the stairs to the standard U-shaped form in a square cage beside the narthex. The greater innovation of the Toledo Alcázar plan, due to Covarrubias but implemented after he had departed from the site by Villalpando and Juan de Herrera, was the doubling of the U-shaped staircase to form an E rather than an H: on axis with the entrance beyond a rectangular court, a single flight leads to a landing from which opposed flights lead at 90 degrees to an intermediate landing and there turn through another 90 degrees to complete the ascent in parallel to the original flight. The form seems first to have been projected for the Monastery of S. Miguel de los Reyes in Valencia in 1546.

5.30h

the now-ageing master had helped to develop at the Hospital de Santa Cruz (AIC4, page 867), is retained but doubled, first over an H-shaped plan in the dislocated spine of Madrid, then over an E at the culmination of the axis in Toledo. The latter was the precursor of the 'Imperial' type which was to have the most spectacular future throughout Baroque Europe – and beyond.

›**5.31 PROJECT FOR A RUSTICATED PORTAL:** from Villalpando's Spanish Serlio, reproducing the original of Book IV, 5.11.

Alonso da Covarrubias was replaced in royal favour by Francisco de Villalpando in 1553, the year work began on the court and staircase in the Toledo Alcázar. That was the year after Villalpando (c. 1510–61) had published Serlio's Books III and IV in Spanish. The dedicatee was Prince Philip, effective ruler of Spain from 1551, who had studied the language of Antique architecture over the previous decade through Vitruvius and his modern commentators, notably Diego de Sagredo: his extensive travels throughout the Habsburg dominions, especially in Italy, were complemented by his knowledge of Serlio and a rigorous grounding in geometry.

SERLIAN DEVELOPMENTS

Covarrubias's Puerta de Bisagra is the boldest Toledan example of Serlian inspiration after Villalpando's promotion of the cause: it follows closely one of the reproduced illustrations.**5.31, 5.32a** The royal interest would have been in precept as much as motif but the initial indications of the Spanish Serlio's impact are provided by motifs relieving the works of Villalpando's circle in the erstwhile royal

›**5.32 SERLIAN INFLUENCE IN THE TOLEDO OF COVARRUBIAS:** (a) Puerta Bisagra (1559); (b) Colegio de Infantes, portal (1555).

Francisco del Corral, who took the name of his birthplace of Villalpando near Zamora, was a metalworker with siblings involved in other decorative arts, including stuccowork: the embellishment of the Capilla de los Benavente in the church of S. María at Medina de Rioseco (from 1544) is among the most lavish of the legacies of his brother Jerónimo. Francisco may have been in Italy in the mid-1530s but was in Valladolid by 1540 and was taken from there to Toledo by Archbishop Tavera to produce the cathedral's chancel grills, pulpit and altar furniture. His architectural career began under Covarrubias as supervisor of work on the court and staircase of the Alcázar in 1550.

Serlian certainly is the caryatid portal attached by Villalpando to Covarrubias's Colegio de Infantes (see Book IV.7, folios 43, 44). Resolutely Serlian, in his rusticated mode, is the treatment of the arch of the Puerta de Bisagra – under its emphatic Spanish Habsburg heraldic superstructure (see Book IV, folio 40, for example). Architectonic gravitas was not the invariable characteristic of the old master's latest works, but if recalling something of his earlier taste for ornament he never let it weaken the architectural armature – as in the Puerta de la Presentación of the Toledo cathedral cloister (1565).

Hernán González de Lara, a stone-mason apprenticed to Covarrubias, supplanted his master at the hospital in 1550 and altered the balance of the plan by redesigning the chapel. He went on to succeed Covarrubaias as master of works at Toledo cathedral in 1570. Primarily a technician, he collaborated with Juan Bautista Monegro on the design of the house of Don Fernando de la Cerda.

The private patrons of Villalpando's Toledan circle included the royal secretary Diego de Vargas (1558), whose house was realized by Serlio's translator over the plan of Luis de Vega, and Don Fernando de la Cerda (brother of the Duke of Medinaceli) whose house of c. 1570, planned by Lara (1512–75), is now incorporated in the Carmelite convent.

›5.33 HERNÁN RUIZ II IN CORDÓBA: (a) Palacio de los Villalones (c. 1560), portal facade; (b) S. Pedro (1542).

seat, such as the portal of the Colegio de Infantes (1555).**5.32b**

Serlio, via Villalpando, may be detected as an influence on the mature works of leading contemporary southern architects but was not of more importance in Andalusia than elsewhere. Hernán Ruiz II (c. 1514–69) was hardly even incidentally Serlian in his elevations but radically so in a major planning exercise. He effected his transition to Classicism initially when working in collaboration with Siloé on the church of Madre de Dios at Baena (1532) and under his influence on the Palacio de los Villalones and S. Pedro at Córdoba (1542).**5.33** Siloé or Andrés de Vandelvira at Úbeda, as much as Serlio, still informs the façade of his church in the Hospital de la Sangre, Seville (1558). **5.34a,b**

5.33a

5.33b

As architect of Seville cathedral (from 1558), he achieved the domical vaulting of the Capilla Real, built to cornice level by his predecessor Martín de Gainza, but his principal legacy is the astonishing elliptical chapterhouse: the former has Andalusian precedents associated with the followers of Siloé, but the inspiration for the latter may justly be credited to Serlio.**5.34c–e** At the same time, moreover, Serlio is the obvious source for the pediments and coffering respectively in the adjacent Patio Mariscal and Antecabildo he designed with Asensio de Maeda.**5.34f,g**

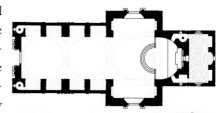

5.34a @ 1:1000

5.34b

5.34c

›**5.34 HERNÁN RUIZ II AND HIS CONTEMPORARIES IN SEVILLE:** (a, b) Hospital de la Sangre (1558–67), plan and church portal; (c–e) Cathedral, Capilla Real vault and chapterhouse (1558–68); (f, g) Antecabildo and Patio Mariscal (1559–69).

Master-mason at Córdoba, in which capacity he completed the vaulting of the chancel, Ruiz went on to the same post in Seville (1558). In that capacity he added the carillon chamber and cupola to the Moorish tower known as La Giralda (AIC3, page 228), completed the Capilla Real and began the chapterhouse.

As noted earlier, the Capilla Real had been built to cornice level by Martín de Gainza when work stopped in 1562 due to concerns over stability and lighting: the domical vaulting completed by Ruiz in the next decade must be seen in the coffered tradition developed by Diego de Riano, Diego de Siloé and Andrés de Vandelvira.**5.19, 5.20h, 5.21a** Planned under the inspiration of Serlio (Book V, folio 4, published in Paris in 1545) soon after his appointment, begun in 1561, Ruiz's chapter-house was Spain's first elliptical space of any pretension and it thus preceded the first important Italian elliptical building – Vignola's S. Anna dei Palafranieri – by some four years.**1.25p, 1.38d** The architect died before confronting the difficult task of vaulting his ellipse: Vandelvira and Francisco del Castillo were consulted and the work was achieved by Asensio de Maeda in 1592. The Antecabildo vault relates to Serlio IV, 12.69, the embellishment of the Patio Marsical to IV, 6.42 and IV, 7.44 in particular.

Contemporary with Ruiz's initial work at the cathedral, the church of the Hospital de la Sangre conforms to the Spanish hall type represented by the royal funerary chapels of Ávila and Toledo, for example, and in particular by S. Pietro in Montorio, Rome – of which the plan is a reformed contraction. The double-storey portico is a latter-day variant on the Siloé-Vandelvira type best represented at Úbeda, with its superimposed rhythmic bays, but it may also be compared with Serlio, Book IV, folio 50.

5.34d

5.34f

5.34g

5.34e

5.35a

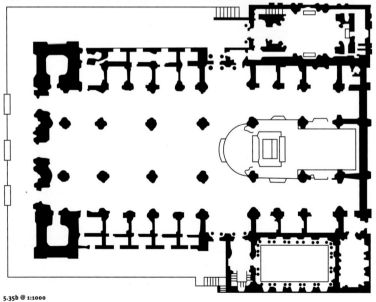

5.35b @ 1:1000

5.35c

(a) crossing, (b) plan,
(c) north aisle to nave, (d) sacristy (from 1555).

The rebuilding of the converted mosque at Jaén
began in 1500. Fears for stability led to demolition from
c. 1530. Vandelvira was called on for the project
adopted in 1534 and executed over the following century. By his death in 1575 only the sacristy, chapterhouse and south transept had been realized – the last
in part. Work does not seem to have been greatly furthered under his successors, notably Francisco del
Castillo, master of works to the bishop. It was resumed
in main part in 1634 when Juan de Aranda and then
Pedro del Portillo continued largely as the existing
structure dictated. The west end was completed from
the 1680s to the design of Eufrasio López de Rojas.

In articulating the sacristy with considerable gravitas, Vandelvira provides his Order with a full entablature and twice raises the arches over it like thermal
windows so that there is no confusion of alternative
structural systems.

It is probable that Vandelvira was abreast of contemporary Italian practice: the permutation of the serliana

5.35d

with pairs of contiguous columns made a prominent initial appearance in the loggia front of Giulio Romano's Palazzo del Te in Mantua before 1530 – as we have seen. As we have also seen, it was adopted by Bartolomeo Ammannati as the central motif in his Roman Palazzo di Firenzi in the early 1550s and was most popular in the Lombardy of Galeazzo Alessi and his followers.[1.47a], [1.85c] It is at least as probable that Vandelvira derived it from Serlio who, in turn, had reproduced it from his master Baldassare Peruzzi's stage-set design:[1.22a], [1.25f,g] approximated in Book IV (6.29, for example), the definitive form of the motif appears often in Book VII (chapter 41ff, for example) which, unpublished in Vandelvira's lifetime, was available to a limited extent in off-print copies.

The impact of Serlio in the south was most marked in the ecclesiastical and secular works associated with the circle of Andrés de Vandelvira: unfortunately, the degree of the latter's personal responsibility in several of these remains undetermined. In 1534, while pursuing the realization of Siloé's scheme for the Sacra Capilla del Salvador at Úbeda with great distinction, he was entrusted with the reconstruction of the cathedral of Jaén and thirty years later began a similar exercise at Baeza (as we have noted): built in place of mosques and medieval in inception, both these works derive their clustered attenuated columns from their Gothic predecessors but recall Siloé at Granada.[5.35, 5.36] Vast, the Jaén project was not fully realized for more than

›5.36 BAEZA: (a–c) cathedral of S. María, nave to east and west, north aisle detail; (d) Fuente de S. María (1564); (e) Casa del Corregidors (1560s?), façade.

Baeza's cathedral was originally built between the 12th and 14th centuries on the site of a mosque converted in 1147. Renovation in Renaissance style began in 1529 but much of the new work collapsed in 1567. Vandelvira was commissioned to rebuild the nave in triple-aisled hall form over the old foundations: his Classicism informs the structure from the transept west and, in its full floridity, the frontispieces of the chapels of S. Jose and S. Miguel to the east of the north portal.

5.36a

a century but Vandelvira's strategy was sustained – reputedly. Much of the more modest Baeza scheme was executed before its author's death in 1575. The covering of the transept, with domical and canopy vaults rather than the networks of ribs which distinguish the sanctuary, was then in train. Thereafter under the direction of the master's associate, Alonso Barba, the canopy vaults over the rest of the nave and aisles were treated to a variety of Classical mouldings and instead of the single lights of the easterly bays, the serlianas of the rest of the clerestory belong to the post-Villalpando era.

The serliana motive is directly derived from its eponymous source by the architect of the Casa del Corregidors

5.36c

5.36b

5.36d

5.36e

Between his death in 1575 and the completion of construction c. 1593, Vandelvira's scheme seems to have been respected in the main by his successors: his assistant Alonso Barba, who directed the master-mason Cristóbal Perez and was rather more remotely overseen by Francisco del Castillo. The form and embellishment of the nave vaults relate to the master's authenticated late work elsewhere, notably in the chapel of the Santiago hospital at Úbeda (see below). The Jesuit mathematician and philosopher Juan Bautista Villalpando seems to have been consulted on the geometry (and added the north portal, as we shall see).

The architect of the bizarrely ill-proportioned fountain is identified as Ginés Martínez (died c. 1606). The similar realization of embellishment – especially the atlante and the cartouches as well as the serliana – prompt the attribution of the Casa del Corregidor to Martínez perhaps as executive architect: the canonical proportions of the whole, the refinement of the portal Order and the incorporation of the anthropomorphic motif have suggested Vandelvira as the originating master.

of Baeza and the Fuente de S. María in the plaza beside the cathedral there: the former, applied to existing structure, is somewhat erratic in its ordering and the fountain arch is peculiarly ill-proportioned in its present state but the inception, if not the execution, of both is traditionally credited to Vandelvira. The latter certainly developed it with gravitas in the sacristy of the cathedral at Jaén: across his prolific career, after mastering the master's ordered opulence, he developed increasing sobriety of style with reference to the contemporary Italian mode.**5.35c**

Vandelvira is documented as having been retained in Úbeda by the successors of Francisco de los Cobos, for whom he worked on the Sacra Capilla del Salvador: Francisco Vela and Juan Vázquez de Molina had him design their palaces (before and shortly after 1560 respectively) and Don Diego de los Cobos, the bishop of Jaén, who was employing him on his cathedral, likewise called on him for the Hospital de Santiago (built from 1562).**5.37** The earliest of these, the Palacio Vela de los Cobos, is comparable to the recent work of Rodrigo Gil de Hontañón in Léon – if not Covarrubias at Alcalá – especially in the arcaded attic gallery, the relief of the plane surfaces below with bold pedimented windows and the portal with attached columns supporting heraldic sculptures. Next, the Palacio Vasquez may be seen as revising Serlio, Book VII, chapters 12 or 60 in terms of chapter 50 (though as yet unpublished): it is without sculptural embellishment except, notably, for its author's favoured atlantes. And, finally, the Siloan floridity of his Sacra Capella del

›5.37 VANDELVIRA, HIS PREDECESSORS AND THE SECULAR COMPLEX IN ÚBEDA: (a) Casa de las Torres, entrance front; (b) Palacio Vela de los Cobos, street front; (c, d) Palacio Vázquez de Molina (from 1562), façade and cortile; (e–h) Hospital de Santiago (1562–76), façade, court and chapel interiors; (i) former Casas Consistoriales (early 17th century after an anonymous earlier project).

Plateresque persisted at least to the eve of Vandelvira's era at Úbeda: the Casa de las Torres is referred to in a document of 1544 and, though not necessarily finished by then, was probably begun at least a decade earlier by an unknown architect for Andrés Dávalos de la Cueva, whose family was recognized as noble in 1532.

The earliest secular work attributed to Vandelvira failing other likely contenders is the Palacio del Deán Ortega, in execution before 1550. Tradition – of southern and western Castille, at least – contributed the corner window: the Classicizing form was supposedly introduced to Úbeda in details of fittings sent from Toledo by Luis de Vega for Deán Ortega. Before the end

5.37b

5.37a

5.37c

of the decade, Vandelvira used it more extensively for Francisco Vela de los Cobos. The portal and window aedicules of the latter's house were specified as models for the palace of his son-in-law, Francisco de Molino y Valencia, built shortly after Vandelvira's death in mid-1575 – and now called after its later owner, the Marques de la Rambla.

The Vázquez palace façade may be compared with Serlio Book VII, chapter 12 (see above): the herm or atlante was a feature of Vandelvira's earliest independent work in Úbeda, the Sacra Capella del Salvador. The uncanonical combination of arch and column in the courtyard here, as in the nucleus of the Santiago complex, avoids the sophistication of the serliana (employed within the Santiago chapel) and even of Siloé's much earlier Salamanca exercise in favour of tradition – as do many of its contemporaries elsewhere.

5.37d

5.37e

5.37g

5.37f

5.37h

Salvador style is entirely banished from the Santiago Hospital: the vaulting of the chapel furthers the Baeza process and a serliana of the doubled-column type (as in Book IV, 6, 27) sustains the musician's gallery but Serlian variety is rejected for the cortile in favour of retrogressive colonnaded arcades in conformity with local practice. The austere façade is relieved mainly by an aedicule framing a relief of the Moor-slayer – with its dependent inscriptional and heraldic elements – above the unarticulated portal.

5.37i

Arcades carried on doubled columns again distinguish the elegant loggias of Úbeda's former Casas Consistoriales: developing the form of Vandelvira's Santiago Chapel trascoro, the building played a prominent part in a programme of civic enlightenment realized from c. 1604. Vandelvira was involved in renovating the building in the 1560s but the late date of its contextual exercise has prompted the attribution of the loggia to his successor as principal architect in the orbit of Jaén, Francisco del Castillo (1528–86). However, the latter, who had worked with Vignola and Ammannati on the Villa Giulia in Rome in the early 1550s, looked beyond Serlio to the latest Italian trends in inventing the Mannerism of his firmly attributed works.

5.38a

›5.38 FRANCISCO DEL CASTILLO AND HIS
FOLLOWERS: (a) Martos, portal of the ayuntamiento
(former Carcel, 1577); (b) Granada, Real Chancilleria:
façade (1587); (c) Córdoba, S. Pablo, entrance front
(anon., 1580s?); (d) Baeza University and S. Juan Evangelista, entrance front (architect unknown, between
1574 and 1593).

Castillo applied a rusticated Order of the Serlian
type (reproduced by Villalpando; see above, page 698)
to lend appropriate strength to the portal of the Carcel
de Martos – where he worked extensively – but the
invasion of its pediment by a descending oculus is not
representative of Serlio's approach to the juxtaposition
of forms.

5.38b

5.38c

The Grenadine Real Chancillería was ordered in 1531 by the King-Emperor Charles: the plan is attributed to Siloé but the existing courtyard of c. 1540, with its arches rising directly from uncanonically elongated Tuscan columns, is difficult to reconcile with that master's much more sophisticated earlier work at Salamanca. The building was not completed until the 1580s when the façade was added by Castillo. Minor elements in the design may be seen as Serlian but the broken pediment is characteristic of later Italian Mannerism – and, of course, Spanish portals had been framed by canonically superimposed Orders at least since the early career of Siloé.

Castillo trained in Rome where he worked with Vignola on the Villa Giulia (see pages 172f): he was thus at the Mannerist well-spring and doubtless knew Vignola's Porte di Michel Angelo but his Grenadine graft is aware of Alessi's work in Philip II's Milan (see page 266).

The university in Baeza was being built while Castillo was active in the region but there is no evidence connecting them. The mannerisms, especially in the treatment of the voussoirs, are related to the work elsewhere (Mengíbar and possibly Ibros) of Alonso Barba who was completing Vandelvira's cathedral at the time. In the absence of connecting evidence here too, the work is attributed to an unknown local architect. So too is the Mannerism of S. Pablo in Córdoba: the juxtaposition of a tall central element, representing the nave, and a pedimented temple front embracing the aisles, suggests distant awareness of Palladio – but the primal authority of a colossal Order in the central zone cedes to bifurcation with reference to Serlio for the rustication.

Around the turn of the century, courses diverted by various mannerisms were pursued by the local masters, most notably Francisco de Castillo at Granada, Alonso Barba (c. 1525–95) in and around Baeza and, in the next generation, Alonso de Vandelvira (1545–1625) in the orbit of Jaén and in Seville where his main contemporary was Hernán Ruiz III (c. 1540–1606). There are the unidentified too, of course, like the author of the façades of Baeza University or S. Pablo in Córdoba. And there were foreigners, especially stuccadores like those who embellished the sanctuary vault of the Cordovan cathedral.**5.38–5.40**

5.38d

5.39a

5.39b

5.39c

›5.39 ANDRES DE VANDELVIRA'S HEIRS:
(a) Baeza cathedral, north portal (1593); (b) Seville, portal of the Monastery of S. Isabel (1609); (c) Úbeda, S. María de los Reales Alcázares (1604–12).

The Baeza cathedral portal was projected by Francisco del Castillo but revised and executed by the Jesuit priests Jerónimo del Prado and Juan Bautista Villalpando: it follows the central west frontispiece of El Escorial in flanking the upper Order with obelisks (as we shall see) but Doric is eschewed for the pilasters and the central relief panel recalls the motif popular with Andrés de Vandelvira. The latter's son, Alonso, followed his father in this and in the disposition of an elegant Order of Corinthian columns to the portal of S. Isabel in Seville. So too did the author of the main portal of S. María de los Reales Alcázares in Úbeda: identified as Martín López de Alcaraz, he had the masterpiece of the elder Vandelvira clearly in his sight from the site.

›5.40 CÓRDOBA, CATHEDRAL OF NUESTRA SEÑORA DE LA ASUNCIÓN: choir vault (c. 1600).

Hernán Ruiz II's work on the nave extended to the crossing under the direction of Juan de Ochoa. In the choir the Mannerist stuccowork is attributed to Roman stuccadores working for the cathedral canon Pablo de Céspedes who had studied in Italy.

5.40

ARAGÓN

Meanwhile, the most easterly of King Philip's Iberian domains, Aragón, was relatively slow to achieve a mature Renaissance Classicism though it was more exposed than the hinterland kingdom to direct influence from Italy and France. Yet it had hardly lagged behind Castile in adopting the Plateresque fashion, as Gil Morlanes II's S. Engracia portal in Zaragoza admirably demonstrates. In the same city Gil Morlanes I's Lonja (mercantile exchange) well represents the persistence of tradition into the fifth decade of the century: it was sustained even into the next

›5.41 ZARAGOZA: (a) S. Engracia, portal (1512–15); (b, c) Lonja, exterior and interior detail (1541–51); (d) Casa de los Morlanes (c. 1555), exterior detail.

S. Engracia was founded ex voto (for the cure of cataracts) by Juan II of Aragón (1398–1479), father of Ferdinand II, over the subterranean shrine of the early Christian martyr. The older Morlanes's church was destroyed by the French in 1808 but the portal was salvaged and incorporated in the later-19th-century rebuilding.

The Lonja (mercantile exchange) was commissioned by Don Hernando of Aragón (1498–1575, son of Ferdinand II's illegitimate son Alonso), who was archbishop of Zaragoza at the time and later viceroy in Barcelona. The younger Morales realized the interior over the plan of Juan de Sariñena.

The homogeneous block of the palace, attributed to Morlanes for his noble kinsmen, is typical but the fenestration is not: the herms may have been inspired by works like the Toulouse Hôtel Beringuier Maynier of the previous decade or by Perino del Vaga's legacy in Genoa: Serlio used the motif in his chimneypiece design Book IV, folios 43 and 58.**2.34a, 1.83c, 1.25d**

5.41a

5.41d

5.41b

5.41c

decade for the trascoro of the cathedral, for example – but that was the work of the sculptor Arnau de Bruselas to the designs of the painter Jeronimo Vallejo. By then, on the other hand, Nicolas Bachelier's Tolosane Mannerism – or its equivalent in the Flanders of Cornelis Floris and Hans Vredeman de Vries – was being grafted on to local Moresque tradition in Zaragozan palaces like the one known as the Casa de los Morlanes, with its herm-supported window aedicules: as we have seen, that motif was popular in the circle of Vandelvira by mid-century. And in mid-century Barcelona, the court galleries of Antoni Carbonell's Palau del Lloctinent may best be compared with recent Lombard practice – if not the plainer works of Covarrubias – rather than anything recommended by Serlio in Villalpando's recent publication.**5.41, 5.42**

The Spanish edition of Serlio – furthering familiarity with its Italian and French versions – provided readily assimilable precept and design resource but it did not obviate the influence of the local masters – or local tradition – and it did not provoke the development of a pattern-book Mannerism comparable to the work of J. A. du Cerceau in Valois France. The future King Philip II may have preferred Serlian Villalpando to the earlier Renaissance sobriety of the mature Covarrubias, at first, but orthodox rationalism would promote extreme austerity at his preferred seat.

5.42

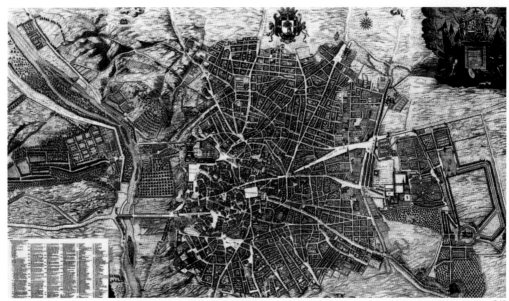

›**5.43 MADRID:** plan (Pedro Teixeira, 1656).

5.43

4 ASCENDANCY OF MADRID AND THE SPANISH ESTILO DESORNAMENTADO

Madrid was established as Spain's capital by royal decree in 1561 – but not as the sole location of the court. Though subject to extremes of temperature, the site offered more scope for development than Toledo and was central – which naturally appealed to a rationalist king bent on consolidation and centralization of power. Unlike Toledo, moreover, it was unencumbered with feudal magnates: they had already been denigrated by the roles allotted to them under the Burgundian court etiquette introduced to Spain in 1547. However, the new king could better defy them and the power they had wielded over his peripatetic predecessors – notably the weak late Trastámaras and the often-absent Emperor Charles. His objective was the development of his proto-modern bureaucratic state and the determination of a centre for a sedentary court after his definitive return to Spain from his decisive victory over the French at Saint-Quentin in 1557.**5.43**

5.44a

5.44b

›**5.44 LUIS DE VEGA'S LEGACY,** at (a) El Pardo (begun 1547); (b) Valsaín (from c. 1552, largely destroyed by fire in the late-18th century) as recorded in anonymous 17th-century mural paintings at El Escorial.

Luis de Vega was the designer, his nephew the master of works. Under him, both El Pardo and Valsaín developed into sprawling complexes about enclosed courts, as usual, but with overt reference to northern modes, especially at roof level. Valsaín was first, El Pardo followed. El Pardo was a traditional, alcázar-like rectangular block with corner towers. Valsaín, in contrast, was notable for the introduction of adjuncts with loggias open to the sylvan setting (after which it was called 'El Bosque'): Prince Philip, who gave specific instructions on the finishing of his colonnaded galleries, would have encountered the form in Flanders, Italy – and Serlio, who also informed the rusticated portals.

Philip had gravitated to Madrid as regent several times between 1539 and 1552 and early in his reign he revived his father's ambitions for the extensive summer palace at Aranjuez, not far off to the south, as well as the hunting boxes at Valsaín and El Pardo to the north.**5.44** The young patron prompted the introduction of high pitched roofs in the Flemish manner and towers with concave pyramidal roofs and spires or onion-domed cupolas of the type common in the Habsburg's imperial domains of central Europe (see above, pages 407ff, 442). The late king-emperor's master of works Luis de Vega (active c. 1520–62) was retained at these established sites – and in brief succession to Francisco de Villalpando at Toledo – in collaboration with his nephew Gaspar. The latter (active c. 1545–76 primarily as a technician) was Villalpando's brother-in-law and had been appointed to head the body constituted in 1552 to supervise royal works, the Junta de Obras y Bosques.

To the north-west of the new capital, in the foothills of the Guadarrama, King Philip embarked on his greatest architectural exercise within the year of the resettlement: the vast monastery-palace at El Escorial, dedicated to S. Lorenzo in recognition of the Spanish victory at Saint-Quentin on that saint's feast day. It was to be consigned to the Jeronymite Order to whose houses Spanish rulers usually resorted when in need of accommodation beyond their established seats – and to whose ministrations at Yuste the king-emperor had consigned himself on his abdication and retreat. The foundation was conceived primarily as the shrine of Philip's parents and the necropolis of their dynasty, where multiple masses would be sung in perpetuity for the repose of their numerous souls: for the repose of the living king a small extension became the preferred retreat but the complex as a whole would surpass anything pursued to completion in Renaissance Europe.

JUAN BAUTISTA DE TOLEDO AND ITALIAN OPPOSITION

Established masters had been retained at established sites but for the work at the new site of El Escorial, King Philip turned to new talent: as he sought to elude the power of the old nobility in his new seat, so he sought to curtail the dominance of the medieval master-builders and their guild over architecture. He chose Juan Bautista de Toledo (c. 1515–67), a Spaniard who had trained in Italy – under Michelangelo at S. Pietro no less – and who went on to serve the Spanish viceroy in Naples, primarily as a military engineer. Recalled by the king in 1559, he was appointed principal royal architect after the death of Francisco de Villalpando in 1561. His earliest works in that capacity were at the Madrid Alcázar and Aranjuez: the former has disappeared entirely, the latter has been obscured by later additions and alterations. His most lasting legacy was a rigorous technical system of architectural education – and the austere style of the Escorial, more military than civil, stripped of all superfluous ornament in determined rejection of the Plateresque past.

That style, subsequently known as *estilo desornamentado*, asserted the primacy of order over ornament under the guidance of Vitruvius: of the symmetry derived from the human body, extruded with absolute regularity as utility required in a building project; of proportion derived from the Classical Orders which, distinguishing the masculine and feminine modes in skeletal structure, should prevail whether loadbearing or agents of articulation imposed on a wall. As we have seen, Portugal was in the van with its *estilo chão* and Alonso de Covarrubias had approximated such a style in his late work, especially after the advent of Bartolomé Bustamante from Italy. And it was Italian example which governed the process of evolution: the strictly canonical application of the Orders apart, this ran to the abstract order of panelled façades like those of the Roman Palazzo Alberini Cicciaporci or the more immediately relevant Farnese palazzi at Caprarola and Piacenza (see above, pages 174f, 178). The return of Juan Bautista reinforced the tendency towards severity along the lines promoted by Vignola to counter Michelangelesque complexity and it was furthered by the intervention of Vignola's colleague – and critic – in the service of the Farnese, Francesco Paciotti (1521–91).

Paciotti of Urbino had been employed primarily by the Farnese on the fortification of their Italian seats – and on the assessment of Vignola's plans for Caprarola. Having accompanied his patron to King Philip's court in Flanders in 1560, he was retained there as military engineer and ordered to Spain the next year to double Juan Bautista – indeed to assess his plans for El Escorial. He returned to Italy and fortification in September 1562, after submitting his report and perhaps projecting the abstract tectonic façade of the Madrid church of Las Descalzas Reales.**5.45** By early the following year he had translated his criticism

›5.45 MADRID, CHURCH OF LAS DESCALZAS REALES: façade.

The convent was founded in 1559 by Archduchess Juana de Austria in a former palace. The authorship of the church's façade is disputed: its rectilinear panelling is framed by abstract pilaster strips in the assertively mural manner of Vignola's subsidiary elevations of the Farnese palaces at Caprarola and Piacenza – the schemes for both of which were assessed by Paciotti. This approach to articulation was to characterize the severe style developed by the architects of Philip II.

of Juan Bautista's scheme for the basilica into one of his own which he forthwith sent to Madrid: reputedly centralized and wholly rectangular, it has been lost with most of the other important drawings from the evolutionary phase of El Escorial.

Paciotti had recommended that the king seek advice on the basilica's design from the Italian profession at large. Spanish agents in Italy were specifically instructed to report on the latest developments in ecclesiastical architecture and, indeed, to solicit designs from the leading architects – whose number naturally included Vignola, Alessi, Tibaldi and Palladio. After his death in 1567, Juan Bautista's scheme and a collection of Italian alternatives were submitted for assessment to the Florentine Academy of Art and Design: Vignola was to produce a synthesis. The outcome was not transmitted to Spain until 1573 by when, as the king affirmed, it had been superseded by events. In the meantime both Vignola and Alessi had been invited to the Spanish court: both declined on grounds of age. However, Alessi, who died in 1572, had already exerted fundamental influence on the definitive design by proxy through his Genoese masterpiece, the church of S. Maria di Carignano of 1552 (see above, pages 260f).

As we have had cause already to observe, Genoa was the major point of contact between Spain, its Lombard dominion and Burgundy. Embarking for the voyage from there in 1562, when Alessi's great work was nearing completion, was the Bergamese painter and decorator Giovanni Battista Castello (c. 1509–69) who had been called to the king's service in Madrid specifically to work on architectural models. Five years later he replaced Juan Bautista in charge of work at El Escorial.

The king's great project was furthered slowly under the direction of Castello whose preoccupation elsewhere gave the master-masons, led by Pedro de Tolosa, the chance to

5.46a

›5.46 VISO DEL MARQUÉS, PALACIO DEL MARQUÉS DE SANTA CRUZ, from c. 1564: (a) entrance front, (b) vestibule vault (with patronage portraits), (c, d) courtyard and naval fresco detail, (e–h) staircase and gallery details, (i, j) antechamber vaults, (k) chapel interior, (l, m) salon interiors.

Don Álvaro de Bazán (1526–88), was captain general of the Navy: entrusted by Philip II with the galleys of Naples, he commanded the reserve division at Lepánto and saved Giovanni Andrea Doria, the Genoese commander of the main force, when he was out-manoeuvred by the Turks. His Italianate palace is unique in Spain.

5.46d

5.46b

reassert themselves. Castillo was busy deploying his main talent on the interior decoration of El Pardo in lavish fresco. Three years before his promotion at El Escorial, moreover, he had begun his most important surviving work, the palace of Don Álvaro de Bazán, Marquis of Santa Cruz, at Viso del Marqués. Consummate in its synthesis of the traditional Spanish castle form and the grandest modern Italian domestic style, its lavish internal embellishment was completed by Genoese craftsmen after its inventor's death in 1572.**5.46**

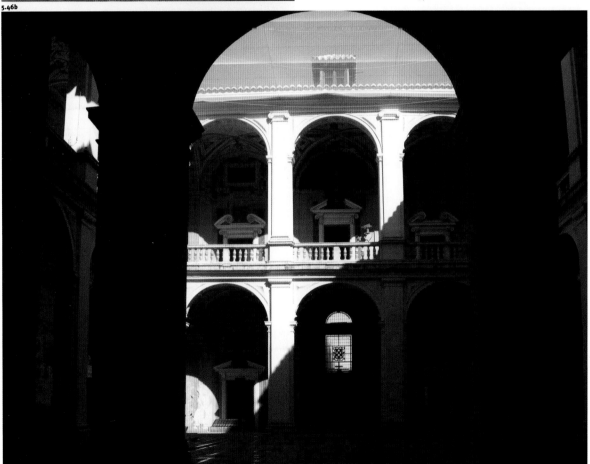

5.46c

5.46e

5.46f

5.46g

5.46h

5.46i

›ARCHITECTURE IN CONTEXT »FROM THE HIGH RENAISSANCE TO MANNERISM

5.46j

5.46k

5.46l

5.56m

5.47a

5.47b

›**5.47 TOLEDO ALCÁZAR,** as completed by Juan de Herrera from 1572: (a) south face (rebuilt after extensive war damage in 1936), (b) imperial staircase (pre-Civil War photograph), (c) general view in context.

Commissioned in the late-1530s to refashion the Alcázar, Alonso de Covarrubias projected the patio and the south wing, with its great staircase, in 1550, as we have noted. Two years later he presented alternative models for the staircase in proto-imperial form but differing width vis-à-vis the patio. After Francisco de Villalpando's access to the site, the larger project was developed to the whole width of the patio gallery and the construction of the ramps began accordingly. Beyond finishing the latter, Herrera designed the cage with its Order of Corinthian pilasters applied to an abstract grid: his completed wing's external face is articulated with superimposed Orders in complement to Covarrubias's north front and in contrast to the unarticulated surfaces east and west.

5.47c

ADVENT OF JUAN DE HERRERA

The renewed vacancy at the head of the king's building service was filled – unofficially, at first – by Juan de Herrera (1530–97). He was from a minor noble family and had a classical education at Valladolid. He attended Prince Philip in his Italian and Flemish domains from 1547 to 1551, served in the army for several years from 1553 and studied engineering and architecture in Italy when Vignola was in the ascendant. As early as 1563 he had been appointed to secondary responsibility for the king's works as Juan

›5.48 ARANJUEZ, ROYAL PALACE, from the 1560s, badly damaged by fire in the 1660s, reconstructed by Pedro Caro Idrogo from 1715 and extended into two wings from 1778 (detail of early 17th-century mural in El Escorial).

The vineyard and its estate house at Aranjuez – originally built by Lorenzo Suárez de Figueroa in 1387 – were bought by the Catholic Monarchs and amplified by their grandson from 1534 as a base for hunting. Renovation and extension of the old building as a summer residence were projected in 1544 but not pursued until after the accession of Philip II. Advanced dilapidation prompted the projection of a new palace in 1557 by Luis and Gaspar de Vega but work was again delayed until the early 1560s: Vega's plans died with him in 1562 and the palace was to be transformed on an altogether larger scale by his successors – Juan Bautista de Toledo and Juan de Herrera.

Juan Bautista's scheme, implemented no further than the chapel wing, was furthered from 1571 with modifications at least to the west range of the main quadrangular block: this was elevated above all the other ranges as later at El Escorial. The articulation of the brick façades with an abstract Order of pilaster strips in white stone derived from Juan Bautista's chapel. The towers derive from the same source but their lead roofs are Herrera's: the absence of towers from the corners of the main block responded to the modernization of the traditional alcázar morphology retained at El Pardo and Valsaín.

Bautista's assistant in collaboration with Juan de Valencia. While accelerating work on El Escorial in the last years of his flagging superior, he pressed ahead with the latter's enlarged project for Aranjuez – ultimately enlarging it still further – and with the completion of the imperial staircase wing of the Toledo Alcázar from the base level provided by Covarrubias and Villalpando.**5·47, 5·48**

Supported by intermittent royal decrees, Herrera had regained the initiative from the master-masons by 1576 – four years after he had been entrusted with prime responsibility. Groomed as he was to follow the king's will already impressed on Juan Bautista, orthodoxy reigned in architecture as it did in religion: faith and taste conformed in severity. In its essentially rationalist aesthetic, at least, the orthodoxy was Augustinian. It was articulated by the Jeronymite Fray José de Sigüenza (1544–1606), the royal librarian, ultimately prior, at El Escorial who witnessed and chronicled the evolution of the great project from 1567: beauty lies in order, in regularity, indeed in symmetry, and in proportion – in number, not in applied ornament.**5·49**

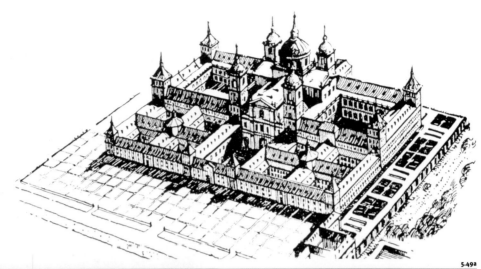

5.49a

5.49b

El Escorial

The vast rectangular, multi-courtyard scheme was due in inception and partial execution to Juan Bautista de Toledo: based on the grid-iron on which S.
Lorenzo was grilled, it is hardly less rationalist in its pure geometry than the
new palace in the Alhambra at Granada but follows the Spanish royal tradition of combining palace, mausoleum and monastery: the arrangements
made for the king-emperor at Yuste provided the immediate, if limited, precedent. It was originally conceived to accommodate the fifty monks deemed
necessary to provide perpetual divine services for the royal incumbents of
the necropolis and their venerators: the number was doubled in 1564, neces-
sitating the addition of an extra storey to the ranges framing the western
courts of the complex, raising their height to that of the eastern sectors.

5.49c

The complex has been seen as emulating the Palace of Diocletian at
Split (AIC1, pages 654f) and even – for those given to the abstruse – as an
ideal interpretation of the Biblical description of Solomon's Temple (reconstructed by J.-B. Villalpando towards the end of the century, but conceived
earlier under the influence of Juan de Herrera). More plausibly, perhaps, it
may be seen as amplifying Antonio Filarete's ideal scheme for the
Milanese Ospedale Maggiore which had already been followed in part at
Santiago de Compostela and for the Hospital de Santa Cruz at Toledo (AIC4,
pages 761, 867). Beyond that, however, the immediate Spanish precedent
was Covarrubias's Tavera Hospital at Toledo as developed after the intervention of Bartolomé Bustamante which, as we have seen, aspired to perfect the double-courtyard scheme of the Madrid Alcázar. Beyond that, too,
is enlargement on the memory of the ideal alcázar – four-square with
square corner towers.

The walls of the south front had been completed, in the austere style
which was to characterize the exterior of the whole complex, before Juan
Bautista's demise. He had built the infirmary's 'Gallery of Convalescence'
(or 'Sun Corridor'), with its gracious serlianas, beyond the south-west corner of the complex. He had designed the courts within in 1565: a grand one
centred on a fountain and overlooked by the principal friars' cells in the
south-eastern sector; in its south-western counterpart, a quartet of small
ones surrounded by lesser cells, dormitories for novices and service
spaces. The main one, dedicated to the Evangelists, was to be framed by

5.49d

›5.49 EL ESCORIAL, PALACE-MONASTERY OF S. LORENZO: (a) overview as devised by Juan Bautista and followed by Juan de Herrera from 1572, (b, c) south front and infirmary 'Gallery of Convalescence', (d) Courtyard of the Evangelists, (e) section through basilica as projected by Juan Bautista, (f–i) overview, sections and plan as realized by Herrera, (j, k,) exterior frontispiece and interior façade of entrance wing, (l, m) basilica front, project drawing and general view, (n–q) basilica interior, dome, engraved record of sanctuary and royal tribune, (r, s) king's bedroom and plan with sight lines to high altar, (t, u) sacristy, engraved record of altar end and general view, (v) main staircase, (w) Gallery of Battles, (x, y) library, general view and detail of bay decoration, (z) general view from north-west.

superimposed galleries inspired by Antonio da Sangallo's work for the Farnese in Rome: a decade of work on these began under Castillo in 1569, ostensibly to Juan Bautista's plan, but within two years the western range had been revised by Herrera to incorporate an imperial staircase instead of the traditional open-centred one devised by Juan Bautista. The king's protégé was then also concerned with the completion of the prototype introduced to the Toledo Alcázar by Covarrubias and furthered by Villalpando.

The king had made his will perfectly clear to Herrera: 'simplicity in construction, severity over all; nobility without arrogance, majesty without ostentation'. And he was to have his favoured slate roofs and spires, characteristic of Flanders and Austria but adopted for Valsaín and the Toledan Alcázar in the late-1550s. However, the change of scale in 1564, accommodating the extra monks by elevating the western half of the south range to match the eastern half and suppressing the intermediate tower, pressed rationalism to monotony in the most exposed face of the whole complex. The king occupied provisional accommodation there from 1571: whether from within he could see nobility without arrogance, it was certainly simple and severe and that was Herrera's inheritance.

Beyond the frontispiece in the centre of the western entrance front and its pendants serving the monastic and collegiate zones, the king's new architect applied an abstract Order for minimal relief to virtually all available surfaces, especially the north front and the west-central atrium. At the head of the latter he realized his master's ideal most assertively in his revision of the façade and superstructure of the great church, the central element in the vast Laurentian scheme.

Francesco Paciotti had found Juan Bautista's design for the basilica wanting both aesthetically and structurally: the proportions were too squat in the main body, too attenuated in the dome, the supports were not substantial enough and the curved elements would not readily accord with the essentially rectilinear grid of the complex as a whole. Italian revisions were set aside, as we have noted, and the king instructed Herrera to proceed on his own terms. However, Alessi's imprint is detectable in the actual building: the Greek cross plan, the colossal Order and the dome all derive from S. Maria di Carignano (see above, pages 260f) – and the simplification of Bramante's centralized scheme for S. Pietro in the Vatican (see AIC4,

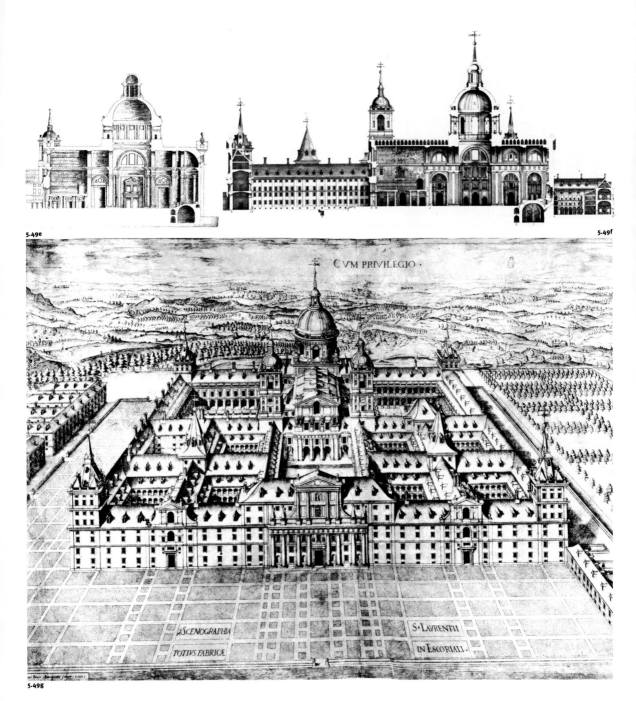

5.49e

5.49f

CVM PRIVILEGIO.

SCENOGRAPHIA
TOTIVS FABRICÆ

S. LAVRENTII
IN ESCORIALI.

5.49g

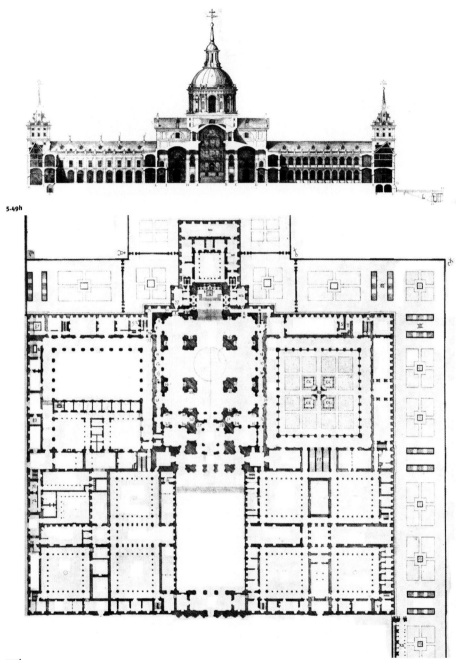

5.49h

5.49i

5.49j

5.49k

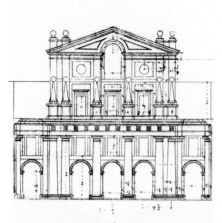

5.49l

page 836). The apsidal arms of the Roman model, originally retained by Juan Bautista, were suppressed in accordance with Paciotti except for the sanctuary: this is clear in a sectional drawing identified as a response to the criticism by Juan Bautista's office.**5.49e** There is a narthex as in Sangallo's late Petrine project and, closer to home, in the Tavera hospital chapel at Toledo (see pages 142f, 694f) – but not in Juan Bautista's revised section. Sangallo had incorporated a centralized ante-church. Herrera retained an ante-space sotocoro and the choir is raised above it in accordance with Spanish tradition. The king specified that the main space was to be reserved exclusively for use as the palatine chapel but that the choir platform was to be large enough to accommodate him when he chose to join the monks in their sung devotions there and, equally, that the sotocoro was to be large enough for the congregation of the public confined to it.

5.49m

Structurally and formally the intrusion of the choir gallery was anathema to Paciotti : specifically, he objected to the way it cut across the colossal Order of the nave, to the flattened ovoid vault and the cave-like darkness of the lower space – but provided no alternative to honouring the vernacular. In his criticism of the proportions overall, Paciotti had been scathing about the pedestals over which Juan Bautista had raised his Doric Order: the dimensions required for them and their bases were incompatible with those of the secondary Order of the subsidiary arcades, let alone the tertiary Order of the sotocoro. The proportions are adjusted with the suppression of the pedestals in the section attributed to Juan Bautista. The result is inconsistency in the height – and therefore, of course, the proportions – of the pilasters rising from the different levels of nave and sanctuary. Unfortunately, this flaw was sustained by Herrera though the Italian's prescription of 1:2 proportions for the nave was adopted. The raising of the sanctuary was propitious in itself, of course, but it also responded to the location of the royal mausoleum in the crypt below. Addressed by the entourage of

5.49o

5.49n

5.49p

5.49q

5.49r

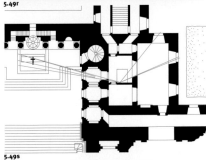

5.49s

5.49u

king and emperor in prayer in paired groups in the loggias over their ceno-taphs, the sacramental high altar, with elevated window for displaying the host, furthered a Spanish tradition which seems to have originated in the domains of the patron's great-grandfather, King Ferdinand.

In the generally austere granite context inherited from Juan Bautista, Herrera's application of the Orders is emphatic and strictly canonical though rising through several storeys on the Roman church-like fron-tispieces of the main façade. Beyond the deep atrium, the narthex portico – prefigured by Juan Bautista if the section referred to above is correctly attributed to his office – has a particularly powerful Order of colossal Doric columns which, with Albertian scrupulousness in respect for coherence, is echoed by the pilasters of the nave. The chilling severity is relieved only by the sumptuous marble and bronze retable produced by the Milanese Gia-como Trezzo in collaboration with the sculptors Leone and Pompeo Leoni: while the gilding of the bronze is lavish, there is minimal ornament extra-neous to the superimposed Orders framing the iconic paintings provided by Federico Zuccaro and Pellegrino Tibaldi. Behind the great entablature of the frontispiece (and sections of its columns) is the elongated library – as frescoed by Tibaldi, quite the most splendid space in the whole complex except for the basilica, its sacristy and chapterhouse.

5.49t

5.49v

5.49w

5.49z

5.49Y

5.49X

From his emergence to predominance at the site in the early 1570s, about the time the king took up residence in his temporary apartment, Herrera's involvement spanned the realization of about two-thirds of the enclosing fabric. Work began in 1573 on the northern third of the complex, destined to provide accommodation for the royal family to the east, refectories and kitchens in the centre, a seminary to the west. Construction of the church was in train in 1574 and the structure was completed in 1582, the interior two years later. The central section of the west front, containing the main entrance and the great library, was begun in 1576. Masonry of the main complex as a whole was largely complete by 1584 – though ancillary buildings would ultimately line the external concourses. In 1585 the king moved into his definitive accommodation in the adjunct framing the sanctuary, the queen into the east range of the northern sector. One year later the remains of the King-Emperor Charles, Empress Isabella and numerous other members of the family were interred in a provisional vault below the sanctuary. Though the burial crypt did not achieve its final form as the dynastic pantheon until the middle of the next century (to the design of Giovanni Battista Crescenzi), the purpose of the exercise had been fulfilled and the cycle of perpetual masses begun.

›**5.50 VALLADOLID, CATHEDRAL OF NUES-TRA SEÑORA DE LA ASUNCIÓN,** from 1578–86: (a) model, (b) plan, (c) west front, (d–f) side elevation, longitudinal and lateral sections (project drawings from Herrera's studio).

The double-square plan is thoroughly modular (in the terms of the time, the 10-foot module is the basic dimension of the square pier). There are four square corner towers but no semi-circular extrusions, and the colossal work was even to have been crowned with a square drum and dome over the central crossing. Construction directed by Diego de Praves and his son was largely from 1588: it had reached cornice level by the death of its royal patron ten years later and little more than half was to eventuate. The upper part of the west front was added by Alberto de Churriguera from 1730.

5.50b @ 1:2000

ESTILO DESORNAMENTADO AT LARGE

Various churches have been attributed to Juan de Herrera in virtue of an austere style reminiscent of S. Lorenzo de El Escorial: certainly his major authenticated excursion into the field of religious architecture also set the Philipine standard to be followed by others with varying degrees of accuracy. This was the revision of the scheme for the great cathedral of Valladolid which had been projected over a collegiate foundation as early as 1527 by Rodrigo Gil de Hontañón in his usual late-Gothic style. The scale of Hontañón cathedrals elsewhere, most notably Segovia and Salamanca, was to be sustained over the double-square plan evolved by Herrera between 1578 and 1586: directed by Diego de Praves (1556–1620), construction had reached cornice level at the death of Philip II in 1598 when it languished.**5.50**

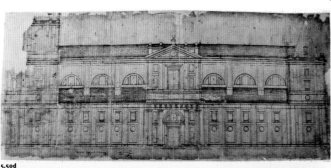

5.50d

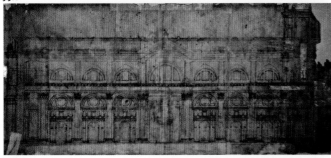

5.50e

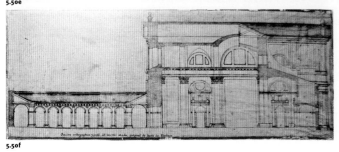

5.50f

5.50c

5.51a

5.51c

5.51b

>5.51 VALLADOLID, PLAZA MAYOR: (a, b) general views (suites of tiles representing festivities in the square before the reconstruction of the civic authority's building in the late-19th century); (c) Casa Consistorial (19th-century photograph of building begun in 1561 and augmented with a central tower in 1833).

Evolved between 1561 and 1577, the design of the Casa Consistorial (ayuntamiento) was attributed to Juan de Escalante with modifications by Herrera: it was built from 1585 by Diego de Praves who was the master's understudy at the cathedral. By 1879 it was dilapidated and replaced between 1892 and 1908.

CIVIC WORKS

Preoccupied throughout his career with El Escorial and work on the king's other palaces, Herrera was nevertheless responsible for several major civic works which established his *estilo severo* permutation of the *estilo desornamentado*. These included, above all, the plan for Madrid. The scheme was developed from Juan Bautista de Toledo's plans for rebuilding the centre of Valladolid after it was destroyed by fire in 1561: the essential element there was the rectangular Plaza Mayor which was addressed by the ayuntamiento from the north and crossed east–west by parallel arteries wide enough for efficient circulation, healthy ventilation and scenographic vistas. Realization was pursued by local architects – Francesco de Salamanca, Juan Sanz de Escalante, Juan de Nantes and Diego de

›5.52 TOLEDO, AYUNTAMIENTO, from 1574: view from north-east.

The new building of the civic authority was commissioned from Herrera in 1574: he followed the format established at Valladolid in the previous decade but supervised work only on the periphery of the ground floor with its arcaded bays framed by attached columns. Completed over the next generation, the upper floors and towers were the work of Nicolás de Vergara el Mozo, Juan Bautista Monegro, Teodoro Ardemans and El Greco's son Jorge Manuel.

Praves – overseen by Herrera.**5·51** The last then applied the broad principles as architect-in-chief on the urban planning board established for Madrid early in the 1580s. As we shall see, a revised scheme was implemented in the first decades of the new century and subsequently reworked. However, with his rationalization of the traditional Spanish porticoed main space and axial arterial colonnaded streets, Herrera's intervention in the planning of the capital provided the prototype for the urban renewal initiated by his king in Spain and its American colonies.**5·52**

5.53a

5.53b

Herrera's plan for the Lonja was executed between 1585 and 1598 by Juan de Minjares. The concept departed from the type of the single great hypostyle space – well represented in Catalonia and Aragón – in favour of perpendicular halls, reached by an imperial staircase, on the upper floors of a quadrangular building. The grandeur of the staircase and the vistas through its galleries are typical of Herrera. So too, of course, is the austerity of the external ordonnance – the doubling of the pilasters responding to loadbearing cross walls – but this is complemented by the rich variety of coffering adopted for the domical bays of the main halls.

5.53d

5.53e

5.53c

The Iglesia del Sagrario was begun by the master-mason Miguel de Zumárraga and continued after his death in 1630 by Fernando de Oviedo. The retable of the Capilla de S. Pedro in the cathedral was constructed by Diego López Bueno to hold the icons of Francisco de Zubarán: these, including the central masterpiece depicting the Assumption over the image of S. Peter as the first pontif, had been installed by 1630.

5.53f

5.53g

Herrera took his style south to Toledo. He produced the designs for the Plaza de Zocodover and the ayuntamiento but his involvement in construction was limited.**5.53** Further south, beyond the seats of the king, his major secular exercise was the Lonja of Seville (1582): instead of the traditional hypostyle hall, he provided a succession of domed galleries framing a court and served by a magnificent imperial staircase.

A late echo of Herrera's style is discernible in the Iglesia del Sagrario attached to Seville cathedral from 1618. And even within that cathedral, in the next decade, the essentially architectonic approach to the design of the great retable in S. Lorenzo de El Escorial was still current – though not without the odd Mannerist flourish. However, despite the prestige of the Lonja and its architect, the *estilo severo* failed to prevail in Andalusia.

5-55

›**5.54 TOLEDO, TAVERA HOSPITAL CHAPEL,** crossing exterior (1624).

The south largely excepted, the Philipine *estilo desorna-mentado* was widely influential – too widely for more than a summary notice here. Exemplary in the orbit of Val-

›**5.55 CIUDAD RODRIGO, CAPILLA DE CER-RALBO,** begun under the direction of Juan de Valencia in 1588: exterior from the south-east.

›**5.56 THE HERRERAN SECULAR COURT C. 1580:** (a) Alcalá de Henares, University; (b) Zafra, alcázar.

5.56a

5.56b

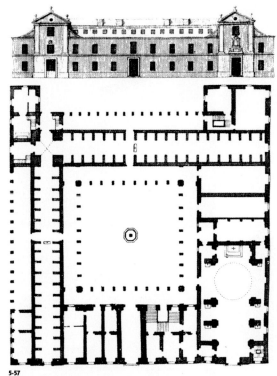

5·57

›5.57 MEDINA DEL CAMPO, HOSPITAL, from 1593: plan and main elevation (17th-century record).

The complex, founded by the banker Simón Ruiz, was begun by Juan de Tolosa in 1593 and finished by Juan de Nates from 1598.

›5.58 VILLAGARCÍA DE CAMPOS, S. LUIS: west front (after 1580).

The church served the Jesuit college founded by Doña Magdalena de Ulloa, widow of Don Luis de Quijada, tutor of John of Austria, the natural son of King-Emperor Charles.

ladolid is the hospital at Medina del Campo, attributed to Juan de Tolosa, and the church of S. Luis at Villagarcía de Campos attributed to Pedro de Tolosa who was the master-mason at El Escorial under both Juan Bautista de Toledo and Juan de Herrera.**5·57, 5·58** Further west, the Capilla de Cerralbo in Ciudad Rodrigo may be singled out as another representative of ecclesiastical works built to Herrera's plans or in his style.**5·55** In Toledo, Nicolás de Vergara el Mozo (c. 1540–1606) and Juan Bautista Monegro furthered work on the ayuntamiento, the cathedral's chapel of the Virgen del Sagrario, the church of S. Pedro Martír and the revision of Bustamante's chapel of the Tavera hospital – which sustained the *estilo desornamentado* in the extreme when built by Hernán González de Lara from 1624.**5·54** In Alcalá, the Sangallan ordonnance of El Escorial's Courtyard of the Evangelists reappears with less gravity in the great court of the university. Another variant of that formula, the patio inserted into the alcázar at Zafra for the Duke of Feria is a fine example of work commissioned by grandees close to the court and therefore able to prevail upon the royal architect at least for a sketch.**5·56**

5·58

5.59b

5.59a

5.59c

ASCENDANCY OF THE MORA

Herrera was succeeded in the late-1580s by Francisco de Mora (1553–1610): trained at El Escorial from 1579, he was primarily involved with the ancillary buildings, notably the main service building known as the Casa de la Compaña (from 1593). With the capital relocated at Valladolid in 1601, he was engaged on the extensive refurbishment of the royal palace and several residences for grandees there, notably for Fabio Nelli, an important banker of Sienese origin (born 1533), to whom the court was indebted.**5.59, 5.60**

The new king and queen commissioned Francisco de Mora to build churches for the convents of the Discalced Carmelites (thenceforward the Descalzas Reales) at Valladolid and Ávila: the latter is the finest example of the

›5.59 CARMELITE WORKS OF FRANCISCO DE MORA: (a, b) Valladolid, the Descalzas Reales, exterior and interior; (c) Ávila, S. José, façade (from 1607).

The Valladolid church is a simple hall of four bays with a dome before the sanctuary. The Herreran retable is due to Gregorio Fernández (c. 1612).

›5.60 VALLADOLID, POST-HERRERAN FAÇADES: (a) Vera Cruz (from 1595); (b) S. Agustin (c. 1619); (c) Palace of Fabio Nelli (Juan de la Lastra, Pedro de Mazuecos and Diego de Praves; from 1576 and 1595).

5.60a

kind; the former was completed after the return of the court to Madrid by Diego de Praves. Principally responsible for furthering work on Herrera's great cathedral and ayuntamiento, Diego depended on the master in his several independent works, notably the façades of the basilican Vera Cruz and Augustinian churches (from 1595 and 1619 respectively). Incorporating the triumphal-arch motif, the centres of both these works relate to the frontispieces of Herrera's cathedral. Well into the 17th century too, retable design was often centralized on superimposed triumphal-arch motifs when it progressed beyond a regularly repetitive ordonnance. 5.27f, 5.37g, 5 59h, 5 63e

5.60b

5.60c

5.61a

5.61b

›**5.61 LERMA:** (a, b) ducal palace (1601–17), view from river and town plaza; (c) the Dominican convent church of S. Blas (from 1613).

5.61c

Apart from the royal projects at Valladolid, Francisco de Mora's major work was for Philip III's favourite, Francisco Gómez de Sandoval (1552–1625), Duke of Lerma, at his eponymous seat. That exercise (begun in 1601) was revised and completed by Francisco's nephew and pupil, Juan Gómez de Mora (1586–1648). It was linked by a passage to the collegiate church of S. Pedro Apostol and shared the plaza with the Dominican convent of S. Blas: the Mora are credited with the construction of the latter (from 1613) and the renovation of the former (consecrated 1616). **5.61**

5.62a

5.62b

›**5.62 MADRID, MONASTERIO DE LA ENCAR-NACIÓN,** from 1611: (a) exterior, (b) interior.

›**5.63 ALCALA DE HERNARES:** (a–c) Bernardas church (from 1618), section, plan and interior detail; (d, e) S. María la Mayor (formerly the Jesuit church, from 1602), exterior and interior.

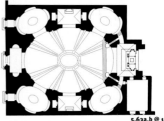

5.63a,b @ 1:500

5.63c

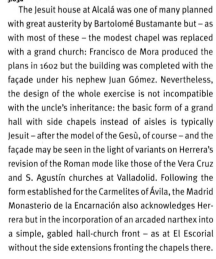

5.63d

The Jesuit house at Alcalá was one of many planned with great austerity by Bartolomé Bustamante but – as with most of these – the modest chapel was replaced with a grand church: Francisco de Mora produced the plans in 1602 but the building was completed with the façade under his nephew Juan Gómez. Nevertheless, the design of the whole exercise is not incompatible with the uncle's inheritance: the basic form of a grand hall with side chapels instead of aisles is typically Jesuit – after the model of the Gesù, of course – and the façade may be seen in the light of variants on Herrera's revision of the Roman mode like those of the Vera Cruz and S. Agustín churches at Valladolid. Following the form established for the Carmelites of Ávila, the Madrid Monasterio de la Encarnación also acknowledges Herrera but in the incorporation of an arcaded narthex into a simple, gabled hall-church front – as at El Escorial without the side extensions fronting the chapels there.

5.63e

Several ecclesiastical works, including the Jesuit church in Alcalá de Henares, are variously attributed to the Mora – uncle, nephew or both. In his earliest independent work, the Madrid Monasterio de la Encarnación (from 1611), the nephew acknowledges the influence of the uncle's S. José in Ávila – at least for the façade – but before the decade was out he had made a novel excursion of Roman inspiration for the Bernardas church of Alcalá de Henares – in the elliptical plan if not the austerity (see page 292).**5.62, 5.63** At the same time El Escorial derivation is still plain in works like the vast Jesuit college at Salamanca (La Clerecía): naturally, the church of that great complex is of the Gesù type (see page 184).**5.64** Closely related to the latter, S. Ildefonso at Toledo is attributed primarily to Juan Bautista de Monegro, master-builder of the cathedral, and the Jesuit brother Pedro Sánchez (from 1629). The façades of both these important Counter-Reformation works belong to another era and will be dealt with in that context.

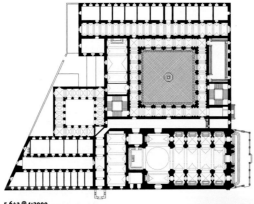

5.64a @ 1:2000

›**5.64 SALAMANCA, LA CLERECÍA,** from 1617: (a) plan, (b) exterior of monastic buildings, (c) south transept front, (d) interior of church, (e) detail of dome.

The former Royal College of the Holy Spirit of the Society of Jesus was founded under the auspices of Margaret of Austria, Phillip III's queen, reputedly in atonement for the Inquisition's incarceration of S. Ignatius Loyola in the cathedral tower. Juan Gómez was responsible at least for the distribution of the main elements on which work began in 1617. On the suppression of the Society in 1767, the complex was assigned to the clergy of S. Marcos (from which it takes its popular name) and was subsequently occupied by the Pontifical University.

5.64b

5.64c

5.64e

5.64d

Juan Gómez had succeeded Francisco as principal royal architect early in 1611. His work on the palaces included the renovation of the Madrid Alcázar, the revision of Herrera's plans for Aranjuez and continuation of the ancillary

5.65a

5.56b

The regular geometry essential to the *estilo desornamentado* was the ideal governing Herrera's intervention in the planning of Madrid but it was unrealizable by the late 1580s. The settlement of the court there had led to a population explosion (from c. 2500 in 1560 to some 15,000 sixty years later). This entailed rapid unplanned expansion east of the alcázar as westward growth was inhibited by the precipitous fall of the site to the River Manzanares. By the mid-16th century some order had been introduced to the southern sector with the construction of the Plaza de S. Salvador (later de la

5.65c

Villa) as punctuation to the main east–west artery, the Calle Mayor, but further south the Calle de Segovia led out to the main western bridge from organic confusion.

South of the widened westward extension of the Calle Mayor, Herrera planned to insert a divided plaza into an incomplete grid crossed to the east of the north–south axis by the first stretch of the road to Toledo and diagonally by the main south-east artery. Implementation was slow before the death of the king in 1598 and halted with the removal of Philip III's court to Valladolid in 1601: it waited another decade after the court's return in 1606. Then Juan Gómez de Mora's revision concentrated on the rectangular main part, the

buildings at El Escorial. However, he was primarily responsible for the realization – and inevitable revision – of the scheme for the Plaza Mayor in Madrid inherited through his uncle from Herrera. His other civic works included the conception, at least, of the capital's Cárcel de Corte (court gaol) and Casas Consistoriales (town hall) – where, as elsewhere, Alonso Carbonell (1583–1660) was the executive master. With these works, especially the urban projects for Madrid, the *estilo desornamentado* was sustained well into the reign of Philip IV (1621–65).**5.65**

5.65d

5.65e

Plaza Mayor, which retained its original perimeter defined by buildings uniform in the repetitiveness of their articulation – like Vignola's work at Bologna. The dominant building on the site had been the Casa de la Panadería where, as the name asserts, bread was produced. Its replacement retained the name but accommodated the king and his entourage when they came to witness major civic events: the association of king with bounty hardly needs explaining.

The Cárcel de Corte façade is a reduced revision of the south front of the Alcázar then being elevated by Juan Gómez. The latter is now generally credited with the design against the insubstantiated attribution to Giovanni Battista Crescenzi: Carbonell, master of works, collaborated with José de Villareal and others after the dismissal of Juan Gómez in 1636.

The project for the capital's ayuntamiento, the Casas Consistoriales, follows the prototypical form of its equivalent in Toledo but reiterates Herrera's abstract ordonnance. Juan Gómez is credited with the design which was probably conceived c. 1630 but executed from c. 1644: after his death in 1648 the work was furthered by Carbonell as master-mason in collaboration with José de Villareal. The Tuscan colonnade on the Calle Mayor façade was added by Teodoro Ardemans in 1696.

›**5.66 MADRID, THE ROYAL PALACE OF BUEN RETIRO:** (a, b) plan and overview c. 1640, (c) garden context (Teixeira, 1656).

The royal quarters of the Monastery of S. Jerónimo el Real, built from 1561 for Philip II by Juan Bautista de Toledo, were occupied by the young Philip IV in the first month of his reign and occasionally thereafter as a place of religious retreat or the starting point of royal entries into the capital. After the birth of Prince Baltasar-Carlos late in 1629, the apartment was amplified to accommodate the nuclear royal family during the ceremony of homage to the future king. That took place early in 1632 and by mid-year it had been decided to develop the complex into a palatial villa set in an extensive park: perpendicular wings framing gardens, with zoo and aviary, had materialized by the end of 1633. Thereafter further dependencies were added somewhat haphazardly until 1640 when the complex

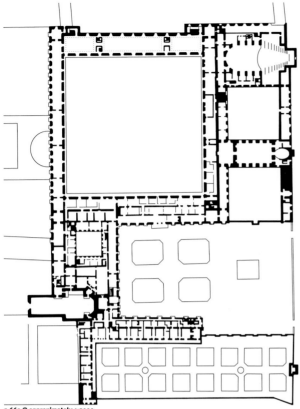

5.66a @ approximately 1:2000

PHILIPPINE POSTLUDE

At El Escorial, particularly in the royal burial crypt below the sanctuary of the great basilica, Juan Gómez had to collaborate with the immigrant Roman decorator Giovanni Battista Crescenzi (1577–1635) – whom he despised but who was preferred by the prime minister, the Count-Duke of Olivares, perhaps because the Moras were associated with the fallen Duke of Lerma. Crescenzi was also entrusted with the development of Philip IV's new Buen Retiro palace in the curtilage of S. Jerónimo on the eastern edge of the capital (from 1633). Furthered by Alonso Carbonell as master of works, that extravagant exercise in monastic extension for royal retreat also sustained the *estilo desornamentado* – at least on the much-derided exterior of the wings framing the main court. At the instigation of Olivares, impatient in his determination to glorify his patron, these were built in haste mainly of humble brick: their shortcomings were to be obliterated by the magnificence of the interior and Diego Velázquez, in particular, served the cause with unsurpassed genius.**5.66**

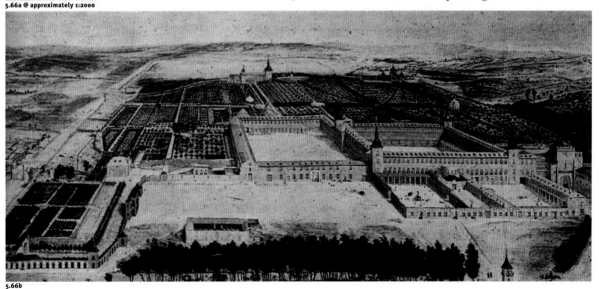

5.66b

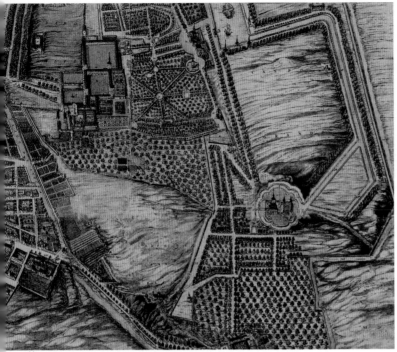

5.66c

embraced the open garden court partly formed in 1633 and two large enclosed courts to its north for tournaments, bullfights and other grand public festivities: these were overlooked from the main royal reception room, the Salón de Reinos (Hall of the Kingdoms) in the intermediate wing. As dependencies of the central court's east wing, moreover, a ballroom and theatre had been added from 1637. The gardens also proliferated rapidly, and no less haphazardly without the controlling conception of an integrated whole: by 1640 there were canals, a lake, an orchard, a ball-court, a riding school and numerous hermitages for both religious and secular retreat – that is, for meditation and for picnics.

The brick exterior is relieved only by stone for the frames of doors and windows. In compensation, the interior was endowed with a major art collection: in particular, paintings were commissioned from Rubens and the leading masters of Rome, including Claude Lorrain, Nicolas Poussin and Giovanni Lanfranco. For the long side walls of the Salón de Reinos a commemorative series of Spanish military triumphs was commissioned from the leading Spanish artists, including Francisco de Zuburán and Diego Velázquez: the former produced a stunning series of the labours of Hercules to hang between the major battle scenes; the greatest of the latter was 'The Surrender of Breda'. Velázquez also rose supremely to the occasion with his two pairs of royal equestrian portraits – the king and his queen (Elizabeth of France) and his parents (Philip III and Margaret of Austria) – which were hung on the end walls. The palace was unprogressive in style but the greatest of its paintings belong to a new era (and will be dealt with accordingly).

After fire ravaged the Madrid Alcázar in 1734, king and court were based primarily at Buen Retiro until the new palace on the Alcázar site was ready for them to occupy in 1764. The poor quality of the old building led to rapid dilapidation and it barely survived occupation by the French army from 1808.

Juan Gómez fell from grace in 1636 – in the shade of prime-ministerial disfavour – which cloaked the machinations of Crescenzi. As the latter had not lived to see his triumph complete, the post of principal royal architect was given to Diego de Praves's son Francisco who had translated the first of Palladio's *Quattro Libri* and dedicated it to the count-duke. After the new master's death within a year, the vacuum was mainly filled by Carbonell until 1643 when Olivares fell: Juan Gómez was then reinstated. In his place, meanwhile, Carbonell played a considerable part in furthering the main projects of his erstwhile superiors. The Cárcel de Corte and Casas Consistoriales apart, these included a hunting lodge in the park of El Pardo, known as La Zarzuela, which was destined to become the favoured residence of later kings.**5.67** They also included the prescribed residence of the deceased kings.

›5.67 EL PARDO, THE ROYAL HUNTING
LODGE OF LA ZARZUELA: entrance-front project
(1634).

Juan Gómez was the architect with Carbonell as executive master, as usual: the latter took control during the former's disgrace. The building contract was let in 1635, roofing began two years later and the gardens were also being planted then. Interior decoration was dominated by a suite of landscapes and hunting scenes provided by assistants of Rubens in Antwerp. The building has been much altered, particularly by its expansion into a palace for King Charles IV in the late-18th century and again in reconstruction after severe damage in the civil war of the 1930s.

The royal burial crypt – the 'Pantheon' – below the sanctuary of the basilica at El Escorial had been replanned by Crescenzi as an octagon for embellishment in marble and gilt bronze. Not inappropriately – if not particularly brilliantly – the work departed from the *estilo desornamentado* in favour of proto-Baroque opulence: completed under Carbonell's supervision in 1654, it marked a turning point in official taste which was to be of great appeal – not least, of course, to ecclesiastical patrons.**5.68**

5.68a

5.68b

›5.68 EL ESCORIAL, ROYAL BURIAL CRYPT
(PANTHEON): (a) north–south section after the design of Giovanni Battista Crescenzi (engraved by Pedro de Villafranca, 1654), (b) view of south range.

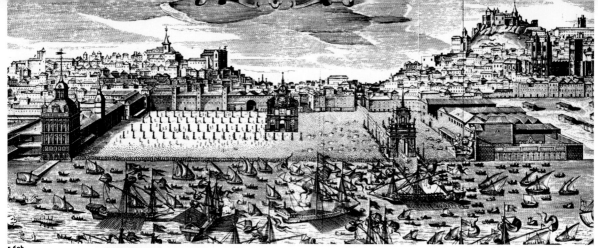

5.69b

5.69a

5 PORTUGAL DURING THE HABSBURG INTERREGNUM

The *estilo desornamentado* penetrated into Portugal – or rather, it contributed added gravitas to the *estilo chão* already prevalent. Juan de Herrera and Francisco de Mora were in Lisbon in the train of Philip II who went there in 1580 to mount the Portuguese throne which he had inherited on the death of his childless nephew, Dom Sebastian (1554–78?), in ill-conceived crusade against the Moors in North Africa. The Spanish architects were to be supported by the Bolognese immigrant Jesuit Filippo Terzi, a military engineer under contract to the defunct regime.

The major ecclesiastical work of the new era was the Augustinian monastery of S. Vicente de Fora. Herrera

›5.69 LISBON, SECULAR WORKS FOR THE HABSBURG SUCCESSION: (a–d) Paço da Ribeira in the early 16th century, after 1581 (engraved and in tiles, pages 638–639), and after damage in the earthquake of 1755; (e–g) simulated triumphal arches erected to mark the state entry of Philip III (1619) by the Italian nation, the mintworkers and the Flemish nation.

On his arrival in Lisbon, Philip II commissioned Filippo Terzi to build a palace in the capital's central riverine defence complex where Dom Manuel I had a pavilion rising from the battered masonry: the new end pavilion of five bays terminated a lower wing stretching inland from the river. The precise configuration of the Manueline complex is unknown but Terzi was doubtless constrained by it: neither the form nor its context is precedented in Spain. Moreover, the extraordinary square dome of the main block suggests awareness of late developments in France – specifically at the château of Verneuil where, as recorded by du Cerceau, the corner pavilions contained apartments.[2.48c,d]

5.69d

5.69e–g

The state entry of Philip III into Lisbon in 1619 was modelled on those accorded to his predecessors by the burghers of Flanders in quest of confirmation of their privileges and, as we have seen, there were important modern and medieval French precedents. The simulated triumphal arches are mainly Flemish in their prolixity of ornament – though that was matched by the festive works of the late-Valois and even by the early royal commissions of Henri IV's regime, as we have also seen. The mintworkers' variant betrays the seduction of the du Cerceaux (in works like the court front of the château of Charleval) but it is also almost worthy of a latter-day Italian Mannerist in its artfully unresolved conflict between the integrity of the whole and the discretion of the parts: the pedimented aedicules supported by the twin columns of each pier assert vertical continuity at the sides while horizontal linkage across the largely void centre is left solely to the recessed cornice moulding.

produced the first project of its great church at his master's instigation: it followed the fully developed scheme of Alberti's masterpiece at Mantua, with rhythmic bays and domed crossing (AIC4, page 750). Schooled by the king's principal Spanish architect, Terzi was appointed to corresponding responsibilities as master of the royal works in Lisbon in which capacity he rebuilt Dom Manuel I's palace by the river, the Paço da Ribeira (from 1581). Naturally he had the assistance of the native architects, notably Baltasar Álvares (Alfonso's nephew, active c. 1570– 1620).**5.69, 5.70**

THE PALATIAL CHURCH AND THE ESTILO CHÃO

S. Vicente's twin-towered three-storey façade is of the 'palace' type: its articulation with superimposed Orders defining the five bays of its two coterminous storeys is

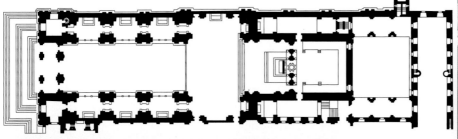

5.70a @ 1:1000

5.70b

5.70c

›5.70 LISBON, S. VICENTE, built from 1582 in place of the mid-12th-century Romanesque church which was the prime monument of the Reconquest: (a) plan, (b) south flank to cloister, (c) west front (finished 1629), (d) interior of nave, (e) crossing, (f) sanctuary.

Baltasar Álvares apart, Portuguese architects involved with Filippo Terzi have been identified as Leonardo Turriano and the brothers Pedro and João Nunes Tinoco. Álvares is given prime credit for the execution of the façade: developed from the Portuguese late-medieval tradition with limited variation in plane and the regular repetition of dry academic Classical detailing, it provided the prototype for many successors in Portugal and Brazil. As to the basilica at El Escorial – and earlier works like S. Mamede or Nossa Senhora da Graça at Évora – entrance is through a narthex sotocoro. Alberti's S. Andrea at Mantua is closely followed in the great tunnel-vaulted interior, with its arcaded chapels separated by twin pilasters: these are hardly less severe than those of the work at El Escorial but their capitals are uncanonical and the frieze of paired brackets alternating with triglyph blocks derives from Serlio. That variarion responds to projection of the frieze (but not the cornice) over the pilasters in support of the flattened transverse arches which provided zones of variation in the coffering of the vault: beyond that, the bracketed dome is quite idiosyncratic. A retrochoir is entered from either side of the high altar as in Palladio's S. Giorgio Maggiore in Venice.[1.79b] Beyond is the royal necropolis.

Terzi is also reputed to have worked for the Augustinians on the centralized church of Serra do Pilar at Oporto and on the Misericórdia at Coimbra where the model for his cloister was Diogo de Torralva's masterpiece at Tomar.

5.70d

5.70e

5.70f

›ARCHITECTURE IN CONTEXT »FROM THE HIGH RENAISSANCE TO MANNERISM

clearly related to Terzi's work on the palace. Reduced to three bays of one great storey and an attic, the formula was, of course, that of the triumphal arch. Appropriately enough, it was the Italian community which demonstrated this most clearly in their contribution to the series of simulated monuments marking the stages of Philip III's state entry into his Lusitanian capital in 1619.**5.69d**

The 'palace' mode of church façade was widely adopted in the homeland and Brazil: its somewhat dry Classicism, limited in its planar variation, admitted a considerable

5.72a

5.72b

›**5.71 PORTALEGRE CATHEDRAL:** (a) interior to sanctuary, (b) west front (from 1581?);

›**5.72 PERMUTATIONS OF THE TWIN-TOWERED FAÇADE IN THE ESTILO CHÃO:** (a, b) Lisbon, S. Catarina dos Livreiros (from 1572), section and west front; (c) Vila Viçosa, Augustinian church (from 1635 to the 1680s).

Entrance to a narthex below a choir gallery was common – if not invariable – well before the era of El Escorial. Entrance directly into the church was normally through triple portals as to S. Antão in Évora or the cathedrals at Leiria and Portalegre. More engaging was the triple-arch narthex of Terzi's S. Vicente or the alternative serliana of works like S Mamede in Évora, S. Maria da Graça in Setubal or S. Catarina dos Livreiros in Lisbon (and many other churches). Instead, the anonymous Braganza basilica of the Augustinians in Vila Viçosa has a single great arch supporting the choir gallery like a bridge: similar examples include Viseu cathedral (after 1635) and Nossa Senhora do Carmo (c. 1670) in Évora. Towers – rarely absent – may project to frame the façade (as in the examples illustrated here), they may be in the same plane (as in the major Jesuit works) or they may be recessed (as in the major Benedictine works).

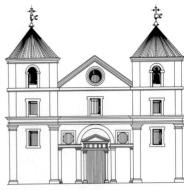

5.72a, b

degree of elaboration. It is at its most robust in its early manifestation at Portalegre. the cathedral there may precede S. Vicente but Herrera was at the site early in 1581, long before the building was nearing completion. Variations of scale and assertiveness range across many works from Alfonso Álvares's lost church of S. Catarina dos Livreiros (Lisbon, 1572) to the mid-17th-century Augustinian church of Vila Viçosa, the later-17th century Nossa Senhora do Carmo at Évora and beyond.**5.72, 5.72**

5.72c

5.73a

5.73b

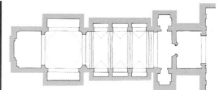

5.73c @ 1:1000

›**5.73 ÉVORA, CARMELITE COMMISSIONS IN THE MATURE ESTILO CHÃO:** (a–c) Nossa Senhora do Carmo (from 1670), interior, entrance front and plan; (d) Remédios convent church of the Discalced Order (from 1601), view from south-east.

The Remédios church in Évora is attributed to Francisco de Mora, and has the severity of the late-16th-century Herreran School. Viewed from the sunken forecourt, the façade of Nossa Senhora do Carmo is palatial: it was built on the site of a Braganza palace and retains the latter's portal beyond the great narthex arch. The vaulted hall overlooked by galleries recalls the Espírito Santo (in the same town) but the shallow chapels are not interconnected.

5.73d

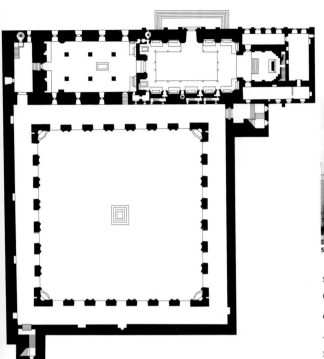

›5.74 ÉVORA, S. CLARA-A-NOVA (from 1649:
(a) longitudinal entrance front to street , (b) plan.

5.74a

The Carmelites were active across the generation spanned by their unattributed churches at Coimbra and Oporto (from 1597 and 1619) or their Discalced Sisters' convent church of the Remédios in Évora (from 1601). Attributed to Francesco de Mora, that plain work is related in style to S. Clara-a-Nova in the same city: entered on the long street front through twin Herreran portals below powerful buttresses, the latter stands as a prime example of planning for an enclosed female order with public space interposed between the nuns' choir and the sanctuary. Repeated for the Carmelites of Coimbra, the approach was common in Iberia and its colonies.**5.73, 5.74**

The *estilo chão* is nowhere plainer than on the exterior of the important Lisbon suburban church of S. Domingos de Benfica (generally unattributed and insecurely dated to the late-16th century). A hall with side chapels, domed crossing and retrochoir, its conception is rather Venetian than Roman – and that was uncharacteristic of Portuguese architecture. The mainly rectilinear plain surfaces are relieved only with abstract pilaster strips at the corners and moderate embellishment to window or portal frames – notably the variation on the thermal-window type which

›5.75 LISBON, BENFICA, S. DOMINGOS, late-16th century?, restored after the earthquake of 1755: (a) west portal, (b) exterior from south-east, (c) interior from nave through screen to retrochoir.

The date and the degree of post-earthquake rebuilding have eluded determination. Unusually in Portugal, the extension of the plan beyond the broad nave into an elongated sanctuary and retrochoir recalls such Venetian works as Sansovino's S. Francesco della Vigna or – as it is vaulted over a thermal window – even the great screened churches of Palladio.

5.75c

›5.76 BENEDICTINE COMMISSIONS IN THE MATURE ESTILO CHÃO: (a) Lisbon, S. Bento (from 1598); (b) Oporto, S. Bento da Vitoria (from 1604), general view in context; (c) Coimbra, S. Bento (from 1634), plan; (d) S. Tirso abbey church (1659–79), façade.

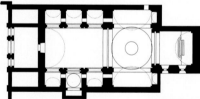

5.76c @ 1:1000

lights the retrochoir from the east. Inside blue and white tiles provide visual – if not tactile – relief in the manner idiosyncratic to Portugal but rare there is the spectacular gilt serliana which screens the monks' choir from the sanctuary in distant homage to Palladio.**5.75**

The continuing emphasis on single-nave volumes largely absolved the Portuguese from wrestling with the problem of designing a unified Classical façade for the compound basilican form. Thus, despite the retention of

The Lisbon church – begun c. 1615 but destroyed in clearing the site for the parliament building in 1876 – is credited to Filippo Terzi and Baltasar Álvares: nearer to home than Palladio – or even Antique Rome – the gable's thermal window most probably came from Genoa via El Escorial. Founded in 1576 and 1598 respectively, ostensibly under the direction of the Álvares uncle and nephew, the Coimbra and Oporto works were furthered from 1604 by Diogo Marques

5.76a

5.76b

Lucas who had trained with Terzi and Álvares. Baltasar's Lisbon façade scheme was developed, in receding stages with Italianate volutes, for the Oporto work on the completion of the nave in the mid-1640s. The early medieval abbey church of S. Tirso, the headquarters of the order in Portugal, was rebuilt on the Lisbon lines by the Milanese Fra Giovanni Turriano.

5.76d

side chapels, they usually ignored the various Italian modes and produced their own variants of the palace-façade type rising to the height of the nave throughout – often, but not always, between twin towers. The Benedictines preferred coterminous superimposed Orders with a great thermal window, above all, to admit the maximum top lighting through towerless fronts on narrow streets.**5.76** The principal survivor is S. Bento da Vitoria in Oporto, attributed to Baltasar Álvares's pupil Diogo Marques Lucas: it recalls earlier Évoran efforts like the Espirito Santo, with its fenestrated galleries, and S. Mamede with its choir tribune over the narthex. The similar work in Lisbon, attributed to Álvares, is lost – except in engraved records. Among the variants, the Benedictine abbey churches at Tibaes and S. Tirso (begun 1628 and 1679 respectively) may be singled out. The façade of the original Carmelite church in Oporto (begun 1619) belongs to the same type but it was altered in the mid-18th century during the construction of its neighbour for the Carmelites' third (lay) order – as we shall see.

5.77a

JESUIT STYLE

The Counter-Reformation orders inspired vigorous campaigns of new building – or renovation – in the first decades of the 17th century.**5.77** The domed crossing of the Roman Gesù (pages 184f)– and the ideal completion of the Mantuan S. Andrea (AIC4, page 749) – adopted by Herrera and Terzi for S. Vicente de Fora, were often repeated by the Portuguese, especially in large-scale works. The Jesuit architect – possibly Baltasar Álvares – came closest to the ideal emanating from the order's Roman headquarters at Coimbra (from 1598 in the former Colégio das Onze Mil Virgens, now the Sé Nova), Oporto (S. Lourenço, known popularly as 'Grilos', from 1614) and Lisbon (S. Antão from 1613, destroyed). The façades of both surviving works – and their several relatives – substantiate innovative variations on the palace type: a triad of pediments crowning overlapping attic bays before or between twin towers distinguishes the Sé Nova of Coimbra and the Grilos of Oporto.**5.77b–f** While the latter was under construction, the formula was adopted by the mintworkers for their contribution to Philip III's entry into Lisbon.**5.69d**

›5.77 JESUIT DEVELOPMENTS FROM THE ESTILO CHÃO: (a) Vila Viçosa, S. Bartolemeu (formerly S. João Baptista, begun 1635), portico; (b, c) Coimbra, the former Colégio das Onze Mil Virgens, now the Sé Nova (from 1598), west front and plan; (d–f) Oporto, S. Lourenço ('Grilos', from 1614), plan, west front and interior; (g) Santarém, Seminário (1676), west front; (h) Ponta Delgada (Azores), Collegiate church of Todos-os-Santos (from 1657, façade from 1740), west front.

The influence of Herrera, through Terzi, is apparent in the unattributed, incompletely resolved work at Vila Viçosa. The plans for both the Sé Nova of Coimbra and S. Lourenço at Oporto are generally attributed to

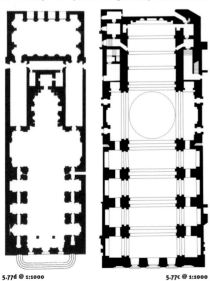

5.77d @ 1:1000   5.77c @ 1:1000   5.77b

5.77e

5.77f

Baltasar Álvares, the former under the influence of Terzi's S. Vicente but without the heterodox detail of the latter's interior. In both cases, however, the building history is far from complete. Responsibility for the radical change of style above the main cornice of the Coimbra façade has yet to be determined. The projection of the superimposed Orders of the Oporto work is bold throughout – suggesting unbroken responsibility.

As we have noted, the arch erected by the mintworkers for the royal entry of 1619 may be related to various works published by J.-A. du Cerceau in his *Les plus excellents bastiments de France* (1576): the central zone, largely void, was devoid even of a residual Order. That arch and the great Jesuit façades of Coimbra and Oporto were essentially different in this respect: both the latter are crowned with central pediments (precociously double-curved) carried on putative Orders rising from the inner pilasters of the lateral aedicules. Heterodox Antique precedent for syncopation in ordonnance (projection of the entablature of an upper Order over a recession in the entablature of a lower Order) is provided by the Library of Celsus at Ephesos and elsewhere in Ionia (AIC1, pages 603f). A modern precedent was provided by S. Giorgio dei Greci in Venice: whether or not the Greek community in Venice – or its architect –

5.77g

5.77h

knew of ancient Ephesos, a variant was ready to hand in the Porta dei Borsari at Verona. How any of this may have been known to Baltasar Álvares is not determinable but the eclecticism of both the Coimbra and Oporto works suggest the intervention of a well-travelled Jesuit collaborator.

The structure of the Jesuit church in Ponta Delgada was finished in the 1670s but funds were not available for furnishing the interior or articulating the façade until the first quarter of the new century: the gilding of the sculpture in the sanctuary was incomplete when the order was suppressed in 1769.

Responsibility for the Portuguese Jesuit style has yet to be conclusively determined. The colossal Tuscan Order of the Oporto and Coimbra works recalls S. Vicente but there is no arcaded narthex and the bold strapwork of the Grilos's volutes betray an awareness of northern pattern-book Mannerism quite foreign to the great Augustinian commission in Lisbon. Exaggeration of the volutes is furthered in the later related church of the Jesuit seminary at Santarém (1676).**5.77g** The latter's great hall conforms to the Jesuit's Lisbon prototype, S. Roque, with its colossal Order of Doric pilasters and its balustraded tribunes, but variations on the Roman Gesù model were preferred for the Grilos and at Coimbra – not without Terzian severity. An even simpler variant was adopted by the order in the 1650s for their collegiate church in Ponta Delgada (Azores): the palace-type façade, not completed until the mid-18th century, combines extravagant volutes with the thermal window characteristic of earlier Benedictine works.**5.77h**

The mintworkers' arch cedes little to its northern models in prolixity of ornament, as did few of its companion pieces – the Flemish nation's contribution in particular, of course. Though they draw back from outright flirtation with syncopation in the articulation of load and support, the mintworkers seem to have been aware of Italian Mannerist games with structural logic – like the 'Grilos' exercise. That is rare, however. The logic of Bramante's rhythmic bay prevails in most of 1619's other ephemeral entry arches and the church façades which follow them in the next generation: the three-storey pile forming the west front of Viseu cathedral is a prominent example but in it, significantly, Franco-Flemish Mannerist exuberance is subjected to a measure of Herreran discipline and there is not the slightest awareness of the major stylistic development then under way in Rome.**5.78**

RETABLES

Naturally the several approaches to the design of Philip III's arches, High Renaissance or Mannerist in style, are well represented in the retables of the following decades. The norm had been the canonical superimposition of Orders framing iconic panels, as in Spain: repetitive in its rhythms, a rare example from late in the 16th century is the work by Gaspar and Domingos Coelho which dominates the sanctuary of Portalegre cathedral.**5.72a** An even rarer survivor of Lisbon's 1755 catastrophe, the high altarpiece of S. Roque (late-1620s) is an outstanding example incorporating the triumphal-arch motif for its varied rhythm.**5.79a** A decade later, the earliest chapel altars in the same church further varied the theme.**5.79b,c** Beyond that, variation in plane and elevation is announced in works like the high altar of Nossa Senhora do Carmo in Évora in the 1630s: the projection of repeated columns carrying arches reiterated as aureoles was to be characteristically Portuguese.

5.78

›5.78 VISEU, CATHEDRAL: façade (from 1635).

The retable façade is attributed to Juan Moreno from Salamanca: it was inserted into the late-medieval context after storm damage.

›5.79 FROM HIGH RENAISSANCE TO PROTO-BAROQUE IN THE RETABLES OF S. ROQUE, LISBON: (a) high altar, (b) S. Anthony, (c) S. Roque.

The church of S. Roque survived the 1755 earthquake largely unscathed: its superb set of altarpieces constitute an invaluable record of developments in architectural embellishment over the century from the late-1630s when most of them were first installed. The chapels of S. Anthony and S. Francis Xavier (opposite one another in the second bay of the right and left flank respectively) represent the mid-17th-century transition from superimposed aedicules to the single Order of a proscenium: the former is the richer, with residual Mannerism in the pediment, but has been restored several times since the earthquake. The chapel enshrining S.

Roque (in the third bay right) represents an early stage of Solomonic embellishment in gold on white.

The first of the Solomonic series in S. Roque may be seen as proto-Baroque. It would be churlish not to go further in the definition of its followers, the most spectacular members of the series: the first on the right flank dedicated to 'Our Lady of the Doctrine', the one enshrining the image of the Assumption (now dedicated to the Sacrament) further along the south flank, and the one dedicated to piety – the most overtly theatrical conception. As all these were extensively embellished in the age of gold initiated by Dom João V soon after his accession in 1706, they will be revisited in that context – as will the most valuable of all the chapels, the one commissioned by the king himself late in his reign and dedicated to S. John the Baptist.

›5.80 COIMBRA, SÉ NOVA: (a, b) mid-17th-century side-chapel altar retables.

5.79b,c

And, of course, variation invited Mannerist complexity, if not wilful ambiguity, in the relationship between load and support – as in the various mid-century altarpieces in the Sé Nova at Coimbra.**5.80**

5.80a

5.80b

5.81a

PALACES

Over the sixty years of Spanish Habsburg rule, Filippo
Terzi's elementary grid was not to cede to foreign fashion
in the articulation of the grandest of palace fronts, like the
one at Vila Viçosa from which the Duke of Braganza, João

5.81b

IV, emerged to take the crown from Philip III. There was limited spatial variety, but the grandest rooms were rectangular and followed the Portuguese precedent of plain walls supporting the canted coves of timber ceilings painted with heraldic devices, historic figures or even the illusionistic extension of space.**5.81, 5.82**

Mannerism may have infiltrated the church façade, especially for the Jesuits, but the *estilo chão* continued to inform domestic architecture in general, except for portals: two mid-17th examples from the upper echelons of

›5.81 VILA VIÇOSA, BRAGANZA PALACE, begun 1512, extended north from 1537, south from 1571, renovated from 1706: (a) façade detail of revetment (1601), (b) principal audience chamber with traditional canted timber ceiling (dynastic images added for João V by the Italian Domenico Dupra in the early 18th century), (c) re-evocation of 17th-century garden.

5.81c

5.82a

5.82b

5.82c

mid-17th century society, the Azurara and Almada palaces, retain pilasters only at the corners despite the latter's much greater extent. Façades of town houses tended to conform to the line of street or square. Suburban or country residences often had wings framing an entrance court, like the grandest French houses of town or country. Prominent examples on the former outskirts of the

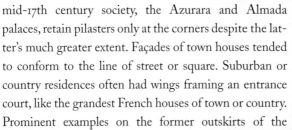

5.82d

5.82e

›5.82 LISBON, MID-17TH CENTURY PALACES: (a–c) Azurara (now Museum of Decorative Arts): entrance front, dining room and bedroom; (d, e) Almada (now Independence Palace), entrance front and courtyard.

The Almada portal incorporates the piano nobile window in the manner familiar in Spain at least since the era of Roderigo Gil de Hontañón: the rather later heraldic formula developed by Covarrubias in the spirit of Serlio is followed for Azurara. The Piedade church at Santarém is among several mid-17th-century churches to adapt the same formula. Flemish variants are represented not least by several of the arches erected for Philip III's entry into Lisbon in 1619 (see pages 406 and 761).

5.83a

›5.83 LISBON, 17TH-CENTURY SUBURBAN PALACES: (a) Azambuja entrance (from 1660; the building, noted for its triumphal-arch entrance clearly derived from Vignola's Arci di Michel Angelo,[1.32e] is now the Spanish Embassy); (b) Galveias, entrance;

metropolis include the Azumbuja, Galveias and Fronteira palaces.**5.83** The last was built from 1670 by the general Dom João de Mascarenhas who assisted the launch of the new Braganza era on the battlefield and was rewarded with

5.83b

5.83c

5.83e

(c–l) Fronteira (after 1670), entrance front, general view across Italianate garden, Battle Room, detail of tiled dado, chapel interior, portico and terrace, Grotto of Venus interior and exterior, Basin of the Knights, general view and detail of Mascarenhas portraiture – ironically, in the manner of Velázquez.

The site on the northern slopes of Monsanto was awarded to Dom João de Mascarenhas in 1670 as part of the reward for his role in re-establishing an independent Portuguese monarchy: the building was begun within two years. Apart from the loggia façade designs in Serlio's fourth book,[1.25f,g] a more recent source was Rubens's *Palazzi Moderni di Genova*, specifically the engraved elevation of the Villa Sauli (c. 1622) which was itself influenced by Serlio.[3.106e] Much of the interior decoration is from the 18th century – or later – but original is the splendid dado of blue and white tiles in the Battle Room depicting episodes in the expulsion of the Spanish.

the marquisate of Fronteira: that elevation and the end of the old era were marked in an early 17th-century Genoese permutation of Serlian style to address an Italianate garden whose primacy in Portugal is challenged only by the royal one at Vila Viçosa.

5.83d

5.83f

5.83g

5.83h

5.83i

5.83l

5.83j

5.83k

›ARCHITECTURE IN CONTEXT »FROM THE HIGH RENAISSANCE TO MANNERISM

5.84a

5.85a

›5.84 PORTUGUESE ON THE SEA ROUTE TO INDIA AND BEYOND: (a) map of Guinea (with Mina above Cape Corco); (b) map of the Indian Ocean from East Africa to the East Indies; (*Voyages of Alfonso de Alburquerque from the Red Sea to Java*, Pieter van der Aa, Leiden 1707); (c) Alfonso de Albuquerque.

Attracted by the prospect of trade in gold and ivory, the Portuguese reached the so-called Gold Coast of West Africa (now Ghana) c. 1470. Pursuing further African trade, but not content with it, they were bent primarily on finding a sea route to India which would eclipse the traditional one dominated by hostile Muslims in West Asia and rival Italians in the Mediterranean (AIC4, pages 250f). Bartholomeu Dias had rounded the Cape of Good Hope early in 1588. In his wake, then pushing further up the east coast of Africa than any previous European navigator, Vasco da Gama put into Mombasa late in 1497 and set off across the Arabian Sea, reaching Calicut on the Keralan coast of the sub-continental peninsula in May 1598: from there trading posts were established on both coasts (see also above, pages 46f).

Alfonso de Albuquerque, appointed governor of Portuguese India in 1509, won Goa from the sultan of Bijapur on S. Catherine's Day (25 November) the following year. On his way to his post, he had taken Muscat in 1507 from a Persian governor and returned to use it as a base in his successful campaign to take Hormuz in 1515 (dying at Goa thereafter): meanwhile, in 1511, he took Malacca (on the south-west coast of the mainland of modern Malaysia). From there Portuguese navigators, followed by merchants and missionaries, set out for the Indies (Indonesia), China and Japan – as we have noted in the historical context.

›5.85 PORTUGUESE FORTS ON THE SEA ROUTE TO THE EAST: (a) Mina (Elmina, Ghana), Fort S. Jago (from 1482); (b–d) Mombasa (Kenya), Fort Jesus (from 1593), view from the sea and details of oblique access way; (e) Muscat (Oman), Al-Mirani Fort protecting the entrance to the harbour.

Skirting the coast of West Africa c. 1470, the Portuguese did indeed find evidence of the extraction and trade of gold and set up a trading post which they christened Feitoria da Mina – transliterated by the locals as Elmina. Within a decade the trade was lucrative enough to attract royal protection: soon after his accession in

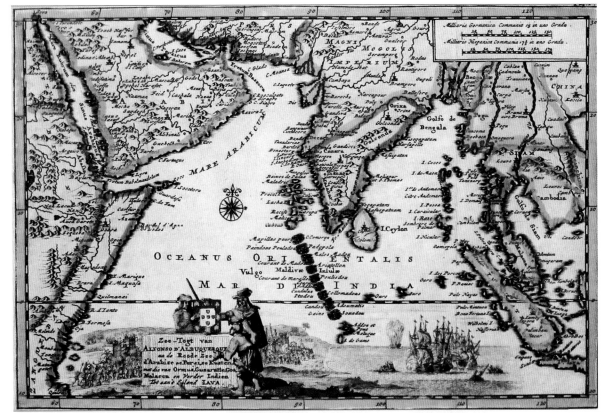

5.84b

1471, Dom João II decreed the dispatch from Portugal of all the men and materials for the construction of a fort to be called after the Portuguese patron S. George. The first permanent European building below the Sahara, it was a landmark in prefabricated masonry construction but not innovative in design: a basic rectangular plan was enhanced with the triangular form of bastion which Italian 15th-century engineers had shown to be the most efficient for deflecting cannon balls. It withstood local and foreign hostility until 1637 when it fell to the Dutch who repaired the damage they had inflicted on it and further strengthened it.

The significance of Mombasa as a way station was not lost on Vasco da Gama's followers. Their attempts to take it began in 1502 and had succeeded by 1528: founded thereafter in the pragmatic manner of Portuguese response to the configuration of strategic sites

5.84c

PORTUGUESE ABROAD

The most distinctive Manueline motifs were imported into Portugal by her maritime adventurers who had reached India at Calicut in 1498.**5.84** The evolved style was re-exported to all the stations along the route and made its mark at the seat of the Viceroy of the Indies at Goa and its outposts. However, in all the worldwide chain of maritime stations and trading posts, the first Portuguese builder was naturally the military engineer responsible for fortification and utilitarian accommodation for men and stores: the gates proclaimed the new masters. And mastery of the sea route to the east across the Indian Ocean, guarded by the chain of forts on African and Arabian

5.85b

5.85c

5.85d

territory, promoted the Portuguese to influence at the seats of local potentates, most notably the emperors of Ethiopia and the sultans of Oman.**5.85–5.87**

elsewhere, Fort Jesus was perfected from 1593 by the Milanese engineer Giovanni Battista Cairati – to the order of the joint Spanish-Portuguese King Philip II.

5.85e

The Portuguese held Muscat from 1507 until they were overwhelmed by the forces of the imam of Oman in 1650. The forts, covering the entrance to Muscat harbour from opposite promontories, were developed from c. 1587, again by Cairati: the Omanis have renovated them several times. (See also AIC3, page 141.)

›5.86 ETHIOPIA, GONDER: CASTLE OF FASILEDES, c. 1640: general view.

Portuguese Jesuits were at the peripatetic court of Ethiopia around Lake Tana from c. 1610. They converted Emperor Susenyos to Catholicism from Ethiopian orthodoxy in 1622 but ten years of turmoil led to their patron's replacement by his son Fasiledes. He settled at Gonder and, though rejecting the Jesuits' religious teaching, retained their advice on the novel building of a permanent palace: its style may be compared with early Portuguese work at Goa – if also with Muslim work on both coasts of the Red Sea and in India (see, for instance, AIC3, page 478, and also below, page 788).

5.86

5.87a

5.87b

5.87c

›ARCHITECTURE IN CONTEXT »FROM THE HIGH RENAISSANCE TO MANNERISM

5.87d

›5.87 PORTUGUESE IN GOA AND BEYOND:
(a) engraved view of Old Goa (mid-18th century); (b)
Fort of Reis Magos guarding the estuary of Goa's Man-
dovi River (from 1551); (c) 'Arch of the Viceroys' at the
former capital's landing stage (1596, reconstructed
1954); (d) Arch of Alfonso de Albuquerque, Malacca,
Malaysia (c. 1520).

Founding a European settlement at Goa after his
defeat of the Bijapuri forces in 1510, Alfonso de Albuquerque promoted religious tolerance, respect for local
traditions (except *sati*, the immolation of widows) and
the preservation of local government, which gained the
support of the enclave's Hindu population – but not the
Muslims. He had intended the port to be a naval base
and administrative hub rather than a fortified trading
factory. Much expanded over the two decades after its
establishment as the capital of Portuguese India,
transferred from Cochin in 1530, it was the seat of the
viceroy whose charge extended west to the Persian
Gulf and east beyond Malacca, Indonesia and China:
they contracted with the imperial authorities to rent a
permanent commercial establishment at Macau in
1557.

The religious orders were quick to follow in the wake
of the navigators and traders. As the material motif
of colonization was enrichment from trade, the moral
rationale was the salvation of souls: like their Spanish
brothers in the earliest Mexican *conventos*, as we shall
see, they enrolled local craftsmen in their missionary
endeavour and the result was a Eurasian hybrid in devotional art – like the Manueline style itself.**5.87, 5.88** The
first Dominican friars arrived in the year of conquest,
1510 but the Franciscan brothers established the first permanent mission in 1517 and a Franciscan, João de Albuquerque, was appointed to the bishopric after it was
established in 1534, four years after the capital of Portuguese India was moved to Goa from Cochin (now
Kochi). Francis Xavier arrived in 1542 and established a
seminary in a former Franciscan college, rededicating it
to S. Paul. The see was raised to an archbishopric, with
jurisdiction over Portuguese Asia as far as Macau, in 1557.
The Inquisition arrived three years later.

In their enclaves along the west coast of the Indian
peninsula from Daman and Diu to Cochin and around to
São Tomé near Madras, the many churches and monastic
buildings left by the Portuguese bear testimony to a zeal
for the Christianizing mission. Naturally, few match in
grandeur the great structures of Goa, where the full range
of post-Renaissance European Classicism and its Mannerist and Baroque permutations are admirably represented. Little survives of the palace but the great churches
are well maintained and the 'Arch of the Viceroys' (1596)
still marks the spot where new pro-consuls were received
on their arrival from Europe: distantly recalling Serlio, it
is attributed to the colony's chief engineer, Julio Simão
who was born in Portuguese India (c. 1565), was appointed
by Philip II to his post in Goa and flourished there for a
quarter of a century from the 1590s.

Outstanding among 16th-century ecclesiastical foundations are the votive chapel of Nossa Senhora do Rosário, the oldest to survive intact, the Franciscan monastic complex of Espírito Santo (founded in 1521, rebuilt except for the lower part of the façade from 1661), the Bom Jesus (built for the Jesuits from 1594) and the cathedral of S. Catarina, seat of the primate of the Indies (founded by the Dominicans in 1562, completed in the 1630s). Prophetic of colonial practice, at least two of these are associated with Simão and clearly reveal the influence of the pattern book – the publication of various engraved plans, sections, elevations and details, sometimes from seminal buildings, often from the imagination of the compiler, which was frequently the mainstay of the provincial and colonial designer. Certainly, however, the decorative complexities of the Mannerism so characteristically promoted by the pattern book were far from foreign to the Indian builders who worked for these designers. The style is still evident well into the 17th century in important works outside the capital, most notably the churches of Nossa Senhora da Immacolata Conceição at Panaji (Panjim), of the Espírito Santo at Margao, of the Salvador do Mundo at Loutulim and of Santana at Talaulim. The most elaborate variation is all that remains of the church of S. Paul in far-off Macau.**5.89**

>**5.88 THE CHRIST CHILD AS GOOD SHEP-HERD** (Goa, c. 1600; Boston, Museum of Fine Arts).

>**5.89 OLD GOA:** (a) Nossa Senhora do Rosário (built in 1543 to mark the spot from which Albuquerque directed his victorious forces against the Bijapuris); (b, c) S. Francisco do Assis (from 1521), general view with cathedral in background and detail of west portal; (d–h) cathedral of S. Catarina (from 1562), east front general view and model, view from south-west, Chapel of the Blessed Sacrament, nave to sanctuary; (i, j) Bom Jesus, view from the north-west, interior to sanctuary (from 1594); (k) Margao (Margaon), Espírito Santo (from 1564, reworked 1675), entrance front; (l) Loutolim, Salvador do Mundo (from 1586), entrance front; (m) Talauli (Talaulim), Santana (from the late-16th century, façade completed 1695), model.

5.88

The first great churches of Goa

The church of the Holy Spirit (Espírito Santo), adjacent to the cathedral, has been much rebuilt over its 16th-century foundations: the major element surviving from the original work is the splendid trefoil Manueline portal. This provides central emphasis otherwise lent only by the slight widening of the middle zone of the three-storey façade in which, though the proportions are hardly canonical, the regular repetition of pilastered bays in clearly defined ranges is typical of the provincial early Renaissance. The plan, of hall-like nave with subsidiary chapels and minimal transepts but no aisles, conforms to the ultimately Albertian reformation of the basilican prototype later

5.89a

5.89b

5.89c

expanded for the post-Tridentine congregational churches of the Jesuits – here as in Europe and colonial America. The majestic space and its opulent fittings, which date from the 17th century, will be revisited in due course.

The cathedral, begun for the Dominicans and dedicated to S. Catherine of Alexandria in virtue of the Portuguese victory over the forces of Bijapur on her feast day in 1510, is unexcelled in scale in all the colonies. The work, begun by Ambrosio Argueiro in 1562, progressed after the turn of the new century under the direction of Julio Simão: it was completed c. 1630. Approximating canonical proportions, the large basilican façade is set slightly forward of twin towers in a synthesis of Albertian and Portuguese elements which predate the invention of the palace-façade type in the motherland (see above, pages 762f). The cool, Classical barrel-vaulted interior may also be seen as a synthesis between the traditional basilica and Vignola's Roman Gesù formula of an expansive hall flanked by shallow transepts and chapels. Dominated by a sumptuous retable in the Iberian Renaissance manner, it has the impressive scale of S. Lorenzo at El Escorial or, more particularly, S. Vicente in Lisbon.

5.89d

5.89f

5.89e

5.89g

5.89h

›ARCHITECTURE IN CONTEXT »FROM THE HIGH RENAISSANCE TO MANNERISM

5.89i

5.89j

5.89k

Rich, if hardly Plateresque, the façade of the Bom Jesus incorporates much leathery scrollwork and oddly proportioned superimposed pilasters at variance with the canonical four-storey sequence from Doric at the base to Composite at the top: nevertheless, the work is attributed to Simão. The churches at Margão, Loutolim and Talaulim also prefer variations on the Bom Jesus formula to colossal Orders. Distant echoes may be detected here of the early 17th-century Jesuit masterpieces in Oporto or Santarém, if not of Filippo Terzi's less mannered palace-façade prototype. However, extruded from Alberti's project for S. Francesco at Rimini, the façades of Talaulim and Loutolim sustain the pattern-book mentality in a mode which bears a strange, if passing, resemblance to the work of Mauro Codussi's late-15th-century Venetian school (AIC4, page 802). The impressive halls of these works clearly respond to Counter-Reformation Jesuit requirements, except perhaps for the quaint timber roof of the Bom Jesus.

5.89l

5.89m

PERNAMBUCO

At Goa there were the great land powers of the Mughals and their clients in the offing with sophisticated firearms. On the other side of the world the threat was largely from rival colonialist warships: by the end of the 16th century a string of fortresses protected all the trading settlements along the long coast of Pernambuco (Brazil), the eastern-most extension of the Americas, east of the meridian drawn 370 leagues west of Cape Verde and therefore conceded to Portugal by the Spaniards in the Treaty of Torde-sillas (1494). Numerous, these were not individually as impressive as the forts of Portuguese Africa or India – as those of Mombasa or Diu in particular. Urban building was modest too, of course. Little survives from the first century of settlement and the rest is best dealt with in the general context of Iberian colonization in South America.

5.90a

5.90b

6 THE SPANISH AMERICAS

5.90d @ 1:1000

Little survives from the first phase of missionary church building in New Spain. The oldest buildings of note in Spanish America, not surprisingly, are to be found in Santa Domingo on the island of Hispaniola where Columbus made his landfall and the first colony was established. Founded in 1502 and the centre of colonial administration for the 'Indies' until the middle of the 16th century, it

5.90c

(c. 1509), plan and view from river; (f–h) Casas Reales, river front, audience hall and court gallery; (i–l) cathedral of S. María la Menor (from 1514), north entrance, west front (completed 1542), interior and plan.

Founded in 1496, destroyed by hurricane in 1502, rebuilt on a slightly different site, Santo Domingo is the first European city of the Americas. The major surviving colonial secular works include the Ozama fortress, the governor's palace (begun by governor Nicolás de Ovando in the first decade of colonization) and the

5.90e

5.90f

5.90g

5.90h

restored 16th-century palace of the crown court (now the Museo de las Casas Reales) and the Alcázar de Colón built by Christopher Columbus's son Diego, viceroy from 1509. The major religious building is, of course, the cathedral of S. María la Menor. Of comparable significance are the remains of the Monastery of S. Francisco built under the patronage of Ovando for the first of the mendicant orders who arrived in 1508.

5.90i

retains the New World's pioneering ecclesiastical and governmental monuments. The primary cathedral of the Americas, S. María la Menor (begun c. 1514), is a hall church of the Poitevan type, with aisles approximating the height of the nave: Gothic rib vaulting is carried on cylindrical piers of quasi-Romanesque gravitas but the west front is Plateresque.**5.90**

5.90j

5.90k

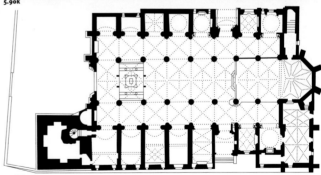

5.90l @ 1:1000

Sacked by Francis Drake in 1586, Santo Domingo was overtaken as the principal port and administrative base of the Indies first by Santiago de Cuba, then by Havana (founded 1519). Designated as a city by royal charter in 1592,

Havana's greatness developed from 1561 when the Spanish crown decreed that the ships of the treasure fleet would assemble there and proceed home in convoy. The fortification of the headlands at the mouth of the splendid harbour, dating from the early 1580s, initiated a scheme for the comprehensive defence of all the major Spanish colonial ports designed by the Italian military engineer, Juan Bautista Antonelli (1550–1616). Major extensions to these fortifications were commissioned in the 1630s.**5.91 5.94**

5.91b   5.91c

Spanish-American fortifications

Havana was defended from 1538 with a fort on the the western shore of its excellent bay: too far from the estuary, it failed to withstand a French attack in 1555 and was rebuilt as the Castillo de la Real Fuerza on a grander scale over a stellar plan in accordance with the latest developments in Europe. It was not finished until 1577 and became the governor's residence when the need for a fortress protecting the harbour's entrance was realized a decade later. Fifty years later construction was well under way on the city walls and their several bastions.

5.91a

›5.91 HAVANA, COLONIAL FORTIFICATION:
(a) late-16th-century map of town and harbour showing narrow estuary to the north; (b) Castillo de la Real Fuerza (1555; the bell tower, crowned with the statue known as La Giralda after the similar statue on the great tower of Seville, dates from 1632); (c) estuary forts with Castillo de S. Salvador de la Punta (foreground) and Castillo del Morro (from c. 1590).

Meanwhile, in 1581, Juan Bautista Antonelli – who had worked for King Philip II in north Africa and Spain – was called upon to project the fortification of the Straits of Magellan against English incursions. Despite the failure of that exercise, five years later he was commissioned to fortify the major Spanish colonial port of Cartagena de Indias – also against the raids of English 'pirates' – with integrated defence works dependent on the fortresses of S. Felipe de Barajas, S. Sebastián de Pastelillo and S. Fernando. The impressive result prompted similar schemes to fortify the other major Spanish colonial bases around the Caribbean and along the coast of

South America. That began on both sides of the isthmus of Panama and continued at Veracruz on earlier foundations. It culminated in 1589 with Antonelli's Castillo del Morro at the eastern entrance to Havana Bay and the extension of the defences to the opposite western headland with the Castillo de S. Salvador de La Punta. The Fortaleza de S. Carlos de la Cabaña was added half-way along the east bank of the narrow estuary in the late 1760s to extend the protection provided by El Morro.

Veracruz, Mexico's principal colonial port, was founded on the island of San Juan de Ulúa at the outset of the conquest as its principal bridgehead. Its fort, protecting the shipping roads and the walled settlement on the mainland opposite, was a key element in Antonelli's campaign of the 1580s. It was renovated in the mid-18th century. The result is recorded in the 19th-century engraving shown here but the Italian post-Renaissance ideal was to confront potential hostility with a radial arrangement of triangular bastions over a polygonal plan: its publication was widespread by Antonelli's time, no longer as an adjunct to an architectural treatise (as it had been in the previous century; see, for instance, AIC4, pages 765f) but in dedicated military-engineering manuals. Italians were the acknowledged experts in the field throughout Europe and its colonies, not least due to Habsburg patronage.

Naturally formal perfection – in star or other regular shapes – ceded to the dictates of the site. Not without the informal disposition of triangular bastions, but essentially pragmatic in conception, the most impressive of all Spanish South America's military installations protects Corral Bay and the mouth of the south-central Chilean Valdivia River. Named after Pedro de Valdivia (c. 1500–53), the conquistador who worked his way down the coast from Peru where he had been one of Francisco Pizarro's principal lieutenants, the settlement was founded by the Spanish conquistadors in 1552 but lost to the Dutch in 1643. Soon regained, the splendid harbour was protected by a phenomenal series of integrated forts (begun in 1645): the largest, S. Sebastián on the northern headland, was complemented by others on the southern shore (Niebla) and the central island of Mancera. They were backed by a series of defence works facing inland against hostile Indians.

›**5.92 VERACRUZ (MEXICO):** overview with S. Juan de Ulúa foreground (early 19th-century record).

›**5.93 CARTAGENA DE INDIAS (COLOMBIA):** late-16th-century map of town and harbour with harbour entrance fortifications (right), town and its defences (centre).

›**5.94 VALDIVIA (CHILE):** (a) map of bay; (b) general view from the fort of S. Sebastian de la Cruz on the northern headland to the central island of Mancera; (c) Niebla from the entrance channel; (d) S. Sebastián from the sea.

5.94a

5.94b

5.94c

5.94d

›ARCHITECTURE IN CONTEXT »FROM THE HIGH RENAISSANCE TO MANNERISM

›5.95 MEXICO CITY: overview c. 1628.

MEXICO

Other than the bases of fortification, little of major significance from the 16th century survives in hurricane-torn Cuba or the other islands of the Antilles – with the partial exception of Santo Domingo. By mid-century the focus of attention had shifted from there to the mainland of New Spain (modern Mexico, ultimately extending well into the southern United States of America). Economic immigrants, attracted by generous land grants, followed quickly on the messengers of Christ whose establishments were the nuclei of new towns often, but not always, on the sites of destroyed native settlements. As in the case of Mexico City itself, the planning of these settlements often followed formal principles ancient to both Central America and Europe – but rarely revived even in Italy until later in the 16th century (AICI, pages 322f).**5·95** Naturally, little from the earliest years of the Spanish capital survive: the seat of conquistador Hernán Cortés's administration had been transformed before the end of the century but some

The Aztec city – formed definitively in 1473 with the union of Tlatelolco and Tenochtitlan, was destroyed to break morale – unsuccessfully – but surrender was forced in August 1521. From nearby Coyoacán, the conquered were ordered to clear the site of their former capital: because of its prestige, strategic value, security and subsisting infrastructure, restoration was decreed early the next year. The peripheral sectors of the original urban complex were assigned to Indians, the conquistadors retained the centre of Tenochtitlan where four main arteries converged at right angles on the central plaza (Zócalo) which had been a centre of trade addressed by the main Aztec temple and palaces (AIC1, page 323). Entrusted with its development late in 1523, the mason Alonso García Bravo imposed a grid of seven north–south and east–west streets on the existing order: with a huge force of Indian labourers under the supervision of another Spanish mason, Martín de Sepulveda, work was advanced by 1530.

The first of the Spanish buildings to be occupied was, naturally, Hernán Cortés's headquarters as governor on the site of the palace of the father of the defeated Aztec ruler Montezuma II along the western side of the Zócalo: after the conqueror left for Spain in

1528, it was superseded by a grander palace on the site of Montezuma's own residence, which became the viceroy's house in 1562. Thus, soon to be dominated by the cathedral, the Zócalo retained its Aztec significance as a centre of government while also continuing to serve as the main market centre. The isolated island site was not thought to need fortification.

›5.96 CUERNAVACA, HOUSE OF CORTÉS,
from 1533, altered: general view

As Marqués del Valle de Oaxaca, Cortés held sway over the valley of his title (somewhat tenuously in the 1520s) and the Valle de Morelos (from 1521), the heartland of the Tlahuica Aztecs west of the Mexican Basin seat of their overlords and a major way station to the Pacific coast. The conqueror's palace was built over the Tlahuica ceremonial precinct: he preferred it as his seat until his final departure for Spain in 1540. The quasi-military front is curiously breached by the central loggias in the manner of the Alcázar de Colón at Santo Domingo.

compensation is provided by the remainder of his house at Cuernavaca which enlarged on the formula adopted by Diego Colon at Santo Domingo.**5.96**

The Franciscans, Dominicans and Augustinians were the first of the reformed and reformatory religious orders in the field: members of the Observant branch of the Franciscans arrived as early as mid-1524, the Dominicans followed two years later, the Augustinians in 1533: Carmelites, Mercedarians and Jesuits followed in 1572, twenty years after their intervention in Brazil. Late in the field, but dedicated to education, the Jesuits were not long in eclipsing the mendicants who approached decadence after several generations of privilege in colonial ecclesiastical affairs. At

the outset, however, the pioneering friars were fervent in the conviction that God had revealed the western – or was it eastern? – continent of untold millions of pagans to Spain for salvation. Mass conversion supervened in multitudinous baptism ceremonies and the sacrament was administered to congregations of thousands: it is claimed that more than five million Indians were saved in the fifteen years after the arrival of the first evangelist.

The conquistadors brought rapacity to expansion throughout the former Aztec empire, the missionaries followed with compassion and a conception of utopia informed by the humanism of Erasmus and, particularly,

Thomas More. The missions, which cared for those in need of physical as well as spiritual salvation and initiated schooling, emulated the simplicity of the early church in sentiment and shelter. This was usually in the precinct of a raised temple: its former hierarchy converted and confirmed in their traditional authority, the late pagan community of that temple became a parish run on native lines with native intermediaries between it and the immigrant priests. The earliest of these were in the metropolis and other major centres of Indian settlement, beside the town square of course: naturally, however, the earliest surviving friary buildings are remote from large towns.

By mid-century friaries were proliferating throughout the former Aztec empire: the Franciscans had radiated out from the capital but tended to leave the north to the Augustinians and the south beyond Puebla to the Dominicans. Though devised as bases for extroverted evangelical activity, rather than retreat, they had the three components standard to monastic communities the world over: cloistered housing for the members of the order; the church (or 'temple') for the regular performance of the rites and preaching to the elect; the precinct for mass congregation (patio, or atrio). Descended both from the ancient Roman temenos and the typical Aztec sacred complex, the last was bounded by square pavilion shrines (posas), centred on a cross and focused on the presentation of the Host, on teaching or the performance of passion plays, in an open exedra chapel.**5.97–5.99**

The Indians did the building, of course: they knew all about loadbearing masonry and how to secure it from earthquakes but needed training in the techniques of vaulting space. For practical as well as evangelical reasons, thus, the patio and its exedra usually appeared first, the essentially utilitarian facilities for the monks (the convento) next, the church last: the house of God, that nec-

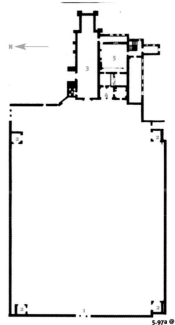

5.97a @ 1:1500

›5.97 FRANCISCAN MISSIONS, from c. 1540: (a) Puebla, Calpan, S. Andrés (from 1548), plan of complex with (1) entrance to atrium, (2) posas, (3) church, (4) portal to monastic quarters, (5) cloister; (b–e) Huejotzingo, S. Miguel Arcángel (from mid-1540s), general view of compound, church portal detail (completed c. 1564), north-west posa (dated 1550), monastery portal and north-east posa; (f) Tlaxcala, S. Francisco, interior with artesonado roofing; (g) Puebla, S. Francisco, vault; (h, i) Cholula, Capilla Real (open chapel from c. 1560), interior detail and plan.

Founded by the first contingent of Franciscan friars in the centre of territory alien to the Aztecs, S. Miguel predates the order's main house in the metropolis: the primitive facilities of the late-1520s were replaced twenty years later – about the time work began at Tepeaca. In accordance with local practice – and Alberti (AIC4, pages 734f) – the first necessity was the precinct raised on a platform above the level of mundane life, walled, gated and endowed with posas. At Huejotzingo the inner faces of all four posas are arcaded over clustered colonettes: angels in the spandrels are framed with the Franciscan rope moulding – in the manner of a Mudéjar *alfiz* – below a heraldic frieze.

Stoutly buttressed, crenellated, meagrely fenestrated, the churches at Calpan and Huejotzingo are
exemplary in their defensive aspect – though the
motive was probably primarily display. S. Miguel was
begun at about the time the posas were completed
(1550), the convento somewhat earlier: as usual, the
cloister adjoined the church to its south. Not unusually,
the entrance to the convento was embellished with a
variety of unorthodox motifs but, of course, not in competition with the neighbouring church portal. The latter, of masonry set into the revetment of rubble walls
below the choir-gallery window, is also unorthodox in
its attenuated colonettes, the striated capitals of its
piers and the convoluted profile of its lintel arch – an
echo from the late-Isabelline homeland which was
heard also at Tepeaca and other contemporary sites.
Surmounted by an arched opening, the north portal
takes unorthodoxy to bizarre extremes with its combination of floral, vegetal, geometric and heraldic motifs
in the Portuguese Manueline manner. A different
extreme, reminiscent of a Cordoban mosque, was
taken by the hyperstyle open chapel of Cholula.

Except for the sacristy portal in S. Miguel, the interiors are relatively uncluttered. Timber roofing was not
uncommon, as at Tlaxcala where it recalls the artesonado tradition of post-Moorish Spain (AIC4, pages 373ff,
458): such survivals are relatively rare. Naturally, groin
vaulting fared better: it is ribbed over corbels above the
low arcading at Tepeaca, over slender colonettes at
Huejotzingo; in both, the rib patterns are varied for the
eastern sanctuary bay and the western choir gallery –
which, as usual, is carried over an interior narthex. S.
Miguel's magnificent retable was produced by the

essarily replaced some form of primitive shelter in the second generation of development in masonry in worthy scale
and style.

Via Santo Domingo, the mendicants brought with them
the idea of the church as one large volume, rectangular but
for the polygonal apse: either vaulted in masonry or with
a timber ceiling, essentially it presented the preacher in
clear view and acoustics. With thick battered walls, sometimes crenellated, it was usually severe outside in part as a
defensive base, in part to impress with militant might, in
part to counter the awe inspired by native religious structures. With or without the intermixture of Plateresque and
Mudéjar motifs, embellishment prevailed on the portal
and the interior – both manifestations of the threshold of

5.97c

5.97d

5.97b

5.97e

5.97f

5.97g

5.97h

5.97i @ 1:1000

Fleming Simon Pereyns and dated to 1586: by then more sophisticated than its context, it might be described as High Renaissance with late-Plateresque moulding of the columns.

›**5.98 AUGUSTINIAN FOUNDATIONS,** from c. 1550: (a–c) Acolman, S. Agustín, plan of church and monastic complex, general view with portal (dated 1560), cloister; (d–j) Actopan, S. Nicolás, cloister, general view with portal, north flank with open chapel, interior to coro and sanctuary, monastery staircase and refectory.

The early Franciscans had founded the Acolman mission as a base for conversion in the vicinity of the major ancient cult centre of Teotihuacan (north of Mexico City) but ceded it in 1539 to the Augustinians who were

5.98b

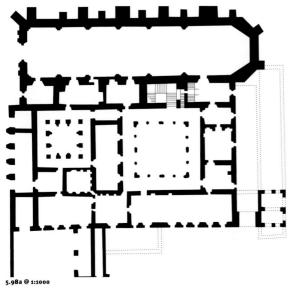
5.98a @ 1:1000

5.98c

5.98d

already present further north at Actopan. Most of the buildings at both sites are the legacies of campaigns begun about 1550. The platforms and, therefore, the patios have been lost in part but their open chapels survive: the one at Actopan is exceptionally expansive and decorated with a coffering design derived from Serlio over iconic images ranging from the Creation to the Last Judgement.

5.98e

5.98f

On the south side of the church, each convento has an arcaded entrance. The one at Acolman, which may be due to the Franciscans, has five unadorned bays beyond which are two cloisters – the outer one of little architectural distinction, the inner one of quasi-Romanesque gravitas but with timber ceilings at both levels. The cloister at Actopan is a much more elegant, more sophisticated, combination of Gothic arches and vaulting below, Renaissance ones and timber ceilings above: the entrance, to the left of the unique tower, is through a three-bay triumphal arch which marks a distinct advance over the loggia at Acolman. Beyond Actopan's cloister is an open-cage staircase of the kind invented in Spain earlier in the century. Beyond that is 16th-century Mexico's most splendid refectory: like the atrio exedra, the latter's tunnel vault is magnificently painted to represent coffering in a Serlian mode.

5.98g

The portal and choir-gallery window aedicule at Acolman echo the Plateresque style of the early 16th-century homeland, Alonso de Covarrubias in particular (see page 640). Covarrubias's later, more Serlian, style may have been known to the designer of the portal at Actopan, despite the uncanonical proportions of the outer Order, and he was adventurous in his attempt at enhancing semi-circular recession illusionistically. Actopan's nave is vaulted, like the refectory: that was usual for the Augustinians but the sanctuary has late-Gothic rib vaulting and that too was the order's norm.

5.98i

5.98h

5.98j

5.99a

5.99c

5.99a @ 1:1000   5.99d

5.99e

›5.99 DOMINICAN FOUNDATIONS, from the late-1550s: (a–e) Teposcolula, SS. Pedro y Pablo, from west, open chapel plan and details, Chapel of S. Gertrudis; (f) Tepoztlán, church portal; (g, h) Yanhuitlán, general view and cloister; (i) Coixtlahuaca, Monastery of S. Juan Bautista, church façade.

Drawn to the cities of the Zapotecs and Mixtecs in the mountainous area around Oaxaca, the Dominicans have left substantial remains of their mission bases established by 1538 in the vicinity of Mixtec Teposcolula and Yanhuitlán. The former is most notable for the extraordinary hexagonal atrio chapel, buttressed on the diagonals within a loggia: the disparity of scale between the latter and the convento entrance, with its inner arboreal column, is striking. Between the two, the portal to the church is intermediate in scale: its triumphal-arch motif – Plateresque in detail – extends across the whole

5.99f

5.99g

twin-towered façade (now missing the southern belfry) and is echoed at the level of the choir gallery. The motif reappears in graver form, with unfluted Doric columns, between the towers of Yanhuitlán: despite delicate surface relief, the triple-height retable-type composition suggests some knowledge of the *estilo desornamentado* – and, perhaps, realization at a later date than the rest of the church or than the similar, but wholly uncanonical, exercise at Coixtlahuaca. Both these churches are single-volume halls, vaulted in Gothic style except for the artesonado ceiling of the narthex. Teposcolula was once vaulted and, not unusually for the Dominicans, incorporated a transept.

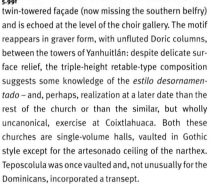

5.99h

5.99i

heaven. Masters of ornament in all the local materials, the native artisans would vie with one another on behalf of their community if licensed to do so – and quickly adapted to European modes. The Augustinians were the most assertive of the divine sanction for the embellishment of sanctified form: the Dominicans were not prepared to be eclipsed; even the austere Franciscans admitted some display of riches as witness to the glory of their faith – rather than self-indulgence.

By 1530 the conquistadors had advanced so far that it had become necessary to divide New Spain for administrative purposes: in the first phase the western region was distinguished as New Galicia with its capital at Compostela. To the south, the Zapotec city of Oaxaca had been occupied by Cortés as the centre of his private fiefdom but the crown, determined to extinguish this precedent, asserted its authority there in 1529 and refounded the town as Antequera. The year before, the principle had been affirmed in practice and in name with the foundation of Villa Real as the centre of Spanish expansion in Chiapas in the far south. Reinforcing the principle, in 1531 Puebla was founded by royal warrant as a way station to Veracruz, the main port on the Caribbean: both ultimately were endowed with provincial responsibility. Ten years further on, Mérida was founded by a conquistador in the name of the crown as a centre of administration in the Yucatán. Also dating from the early 1540s are Valladolid (modern Morelia) and Guadalajara which supplanted Compostela as capital of Nueva Galicia in 1560.

The capital and the main provincial towns, some new, many rebuilt on established sites to satisfy European needs, quickly expanded in the second half of the 16th century on the formal lines familiar to the natives: a central plaza in a grid of streets was required by royal warrant well before mid-century and a thoroughly detailed formula for the

5.100

›5.100 MÉRIDA, PALACIO DE MONTEJO: façade (c. 1549).

Built with Indian labour for the first governor of the Yucatán, Francisco de Montejo, the house was finished in the year in which its patron was summoned home. The interior has not survived in its original form. Among various allegorical motifs of more or less naïve conception, the profusion of portrait heads on the portal includes the patron and his sovereigns – the King-Emperor Charles and Isabella of Portugal – and even more primitive representations of conquistadors trampling on defeated Indians.

5.101a

5.101b

›**5.101 PUEBLA, CASA DEL DEÁN,** c. 1580: (a)
façade, (b) frescoed reception room.

The patron, as the name implies, was the dean of the
cathedral, Tómas de la Plaza, who held the office for a
quarter of a century from 1564. The format of piano
nobile over shops – traditional since Ancient Rome –
and rooms ranged all round a court was to be typical of
the aristocratic colonial house, at least until affluence
encouraged greater vertical as well as horizontal
expansion.

›**5.102 FROM PLATERESQUE TO HIGH
RENAISSANCE IN THE FRANCISCAN RET-
ABLE:** (a) Huejotzingo, S. Miguel Arcángel (before
1586); (b) Xochimilco, S. Bernardino (after 1590).

The Xochimilco convento was founded in 1525, at
the outset of Franciscan activity in New Spain. The
single volume of the nave was endowed with a retable
towards the end of the 16th century: unattributed, it is
Mexico's finest surviving representative of the type in
High Renaissance style – though not without broken
pediments and Mannerist embellishment to the lower
drums of the superimposed Orders. Slightly earlier, the
irresolutely canonical retable of Huejotzingo (with
paintings signed by Simon Pereyns in 1586) retains
Plateresque 'candelabra' columns in its upper register.

constitution of cities decreed in 1573. Apart from government buildings, all the major settlements had numerous
conventos and these supported equally numerous schools
and hospitals – much rebuilt, but originally modelled on
their counterparts in the homeland (AIC4, page 867), the
greatest of the latter were the most prominent of all colonial urban facilities. Naturally, few significant houses survive unscathed from the 16th century: the Palacio de
Montejo in Mérida (late-1540s) and the Case del Deán in
Puebla are particularly notable for marking the transition
from a late efflorescence of the Plateresque in the colony
to a purer Renaissance style.**5.100, 5.101** In contemporary
ecclesiastical work, especially retable design, that trend is
represented from Huejotzingo to Xochimilco (1590).**5.102**

5.102a,b

Where the state led in establishing centres of provincial
authority, the Church followed in establishing bishoprics
– and the presence of the Inquisition. Beside cathedrals
there were, of course, to be palaces for the prelates as well
as for the civil governors – few of which retain much of their
16th-century appearance. The bishop, usually chosen from
a mendicant order, was seated provisionally in a mendicant
church, as, for instance, in S. María de Gracia at Guadalajara or the house of an order favoured by the founder – such

as the Mercederians of Cortés's chaplain, Fray Bartolomé de Olmedo, in Oaxaca. As early as 1524, however, the first metropolitan cathedral was built on the site of the Aztec temple in the heart of their capital: it was replaced from 1563 during a spate of great cathedral building in the high Philippine age – when returns from the discovery of silver in 1546 were being fully realized. This extended from Guadalajara and (later) Morelia, north-west and west of Mexico City, south-east via Puebla to Mérida in the Yucatán peninsula.**5.103–5.106**

›5.103 MÉRIDA, CATHEDRAL OF S. ILDE-FONSO: (a, b) plan and section, (c) interior, (d) façade (dated 1599).

The ambitious Bishop Toral launched the programme for the construction of a great cathedral only twenty years after the foundation of the town. On the east side of the Plaza Mayor, occupying the site of a Mayan temple, it was designed by an unknown architect on the model of Santo Domingo cathedral: Pedro de Aulestia and Juan Miguel de Agüero were responsible for directing works between 1561 and 1598. The largest church in the Yucatán peninsula, its façade shows few architectural features of particular merit. The geometry of the interior, following Renaissance precept, extrudes the square of the aisle bays into the golden section rectangles of the nave bays – except for the square crossing bay with its circular dome. The latter, the oldest in Mexico, is ascribed in an inscription to Juan Miguel de Agüero and dated to 1598.

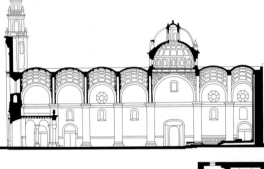

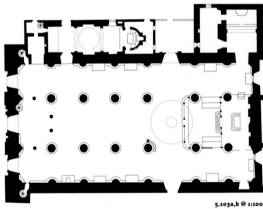

5.103a,b @ 1:1000

5.103c

Primary cathedrals

The two cathedrals at the extremities of our sample, Mérida and Guadalajara, were the simplest of the Philippine rebuilding exercises (from 1563 and 1571 respectively). They are of the hall-church type, rising over elementary basilican plans, like the cathedral of Santo Domingo but without the polygonal apse, extended side chapels or Gothic profiles. However, the domical vaults of Guadalajara are ribbed in the late-medieval manner though the earlier work at Mérida has a network of ribs simulating coffering: the cylindrical piers of Santo Domingo are retained for Mérida but Guadalajara has clustered Doric columns and impost blocks.

Between twin towers of greatest austerity at Mérida, the severe fronts of both works are elementary in their articulation: at Mérida, colossal Tuscan pilasters support a great blind arch representing the nave, over the arms of the patron, the choir-gallery window and a portal in the form of a minor –

5.103d

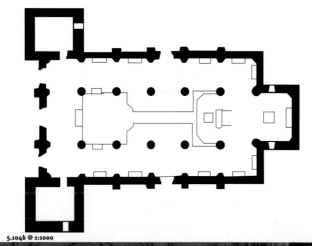

5.104b @ 1:1000

5.104a

›**5.104 GUADALAJARA:** (a) S. María de Gracia, exterior (from 1572); (b–d) cathedral of Nossa Senhora de la Asunción, plan, interior and west front detail.

The church of S. María de Gracia was founded in 1541 for Dominican sisters but was transformed from adobe to masonry after a fire thirty year later. With entrances in the long street front, in conformity with the Iberian practice for the church of a female order, it is the city's principal representative of the typical 16th-century mixture of Renaissance and Gothic styles – the latter in the vaulting, of course, the former in the articulation of the portal and the nave arcades. After the

5.104c

5.104d

provincial capital was established in Guadalajara in 1560, It served as the seat of the bishop while the cathedral was being constructed.

The Franciscan Fray Pedro de Ayala, second bishop of Nueva Galicia, obtained permission to build the definitive cathedral early in the year after the relocation of the provincial seat: planning by an unknown architect was advanced by 1568, work directed by the master-mason Martín Casillas was under way by 1576 and had reached the springing of the vaults by the end of the century. These were to be resolutely Gothic on the recommendation of Diego de Aguilera who was currently employed on the metropolitan cathedral. The sacrament was translated from S. María de Gracia to the completed cathedral in 1618

The retables date from after c. 1700. The façade pediment, towers and the crossing dome were reconstructed after earthquake damage in the 19th century.

and somewhat crushed – triumphal arch; at Guadalajara the façade is abstract in its articulation below a broad semi-circular pediment, except for the portals which echo the configuration of Mérida but play a much greater part.

The replacement of the metropolitan cathedral was, naturally, the grandest of its era: also conceived as a hall church, it was begun over a plan derived from Andrés de Vandelvira's work at Jaén – ultimately Diego de Siloé's at Granada – but the nave was raised to a clerestory and extended east to centralize the domed crossing under the inspiration of Herrera's contemporary work at Valladolid.**5.35b, 5.50b** The change was

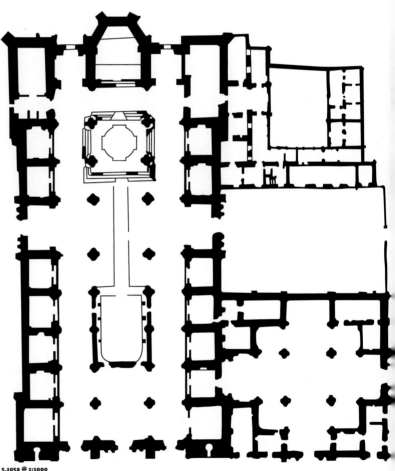

>**5.105 MEXICO CITY, CATHEDRAL OF NUESTRA SEÑORA DE LA ASUNCIÓN,** from 1573: (a) plan, (b) interior, (c) west portal, (d) general view from south-west (as completed in the late-17th and 18th centuries).

The first cathedral was begun in 1524 on Cortés's orders under the direction of Martín de Sepúlveda. Basilican in plan, it was completed in 1532 for Juan de Zumárraga, the first bishop. A century after its foundation, it succumbed to the completion of the north-east section of the definitive cathedral. Commissioned from Valladolid in 1544, that was built in stages from 1573 to 1813, initially under the direction of Claudio de Arciniega. The church was dedicated in 1656 and again in 1667 after vaulting was completed by Luis Gómez de Trasamonte. The latter began the articulation of the

5.105a @ 1:1000

5.105b

5.105c

due to the Andalusian architect Claudio de Arciniega, master of works from 1584, and he may have influenced similar changes to the cathedral project at Puebla: begun after 1575 on plans attributed to Francisco Becerra, that was evidently not too far advanced a decade later for thoroughgoing revision along the lines of Valladolid – in plan. Vandelvira and Siloé still echo – distantly – through the attenuated Doric arcades which carry ribbed groin vaulting over the nave and domical vaulting over the aisles in both works: the proportions are more attenuated in the metropolitan work, the ribbing of the nave vaults thin; there is more gravitas in the Puebla clerestory lunettes with their oculii and this was enhanced by the coffering of the vaults in the 19th century when the main retable was also revised.

Like Siloé's Granadine masterpiece, followed by Vandelvira, the metropolitan and Puebla cathedrals both have superimposed triumphal-arch motifs, with strictly canonical Orders, on their principal and subsidiary

main front (facing south) which was furthered from 1672 by Rodrigo Diaz de Aguilera. The side portals of the late-1680s are due to Cristobal de Medina. Begun in the latter's time, the towers were completed only in 1791 to the design of José Damián Ortiz de Castro for their top storey. The clock turret and the revetement of the dome date from early in the 19th century. Meanwhile, the Sagrario church was added to the cathedral's east and the interiors of both were equipped with the spectacular retables which we shall return to in due course.

A fire in 1962 destroyed a significant part of the cathedral's interior. Moreover, founded on soft clay, the structure has chronic subsidence problems addressed in reconstruction work beginning in the 1990s.

5.105d

5.106a

5.106b

›5.106 PUEBLA, CATHEDRAL OF NUESTRA SEÑORA DE LA IMMACULADA CONCEPCIÓN, from 1575: (a) west front, (b) interior (redecorated in the 19th century), (c) Retable de los Reyes (from 1646), (d) plan.

A project for the cathedral was submitted to the chapter early in 1557 but construction to the designs of Francisco Becerra – with Juan de Cigorondo as master of works – was delayed for nearly twenty years. In parallel with work on the espicopal place (habitable from 1619 but comprehensively altered in the late-18th century) progress at the cathedral site was slow and came to a halt in 1626. In 1634, Juan Gómez de Trasmonte, master-mason on the metropolitan project, modified the design of vaults and dome, and construction was furthered vigorously from 1640 when Bishop Juan de Palafox y Mendoza arrived with orders to finish it. It was consecrated in April 1649 but not entirely completed

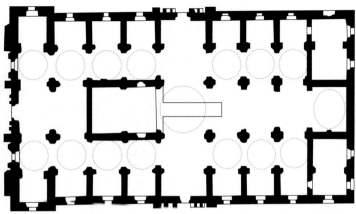

5.106d @ 1:1000

5.106c

until 1690: the dome, supported on its octagonal drum by extraordinary flying buttresses, dates from the 1640s but the towers were not completed until 1680 and c. 1770 (north and south respectively). The late-17th-century north portal, with its superimposed pilasters and all the Habsburg kings from Charles to Philip IV, is due to Diego de la Sierra and will be revisited in due course. The interior was redecorated along Neoclassical lines in the early 19th century: many of the altarpieces were reworked then too but due respect was paid to the ordonnance of the sanctuary Retable de los Reyes attributed to the Sevillian master Juan Martínez Montañés.

Protracted in implementation, the towers and domes of Puebla and the metropolitan cathedral belong to a new era but the interiors and frontispieces of both buildings are conservative of 16th-century Philippine modes.

façades – and a didactic panel in place of the choir-gallery window in the capital's work. Both entrance fronts are expansive: Puebla's is overtly basilican between its recessed towers and still essentially High Renaissance. The frontispiece makes less impact in the metropolitan work where horizontality is asserted by the continuous plane and cornice to either side. For the west portal of the latter, the Siloan frontispiece formula is revised in the French mode of Classicizing aspiration but with a measure of post-Herreran severity which cedes to Solomonic display at attic level (c. 1688). Both cathedrals retain the Andalusian form of dome with octagonal drum, innovatively at Puebla – where a sense of insecurity prompted bizarre diagonal buttressing. Both were much altered in protracted construction which takes us well beyond the Habsburg era and its typical styles.

The dome was introduced to central Mexico at Puebla, for the cathedral and perhaps a decade earlier on the less-ambitious scale of the church of S. Teresa. Circular, indeed centralized, forms were rare in planning – throughout the Spanish colonies. Well before the Pueblan or metropolitan cathedrals were completed (c. 1660), however, the complex basilica with domed crossing, or the Roman Gesù variant with linked chapels, had superseded the simple rectangular volume of the typical mendicant church at the level of the richer parish and even for mendicant

5.107a

conventos rebuilt or newly founded in the main towns: S. Domingo in Mexico City is a prominent example but the aisled basilica was sustained by the capital's Jesuits for S. Ignacio (La Profesa, now dedicated to S. Felipe Neri). On the other hand, female orders were usually served by

›5.107 MEXICO CITY, CONCEPTIONISTS AND CISTERCIANS: (a) La Encarnación (from 1639), side front; (b, c) Regina Coeli (from 1650s), side front and interior; (d) Nuestra Señora de Valvanera (from 1667), portal; (e) S. Bernardo (consecrated 1690), view from south-east.

5.107b

5.107c

The Regina Coeli was founded by the Conceptionists in 1573, the church dates from 1655: Miguel Custodio Durán renovated it from 1731, introducing major new retables and adding the important Chapel of the Purísima Concepción for Buenaventura Medina Picazo. Nuestra Señora de Valvanera (popularly known as Balvanera) was also founded in 1573 – for an order dedicated to the infant Jesus – but rebuilt under its present dedication for the Conceptionists from 1667. La Encarnación was founded twenty years later but rebuilding began a generation earlier.

In all three cases the entrance is through portals on their elongated sides. These represent variations on the heraldic type of Covarrubias or the Vandelvira succession, not without Villalpando-Serlian orthodoxy in the treatment of their pilaster Orders: an iconographic panel is retained for the grander of the two Regina Coeli frontispieces but Valvanera has a window in its upper level after the example of La Encarnación's twin compositions.

Founded in 1636, consecrated in 1690, S. Bernardo is entered on axis with the altar: between *tezontle* piers with assertive stone quoins, its frontispiece is also of the heraldic type, with the triumphal-arch motif defining the lower level, but the canonical Orders are of engaged columns on both levels.

5.107d,e

unaisled halls set parallel to the street as in Iberia. Prominent examples in Mexico City included the Conceptionist convent churches of La Encarnación, Nuestra Señora de Valvanera, Regina Coeli and the latter's sister Cistercian foundation of S. Bernardo.**5.107**

After the intervention of Claudio de Arciniega and Francisco Becerra, in particular, it was usual for church commissioners to employ professional architects. They generally worked under the inspiration of the Counter-Reformation promoted by the Council of Trent: the Guild of Masons and Architects was instituted in 1599 to regulate practice – though its prescriptions did not necessarily run to priestly architects working for their orders. Serlio (via Villalpando), other pattern books and treatises were indispensable.

The superimposition of canonical Orders, usually in a permutation of the triumphal-arch motif, prevailed in portals until the end of the Habsburg era – and even beyond: apart from our metropolitan examples, the Mercederians in Puebla and Guadalajara, or the Augustinians in Guadalajara and Oaxaca may be singled out as representative.**5.108** The Dominicans of Puebla and Oaxaca commissioned churches of the extended Gesù type c. 1570: their construction over three or four decades coincides with the first phase of work on the greatest of the cathedrals, anticipating the adoption of the triumphal-arch form of frontispiece for the latter by nearly three-quarters of a century.**5.109** The one at Puebla is Herreran in its gravitas: its Oaxacan contemporary is richer in sculptural relief but that is strictly subservient to the architecture. Quite to the contrary, the chief glory of both complexes is the decoration of their rosary chapels: though still essentially Mannerist, this anticipates the wilder excesses of the Baroque

›**5.108 CONSERVATIVE AUGUSTINIANS:** Oaxaca, S. Agustín, church front.

The foundation dates from 1586: the church – with its splendid façade relief of the dedicatee as a mainstay of the Church – was rebuilt from 1699.

›**5.109 INNOVATIVE DOMINICANS:** (a) Mexico City, S. Domingo (from early 1680s), general view from south; (b, c) Puebla, S. Domingo (1571–1611), façade and interior towards sanctuary; (d–g) Oaxaca, S. Domingo de Guzmán (1575–1675), model, plaza front, interior to sanctuary, details of coro vaulting.

The capital's original church of S. Domingo served the *primo convento* of New Spain, founded in 1526. A substantial rebuilding was consecrated in 1590. Further rebuilding was begun just under a century later and consecrated in the fourth decade of the new century. The lower drums of the columns, projecting

5.108

5.109a

through two planes to the triumphal-arch motif, are treated to florid relief ornament in the late-16th-century French Mannerist manner below an incompletely resolved – or mutilated – tripartite pediment.

The Puebla Dominicans began the construction of their definitive convento c. 1570: the church was nearing completion forty years later; the façade is dated 1611; the earliest record of work on the Capilla del Rosario is dated 1632 but it was probably unfinished on dedication in 1690. The Oaxacan brothers founded their convento in 1570 and began their church five years later: construction, punctuated by recurrent earthquake damage, was protracted over more than a century: the portal of the residential block is dated 1575; the nave decoration was complete by 1665, the façade ten years later. The celebrated Capilla del Rosana was still being decorated well into the 18th century.

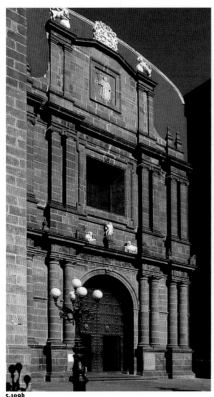

5.109b

5.109c

5.109d

For their façade, the Pueblans adopted the triumphal-arch type of the cathedral's double-storey frontispiece: the columns are doubled for the expansion of the composition to cover the whole front between the towers but there is scant sculptural enrichment. For Oaxaca they commissioned a three-storey version without doubled columns but with varied rustication and high-relief sculpture subjected to the architecture: it was recessed behind the plane of the towers in the manner of the earlier Dominican establishments at Coixtlahuaca or Teposcolula.

Stuccoists, probably imported from Spain early in the second decade of the 17th century, worked at Puebla under the direction of Pedro García Durango and Francisco Gutiérrez. They began with geometric ribbing and progressed to low relief strapwork of French or Flemish inspiration in the sanctuary bay. The decoration of the latter was largely complete by 1630.

– in both its imported and native popular manifestations, as we shall see in that context.

The Dominicans of Oaxaca have lost their original high-altar retable. The Pueblan survivor is distinguished by the curvilinear projection of its clearly articulated bays: it was renovated and endowed with its lower

5.109e

5.109g

Solomonic Order from 1688 by a master from the metropolis identified as Pedro Maldonado. That Order was introduced to the colony by Juan Martínez Montañés: called over from Seville by Puebla's Bishop Juan de Palafox y Mendoza to produce the retable of the Capella de los Reyes in the apse of the cathedral, he transformed the piers of the triumphal-arch motif with superimposed Solomonic aedicules (c. 1648). This departure from the regular beat of High Renaissance rhythm – as at Xochimilco – was the key to the progressive development furthered by the Pueblan Dominicans forty years later.**5.102a, 5.106c, 5.109f**

5.109f

CENTRAL AMERICA

Ravaged by earthquakes, Central America is not rich in 16th- or early 17th-century remains: an exception is the church at Rabinal (from c. 1572), with its basilican façade, its Serlian rustication, its Vignolesque portal and its several broken pediments. Rabinal is an outpost. The first seat of the Spanish governor in Guatamala (which then extended throughout Central America) was at Cuidad de Santiago de los Caballeros (known as Ciudad Vieja) but it succumbed in 1541. The town moved to the Valle de Panchoy but was destroyed in 1590, again a century later and in 1773: thereafter Guatamala City was founded as the capital and Santiago became Antigua. As in Mexico, Gothic and Plateresque survived well into the 16th century. The most prominent monuments were rebuilt in the second half of the 17th century but are still essentially Mannerist – or High Renaissance – rather than Baroque. A major example is the basilican cathedral of S. José, its façade emblazoned with superimposed triumphal arches.**5.110**

5.110a

›**5.110 GUATEMALA ANTIGUA:** (a) chalice (c. 1560; Boston, Museum of Fine Arts); (b) cathedral of S. José, façade, (c–e) church of Nuestra Señora de la Merced, façade, interior and cloister fountain.

The original cathedral was built c. 1540 but, often damaged by earthquake, was replaced from 1669. Extensive rebuilding followed substantial damage in the earthquake of 1773. The Merced church was also founded in the 1540s, renovated after the recurrent earthquakes and rebuilt in its present stout form in 1767 to withstand earthquakes – which it did six years later.

5.110b

5.110e

5.110c

5.110d

More or less canonical variations on the triumphal-arch motif persisted on the façades of the many churches constructed or reconstructed after Antigua's recurrent earthquakes, well into the 18th century. They are generally categorized as Baroque but are so only in the most superficial of that style's characteristics: superfluity of ornament. The most celebrated example, the stocky Nuestra Señora de la Merced (late-17th century) with the squat towers typical of an earthquake-prone area, is richly chased on every surface of its frontispiece but the superimposed triumphal arches are essentially Classical and the mannered articulation of the towers suggests distant acquaintance with Wendel Dietterlin.

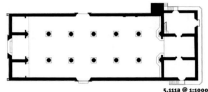

5.111a @ 1:1000

›5.111 ISLA MARGARITA, CATHEDRAL OF LA ASUNCIÓN, from c. 1590: (a) plan, (b) exterior, (c) interior.

5.111b

5.111c

›5.112 CARTAGENA DE INDIAS: (a, b) cathedral (from 1575) exterior and interior; (c) S. Domingo exterior (later 16th century); (d) Augustinian monastery of La Popa, cloister (late-16th century).

An aisled basilica with clerestory and polygonal apse, Cartagena de Indias cathedral was built over the decade from 1575 in place of a primitive structure founded at the outset of the settlement: the master-mason is named as Símon González. Badly damaged in the assault on the town by Francis Drake in 1586, repairs were interrupted by the collapse of the roof in 1600 but completed in 1612 – except for much later work on the belfry. The main portal is reminiscent of developments in the Jaén region of Andalusia after Vandelvira (see page 712): the side portal is Herreran in its canonical austerity. The frontispiece of S. Domingo is a less accomplished essay in Herrera's Valladolid mode.

NEW GRANADA AND PERU

Nuevo Reino de Granada, the northern Andean region of South America, was won a generation later than New Spain: the primary coastal settlements on the Caribbean were not established until c. 1530. There – at Coro and Isla Margarita in modern Venezuela, as well as Cartagena in Colombia – colonnaded basilicas of the S. Domingo type were still being built or rebuilt at the end of the century – though no longer with Gothic vaulting. Meanwhile, at Tunja in the highlands near Bogotá, the cathedral was being built in this antique style a generation after the founding of the town in 1539.**5.111–5.113**

5.112d

5.112b

5.112a

5.112c

5.113a

5.113b

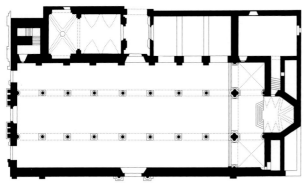

›5.113 TUNJA (COLOMBIA), CATHEDRAL OF SANTIAGO, from c. 1555: (a) exterior, (b) interior, (c) plan.

Tunja cathedral was begun after its primitive predecessor was destroyed by fire in 1554. The columns of the aisled basilica were originally Gothic shafts. In pure Herreran contrast, the portal was inserted into the attenuated Tuscan ordonnance of the façade by the master-builder Bartolomé Carrión towards the end of the century.

As in New Spain, the mendicants followed the conquistadors into the hinterland of New Granada. The Franciscans had penetrated the continent as far to the south-west as Santiago del Nuevo Extremo (Chile) by 1553, just over a decade after its foundation by the conquistador Pedro de Valdivia. Two years earlier the first contingent of Augustinians arrived in Peru from Spain. They were followed within four years by the Mercedarians and two years later still by the Dominicans. The Jesuits arrived at the end of the century. Permanent settlement in the south-east (in modern Argentina), cut off from the rest of Spanish America by the Andes and Brazil, was not established until the middle of the century.

The premier ecclesiastical complex at the extremity of Spanish America is the monastery of S. Francisco in Santiago: the church was unsurprisingly a somewhat primitive hall with rough-cast walls and timber roof.**5.114a** A generation earlier, however, the Franciscans were the first to leave an architectural mark of the first order far to the

›5.114 FRANCISCANS AT THE CONTINENTAL EXTREMITIES: (a) Santiago de Chile, S. Francisco (from 1572, aisle arcades and skylight introduced mid-19th century, redecorated), interior; (b, c) Quito (Ecuador), S. Francisco, plaza front and interior; (d, e) Bogotá (Colombia), S. Francisco, interior and plaza front.

5.114a

5.114b

north in Quito (in modern Ecuador). Their monastery was founded c. 1535 on the site of the raised palace of the late Inca: their great church was complete with its façade after 1580. At least in its inception (c. 1550) the work was due to the Flemish friar Jodoco Ricke but it may have been adapted to reflect Counter-Reformation practice in Rome. The church is basilican with interconnecting chapels flanking the nave in the Vignolan manner but, as we have noted, that was familiar to the late-medieval Franciscans and through them to Alberti: the Roman type of basilican façade is superimposed on a twin-towerd mass, with Serlian rustication to the side bays and a frontispiece of superimposed Orders in the French style.**5.114b–e**

5.114c

Quito was founded in 1536, the Flemish friars Jodoco Ricke and Pedro Gosseal founded the convento soon after: the initial plans may have been sent from Spain or they may have been due to them. Work began on the church in 1550: consecrated in 1605, it was finished in

5.114d

1680 after the successive intervention of local architects Jorge de la Cruz and Antonio Rodríguez who understood the earthquake-prone terrain and
traditional construction techniques. The façade is a
basilican exercise after Serlio, but with applied
columns supporting a semi-circular pediment, superimposed on the twin-towered structure common in
Spanish America – yet the rustication belongs to
both. Over the clerestory, the timber roof was redone
and the rich embellishment restored after earthquake
damage in 1755. The retable is late-Baroque but the
one in the much simpler Franciscan church in Bogotá
(finished in 1622 but restored after the earthquake
of 1785) is hardly inferior to the work revised by the
Mexican master Pedro Maldonado for the Pueblan
Dominicans.**5.109f**

5.114e

5.115a

5.115b

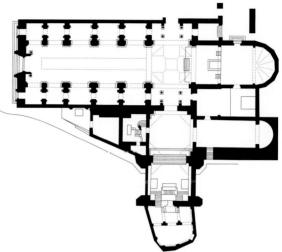

5.115c @ 1:1000

›**5.115 EARLY MISSION CHURCHES IN NEW GRANADA:** (a–c) Quito, S. Domingo, interior, exterior and plan; (d) Quito, S. Agustín (from 1606), entrance front; (e) Bogotá, S. Agustín, interior as decorated by the 1630s.

The interior elevation of Quito's S. Domingo is articulated with a Doric Order of coupled pilasters framing the chapel arcades but the chancel arch is pointed, as at S. Francisco, and there is an intricate Mudéjar ceiling. In the same city, S. Agustín (reputedly planned by Francisco Beccara in the early 1580s but executed by Juan de Corral from 1606) is more austere inside, with an abstract ordonnance of Tuscan derivation – but no canonical cornice – supporting the semi-circular transverse arches between groin-vaulted bays: the network of ribs on the choir vault is anomalous. For both churches, the frontispieces were extracted from the basilican context. Over a flattened arch flanked by meagre columns, the triumphal-arch motif survives only to frame the coro window on the upper level of S. Domingo. S. Agustín's frontispiece (inscribed as completed in 1669) is more robust in its ordonnance, with columns progressing through two planes on both levels, but the complexity of the broken pediment is highly mannered.

The interior of Bogotá's S. Agustín – an arcaded basilica with limited clerestory – runs to a distant echo of Serlio on the timber vault.

5.115d

The Augustinians and Dominicans were present in Quito from mid-century but did not begin work on their definitive churches until thirty years later. The Spanish architect Francisco Becerra, whom we have already encounterd in connection with the cathedral at Puebla, has been associated somewhat unconvincingly with S. Domingo, rather more plausibly with S. Agustín – but neither was complete until well into the 17th century. The former is highly eclectic, the latter more Classical in its geometry and abstract ordonnance. In the S. Domingo frontispiece the relationship of solid to void, of simplicity to complexity, is unorthodox – to say the least. S. Agustín's frontispiece is much bolder in its ordonnance: columns are engaged to diminishing planes in the manner not unfamiliar to contemporary Europe, but here the exercise generates little of the movement essential to the Baroque.**5.115**

5.115e

The Jesuits had arrived in New Granada by the end of the 16th century. They had begun their infiltration of the continent in Brazil in the 1550s, spread south (into modern Paraguay and Argentina) by the 1580s and north-west into the Andes colonies. Between Córdoba in Argentina

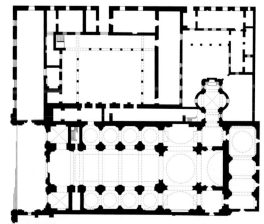

5.116a @ approximately 1:1000

5.116b

5.116c

›**5.116 EARLY JESUIT CHURCHES AT THE EXTREMITIES OF THE CONTINENT:** (a–c) Bogotá (Colombia), S. Ignacio (begun 1610, consecrated in 1635), plan, façade, detail of nave vaulting; (d) Quito, La Compañía, interior (from c. 1605, revised 1636); (e) Cartagena de Indias (Colombia), S. Pedro Clavier (c. 1695–1717), façade; (f–h) Córdoba (Argentina), La Compañía de Jesús (from 1645, vaulted from 1667), entrance front, interior to sanctuary and detail of dome.

The architect of S. Ignacio in Bogotá, the Tuscan Jesuit Juan Bautista Coluccini (1569–1641), departs from the Gesù model in the elaborate Mudéjar motifs of the tunnel vaulting and the abstract interpretation of the triumphal-arch motif central to the façade – and supporting a diminutive attic. This abstraction derives from the Tuscan Order of works like the façade of the cathedral at Tunja.

The Jesuit church at Quito was begun in 1605 under the direction of brothers named Madrigal. It was revised in 1636 by Marcos Guerra who had previously practised in Naples: the profusely decorated main body is a variant of the Neapolitan variant of the Roman Gesù formula. The most arresting façade dates from a century later – and will be encountered in due course.

La Compañía in Córdoba is attributed to the Jesuit father Bartolomé Cardenosa: it lacks a façade and the side chapels of the Gesù model, but not the domed crossing. It is distinguished by the transverse arches of its extraordinary timber vaulting: that is credited to the Flemish former shipbuilder Philippe Lemaire who derived the mode from Philibert de l'Orme (*Nouvelle Inventions pour bien bastir et à petits frais*, 1561).

The Jesuit church and college in Cartagena de Indias is dedicated to S. Pedro Claver, the 'Apostle of the

and Bogotá in Colombia, naturally, they followed the model of their Roman headquarters in laying out their many churches. The sequence of surviving buildings does not follow the Society's progress from south to north: Quito's Compañía and Bogatá's S. Ignacio were founded in the first decade of the 17th century, for example, Córdoba's Compañía de Jesús thirty years later; half-way between, Arequipa's La Compañía (Peru) was built over a century from 1590 – except for the façade – and the great Jesuit church in Cusco (also Peru) replaced the building destroyed in the earthquake of 1650. Back in Colombia, Cartegena de Indias's S. Pedro Claver may be taken as representative of Jesuit work completed in one generation at the end of the Habsburg era.**5.116**

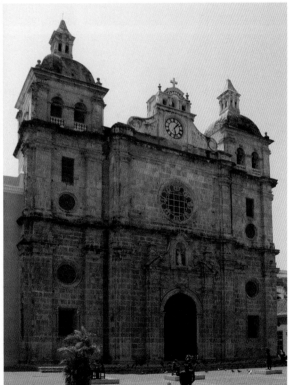

5.116d
Negroes'. The scheme, attributed to Juan Mejía del Valle, follows the order's Roman prototype – even to the tribunes above the chapels, but with the usual Iberian coro gallery within the main entrance. That layering of space is expressed – at least in principle – by the double-storey front to the nave with Tuscan austerity appropriate to the ethos of the dedicatee. Restrained from Italianate basilican expansion by stout towers with squat arcaded belfries, the morphology recalls the Jesuit church of Cusco in Peru and, indeed, the Grilos of Oporto without the Mannerist complexity.**5.56.e, 5.117d** The pediment was added in the 19th century. The original low dome, drumless on the interior, was replaced by a pseudo-Baroque one in the 1930s.

5.116e

5.116f

5.116h

5.116g

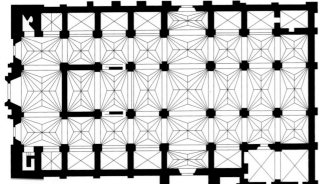

5.117a @ 1:1000

PERU

The busy Francisco Becerra went south from Quito to advise, or supersede, Juan Miguel de Veramendi on building the cathedrals of Lima and Cusco (from 1582, revised before the end of the century). There are earlier remains in Peru – usually of Franciscan or Dominican foundations – but none of significance matching the works initiated by Becerra. The hall-church model was again Andrés de Vandelvira's Jaén cathedral, in rectilinear plan and section at least; as in Diego de Siloé's great work at Granada, Gothic rib-vaults rise to pointed profiles between semi-

5.117b

circular transverse arches but they are carried on Tuscan pier pilasters with entablature blocks of much more Herreran gravitas in Cusco than in Lima – or, indeed, Granada. Again too, the central frontispiece in Lima's twin-towered façade derived from Vandelvira's translation of Siloé's superimposed triumphal-arch formula.**5.20b** Reconstructed after the earthquake of 1651, Cusco's façade is innovative, even in European terms: indeed, it may be seen to represent the most significant development in Spanish ecclesiastical architecture in the lean years of Philip IV's reign.**5.117–5.119**

The initial design of Cusco cathedral is attributed to Juan Miguel de Veramendi who was called in from Sucre (Bolivia) but was replaced within a year. The present building owes its inception to the revisions of the 1580s further revised at the end of the century. In 1603 the viceroy appointed Bartolomé Carrión

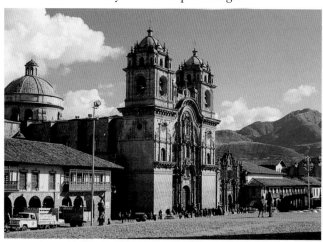

Proto-Baroque in Cusco

Cusco was founded by the conquistador Francisco Pizarro on the old Inca capital in 1534. The cathedral's construction began in 1559 on the foundations of the Inca Viracocha's palace to obliterate Inca tradition: the present building dates largely from the first half of the following century. The façade frontispiece apart, repairs rather than rebuilding seem to have followed the earthquake of 1651. That devastated much else in the city, including the neighbouring Jesuit church: founded in the late-16th century on the site of the palace of Inca Huayna Cápac, the near neighbour of Virachocha, the church of La Compañía de Jesús was rebuilt on the Gesù model, of course: the façade belongs to a different world.

5.117c

5.117d

5.117e

(the author of the frontispiece at Tunja) who further modified the design as building progressed. The nave was vaulted and the façade begun under the direction of Francisco Domínguez de Chávez from 1649, without significant disruption by the earthquake of the following year but probably with revisions to the design of the frontispiece. Finished in the mid-1650s, except for interior embellishment, the church was consecrated in 1668.

The replacement of the first Jesuit church, on the prestigious plot near the cathedral, was begun immediately after the catastrophe of 1650: it was finished in 1668. Authorship is attributed – not without dispute – to the obscure Flemish Jesuit father Jean-Baptiste Gilles (Juan Bautista Egidiano): there is documentary evidence for work on the frontispiece and towers by one Diego Martínez de Oviedo. The college building was added to the south flank, the Loreto Chapel to the other side, in the 18th century.

In contrast to the cathedral, where width counters height and the frontispiece is two-tiered, the Compañía has a triple-height retable frontispiece compressed between its twin towers. The type was not uncommon in Spain, where it developed from Franco-Flemish practice, but the aspiration to exceed the height achieved by the superimposition of columns and pilasters is furthered in a highly original manner here: the main arch, representing the full width of the nave, is broken and a higher one, representing the width of the portal, is interposed to produce a trilobed profile in amplification of the fragmentation and interpenetration of arcuate elements in each of the storeys below. Superimposition of Orders on both the horizontal and vertical planes had its contemporary parallel in the homeland: the accumulation of fragmented architectural elements is well in advance of developments there – and certainly of conservative Mexican practice in the last Habsburg reigns.

There were many variants of the Compañía retable-façade formula. One of the more elaborate of them is El Belén: the broken pediment of the lower zone is replaced by an extraordinary rectilinear tablet framed in the Mudéjar *alfiz* manner (AIC3, pages 200, 213, etc.). Among the more elementary is the façade of La Merced, also reconstructed after the 1651 earthquake: the multiplicity of columns is avoided and the triumphal-arch motif remains the essential element; its columns, applied in a single plane, are carried over to the splendid arcaded cloister – in high Classical regard for consistency countered by the quixotic patterning of the shafts in place of canonical fluting.

More elaborate homage to the achievement of the Cusco Jesuits was paid by builders as far afield as Lima, the metropolis on the Peruvian coast, and Sucre on the high plateau of Bolivia. The principal manifestation there is the portal of the cathedral (1680s). In Lima, the mode is best represented

5.117f

The Merced complex, also destroyed in 1650, was rebuilt from 1653: the church, due to the architects Alonso Casas and Francisco Monya, was completed in 1675 (the date of the façade inscription). The single-volume church of El Belén (on the outskirts of town) was begun at the end of the century: its twin-towered façade echoes the compressed form of the Compañía but with unrelieved towers.

5.117g

5.117h

5.118b

5.118c

5.118a

by the frontispiece of the Franciscan church: rebuilding (from 1656) is credited to the Portuguese Constantino de Vasconcelos and Manuel de Escobar but they worked within the Spanish context of the Andean colonies. Apart from advance on Cusco for their retable frontispiece, they surpassed the example of their Franciscan confrères at Quito in rusticating the towers: the former is more daring in interpenetration, more consistent in fragmentation, than at Cusco; the rustication is more subtle in its variation than at Quito, to assert the integrity of the framing masses. Their cloister too, with the alternating rhythm of major and minor arches – and ellipses – on its upper level, presents an instructive comparison with the essentially High Renaissance repetitive articulation preferred at La Merced.

›5.118 LIMA, DEVELOPMENT OF THE CUSCO STYLE: (a–f) S. Francisco (from 1656), cloister and tiled gallery, stairs with artesonado vault (restored most recently after earthquake damage in 1940), church interior and sacristy portal (1729), general view from forecourt; (g) parish church of S. María Madalena, front (late-17th century, restored).

An earlier church on the Franciscan site (finished in 1624) was due to Brother Miguel de Huerta who also contributed much to the monastery, especially the staircase with its artesonado vault and the cloister – at least in inception. That church succumbed to earthquake within a generation. Its replacement was begun by Constantino de Vasconcelos in 1657: after his death

5.118d

in the late-1660s, the main body was completed (c. 1672) by his assistant, Manuel de Escobar, who was in turn assisted by the Franciscan brother Carlos de la Concepción. The retable façade and towers date from later in the century – the former, at least, in accordance with Vasconcelos's scheme. The sacristy portal, signed by Lucas Meléndez, is dated 1729 and represents the last phase of the development of the design process introduced in Cusco eighty years earlier.

5.118f

5.118g

5.118e

5.119a

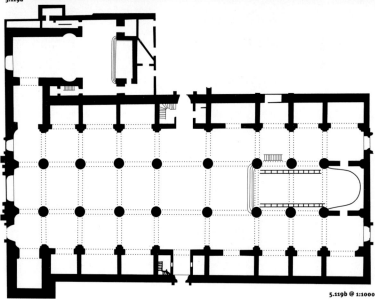

5.119b @ 1:1000

›**5.119 LIMA, CATHEDRAL,** from 1582: (a) interior, (b) plan, (c) west front.

The first church on the site was founded by Francisco Pizarro in 1535. A second rebuilding was projected in the late-1560s and begun early in the next decade by the master-mason Alonso Beltrán. Called in to further the work on both the viceroy's palace and the cathedral, Francisco Becerra proposed a new scheme for the latter: scaled down from the Jaén model,**5.35b** work on it was advanced by 1604 when the sanctuary was dedicated. The groin vaulting of Becerra's nave was unarticulated: the antiquarian ribs were added in reconstruction after earthquake damage in 1609 and again (in stuccoed timber) following further damage in 1677 and 1746. The lower storey of the frontispiece is dated 1626, the upper 1722: the latter respects the scheme of Juan Martínez de Arrona on the whole (recorded) except for the semi-circular pediment. Much modified, the belfries date largely from the 19th century.

5.119c

Much in the Cusco school and its Lima derivative is Mannerist in motif – Wendel Dietterlin is more likely than Bernardo Buontalenti as the source – but the dynamic motive takes us to the threshold of the Baroque. In the variant devised for the cathedral, had the concave curves of the side bays been countered with convexity in the centre we would have crossed that threshold. That, therefore, remains for another volume.

GLOSSARY

ABACUS flat slab forming the top of a capital.

ADDORSED 'back to back' (of, for example, columns).

ADOBE mud or mud brick.

AEDICULE ornamental niche housing a sacred image, for example.

AISLE side passage of a church or temple, running parallel to the nave and separated from it by columns or piers.

ALCÁZAR any of a series of palaces built by the Moors in Spain. From Arabic *al qasr*.

ALL'ANTICA 'in the manner of the ancients'; that is, drawing on the repertoire of Classical forms in Renaissance architecture.

ALTAR focus of attention in religious ritual; the communion table in a Christian church.

AMBULATORY semi-circular or polygonal arcade or walkway surrounding, for example, a sanctuary.

AMPHITHEATRE more or less circular theatre, with banks of seats surrounding the performance space.

ANDRONE dining room in a private house, reserved for the use of the master of the household.

APSE semicircular domed or vaulted space, especially at one end of a basilica, hence **APSIDAL**, in the shape of an apse.

ARCADE series of arches supported by columns, sometimes paired and covered so as to form a walkway. Hence **BLIND ARCADE**, a series of arches applied to a wall as decoration.

ARCH, CUSPED composed of two or more arcs with a cusp at their intersection.

ARCH, DIAPHRAGM in which the area from springing line to apex is made blind with an infill.

ARCH, OGEE composed of two cyma reversa mouldings meeting head to head at the apex.

ARCH, STILTED in which an interpolated pier raises the springing line above the impost.

ARCHITRAVE one of the three principal elements of an entablature, positioned immediately above the capital of a column, and supporting the frieze and cornice.

ARCUATE shaped like an arch. Hence (of a building) **ARCUATED**, deploying arch structures (as opposed to trabeated).

ARTESONADO coffered ceiling formed of decorative wood panels and interlaced beams.

ASHLAR masonry cut and laid to present a smooth finished surface (as opposed to, for example, Cyclopean or rubble construction).

ASTYLAR without columns.

ATLANTE element in the shape of a male figure, used in place of a column.

ATRIUM entrance-hall or courtyard, often open to the sky.

ATTIC shallow storey above the main Orders of a façade, or a wall at the top of the entablature concealing the roof.

AULA REGIA public audience chamber or throne room in a royal or imperial court.

AYUNTAMIENTO Spanish muncipal authority, hence the building housing it.

BALDACHINO canopy raised on columns over an altar or tomb.

BALUSTER short column or pillar, usually bulbous towards the base, supporting a rail.

BALUSTRADE a row of balusters supporting a rail.

BAPTISTRY building, adjunct to a church, dedicated to baptism.

BARCHESSE the wings of a villa devoted to agricultural functions.

BASILICA church, temple or other public building, consisting principally of a colonnaded rectangular space with an apse at one end, generally enclosed by an ambulatory, or having a central nave and side aisles, and lit by a clerestory.

BASTION structure projecting from the angle of a defensive wall enabling enhanced vision and mobility for a garrison.

BATTERING reinforcement of walls and column bases by building sloping supporting structure.

BAY one of a series of compartments of the interior of a building, the divisions being created by piers or columns, for example.

BELFRY bell tower or the particular room in a bell tower where the bells are hung.

BELVEDERE open-sided roofed structure, freestanding or situated on the roof of a building, placed so as to command a view.

BEMA sanctuary of a church, especially Byzantine.

BOSQUET (from Italian *boschetto*, a little wood), in French gardens, a formal arrangement of trees.

BOSS ornamental projection at the apices where the ribs of a vault meet.

BOZZETTO a small sketch model for a sculpture or a building.

BRODERIE in French formal gardening, a parterre using paths and beds to form an embroidery-like pattern.

BURGFRIED German castle keep; also, the productive area administered from a castle.

BUTTRESS support, usually stone, built against or adjacent to a wall to reinforce or take load.

CAMPANILE bell tower, usually freestanding.

CANOPY roof for a niche or statue, often supported by slender poles.

CANOPY VAULT, *see* **VAULT, CANOPY**.

CAPPELLA chapel.

CAPITAL top part of a column, supporting the entablature, wider than the body of the shaft, usually formed and decorated more or less elaborately. The part of the column which, taken together with the entablature, forms the major defining element in the Greek Orders of architecture – Doric, Ionic and Corinthian.

CARYATID female figure used as a support in place of a column.

CASINA a small summer house or kiosk.

CASINO a country house, typically a house for summer occupation.

CATHEDRAL large church, serving as the focal point for a bishop in his diocese.

CAVEA the seating within a theatre.

CAVETTO concave moulding with a quarter-circular cross-section.

CENTRALIZED PLAN building design in which the structure is symmetrical in plan around the centre, allowing for reflection about both 90- and 180-degree axes.

CHANCEL part of a church where the clergy and choir are ranged, separated by screen or railing from the main body of the building.

CHANTRY CHAPEL chapel dedicated to the chanting of masses to save the soul of the sponsor.

CHAPEL subsidiary space having its own altar, situated within a larger church or cathedral.

CHAPTER assembly of canons in a cathedral or abbot and senior monks in a monastery, responsible for managing institutional affairs.

CHAPTER HOUSE room or building within or adjacent to a monastery or cathedral, in which the chapter meets.

CHÂTEAU a large country or manor house; at one extreme, a palace.

CHEVET apse at the east end of a church wherein there is an ambulatory with chapels or miniature apses radiating off it.

CHEVRON decorative moulding composed of a zigzag pattern.

CHIAROSCURO the use of light and shadow in a painting, creating the illusions of depth and volume, often to dramatic effect,.

CHOIR area of a church near the altar, in which the choir (singers) sit.

CIBORIUM canopy raised on columns so as to form a covering above an altar or tomb, for example.

CLERESTORY windowed upper level, providing light from above for a double-storey interior.

CLOISTER covered arcade, often running around the perimeter of an open courtyard.

COFFERING decoration of a ceiling or vault, for example, with sunken rectangular or other polygonal panels.

COLONNADE line of regularly spaced columns.

COLONNETTE small column, decorative and/or functional.

COLORE in art, compositional coherence achived through the painterly application of pigment, developed in Venice by Giovanni Bellini and his followers.

COLUMN vertical member, usually circular in cross-section, functionally structural or ornamental or both, comprising (usually) a base, shaft, and capital.

COLUMN, ENGAGED column which does not stand completely proud of a wall, either having stone ties or being partially sunk into the wall, though not so much as a pilaster.

CONCINNITAS beauty of style achieved through the skilful and harmonious joining of elements.

CONSOLE a **CORBEL** or bracket, often with a scroll-shaped profile.

CORBEL support bracket, usually stone, for a beam or other horizontal member. Hence **CORBELLED**, forming a stepped roof by deploying progressively overlapping corbels.

CORINTHIAN ORDER *see* **ORDER, CORINTHIAN**.

CORNICE projecting moulding forming the top part of an entablature. More generally, a horizontal ornamental moulding projecting at the top of a wall or other structure.

CORO choir in a church.

CORPS DE LOGIS principal part of a major building, as distinct from its wings, subsidiary blocks, colonnades or **PAVILLONS**, etc.

CORTILE an internal court, open to the sky and surrounded by an arcade.

COVE/COVING curved concave moulding forming or covering the junction between wall and ceiling.

CRENELLATION indentation in a parapet.

CROCKET carved ornament usually in the form of a curled leaf.

CROSSING the area where the transept of a church crosses the nave and chancel, often surmounted by a tower.

CRYPT underground chamber, often beneath the chancel of a church.

CRYPTO-PORTICUS concealed or sunken passage or arcade.

CURTAIN WALL defensive wall of a castle.

CUSP projection formed between two arcs, especially in stone tracery, hence **CUSPED**.

CYCLOPEAN masonry made up of massive irregular blocks of undressed stone.

CYMA RECTA wave-shaped moulding, usually forming all or part of a cornice, the upper part being convex and the lower concave.

CYMA REVERSA wave-shaped moulding, usually forming all or part of a cornice, the upper part being concave and the lower convex.

DADO the middle part, between base and cornice, of, for instance, a pedestal, or the lower part of a wall when treated as a continuous pedestal.

DIAPERWORK repeated pattern in brick or tile, for example, often involving diamond shapes.

DIAPHRAGM ARCH, *see* **ARCH, DIAPHRAGM**.

DISEGNO draftsmanship; also the ability to create through drawing.

DOME more or less hemispherical roof or vault, hence domical.

DONJON French term denoting the keep or main tower protected by the walls of a castle.

DORIC ORDER *see* **ORDER, DORIC**.

EAVES the part of a roof which overhangs the outer face of a wall.

ENCEINTE the whole fortified area of a castle.

EN ECHELON disposed in parallel, like the rungs of a ladder.

ENFILADE a suite of rooms with their doorways aligned – thus creating a vista – and typically embodying a hierarchy from public to private.

ENGAGED COLUMN, *see* **COLUMN, ENGAGED**.

ENTABLATURE that part of the façade of a church, etc., which is immediately above the columns, and is generally composed of architrave, frieze and cornice.

ESTILO CHÃO austere Portuguese architectural style of the 16th century characterized by the use of simple Classical forms and absence of decoration.

ESTILO DESORNAMENTADO 16th- and early 17th-century Spanish architectural style reacting to the excessive decoration that characterized the **PLATERESQUE** style. In contrast, the *estilo desornamentado* was functional and emphasised order over ornament and symmetry – under the guidance of Vitruvius.

EXEDRA recess, usually apsidal, containing seats.

EXONARTHEX extension to the narthex of a church, formed by the aisles.

FAN VAULT, *see* **VAULT, FAN**.

FILIGREE decorative work formed of a mesh or by piercing material to give the impression of a mesh.

FINIAL ornament at the top of a gable or roof, for example.

FLAMBOYANTE ARCHITECTURE highly decorative late-Gothic style developed in France in the late-14th and 15th centuries.

FLUTING decorative vertical grooves incised on a column.

FLYING BUTTRESS an arch and more or less freestanding buttress which together take the load of a roof, for example.

FONT freestanding basin, usually of stone, sited in a church for use in the Christian baptism ritual.

FORUM central open space of a town, usually a marketplace surrounded by public buildings.

FRESCO method of painting done on plaster which is not yet dry, hence also the resultant artefact.

FRIEZE the middle part of an entablature, above the architrave and below the cornice. More generally, any horizontal strip decorated in relief.

FRONTISPIECE principal entrance and its surround, usually distinguished by decoration and often standing proud of the façade in which it sits.

GABLE more or less triangular vertical area formed by the ends of the inclined planes of a pitched roof.

GALLERY upper storey projecting from the interior of a building, and overlooking the main interior space.

GISANT funerary sculpture with recumbent figure of the dead person.

GLACIS slope or ramp in front of a defensive wall.

GOLDEN SECTION architectural proportions thought to produce an effect particularly pleasing to the eye, whereby, for example, the ratio of width to length equals the ratio of length to (width plus length).

GOTHIC ARCHITECTURE style featuring pointed arches, rib vaults and flying buttresses, which prevailed in Western Europe roughly from the 12th century to the 16th.

GREEK CROSS cross with four arms of equal length.

GRISAILLE a painting in monochrome, or near monochrome, restricted to variations in tone to define form.

GROIN rib formed at the intersection of two vaults.

GROIN VAULT, *see* **VAULT, GROIN**.

GROTTESCHI 'grotesques', motifs employing mixed human, animal and vegetable forms derived from the decoration of Ancient Roman grottoes rediscovered in the Renaissance.

GUTTAE projections, more or less conical in form, carved beneath the triglyphs of a Doric entablature.

HALL CHURCH church in which nave and aisles are of equal height, or nearly so, often under a single roof.

HERM sculpted pillar with a male head (usually of Hermes) and sometimes his torso above a plain section. In Ancient Greece these were used as markers of territory; in Renaissance architecture often applied as a decorative element.

HIPPODROME arena for horse-racing and, subsequently, for other sporting events.

ICON image of a sacred subject, often acquiring sacred significance in its own right. Hence **ICONIC**, possessing sacred significance.

ICONOSTASIS screen separating the nave from the sanctuary in a Byzantine church, latterly used for placing icons.

IGNUDO -I Michelangelo's term (from Italian 'nudo', 'naked') for the many seated idealized male nudes incorporated in the frescoes for the Sistine Chapel ceiling.

IMPOST structural member – usually in the form of a moulding or block – at the top of a pillar, for example, on which an arch rests.

IN ANTIS a portico in which the columns align with the flanking walls rather than projecting beyond them.

INSULA Roman apartment building, with shops and other businesses at street level and housing on several floors above.

IONIC ORDER *see* **ORDER, IONIC**.

JAMB side of a doorway or window frame.

JOISTS horizontal timbers typically supporting a floor.

KEEP main tower of a castle, providing living accommodation.

LADY CHAPEL chapel dedicated to the Virgin Mary.

LANCET arch or window rising to a point at its apex.

LANTERN TOWER windowed structure lighting an interior, situated on a roof, often at the apex of a dome.

LATIN CROSS cross with one arm longer than the other three.

LIERNE short intermediate rib, often non-structural.

LINTEL horizontal member over a window or doorway, or bridging the gap between two columns or piers.

LOGGIA gallery open to the elements on one side.

LUNETTE semi-circular window or recess, usually at the base of a dome or vault.

MACHICOLATION gallery or parapet projecting on corbels from the outside of defensive walls, with holes from which missiles might be dropped or thrown.

MANIERA literally 'style' but associated with a self-conscious style of painting that displayed technical virtuosity with value placed on qualities such as grace and innovation.

MANUELINE ARCHITECTURE late-Gothic style developed in Portugal (and named after King Manuel I, 1495–1521) in which maritime imagery and Spanish, Italian and Flemish influences were brought together with singularly lavish results.

MAUSOLEUM building providing a monumental carapace for a tomb.

METOPE originally the space between the triglyphs in a Doric frieze, and subsequently the panel, often carved in relief, occupying that space.

MINSTER cathedral or major church attached to a monastery.

MONASTERY buildings providing accommodation for a community of monks or nuns.

MOSAIC decoration formed by embedding small coloured tiles (tesserae) in cement.

MULLION vertical element forming subdivisions of a window.

MULTIFOIL much subdivided basically arcuate or circular form of ornament.

NARTHEX chamber adjunct to the nave of a church.

NAVE central body of principal interior of, for example, a church.

NYMPHAEUM originally – in Classical Greece and Rome – a sanctuary dedicated to water nymphs; later a structure or area with water features treated more or less elaborately.

OCULUS circular window in a church, for example.

OGEE ARCH, *see* **ARCH, OGEE**.

ORATORY small room for prayer; in a Benedictine monastery, a communal prayer room.

ORDER defining feature of Classical architecture, comprising a column – itself usually composed of base, shaft, and capital – together with its entablature.

  CORINTHIAN an evolution from the Ionic Order, characterized by the replacement of the capital volutes with a more elaborate and deeper decorative arrangement. Later Corinthian columns evolved so as to be even taller relative to their base diameters than the Ionic. The entablature retained the comparatively light characteristics of the Ionic.

  DORIC the oldest and most simply functional of the Greek Orders of architecture, characterized by a fluted and tapered column without a base, topped by a usually plain capital, surmounted by a relatively high entablature made up of architrave, frieze, and cornice.

  IONIC slightly later and more elaborate order than the Doric, featuring fluted columns with bases and characteristically topped by a capital with scrolled volutes. The columns typically are taller relative to their base diameters than are the Doric, and are correspondingly less acutely tapered. The entablature is less tall than that of the Ionic, being originally composed of architrave and cornice only, though a frieze became usual later.

ORIEL window in a projecting bay supported by a bracket or corbel.

PALATINATE area ruled by a count palatine.

PALAZZO in Italy, a mansion or other large and imposing building.

PARAPET low wall, often protecting walkway at the top of an outer wall, originally for defensive purposes.

PARTERRE gardens inspired by embroidery patterns using flat-topped hedges of uniform height to mark out a series of ornamental flowerbeds planted symmetrically. *See also* **BRODERIE**.

PATIO outdoor space; a forecourt or courtyard.

PAVILION usually a free-standing structure used for recreation and situated some distance from a house or other major building. However, the term is also often used to translate French **PAVILLON**; *see below*.

PAVILLON In a symmetrical building or range of buildings, *pavillons* are outstanding attached structures that provide emphasis at the extremes or the centre of a façade, for example.

PEDESTAL base supporting, for example, a column or statue.

PEDIMENT triangular area of wall, usually a gable, above the entablature, enclosed above by raking cornices.

PENDENTIVE curved concave triangular member used at the corners of a square or polygonal structure so as to enable reconciliation with a domed roof.

PFALZ palatinate in south-west Germany.

PIANO NOBILE main, usually the first, floor of a large house or palazzo, site of the important reception rooms.

PIER supporting pillar for wall or roof, often of rectangular cross-section and/or formed from a composite mass of masonry columns.

PILASTER pier of rectangular cross-section, more or less integral with and only slightly projecting from the wall it supports.

PINNACLE slender ornamental termination at the top of a gable or buttress, for example, often in the shape of a miniature turret.

PLATERESQUE intricate and decorative stonework, from the Spanish *plata* (silver).

PLINTH rectangular base or base support of, for example, a column or wall.

PODIUM continuous base or pedestal consisting of plinth, dado and cornice, to support a series of columns.

PORCH covered entranceway to a building.

PORTA COELI entrance to a sacred building, literally 'gate of heaven'.

PORTAL doorway, usually on the grand scale.

PORTE-COCHÈRE open porch large enough to shelter a vehicle; originally an entrance to a building through which a coach could be driven to reach an enclosed courtyard.

PORTICO entrance to or vestibule of a building, often featuring a colonnade.

POSA in New Spain, etc., a small chapel at the corner of a courtyard.

POST vertical element in, for example, a trabeated structure.

PRESBYTERY area reserved for clergy, at the eastern end of a church, in which the main altar is situated.

PULPIT raised structure in church, from which the preacher addresses the congregation.

QUADRATBAU choir which is square in plan.

QUADRATURA ceiling paintings using severe perspective techniques such as foreshortening and with elaborately painted architectural settings; more generally simulated architectural features.

QUADRO RIPORTATO framed paintings in normal perspective incorporated into a ceiling fresco, often combined with illusionistic techniques.

QUATRALOBE area composed of four interlocking circular segments.

QUATREFOIL having a shape composed of four subsidiary curves.

QUINCUNX structure composed of an agglomeration of five elements, four being identical and disposed so as to form more or less a hollow square, its centre being filled by the fifth.

QUOIN external corner of a building, where the stones thereof are arranged to form a key pattern.

RAADHUIS town hall.

RAMPART defensive earthwork, usually surrounding a fortress or citadel, often with a stone parapet.

RAYONNANT style of tracery in which the pattern radiates from a central point.

REFECTORY communal dining hall in a monastery or convent.

RELIEF carving typically of figures, raised from a flat background usually by cutting away more (high relief) or less (low relief) of the material from which they are carved.

REREDOS carved or painted screen in wood or stone, rising from behind an altar.

RETABLE carved screen or reredos rising above and behind the altar, especially in the Spanish tradition.

RETROCHOIR the area behind the high altar in a large church.

REVETMENT decorative reinforced facing for retaining wall.

RIB raised band on a vault or ceiling.

RIB VAULT, *see* **VAULT, RIB**.

RICETTO a vestibule, originally a defensible area protecting a settlement.

ROTUNDA circular room or building, usually with a domed roof.

RUSTICATION exterior ornament, often but not necessarily restricted to the lowest storey of a Classical building, in which masonry is given the appearance of strength (or roughness) by the use of projection and exaggerated chamfered or otherwise recessed joints.

SACRISTY room in a church for storing valuable ritual objects.

SALA a room.

SALA TERRENA formal and extensive room, often highly decorated, with garden access through one side.

SALONE a formal room.

SALOTTO a drawing room or salon.

SANCTUARY the most sacred part of a church, usually where the altar is situated.

SARCOPHAGUS coffin or outer container for a coffin, usually of stone and decorated with carvings.

SCAGLIOLA a composite material resembling marble and used in the manufacture of sculpture and architectural elements.

SCENAE FRONS the flat wall forming the back of the stage in a semi-circular Roman theatre.

SCENOGRAPHIC effecting a representation in perspective.

SCOTIA concave moulding on the base of a column, often between two convex torus mouldings, thus providing an apparently deep channel between them.

SCREEN partition separating one part of an interior from another.

SCREEN WALL false (i.e. non-structural) wall to the front of a building, masking the façade proper.

SÉ cathedral

SERLIANA (after Serlio but probably an innovation by Bramante) used of windows and doors (or a blind feature) in a tripartite arrangement, the central opening with a semi-circular arch supported by columns. This central feature is taller than the narrower, usually flat-topped, openings to either side of it.

SFUMATO in painting and drawing, the use of fine shading to produce subtle gradations of tone.

SGRAFFITO Italian term meaning 'to scratch', a decorative technique in which a plaster layer is scored to reveal a contrasting colour.

SHAFT more or less cylindrical element of a column rising from the base to the capital.

SOCLE shallow plinth supporting, for example, a piece of sculpture.

SOFFIT the underside of an architectural element in, for example, a cornice or architrave.

SOLAR a room for sleeping or private family use; initially at the end of the great hall but later usually on the top floor of a house.

SOTOCORO below the choir.

SPANDREL triangular space formed by the outer curve of an arch and the horizontal and vertical elements of the (often virtual) rectangle within which the arch sits.

SPIRE elongated conical or pyramidal structure forming the apex of a tower.

SPRINGING the point at which an arch springs from its support.

SQUINCH arch placed across the corner of a square structure so as to form a polygon capable of being roofed with a dome.

STADTHUIS city or town hall.

STANZA a room or apartment.

STILTED ARCH, see **ARCH, STILTED**.

STRINGCOURSE projecting horizontal course of structural elements or moulding.

STUCCO plaster, especially used where decoration is to be applied.

STUDIOLO a small room used as a more-or-less private retreat.

TABERNACLE niche or cupboard, usually housing the consecrated host or sacred relic.

TEMPIETTO a small temple.

TESSERA small tile made of marble or glass, for example, used in conjunction with others to form mosaic.

THERMAE public baths, usually divided into frigidarium, tepidarium, and calidarium.

TIE-BEAM horizontal beam preventing two other structural components from separating.

TIERCERON subordinate rib set between the main members of a rib vault.

TORUS large moulding, typically at base of a column, of more or less semi-circular cross-section.

TRABEATED structurally dependent on rectilinear post and beam supports.

TRACERY pattern of ribs or bars inset to ornamental effect into a window or on to a panel.

TRANSEPT that part of the interior of a large church or cathedral which crosses the nave or principal interior space at right angles.

TRANSOM cross-bar or lintel, especially of a window.

TRASCORO part of the choir behind the main body of the choir or altar (**RETROCHOIR**)

TREFOIL having a curved shape composed of three subsidiary curves.

TRIBUNE vaulted apse, often the site of an altar or throne, or a semi-circular recess behind the choir of a church, or a vaulted gallery over an aisle and commanding the nave.

TRIFORIUM arcaded corridor facing on to the nave or chancel of a church, situated immediately below the clerestory.

TRIGLYPH block carved with vertical channels, used in a Doric frieze.

TRIUMPHAL ARCH originally a monument commemorating a victory, often taking the form of a massive rectangle penetrated by an arch.

TUNNEL VAULT, see **VAULT, TUNNEL**.

TYMPANUM an area, usually recessed, formed by a lintel below and an arch above.

VAULT structure forming an arched roof over a space.
    BARREL enclosing a more or less hemicylindrical space.
    CANOPY creating a roof for a niche or tomb.
    DOMICAL enclosing a more or less hemispherical space.
    FAN in which ribs of equal length, spaced equidistantly, are disposed around cones whose closest point of approach creates the apex of the vault.
    GROIN enclosing a space composed of two intersecting more or less hemi-cylindrical shapes.
    RIB composed of load-bearing ribs, carrying the material which fills the spaces between them.
    TUNNEL enclosing a more or less hemi-cylindrical space.

VESTIBULE originally the courtyard in front of the entrance to a Greek or Roman house; hallway to a building; space adjunct to a larger room.

VIGNA a vineyard.

VILLA freestanding house, originally Roman country house.

VOLUTE scroll or spiral ornamental and/or support member, characteristic of Ionic capitals.

VOUSSOIR wedge-shaped stone deployed in building an arch. Hence **VOUSSOIR ARCH**, where such stones are used.

WARD castle courtyard, bailey.

WESTWORK entrance hall and superstructure at the west end of a Romanesque or Carolingian church.

XYSTUS originally the portico in front of a gymnasium, where exercise could be taken in poor weather; later a term designating the open area for promenading in front of a portico.

FURTHER READING

This set of volumes, *Architecture in Context*, is based on a survey series of lectures covering the whole spectrum of architectural history developed over a quarter of a century at the Canterbury School of Architecture. It is therefore impossible, even if it were desirable, to enumerate all the books that I have consulted and, in one way or another, depended on, over that period. Beyond students of architecture, for whom this whole process was initiated, I hope that the present work will provide the general reader with a broad but also reasonably deep introduction to the way our environment has been moulded over the past five thousand years. With this in mind, rather than a bibliography, I hope it will be useful if I provide a rough guide to how I would go about developing a course in further reading, were I starting now.

First, I would consult the *Grove Dictionary of Art* and the *Macmillan Dictionary of Architecture*, as much for the bibliographies attached to each section of each subject as for the individual articles – inevitably some are better than others as different authors naturally bring different standards of scholarship to bear on their products. *A World History of Art* by Hugh Honour and John Fleming (London 1984, sixth edition 2002) is unsurpassed in the field of general introductions.

Second, for greater depth and breadth, I would consult the relevant volumes of *The Pelican History of Art*: now published by Yale University Press, many of these have been updated or, where the text is an historical document in itself, edited with minimal corrections. The quality in these works is in general much more even as each self-contained subject is usually given to one scholar of outstanding academic record. Again, the bibliographies appended to each volume will be an invaluable guide to even broader and deeper reading. Taschen (under the indefatigable editorship of Henri Stierlin) has published a lavishly illustrated multi-volume series that has perhaps been over-ambitious and therefore remains incomplete.

Third: specific histories of architecture. As any student of the subject knows, the inescapable primer is the work first published in 1896 by Sir Banister Fletcher as *A History of Architecture on the Comparative Method*: that was essentially a catalogue arranged roughly chronologically by area – starting with ancient Egypt and Mesopotamia – but as the method was gradually superseded more room was found in the later 20th-century editions for essential analysis. Beyond that, from my view in the 1970s the most useful general survey of architectural history was the multivolume series initiated by Electa in Milan, edited by Pier Luigi Nervi and pub-

lished in English by Abrams (and later by others): it had its flaws, not least in the relationship of text to illustrations even in the fine account of Renaissance architecture by Professor Peter Murray. The range of scholars involved was impressive (notwithstanding some flagrant political bias) and, despite their age, some of the material not otherwise easily available is still essential reading.

In particular I would recommend the following monographs and their bibliographies: Michael Levey, *High Renaissance* (Harmondsworth 1975); John Shearman, *Mannerism* (Harmondsworth 1967); Rudolf Wittkower, *Architectural Principles in the Age of Humanism* (New York 1965); Hanno-Walter Kruft, *A History of Architectural Theory* (London 1994); Henry A. Millon and Vittorio Magnago Lampugnani (eds), *The Renaissance from Brunelleschi to Michelangelo: The Representation of Architecture* (Milan 1994); Christoph Luitpold Frommel, *The Architecture of the Italian Renaissance* (New York 2007); Colin Rowe and Leon Satkowski, *Italian Architecture of the 16th Century* (New York 2002); James S. Ackermann, *The Architecture of Michelangelo* (Harmondsworth 1961,1970), and *Palladio* (Harmondsworth 1966); Lionello Puppi, *Andrea Palladio: The Complete Works* (New York 1975); Guido Beltramini, Antonio Padoan and Howard Burns, *Andrea Palladio: The Complete Illustrated Works* (New York 2001); Howard Burns (ed.), *Andrea Palladio 1508–1580: The Portico and the Farmyard* (London 1975); Douglas Lewis (ed.), *The Drawings of Andrea Palladio* (Washington DC 1981); Louis Hautecoeur, *Histoire de l'Architecture Classique en France*, tome 1 (Paris from 1943) and *Histoire du Louvre* (Paris n.d.); David Thomson, *Renaissance Paris* (Berkeley and Los Angeles 1984); Anthony Blunt, *Philibert de l'Orme* (London 1958); Rosalys Coope, *Salomon de Brosse* (London 1972); Jean-Maris Pérouse de Montclos, *Histoire de l'Architecture Française* (Paris 2003) and *Fontainebleau* (London 1988); Henry-Russell Hitchcock, *German Renaissance Architecture* (Princeton 1981); William Craft Brumfield, *A History of Russian Architecture* (Cambridge 1993); Peter Kidson and Peter Murray, *A History of English Architecture* (New York 1962); Mark Girouard, *Elizabethan Architecture* (New Haven and London 2009); Giles Worsley, *Inigo Jones and the European Classicist Tradition* (New Haven and London 2007); John Harris and Gordon Higgott (eds) *Inigo Jones: Complete Architectural Drawings* (New York 1989); George Kubler, *Building the Escorial* (Princeton 1982) and *Portuguese Plain Architecture* (Middletown CT 1972); Víctor Nieto, Alfredo J. Morales and Fernando Checa, *Arquitectura del Renacimiento en España, 1488–1599* (Madrid 1989); Jonathan

Brown and J. H. Elliott, *A Palace for a King: The Buen Retiro and the Court of Philip IV* (New Haven and London 1980); Xavier Bray (ed.), *The Sacred Made Real* (London 2009); Manuel Toussaint, *Colonial Art in Mexico* (Austin and London 1967); Joseph Armstrong Baird, Jr, *The Churches of Mexico 1530–1810* (Berkeley 1962); James Early, *The Colonial Architecture of Mexico* (Albuquerque 1994); Damián Bayón and Murillo Marx, *History of South American Colonial Art and Architecture* (Barcelona 1989).

My own dependence on the contributors to the series cited above and to the authors of the individual monographs in the abbreviated list will be apparent to even the most cursory reader. I apologize that it is far too wide-ranging individually to acknowledge here.

INDEX

Córdoba (Argentina): La Compañía de Jesús 839, *840*

Corinthian Order: Austria *432*; England *593*, 625; France 246, *313*, 330, *334*, 340, 350, 393, *393*; Germany 413, 446, *448*, 475, 477, 506, 507; Italy, civic building 235; Italy, ecclesiastical 129, 243, *261*, 271; Italy, palace 135, 211, 212, *213*, 231, 244, *266*; Spain 529, 660, *697*, *712*, *724*

Cornelius Floris II 416–17; Frederiksborg Castle *553–7*; funerary monuments *416*; Oude Stadhuis, The Hague *419*; Philip II, entry into Antwerp 416, *416*, 420; Rathaus, Cologne *417*, 417–18; Stadhuis, Antwerp 417–19, *418–19*

corps de logis 300, *302*, *306*, 337, 340, *351*, 352

Correggio (Antonio Allegri da Correggio) 31–2, *31–3*

Cortés, Hernán *802–3*, 802–3, 812

Cortona, Domenico da: Hôtel de Ville, Paris *313*, 313

Coulommiers: Château *390–1*

Counter-Reformation orders 269, 290, 294–5, 523, 770

courtyard houses *564–5*, 565

Cousin, Jean *326*

Covarrubias, Alonso de: Alcázar, Madrid *692–3*, 695–6; Alcázar, Toledo 696–7, 697, *724–5*; Archbishop's Palace, Alcalá de Henares 690, *691*; Archbishop's Palace, Toledo 695–6; Cathedral, Sigüenza 688, *688*; Cathedral, Toledo *688*; Colegio Fonseca, Salamanca *680–1*, 681; commissioned tombs *648*, *649*; Hospital de Tavera, Toledo *694*, 697; Hospital of S. Juan Bautista 695; Hospital of Santa Cruz, Toledo 641–2, *642*, 650; Monastery of S. Bartolomeo, Lupiana 690, *690*; S. Benito Abad, Yepes 688–9, 689

Coverdale, Miles 65, *65*

Cranmer, Thomas 64–5

Crescenzi, Giovanni Battista 756–7, *757*, *759*

Cricoli: Villa Trissino *227*

Crivelli, Andrea *432*

Cromwell, Thomas 63, 64–5, 66

Cruz, Jorge de la *835*

Cuernavaca: House of Cortés *803*

Cuidad Rodrigo: Ayuntamiento 691, *691*; Capilla de Cerralbo *744*, *745*

Cusco: Cathedral 841, *841*, 842; El Belen *844*, *844*; La Compañía de Jesús *842–3*, 843; La Merced *844*, 844

da Udine, Giovanni *19*, 116, *118–19*

de l'Orme, Philibert 327–8; Anet Château 328–9, *329–33*; Château, Saint-Maur-des-Fossés 328, *328–9*; Château Neuf 333, *333*; Hôtel Bullioud, Lyon *327*; Hôtel des Tournelles *346*; *Nouvelles Inventions pour bien bastir et a petit frais 344*, *344–5*; S. Étienne-du-Mont *333*, 333; Tuileries 346–7, *346–7*, 362

Deene Park (Northamptonshire) *570–1*

Delft: Nieuwe Kerk *549*

della Robba, Girolamo *312*

dell'Allio, Domenico *441*

Denmark 553, *553–7*, 556–7

Devotio Moderna 51, 53

Dietterlin, Wendel *490–3*, 491, 575

Dijon: Maison Milsand *348*; S. Michel *308*

Dillingen: Studeienkirche Mariä Himmelfahrt *520*

disegno 10, 25

Domenichino: Villa Ludovisi *285*

domical vaulting 818

Dominican Republic: Santo Domingo 794, *794–7*

Dominicans 82, 94–5, *532*, 786; Mexican missions 803, 804, *810–11*, 812, 824, *824–5*; South American missions 833

Donatello (Donato di Niccolò di Betto Bardi) 5, *6*

Doric Order: England *581*, 586, 592, *593*; France 330, 340, 350, *351*, 353, 356, 364, 389, *397*, 413; Germany 477, 495, *517*, *519*, India *793*; Italy, civic building *132*, 133, 218, 221, *235*; Italy, ecclesiastical *17*, 145, 215, 261, 275, *276*; Italy, palace 122, *135*, *150*, *158*, *175*, 212, *213*, *266*, 273; Italy, town house 121; Italy, villa *172*, 214, *249*, *263*; Mexico *811*, 815, 818, *836*; Portugal *773*; Spain 670, 696, *712*, 734, 735

Drake, Francis 797, *830*

Dresden: Residenzschloss 449, *449–52*, 451

du Cerceau, Jacques I Androuet 363–5, 399, *400*, 401; Charleval Château 369, *369–70*; Hôtel de la Reine *364*; Hôtel de Nevers 365, *366*; *Les plus excellents Bastiments de France* 363–4, 367, *368*, 772; *Livre d' architecture* 364, *364–6*; Verneuil Château *368–9*

du Cerceau, Jacques II Androuet: Louvre *379–80*; Montceaux-en-Brie Château *376*; Tuileries *379*

Dubois, Ambroise *374*, 374–5

Duca, Giacomo del *290–1*

Dupérac, Étienne *331*; Château Neuf *377*

Dürer, Albrecht 3, *40*, *52–3*, *425*, 433

Écouen: Château *356–8*, *357–9*

education: secular 51–2

Edward VI, King 66–7, *70*

Effiat: Château *388–9*

Egas, Enrique 650

Egkl, Willhelm 503, *505*

El Escorial 717–20, *727–37*, *728–9*, *733–5*, 737, *757*, *759*

El Pardo: Hunting Lodge *717*, 717, *721*, *759*

Elizabeth I, Queen 71, 90, *91*, 562

Elvas: Nossa Senhora da Consolação *658*, *659*–60

England: conflict with Spain 90–1, *91*; Protestant reform 62–7, 72

Erasmus, Desiderius 53, *53–4*, *803*

Escobar, Manuel de *845–7*, *846*

estate houses *230*, 230, *232–3*

estilo chão: Classicism and *656–62*, *656–65*, 664; domestic architecture 777–8; palatial church and 760–1, *760–9*, *764–5*, *767–9*

estilo desornamentado 718, 740, 744, *753*, 755

Estremoz: S. Maria do Castello *659*

Ethiopia: Castle of Fasiledes, Gonder *785*

Europe: politics of 41–6

Évora: Espírito Santo 661–2, *663*; Nossa Senhora da Graça 662, *663*; Nossa Senhora do Carmo *766*, *774*; Remédios church *766*, *767*; S. Antão 660, 661; S. Clara-a-Nova *767*, *767*; S. Mamede 662, *663*

Exton (Rutland) *613*

Fawsley (Northamptonshire) *574*, 590, *591*

Ferdinand I, Emperor 42–3, *43*, 56, 72, *433–5*, *437–8*

Ferdinand II, Emperor *517*
Fère-en-Tardenois: Château *354*
Ferrabosco, Pietro 434, *434–5*
Filippi, Giovanni Maria 509, *524, 525*
firmitas 204, 257
Flamboyant *412*; Flanders 419, 424; France 298, 301, 303, *303, 304, 354*; Germany 474; hybrid styles *407, 410, 642, 648*
Flanders: Classicism 413–21, 424; Counter-Reformation period 532–6, *532–45*, 539, 541–3; Renaissance style 405–7, *405–12, 409*
Florence 204–5; Accademia delle Arti del Disegeno 193; Boboli Gardens 206–7, *207*; Cathedral of S. Maria del Fiori 5–6; Fortezza da Basso *139*; Palazzo della Signoria 5–6, *6–7*, 194; Palazzo Griffone *200*; Palazzo Montalvo *200*; Palazzo Pitti 197–9, *200*; Palazzo Vecchio 194, *194–5*; Piazza della Signoria *30*; Ponte Santa Trinita *198–9*; S. Giovanino *200*; S. Lorenzo *104–9*; Uffizi *196*, 197
Florentino, Francesco 674–5, *675*
Florentino, Jacopo 674
Florentinus, Franciscus *430–1*
Floris, Frans 89, *89*
Fontainebleau: Château 304–5, *304–5, 320–5, 343, 343, 371, 374–5, 378*
Fontaine-Henry: Château *307*, 307
Fontana, Domenico 277, *279–81*, 280
Fontana, Giovanni *286*, 288
Fouquet, Jean 299–300, *300*
Francart, Jacob 534, *534–6, 537*
France: anti-Classicism 362, 364; early Bourbon patronage 371–5, 377, 379–81, 384–7; Flamboyant 303, *304*; graphic art 298–9, *309*; High Renaissance 327–8; Italian Classicism 316, 318; new nobility and Italian influence 300–2; religious war 75–7; Valois to Bourbon 91–3
Francini, Alessandro 377, *378, 396*
Francini, Tommasco 377, *396*
Franciscans: Indian missions 787–8; Italian churches 216; Mexican missions 803, *804–7*, 812, *813*; Russian churches 520; South American missions 833–4
François, Gatien *312*

François I, King 42, 44, *44–5*, 67–8, 313, *327*, 334, 568
Franke, Paul 521, *522–3*
Frascati: Villa Aldobrandini 287, *288*; Villa Mondragone *286*
Frederick II, King of Denmark 553, 556
Freiburg Münster *495*
Fréminet, Martin *375*
funerary monuments: Elizabethan 574, 591, *591*; Jacobean *611*; Spanish Neoclassical *648*, 648–9

gable 424, *424*, 426, 468, 470, *470, 472–3*
Gadier, Pierre *312*
Gaenza, Martín de *678*
Galilei, Galileo *30, 30*
gardens: Flanders *411*; France 305, 331, 359, 369, 377–8, 395–6; Italy 186–91, *186–91*, 206–7, *206–7, 285–8*; Portugal *777*; Spain 757–8; Tudor England 566–7, *567*
Gaultier, Germain *396–7*
Gdańsk *470–1*; Arsenal *472–3*
Genga, Girolamo 130
Genoa: Palazzo dell'Università *265*; Palazzo Doria Tursi *264–5*; S. Maria Assunta, Carignano 260, *260–1*; Strada Nuova *263–4*; urban planning 263, *263–4*, 265
Germany: clerical funerary monuments 494–5, *494–5*; French Classicism 484–5; Gothic style dominates 425–7; interiors *488–9*, 489; Italian Classicism 444–56; Mannerist style 474–5; protestant reform 54–8; Renaissance style 428–9, *428–9*, 469; Wendel Dietterlin 490–3, *491*
Ghana: Fort S. Jago, Mima *782–3*
Ghent: Kasteel Van Ooidonk *410*
Giambologna *30, 30–1*, 202
Gil de Hontañón, Rodrigo: Cathedral, Astorga 683, *683*; Cathedral, Santiago de Compostela 685; Chapel of Las Bernardas de Jesús, Salamanca 683, *683*; Colegio Fonseca, Salamanca *680–1*, 681; Gómara Palace *687*; Guzmán Palace, León 686, *686*; Medina da Rioseco *682–3*; Medina da Rioseco, Santiago *682*; Monterrey Palace 684, *685*, 686; University, Alcalá de Henares 684, *684*
Gil Morlane I 714, *715*

Gil Morlane II 714, *714*
Giocondo, Fra 17, *18*, 18
Giulio Romano 38–9, 111; Casino Turini *112–13*; Cortile di S. Damaso 19; Mantua Cathedral 128–9, *129*; Mantua residences 128; Palazzo de Te 121, *122–7*, 123; Palazzo Maccarani 120, *121*; Sala di Costantino *20*; Villa Farnesia *118–19*
Giunti, Domenico 267–9, *267–9*
Goa: Bom Jesus 788, *792, 793*; Cathedral of S. Catarina 788, 789, *790–1*; Espírito Santo, Margao 788–9, *792*; Nossa Senhora de Rosário 788, *788*; Portuguese buildings 786–7, *786–7*; S. Francisco do Assis *789*; Salvador do Mundo *793*; Santana *793*
Gonzaga, Federigo *121*
Goujon, Jean 334, *334–5*, 336, 342
Granada: Alhambra Palace 669, *669–71*, 671; Church of the Monastery of S. Jerónimo *675*, 675; Metropolitan Cathedral of the Incarnation 672–3, *672–5*, 675; Real Chancilleria *710–11*
Graz: Landhaus *441*; Schloss Eggenberg 515, *516–17*
great halls 561, *562*, 563
Greco, El (Doménikos Theotokópoulos) 73, *79*, 95
Greenwich: Charlton House 598, *598, 599*; Queen's House 618–22, *620–1*
Grigi, Guglielmo dei 208, *208*
groin-vaulting 241, 659–60, 805, 818
Grosbois: Château *386–7*
grotteschi 223
Grünewald, Matthias *52–3*
Guadalajara: Cathedral 814–15, *816–17*, 817
Guatemala: ecclesiastical buildings *828–9*, 828–9
Gucci, Santi 463
Guild of Masons and Architects 823
Guise, Henry, Duc de 76, 92
Gustavus II Adolphus, King of Sweden *545*
Güstrow: Schloss 474, *474*

Habsburg Empire: administration of 71–3; expansion through marriage 42–3, *42–3*; Reformation, consequences of 58, 68–70, 98–100; war with France 44, 66–7

Primaticcio, Francesco 321–2, 324–5, *342–3*, *342–3*
printing 373
protestant reform: advocates of 53–6; England 62–6, 72; Germany 54–8; Scandinavia 58
Puebla: Casa del Deán 813, *813*; Cathedral 818, *820–1*, 821, 827; S. Domingo 824, *825–6*, *826–7*

Quadro, Giovanni Battista 462–3, *462–4*
Quijano, Jerónimo 679, *679*
Quito: La Compañía 839, *839*; S. Agustín *836–7*, 837; S. Domingo *836*, 837; S. Francisco 834, *834–5*

Raimondi, Marcantonio 7
Raphael 9–10; 'Baptism of Constantine' 21; 'Battle of the Milvian Bridge' *20–1*, 21; Casino Turini *112–13*; Cortile di S. Damaso *18–19*, 19; 'Expulsion of Heliodorus From the Temple' 14, *14–16*; 'Healing of the Lame Man' 13, *15*; 'Incendio del Borgo' 16, *16–17*, 18; 'Madonna of the Fish' 23, *24*; 'Massacre of the Innocents' 7, *7*; Palazzo Branconio dell'Aquila 110–11, *110–11*; portrait of Baldassare Castiglione *12*; S. Maria del Popolo *12–13*; Sala di Costantino *20*, 21; 'School of Athens' *9*; Sistine Madonna *10–11*; Stanza di Eliodoro *12–16*, 18; 'The Three Graces' *119*; 'Transfiguration' *20*, 23; Villa Farnesia *118–19*, 119–20; Villa Madama *112–14*
Raynham Hall (Norfolk) *634–5*
Reigate Priory *565*
Rennes: Palais de Justice *396–7*
retable 735, *743*, *774–5*, *774–5*, 843
Rheims: Hôtel de Ville *402*
rhythmic bays 105, 129, *172*, 275, *346*, 353
Riaño, Diego de *678–9*, 679
rib vaulting 795, 841–2
Ridinger, Georg *482–3*, 483
Rodez: Cathedral *352–3*
Rodríguez, Antonio *835*
Rome *83*; Aqua Felice fountain *278*; Campidoglio *164*, 164–5, *166–7* 167; Casino Turini *112–13*; Castel Sant'Angelo *138–9*; Il Gesù 184, *184–5*; Palazzo Aldobrandini *284–5*; Palazzo Borghese 179, *282–4*; Palazzo Branconio

dell'Aquila 110–11, *110–11*; Palazzo de Baldassini 146; Palazzo del Quirinale *281*; Palazzo Farnese 148, *148–51*, 150–1; Palazzo Firenze *201*; Palazzo Gaddi 131, *131*; Palazzo Laterano *279*; Palazzo Maccarani *121*; Palazzo Massimi alle Colonne 152–3, *153*; Palazzo Spada *180–1*; Piazza dei Conservatori 165, *166–7*; Piazza della Signoria *202–3*; S. Andrea della Valle 289, *291*; S. Andrea, Via Flaminia *182–3*; S. Anna dei Palafrenieri *182–3*; S. Giovanni dei Fiorentini 162, *162*; S. Maria ai Monti 289, *290*; S. Maria del Popolo *12–13*; S. Maria dell'Orto *183*; S. Maria in Trivio *290–1*; S. Maria Maggiore 162, *162*, *280*; urban planning *139*, 139, 162–4, *163*, *278*, 278–9; Villa Borghese *286–7*; Villa Farnesina *118–19*; Villa Giulia 171, *172–3*; Villa Ludovisi *285*; Villa Madama 112–14, *113–17*, 116, *116–17*; Villa Mattei *285*; Villa Medici *201*; Villa Peretti *281*; The Zecca *147*
Roskilde Cathedral *416*
Rosny: Château *386*
Rosso Fiorentino 26–7, *27–8*, 28–9, 33; 320–2
Rothenburg ob der Tauber *468*
Rouen: S. Maclou *334*; Tomb of Louis de Brézé *334*
Ruão, Jerónimo de 650–2, 652, 661, 664, *664–5*
Rubens, Peter Paul 6, *97*, 375, *532*, *540–1*
Rudolf II, Emperor *98–100*, 98–100, 433, 509
Ruiz, Hernán II *699*, 699, 700, *700–1*, *712–13*
Rushton, Triangular Lodge *600–1*
Russia 86–7

S. Carlo Borrmeo 79–80
Sagredo, Diego de 666–7
Saint-Germaine-en-Laye: Château *314–15*; Château Neuf 333, *333*, 377
Saint-Loup-sur-Thouet: Château *387*
Saint-Maur-des-Fossés: Château 328, *328–9*
Salamanca: Catedral Neuva 644–6; Chapel of Las Bernardas de Jesús *683*, 683; Colegio Fonseca *680–1*; La Clerecía *752–3*; Monterrey Palace 684, *685*, 686; S. Esteban 642, *647*, 648
Salvaterra de Magos: Chapel of Infante Dom Lúis *658–9*, 659
Salviati, Cecchino *294*

Salzburg: Cathedral *530–1*; Schloss Hellbrunn 514, *514*
Sambin, Hughes *348*
Sangallo, Antonio da 131, 139, 146–7, 151; Fortezza da Basso *139*; Palazzo de Baldassini 146; Palazzo Farnese *148–51*; S. Pietro 140–2, *140–5*, 144–5; S. Spirito, Sassia 146, *146*; Vatican Palace *180*; Villa Madama *114*; The Zecca *147*
Sanmicheli, Michele 131, 209, 214; Palazzo Bevilacqua 135, *135*; Palazzo Grimani *210*, 211; S. Bernardino *136–7*, 137; Sanctuary of the Madonna di Campagna 137; Venice, portals of *132–3*, 133; Verona, palaces *134–5*; Villa la Soranza *214*
Sansovino, Iacopo 209, *211*; commissioned tombs 215, 648; Libreria Marciana and Loggetta 218, *218–22*, 222; Palazzo Corner della Ca' Grande *212–13*; Palazzo Dolfin *211–12*, *212*; Palazzo Gaddi 131, *131*; Piazza S. Marco 217–18, *218–19*; S. Francesco 215; S. Francesco della Vigna *216*; S. Giorgio dei Greci *217*, 217; Scuola Grande della Misericordi *217*, 217; Villa Garzoni *214*, *214*
Santarém: Seminário 772, *773*
Santiago: Medina da Rioseco *682*, *682–3*
Santiago de Chile: S. Francisco *833*, 833
Santiago de Compostela: Cathedral *685*
Santo Domingo: Casas Reales *795*; Cathedral of S. María la Menor *797*
Sarto, Andrea del 23, *24*
Sassia: S. Spirito 146, *146*
Savot, Louis *401*
Saxony, Electors of 55, *56*, 69, 427
Scamozzi, Vincenzo *236–7*, 254, *255*, *530*
Scarpagnino (Antonio Abbondi) 208, *208–9*
Schallaburg: Schloss *440*
Scherpenheuvel: Onze-Lieve-Vrouwekerk 535, *535*
Schloss Hovestadt *481*
Schmalkalden: Schloss Wilhelmsburg *486–8*
Schmalkaldic League 57, 64, 68
School of Fontainebleau 321–2, 327, 374, 569
Scorel, Jan van *59*
screens: choir 533, *533*; hall *576*, 577, 581, 591, *592–3*
serliana 211, 235